Even the Angels Must

AGAIN

Jan S. Doward

Edited by Jerry D. Thomas
Designed by Michelle C. Petz
Cover and inside art by Thomas Dunbebin

Copyright ©1998 by
Pacific Press® Publishing Association
Printed in the United States of America
All Rights Reserved

ISBN 0-8163-1408-X

98 99 00 01 02 • 5 4 3 2 1

Contents

Introduction to Unexpected Humor

Somehow, it never seemed to me that for all his wisdom, Solomon caught the full significance of an out-of-sync time for laughter. In his famous comment about the seasonal things of life, he simply stated there's "a time to laugh." But it's a lot more hilarious when it's not time. It always seems funnier when humor comes at right angles to a solemn, worshipful situation.

I think I first came to this realization after choking and crying as I desperately tried to suppress my laughter during a church service several years ago. It happened in a small country church—one of those compressed sanctuaries in which the pulpit and pews fit tightly together, not so much for good eye contact, but merely to crowd in more people. It was a hot summer day, and all the windows stood open for the sorely needed cross ventilation. The staid Scandinavians who made up the bulk of the congregation sat impassively listening to their favorite old-time lay preacher intoning some sure and comfortable theology.

In the midst of his sermon, Mr. Swanson sagely asked a rhetorical question. I can't recall what he actually queried, but I distinctly do remember that as, if in answer, a cow mooed right on cue. The bovine sound effects came through the open window behind the pulpit.

This set me up. I put my hand to my mouth, but more was to follow. Swanson, hard of hearing as he was, only leaned forward in the pulpit and cupped his ear.

"How's that again, brother?" he asked seriously.

I couldn't hold it! Grabbing my handkerchief, I stuffed it in my mouth. My wife nudged me. But it was no use. I knew she had better control and would somehow save her laughter for later when she could have a good belly laugh at home. Not me. I suffered intense gagging and tears. My head grew hot, and I sensed my face was red from the effort of holding in check the happy sounds I wanted so much to make. What made it worse was the fact that all the saints sat soberly looking straight ahead, sedately listening as if nothing had ever happened.

Since that time I've been on the lookout for others who have experienced similar moments, moments when laughter has irreverently elbowed its way into worship. I've asked evangelists, pastors, and church-goers in general all over the country to share with me. Laughter knows no denomina-tional barriers, but I have always hastened to add in my quest that I definitely do believe in reverence. It's just that I have a sneaking hunch even the angels sometimes must bend over in laughter over the unexpected.

The Hazards of Baptism

My friends and family know I'm always on the prowl for true, unpublished stories. One day my youngest daughter phoned.

"Dad," she laughed, "you'd have cracked up today in our church. During a baptism, one of the older ladies lost her wig! The pastor picked it up like some drowned rat and handed it to her as she stepped out of the water. We had to sing about two dozen hymns before she'd come out to meet the congregation. It was too funny!"

I imagined it was! Baptisms, I've discovered, have a special built-in mechanism for potential humor.

I can only visualize what I would have suffered had I been attending the little Southern Baptist church in back-country Georgia during a morning they had scheduled a husband-and-wife immersion.

From what I was told, it was one of those cozy arrangements in which the deacons have to move the pulpit and lift the floorboards to expose the baptistry. Sheets were hung over wires to form a "dressing room" on each side of the baptismal tank. The husband had already been baptized and returned to change into his clothes, when his overweight wife descended the rickety stairs to the water. But the last step cracked and collapsed on her. As she lunged forward, staggering past the pastor, her arms wildly thrashed about for something to grasp. She caught the sheet on the opposite side and tore it down, exposing her shocked husband to the whole congregation. As he stood there in the buff, he made a quick and stunning decision. Diving headfirst into the baptistry, he disappeared from sight.

I can only imagine how many hymns they had to sing to bring the congregation back into line after that performance!

• • • • •

Uninvited persons in the baptistry are unusual. But when it does happen, the ceremony takes on new meaning.

With the pulpit moved to one side and the floorboards lifted, this particular church's fairly wide platform was much narrower. But the old gentleman slated to offer the benediction chose to remain in his seat on the rostrum during the baptism anyway. At least he intended to remain in his seat!

With so many being baptized that day, the elder grew weary of his straight-back position and began leaning his chair against the wall. As time passed, he started teetering the chair slightly. But once, the teeter wasn't slight enough. In a flash he was up-ended. With legs extended upward and hands frantically grasping for invisible handles, he went fully clothed into the baptistry.

For those in the congregation who had temporarily glanced away, it seemed like a fantastic disappearing act!

• • • • •

> The first rule for rural church baptisms is to notify all participants when the floorboards are removed. The second is to maintain composure at all costs if they aren't.

One little deaconess, whose sole job was to supply towels to both curtained-off "dressing rooms," began her duties in earnest as she passed back and forth with armloads of towels. But between one of her passes across the front, when her back was turned, the deacons lifted the floorboards!

Without a glance, the deaconess turned and headed back the way she had come. But this time, her path led straight into the water. She didn't resort to water-walking, and she didn't scream or back away. She went right on in without so much as a flicker

on her firm facial expression. Resolutely wading across the baptistry, she never lost stride. Still holding the towels high, she climbed the steps on the opposite side and continued her duties as if nothing had happened. It would be hard to match that for total composure!

•　•　•　•　•

Somehow those rural churches with the hidden baptistry beneath the rostrum never seem to lend themselves to the sanctity of a baptism. At least the preliminaries can certainly be distracting.

During one morning service, I watched in dismay as the deacons grunted and strained to slide the pulpit to one side and lift the floorboards. The clouds of steam that rose from the baptistry led one of the deacons to lean over to test the water.

"Ouch!" His loud cry shattered the sanctuary. Before the congregation could recover from that outburst, he grabbed a huge paddle from the adjoining room and began stirring the water vigorously.

From that moment on, my mind kept fighting to focus on reverence instead of conjuring up all sorts of scenarios of a blistered minister and lobster-red candidates emerging from the baptistry one by one.

• • • • •

But small country churches certainly don't have a corner on potentially humorous situations. Let me share something that happened recently in a plush suburban setting. This church had installed a glassed-in section in the lower part of the baptistry so that the congregation could witness the underwater activity during immersion.

Apparently, bubbles and bloated faces are more meaningful for many folk, adding a special dimension to the sacred rite. But this time, the whole congregation was afforded far more visual excitement than was originally scheduled.

The first man baptized arose from the water totally confused and headed up the stairs to the ladies' dressing room. By the time he realized his mistake, another candidate had taken his place in the water. He patiently waited behind the curtain for the right moment. Just as the next party slipped under, he went into action. But the audience never saw the baptism. Their wondering eyes beheld only a black-robed body desperately swimming underwater across the baptistry!

• • • • •

Communication is absolutely vital for any baptism. The candidates must understand what to expect or they can conceivably take all sorts of poses, postures, and appearances before the plunge. The problem is compounded when there is a language barrier.

One Russian couple presented themselves for the ceremony in a very dignified church. He could understand a little English, but his wife could not grasp one word.

She entered the baptistry first and immediately held her hands in front of her, palms together, poised as if about ready to take a dive.

"Will someone please go get this lady's husband so he can tell her what to do," the minister pleaded.

Suddenly called from the men's dressing room to go interpret, the anxious husband rushed out onto the rostrum clad only in his long johns.

That otherwise conservative congregation had a most difficult time suppressing their amusement. After all, how often did they witness that sort of display during church?

• • • • •

Every minister has his own preference for baptismal attire. Some wear weighted robes while others prefer old suits that obviously keep on shrinking. But I heard the story of one preacher who preferred hip boots. Since he was a short man, those fishing waders gave him a rather compressed look—as if somehow, his head and shoulders had been jammed into his legs. But the appeal of wearing those waders held him firmly. They held him even firmer during one evangelistic tent meeting.

A portable tank was placed near the front of the tent, but the attendant responsible for placing the false bottom in the tank forgot his duty. When the hip boot evangelist climbed into the tank he sank clear to his chin. With the waders filled to the brim, he was literally riveted in place.

"Would someone please pull the curtains and get me out of here!" he cried.

Imagine the effect on the waiting audience after that sort of introduction to the baptismal ceremony!

• • • • •

Shortly after a successful Vacation Bible School, a Kentucky Baptist church scheduled a baptism, mainly for children. As one little fellow stepped into the baptistry, he found himself up to his chin in water. Overwhelmed by the depth, he immediately began dog-paddling across the glassed-in baptistry—much to the amusement of the congregation. He tried to turn back when he reached the pastor, but then decided to swim to the other side. Instantly, the pastor's arm shot out like a shepherd's crook and pulled him back.

"If I can catch them, I can baptize them!" the pastor quipped to the audience.

The little boy just beamed with delight as the entire congregation roared with laughter.

•　•　•　•　•

Due to a large number of candidates preparing for baptism, a well-known evangelist decided to use a local swimming pool instead of a church baptistry. One of the many candidates lined up at the shallow end of the pool that day was a heavy-set woman who secretly held a very morbid fear of being immersed. It was one thing for her to talk about the rite in the dry setting of some church but quite another when the moment arrived in the pool. The very thought of having her head and upper torso under water was too much. Suddenly she startled everyone, including the evangelist, by raising both her hands above her head and pleading in a loud voice.

"Oh, save me from the water! Oh, save me from the water!"

To say that the occasion was a memorable one would be a vast understatement. For the evangelist to secure her hands, then get her entire body immersed and lifted upward without being pulled clear under himself in the struggle was a major accomplishment that few who witnessed it will ever forget.

• • • • •

Shall we gather at the river? Yes, indeed! Nature has a way of enhancing the beauty of baptism. But it also has a way of totally shattering the sanctity of the rite, causing wild thrashing and splashing at the most inopportune moments. Smoothness of operation depends on water temperature and the clearness of the stream or lake. Blue lips and chattering teeth are only one aspect of the inherent dangers. The prospects of either the candidate or the officiating minister suddenly disappearing down some hidden hole always lurk as a distinct possibility. And the danger of these natural hazardous possibilities is often in direct proportion to the size of the person being baptized.

As one very obese lady presented herself for a river baptism, the deacons whispered their concern to the minister. Since she tipped in close to 300 pounds, they would certainly be willing to assist the pastor in both the lowering and lifting.

"Oh, I believe I can handle this without any problem," the pastor graciously smiled. "Once in the water her weight will not be much of a factor."

He was SO wrong! As he dipped her under the water, the sheer weight of her huge frame yanked him off his feet. He too plunged beneath the dark depths. About fifteen feet downstream, the pastor surfaced, arms waving as he gulped for air. The chunky candidate had apparently settled on the muddy bottom. Fortunately, the deacons were right on hand to follow the tell-tale bubbles and hastily waded to her rescue.

Many songs were sung before order was restored among the congregation lining the shore. Perhaps a little prayer session helped too!

• • • • •

Church Bloopers

Spoonerisms are such great blessings because they allow the whole audience to laugh spontaneously without fear of frowns. The accidental transpositions of sound always seem funnier when said at some large assembly. Maybe it's because there are more people laughing and it takes longer to settle everyone down.

At a great ecclesiastical gathering in the Midwest a few years ago, the keynote address speaker began with . . . "Here we stand, puke and weany men that we are . . . I mean weak and puny men . . ."

It is doubtful anyone remembered much of anything else that evening.

• • • • •

The tongue can do marvelous things even with simple messages. One person who was given the assignment of announcing the hymn number became rattled once his tongue got tangled on the initial effort.

"We will now sing nymn humber . . . I mean hum nymber, er, er . . . num hymber . . . Oh, just sing 175!" he finally blurted out. It was probably a good thing that the organ could help drown out most of the snorts and snickers once 175 was under way.

• • • • •

A spoonerism is funny enough when a speaker recognizes it and attempts to correct it. But when he or she continues without the slightest hint as to why everyone is so highly amused, it adds a special touch that creates even more humor.

One minister who had gained a reputation for his slips of the lip attempted to generate enthusiasm at a youth song service and happily exclaimed, "It's such a beautiful day today I think we ought to have a sitting fong!"

Whatever fitting song was selected came laced with grinning amusement that kept a perplexed look on the puzzled pastor's face as he led the group in singing. This look, in turn, kept the youth hanging happily onto his every word in keen anticipation of another possible blooper. That pastor may never know what he said that kept his listeners so riveted to his message!

• • • • •

A simple word or phrase blunder can be just as devastating as any spoonerism. One Baptist preacher, while waxing eloquent in his closing remarks exclaimed earnestly, "Now if you can get that into your heads, then you'll have it in a nutshell!"

Few, of course, ever remembered much of the sermon but most would never forget the ending.

• • • • •

A popular TV preacher, noted for his dignified demeanor and articulate delivery on camera, once had to make a quick recovery from a slip during an out-of-studio meeting. In an effort to show his audience the connection between several Bible verses he said in his typical cathedral voice, "Now let me give you a co-text (which sounded like Kotex). I mean companion text."

• • • • •

Every business organization, government agency, and scholastic discipline has its own in-house terminologies which are totally meaningless to the general public. The various denominations are no exception.

One evening a Seventh-day Adventist evangelist got carried away with his personal background in church work. Without explaining the exact meaning of the church's organizational structure, he proclaimed with a flourish, "I was a Union officer at one time."

Puzzled, a little sixth-grade girl leaned over and whispered to a friend of mine, "I didn't think he was old enough to be in the Civil War."

• • • • •

One of the most classic bloopers on file occurred in a Christian college testimonial meeting. A tearful freshman concluded his personal testimony with a memorable request.

"Please pray I'll not be found sleeping with the five foolish virgins when Jesus comes," he sobbed.

The student body has long since scattered, but whenever any of them chance to meet, a simple mention of that moment still brings howls of laughter.

• • • • •

Announcements can always hold their own when it comes to blunders. And they often go uncorrected, which leaves the audience in a state of bewilderment and curiosity.

Prior to the eleven o'clock service, a Mrs. Hand requested the pastor to remember her ill husband during the morning prayer. The good man agreed but when the time came, he went to the pulpit and informed his waiting flock of a very serious matter.

"Sister Husband would like the congregation to pray for her hand."

• • • • • •

Sometimes the introduction of a guest speaker can get so sticky that it is the better part of wisdom to let it go and allow the visiting preacher the honor of any correction.

He was supposed to be introduced as Pastor Brazee; but when the announcer came to his part, he smiled and said in gracious tones, "We are happy to have with us this morning. Pastor Brassiere."

I've always been glad I didn't do it or I'd have had to leave the rostrum very quickly on an emergency call!

• • • • •

Nervousness before a large audience is often the cause of some verbal mistake.

During one jammed Seventh-day Adventist camp meeting there were over 20,000 people present. On the platform was a church official named Elder Belleau (pronounced Bellow), who was slated to offer the morning prayer. But the nervous ministerial intern, whose only job for the occasion was to introduce the church leader, got up before that great concourse of people and solemnly announced, "Elder Pray will now bellow."

It took more than thirty minutes of singing to bring that congregation back to some semblance of prayful attitude. Each time it seemed the proper moment had arrived, a ripple of laughter would begin somewhere, and off they'd all go again. Truly a great moment to remember!

• • • • • •

Getting carried away with the sweep of some great concept often can lead to marvelous wording and confusion.

I once attended a meeting in which the enthusiastic preacher requested all those old-timers, born before the turn of the century, to stand. Since his sermon was on last-day prophecies, he hoped to emphasize how these folks had actually seen many things fulfilled.

It took a little effort but one by one over the audience the white-haired ones managed to struggle to their feet. The preacher then meant to say, "You have seen many prophecies fulfilled," and then politely ask them to be seated. But instead, his mind leaped forward anticipating his next point, and in a loud voice he grandly proclaimed, "YOU HAVE BEEN SEATED!"

The dear old saints blinked in stunned confusion. Slowly, however, it dawned on them that the preacher, caught up in his own grandiose oratory, was continuing without further need of their participation and they gradually slipped into their seats.

Fortunately for me, enough commotion was created to cover my own amused sound effects.

Exciting Evangelism

Some evangelists have a real knack for the highly dramatic and sensational. But this can lead to goofs, which do far more than enhance the quality of any meeting.

One evangelist I know felt it was imperative to illustrate eternal fire. His visual aid was designed to awaken even the most lethargic. Placing about a quarter inch of gasoline in the bottom of an old-fashioned washtub he struck a match at the appropriate time.

Whoosh!

"Eternal fire" burst forth, sending dark smoke to blacken the newly painted church ceiling. Somewhere behind the ominous fury of flames and smoke, the evangelist desperately tried to make his point in spite of the commotion of the fire and apprehensive audience. It seems that he had never practiced this performance because two deacons leaped to their feet and quickly carried "eternal fire" outside the church.

The audience never forgot the visual aid even if they couldn't remember what it was supposed to illustrate. But I've often wondered what the neighbors thought as they witnessed that washtub ablaze in the churchyard. It was certainly an exciting way to attract attention—but not necessarily to the preaching service.

• • • • •

Unexpected audience participation always holds immeasurable possibilities of added thrills not on the evangelistic program.

One evangelist, caught up in the sensational arts, decided that the most effective method to establish the sureness of Daniel's prophecy that Europe would never be united was to bring back former world leaders from the "grave" and have them give their "testimony" over the PA system. On cue, his assistant backstage was to speak into a microphone placed on the bottom of a bucket to give the voice that eerie tomb-like resonance. But the assistant didn't get very far into his act before things got out of hand.

"I am Napoleon," he said slowly. "I am speaking from the grave tonight . . . I tried to unite . . ."

"EEEEYOW!" a woman on the front row screamed. Throwing her hands heavenward, she slipped out of her seat and slumped to the floor in a dead faint.

Since medical assistance was necessary, all eyes were riveted on the activity up front and the evangelist never could get his momentum back.

• • • • •

> When any evangelist hankers to use an illustration borrowed out of biblical times he had better use the real thing. Substitutes can cause embarrassment.

One very demonstrative young preacher decided to reenact that moment when the prophet Jeremiah broke the "earthen bottle" as a symbol of how Israel would be broken in his day. Instead of using a clay jar as the prophet did, the evangelist tried to smash an old-fashioned glass milk bottle.

"As this bottle is shattered so was ancient Israel!" he proclaimed with finality.

But when he vigorously threw the bottle to the floor, it happily bounced back and came to a rest atop the piano. While it was fortunate for those on the front row that it didn't break, it now stood serenely perched on the piano and no amount of enthusiastic audio report of how Israel was shattered could counteract the reality of that visual aid quietly resting right before everyone's eyes.

• • • • •

For sheer visual excitement, it would be hard to match the efforts of one Southern California evangelist. He attempted to depict the dream of Daniel 2 where the stone struck the great image and shattered it. Timing, however, is absolutely essential in pulling off any creative visual aids. Miscues are disastrous. His was disastrous!

The evangelist had rigged up a wire running from high in the balcony clear to the theater stage where he had placed a large plywood break-away image all painted according to the biblical description: head of gold, chest of silver, belly of brass, legs of iron, and feet of iron and clay. A pulley was secured on a wire from which hung a large, weighted papier-mâché "stone" several feet in diameter.

A local church volunteer was to station himself way up in the balcony and release the "stone" on cue for the grand climax.

"Now when you hear me read that text from Daniel 2:34 'a stone was cut out without hands, which smote the image upon his feet that were of iron and clay, and brake them to pieces,' you release the 'stone' down the wire. OK?"

The old man nodded. It was simple. Hear the text and release the "stone." Nothing to it.

On opening night the theater was filled. The magic of the moment swept the evangelist up in an ecclesiastical euphoria. Suddenly breaking from his usual format, he decided to open his Bible and dramatically read the whole section of Scripture as an introduction. Without thinking of the consequences, he inadvertently read verse 34 and kept right on reading.

The man in the balcony sat up with a start. The text! Since that was his cue, he immediately let fly the "stone" which vaulted over the heads of the audience to its target. The evangelist looked up just in time to see the "stone" heading right for the image. Holding out his hand like some cop trying to stop traffic he shouted.

"Not NOW, brother! NOT NOW!"

But it was too late. The "stone" struck the

image, sending the break-away parts in all directions just as it was scheduled to do for the finale.

For those on the evangelistic team, it must have been a howler. For those in the audience not familiar with the specifics of Bible prophecy, it must have been a startling experience.

• • • • •

Most evangelists roam the platform. With their penchant for prancing and pacing, few remain behind the pulpit very long. I've only seen one who stayed very close to the pulpit and he was a man with a very dry throat. Placing four glasses of water on the pulpit, he accomplished one of the most marvelous physical feats I have ever seen— he grabbed each of those four glasses in turn and swallowed the water they contained without the slightest cough, choke, or pause in his sermon.

• • • • •

Most speakers drift, however. And thanks to the cordless microphone, they can roam to their heart's content without getting tangled in some trailing cord. But one evangelist I know got far more action than he ever anticipated.

For his subject of Bible prophecy from Revelation, three giant-sized plywood angels were strung on wires. Each was to be sent flying through the "midst of heaven" by an off-stage assistant. With an appropriately-timed yank on a pulley, the assistant could send the "angels" flying one after another in a sort of three-layered angelic pattern. It was impressive, to say the least.

It became even more impressive one evening when the assistant accidentally sent all three flying at once. The evangelist who expected to speak at some length on the meaning of each separate "angel" suddenly found himself doing a lot of fancy dancing while ducking and dodging as those "angels" flew, one after another. That evening's clever choreography was really extra special because few would ever see again such unrehearsed gyrations accompanied by some of the fastest moving spotlights on record.

• • • • •

Sleeping during religious services has always carried inherent humor. A variety of these actual sleeping occurrences have filtered through to me over the years, including cases where those responsible for closing the service suddenly awoke from slumber, abruptly jerked to a standing position and with raised hands, prematurely asked the congregation to "rise for the benediction."

But the one I like best happened right in the audience during a large evangelistic tent meeting in Southern California several years ago. Without any of the typical snoring, an old man quietly snoozed on the front row, totally oblivious to his surroundings. But while he slept, a fuse blew, plunging the audience into darkness. Only the public address system remained on. The evangelist never lost a beat.

"So long as you can still hear my voice, I'll keep right on preaching," he explained. "My attendants will get the lights fixed shortly."

He wasn't far along in his "dark" discourse when the old man awoke. Hearing the preacher's voice, but seeing nothing aroused all his dormant energies.

"Oh, pray for me! I've gone blind!" he shouted loudly.

Two teen-age girls seated behind the old man got so tickled at the sudden interruption that they quickly dropped to the ground and crawled under the tent wall to laugh it off outside. I'm afraid if I had been there, I'd have had to join them.

• • • • •

Public address systems often amplify far more than singing or sermons, though. An evangelist friend of mine consistently wears a cordless mike during his meetings. Once, however, he forgot to turn it off when he recessed to the men's room during the song service. Interspersed throughout the singing, sounds could distinctly be heard in the auditorium—the sound of whistling, of the urinal flushing, of the washbasin filling, and of paper towels pulled from the holder and crumpled.

When my friend returned to the platform, he whispered to one of his associates, "How's it been going?"

The associate pointed toward the lapel mike and whispered back, "You ought to know; you were on!"

More Than Music

Music is supposed to be as much a part of worship as prayer and preaching. Yet for all of its possibilities, it can become the source of some highly entertaining episodes.

A local church orchestra conductor made the mistake of inviting me to play my trumpet with his musical group. It is true I once tooted the trumpet in a high school band, but since those distant, hazy days I

have only played for my own amazement
and amusement. But at the time, I felt
relatively sure I could handle most well-
known hymns without too much difficulty.
I always felt that if I could hum the tune,
then with a little practice I could play the
hymn. The problem was I can't ever
remember practicing together.

On the opening performance during
church service, the orchestra seemed to
struggle through the first hymn. The
blending of the instruments never did come
off right. It sounded a bit wheezy and off-
key, sort of like a New Year's celebration at
times. At best, the trumpet is not a subdued
instrument and during the first rendition I
could easily be heard above the woodwinds
or whatever else happened to be there that
morning.

Then the conductor made a startling
announcement.

"We will now play the hymn right across
the page, number 398."

"Hymn 398!" I gulped. "I just played that!"

The orchestra sounded so much better on
the next piece.

•   •   •   •   •

Through the years, I have had a part in creating just enough musical disasters to avoid filling out any questionnaires for latent church talent. Memories that range from playing the wrong piece to shouting "Stop! Stop!" when I ran out of breath during a congregational sing-a-long with my trumpet have etched deeply into my mind the need for staying musically incognito.

Knowing this, my youngest daughter and her husband once tried to trick me into joining a newly forming church orchestra. When the questionnaire was distributed I discreetly passed mine on without so much as blinking. But unbeknown to me, they took one and filled in my name, address, and phone number, and printed "Trumpet" on the instrument line. Then came the clincher.

"When would it be the best time for you to practice?" the questionnaire asked.

They filled in: "I don't need to practice!"

They only confessed to this diabolical scheme when the call to join never came.

Obviously, I was far and away too talented for any local church orchestra.

• • • • •

Caution should always be the watchword for purchasing so-called musical bargains. One church to which I belonged several years ago rushed into buying a used organ simply because a musically inclined minister transferring to a new location wanted to unload his personal instrument. He admittedly purchased the organ originally from a skating rink and that should have warned the unwary congregation. But they were taken with the notion of getting such a large-size organ for such a whale of a discount. The sales pitch was tremendous and even backed by a recital that seemed to captivate most folk. Yet the recital never brought out the fullest extent of the organ's possibilities. That was left for a guest organist several weeks after the purchase was finalized.

Everything went smoothly during the worship service until the conclusion of the morning prayer. While the congregation

was still on its knees, the organist—
intending to provide the special meditative-
mood music—accidentally activated the
wrong buttons. Wafting over the sanctuary
was the distinct sound of trap drums,
tambourines, castanets, and cymbals in a
sort of syncopated beat that was very
noticeable with the Bach-type music we had
been hearing.

I wish now that I had peeked because I am
sure the guest organist must have been
frantically fumbling with all the stops and
buttons or whatever other gadgetry was on
the panels. But once triggered, the only way
to stop the jazzy percussion section would
be to hit the off switch or pull the plug. But
that, of course, would have made the
muffled snorts and snickers passing through
the congregation seem even louder.

• • • • •

Organ preludes, interludes, and postludes
are traditionally designed for reverence.
The temptation, however, to use this
convenient musical cover to carry on a
conversation is too much for some.

One organist glanced down in disgust at two ladies near the front row who were caught up in very animated whispering. Determined to grab their attention and lift their souls to more sacred matters, he increased the volume. Utterly oblivious to their surroundings and what had happened, the women only raised their voices accordingly. Square-jawed and determined not to be outdone, the organist stepped up the volume even further. The organ swelled to a great crescendo, yet the women vigorously pursued their conversation.

By the width of their mouths and the lively gesturing, the organist suspected they had resorted to shouting. In total abandonment, he grimly departed from the musical score and jammed everything to a halt leaving the women's loud conversation suspended for all to hear. In the sudden silence of the sanctuary, the startled congregation heard a most vociferous but fascinating culinary remark.

"BUT I FRY MINE IN LARD!"

Music can be such a blessing when rightly used!

• • • • • •

Unrestricted volunteering of musical talents can pose problems of unusual dimensions. To have singers, for instance, suddenly decide to share their unscheduled talent is rare, but when it does happen, few in the congregation ever forget it.

The minister of a large college campus church was well into his sermon when a woman far up in the balcony decided it was time for her to share her singing ability. Leaving her seat, she made her way downstairs and into the main sanctuary. Striding with determination right up to the rostrum, she informed the startled minister of her intent.

"I want to sing!" she declared.

The time for special music had long since passed, but the poor preacher—not knowing what else to do—stepped aside and allowed the eager singer to use the pulpit for her a cappella rendition. When she finished, the minister went right on with his sermon, but in the back of his mind was a determination to secure church board action to curtail any future spontaneous performances.

•   •   •   •   •

Fortunately, she at least sang a religious song. The congregation in a small northwest country church, however, was not so lucky. An elderly member suddenly became inspired to sing, but to the astonishment of everyone that Sabbath morning he shared, "Down by the Old Mill Stream"!

Regardless of whatever else was heard that day none could erase the memory of listening to those words of the old love song, "You were sixteen, my village queen, down by the old mill stream!" What this had to do with worship remains a mystery to this day.

•   •   •   •   •

What musicians wear often makes more of an impression than their music. I cannot remember one piece a student organist played that morning in the college chapel but I distinctly do recall seeing her reaching for the foot pedals in her pajamas!

She had obviously overslept and had rushed from the women's dorm clad only in her coat and pjs. Thinking nobody would notice anything unusual, she had played with total abandonment, displaying her enormous talents. The organ, however, was located in the balcony and all those seated at a certain angle below could look up and behold legs draped in silky bright pink.

I suppose with a little creative selectivity, certain hymns and gospel tunes could have been used to accompany this sort of appearance.

• • • • •

Proper dress is so important to musicians that any discrepancy just prior to a performance can cause sheer panic. Several years ago, a choir director discovered his pants sadly sagging in the rear moments before a sacred concert. He had lost both buttons that held his suspenders! One of the astute local townsfolk, however, volunteered to meet the emergency by supplying him with an old-fashioned horse blanket pin. The director's trousers held firmly enough but every time he lifted his arms while conducting, his coat would part in the back exposing that giant-sized safety pin.

A few fervent "Amens" would have helped to cover the continued audience amusement.

• • • • •

In the days when choir directors waved batons and women wore their hair in buns, a certain dignity and solemnity pervaded performances. But musical numbers could get positively dramatic.

One director let his baton slip during a lively hymn and it sailed like a dart to its target—the organist's hair. It struck with such force that it remained in her bun during the rest of the rendition. Whatever exciting selection was being sung that day could have been enhanced with a special stirring arrangement of that old gospel song, "The Fight Is On!"

• • • • •

> Singing from memory always has inherent hazards. The human mind is quite capable of going totally blank even with familiar words.

While singing "The Lord's Prayer" during a wedding, a friend of mine succumbed to a lapse of memory as he approached the finale. To the dismay of the pianist accompanying him, he repeated—like some broken record—"For Thine is the kingdom . . . is the kingdom . . . is the kingdom . . ." Such recycling while groping for the right words would certainly awaken even those dreamy-eyed patrons and relatives who never seem to listen much during a wedding.

• • • • •

> Hunger and boredom often drive people to do the strangest things. Musicians are no exceptions, especially if they are youthful.

One teenage choir member, feeling the Sunday morning service was dragging too

much, began thinking of his stomach. This activated his memory of a bag of potato chips in his car. Since he sat where the audience was not fully visible, he slipped from his seat and inexorably began crawling to the nearest exit. Once outside, he ran to the parking lot, retrieved the bag of chips and hastily returned. Placing the bag between his teeth he dropped to his knees and ever so carefully pushed open the door. While concentrating on the carpet ahead of him so as not to make a sound, he inched his way on all fours to find his choir seat.

Suddenly the whole congregation stirred. Glancing up, he discovered to his horror that he had accidently taken the wrong door and was midway out on the platform!

It is very doubtful that any musical selection could have erased that sight in the minds of the congregation. At least, none was found that Sunday morning.

• • • • •

> Selecting the wrong door has always been loaded with definite but distinctive possibilities for disaster.

In the days when men wore collar buttons, one young choir member lost his just prior to a religious college performance. With everyone else nearly ready, he frantically searched all over the dressing room but to no avail. Finally in desperation, he burst into what he thought was the men's room to ask for help. "Do any of you happen to have an extra collar button?" he loudly pleaded. But to his dismay, he had opened the wrong door and was standing in full view of the audience clad only in his shirt and shorts.

The ensuing laughter prevented him from making his appearance for the first number of the sacred concert even though he had found a button stud at the last moment.

Sneaking in later to blend with the rest of the choir took a certain amount of finesse, of course.

• • • • •

One singer I know sat near the front of the church and prepared to share his talents with the congregation. His wife and two-year-old daughter were sitting in the same pew. That is to say, his daughter was standing in the pew next to him, so she could be as tall as he was.

Then the girl had a wonderful sharing idea. Taking the bright red ribbons out of her own hair, she neatly stuck them into her daddy's thick curly hair.

Not feeling the touch of her tiny fingers, the singer stood up for his song with both ribbons showing nicely. For him, the constant smiles spread across the congregation during his solo were a great mystery. Not until he sat down did he learn of those bright red decorations in his hair!

People may have forgotten the song he sang that day, but they will never be able to erase the mental image of those visual aids in the singer's hair!

•   •   •   •   •

Those Embarrassing Moments

When it comes to embarrassing moments in church, I personally have achieved my share. In fact, I can easily identify with those who have reason to blush.

Once I enthusiastically taught a Bible class which was delightfully spellbound and smiling throughout my entire arm-waving teaching. I was almost inclined to believe I had achieved the level of a master teacher until I later discovered the cleaner's tag conspicuously stapled to my sleeve!

• • • • •

I've even walked right into a church sanctuary with red suspenders dangling down my sides. I would have made it clear to the front of my waiting class except that my dear wife luckily spotted me first. Her whispered concern over my absent-mindedness sent me back-peddling to the nearest men's room where I solemnly vowed never to wear suspender's again. Then and there I pledged conversion to a belt!

• • • • •

Belts may seem superior to suspenders, but they aren't always a sure thing for support either. Not if you're terribly overweight anyway. One of the most mortifying experiences on record happened to a very heavy-set preacher before a youth audience. He wanted to show the young people that the gospel was really like a life preserver and intended to wear one around his waist at the height of his sermon on salvation.

The problem was he couldn't find a genuine preserver but had to settle for a brightly colored, child's plastic inflatable ring. He pulled this out from behind the pulpit at the appropriate time, and while blowing it up paused to pant out the great spiritual lesson. Then slipping the plastic ring over his head and shoulders, he wiggled it down to his chest. As he maneuvered it further down to his waistline, the ring fit so tightly that he was forced to squirm and twist to get it into place.

Finally in desperation, he inhaled as much as possible and pushed the ring down. At that precise moment, his pants fell off! Obviously he could not see over his tummy, and with all the bodily contortions and the snug fit, he was totally unaware of what had happened. The unexpected roaring laughter of the entire student body did alert him that something was dreadfully amiss, but this only created a puzzled expression on his face which punctuated his predicament and generated still more laughter.

One can only imagine the added hilarity

when he tried to take a step with his trousers tangled around his ankles and that inflated ring around his waist. Ah, what tremendous truths can be taught with such simple devices!

• • • • • •

Skirt fasteners can be just as hazardous as any belt though. While reaching for a high note, one singer discovered that reality. Her skirt fastener, unable to bear the strain, let loose. Her skirt settled in a heap on the floor. Fortunately, she had chosen to stand behind the organ that morning. After completing her musical number in her slip, she stooped over, gathered up her skirt and discreetly exited through the door directly behind her.

Only the men on the rostrum witnessed the performance, and one wonders if they had as much composure as the lady singer.

• • • • •

No one could ever fault an elderly southern lay preacher for his thorough Bible preparations but sometimes his personal appearance seemed in need of improvement. Once while he was seated on the rostrum awaiting the time to preach, a deacon whispered to him, "Your shirt tail is hanging out."

The old gentleman nodded a thank you and while looking straight ahead proceeded to tuck in the exposed tail of his shirt. The problem, however, was that he tucked in more than what he was wearing. When he got up to speak he pulled down the American flag!

• • • • •

At another service this same elderly gentleman got a message about his appearance.

"Your fly is open," the deacon seated next to him whispered.

Sure enough. So with a quick, discreet zip the old preacher closed the embarrassing gap. But in so doing he inadvertently caught the end of his necktie. When it was time to speak, he tried to get up but found himself frozen in a sitting position, unable to straighten.

• • • • •

Pastors are supposed to be trained in the fine art of friendly greetings. The warm handshake, the shoulder or arm squeeze, the pat on the back and smiling face are all part of the well-disciplined schooling to make folk feel welcomed in church. But while pressing the flesh has a long-standing tradition of success, head-patting has its special perils.

One dignified associate minister of a large city Christian church took his cue to greet the elderly ladies gathered in the church lounge Sunday morning. As he approached one dear old saint on the sofa, he smiled broadly.

"Well, good morning, Mary," he said, bending over to gently pat her on her head. But as he walked away the buttons on his coat sleeve somehow caught her wig and he walked off with it attached. Neither Mary nor the minister were aware of what had happened. She sat there smiling in the bald, still pleased with the little head blessing but unconscious of why all the other ladies were laughing so much.

"What's so funny?" she asked.

But none could stop laughing long enough to tell her.

Meanwhile, one of the deacons caught the minister down the corridor and asked him a profound question before he entered the sanctuary.

"Just what is that wig doing on your sleeve?"

Returning the wig and explaining the whole situation to dear Mary required a great deal of diplomacy. It's doubtful any young buck fresh out of the seminary would come equipped to handle that sort of problem. But then, head-patting probably wasn't on any of the school's curriculum anyway and the gesture might never occur to a ministerial intern, however gifted.

• • • • •

Children on the loose in church can create more havoc and embarrassment in less time than just about any single thing known to man. Parents, parishioners, and preachers alike cringe when some child escapes to unknown parts in the sanctuary during the worship service.

How well I remember being startled beyond my wits when a toddler who had crawled from the rear of the room suddenly emerged from under the pew directly in front of me while I was preaching. It was one of those tight little country sanctuaries and the effect was dramatic.

I quickly leaned over the pulpit and pointed downward.

"Whose is it?" I blurted out.

Then another question pressed for an answer as I fumbled with my notes: Where was I?

• • • • •

Easter Sunday is traditionally associated with the solemn dignity of a very special service. But back at the turn of the century, the congregation of a large Baptist church in Michigan was totally stunned by the results of one active three-year-old on the prowl—

her plan: to pick a bouquet of pansies from a lady's bonnet.

At best, little Lucile was never known for her quiet behavior during church services. Her wealthy father had lavished gifts on the church right down to the beautiful stained glass windows. But his little daughter gave also. Her impromptu acts and speeches during Sunday services provided embarrassment not only for her entire family but the whole congregation as well.

On that particular Easter Sunday, she made a promise though.

"I'll be good."

Her parents doubted that but Father held her on his lap, where for a little while, she seemed content. Her snappy eyes darted around the congregation searching with intensity for some fresh idea. Finally, she spied a woman wearing a bonnet filled with what looked like pansies. Back in those days, designers didn't garnish women's headgear with a few imitation flowers but often placed a mini-garden aloft. Lucile's little hands itched to pick those pansies. "Me sit on the floor," she whispered to her father. Thinking she was weary of his lap, he allowed her to slip from his grasp.

Instantly, Lucile began crawling under the pew, crossed the aisle, and positioned herself directly behind the woman with the big Easter bonnet. At first, she tried picking her bouquet gently but when none came loose, she gave the flowers a big yank. Not only did the whole bonnet come off but the wig securely pinned to it came also, exposing a shiny bald head.

In a high-pitched voice that could easily be heard clear to the back row of the balcony, Lucile yelled "Mama! Mama! Come quick! I've scalped her!"

But Lucile's piercing voice was instantly followed by another only slightly lower in tone. Grabbing her head in her hands, the woman let fly a volley of profanity that sent shudders throughout the horrified congregation. While the oaths were still fresh on her lips, she churned in a flurry of fast footwork down the aisle and out of the church never to return. She even left town without a forwarding address!

One can only visualize the minister later

standing by the church door after the service with a frozen door-to-door salesman smile pasted on his face. Picture the parishioners passing by and—between stifled laughs—shaking his hand and telling him how nice his Easter sermon was. The truth was, all any of them would ever honestly remember was the scalping episode.

• • • • •

Unfortunately, children never seem to plan their escapes at a time when the congregation is standing to sing. If somehow they could cue their exploratory trips to such times, it would provide a nice cover for parents to pursue with some semblance of dignity and without disturbing too many people.

I'm sure a friend of mine certainly wished his little son had held off for a long six-stanza hymn. Jimmy slipped loose one morning in a large religious gathering. The challenge of negotiating through that forest of legs intrigued Jimmy, and off he scooted

for the front row. His father followed up the aisle in a half-crouch position peering down each row and wistfully calling, "Jimmy . . . Jimmy!"

But Jimmy was long gone. I could measure his progress by the way people jerked to attention as he passed below them. Women especially seemed vulnerable, emitting little frightened squeaks as they half leaped to their feet when Jimmy grabbed their legs as he worked through the unusual obstacle course.

My poor miserable friend finally retrieved his small son way up front near the rostrum. The long trek back with Jimmy in tow was an agonizing experience. It is doubtful he remembered who spoke that day or even the special music. I know I can't!

• • • • •

> Children are not the only ones who can cause embarrassment in church. It can range through every age, depending on the personality, perception, or functioning faculties.

One day a devoted son-in-law graciously consented to take his dear wife's elderly mother to church. Since she was hard of hearing, he carefully escorted the ninety-year-old lady down the aisle to the section where earphones were attached to the back of the pews. Once she was seated and the earphones adjusted, everything seemed ready for worship. But the timing was off. Right then the minister requested that the congregation bow their heads for a moment of silent prayer. Everyone obeyed except this elderly soul who cocked her head and frowned. Then in her own penetrating voice she shattered the sanctity of the meditation.

"I can't hear a thing!" she exclaimed loudly.

No, indeed!

• • • • •

Stray pets on the loose in church can cause a variety of exciting events which may or may not blend well with the worship service.

A stunned Methodist minister suddenly became very red-faced one Sunday morning when his friendly collie ambled in from the next door parish. The pastor might have adapted this into some appropriate illustration of a warning about leaving gates and side doors open, or even the positive aspects of living in balmy California, but the sermon was not in progress at that juncture. Instead, a large number of the congregation were quietly kneeling at the Communion rail; and the dog, seeing all those beautiful, shining countenances at his level, tail-wagged happily down the line, licking faces as he went.

Regardless of the minister's embarrassment, how warm and touching can a Communion get anyway?

• • • • •

What began as an enlightening vespers designed to show the close relationship between health and spirituality turned into a tense and embarrassing verbal shoot-out which prompted me hastily to close the meeting.

I had arranged with a physician who specializes in this topic to speak, then open the floor for discussion. It was during the latter part of this period that an oversized woman stood to her feet.

"You spoke about obesity tonight but my doctor tells me that I have glandular problems and have to be obese."

Tightening his grip on the platform microphone, the doctor said firmly, "There were NO obese people in the concentration camps!"

The large lady shot back, "I demand an apology!"

"And I'm not giving one!" the doctor snapped.

Everything happened so rapidly I hardly had time to sort matters out, but I quickly suggested we stand for the closing hymn. Fortunately, I had pre-chosen a peaceful one, because under the pressure I could have inadvertently gone to the listing of hymns for "special occasions" and taken the old rallying one, "Sound the Battle Cry"!

• • • • •

Few visiting church dignitaries ever have the attention of monkeys as well as people at a worship service, but a church leader from the U.S. preaching in southern India certainly did.

In an open-air meeting, the primates were chattering and swinging from limb to limb in the nearby trees of a grove while the speaker urged the local congregation to be active in missionary work among their own families and villages. In the middle of his sermon, he asked a rhetorical question:

"Who will go to spread the gospel?"

To drive his point home, he repeated, "Who? Who? Who?"

Suddenly the monkeys in the trees came alive. In unison, they echoed back, "Whooo . . . whooo . . . whooo!"

And who among that crowd of people could help but respond after that performance?

• • • • •

For all the advertisements extolling the virtues and advantages of adhesives for false teeth, those who wear them know the embarrassment of possible looseness and the sound effects of clatter.

One elderly preacher never seemed to find the right "stickum" and his sermons were invariably punctuated with a distinctive clicking and clacking sound. One morning, however, he lost his teeth altogether! At the height of his sermon, they flew right out of his mouth! Still, he may have been old, but he was quick. With a quick wide-open jaw, he instantly caught his escaping teeth

midair and went right on preaching.

Those who witnessed this fine reactionary performance almost wished for an instant slow motion replay to see just how he actually snapped those teeth back in place so quickly.

• • • • •

When a white preacher is to be a guest at a black church, the chances of committing some public "faux pas" increases tremendously.

A friend of mine desperately wanted to make a good impression in his opening remarks. The only thing he could think of off-hand was the fact that the ushers and usherettes were dressed sharply in white, including white gloves.

"Everyone looks so nice this morning," he said as he smiled at the black congregation. "White is my favorite color!"

It's always much safer to stick with well-prepared notes.

• • • • •

A visiting white speaker I know brought an

entire black congregation into gales of laughter one morning all because of a cultural misunderstanding.

After the sermon, the black pastor sitting next to him leaned over and whispered, "Open the doors of the church."

Now that expression is not a familiar one to most white folk. The guest preacher never linked opening the doors of the church with an altar call.

Raising his eyebrows, the guest speaker whispered incredulously, "You mean that?" The black pastor nodded.

Without further prodding, the white preacher left his seat during the closing hymn and resolutely walked to the rear of the church to open all of the doors. A deacon standing back there caught the significance of what had happened and suggested to the guest speaker that he not return to the rostrum. But instead the preacher squared his shoulders and stalked back down the aisle. As the closing hymn ended, he stepped to the pulpit mike to make his announcement.

"The doors of this church are now

officially opened!" he declared emphatically.

The congregation came unhinged with laughter leaving the white preacher confused and rapidly glowing red.

• • • • •

> Carefully listening to directions is so important, yet when pressed for time, the brain can easily short-circuit causing a variety of delicate situations.

One guest speaker, already a bit late for his appointment, asked a deacon directions to the men's room.

"Downstairs," he pointed. "Second door on the right."

The visiting preacher thanked the deacon and hurried below knowing he had only a few minutes before he was expected to join the local church leaders in the minister's study prior to going onto the rostrum.

Doors? The downstairs hallway seemed a maze of them. But at that moment the guest preacher had other priorities. The fine distinctions of choosing the proper door didn't register nor did he even bother to read the sign as he took the first door on the right. It only took a glance to see that he had entered the wrong rest room, but the sound of the door opening behind him drove him at top speed into one of the stalls. He just sat there with his legs hoisted high for fear that the woman might see his trousers.

More women came. Some even began rattling the stall door to hurry whoever was on the other side. Since there was only one other facility, it didn't take long for the traffic to back up. Soon the ladies' rest room was jammed with irate females who were becoming increasingly distressed over the delaying party in the first stall. It was bad enough hearing all the muttering and cutting comments without being so cramped that his legs seemed about to collapse and fall to the floor.

The guest speaker scarcely breathed for fear that one of the younger set might crawl underneath or peek over the top and reveal the stark truth. Precious minutes fleeted away until finally, after sweating it out about as long as he thought he could endure, the rest room eventually was empty again.

Those waiting for him in the minister's study simply could not imagine what was detaining him since he had been seen talking to the deacon in the foyer earlier. Finally when he did show up, he offered no explanation for the delay.

After all, why add further embarrassment with a detailed description of the shattering experience?

• • • • •

Fortunately for the young ministerial intern, the Adventist camp meeting congregation would never be privy to his plight in the men's room. It happened during camp pitch time a few days before the great gathering . The rest rooms were all being refurbished and he, not noticing the "wet paint" sign, sat down and was promptly stuck with a new type of highly adhesive paint. At first he thought he could wiggle free but soon it became apparent he was glued to the toilet seat. His cries for help were finally heard and several of the other interns arrived to unbolt the seat that still remained attached to him. Draping a blanket over his back to hide the embarrassing attachment, they drove him in a pickup truck to the local Adventist doctor.

When the good doctor unveiled the problem he couldn't keep from laughing.

"I've seen a lot of these, he said, "but I've never seen one framed before!"

• • • • •

In spite of repeated Scriptural revelation, it is difficult to imagine the impact of a resurrection from the dead. Yet one Sunday morning near the turn of the century while my grandfather was preaching, he and all his parishioners momentarily may have conceived they witnessed one right before their very eyes.

Back in those days funerals were often held in churches and the funeral paraphernalia sometimes remained in the vestibule behind great folding doors that led to the main sanctuary.

My dad and his brother Al discovered a

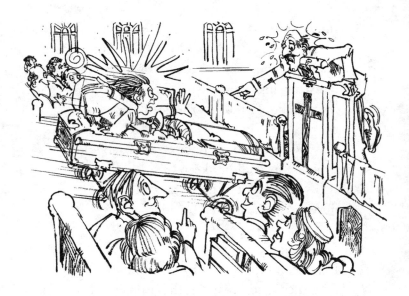

casket on rollers that Sunday morning and decided to have some fun rather than listen to their father preach. Dad suggested Al climb aboard the casket and he would push him around for a nice ride. Now as far back as I can remember, Uncle Al was huge. In school, the boys were known as Big Doward and Little Doward. It always seemed to me that Dad had more wit than weight. So that bright Sunday morning Al snuggled down in the silk-lined casket while his little brother wheeled him around making figure eights and all sorts of exciting maneuvers only a preacher's son could imagine. Al sat there grinning from ear to ear. But suddenly my dear Dad had a tremendous burst of inspiration. Why not send Al down the main aisle?

Before Al could change his mind and climb out, Dad quickly flung open the center folding doors and shoved the casket as hard as he could. I never learned what Grandfather's subject was that morning. Hopefully it was something appropriate because as Al sat bolt upright in that casket, he sailed directly down the aisle and struck the pulpit with such force that it startled all the dear saints.

Later that same Sunday, Grandfather did a little laying on of hands, and not in ordination either!

Yet as I have reflected on what happened, I've wondered if any spirited evangelist has ever thought of that idea for a live illustration.

• • • • •

Toilet paper ads invariably make their pitch

in favor of tissue softness. You seldom hear anything about the strength of the paper or its ability to withstand violent tugs and strains. Yet it is this very ability that permitted my father to make his unique appearance with the rest of the deacons prior to Communion service that memorable Sunday morning.

Dad had tried to coordinate his urgent visit to the men's room with the weekly entrance of the deacons to serve Communion. Since he was last in the two dozen deacon line-up, it seemed simple enough. There would be time for him to hurry up from the basement stairs and get in line with his partner in the narthex.

It was always such an impressive and dignified ceremonial entrance. The great pipe organ would fill the cavernous church with some pompous tunes while the deacons would march two by two down the long sloping aisle to the rostrum and peel off to flank the ornate Communion table with a dozen deacons on each side.

The organ started to play that morning as the deacons straightened their coats and ties and squared their shoulders preparatory for the grand entrance, when one of them glanced over at Dad at the last moment.

"Doward, what's that trailing behind you?" he whispered.

Somehow the toilet paper had hooked on Dad's suspender buttons and remained intact as he headed for the line-up. Yards and yards of the strong paper came off the roll. Nothing broke.

He had a line running all the way from the narthex to the men's room in the basement where still a remnant of the roll remained.

At that time, I was glad his deacon colleague had spotted the trouble and saved so much embarrassment. But years later, I've often wondered about the effect if Dad had made it all the way to the front. It certainly would have been a Communion service few would ever forget.

•　•　•　•　•

Old fashioned churches with belfries have always held a special appeal. The sound of a church bell ringing clear on a Sabbath morning holds a charm that evokes the very essence of poetry. But the person on the inside—assigned to the pulling of the rope—can turn the occasion into an embarrassing bit of personal prose.

In a church where I attended, a diminutive deacon energetically pulled so hard one Sabbath morning that the heavy bell swung clear over. Rather than let go his grip, he clung tenaciously to the end of the rope and was yanked clear to the ceiling. The folk in the lobby who witnessed this fascinating zipping-to-the-top then dropping-to-the-floor episode had a most difficult time entering the sanctuary with a straight face.

• • • • •

Postscript

The toughest test of self-control during those moments of unexpected humor occurs when everyone is watching.

I was asked to be the guest speaker at a statewide religious meeting in Iowa a few years ago. The meeting took place in a high school auditorium where the stage backdrop composed of long, colored burlap strips hung from the ceiling. It actually did resemble solid paneling.

Just as I was introduced, I happened to glance toward the left-hand wing. At that precise moment, a stage attendant tried to lean against what he thought was the wall. He flopped clear out of sight. All I could see were two feet sticking out from under the burlap. It was like a typical Hollywood sight gag.

Suddenly I was on! Nobody in the audience saw the accident except those in the balcony to my far right, and they were in stitches, which didn't help me a bit. Just glancing toward them almost triggered spasms of laughter from me. What to do? I adjusted my notes and then spied the grain of wood on the podium. Oh, how I studied that wood! Concentrate! Every ounce of my energy was momentarily diverted to that wood!

Later when I could reflect on the occasion it occurred to me to make a slight personal adjustment to Solomon's wise words. "When it's not time to laugh but it's funny anyway, concentrate on something else." Sometimes it's the only way out.

A few years after this little book was first published I received a long-distance call from a very upset lady who thought I had transgressed by relating any humor that happened in church.

"I'm sorry you feel this way, but these were all stories I have collected through the years. None were made-up, I did not relate any contrived humor or tell jokes, " I explained.

She still was not satisfied, so I continued. "Well, just what would you do if some unexpected funny thing happened during a religious service?"

"I might smile, " she answered firmly, "but I wouldn't laugh."

I felt extremely sorry for the woman. "You know," I said, "we were made for laughter, not for tears. Tears came after the entrance of sin."

That seemed to help a bit and we parted in at least a somewhat state of good will. I really hope she thought about God's gracious gift of pure, unadulterated laughter.

"It was so funny, I almost split in half trying not to laugh out loud in church!"

Have these stories reminded you of things you've seen? If you've witnessed a hilarious incident in church, write it down and send it in! We're collecting stories for a possible second book like *Even the Angels Must Laugh Again*. If you have a story to share, send it to:

Angels Must Laugh Editor
Pacific Press
PO Box 5353
Nampa, ID 83653

Or send it by e-mail to:
jertho@pacificpress.com

While we cannot acknowledge receipt of your story, each person submitting a story that is used in the book will receive a free copy of the book when it is published.

Share your laughter . . . and your love for your church family!

Clinical Management
of Neurogenic
Communicative
Disorders

Clinical Management of Neurogenic Communicative Disorders

Second Edition

Edited by

Donnell F. Johns, Ph.D.

Associate Professor of Surgery, Department of Surgery, Director of Clinical Research, Division of Plastic Surgery, and Clinical Associate Professor of Otorhinolaryngology, Southwestern Medical School, The University of Texas Health Science Center at Dallas; Clinical Attending Staff, Parkland Memorial Hospital, Baylor University Medical Center, and Children's Medical Center, Dallas, Texas

Little, Brown and Company
Boston/Toronto

For Carol Jean and Bridget Clare

Contents

Contributing Authors

Sara Haynes, M.S.
Chief of Speech-Language Pathology and Faculty Associate, Callier Center for Communication Disorders, University of Texas at Dallas, Dallas, Texas

Audrey L. Holland, Ph.D.
Professor of Communication and Research Assistant Professor of Psychiatry, University of Pittsburgh, Pittsburgh, Pennsylvania

Donnell F. Johns, Ph.D.
Associate Professor of Surgery, Department of Surgery, Director of Clinical Research, Division of Plastic Surgery, and Clinical Associate Professor of Otorhinolaryngology, Southwestern Medical School, The University of Texas Health Science Center at Dallas; Clinical Attending Staff, Parkland Memorial Hospital, Baylor University Medical Center, and Children's Medical Center, Dallas, Texas

Leonard L. LaPointe, Ph.D.
Professor and Chairman, Department of Speech and Hearing Science, Arizona State University, Tempe, Arizona; Consultant, Audiology and Speech Pathology Service, Veterans Administration Medical Center, Phoenix, Arizona, and Veterans Administration Outpatient Clinic, Los Angeles, California

John C. Rosenbek, Ph.D.
Adjunct Professor, Neurology, University of Wisconsin Medical School; Chief, Audiology-Speech Pathology, Veterans Administration Hospital, Madison, Wisconsin

Robert T. Wertz, Ph.D.
Adjunct Associate Professor, Department of Neurology, University of California at Davis, Davis; Chief, Audiology and Speech Pathology, Veterans Administration Medical Center, Martinez, California

Mark S. Ylvisaker, M.A.
Clinical Instructor, Department of Communication Disorders, University of Pittsburgh; Director, Speech-Language Therapy Department, The Rehabilitation Institute of Pittsburgh, Pittsburgh, Pennsylvania

Preface

More than a decade has passed since the writing of the first edition of *Clinical Management of Neurogenic Communicative Disorders*. The second edition is in response to the needs and demands of the academic community and practicing clinicians for an updated, practical, state-of-the-art guide for the evaluation and management of an increasing number of patients with neurogenic communicative disorders. The contributing authors are recognized scholars and authorities in the field, but, just as importantly, they are everyday practicing clinicians. Therefore, this second edition focuses on practicality. It provides a comprehensive review of the neuropathologies to serve as a textbook, and, at the same time, it presents practical guides to effective treatment strategies for the various neurogenic communicative disorders to serve as a therapeutic manual as well. A major thrust of this edition is to provide a source of information for thorough evaluation and proposed solutions to the perplexing problems presented by those patients with communication disorders as a result of neurologic impairment. To this end, representative case presentations are included, as well as a wealth of specific techniques contained in the text and appendixes. The clinical utility of this second edition is enhanced by an expanded number of photographs, charts, and forms.

I have been extremely privileged to be associated with the esteemed clinical scholars who contributed to this book; it could not have been accomplished without their timely suggestions and collective amicable cooperation. As a token of my appreciation, I would like to offer "Please put the ghosties in the refrigerblator." Domi vobiscum.

It is indeed a pleasant chore to recall help received from others: To Barbara Ward, former Allied Health Editor, Little, Brown and Company, for her cheerful cajoling and insistence in launching this edition; to Joyce I. Connell, Assistant Allied Health Editor, Little, Brown and Company, for her understanding, patience, and guidance; to Cynthia J. Baron, Book Editor, Little, Brown and Company, whose dogged persistence made it possible to avoid some of the stylistic hazards an author can put in the reader's way; and to Fritz E. Barton, Jr., M.D., Professor and Chairman, Division of Plastic Surgery, Southwestern Medical School, The University of Texas Health Science Center at Dallas, for his consistent support and for allowing me the time and freedom for this undertaking. My personal thanks are extended to Diane G. Woodley, Administrative Assistant, Division of Plastic

Surgery, Southwestern Medical School, The University of Texas Health Science Center at Dallas, for her valued assistance and pleasant demeanor throughout this sometimes arduous process and for generally keeping me humble and in my place. Finally, my thanks go to Dr. Frederic Louden Darley, who continues to serve as an inspiration to me.

D. F. J.

1

Neuropathologies of Speech and Language: An Introduction to Patient Management

Robert T. Wertz

Organization

Those who suffer speech or language deficits subsequent to neurologic damage display a variety of impaired listening, reading, speaking, and writing skills. These deficits can be consolidated under the general label *neuropathologies of communication* for convenience. Within this general classification exists a variety of behaviors that result from damage in different parts of the nervous system, have various causes, and, most important, necessitate different approaches to patient management. Speech pathologists are charged with providing these different approaches. Specifically, they must formulate definitions, make appropriate appraisals, arrive at diagnoses, state prognoses, and develop treatment programs for at least five different disorders—aphasia, the language of confusion, the language of generalized intellectual impairment, apraxia of speech, and the dysarthrias. The discussion that follows is an introduction to the steps involved in managing patients who demonstrate these neuropathologies of speech and language.

Some may quarrel with limiting the disorders to five; certainly, there are others. Myers [171] has called our attention to communication deficits demonstrated by patients who have suffered right hemisphere brain damage. Hagen [91] has discussed the speech pathologist's role in managing those who suffer closed head injury, and Ylvisaker and Holland expand this in Chapter 5. This introduction, however, will be confined to the five traditional disorders we have had sufficient experience with; the ones for which our data indicate we have something to offer our patients.

The task is twofold. First, the data are organized in terms of possible approaches to classifying and differentiating among the disorders; the confusion created by coexisting disorders and similarities among disorders is eliminated; and the data necessary for patient management (biographical, medical, speech, and language) are gathered and evaluated. Second, a definition, localization, cause, appraisal technique, diagnosis, prognosis, therapeutic focus, and a clinical example are given for each disorder. The intent is to provide sufficient background for the beginner, before he or she has had clinical experience; to provoke the experienced clinician to reappraise his or her approach in managing patients with neurologic disorders; and to inform medical and allied health professionals about the speech pathologist's role in rehabilitating them.

The Territory

Establishing the boundaries of the territory covered by neuropathologies of speech or language or both can be done in several ways. Limits can be set by defining the disorders, specifying the site of the lesion or damaged system causing the abnormal speech and language behavior, listing specific neurogenic disorders that disrupt communication, constructing a model that categorizes these disorders, or presenting performance profiles on measures designed to detect the disorders. A brief discussion of each approach follows.

DEFINITION. Defining neurogenic speech and language disorders is the same as defining anything else. A label (e.g., *aphasia*) is stated and its precise meaning is given. Before long the label is sufficient to trigger the definition in the listener's mind, and he or she will fill in the implied definition when the label is given. Frequently, however, several different labels may represent a single definition, which creates confusion. For example, Johns and LaPointe [118] list approximately 20 terms or phrases used to represent apraxia of speech. While there is remarkable similarity among the definitions, the labels are extremely divergent. Therefore, care is

exercised in defining the five disorders considered here. Table 1-1 shows definitions for the neuropathologies of speech and language identified by Darley [48].

Aphasia, the language of confusion, and the language of generalized intellectual impairment are *language disorders*; and apraxia of speech and the dysarthrias are *motor speech disorders*. This difference—language disorder versus motor speech disorder—is crucial in patient management. Although there is nothing magic about the word, or words, that constitute a label, there is something important about what a label implies, since the implications of labels and definitions (such as those listed in Table 1-1) dictate what is done in patient management. For example, therapies that are appropriate for aphasia are inappropriate for apraxia of speech [262].

LOCALIZATION. A second approach to organizing the data is to classify each disorder according to the neuroanatomic area or system involved (Fig. 1-1). For example, aphasia, the language of confusion, the language of generalized intellectual impairment, and apraxia of speech result from a lesion or lesions in the cerebral hemispheres, specifically

Table 1-1. Definitions for five neuropathologies of speech or language or both

Neuropathology	Definitions
Aphasia	Impairment, due to brain damage, of the capacity to interpret and formulate language symbols; a multimodal loss or reduction in decoding conventional meaningful linguistic elements (morphemes and larger syntactic units); disproportionate to impairment of other intellectual functions; not attributable to dementia, sensory loss, or motor dysfunction; manifested in reduced availability of vocabulary, reduced efficiency in applying syntactic rules, reduced auditory retention span, and impaired efficiency in input and output channel selection.
Language of confusion	Impairment of language accompanying neurologic conditions; often traumatically induced; characterized by reduced recognition and understanding of and responsiveness to the environment, faulty memory, unclear thinking, and disorientation in time and space. Structured language events are usually normal and responses utilize correct syntax; open-ended language situations elicit irrelevance, confabulation.
Language of generalized intellectual impairment	Deterioration of performance on more difficult language tasks; reduced efficiency in all modes; greater impairment evident in language tasks requiring better retention, closer attention, and powers of abstraction and generalization; degree of language impairment roughly proportionate to deterioration of other mental functions.
Apraxia of speech	An articulatory disorder resulting from impairment, as a result of brain damage, of the capacity to program the positioning of speech muscles and the sequencing of muscle movements for the volitional production of phonemes. No significant weakness, slowness, or incoordination of these muscles in reflex and automatic acts. Prosodic alterations may be associated with the articulatory problem, perhaps in compensation for it.
Dysarthrias	A group of speech disorders resulting from disturbances in muscular control—weakness, slowness, or incoordination—of the speech mechanism due to damage to the central or peripheral nervous system or both. The term encompasses coexisting neurogenic disorders of several or all the basic processes of speech: respiration, phonation, resonance, articulation, and prosody..

Source: Adapted from F. L. Darley, Aphasia: Input and output disturbances in speech and language processing. Presented in dual session on aphasia to the American Speech and Hearing Association, Chicago, Ill., 1969.

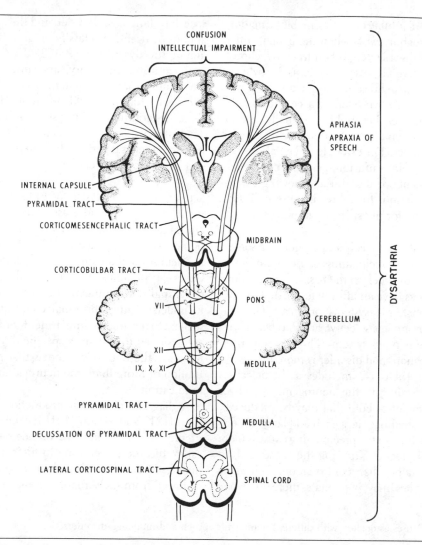

CONFUSION
INTELLECTUAL IMPAIRMENT

APHASIA
APRAXIA OF
SPEECH

INTERNAL CAPSULE
PYRAMIDAL TRACT
CORTICOMESENCEPHALIC TRACT

MIDBRAIN

DYSARTHRIA

CORTICOBULBAR TRACT

V
VII

PONS

CEREBELLUM

XII
IX, X, XI

MEDULLA

PYRAMIDAL TRACT
DECUSSATION OF PYRAMIDAL TRACT

MEDULLA

LATERAL CORTICOSPINAL TRACT

SPINAL CORD

Fig. 1-1. Localization of neuropathologies of speech and language, showing the language of confusion and the language of generalized intellectual impairment, resulting from bilateral hemispheric lesions; aphasia and apraxia of speech, resulting from unilateral left hemisphere lesions; and dysarthria, resulting from upper motor neuron, lower motor neuron, extrapyramidal, or cerebellar involvement.

cortical damage. Aphasia and apraxia are associated with unilateral left hemisphere lesions, whereas confusion and generalized intellectual impairment usually result from bilateral damage. Dysarthria, depending on the type, can result from impairment of the upper motor neuron system, the lower motor neuron system, the cerebellum, the extrapyramidal system, or combinations of these.

By classifying neurogenic speech and language disorders in terms of neuroanatomic localization, assumptions can be made about which disorder is most likely to be present. For example, if a patient is known to have sustained a left hemisphere cerebrovascular accident (CVA), one can speculate that the subsequent speech and language disorders, if they occur, will be aphasia, apraxia, or both. Confusion, generalized intellectual impairment, or a significant dysarthria is not common following a unilateral left hemisphere lesion. Similarly, the language disorders (aphasia, confusion, and generalized intellectual impairment) or the motor speech disorder (apraxia of speech) is not anticipated when involvement is localized to the lower motor neuron system. Thus the problem, if present, is dysarthria.

Localization as a means of classifying speech and language disorders breaks down when the injury is diffuse. Massive trauma or metastatic neoplasms may involve several neuroanatomic areas and systems, and the resultant speech and language disorders may be a jumble of unclassifiable symptoms. The same situation exists when the patient suffers from certain diseases (e.g., Huntington's chorea) that involve several areas or systems, or when a patient has a mixed disorder (e.g., a patient with Parkinson's disease who suffers a cerebrovascular accident in the left hemisphere). Finally, the location of the lesion does not automatically indicate a specific disorder. For example, bilateral cerebral damage may yield confusion, generalized intellectual impairment, or dysarthria. Knowing the location of the lesion, therefore, is more indicative than diagnostic for the speech pathologist.

CAUSE. Classifying speech and language disorders according to the precipitating cause is similar to classifying the disorder on the basis of localization. Many disorders have an affinity for disrupting specific neuroanatomic systems or areas. Unfortunately, others are less selective and can occur anywhere in the nervous system. Thus a comparison of cause, location, and disorder is more interesting than useful. Table 1-2 includes a list of causes classified according to the neurogenic speech or language disorder or both that may be produced.

Classifying neurogenic speech and language disorders on the basis of the precipitating cause is more general than precise. Knowing the cause leads to assumptions rather than confirmation. Too many pathologic states may precipitate more than one speech or language disorder; and the cause is probably most useful in classifying and differentiating among the dysarthrias [50–52]. Even here, however, caution is necessary, since disorders that may affect more than one system or area (e.g., CVA, neoplasm, trauma) yield different types of dysarthria, depending on the system or area involved. The influence and significance of the cause will be elaborated as it pertains to each of the five speech and language disorders later.

SPEECH AND LANGUAGE MODELS. Constructing a model to explain and classify neurogenic speech and language disorders has been a popular pastime. Some models [32] are used in an attempt to explain the neural mechanisms active in communication. Others [190] are used to diagram the author's view of normal communication and to serve as an aid in understanding abnormal communication subsequent to neurologic impairment. Still others [257] are designed to explain a specific disorder. Unfortunately, there are few models that permit classification of more than one neuropathology of communication.

A diagram of speech production proposed by Kent [121] and Hixon [101] has been adapted in Figure 1-2 to classify five neurogenic communication disorders according to their oral-expressive manifestations. Speech and language behavior can be traced from the semantic, syntactic, and lexical

Table 1-2. Causes associated with different neurogenic speech and language disorders

Cause	Speech and language disorders				
	Aphasia	Language of confusion	Language of generalized intellectual impairment	Apraxia of speech	Dysarthria
Cerebrovascular accidents	+	+	+	+	+
Neoplasm	+	+	?	+	+
Trauma	+	+	?	+	+
Infection	+	+	?	+	+
Diffuse CNS disease, e.g., Alzheimer's, Pick's, Jakob-Creutzfeldt	?	?	+	?	+
Metabolic disorders, e.g., myxedema, Wilson's	−	?	+	−	+
Deficiency diseases, e.g., Wernicke-Korsakoff's, pellagra	−	?	+	−	+
Toxins and drugs	−	+	+	−	+
Other diseases, e.g., multiple sclerosis, muscular dystrophies	−	−	−	−	+

+, associated with cause; −, not associated with cause; ?, association debatable.

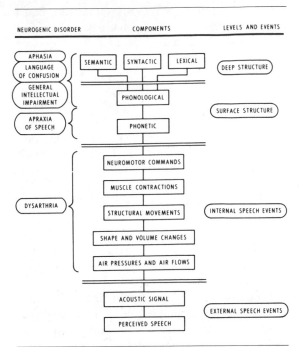

Fig. 1-2. Components and levels and events involved in different neuropathologies of speech and language. (Adapted from R. D. Kent, Study of vocal tract characteristics in the dysarthrias. Presented to the Veterans Administration Workshop on Motor Speech Disorders, Madison, Wis., 1976; T. Hixon, Respiratory-laryngeal evaluation. Presented to the Veterans Administration Workshop on Motor Speech Disorders, Madison, Wis., 1976.)

components (the deep structure of language) through the phonologic and phonetic components (the surface structure of language) to at least five other components that exist as internal speech events and, finally, to an acoustic signal, or perceived speech (external speech events). The path begins in the patient's cortex and ends in the clinician's laboratory instrument or ear. Aphasia, the language of confusion, and the language of generalized intellectual impairment will occur whenever a lesion or lesions disrupt the linguistic structures— both deep and surface. Apraxia of speech is a motor speech disorder that results when a pathologic process interferes with the phonetic component of surface structure. Dysarthria, another motor speech disorder, reveals itself as a result of abnormal internal speech events. The primary means of detecting the oral-expressive manifestations present in any of the five disorders is by instrumental analysis of the acoustic signal or by making perceptual judgments.

Obviously, the model is multidimensional. Three

separate processes—language, motor speech, and acoustic-perceptual—are linked. The first two processes are generated by the patient, and the last is observed by the clinician. Further, the model is limited to classifying oral output only. Similar representations could be constructed for writing and gesturing.

The model does have several useful clinical features. It demonstrates how different disorders may be observed. Language problems, the most internal of all pathologic processes, can be observed only in external events—how the patient gestures, talks, and writes. The same is true of apraxia of speech. Disrupted phonetic components are observed in the patient's speech. Dysarthria, however, may be observed externally as perceived speech or acoustically by analysis of the patient's speech and also internally by electromyography of muscle activity, cinefluorography of structural movements, transducer recordings of shape and volume changes, and manometric or respirometer recordings of air pressures and flows. Further, the model permits differentiation among disorders. For example, differences in the semantic, syntactic, lexical, and phonologic components assist in differentiating aphasia from confusion and generalized intellectual impairment. Apraxia of speech can be distinguished from dysarthria by observing impairment of the phonetic component in the absence of any deficits in the internal speech events of muscle contractions, structural movements, shape and volume changes, and air pressures and flows.

BEHAVIORAL PROFILES. Constructing a behavioral profile based on how a neurologically impaired patient performs on a speech and language test is another approach to organizing the data. A test of speech and language abilities is administered, the patient's performance is graphed or categorized, and, depending on the configuration of the graph or the description of the category, the patient is given a diagnostic label. This is similar to constructing a model. An attempt is made to differentiate among disorders based on the speech and language behavior displayed. Unlike models that arise from a heuristic, clinical, or theoretical position, differentiation according to behavioral profiles or categories is usually data-based. However, as in the model approach, most efforts are designed to differentiate within a disorder. Few schemes permit differentiation among disorders.

Schuell [218], Wepman and Jones [256], Luria [154], Goodglass and Kaplan [85], and Kertesz [128] have developed behavioral profiles for categorizing different types of aphasia. Johns and Darley [117] list behavioral criteria for differentiating apraxia of speech from dysarthria. Darley, Aronson, and Brown [50–52] use perceptual speech characteristics to categorize different types of dysarthria.

Few approaches permit classifying more than two different neurogenic speech and language disorders according to behavioral profiles. Halpern, Darley, and Brown [92], however, used performance on an adaptation of Schuell's [220] short examination for aphasia to compare aphasia, the language of confusion, the language of generalized intellectual impairment, and apraxia of speech. Five speech and language behaviors—reading comprehension, auditory retention span, fluency, writing to dictation, and relevance—appeared to differentiate among the four disorders. Salient speech and language features for each disorder were impaired auditory retention span and fluency in aphasia; impaired reading comprehension, writing to dictation, and relevance in the language of confusion; impaired reading comprehension in the language of generalized intellectual impairment; and fluency in apraxia. The authors say their groups were not equal in the extent of cerebral involvement or the severity of speech and language deficits.

Porch [187, 190] has developed a system for plotting speech and language performance by aphasic patients. The data are furnished by the patient's performance on the Porch Index of Communicative Ability (PICA), a battery of 18 gestural, verbal, and writing subtests that employs a 16-point multidimensional scoring system. A mean score for each subtest is plotted according to the difficulty of the tests (ranked response summary) or the mode of expression (gestural, verbal, graphic) necessary for performance (modality response summary). Based on the performance of 280 aphasic patients, Porch has developed behavioral profiles that represent aphasia, aphasia resulting from bilateral damage, aphasia with severe formulation difficulty, aphasia with dysarthria, aphasia with impaired verbal monitoring, aphasia complicated by illiteracy, and an aberrant pattern.

Figure 1-3 shows PICA modality response profiles for patients diagnosed as displaying aphasia, the language of confusion, the language of generalized intellectual impairment, apraxia of speech, and dysarthria. Each patient's diagnosis was based on a variety of information (biographical data, medical history, and examination) and a battery of speech, language, and intelligence measures. Thus the PICA profiles constitute only one piece of information in each patient's appraisal. However, since the different patterns assisted in making each diagnosis, they serve as an example of how behavioral profiles are used to differentiate among neurogenic speech and language disorders.

Behavioral profiles, like other ways to organize data, are more indicative than definitive. Profiles from patients showing different speech and language disorders do differ; however, at present, these differences are not sufficiently distinct to permit a differential diagnosis based on the profile observed. Refinement in testing methods and acquisition of empirical data may improve this approach.

Confusion among Disorders

Two major sources of confusion hamper differentiation of neurogenic speech and language disorders. First, some patients have coexisting disorders. For example, it is common for a patient to demonstrate apraxia of speech with coexisting

---

Fig. 1-3. A. PICA modality response summary for an aphasic patient. Language deficits are present in all communicative modes: auditory comprehension, subtests VI and X; reading, subtests V and VII; speaking, subtests I, IV, IX, and XII; and writing, subtests A to F. **B.** PICA modality response summary for a patient demonstrating the language of confusion. Little difficulty was displayed on gestural and verbal subtests; however, unusual responses were given on graphic subtests. Poorer performance is seen on easier subtests, C to E, than on B, a more difficult subtest. Irrelevance and confabulation characterized many responses, e.g., writing brand names instead of copying printed words on subtest E. **C.** PICA modality response summary for a patient demonstrating the language of generalized intellectual impairment. Deficits are seen on the two reading tasks, subtests V and VII, and on all writing tasks. The patient was premorbidly literate and had adequate visual acuity. **D.** PICA modality response summary for a patient showing apraxia of speech with mild to moderate aphasia. Verbal responses were characterized by numerous self-corrections, phonetically related responses, and distorted responses. **E.** PICA modality response summary for a patient showing severe dysarthria. Auditory comprehension, subtests VI and X; reading, subtests V and VII; and writing, subtests A to E, were essentially normal. All verbal responses were either unintelligible or partially intelligible related responses. (All PICA forms are from B. E. Porch, *The Porch Index of Communicative Ability*. Palo Alto, Calif.: Consulting Psychologists Press, 1967. Reproduced by special permission of the publisher.)

Porch Index of Communicative Ability

MODALITY RESPONSE SUMMARY

Name R. S.   Case No.

Age 58   Birthdate 1/19/17   Sex M   Race   Handedness ®️ L Used

Diagnosis CVA Left Hemisphere   Onset 5/29/75

Date   Overall   Gestural   Verbal   Graphic

Date   Overall   Gestural   Verbal   Graphic

Date 8/6/75   Overall 10.64   Gestural 12.73   Verbal 11.20   Graphic 7.50

GESTURAL   VERBAL   GRAPHIC

II III V VI VII VIII X XI I IV IX XII A B C D E F

Published by

CONSULTING PSYCHOLOGISTS PRESS

577 College Avenue   Palo Alto, California

Note

A

Porch Index of Communicative Ability

MODALITY RESPONSE SUMMARY

Name C. H.   Case No.

Age 62   Birthdate 8/12/12   Sex M   Race   Handedness ®️ R Used

Diagnosis Postsurgical - Olfactory Groove   Onset Surgery 10/17/74

Meningioma

Date   Overall   Gestural   Verbal   Graphic

Date   Overall   Gestural   Verbal   Graphic

Date 11/1/74   Overall 13.57   Gestural 14.49   Verbal 14.03   Graphic 12.05

GESTURAL   VERBAL   GRAPHIC

II III V VI VII VIII X XI I IV IX XII A B C D E F

Published by

CONSULTING PSYCHOLOGISTS PRESS

577 College Avenue   Palo Alto, California

Note

B

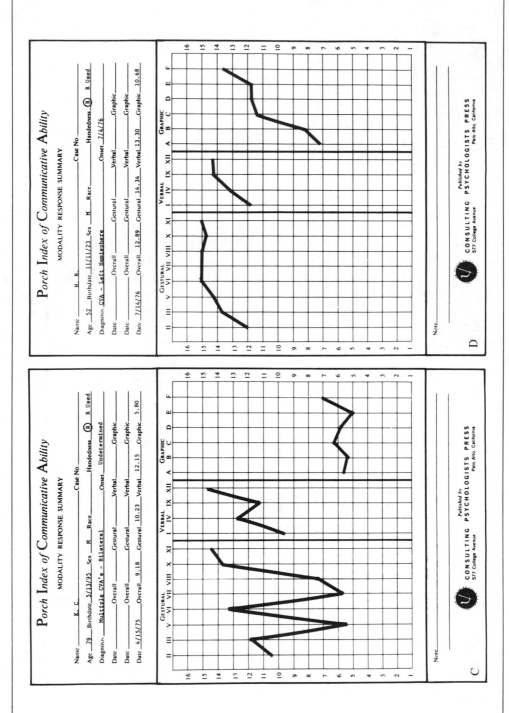

Fig. 1-3 (CONTINUED)

8

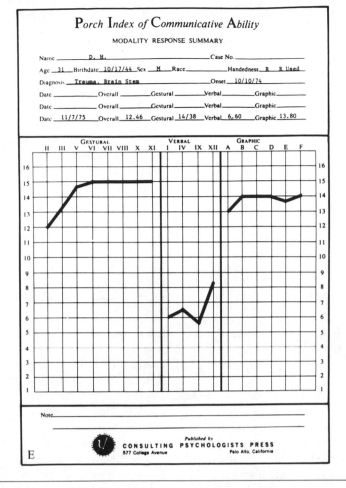

Porch **I**ndex of **C**ommunicative **A**bility

MODALITY RESPONSE SUMMARY

Name _____ D. H. _____ Case No. _____
Age _31_ Birthdate _10/17/44_ Sex _M_ Race _____ Handedness_R_ R Used _____
Diagnosis __Trauma, Brain Stem_____ Onset _10/10/74_
Date _____ Overall _____ Gestural _____ Verbal _____ Graphic_____
Date _____ Overall _____ Gestural _____ Verbal _____ Graphic_____
Date _11/7/75_ Overall_12.46_ Gestural_14/38_ Verbal_6.60_ Graphic_13.80_

Note_____

Published by
CONSULTING PSYCHOLOGISTS PRESS
577 College Avenue   Palo Alto, California

E

Fig. 1-3 (CONTINUED)

aphasia. The motor speech disorder interacts with the oral-expressive manifestations of the language disorder, and the result may be quite different from the verbal deficits observed in either problem alone. Second, many disorders share the same speech and language symptoms. For example, Porch [188] observed that aphasic patients show greater deficits on more difficult communicative tasks than on easier ones. The same may be true of patients demonstrating the language of generalized intellectual impairment. Thus the occurrence of coexisting disorders and the similarity of symptoms among disorders present diagnostic problems.

COEXISTING DISORDERS. The coexistence of neurogenic speech and language disorders has been acknowledged by many. Darley [43, 45] and Mohr [167, 168] give reasonable explanations of the coexistence of apraxia of speech and Broca's aphasia. Aten, Johns, and Darley [7] reported on patients

demonstrating apraxia with, probably, coexisting aphasia observable in their auditory comprehension abilities. Critchley [38] discusses dysarthriclike speech in the demented. Schuell [218] recognized coexisting disorders in at least two of her prognostic groups: (1) group 4, aphasia with scattered findings compatible with generalized brain damage, and (2) minor syndrome B, mild aphasia with persisting dysarthria.

Little empirical evidence exists to document the presence of coexisting disorders. Reports are typically clinical observations or retrospective reviews of a series of cases. Wertz, Rosenbek, and Deal [265] determined the incidence of apraxia of speech alone and in combination with aphasia or dysarthria or both. Data on the 176 adults in their sample are shown in Figure 1-4. Sixty-five percent of the sample demonstrated apraxia of speech combined with aphasia, 14 percent displayed apraxia combined with aphasia and dysarthria, 13 percent had apraxia only, and 8 percent showed apraxia

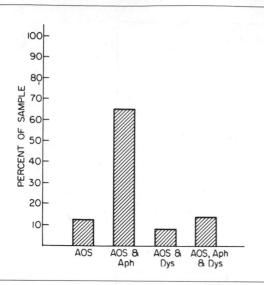

Fig. 1-4. Percent of sample reported by Wertz, Rosenbek, and Deal [265], showing apraxia of speech; apraxia of speech and aphasia; apraxia of speech and dysarthria; and apraxia of speech, aphasia, and dysarthria. Data indicate the common occurrence of coexisting neuropathologies of speech.

and dysarthria. This report indicates that mixed disorders are quite common.

The presence of more than one neurogenic communication disorder creates diagnostic, prognostic, and treatment problems. First, the patient who suffers more than one disorder may have such jumbled speech and language that diagnosis of the specific problems is impossible. For example, a patient with severe aphasia characterized, in part, by limited auditory comprehension may negate diagnosis of a coexisting apraxia of speech. His or her verbal output may be too sparse to obtain a sufficient sample for a diagnosis, or limited auditory comprehension may contaminate all verbal responses elicited on repetition tasks. Second, accurate prognosis is difficult when faced with a "pure" disorder; and the presence of mixed problems makes an accurate prognosis even more difficult. For example, Schuell's prognostic groups [218] do not predict for the patient with aphasia and apraxia of speech. However, she does predict recovery for generalized brain damage, prognostic group 4, which probably results in generalized intellectual impairment as well as aphasia, and for minor syndrome B, aphasia accompanied by dysarthria. Third, the treatment employed is dictated by the disorder. Rosenbek and Wertz [206] suggest that aphasia therapy administered to remediate apraxia is doomed to failure;

coexisting disorders require coexisting treatments. However, the verbal repetition drills that are effective with some apraxic and dysarthric patients are not possible when the patient suffers coexisting auditory comprehension problems associated with aphasia.

Thus confusion exists when neurogenic speech and language problems coexist, and the presence of coexisting disorders is not rare. To make a diagnosis, each disorder is identified, the severity of each is documented, and the contribution of each disorder to the overall communicative deficit is determined. The prognosis depends on whether ultimate recovery can be predicted for each disorder present, as well as for the combined communicative deficit resulting from the interaction between or among disorders. Finally, the treatment involves developing appropriate methods for remedying each of the problems present. The methods that are appropriate to evoke a change in one of the problems must also be applicable within the limits imposed by the coexisting problems.

SIMILAR SYMPTOMS. Additional clinical confusion is created when dissimilar neuropathologies of communication have symptoms that appear to be similar. This occurrence creates a diagnostic dilemma, because patient management varies with different disorders.

The literature offers some help in differentiating disorders that have similar symptoms. Unfortunately, even the best available help does not eliminate all ambiguity. For example, Johns and Darley [117] have listed the articulatory characteristics of apraxia of speech and dysarthria. Application of these characteristics assists in determining whether the motor speech problem observed results from difficulty in programming motor speech movements (apraxia of speech) or from weakness, slowness, incoordination, and a restricted range of movement (dysarthria). Thus apparently similar articulatory deficits can be compared, differentiated, and properly diagnosed. However, LaPointe and Wertz [136] report that the task is difficult because of the similarity of symptoms among the two disorders. More difficulty is experienced when attempting to differentiate apraxia of speech from some of the oral-expressive manifestations of aphasia. Some of the paraphasias described by Goodglass and Kaplan [85, 86] may masquerade as apraxia. Further, reading and writing deficits present in the language of generalized intellectual impairment are similar to those demonstrated by some aphasic patients. Finally, when a patient is disoriented in terms of the time, date, and place, the question becomes: Is he or she displaying symptoms of confusion, dementia, aphasia, or the result of an unplanned vacation into a serious illness that has removed the patient from temporal and physical reality?

Few empirical efforts have been made to differentiate among several different neuropathologies of speech and language. Halpern, Darley, and Brown's [92] report is almost a solitary example of comparing and contrasting more than two different disorders. While they were successful in differentiating among patients displaying aphasia, the language of confusion, generalized intellectual impairment, or apraxia of speech, the report also supports the view that all have some similar symptoms. Their data were grouped into 10 categories—auditory retention span, auditory comprehension, reading comprehension, naming, writing to dictation, arithmetic, syntax, adequacy, relevance, and fluency. Five of these—auditory retention span, fluency, auditory comprehension, writing to dictation, and relevance—assisted in differentiating

among the disorders. The rankings are shown in Table 1-3.

Even though some categories identified certain groups, Table 1-3 indicates a good deal of similarity of symptoms among all the groups. For example, the aphasic and confused language groups were impaired in all 10 categories. The generalized intellectual impairment and apraxia of speech groups were impaired in seven of the 10 categories. Thus all four groups show some degree of impairment in seven of the 10 categories. This suggests a good deal of similarity among disorders and, faced with individual patients displaying a wide range of overall severity, the clinician will find that these similarities may make differential diagnosis extremely difficult.

The Data

Management of patients who have neuropathologies of communication requires systematic collection of biographical, medical, and behavioral data to make a diagnosis, formulate a prognosis, and, if warranted, focus therapy. The data collection process is called *appraisal. Diagnosis*, or putting a

Table 1-3. Language categories useful in differentiating among different disorders[a]

Rank[b]	Aphasia	General intellectual impairment	Apraxia of speech	Confused language
1	Adequacy	Adequacy	Adequacy	Arithmetic
2	*Auditory retention*	*Reading comprehension*	*Fluency*	*Reading comprehension*
3	Arithmetic	Arithmetic	Arithmetic	*Writing to dictation*
4	Auditory[c] comprehension and	Auditory comprehension	Syntax	*Relevance*
5	fluency	*Auditory retention*	Auditory[c] comprehension and	Adequacy
6[d]	Naming	Naming	Writing to dictation	Auditory comprehension
7	Syntax	Syntax	Auditory retention	Syntax
8	*Reading comprehension*	Relevance and	Naming	Naming
9	*Writing to dictation*	*Writing to dictation*	Reading comprehension	*Auditory retention*
10	*Relevance*	*Fluency*	Relevance	*Fluency*

[a]Language categories useful in differentiating among disorders listed in italics.
[b]Rank order is in severity, where 1 is most impaired and 10 is least impaired.
[c]Categories in brackets were equally impaired.
[d]Mean percent impairment.
Source: Adapted from H. Halpern, F. L. Darley, and J. R. Brown, Differential language and neurological characteristics in cerebral involvement. *J. Speech Hear. Disord.* 38 : 162, 1973.

label on the disrupted communication, is made by the clinician. Tests, whether they are medical or behavioral, are not used to diagnose, but rather to appraise. *Prognosis* is an exercise in predicting the future. Based on the diagnosis made, the information collected, and what is known to influence change in the disorder observed, the clinician predicts recovery, or the lack of it. *Focusing therapy* means where therapy begins and what is worked on. All three sources of data—biographical, medical, and behavioral—influence the focus of therapy.

BIOGRAPHICAL DATA. Obvious biographical data include the patient's name and address, the name of a responsible representative, age at onset, years of education, date of onset, and occupational status. Additional useful information is listed in Table 1-4. Some of these data have diagnostic significance. For example, if a patient was premorbidly illiterate, his or her postmorbid reading and writing skills will reflect the lack of education. The clinician must determine whether reading and writing deficits subsequent to brain damage represent severe aphasia, the language of generalized intellectual impairment, or premorbid illiteracy. Further, premorbid speech and language deficits may influence the diagnosis. For example, stuttering is frequently linked with certain neuropathologies of speech [205]. Obviously, stuttering can also exist

in patients who have not suffered neurogenic impairment. It is necessary to know if the stuttering-like behavior observed in a patient who has suffered a neurologic insult existed premorbidly or if it arose subsequent to the damage.

Some biographical information has prognostic significance. For example, age, education, handedness, intelligence, and social milieu may influence recovery from aphasia [47]. Premorbid communicativeness and premorbid and present motivation and cooperation also could be added to the list. Brain-injured patients do not understand, read, speak, or write more or better than they did premorbidly even after lengthy "successful" treatment. Moreover, patients' motivation and cooperation influence their desire for and participation in treatment and thus influence the prognosis.

Biographical information influences the focusing of therapy. For example, education, intelligence, occupational background, and premorbid communicative ability dictate which communicative skills are emphasized, the content of treatment stimuli, and what level of proficiency is strived for. The patient's premorbid language determines whether English or some other more frequently used language should constitute the treatment stimuli. Also, the patient's marital status and living environment influence whether home assignments are included as part of the treatment program.

Table 1-4. Biographical data

Dimension	Sample attributes
Handedness (premorbid and present)	Right, left, ambidextrous
Racial/ethnic group	White, black, Oriental, Spanish-American, American Indian, etc.
Marital status (premorbid and present)	Single, married, widowed, separated, divorced
Occupational status (premorbid and present)	Wage earner, full time; wage earner, part time; retired; student; unemployed
Highest occupational level attained	Professional, executive, managerial, administrative, middle management, clerical, skilled manual, unskilled manual, etc.
Premorbid communicativeness	Superior, high, above average, average, below average, low, uncommunicative
Premorbid intelligence	Superior, above normal, normal, below normal
Premorbid language (list in order of acquisition)	English, Spanish, German, Polish, etc.
Language usage (premorbid and present)	English only language used, English only used but converted from indicated language, English used but infrequent use of indicated language, etc.
Environment (premorbid and present)	Own dwelling with others, own dwelling alone, dwelling of another person, acute hospital, chronic hospital, etc.
Motivation (premorbid and present)	High, above average, average, below average, low
Cooperation (premorbid and present)	High, above average, average, below average, low
Cooperation of persons in living environment	High, above average, average, below average, low
Premorbid speech and language deficits	Stuttering, articulation, hearing, etc.

Source: Adapted from R. T. Wertz et al., Veterans Administration cooperative study on aphasia: A comparison of individual and group treatment. *J. Speech Hear. Res.* 24 : 580, 1981.

MEDICAL DATA. Medical data also have diagnostic, prognostic, and treatment implications. Relevant medical dimensions and sample attributes are listed in Table 1-5. First, the speech pathologist wants to know the patient's complete neurologic diagnosis, including the specific cause, location, and extent of the lesion; previous neurologic episodes; and other major medical diagnoses. Second, a report of visual, auditory, and tactile acuity is essential. Third, information on reflexes; signs of brainstem involvement; presence of limb weakness, spasticity, and incoordination; and clinical data, including x-ray, electroencephalogram (EEG), brain scan, computed tomography (CT) scan, positron computed tomography, nuclear magnetic resonance, lumbar puncture, angiogram, and others, may be important. Finally, knowledge of the patient's medications, their effects, and whether they are administered to control seizures is necessary.

The cause, location of the lesion, and presence or absence of brainstem involvement influence diagnosis. For example, massive head trauma, metastatic neoplasm, and infection may imply bilateral involvement, which indicates the language of confusion or the language of generalized intellectual impairment. A single unilateral left hemisphere CVA probably limits the diagnosis to aphasia, apraxia of speech, or a combination of the two. Brainstem involvement might imply coexisting dysarthria. Laboratory data offer support for the location and extent of the patient's lesion.

The cause, coexisting major medical disorders, and a history of previous episodes have prognostic relevance. Eisenson [67, 69] reported that patients with nonpenetrating head trauma have a better prognosis than those with neoplasms or cerebrovascular lesions. Further, patients in good health and physical condition immediately after onset have a better chance of improvement than those who have persisting illness or physical limitations. Fi-

Table 1-5. Medical data

Dimension	Sample attributes
Present cause	CVA, trauma, neoplastic, infectious, etc.
Coexisting neurogenic diagnoses	Previous CVA, vasculitis, metastases, neurogenic diseases (e.g., multiple sclerosis, Parkinson's disease), etc.
Coexisting major medical problems	Pneumonia, cardiac conditions, respiratory conditions, diabetes, etc.
Complete diagnosis	Thrombosis of middle cerebral artery with right hemiplegia, hemisensory defect, hemianopsia, expressive aphasia; etc.
Localization of lesion	Left hemisphere or right hemisphere (frontal, temporal, parietal, occipital); bilateral; brainstem; cerebellar; etc.
Vision	Acuity: right and left eyes (20/20, 20/30, etc., corrected and uncorrected)
	Field abnormalities: right and left (homonymous hemianopsia, superior or inferior quadrant, monocular central or paracentral scotoma, etc.)
Hearing	Acuity: right and left (conductive, sensorineural, mixed; severity; duration; etiology; aided or unaided)
	Discrimination: right and left (percent impaired, aided and unaided)
Reflexes	Right and left; upper and lower extremities; increased, decreased, normal; abnormalities (e.g., snout, jaw); etc.
Signs of brainstem involvement	Right and left: facial weakness (upper, lower, total), facial sensory loss, nystagmus, dysarthria, dysphagia, etc.
Limb involvement	Right and left, upper and lower: weakness, spasticity, coordination, involuntary movements.
Sensory deficit	Right and left, upper and lower: vibratory, position, superficial (pain or touch), discriminatory (stereognosis—figure writing), double simultaneous stimulation (extinction)
Gait impairment	Ambulatory, nonambulatory, ataxic, etc.
Neurologist's estimate of language impairment	Severity (none, mild, moderate, marked, severe); type (Broca's, Wernicke's, etc.)
Mental status	Mood abnormalities (depression, anxiety, euphoria), intellectual impairment
Laboratory findings	Skull x-ray, EEG, brain scan, CT scan, PET scan, NMR, spinal tap, angiogram, ECG, etc.
Medications	Types, dosage, duration

Source: Adapted from R. T. Wertz et al., Veterans Administration cooperative study on aphasia: A comparison of individual and group treatment. *J. Speech Hear. Res.* 24 : 580, 1981.

nally, patients who have suffered a single episode have a brighter prognosis than those with a history of multiple episodes.

Peripheral auditory, visual, or tactile involvement will dictate which sensory modalities are stimulated in treatment and, therefore, influence therapy's focus. Visual-field abnormalities require teaching patients to learn to attend to the involved peripheral area. Certain medications have a sedating effect and may require special stimulation techniques to improve attention. Mental status, including mood abnormalities and intellectual ability, dictates the type of treatment administered and, perhaps, its content. For example, depressed, anxious, or euphoric patients require treatment tasks, criteria for success, and procedures different from those employed with patients demonstrating more stable personality characteristics. Further, intellectual impairment not only has diagnostic significance but also dictates the general approach used— learning versus general facilitation—and performance requirements.

LANGUAGE, SPEECH, AND INTELLECTUAL DATA. The speech pathologist provides language and speech data, and, in the absence of a psychologist or a neuropsychologist, the intellectual data. Table 1-6 lists areas to be appraised, sample tests and tasks for each area, and reference sources for the examples given.

Since the purpose of the initial appraisal is to gather sufficient information to make a diagnosis, formulate a prognosis, and focus therapy, it is more comprehensive than subsequent evaluations made for other purposes (e.g., determining the effects of treatment).

All patients referred for speech and language evaluation should receive one or more of the tests listed in Table 1-6 under General Language Ability. Goodglass and Kaplan's [85] Boston Diagnostic Aphasia Examination (BDAE) and Kertesz's [127] Western Aphasia Battery (WAB) are useful to confirm localization information requested by the neurologist and to classify the type of aphasia. The Comprehensive Examination for Aphasia devel-

Table 1-6. Comprehensive evaluation of language, speech, and intellect

Dimension	Sample tests and tasks	Reference
General language ability	Boston Diagnostic Aphasia Examination	Goodglass and Kaplan [85]
	Western Aphasia Battery	Kertesz [127]
	Comprehensive Examination for Aphasia	Spreen and Benton [237]
	Examining for Aphasia	Eisenson [68]
	Language Modalities Test for Aphasia	Wepman and Jones [256]
	Minnesota Test for Differential Diagnosis of Aphasia	Schuell [219]
	Porch Index of Communicative Ability	Porch [187]
"Functional" language ability	Functional Communication Profile	Sarno [216]
	Communicative Abilities in Daily Living	Holland [106]
	Rating of Conversational Ability	Clinician's assessment
Motor speech evaluation	Vowel prolongation, rapid alternating movements, word repetition, sentence repetition, picture description, oral reading, oral-nonverbal movements, serial speech tasks	Darley, Aronson, and Brown [50], Eisenson [68], Goodglass and Kaplan [85], Schuell [219], Wertz, LaPointe, and Rosenbek [262]
Orientation and general information	Time, place, date; autobiographical data, general knowledge	Goodglass and Kaplan [85], Schuell [219]. Clinician's assessment
Nonverbal intelligence	Coloured Progressive Matrices	Raven [195]
	Symbol Digit Modalities Test	Smith [231]
	Wisconsin Card Sorting Task	Grant and Berg [87]
Special tests		
Auditory comprehension	Token Test	DeRenzi and Vignolo [62]
	Revised Token Test	McNeil and Prescott [161]
Verbal fluency	Word Fluency Measure	Borkowski, Benton, and Spreen [26]
Reading comprehension	Reading Comprehension Battery for Aphasia	LaPointe and Horner [113]
Motor speech	Structural functional examination and special systems test	Rosenbek and Wertz [207]

Source: Adapted from R. T. Wertz, Appraisal and Diagnosis in Aphasia: Evaluating the Effects of Treatment. In M. Sullivan and M. S. Kommers (eds.), *Rationale for Adult Aphasia Therapy*. Omaha: University of Nebraska Medical Center, 1977.

oped by Spreen and Benton [237] samples a variety of behaviors and provides some normative data. Eisenson's Examining for Aphasia [68] is comprehensive and is an excellent tool for bedside screening. The Language Modalities Test for Aphasia [256] permits classification by the type of language impairment (e.g., pragmatic and semantic) and is unique in its use of projected stimuli. Schuell's Minnesota Test for Differential Diagnosis of Aphasia (MTDDA) [219] provides an abundance of auditory, visual and reading, speech and language, and writing tasks designed to sample all levels of severity. In addition, the results can be used to formulate a prognosis based on Schuell's five categories and two minor syndromes. The PICA [187] employs a multidimensional scoring system that preserves and quantifies a large portion of the patient's responses. It is sensitive to and is reliable in demonstrating changes in a patient's behavior. Brookshire [28] presents a complete analytic discussion of several of the measures listed in Table 1-6, and Darley [44] provides reviews of several tests for language impairment in adults.

It may be necessary to use parts of different tests to extend one's observations. Selective combining of subtests from different examinations will permit a range of tasks sufficient to sample all levels of severity. Although most of those listed were designed to measure aphasia, each contains subtests that are appropriate for appraising the other four neuropathologies of speech.

A neglected area of appraisal is adequate assessment of the patient's "functional" language ability. There are patients who communicate adequately in the waiting room and, later, in a test situation, tell you one "scratches his sand with a toothbrush." Similarly, the discrepancy between a patient's wife's report of her husband's good auditory comprehension at home and the clinician's knowledge of his marked auditory deficits on a treatment task is difficult to explain. There are many severely involved patients who function well in the real world, and, conversely, some who do well on treatment tasks but cannot find the path from their sixth-floor ward to the clinic on the second floor. We lack tools to measure and explain these inconsistencies.

Sarno's [216] Functional Communication Profile (FCP) is one of the few instruments designed to assess the aphasic patient's functional language ability. By direct observation or a nonstructured interview, the clinician rates five areas—move-

ment, speaking, understanding, reading, and other—on a nine-point scale, ranging from no ability to normal. Percentage scores are obtained for each area as well as for an overall percentage score. The FCP should provide information about how patients interact with others and their environment.

Holland [106] has also provided a measure of "functional" communication. Her Communicative Abilities in Daily Living (CADL) was designed to assess communication used in everyday encounters. Several behaviors—reading; writing; using numbers to estimate, calculate, and judge time; speech acts; utilizing verbal and nonverbal context; role-playing; sequence- and relationship-dependent communicative behavior; social conventions; divergences, the ability to generate logical possibilities; nonverbal symbolic communication; movement-related or movement-dependent communicative behavior; and humor, absurdity, or metaphor—are evaluated. The CADL was validated by comparing clinical performance by a sample of patients with what they were observed to do when followed through their daily routines and environments. A patient's CADL performance can be compared with normative data for normal adults and five types of aphasia—global, mixed, Wernicke's, Broca's, and anomic.

Another method of evaluating functional language ability is the clinician's judgment expressed on a multipoint rating scale. If one is interested in how well a patient converses, for example, conversing with him or her and rating the performance is a rational approach. The Veterans Administration Cooperative Study on Aphasia [260] employed a measure of this type. Patients were engaged in 3 to 5 minutes of conversation, and observers rated performance on a scale of 1 (normal) to 7 (severe deficit).

Two of the neuropathologies of speech being considered here, apraxia of speech and dysarthria, require a motor speech evaluation to detect their presence and severity. Darley, Aronson, and Brown [50] suggest ways of evaluating dysarthria, and Johns and Darley [117] and Wertz, LaPointe, and Rosenbek [262] list procedures for appraising apraxia of speech. Several of the "general language ability" tests [68, 85, 219] include tasks that sample motor speech abilities.

Apraxia of speech should reveal itself during rapid production of combined monosyllables (e.g., /pʌtʌkʌ/), repetition of multisyllabic words, repetition of words of increasing length (e.g., thick, thicker, thickening), oral reading, and picture description. Dysarthria becomes apparent during vowel prolongation, rapid alternating movements, oral reading, and picture description. Regardless of the task or tests employed, patterns of behavior are more important than specific test scores.

Orientation and general information are useful in appraising the presence of confusion and generalized intellectual impairment. These include orientation in terms of time, place, and date; ability to give autobiographical information (e.g., date of birth, home town); and fund of general knowledge (e.g., presidents, present and past; geographic location of large countries). As observed previously, the aphasic patient with impaired auditory comprehension and reduced verbal output may fail these tasks; however, he or she is distinguished by this lack of response. The confused patient is depicted by the misinformation he or she gives, and the patient with generalized intellectual impairment reveals a lack of information.

Appraising intellectual impairment in neurologically impaired adults is difficult. By definition, we expect the patient with generalized intellectual impairment to display intellectual deficits. The association between aphasia and intelligence is not clear. Lebrun and Hoops [142] summarize the lack of consensus in this area. We do not expect patients with motor speech disorders, apraxia of speech, and dysarthria to display coexisting intellectual deficits. However, if the motor speech disorder results from hemispheric involvement, the damage that disrupts speech may also disrupt intelligence. Further, the confused patient may have no intellectual deficit; however, his or her tendency to confabulate, lapse into irrelevance, and misinterpret instructions may result in poor performance on intellectual tests. Finally, aphasic patients' language impairment handicaps them on most traditional intelligence measures. Nonverbal intelligence measures have been the tests of choice for neurologically impaired adults; however, even these are suspect. Performance will probably vary from one nonverbal measure to another, depending on the amount of verbal mediation required or whether the stimuli may be given verbal labels.

A popular measure for estimating nonverbal intellect is Raven's Coloured Progressive Matrices [195]. The tasks require intact visual input, a minimum of auditory comprehension, and a gestural response. The Symbol Digit Modalities Test developed by Smith [231] is equally nonverbal for stimuli and instructions. However, the patient must be able to write numbers or say them. Grant and Berg developed the Wisconsin Card Sorting Task [87], which provides information on patients' ability to formulate a strategy for problem solving, utilize feedback, and improve their performance on subsequent trials.

Special tests are designed to evaluate areas of specific disability or strength. The measures listed in Table 1-6 are limited to auditory comprehension, verbal language, reading, and motor speech abilities. Additional instruments exist or could be designed to explore gestural and writing performance. Auditory comprehension deficits may go undetected on the auditory comprehension subtests contained in general language ability tests. For example, a patient may show no impairment on auditory subtests of the PICA, but he or she may have extreme difficulty with the longer, more complex items in the Token Test developed by DeRenzi and Vignolo [62] or McNeil and Prescott's Revised Token Test [161]. Thus the Token Test demonstrates that it is what it is reported to be, a sensitive test to detect receptive disturbances in aphasia. Similarly, the Word Fluency Measure developed by Borkowski, Benton, and Spreen [26] expands our ability to measure word-finding. The patient is asked to say all the words he or she can think of in 1 minute beginning with a given letter. Patients are limited only by their expressive vocabulary and the temporal confines of the test. The task is useful for evaluating minimally involved patients who demonstrate no difficulty on the verbal subtests of the general language ability tests.

LaPointe and Horner's [133] Reading Comprehension Battery for Aphasia (RCBA) is designed to evaluate the nature and degree of reading impairment in aphasic adults. It can be used with all of the neuropathologies of speech and language to appraise reading ability. Stimuli appropriate for adults are used to determine single-word comprehension on three subtests that contain visually, auditorily, or semantically similar words. Seven additional subtests evaluate functional reading, synonyms, sentence comprehension, paragraph comprehension, factual comprehension, inferential comprehension, and morphosyntactic comprehension. Rosenbek and Wertz [207] have compiled a battery of motor speech tasks designed to evaluate functional use of speech structures and speech systems. These are useful in determining the relative contribution of involvement in respiration, phonation, articulation, resonance, and prosody to the overall severity of dysarthria. For example, integrity of the respiratory muscles can be evaluated by asking the patient to sniff or pant. Similarly, the larynx can be assessed by asking the patient to produce a rapid series of single vowels (e.g., /i-i-i/).

The comprehensive evaluation listed in Table 1-6 is not a prescription. Many useful instruments have been omitted. The purpose is to specify speech, language, and intellectual dimensions that require appraisal in patients with neurogenic speech and language disorders. Further, it is hoped that listing specific areas and abilities requiring evaluation will help clinicians to avoid immersing patients in a psychometric marinade.

Summary
Published observations, speculations, case reports, and empirical evidence have advanced our knowledge of communicative deficits that occur following neurologic impairment to a point where there is a danger of losing sight of the patient amidst a ruck of terminology and theoretical bias. We risk considering the patient as only interesting rather than as a candidate for rehabilitation. Emphasis here has been focused on clinical management of neurogenic speech and language disorders. Thomas, in his *Lives of a Cell* [241, p. 22], tells us, "Somewhere underlying all the signals is a continual music . . .And almost anything an animal can employ to make a sound is put to use." Somewhere behind the insolvable ejaculations of neurologically impaired patients is a music awaiting lyrics. Putting words to the music is the primary task in patient management, and the variety of songs eventually sung is the primary test of its effectiveness.

The Disorders
Primary steps in patient management are appraisal, diagnosis, prognosis, and focusing of therapy. This section contains discussion of each step for all five neuropathologies of speech and language. The ways of organizing the data, including localization, cause, definitions, and behavioral profile, are employed when appropriate. Also, suggestions are given to eliminate the confusion created by coexisting disorders and similar symptoms among disorders. The necessary data—biographical, medical, and behavioral—for patient management are listed; and methods for focusing therapy for each disorder are suggested. Finally, a sample case is offered as an illustration.

Aphasia
Numerous definitions of aphasia exist. For patient management, Darley's definition, given in Table 1-1, is useful because it tells us what aphasia is and what it is not. First, we expect these patients to have suffered brain damage. Because of this damage, they demonstrate difficulties in listening, reading, speaking, and writing. These deficits are obvious in their lack of available words, impoverished syntactic constructions, and inability to understand lengthy or complex auditory and visual messages. Second, we do not expect that their problems result from difficulty in programming muscle movements for producing phonemes, generalized intellectual impairment, or significant motor dysfunction. Thus aphasia is not apraxia of speech, dementia, or dysarthria. One or more of these disorders may coexist with aphasia, but they result in different symptoms and require different therapeutic approaches from those employed with aphasic patients. A theoretical clinical profile of aphasia is shown in Figure 1-5.

LOCALIZATION. The general localization of lesions resulting in aphasia is fairly well established. However, controversy continues regarding the effects of interhemispheric and intrahemispheric lesions on the presence, severity, and type of aphasia. Mountcastle [170] has edited a series of papers that support the concept of two brains, a left and a right brain. Most of us use the left brain for language and the right brain for nonverbal activities. However, the influence of handedness and congenital brain injury on this relation is not totally clear. Further, the effects of lesions in different areas of the left hemisphere continue to be debated. Some investigators [82, 85] emphasize the importance of anterior versus posterior lesions on the type of subsequent aphasia, while others [43, 222] focus on behavior and eschew the influence of localized lesions.

Abundant evidence exists [66, 96, 183, 211] to support the belief that the left hemisphere is typically dominant for speech and language, regardless of an individual's handedness. Right hemisphere language dominance, although uncommon, occurs more frequently in sinistrals than in dextrals. Estimates of right hemisphere dominance range from 10 to 33 percent in the left-handed and from less than 1 to 10 percent in the right-handed. Hecaen and Sauget [97] argue that familial left-handers appear to have bilateral representation of language.

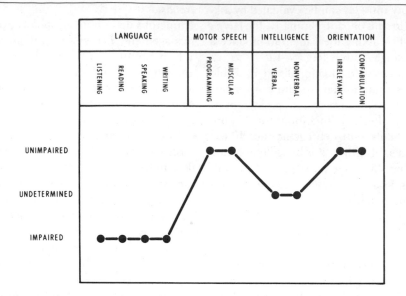

	LANGUAGE				MOTOR SPEECH		INTELLIGENCE		ORIENTATION	
	LISTENING	READING	SPEAKING	WRITING	PROGRAMMING	MUSCULAR	VERBAL	NONVERBAL	IRRELEVANCY	CONFABULATION

Fig. 1-5. Theoretical clinical profile of aphasia, indicating language impairment in all modalities, no motor speech deficits, undetermined intellectual involvement, and a lack of orientation problems.

An additional influence on cerebral dominance occurs in patients who have suffered either congenital left hemisphere damage or have acquired a left hemisphere lesion early in life. Penfield and Roberts [183] suggest that left hemisphere damage incurred before age 2 may induce a shift in language dominance to the right hemisphere. Berry [20], after reviewing early left hemisphere injury and its influence on shift in dominance, concludes that the cutoff age for transfer may be as old as 10 or 12 years.

More controversial than the effects of interhemispheric lesions are the influences of intrahemispheric lesions. Some classify types of aphasia on the basis of where the lesion exists in the left hemisphere, while others are content to describe the behavioral deficits and display little interest in the site of the lesion. For example, Goodglass and Kaplan [85] list eight primary types of aphasia—global, Broca's, Wernicke's, anomia, conduction, transcortical sensory, transcortical motor, mixed nonfluent—and two types, anterior and posterior, of subcortical aphasia. The primary types are identified by salient symptoms that differ among each type and correspond to Geschwind's [81] organization of language in the left hemisphere. Lesions that yield the subcortical aphasias have been identified by Alexander and LoVerme [3] and Naeser et al. [172]. Similarly, Kertesz [128] lists eight spe-

cific types of aphasia—global, Broca's, isolation, transcortical motor, Wernicke's, transcortical sensory, conduction, and anomic. Conversely, Darley [43] and Schuell et al. [222] eschew classifying aphasia into specific types. Both believe aphasia is a general language deficit crossing the four communicative modalities of listening, reading, speaking, and writing; they feel differences among aphasic patients can be explained by severity or coexisting disorders.

Finally, it is necessary to differentiate aphasiclike behavior in dementia and confusion from aphasia subsequent to a unilateral, left hemisphere lesion. Patient management for aphasia resulting from a left hemisphere lesion differs from that employed with demented patients who demonstrate aphasiclike behaviors or patients with language deficits following bilateral damage. For example, the prognosis for recovery for those in the former category is better than for those in the latter. Further, the presence of coexisting disorders is more common in the latter patients than in the former ones. Porch [189] offers PICA profiles for patients who have suffered bilateral damage. He suggests they differ from unilateral left hemisphere–involved patients in three major areas. First, patients with bilateral involvement demonstrate more difficulty on primary visual tasks (e.g., matching identical objects and matching pictures with objects) than they do on primary auditory tasks (e.g., pointing to objects when named and pointing to objects when described by their function). Patients with left hemisphere lesions have more difficulty with the auditory tasks than with the visual ones. Second, patients with bilateral lesions show disproportionately high verbal performance compared to their gestural and written performance. Conversely, patients with left hemisphere lesions, depending on the severity, are better in gestural performance than in speaking and writing. Third, patients with bilateral lesions display disproportionately more involvement in writing compared with their performance in gesturing and talking.

Calling language deficits that result from bilateral involvement aphasia creates confusion. Halpern, Darley, and Brown [92] reported that patients with the language of generalized intellectual impairment typically suffer bilateral involvement and are impaired on most language tasks. They differentiate these patients on the basis of more impairment of reading comprehension in patients with generalized intellectual impairment compared with more impairment of auditory retention in patients with aphasia. Further, Joynt and Goldstein [120] list seven minor (right) hemisphere syndromes—spatial perception and body image disorders, visual perception disorders, constructional disabilities, auditory perception disorders, somatosensory disorders, speech disorders, and motor impersistence—that are not present in aphasia resulting from a left hemisphere lesion. Thus damage in the right hemisphere appears to result in different behavioral deficits from those seen following damage in the left hemisphere. When both hemispheres have been damaged, the interaction among these different deficits creates an extremely confusing clinical picture, and labeling the result aphasia is not useful.

Localization of the lesion that results in aphasia is important when one communicates with medical colleagues. Confusion between neurologists and speech pathologists may result from different orientations to the problem of aphasia and the jargon used to express these orientations. Neurologists are typically trained in lesion-dictated terminology, and speech pathologists tend to use behavioral definitions. The neurologic approach has its roots in the use of speech and language symptoms as localizing signs. In the 1880s, what the patient said and how he or she listened, read, and wrote were extremely important, since the sophisticated instruments and methods used to localize lesions today were nonexistent. This approach persists, and, interestingly, remains fairly accurate. Speech pathologists, being charged with patient management, find it difficult to treat a label (e.g., Broca's aphasia, Wernicke's

aphasia). Rehabilitation is enhanced by definitions, descriptions, and quantified estimates of behavior. Nevertheless, speech pathologists must acquire a knowledge of the neurologic terminology applicable to aphasia. The physician is the primary patient care person, and communication with him or her is essential.

CAUSE. While there is an occasional reference to aphasia existing in a specific neurologic disease— for example, prolonged, monosymptomatic dysphasia in epilepsy [60]—the causes listed for aphasia in Table 1-2 are those most frequently encountered. The majority of aphasic patients have suffered a CVA. The second most frequent source of aphasia is trauma to the left hemisphere. Neoplasms and infection account for the remainder of cases of aphasia. An additional cause might be surgical intervention; however, this is typically done to treat vascular probelms, repair traumatic damage, or remove tumors. The cause is believed to influence patient management primarily through its effects on prognosis [46]. Brookshire [28] presents a clear description of causes resulting in aphasia.

Vascular problems or CVAs that cause aphasia can be classified as thrombotic, embolic, aneurysmal, or hemorrhagic. Another type of vascular cause, hematoma, is confusing because it can be classified as a tumor and typically results from trauma. A hematoma is an accumulation of blood that occurs as a result of hemorrhage. Probably the most frequently encountered type is the subdural hematoma, which results from bleeding into the space between the dural and arachnoid membranes.

Traumatic head injuries are usually subdivided into penetrating, open head wounds, or nonpenetrating, closed head wounds. An increase in the incidence of the former occurs during times of war, and an increase in the latter is occurring as a result of automobile accidents. Nonpenetrating trauma may be accompanied by a contrecoup. Damage occurs to the side of the brain opposite from where impact takes place, when the brain rebounds off the interior surface of the skull. Bruising occurs and may cause problems that coexist with aphasia. For example, if a blow is received to the left hemisphere, aphasia will result because of damage directly beneath the impact, and right hemisphere symptoms may result from a contrecoup. Is it useful to call patients who have suffered bilateral head trauma aphasic? Holland [105] and Ylvisaker and Holland in Chapter 5 suggest it is not, and I agree.

Inflammation resulting from encephalitis and

meningitis may induce aphasiclike symptoms. Typically, these problems are widespread and result in something more than aphasia. Brain abscesses are more localized and may result in aphasia. They tend to destroy brain tissue at the site of the abscess and may create increased pressure within the skull.

Neoplasms vary in type, location, and malignancy. The primary site may be within the brain, or brain damage may result from metastasis of a tumor whose primary site is elsewhere in the body (e.g., kidney). Metastases may result in bilateral involvement (e.g., metastases to both hemispheres) and therefore create something other than or in addition to aphasia. Obviously, the benign or malignant nature of a tumor will have an influence on the patient's prognosis for recovery.

Porch [188] has reported his clinical impressions of recovery for several different causes. He suggests that aphasic patients who have suffered a thrombotic CVA show a gradually increasing recovery curve during the first 6 months after onset. Patients who have sustained a hemorrhage show straight-line recovery during the first 6 months after onset. Patients who have undergone surgical ablation for an arteriovenous malformation (congenital abnormal collection of vascularity) show rapid, straight-line recovery during the first 3 months after surgery. Finally, patients who have suffered nonpenetrating trauma show stair-step recovery that continues up to 18 months after onset. These observations, if they can be documented with empirical evidence, will make a significant contribution to the study of aphasia and management of aphasic patients. A knowledge of the recovery patterns for patients with different disorders will improve prognosis and treatment planning. For example, aphasic patients with thrombotic disorders could be tested monthly. If they do not show continued improvement during the first 6 months, they would have a poorer prognosis, and therapy might be terminated or cut back to maintenance levels. Conversely, the stair-step recovery curve in trauma would indicate continued treatment during the first 18 months after onset, and failure to show month-to-month improvement would not be a reason for terminating therapy.

Halpern, Darley, and Brown [92] report that the cause of the disorder was not useful in differentiating among their patients with aphasia, generalized intellectual impairment, apraxia of speech, and confused language. Five of their 10 aphasic patients suffered from a CVA, four had a tumor, and one had aphasia subsequent to infection. Patients with generalized intellectual impairment had a higher percentage of degeneration, 9 of 10 patients with apraxia had suffered a CVA, and half the patients with the language of confusion had sustained trauma.

APPRAISAL. Complete appraisal includes collection of biographical, medical, and behavioral data. Necessary biographical data have been listed in Table 1-4. These include the patient's social history, interests, and current concerns. Important medical data, listed in Table 1-5, provide complete information on the neurologic status of the patient, including neurophysiologic limitations and any active medical conditions that may influence his or her performance. Measures for collecting behavioral data, listed in Table 1-6, indicate which cerebral processes are impaired and which are intact. Behavioral data are provided, in part, by the speech pathologist. An appropriate battery of measures is necessary to make a diagnosis, formulate a prognosis, and, if warranted, focus speech and language therapy.

To appraise speech and language behavior, a battery of speech and language tests must be selected. To some, tests are a necessary evil; to others, they are simply an evil. Furthermore, there is no single test that is acceptable to everybody. Table 1-7 lists the abilities that require appraisal. Examples of tests that measure each ability are given. As mentioned earlier, a clinician's tools are gathered to satisfy his or her purposes, experience, and biases. Thus Table 1-7 is not a prescription, but a description of measures we have found useful in our clinic.

Table 1-7. Aphasia appraisal battery

Abilities	Possible measures
General language	Porch Index of Communicative Ability
	Boston Diagnostic Aphasia Examination
	Western Aphasia Battery
	Minnesota Test for Differential Diagnosis of Aphasia
Auditory comprehension	Token Test
	Revised Token Test
Reading	Reading Comprehension Battery for Aphasia
"Functional" communication	Communicative Abilities in Daily Living
	Functional Communication Profile
Motor speech	Motor Speech Evaluation
"Nonverbal" intelligence	Coloured Progressive Matrices

Appraising aphasia begins with administration of one or more general language measures. Typically, we administer the PICA and the BDAE. When time permits or when questions persist, we might supplement these with the WAB and the MTDDA.

The PICA evaluates gestural, verbal, and writing abilities with a 16-point multidimensional scoring system. This yields a quantified estimate of a patient's behavior on 18 subtests. When the patient's performance is converted into percentiles, it can be compared with a large sample of aphasic patients, giving an indication of severity. The same essentially homogeneous stimuli are used on 17 of 18 subtests, and the control of stimulus variability permits comparison among the subtests.

While the PICA is appropriate for most patients, it may be weak in detecting minimal involvement. It has demonstrated test-retest reliability and tester reliability. Thus it is sensitive enough to measure change in patients over time without being influenced much by changes in the examiner's scoring or administrative procedures. Test results can be plotted graphically on the ranked response summary and the modality response summary shown in Figure 1-6. The ranked response summary shows the 18 subtests ranked in order of difficulty from left to right along the abscissa and the 16-point multidimensional scoring system, ranging from 1 (no response) to 16 (complex response), along the ordinate. Aphasic patients typically display a gradual increase in performance on the multidimensional scale as they move from more difficult subtests to easier ones. This is not a straight-line function, as can be seen in Figure 1-6. The modality response summary plots performance according to the output modality required for each subtest. Thus a comparison of gestural, verbal, and writing abilities is possible. Using the percentiles provided by Porch [187, 190], overall, gestural, verbal, and graphic severity levels can be obtained. For example, the patient represented in Figure 1-6 shows an overall performance at the 54th percentile, gestural performance at the 55th percentile, verbal performance at the 59th percentile, and graphic performance at the 49th percentile. By observing individual subtests, specific abilities can be appraised. For example, primary auditory subtest (VI and X) and primary reading subtests (V and VII) indicate auditory comprehension and reading abilities. Also, the PICA provides some information in differentiating among neuropathologies of speech and language. Inordinately low verbal performance compared with gestural and graphic performance might indicate severe apraxia of speech or severe dysarthria. Further, depressed scores on the reading and writing subtests may indicate premorbid illiteracy or possible generalized intellectual impairment. The PICA may take too long for some patients, depending on the severity of their condition, and it can be frustrating, since the more difficult subtests are administered first. DiSimoni, Keith, Holt, and Darley [64] report a good deal of redundancy in the PICA, and they suggest it can be shortened without sacrificing its ability to indicate severity. However, Porch [190] contends that reducing the number of items or subtests would sacrifice information that is important to focus treatment. Some recent modifications have been made in the PICA [187]. These include recomputation of the original percentiles, revision of the ranked response summary, and revision of the original modalities into writing, copying, reading, gestural, verbal, auditory, and visual. Clinicians will find both versions of the PICA, new and old, in use.

The BDAE supplements the PICA in several ways. First, it samples a wider range of behavior and, therefore, permits detection of deficits that may not be detected on the PICA. Second, it is designed to classify aphasia into one of the traditional types. Twenty-three subtests are administered to evaluate fluency, auditory comprehension, naming, oral reading, repetition, paraphasia, automatic speech, reading comprehension, writing, and music. The basic battery can be supplemented with subtests to explore a patient's spatial and computational abilities. Overall severity is rated on a 0 to 5 scale, and the rating can be converted to a percentile. The type of aphasia is determined by plotting the patient's performance on the BDAE rating scale profile of speech characteristics and comparing the configuration to patterns that represent specific types of aphasia. The BDAE first appeared in 1972 [86]. Methods for plotting performance were revised in 1983 [85].

Special tests are typically used to provide information on patients who do not demonstrate either deficits or minimal deficits on the PICA or BDAE. Minimal aphasia may not be detected on the general language measures. However, the patient may complain of persisting difficulties not present premorbidly. Moss [169] describes language problems he experienced that were not detected by conventional testing. Minimal aphasia, therefore, may require the speech pathologist either to listen to what

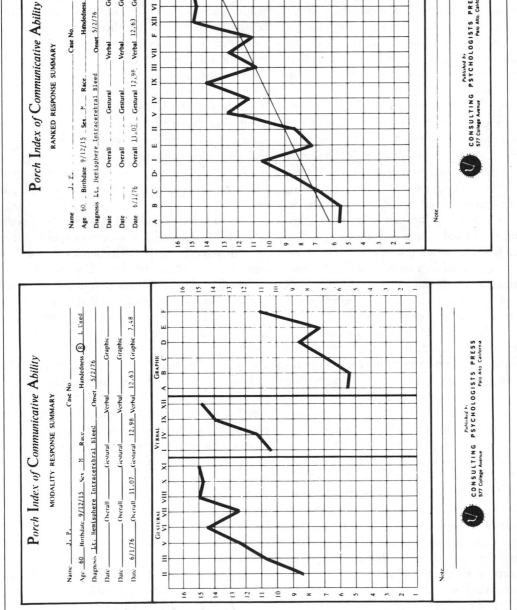

Fig. 1-6. PICA modality and ranked response summaries, showing performance by an aphasic patient. Theoretically, a patient with normal performance would score 15 on all subtests.

the patient has to say about the problem or to employ special tests.

The Token Test, developed by DeRenzi and Vignolo [62], detects mild auditory comprehension deficits by manipulating the length and complexity of the auditory stimuli. Tokens varying along the three dimensions of color, shape, and size are used to eliminate redundancy. The battery is comprised of five parts. The first four gradually increase the length of the auditory stimulus (e.g., "Touch the red circle" is gradually increased to "Touch the small red circle and the large green rectangle"). Part V manipulates grammatical complexity (e.g., "Put the red circle between the yellow rectangle and the green rectangle"). Wertz, Keith, and Custer [261] report that the Token Test detects auditory comprehension problems in patients who have passed both auditory tests on the PICA. Several variations of the Token Test exist. The original one is described here. Boller and Vignolo [25] developed a slightly different form that modifies the stimuli and instructions. Spreen and Benton [237] include the Token Test as part of the Neurosensory Center Comprehensive Examination for Aphasia; Spellacy and Spreen [235] have developed a short form of the test; and McNeil and Prescott [161, 162] have formulated a longer, revised version, the Revised Token Test. So many versions exist that Berry [22] cautions clinicians to state which form of the Token Test has been administered.

LaPointe and Horner's [133] RCBA, described earlier, is used to supplement the PICA and BDAE reading subtests. A patient's performance is plotted in percent correct on each of the 10 subtests. The resulting profile displays reading strengths and weaknesses, and permits detecting where to intervene with treatment. The RCBA's adult-level stimuli make it a fine addition to our appraisal armamentorium and eliminate the previous practice of probing aphasic patients' reading deficits with reading tests more appropriate for children.

During the 1970s aphasiologists found "functional" communication. While it was not lost, the only standardized means of appraising it was the FCP [216]. Holland's [106] CADL now provides an additional tool to measure how patients function on their own. The CADL's content was described earlier. A three-point scoring system is used to determine a patient's "functional adequacy" in a variety of simulated situations and with a variety of stimuli the patient might encounter in his or her passage through each day of being aphasic. Adequacy is determined by *whether* the patient gets the message across, not *how* the patient gets the message across. If the appropriate response is clearly understood, be it spoken, gestured, written, drawn, or licked, it is considered correct. Thus, the CADL permits and encourages the patient to do what he or she can do to communicate. It does not replace the more traditional tests, but it is a valuable supplement.

A motor speech evaluation is administered to aphasic patients to determine the presence of coexisting apraxia of speech or dysarthria. While tests for apraxia of speech [42] and dysarthria [72] exist, we use the motor speech evaluation compiled by Wertz, LaPointe, and Rosenbek [262] in our aphasia appraisal battery. The origin of the battery is spread throughout the literature, and it contains contributions from numerous clinicians. The tasks include conversation; picture description; vowel prolongation; repetition of monosyllables, a sequence of monosyllables, multisyllabic words, words that increase in length, and sentences; multiple trails with the same word; counting forward and backward; repetition of sentences used volitionally; and oral reading. Overall performance is rated on a scale of 1 to 7 to indicate severity, and the types of errors are analyzed to determine the presence of apraxia of speech or dysarthria.

Raven's Coloured Progressive Matrices [195] is used to obtain an estimate of nonverbal intelligence, and it may be supplemented with Smith's Symbol Digit Modalities Test [231]. The Coloured Progressive Matrices include three sets of 12 problems that require the patient to select one of six alternatives to "complete a pattern." It is highly visual and may handicap patients with peripheral or central visual involvement. Scoring is binary. Meager norms are provided in the manual. There is a wide range of performance among aphasic patients on the Coloured Progressive Matrices, and performance does not correlate with the severity of the patient's language involvement. Thus its use is primarily diagnostic. To be aphasic, patients' language deficits must not be explained by their intellectual deficits. Otherwise, the problem is probably generalized intellectual impairment.

The tests listed in Table 1-7, which have been described, constitute a battery that is useful for appraising aphasia and differentiating it from other neuropathologies of speech and language. Administering the measures discussed could take approximately 5 hours. However, not all are necessary for every patient, and all need not be administered before making a diagnosis and initiating treatment.

Enough appraisal to make a diagnosis, state a prognosis, and focus treatment is sufficient.

DIAGNOSIS. Diagnosis of aphasia requires that the clinician compare the appraisal data collected with his or her definition of aphasia and his or her definitions of the other possible neuropathologies of speech and language. Thus diagnosis is a process of inclusion and exclusion. We expect the aphasic patient to have suffered at least one instance of damage to the left hemisphere. Confirmation of this diagnosis is provided by the medical data. We expect the aphasic patient to demonstrate a general language deficit in all communicative modes, including auditory comprehension, reading, speaking, and writing. Confirmation of this is provided by the general language measures (PICA and BDAE), special tests (Token Test and RCBA), and the CADL. We do not expect gross disorientation in terms of the time, date, or location. However, the severity of language involvement may make it impossible to evaluate these areas. We do not expect overt signs of intellectual deficit, which would indicate the language of generalized intellectual impairment. Finally, the patient's oral expressive deficits should be problems of language and not problems of programming speech movements or problems resulting from weak, slow, restricted muscle activity.

Additional requirements in diagnosis may be to label the type of aphasia and to state an estimate of severity. The type of aphasia will vary from that provided by the BDAE (e.g., Broca's, Wernicke's, conduction) to that provided by the Minnesota Test for Differential Diagnosis of Aphasia (e.g., simple aphasia, aphasia with visual involvement, aphasia with sensorimotor involvement). Severity may be stated with an adjective—mild, moderate, marked, or severe—or in terms of a percentile provided by PICA performance.

PROGNOSIS. Prognosis requires making a statement about a patient's potential for improvement, an area in which we are sadly deficient. Prognosis can be made using one of three approaches. First, certain patient variables—biographical, medical, and behavioral—appear to be associated with good and bad prognoses. Second, some clinicians have formulated prognostic categories based on initial test performance. And third, there is the possiblity that recovery from aphasia can be predicted using statistical techniques. All three approaches have been based on retrospective observation of performance by groups of aphasic patients. The task, however, is to make a prospective statement for each patient individually.

Darley [46, 47] reviewed several prognostic variables that are believed to influence recovery from aphasia. These are listed in Table 1-8. The first nine represent biographical, medical, and behavioral factors, and the tenth involves the influence of treatment. Eisenson [66] divides prognostic vari-

Table 1-8. Prognostic variables in aphasia

Variable	Summary
Age at onset	Younger patients have a better prognosis
Premorbid education, intelligence, and language abilities	Undetermined influence on prognosis
Associated defects and health during recovery	Patients with no associated deficits or illness have a better prognosis
Social milieu	Undetermined influence on prognosis
Cause	Nonpenetrating trauma has a better prognosis than penetrating trauma, vascular, tumor, and infection
Site and size of lesion	Small lesions not in the temporoparietal area have a better prognosis
Time after onset	Patients with brief duration of aphasia have a better prognosis
Severity and type of aphasia	Mild aphasia and the absence of significant auditory comprehension deficits and severe apraxia of speech are favorable prognostic signs
Nonlanguage behavior	Awareness, high motivation, and high aspiration are favorable prognostic signs
Length and intensity of treatment	Participation in a longer, more intense treatment program is more likely to achieve prognosis

Source: Adapted from F. L. Darley: Treatment of Acquired Aphasia. In W. J. Friedlander (ed.), *Current Reviews of Higher Nervous System Dysfunction, Advances in Neurology.* New York: Raven, 1975. Vol. 7; The efficacy of language rehabilitation in aphasia. *J. Speech Hear. Disord.* 37 : 3, 1972.

ables into positive and negative categories. The variable approach in prognosis, therefore, defines prognostic virtue by exclusion and inclusion.

The younger the patient, the better the prognosis. While there is no exact cutoff age, most investigators [69, 83, 213, 232, 245, 255] suggest that patients under age 60 have a more favorable prognosis for recovery than patients over age 60. Schuell admits that age influences recovery from aphasia [218], but she cautions that there are individual differences. She cites examples of young patients with persisting severe aphasia and older patients who demonstrated excellent recovery. Basso, Capitani, and Vignolo [10] found age had no influence on either treated or untreated aphasic patients.

The influence of premorbid education, intelligence, and language abilities on recovery from aphasia is undetermined. Eisenson [70] suggested that highly educated aphasic patients had a less favorable prognosis. Conversely, Jones and Wepman [119] report that education has a positive influence on the patient's ability to perform arithmetic operations after the onset of aphasia; and Smith [232] cited more improvement during therapy in patients with more education. Furthermore, Wepman [255] found a positive, significant correlation between premorbid intelligence and posttreatment intelligence; but Sarno, Silverman, and Levita [217] observed that education, occupational status, and premorbid language ability were not related with recovery made in therapy.

Good health is considered a good prognostic sign [69]. Further the absence of peripheral auditory or visual deficits has a positive influence on recovery [5, 67, 232, 244]. Smith [232] and Bateman [11] differ regarding the influence of hemiplegia on recovery. Bateman believed little could be done to improve language in aphasic patients with persisting hemiplegia. However, Smith reports similar gains in both hemiplegic and nonhemiplegic patients during a treatment program.

Social milieu, the location and composition of an aphasic patient's environment, may or may not have an influence on his or her recovery. Stoicheff [239] provides indirect evidence that positive, correct feedback of the patient's performance will influence language ability. Sarno, Silverman, and Levita [217] found no significant effect of the patient's environment on recovery. Of course, attributes within a patient's social milieu may conflict. For example, a seemingly favorable residential location (i.e., home as opposed to a hospital for the chronically ill) may conflict with an unfavorable psychological environment (i.e., an antagonistic or overprotective family). Holland [106] reports CADL performance by patients residing in an institutionalized environment is typically lower when compared with CADL performance by patients living in a noninstitutionalized setting.

The cause of aphasia is believed to influence the prognosis. As mentioned earlier, Porch [188] suggests that different vascular problems recover at different rates, and trauma differs from all vascular problems. Generally, nonpenetrating trauma is believed to carry a better prognosis than penetrating trauma [155]. Butfield and Zangwill [30] and Eisenson [67] reported more improvement in patients who had sustained trauma than in patients who had suffered either vascular or neoplastic disorders. Further, Eisenson [67] reported his clinical observations that single vascular episodes result in a better prognosis than multiple ones. Anderson, Bourestom, and Greenberg [5] concluded that hemorrhagic strokes result in the poorest prognosis when compared with other vascular disorders.

The location and size of the lesion appear to influence the patient's recovery. Penfield and Roberts [183] and Eisenson [67] report that temporoparietal lesions result in more severe and persisting aphasia than lesions in other parts of the left hemisphere. The influence of the size of the lesion is difficult to determine because of inadequate localization data. However, the larger the lesion, the greater the possibility of more severe and persisting aphasia. Yarnell, Monroe, and Sobel [267] and Rubens [210] are consistent in their observations that patients with small lesions, a single lesion, and lesions that avoid the temporoparietal region have a better prognosis than those with large lesions, multiple or bilateral lesions, and damage in the temporoparietal area. It is possible, of course, that a large lesion may miss or invade only the fringes of important speech and language areas, while a small lesion may be located directly in the center of an important area. Porch [189] and Eisenson [67] have observed that patients with bilateral lesions recover differently and have a poorer prognosis than patients with unilateral left hemisphere lesions.

The interval between onset and therapy appears to be a significant prognostic variable, and the data to support this conclusion come from treatment studies. Butfield and Zangwill [30], Wepman [255], Vignolo [245], Sands, Sarno, and Shankweiler [213], Smith [232], Basso, Capitani and Vignolo [10],

Kertesz and McCabe [129], and Wertz, LaPointe, and Rosenbek [262] all report less recovery in patients who entered therapy after a long period following onset. While the specific interval between onset and therapy has not been determined, Vignolo [245] suggests that treatment gains are maximized if patients are seen within 6 months of onset.

There is general agreement that patients with more severe aphasia have a poorer prognosis than patients with milder aphasia. Schuell [218] based her prognostic categories, in part, on the severity of aphasia. Observations by Butfield and Zangwill [30], Wepman [255], Sands, Sarno, and Shankweiler [213], Mitchell [166], and Basso, Capitani, and Vignolo [10] support Schuell's beliefs regarding severity. The presence or absence of specific language deficits may have some prognostic significance; however, the reports are inconsistent. Culton [40] and Schuell [221] believe that inability to point to objects when they are named is a particularly poor prognostic sign. Conversely, Sarno, Silverman, and Levita [217] and Smith [232] report that specific auditory comprehension deficits do not restrict progress in treatment. Vignolo [245] observed that severe anarthria (probably oral nonverbal apraxia with coexisting apraxia of speech) was a bad prognostic sign. Wepman [253] formulated a scale for estimating recovery based on patients' ability to self-correct their utterances. Similarly, Kertesz and McCabe [129] and Lomas and Kertesz [149] have suggested that the patient's type of aphasia will influence recovery. Anomic and conduction types were reported to have the best prognosis. Conversely, Prins, Snow, and Wagenaar [193] found no influence of type of aphasia on improvement.

Nonlanguage behavior characteristics are believed to influence prognosis, although many of these are difficult to measure [254]. Eisenson [69, 70] suggested that euphoria, introversion, feelings of guilt, low level of aspiration, and dependency were all poor prognostic signs. Similarly, Anderson, Bourestom, and Greenberg [5] noted that high motivation and levels of aspiration were favorable prognostic signs. Holland [107] suggests that the way an aphasic patient attempts to solve problems may have prognostic significance. For example, patients who seek alternative solutions following failure, initiate different strategies, and, at least, take a guess may have a better prognosis than patients in whom these behaviors are not observed.

The last prognostic variable, length and intensity of treatment, has been discussed by Darley [46]. He concludes that patients who have longer, more intense therapy typically make more gains than patients who have received shorter, less frequent treatment programs. Thus prognosis, or at least achieving a prognostic prediction, is influenced by the availability, patient's willingness to participate in, frequency, and length of speech and language therapy. Darley speculates that the quality of therapy also has an influence. However, he notes this is difficult to measure and data are lacking. Others, including Basso, Capitani, and Vignolo [10], Deal and Deal [57], and Wertz [258], suggest that treatment early after onset results in more gain than treatment initiated later.

The variable approach for formulating a prognosis is popular. The major problem with this approach, of course, is that variables coexist and prognosis is influenced by the way they interact. Vignolo [245] discussed the problem by questioning whether a younger patient with severe aphasia had a better prognosis than an older patient with mild aphasia. To date, no one has answered this question.

Schuell's prognostic aphasia groups are an example of the second approach for formulating a prognosis [218]. Her retrospective analysis of patients' performance on the Minnesota Test for Differential Diagnosis of Aphasia resulted in the development of specific prognostic groups. These range from a prognosis for excellent recovery of all language skills to a poor prognosis for language that becomes functional in any mode. The procedure requires the clinician to administer the MTDDA, classify the patient's performance in a prognostic group, and follow Schuell's directions for obtaining the prognosis predicted. This is an accurate approach, and Schuell has reported its effectiveness. Unfortunately, it is difficult to classify some patients into a prognostic group.

The third approach, predicting a specific recovery level based on initial test performance, requires statistical analysis. Porch et al. [191] and Porch, Wertz, and Collins [192] have used a stepwise multiple regression analysis to predict change in aphasia as measured by the PICA. Patients were tested at different times after onset, followed, and retested at a later date. A retrospective analysis was done using performance in the early test to determine whether performance on the later test could have been predicted. When predicted performance was correlated with the performance actually obtained, correlations ranged from $+0.74$ to 0.94. All were significant. Deal et al. [59], using the multiple regression formula developed by Porch et al. [191], tested its clinical application. Although group results were significant, less than two-thirds of the sample obtained scores within a -5 to $+5$ percentile range of the score predicted. Thus, the use of multiple regression analyses to predict improvement or the lack of it remains promising but is not yet precise. Further, Sarno, Sarno, and Levita [214] caution that improvement on tests for aphasia may not be observable as a functional gain in the real world.

There has been a good deal of work on developing prognostic tools to predict the aphasic patient's future. However, we continue to lack precision in forecasting how much improvement will occur, when improvement will take place, and what it will permit the patient to do.

FOCUSING THERAPY. Clinicians who treat aphasic patients have done so without an abundance of empirical evidence to support the effectiveness of their efforts. Darley's reviews of the effects of speech and language therapy on recovery from aphasia [46, 47] concluded that treatment is probably effective. However, the evidence to support this contention was sparse. Two recent clinical trials by Basso, Capitani, and Vignolo [10] and Wertz et al. [260] and a plethora of single-case studies have provided empirical evidence that aphasia therapy is efficacious. Of course, every clinician remembers patients that have not been helped and some who have been helped only a little. We continue to seek answers to questions about when to treat, how much, where, and how. Nevertheless, those of us who spend our days with aphasic patients now work under an aegis of evidence indicating that our efforts do some good [57]. Benson's [18] observation is apt, which says that language therapy for the aphasic patient is, without a doubt, efficacious.

Today, treatments for aphasia abound. Chapey's [33] collection contains at least 13 different types of aphasia therapy. Holland [104] has edited a volume that organizes treatment by severity. Linebaugh [145] offers methods for mild aphasia, Horner [110] for moderate aphasia, and Helm-Estabrooks [99] for severe aphasia. A different approach has been compiled by Perkins [185] where clinicians suggest appropriate treatments for specific types of aphasia—Broca's, Wernicke's, global, etc. LaPointe, in Chapter 4, also offers specific methods for treating aphasic patients. The approach here is to present a general orientation for focusing traditional individual treatment.

In focusing therapy the area requiring work is determined, the method of treatment is chosen, and therapy is initiated. Schuell, Jenkins, and Jiménez-Pabón [222] tell us to begin where the patient starts to have difficulty. Porch [188] paraphrases this suggestion into PICA terminology and advocates initiating treatment on the fulcrum of the response curve. Treatment begins, therefore, when the patient begins to experience difficulty not only in accuracy but also in latency, efficiency, completeness, and responsiveness. Treatment tasks are composed of things the patient cannot do and things the patient can do if given sufficient time or additional information. Patients tell us where to begin by their performance on our appraisal tasks, and they suggest what their therapeutic goals should be. These include diagnostic goals (e.g., continued exploration of strengths and weaknesses), treatment goals (e.g., increasing the length of auditory stimuli that can be comprehended without repetition), and counseling goals (e.g., motivating patients to use an alternative mode of communication, such as gesture, until their verbal skills are sufficient to replace gestures).

There are at least two orientations for aphasia therapy. First, aphasia can be viewed as a regressive phenomenon, where language has backed down the ladder of acquisition. This orientation suggests that therapy is an educational undertaking, wherein the clinician teaches what is assumed to have been lost. Jakobson's [116] suggestion that the dissolution of language in aphasia is the reverse of acquisition of language in the child supports this approach. Second, aphasia can be viewed as a disorganization of normal language behavior, and the task of treatment is to reorganize what has been disrupted. Luria [152] suggests that language is reorganized when treatment transfers disrupted function to structures or systems that remain intact. This dichotomy, education versus reorganization, may be artificial, since most of us use a combination of techniques that could be labeled, at times, educational, and at other times, reorganizational. Treatment based on the reorganization hypothesis is more optimistic, since clinicians do not have the time to teach aphasic patients all the language necessary for even low-level functional communication. Thus therapeutic programs that facilitate desired behavior, prevent maladaptive behavior, and reorganize impaired language skills are desirable.

An outline for focusing therapy is given in Table 1-9. Six general dimensions are listed, and each is influenced by the patient being treated. The cli-

Table 1-9. Considerations in focusing aphasia therapy

Dimension	Attributes
Stimuli	Meaningfulness, length, complexity, redundancy, frequency, number present, relatedness
Stimulus modes	Auditory, visual, tactile
Response modes	Pointing, simple gesturing, complex gesturing, writing, drawing, speaking
Temporal relation of stimulus and response	Unison, immediate, delayed, consecutive
Facilitators	Repetition, cue, combined stimulus modes, number of alternatives
Methods	Imitation, matching, selection, completion, intrasystemic reorganization, intersystemic reorganization, type-specific treatment, "functional" treatment

nician makes a decision on the basis of the patient's deficits and needs as well as the patient's desires. A good deal of wasted time, patient unhappiness, and therapeutic failure may be avoided if the clinician follows Schultz and Carpenter's [223] suggestions for selecting a therapeutic model. Briefly, they advise us to reach an agreement with our patients regarding first, whether a change is needed, and second, how that change should be effected. If, for example, the patient views the clinician as a teacher and agrees a change is needed, the clinician has license to construct tasks, and deliberation is reduced to the stimuli used. Conversely, if the patient knows what he or she wants to accomplish and views the clinician as a facilitator, the cognitive type of treatment suggested by Wepman [252] may be more appropriate. Whatever the approach, the clinician and patient must reconcile their differences or little progress will be made.

When asked what worries me about my patients, I usually reply, my therapy. Focusing therapy according to the dimensions listed in Table 1-9 reduces some, but not all, of this concern. Treatment begins with the selection of stimuli, giving consideration to their meaningfulness, length, complexity, redundance, frequency of occurrence in the language, number present in the task, and the relatedness among alternatives. Each of these factors can be spread along a continuum, and the point at which the patient enters the continuum is dictated by both the patient and the task. Treatment tasks should be hierarchically arranged, beginning where the patient first experiences difficulty and gradually becoming more difficult. As a general rule, a treatment task is selected in which the patient can achieve approximately 80 percent accurate responses. The stimuli chosen influence the patient's accuracy, and performance dictates the length, complexity, amount of redundancy, fre-

quency of occurrence, number of alternatives present, and relatedness necessary for success.

Once appropriate stimuli are selected, they must be presented in a specific stimulus mode. Three possibilities are auditory, visual, or tactile. Again, the patient tells us where to begin. His or her proficiency, or lack of it, within a stimulus mode will indicate which ones to use. For example, for some patients, "Point to the pen" is incomprehensible. However, combining the printed word *pen* with the auditory stimulus may help. Thus combined auditory and visual modes of stimulus presentation may facilitate auditory comprehension. However, caution is necessary in the use of multimodal stimulation. Combining modes is appropriate only if it helps patients improve their performance. Some patients perform better when stimuli are presented unimodally.

Once stimuli and stimulus modes of presentation are selected, appropriate response modes are determined. Patients may perform in several ways, including pointing, simple gesturing, complex gesturing, writing, drawing, and speaking; and all of these may be combined with any of the three stimulus modes. For example, if an auditory stimulus is presented, the patient may point to the object, demonstrate its function by simple or complex gesturing, write its name, draw it, or say its name. Typically, the patient will show a range of ability in using different response modes. Also, he or she may point better than gesture, and both responses may be better than spoken or written ones. Thus the response modes and the order in which they are used are determined by the patient's abilities. Note that some patients will violate expectations on pointing tasks; e.g., they appear to understand much more than their ability to point to stimuli indicates. Brookshire [28] discusses this discrepancy in auditory comprehension. If the patient has difficulty performing the somewhat unnatural task of pointing to objects when named but understands lengthy social messages, such as "Put on your glasses, move your chair over to the table, and we will begin," one may avoid using the pointing response mode.

The next consideration is the temporal relation of stimulus and response. A task may require that a patient respond in unison with the therapist, immediately after stimulation, or after a delay, or that the patient produce several consecutive responses following stimulus presentation. Many of us fail to use unison responses, in which the clinician and patient produce the response simultaneously, with severely involved patients. However, producing the stimulus with the patient has the advantage of giving simultaneous auditory and visual feedback, which may be a step lower on the response hierarchy, to those who fail on repetition tasks. Further, in normal conversation the listener must produce appropriate responses following varying intervals after hearing the key words. Thus auditory comprehension tasks can involve presentation of auditory stimuli, inserting a pause, and then requesting a response. This approach can be used with patients who have better auditory comprehension abilities. Finally, asking the patient to make consecutive responses permits him or her to incorporate self-correction and improve performance. Wepman [254] stresses the prognostic significance of self-correction, and Johns and Darley [117] report that patients with apraxia of speech profit from repeating a stimulus three times consecutively.

Next, there is a need to consider which facilitators will be used. A facilitator is an aid the clinician uses to increase the probability of a correct response. Examples of facilitators are stimulus repetition, cues, combining stimulus modes, and reducing the number of alternatives present in the task. Some patients with auditory comprehension deficits profit from a repetition of instructions or stimuli. If a repetition does not elicit the correct response, the clinician may present a cue that will give the patient additional information. For example, a patient who cannot name an object may profit if the instructions are repeated. If the patient is still unable to perform, the clinician may say, "You know what you do with this, what do you call it?" Suggesting the function to the patient may give a cue to its name. Also, combining stimulus modes may help the patient make a correct response if he or she fails when only a single mode

is presented. For example, a patient may be unable to name an object in a sentence completion task but will succeed when the printed name of the object is given. Finally, reducing the number of alternatives in a response matrix may facilitate performance. For example, the patient's accuracy may improve if given five, rather than 10, alternatives from which to select. Facilitators are used to create intermediate steps in a hierarchy. If a patient is having difficulty moving to a sentence completion task after having succeeded on a word repetition task, facilitators, such as repetition, cuing, or combining stimulus modes, may help bridge the gap.

Finally, it is necessary to select treatment methods that are consistent with your philosophy of treatment. If you believe aphasia is a regression in language abilities, you select methods consistent with an educational philosophy of treatment. Appropriate methods would include imitation, matching, and drill. However, one must be careful not to overemphasize the effectiveness of these approaches. If patients improve from continued exposure to stimuli and repetition, they may not need the services of a speech pathologist. In this case, persons around the patient could teach them what they have supposedly lost. Our job is to develop methods that transcend simple repetition of language tasks. Traditional methods of imitation, matching stimuli, selecting among alternatives, and completing responses are appropriate and effective, and they fill specific needs. There are other methods, however.

Luria [152] discusses two methods for reorganizing language in aphasic patients. The first, intrasystemic reorganization, attempts to improve deficits within a communicative system by transferring control either downward or upward within the system. For example, patients who are not able to speak may succeed if the verbal responses are sung or a strong rhythm is employed. In this case, melody and rhythm, two components within the verbal system, are used to reorganize deficient verbalization. Melodic Intonation Therapy (MIT), described by Sparks, Helm, and Albert [233] and Sparks and Holland [234] is an example of this approach. The second, intersystemic reorganization, utilizes a functional system to reorganize behavior in an impaired system. For example, aphasic patients who demonstrate a paucity of speech may facilitate their verbal output by employing appropriate gestures. The approach of Skelly et al. [229] uses American Indian sign (Amerind) gestures to aid verbalization; an example of intersystemic reorganization. It appears to be appropriate for re-organizing verbal output in many aphasic patients.

Benson [18] has suggested the need for treatments appropriate for specific aphasic deficits. As mentioned above, MIT is an example of this approach. Helm [98] has listed selection criteria for patients who profit from MIT. These patients display the characteristics typical of Broca's aphasia. Similarly, Helm-Estabrooks, Fitzpatrick, and Barresi [100] have reported on Visual Action Therapy (VAT), a systematic method of associating objects and their use with action pictures and reduced-size drawings of the objects, which is effective for global aphasia.

Finally, some clinicians have introduced functional treatment where emphasis is placed on language context rather than on language content. Davis and Wilcox [55] have developed Promoting Aphasic's Communicative Effectiveness (PACE), where the patient and clinician convey information in a conversational context, and each uses whatever is necessary—speech, gesture, drawing, writing—to communicate with the other. Aten, Caligiuri, and Holland [6] have described the use of functional treatment in group therapy.

Good treatment is like good writing. Initially, one needs to get rid of clutter. The considerations offered in Table 1-9 for focusing therapy may help. We assume that progression is a process of easing the patient into a world of disarray, and when the patient can handle chaos, treatment ends. However, to reach this goal, treatment must begin with simplicity. After treatment tasks have been formulated, they are administered in therapy, and the tasks are repeated until the clinician feels new ones are appropriate. The treatment is documented systematically and, perhaps, is quantified in much the same way as appraisal.

It is important to keep systematic records of patient performance on treatment tasks. Unfortunately, many clinicians fail to do this. An excellent method for rectifying this oversight is LaPointe's Base 10 Response Form [132]. Examples of its use on two treatment tasks are shown in Figure 1-7. The Base 10 Response Form permits the clinician to describe the treatment task, establish a criterion of desired performance, select a system for scoring patient responses, and chart performance on 10 stimuli during 10 treatment sessions. Systematic use of the form tells us if the task is appropriate, if the patient is succeeding or failing, and when to modify or move on to another task. Figure 1-7 shows two base 10s; one for an auditory-gestural

task and one for a visual-verbal task. Both were scored with the multidimensional PICA system. The auditory-gestural task involved asking the patient to provide the appropriate intersystemic gesture that represented a verb. Optimum performance was set at 8, a cued response, and the patient improved after 10 sessions. Conversely, the visual-verbal task required the patient to say a verb that was represented by a gesture provided by the clinician, and no learning was observed after 10 sessions. The lack of improvement on the visual-verbal task indicated it was not appropriate for the patient. Faced with this lack of improvement, the therapist had to revise the criterion for acceptable response, modify the task by using different facilitators or methods, or drop back to an intermediate treatment task in the verbal hierarchy. Thus systematic documentation of patient performance in treatment forces the therapist to remain on-line and make these decisions.

Documenting a patient's performance on treatment tasks is no substitute for periodic reevaluation. Since the treatment program does not treat all communicative deficits, there is a need for general reevaluation to determine whether treatment is reaching stimuli and areas not treated. None of us has sufficient time to teach all the language abilities a patient needs. Thus we expect generalization.

Wertz [259] lists several chronologic considerations in evaluating recovery from aphasia. These include systematic reevaluations during treatment, follow-up evaluations after treatment, evaluation immediately before and after surgery or change in medication, and as soon as possible after a new onset. Reevaluation of the aphasic patient undergoing treatment is influenced by the frequency, amount, and success of the treatment program being administered. Porch [188] suggests periodic reevaluations at 1, 3, 6, 9, and 12 months after onset. In our clinic, patients who are involved in intensive treatment programs are evaluated on this schedule, and patients seen once or twice a week are evaluated after approximately 30 treatment sessions. There is no rigid rule for when a patient should be reevaluated, except that it should be done.

CLINICAL EXAMPLE. C. W., a 56-year-old man, suffered a left-hemisphere subdural hematoma from a fall on December 4, 1975. He was comatose for approximately 1 week, remained in the hospital for an additional 3 weeks, and returned home 1 month after the accident. He had worked for 20 years in

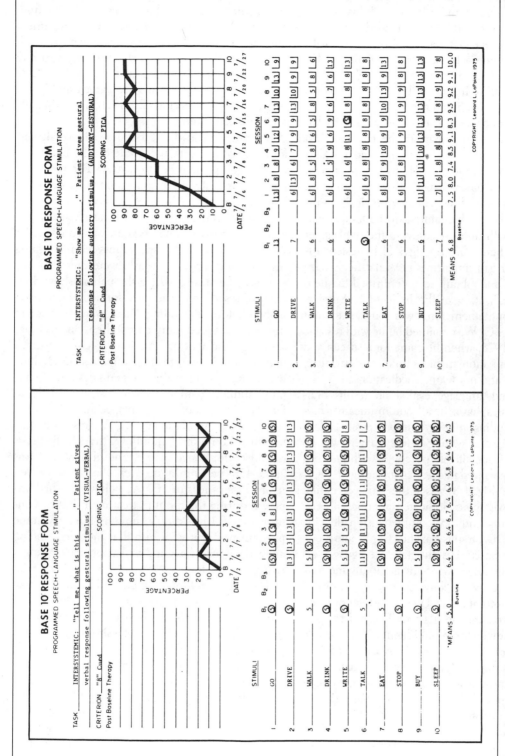

Fig. 1-7. Use of the Base 10 Response Form in aphasia therapy. Little learning resulted from the treatment task shown on the left. Obvious learning was obtained by administering the task shown on the right.

the shipping department of a lumber mill near his home in a rural northeastern community. He had been an avid hunter and fisherman all his life. C. W., who was premorbidly left-handed, had completed 11 years of education. He was married, with two grown children living away from home. He was generally regarded as the "quiet type." He spoke only English all of his life and was thought by his wife to have average intelligence. After his injury, he was not motivated to return to work. His fall produced the only brain injury he had ever had and he suffered no coexisting neurologic disorders or major medical problems. He had no peripheral sensory deficits other than that necessitating the use of glasses for reading. The neurologic diagnosis was a left subdural hematoma in the temporoparietal area, with mild weakness in the right upper extremity. There were no signs of brainstem involvement or gait impairment. Visual fields were intact. EEG and a brain scan confirmed the neurologist's localization of the hematoma. Surgical evacuation of the hematoma was considered but it was not done. C. W. remained home with his wife until June, 1976, when he came for a speech and language evaluation in our clinic. He was alert, ambulatory, and not taking medications.

Speech and language evaluation results indicated marked aphasia in all communicative modalities, including auditory comprehension, reading, speaking, and writing deficits. There was no indication of apraxia of speech, dysarthria, confusion, or generalized intellectual impairment. PICA performance (Fig. 1-8) was at the 32nd percentile, overall; BDAE scores indicated anomic aphasia, with coexisting auditory comprehension deficits, and the MTDDA results classified C. W. into group 1, simple aphasia. His functional language was fluent but contained essentially no nouns and only a few verbs. C. W.'s conversational rating was 5 on the seven-point scale. He gave a total of seven correct answers on the 61-item Token Test, produced no words on the Word Fluency Measure, and scored 18 correct on the 36-item Coloured Progressive Matrices. Motor speech evaluation revealed no apraxia of speech, dysarthria, or oral-nonverbal apraxia. C. W. was oriented for time, place, and date using yes–no responses to multiple-choice stimuli.

Favorable prognostic signs were the patient's relatively young age, his good health and lack of associated defects, a nonpenetrating traumatic injury, and lack of unfavorable personality characteristics. Negative prognostic signs included location of the lesion in the temporoparietal area, a 6-month duration of aphasia, and the patient's geographic location, which prevented him from participating in an intense and lengthy treatment program. We believed the favorable prognostic signs outweighed the negative ones and suggested that the patient enter the hospital for an intensive 1-month treatment program. He agreed and began his treatment trial on June 21, 1976, approximately 6 months after onset.

Reevaluation at this time showed overall performance at the 37th percentile on the PICA and no change on the other measures. The treatment program consisted of 4 hours a day of speech and language therapy, 1 hour of physical therapy, and evening assignments using a Language Master along with written work. The program was conducted 5 days a week, and C. W. spent the weekends visiting his daughter. Treatment tasks were hierarchically arranged, beginning where the patient showed latency of response or the need for additional information before responding. Tasks were designed to treat all areas—auditory comprehension, reading, speaking, and writing. An intersystemic program that combined gestures and verbs was used along with a "natural language" program designed to improve auditory comprehension and, eventually, to facilitate the use of nouns in speech.

After 1 month of therapy, C. W. was discharged to return home for 1 month. Although his PICA overall performance at the time of discharge was at the 45th percentile, no overt changes were seen in any other measure. C. W. believed he had improved during the month's treatment, but he continued to feel he "didn't know nothin'." A home program was sent with him that included reading and writing exercises and verbal practice, using a Language Master.

The patient returned for an additional month of inpatient therapy on August 31. His PICA performance at that time was at the 50th percentile; his Word Fluency performance showed four words produced compared with zero on previous tests; and his Token Test performance had improved to 16 correct items compared with seven items at baseline. A treatment program was instituted farther up the patient's communicative hierarchies. The intersystemic program was intensified using additional verbs and nouns, and the natural language program was replaced with sentence completion techniques and the use of oral spelling to facilitate naming.

At the completion of the month's treatment pro-

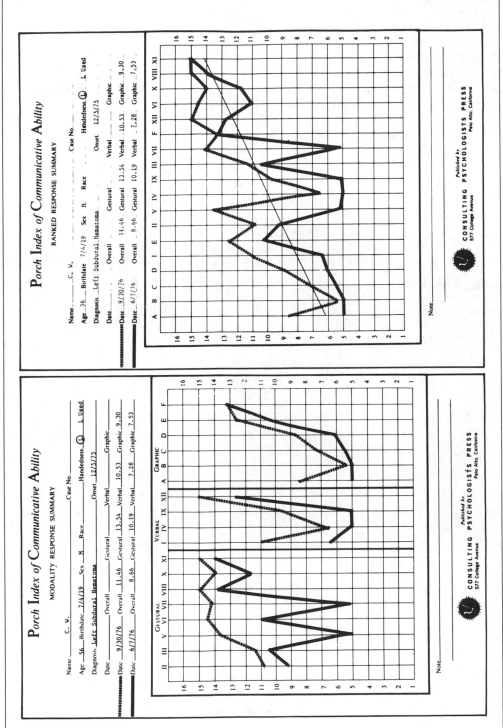

Fig. 1-8. PICA profiles showing pretreatment and posttreatment performance for C. W. Intensive inpatient therapy was administered from June 23 to July 23, followed by a 1-month vacation, followed by another month of treatment administered from August 31 to September 30.

gram, C. W. obtained an overall PICA score at the 60th percentile. His performance on the BDAE and MTDDA had improved, but the type of aphasia and the prognosis remained the same. His Word Fluency performance now showed eight words produced; his Token Test total was 13; and his Coloured Progressive Matrices performance was 24 items correct. C. W. was released for a month's vacation with a new home program. He was to return in a month for additional treatment. At discharge, he informed us "Now, I know somethin'."

C. W.'s PICA recovery curve is shown in Figure 1-9. It shows gradual improvement over a 4-month period following periods of both treatment and no treatment. The patient's "nine-high performance" (mean of his best nine subtests on the PICA) appears to elevate slightly during periods of treatment. This is where therapy has been focused, where the

patient's performance begins to break down; and these are the performances that have shown the most improvement. Figure 1-8 shows his posttreatment PICA profile compared with his initial PICA profile. Considerable improvement can be seen on primary auditory subtest VI and X and on reading subtests V and VII. Improved speaking ability is obvious on all tasks. Giving the functions of objects, subtest I, improved more than naming, subtest IV. We would like to think this shows the influence of the intersystemic verb program. Also, similar gains could be seen in his writing. Subtest A, writing the functions of objects, showed more gains than subtest B, writing the names of objects.

C. W.'s improvement appears to support Porch's [188] suggestion that recovery following trauma continues beyond 6 months after onset. Further, it lends some confidence to the belief that nonpenetrating trauma carries a favorable prognosis. Finally, change in this left-handed patient may support Eisenson's suggestion [66] that left-handers who suffer aphasia have a favorable prognosis. Whether the gains justify the time and effort can

Fig. 1-9. PICA recovery curve for C. W., showing initial performance at the 37th percentile; after 1 month of therapy, performance at the 45th percentile; following a month's vacation, performance at the 50th percentile; and, following an additional month of treatment, performance at the 60th percentile.

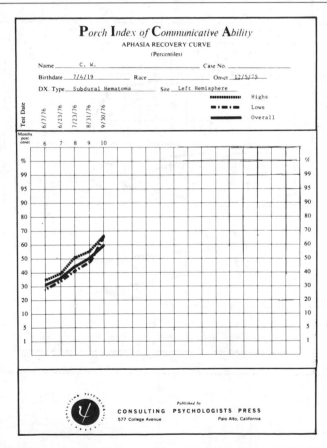

be debated. However, "knowing somethin' " is better than "knowing nothin'."

Language of Confusion

Darley's definition [48], his discussion of differential diagnosis [49], and Halpern, Darley, and Brown's comparison of four neuropathologies of speech and language [92] practically exhaust the literature on the language of confusion. Although most of the information remains in clinical files or is buried in discussions of confusion that exists in other disorders [28, 38, 80, 112, 153, 236], about 6 percent of the total patients referred to our clinic demonstrate the language of confusion.

The problem appears as a language disorder. By definition [48], given in Table 1-1, confusion may follow neurogenic damage, frequently head trauma. The confused patient has difficulty understanding and recognizing his or her environment. The confused patient's memory is faulty, thinking is muddled, and orientation for time and place is incorrect. Structured language tasks useful in detecting aphasia do not, typically, detect the language of confusion. The patient's vocabulary and syntax are within normal limits. In more open-ended language situations, confusion emerges as irrelevance and confabulation. Thus confused patients have little difficulty naming objects or describing their functions. However, when asked "What is a robin?," the patient may respond, as one of Darley's did, "A robin, is a robin, is a robin, is a robin. Gertrude Stein!" Or, if asked "Who was Helen Keller?," the patient may generate answers similar to those provided by our patient, who had never met Miss Keller.

Clinician: Who was Helen Keller?
   Patient: Helen Keller? I know her well. She would come to give a talk and I would carry her slides.
Clinician: Who was she?
   Patient: She? She was a lady who was supposed to be good, but I really didn't think so myself.
Clinician: Did she have any problems?
   Patient: Problems? Oh yes! She had problems, all kinds of problems. But I was too busy carrying slides.
Clinician: What kinds of problems did she have?
   Patient: You name it, and she had it. But she never had any difficulty with her slides. I carried those as you might remember.
Clinician: Did she have problems with her eyes or ears?
   Patient: Oh my, yes! She had problems with her eyes, with her ears, with her nose, with her mouth, with her chin. Lots of problems.

This patient's PICA performance was within normal limits. His confabulation led to our diagnosing the language of confusion.

Figure 1-10 shows a theoretical clinical profile for the language of confusion. Halpern, Darley, and Brown [92] report that their 10 confused patients were moderately impaired in four areas (arithmetic, reading comprehension, writing to dictation, and relevance) and mildly impaired in six areas (adequacy, auditory comprehension, syntax, naming, auditory retention, and fluency). A different sample of confused patients from our clinic indicates a wide range of language abilities. Some are essentially normal, and some show mild to moderate involvement. Therefore the profile of confusion shown in Figure 1-10 lists involvement of listening, speaking, reading, and writing as undetermined. Although we do not expect confused patients to demonstrate motor speech disorders, they may coexist with the language of confusion. However, they are not symptoms of the basic language disorder. Intellectual abilities in confused patients are also undetermined. Some of our patients perform normally on the Coloured Progressive Matrices, while others have a great deal of difficulty with this test. Halpern, Darley, and Brown [92] reported moderate involvement of arithmetic ability in their sample. Generalized intellectual deficit is not part of the symptom complex in the language of confusion. However, confused patients may do poorly on both verbal and nonverbal intelligence tasks either because they ignore instructions and give irrelevant responses and confabulate, or the lesion that results in the language of confusion has also damaged cortical areas necessary for intellectual performance.

LOCALIZATION. Figure 1-1 classified the language of confusion as resulting from bilateral involvement of the cerebral hemisphere. Halpern, Darley, and Brown [92] reported 3 of 10 patients who were classified as having diffuse lesions and 7 who had disseminated (multifocal; diffuse and focal) lesions. Also, 6 out of the 10 showed an EEG with general or bilateral dysrhythmia with delta rhythms. In our clinic 15 patients diagnosed as demonstrating the language of confusion were reported by the referring neurologist to have diffuse, bilateral involvement.

Luria [153] discusses patients with frontodiencephalic lesions who are disoriented in terms of space and time and who confabulate. For example, when asked "Have you met me before?" these pa-

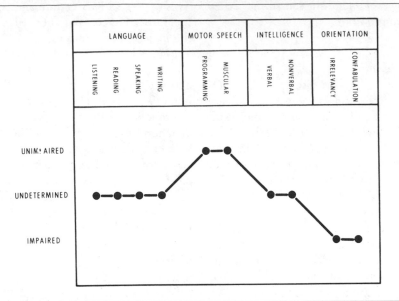

	LANGUAGE				MOTOR SPEECH		INTELLIGENCE		ORIENTATION	
	LISTENING	READING	SPEAKING	WRITING	PROGRAMMING	MUSCULAR	VERBAL	NONVERBAL	IRRELEVANCY	CONFABULATION

Fig. 1-10. Theoretical clinical profile of the language of confusion, indicating undetermined language involvement, no motor speech deficits, undetermined intellectual problems, and impaired orientation characterized by irrelevance and confabulation.

tients reply in the affirmative, give the name of someone else they know well, and set the specific place of meeting. Conversely, Luria states that patients with circumscribed lesions are oriented in terms of space and time. Geschwind [81] mentions confabulatory responses in patients who have disconnection of the sensory association cortex. Rather than expressing an inability to perform, the patient usually gives a confabulated response that is far afield. Sperry and Gazzaniga [236] support Geschwind's observations. Geschwind's report of writing disturbances in acute confusional states [80] does not give precise localization data. However, the causes of confusion in the patients studied indicated diffuse damage, and patients with signs of focal brain lesions were excluded from the study. Brookshire [28] describes a variety of behavioral deficits following lesions in the right hemisphere. Some of these (disorientation, confabulation) suggest the language of confusion. He reports a patient with an apparent right hemisphere lesion who meets several criteria listed in the definition of confusion.

The language of confusion appears to be associated with diffuse, bilateral lesions. Confusion may follow focal or unilateral lesions, but it is transient. Also, either no deficit or another neuropathology of speech or language emerges following the acute stage of confusion.

CAUSE. Causes of the language of confusion include CVAs, neoplasm, trauma, infection, and the effects of toxins and drugs. It is debatable whether true language of confusion is associated with diffuse central nervous system (CNS) disease (e.g., Alzheimer's, Pick's, or Creutzfeldt-Jakob disease), metabolic disorders, and deficiency diseases, or whether patients with these problems appear confused as a result of generalized intellectual impairment. To be consistent with our discussion of localization, the cause must be capable of inducing diffuse damage, typically of rapid onset. Halpern, Darley, and Brown's [92] sample included 8 of 10 patients whose onset was rapid, under 10 days.

A sample of 15 patients in our clinic who had the language of confusion included 7 with vascular damage, typically multiple, bilateral strokes; 1 with bilateral metastases; 5 with bilateral trauma; and 2 with an undetermined cause, diagnosed as "chronic brain syndrome." Halpern, Darley, and Brown's [92] 10 patients were subdivided into 1 who had a tumor, 5 who suffered trauma, 1 who had an infection, and 3 who had a hemorrhage or hematoma. Geschwind's [80] patients with "natural" acute confusion demonstrated delirium tremens, hepatic encephalopathy, Wernicke's encephalopathy, acute alcoholic intoxication, or barbiturate intoxication. He also observed confusion in patients undergoing electroconvulsive therapy and those under the effects of barbiturates given intravenously for general anesthesia. Geschwind reports that acute confusion can occur in any toxic or metabolic disorder of rapid onset, cases of head injury, subarachnoid hemorrhage, or increased intracranial pressure of rapid onset.

Darley's [48] definition suggests that the language of confusion is often induced traumatically. Experience in our clinic supports this observation. Patients who have suffered bilateral trauma are the ones who display the classic definitive symptoms.

APPRAISAL. Appraising the language of confusion requires collection of biographical, medical, and behavioral data. (The specifics in each area have been listed in Tables 1-4 to 1-6.) A thorough knowledge of the patient's educational-social-vocational history also is essential, since it is necessary to have an accurate baseline to compare with his or her possible confabulation. For example, if the facts are that the patient obtained a Master of Arts degree in Education from the University of New Mexico, a report of obtaining a Ph.D. in chemistry in the area of tooth structure by enrolling in two schools at the same time can be considered confabulatory. Medical data provide support for what is known about the cause and localization associated with the disorder. For example, rapid onset, a diffuse or disseminated (multifocal or diffuse and focal) lesion, traumatic cause, and an EEG showing general or bilateral dysrhythmia are neurologic data that support the diagnosis. Behavioral data (e.g., language, speech, intellect, orientation) are necessary to make a differential diagnosis.

The comprehensive evaluation listed in Table 1-6 or the specific battery suggested for aphasia in Table 1-7 provides sufficient information to make a diagnosis and, if warranted, to focus therapy. Tests of general language ability sample auditory comprehension, reading, speaking, and writing and provide data for ruling out aphasia and the language of generalized intellectual impairment. "Functional" language measures give an estimate of how well the patient does outside the clinic, and the conversational rating establishes a situation for obtaining confabulatory and irrelevant responses. The motor speech evaluation either rules out apraxia of speech and dysarthria or identifies them as co-existing disorders. Orientation and general information tasks are probably the most salient measures for diagnosing the language of confusion. Nonverbal intelligence tasks are used to rule out dementia, and they place the confused patient in a situation in which he or she is forced to attend to a specific task. If the patient fails to do so, the

clinician has an opportunity to observe his or her irrelevant responses and contrast these with the out-and-out errors suspected in patients with generalized intellectual impairment. Special tests (Token Test and Word Fluency Measure) provide a sensitive measure of auditory comprehension, which Halpern, Darley, and Brown [92] report is mildly impaired in confusion, and establish an open-ended verbal situation in which the patient may either become irrelevant or confabulate. Unless a coexisting dysarthria is suspected from the motor speech evaluation, there is no need to administer special tests of motor speech ability, such as the Structural Functional Examination.

The most useful tools for detecting the language of confusion are those that give the patient room to show the disorientation, and tendency to confabulate or offer irrelevancies. Biographical information tasks in the BDAE or MTDDA are useful, although clinician-constructed items, such as those contained in the Mayo Clinic Procedures for Language Evaluation [159] are extremely sensitive. Table 1-10 lists sample items from the Mayo and shows representative confused responses provided by our patients. These can be contrasted with the expressed inability to perform demonstrated by aphasic patients and the errors made by patients with the language of generalized intellectual impairment.

Geschwind [80] stresses the importance of using writing tasks to appraise acute states of confusion. Specifically, he suggests tasks that involve writing to command (patients are asked to compose sentences about the weather or their job), writing to dictation (patients are asked to write words and sentences said by the examiner), and copying (patients are asked to copy, in script, a sentence presented in printed letters). Chédru and Geschwind [34] also emphasize the need for appraising writing in confused patients. In addition, they suggest that a complete neuropsychological battery should include evaluation of mood and behavior, disorientation, unconcern toward illness, wordfinding, verbal paraphasia in repetition and oral reading, verbal fluency, spatial ability (right-left recognition), constructional apraxia, calculation, and memory.

Mills and Drummond [164] report that naming errors may signify the language of confusion. By comparing naming errors on high-uncertainty and low-uncertainty stimuli, response time, and semantic analysis of errors, they differentiated confused patients from aphasic patients. Milton, Tun-

Table 1-10. Orientation and general information items used to appraise the language of confusion

Item	Example response in the language of confusion
*Orientation**	
What day of the week is today?	This week, today is Monday.
What month is it?	It was May.
What is the date?	I really don't know. You will have to ask someone else.
What year is it?	1940! Wait a minute. 1951! No! 1963!
Where are you now?	I am in the University of Minnesota.
What city are you in?	Sun Prairie.
What state are you in?	Wisconsin or Minnesota or both.
Why are you here?	To reenroll in school.
General Information	
When do we celebrate Christmas?	The night before.
What is the capitol of the United States?	That would be Madison, Wisconsin.
Who is the president of the United States? (back through F.D.R.)	Dr. Duck! And before him was Dr. Duck himself and then Snixon and Nelson.
Who discovered America? When?	Lief Erickson in the 12th Century.
How many states are there in the United States?	There are still 49.
Who was the first president of the United States?	That would be Benjamin Franklin.
Who was president during the Civil War?	Washington succeeded Franklin.
Who invented Mickey Mouse and Donald Duck?	The inventor of Mickey Mouse was Dr. Duck.
What country is immediately north of the United States?	That would be Canada or Mexico depending on the direction you go?
Who was Helen Keller?	She had a watch from her father, and she would answer him by looking at the watch.

*Evaluation was conducted on January 14, 1975, in the Veterans Administration Hospital in Madison, Wisconsin.
Source: Adapted from Mayo Clinic Procedures for Language Evaluation. Unpublished test.

stall, and Wertz [165] employed a descriptive scoring system to evaluate naming behavior in a confused patient who had suffered bilateral head trauma. Its use permitted differentiation of confusion from aphasia, focusing treatment, and evaluating the efficacy of treatment.

DIAGNOSIS. The primary task in diagnosing the language of confusion is to differentiate it from aphasia and the language of generalized intellectual impairment. Mistaking the language of confusion for apraxia of speech or dysarthria seldom, if ever, occurs, but either may coexist with it and complicate the diagnosis. Specifically, the clinician must be satisfied that the patient's syntax and word-finding abilities are sufficiently adequate to rule out aphasia and that the disorientation, confabulation, and irrelevancy cannot be explained by an intellectual deficit.

Darley's [48] definition specifies the presence of disorientation, faulty memory, unclear thinking, irrelevance, and confabulation on open-ended language tasks. These features can be contrasted with more normal behavior on structured language tasks.

Halpern, Darley, and Brown [92] indicated that confused patients displayed mild to moderate deficits in the 10 areas evaluated. The group mean impairment, 28 percent, was at the upper end of the range of "mild impairment"; and 4 of their 10 patients were within the range of "moderate impairment," 31 to 60 percent. Lack of relevance was the main characteristic that differentiated the group of confused patients from those with aphasia and generalized intellectual impairment. For example, of the 10 areas evaluated, relevance was the third most impaired area for confused patients. Conversely, relevance ranked tenth for aphasic patients and eighth for patients with generalized intellectual deficits. Generally, their confused patients gave bizarre responses, showed unclear thinking, had faulty memory, and made no attempt to correct irrelevant responses.

A series of questions suggested by Darley [49] assists in differentiating confused patients from those with aphasia. First, Is the patient oriented in terms of space and time? Second, Does the patient stay in contact with the examiner? Third, Is the patient aware of his or her inappropriate responses? Fourth,

Does the patient demonstrate vocabulary and syntax problems? If answers to all these questions are no, confusion is a highly probable diagnosis.

Differentiating confusion from a general intellectual deficit is difficult. Both disorders are characterized by moderate difficulty in reading comprehension and arithmetic, and both have mild auditory comprehension deficit. Halpern, Darley, and Brown [92] reported that confused patients had more problems in writing to dictation than the group of patients who had generalized intellectual impairments; however, the latter scored lower on "adequacy" than the former. The main difference was in relevance. Confused patients were highly irrelevant, and patients with generalized intellectual impairment were seldom irrelevant.

PROGNOSIS. The future for a patient displaying the language of confusion is not found in the meager literature existing on the subject. Reports by Geschwind [80] and Chédru and Geschwind [34] on writing deficits in "acute confusional states" imply that change is imminent. Conditions do not remain acute forever.

Probably the best predictor of recovery from confusion is the patient's disorder. If the cause is one that eventually permits recovery from physiologic symptoms and the patient's medical future is bright, then improvement in behavioral deficits would be expected. Conversely, if the disorder is progressive, the prognosis is poor. Somewhere between these two is a guarded prognosis given for patients who are suffering from a disorder that is nonprogressive, but the initial episode is sufficiently severe to result in persisting behavioral deficits that may improve with treatment. Finally, there are patients who have the language of confusion initially, in whom the disorder is evolving, and, when complete, their speech and language behavior will require another diagnosis. For example, we diagnosed the language of confusion in a patient suffering from cerebral vasculitis. His confusion remained chronic for almost a year, and then he suffered a left-hemisphere CVA that resulted in profound aphasia.

Disorders resulting in confusion that imply a favorable prognosis are trauma; operable, nonmalignant neoplasms; infections; and toxic or drug-induced states that have not persisted or resulted in severe destruction of tissue. Disorders indicating a poor prognosis are multiple CVAs; malignant neoplasms; and severe destruction of tissue resulting from the effects of infection, toxins, or drugs.

All these disorders indicate a guarded prognosis when sufficient damage has occurred, the medical condition is static, and the patient is left with chronic behavioral deficits.

FOCUSING THERAPY. Treating the language of confusion may involve one or more of three approaches. First, medical management (medication, surgery, diet, and so on) may combat the effects of the cause and result in elimination or reduction of behavioral deficits. Second, modifying the patient's environment with strong doses of reality that restrict flights into irrelevance and confabulation may serve to improve the patient's orientation and eliminate bizarre behavior. Third, language therapy designed to improve listening, reading, speaking, and writing deficits may be administered with an initial emphasis on highly structured tasks that gradually evolve into more open-ended situations. Unfortunately, few reports on the effectiveness of treatment with confused patients exist.

Medical management of patients demonstrating the language of confusion is dictated by the disorder; surgery or medication or both are employed in some patients who suffer trauma, neoplasms, or infection. Also, reduction of the intracranial pressure may reduce or eliminate the patient's confusion. For example, one of our patients who underwent surgical removal of an olfactory groove meningioma and a postoperative drug program improved his preoperative PICA performance, which was in the 60th percentile overall, to the 80th percentile postoperatively. Before surgery, he believed he was "in the producer's office to cast a medieval farce." One week after surgery, he correctly identified his environment as the "Madison VA Hospital, where I had brain surgery." Withdrawal of medication is the approach used with some confused patients suffering from the toxic effects of drugs. For example, the acute state of confusion associated with bromide intoxication may be relieved by immediate cessation of the drug and administration of sodium chloride; however, the confusion may persist for several weeks. We observed rapid improvement in a confused patient whose Dilantin level was reduced to the therapeutic level from three times that amount. He explained that "if one of those was supposed to be good for me, I figured three or four would work wonders." Finally, combined administration of medication and manipulation of diet reduces confusion in certain deficiency disorders. Pellagra, for example, if caught early, responds to a treatment program that corrects the dietary state and includes large doses of nicotinic acid and thiamine. Similarly, the acute state of confusion seen in Wernicke-Korsakoff's syndrome may improve with bed rest, withdrawal of alcohol, high caloric and vitamin diet, and large doses of thiamine.

Typically, medical management is designed to treat the entire disorder, not just the patient's confusion. There are, however, a handful [36, 78, 197] of reports that have recommended medication to improve confusion in patients with cerebrovascular disorders. Cox [36] summarizes the general opinion that dosages of naftidrofuryl result in observable improvement in some patients' orientation, relevancy, mood, and personality traits. However, no difference was seen between a drug-treated group and a placebo-treated group on specific tests of memory, vocabulary, calculation, and speech. Nevertheless, both groups displayed significant improvement in all areas in a test-retest comparison.

Modification of the confused patient's environment by introducing contacts with reality has been successful with some confused elderly patients [75, 186, 249]. Called *reality orientation*, the approach is reported to be appropriate for patients demonstrating confusion and disorientation because of organic cerebral deficits resulting from arteriosclerosis, trauma, CVA, or excess medication. Phillips [186] described the basic motif. Patients are constantly reminded of their names, where they are, the day of the week, the month, the year, what meal comes next, and so on. This is accomplished by direct interaction with all hospital staff members, individual and group sessions, and the constant presence of a reality orientation board that lists all the essential information. All staff members, custodial personnel through the hospital administration, are involved. There is rigid adherence to the patient's schedule and emphasis on maintaining the same personnel. The basic conditions are a calm environment, a set routine, clear responses to the patient's questions with the same type of questions asked of the patient, clear directions and assistance in guiding patients to and from their destinations if they need it, constant reminders of the date and time, interruption of patients who start to ramble in their speech or actions, firmness when necessary, sincerity, a calm manner when making requests of patients, and consistency.

Beyond the constant reality orientation delivered on a 24-hour schedule by individual staff members, three group settings are provided as a more formal induction into reality. The basic group is comprised of a staff member and 3 or 4 patients who meet daily for a half-hour. Basic orientation information is drilled and cemented into habitual use. If a patient is unable to respond, the information is given to him or her, and the patient is asked to repeat it. When patients show they are ready, they are promoted into an advanced group, where they are expected to perform faster and at a higher level of accuracy. New material is introduced at a more rapid pace, and its complexity is gradually increased. Advanced groups include 6 to 8 patients and maintain the same schedule, a half-hour a day, 5 days a week. On completion of the advanced group, patients are eased into other group programs—special interest, exercise, discussion, crafts, and so on—and "remotivation sessions." The latter meet for 1 hour five times a week. These groups are composed of up to 15 patients and a group leader who uses objects, readings, and records to facilitate discussion among group members.

Folsom [75] reports the effectiveness of reality orientation with elderly veterans, and Phillips [186] cites similar results in community nursing homes. The latter suggests it might be the social interaction with others rather than the actual therapeutic approach that assists the patient in returning to reality. While there is inconclusive empirical support for the effectiveness of either type of treatment, a heuristic explanation is that patients can receive social interaction from friends, family, and ward mates and remain confused. Some, when enrolled in a reality orientation program, become oriented, reduce or eliminate confabulation, and become relevant.

The role of the speech pathologist in focusing and administering treatment for patients who demonstrate the language of confusion is not specified in any published literature. Commonly, the speech pathology service is not the first type of treatment that occurs to the primary care physician faced with a confused patient. Thus referral of confused patients to speech pathologists is not common, and our experience in focusing and administering therapy to relieve confusion is limited. However, since these patients may display specific language deficits, one could argue that intervention with language therapy is a justifiable adjunct to the medical treatment.

Halpern, Darley, and Brown [92] report that arithmetic, reading comprehension, writing to dictation, and relevance are moderately impaired in confused patients. Overall language adequacy, auditory comprehension, syntax, naming, auditory retention, and fluency are mildly impaired. Since these patients demonstrate many of the language deficits present in aphasia, some of the dimensions listed in Table 1-9 for focusing aphasia therapy may be appropriate when developing treatment for confused patients. The primary principle in focusing therapy for confused patients is to control the specificity of the response. Darley [48] suggests that confused patients do fairly well on structured language tasks. They begin to confabulate and become irrelevant when language situations become open-ended. Therefore treatment for the language of confusion is a process of gradually reducing the amount of structure present in the task and, simultaneously, maintaining control over the patient's tendency to be irrelevant and confabulate. Like aphasia therapy, therapy for the language of confusion begins with simplicity and progresses toward complexity. Also, similar to the approach employed with aphasic patients, treatment begins where the confused patient starts to experience difficulties.

Stimuli for confused patients should be meaningful. Listening, reading, speaking, and writing activities are designed, employing stimuli that orient the patient—his or her name, date, location, your name, and so on—and proceed to activities that fill in the patient's biographical background, such as age, occupation, and names of family members. Length and complexity of stimuli are increased as the patient is able to cope with them. The stimulus mode, or modes, is chosen to keep the patient tuned into the task. If the patient has a tendency to wander when auditory stimuli are used, a visual mode or combined auditory-visual modes may be more appropriate. Also, manipulation of response modes is a good way to keep the language tasks structured. There is little room to confabulate when the response requested is pointing or simple gesturing. More opportunity to be irrelevant and confabulate is possible when the patient is requested to produce complex gestures, speak, or write. Therefore treatment begins with pointing and simple gesturing and progresses into speaking, complex gesturing, and writing. Maintaining a tight control over the temporal relations of stimulus and response also assists in structuring the task. Initial tasks may utilize unison or immediate responses, and subsequent tasks introduce increasing amounts of delay. In addition, consecutive responses are a way of reinforcing the orientation. For example,

if a patient is requested to repeat his or her name, the date, or whatever, three times rather than once, control is exercised in keeping the patient tuned into the task. When dealing with a confused patient, one should add immediate knowledge of results to a list of facilitators. The techniques employed in reality orientation that stop the patient if he or she begins to confabulate or become irrelevant and give the patient the correct response are essential. From the beginning, confused patients should be stopped, questioned, and told their responses are inappropriate.

Some methods appropriate for treating aphasia may be appropriate for confused patients, depending on the severity of their disorder. Imitation, matching, and selection among alternatives are good ways to keep the tasks structured. Completion tasks are introduced gradually to provide the confused patient more time to respond. The tasks can be manipulated in terms of concreteness or abstractness gradually, either to introduce more freedom or to maintain restraint in the patient's response. For example, repetition tasks may evolve into naming tasks, which may be followed by sentence completion tasks. These tasks may evolve into using words in a sentence, which may be followed by defining words, and eventually, the patient may be asked to explain analogies or proverbs. This rather simplistic hierarchy of verbal tasks proceeds as the patient demonstrates he or she can control the tendency to confabulate and become irrelevant.

All treatment is focused with strong participation by the patient. We must be constantly aware of what the patient has to tell us about the disorder. For example, one of our patients demonstrated that printed stimuli reduced his tendency to confabulate. In addition, he would rather talk about his own history than drill on stimuli provided by the therapist. Therefore we developed a series of questions about his personal history and used these as the treatment stimuli. Initially, they were printed on cards, shown to him as the therapist read the questions aloud (e.g., "Where did you work?"). The question was repeated in unison with the therapist, and the card was reversed to reveal the answer, which followed the same pattern—shown to the patient while the therapist read it aloud and then repeated in unison. A baseline was taken at the beginning of treatment to determine the patient's ability to provide answers to 50 questions about his history. The treatment paradigm was administered twice daily during half-hour sessions, and performance was measured weekly. At the end of 4 weeks, the patient was 100 percent correct in providing spontaneous answers to all 50 questions; and there was carryover into his conversation with the speech pathology staff and other hospital personnel. He seldom lapsed into confabulation or became irrelevant. When he did (e.g., "Now let's get this straight about the rooms. The girl therapist and I will use it during the day and you can have it at night"), the impetus was usually traced to a change in his daily schedule (e.g., his physical therapy schedule and room had been changed without his being prepared for it). Treatment evolved into presentation of rapid, alternating questions described by Martin [158] on unrelated topics.

A total treatment approach for the language of confusion would involve medical management directed at the cause, reality orientation, and specific language therapy designed to improve specific communicative deficits. The speech pathologist has a role to play in rehabilitating the confused patient's language and can assist in organizing reality orientation by providing instruction and materials to hospital personnel who have contact with the patient.

CLINICAL EXAMPLE. J. M., a 53-year-old high school mathematics teacher, suffered a cerebrovascular episode on August 2, 1972. The neurologic diagnosis was "CVA, left hemisphere and midbrain infarct." He was given a speech and language evaluation on September 27. J. M. was disoriented for time, date, and place. His verbal output consisted of circumlocutions, confabulations, irrelevancies, and neologisms. A PICA, shown in Figure 1-11, indicated overall performance at the 62nd percentile. While language deficits were present, the patient's vocabulary and syntax were too good to be explained as aphasia. His tendency to confabulate and to be irrelevant and his disorientation indicated the language of confusion. J. M. was seen again on October 4, approximately 2 months after onset. His overall performance on the PICA had improved to the 87th percentile. A Token Test revealed marked involvement of auditory comprehension, Word Fluency performance was at the 55th percentile for patients with left hemisphere involvement, and his Coloured Progressive Matrices performance was at the 75th percentile. He continued to demonstrate an inability to follow directions, a good deal of confabulation and irrelevancy, and a lack of orientation for time, date, and place. A daily treatment program designed to improve his orientation, reduce confabulation, and increase his ability to follow directions was instituted. After 4 weeks of treatment, J. M. wanted to return home. He was discharged from the hospital. A home treatment program was designed and administered by a family friend. It included orientation drills, mathematical drills, and exercises designed to improve the patient's ability to follow directions.

J. M. returned for reevaluation on November 22. His PICA overall performance was at the 99th percentile, and his Token Test performance had improved to 59 items correct on the 61-item test. No changes were noted in his scores on Word Fluency or Coloured Progressive Matrices. The patient wanted to return to work, and his school encouraged this. A home program comprised of activities he would be required to do as a high school teacher was sent with him. In addition, arrangements were made for him to grade high school mathematics examinations and to tutor mathematics in the local junior high school.

The patient returned for reevaluation on January 15. His PICA overall performance remained at the 99th percentile, and he obtained a perfect score on the Token Test. No changes were noted in his performance on Word Fluency or the Coloured Progressive Matrices. Reports from the patient's high school colleagues indicated he had performed quite adequately as a tutor in the junior high school and as a grader. Arrangements were made for J. M. to begin teaching part-time in the high school at the beginning of the spring semester.

A final evaluation was obtained on June 13. J. M.'s PICA performance remained at the 99th percentile and no errors were noted on the Token Test. Again, no changes were noted in his scores on the Word Fluency Measure or Coloured Progressive Matrices. The patient was oriented, relevant, and displayed no confabulation. He had taught successfully on a part-time basis during the spring semester and planned to return to teaching full time in the fall.

Figure 1-12 shows J. M.'s recovery curve. Rapid improvement can be seen within the first 3 months after onset. Return of functional language was adequate for the patient to resume his position as a high school teacher. However, a persisting deficit was an inability to remember the names of colleagues and acquaintances. J. M. expressed that he was not "as good as before," but "no one needs to be that good."

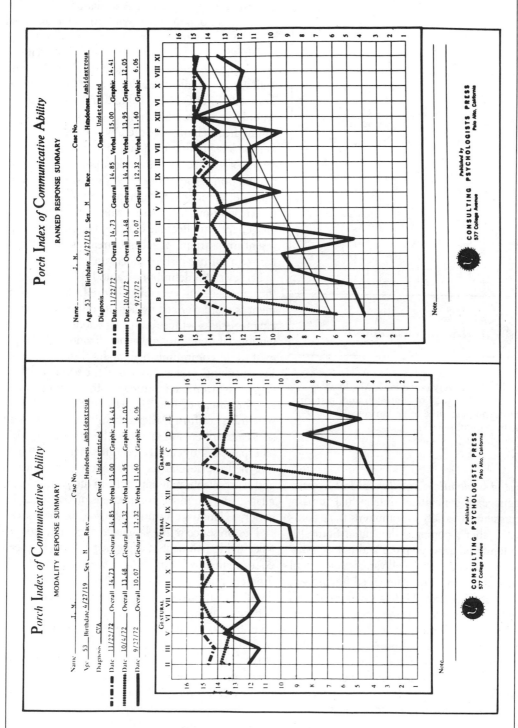

Fig. 1-11. PICA modality and ranked response summaries, showing initial and subsequent performance by J. M., who demonstrated the language of confusion. Initial performance at the 62nd percentile overall improved to performance at the 99th percentile in 2 months.

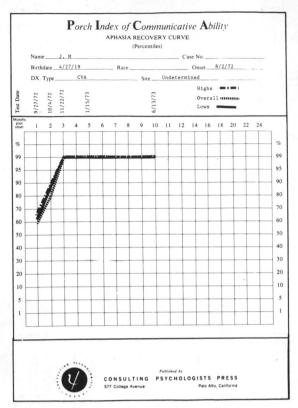

Porch **I**ndex of **C**ommunicative **A**bility

APHASIA RECOVERY CURVE
(Percentiles)

Name _____ J. M. _____ Case No. _____
Birthdate _4/27/19_____ Race _____ Onset _8/2/72____
DX. Type _____CVA_____ Site _Undetermined_

Published by
CONSULTING PSYCHOLOGISTS PRESS
577 College Avenue   Palo Alto, California

Fig. 1-12. PICA recovery curve for J. M. showing rapid recovery in language of confusion from performance at the 62nd percentile to performance at the 99th percentile in 2 months.

Language of Generalized Intellectual Impairment
The language of generalized intellectual impairment represents a variety of symptoms that, combined with others, comprise dementia. Some [9] describe dementia as a symptom and not as a disorder—one that is present in all varieties of mental disturbance that result from impaired function of the cerebral hemispheres. The classic features [209] of dementia may include some degree of disorientation, impaired memory, defective calculation, and labile affect. Wang and Busse [246] report that dementia is the most common clinical syndrome among aged persons; 63 percent of elderly institutionalized patients demonstrate some degree of dementia. The neurogenic etiology and the subsequent language deficits qualify dementia for consideration as a neuropathology of communication. The speech pathologist, therefore, assists in its diagnosis and management.

DEFINITION. Wells [251, p. 8] defines *dementia* as "the spectrum of mental states resulting from disease of man's cerebral hemispheres in adult life." The American Psychiatric Association [4] lists dementia as an organic brain syndrome characterized by impairment in orientation, memory, intellectual function (e.g., comprehension, calculation, knowledge, learning), judgment, and lability and shallowness of affect. Bayles [13, 14] and Bayles, Tomoeda, and Caffrey [16] tell us dementia is the chronic, progressive deterioration of intellect resulting from changes in the CNS. Cummings and Benson [41] define dementia as an acquired syndrome of intellectual impairment produced by brain dysfunction. Horenstein [109] discusses amnestic, agnostic, apractic, and aphasic features in dementia. He cautions that these cannot explain the overall general intellectual deficit. They simply represent impairment of specific areas of the brain as part of a diffuse disease process.

Darley's [48] definition, Table 1-1, specifies that the language of generalized intellectual impairment is characterized by deficits on more difficult language tasks—those requiring retention, close attention, abstraction, and generalization. Problems exist in all communicative modes (listening, reading, speaking, and writing), and the severity of language involvement is similar to that demonstrated in other areas of intellect. Horenstein's [109] observations confirm Darley's definition. The patient speaks less often and says less when he or she does. The patient's utterances become increasingly stereotyped, perseverative, and concrete; abstraction and symbolization disappear from the patient's language; and auditory comprehension is better for concrete language stimuli than for abstract ones.

The presence of the language of generalized intellectual impairment in demented patients has been documented by Ferm [74], who reported that only 5 percent of the demented patients in her sample could communicate adequately. The correlation between the rating of communicative deficit and severity of dementia as measured by a modification of Isaacs and Walkey's test [112] for dementia was +0.82, the highest of all abilities (orientation, recognition of persons, eating, and so on) compared with overall severity. Halpern, Darley, and Brown [92] observed mild to moderate impairment on 7 of 10 communicative tasks in their sample of patients diagnosed as demonstrating the language of generalized intellectual impairment. Thus language is impaired in dementia, and, based on Ferm's results, the severity of impairment may be a good indication of overall severity of dementia.

The clinical profile of the language of generalized intellectual impairment, shown in Figure 1-13, indicates language deficits in all communicative modes, no motor speech disorders, impairment of both verbal and nonverbal intelligence, and undetermined involvement in orientation. There is consensus regarding language disturbance in dementia [48, 74, 92, 108]. Motor speech disorders, apraxia of speech or dysarthria, are not symptoms of the general disorder, but either may coexist [109]. Critchley [38] and Espir and Rose [73] discuss dysarthriclike speech in demented patients, where /s/ and /t/ are interpolated and voice quality becomes high-pitched; however, neither is believed to result from muscular involvement. Intellectual deficit (verbal and nonverbal) is the primary sign of dementia [250]. Although disorientation for time and place may be present [108, 251], the confabulation and irrelevancy seen in the language of confusion are absent.

LOCALIZATION. Kral [130] believes relationships between the site of the lesion and behavior in demented patients are poorly understood. Dementia results from a process that involves either the entire brain (e.g., Alzheimer's disease) or large portions of the cortex (e.g., Pick's disease). Most [9, 90, 251] suggest that dementia results from diffuse involvement of both cerebral hemispheres, and the presence of specific deficits, such as amnesia, agnosia, apraxia, or aphasia, does not permit anatomic inference regarding the location of the lesion [109].

Occasional reports provide specific localization information. Reyes, Chokroverty, and Masdeu's [196] observation of dementia in a patient with Hodgkin's disease and thalamic neuroaxonal dystrophy is an example. Further, Horenstein [108] lists behavioral deficits found in dementia that have localizing significance (e.g., color-form sorting deficits imply frontal lobe involvement). However, he concludes that function in dementia is globally deficient, indicating diffuse damage. Cummings and Benson [41] subdivide dementia into cortical dementias (e.g., Alzheimer's and Pick's diseases) and subcortical dementias in the extrapyramidal disorders (Huntington's disease, Parkinson's disease, and others).

Eight of the 10 patients reported by Halpern, Darley, and Brown [92] who demonstrated the language of generalized intellectual impairment had suffered diffuse lesions. EEG results on demented patients [144] typically show general or bilateral dysrhythmia. Certain localized disorders (e.g., arteriovenous malformations, subdural hematomas, trauma, abscess, tumor) may be diagnosed as de-

Fig. 1-13. Theoretical clinical profile of the language of generalized intellectual impairment, indicating language impairment in all modalities, no motor speech deficits, impaired intellectual abilities, and undetermined orientation problems.

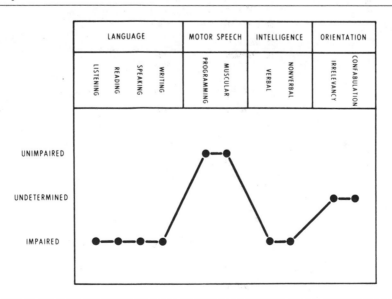

mentia, although the diagnosis is debatable. Thus it is not a question of whether lesions that cause dementia can be localized, but whether localized lesions cause dementia. Perhaps aphasia, the language of confusion, apraxia, and so on would be more appropriate labels for what may appear, initially, as dementia. For the speech pathologist, localization is important if it influences the diagnosis. If the behavioral deficits are clearly dementia, localization is only interesting.

CAUSE. Possible causes of dementia are listed in Table 1-2. Other lists are abundant in the literature [9, 73, 90], and most of them [9, 90] differentiate between causes of presenile and senile dementia. Barrett [9] separates what he calls *primary* causes, those with well-defined cerebral disorders, from *symptomatic* causes, those that represent other disease processes and exert a secondary effect on the nervous system. Many of the latter are, according to Barrett, amenable to treatment. An adaptation of his classification is shown in Table 1-11.

Primary dementias include presenile, senile, Jakob-Creutzfeldt disease, and Huntington's chorea, among others. Alzheimer's disease and Pick's disease are classified as causes of presenile dementia [9, 90, 250]. This indicates that both have their onset before age 65. The primary sign in Alzheimer's disease is intellectual deterioration, which

may masquerade as a psychogenic illness if the patient exhibits anxiety, depression, and paranoia. Eventually, disorientation, memory disturbance, auditory comprehension deficits, and defective judgment develop. Language symptoms appear as intellectual deterioration progresses, and death typically occurs 5 to 15 years after diagnosis. The pathology usually involves extensive areas of the cerebral cortex, although it may be restricted to the frontal or temporal lobes. Pick's disease results from atrophy of the cortex. The behavioral features are essentially the same as those seen in Alzheimer's disease. Familial instances are reported for both disorders.

Senile dementia is similar to Alzheimer's disease. The pathology consists of diffuse cerebral atrophy, senile plaques, and neurofibral tangles. Progression is slower than in Alzheimer's disease, and focal signs, such as aphasia and apraxia, are less apparent. Jakob-Creutzfeldt disease results from rapid disintegration of the neurons in the cerebral cortex. Also, some involvement of the basal ganglia, cerebellum, and anterior horns of the spinal cord has been reported. Behavioral manifestations include personality changes, anxiety, depression, and intellectual and memory deficits. These may progress to include speech disturbances, confusion, and visual hallucinations. The course of the disease is usually measured in months, and most afflicted

Table 1-11. Primary and symptomatic causes resulting in dementia

Primary causes	Symptomatic causes

Presenile dementias
  Alzheimer's disease
  Pick's disease
	Arteriopathic dementias
	  Lacunar state
	  Binswanger's subcortical encephalopathy
	  Granular cortical atrophy

Senile dementia	Cerebral hypoxia
Jakob-Creutzfeldt disease	

Huntington's chorea	Metabolic diseases
	  Myxedema
	  Hypoglycemia
	  Chronic hepatic disease
	  Uremia
	  Wilson's disease

Others
  Parkinson's disease
  Progressive supranuclear palsy
  Spinocerebellar degeneration
  Hallervorden-Spatz disease
	Nutritional diseases
	  Wernicke-Korsakoff syndrome
	  Vitamin B_{12} deficiency
	  Pellagra
	Heavy-metal intoxication (lead, mercury, manganese)
	Drug intoxication
	Normal-pressure hydrocephalus
	Neoplasms
	Trauma
	Infections

Source: Adapted from R. E. Barrett, Dementia in adults. *Med. Clin. North Am.* 56 : 1405, 1972.

patients do not survive the first year. Huntington's chorea is a genetically determined motor disorder. The pathology consists of neuronal loss in the caudate nucleus and putamen as well as neuronal degeneration in the cortex of the frontal lobes. The disease evolves slowly, and survival of 15 to 20 years is not uncommon. The "other category" listed in Table 1-11 does not feature dementia as the primary symptom, but it may be associated with each disorder and is demonstrated by varying degrees of intellectual impairment.

Barrett [9] implies that the symptomatic dementias may have a favorable prognosis. These constitute a host of highly dissimilar problems, including arteriopathic dementias caused by cerebral arteriosclerosis. Three general types are identified— lacunar state, Binswanger's subcortical encephalopathy, and granular cortical atrophy. The lacunar state results from numerous small cavities in the basal ganglia, the white matter, thalamus, deep cerebellar structures, and pons. The cerebral cortex remains essentially normal. Binswanger's encephalopathy results from destruction of the white matter of the cerebral hemisphere and, again, the cerebral cortex is relatively well preserved. Granular cortical atrophy results from numerous small infarcts in the cerebral cortex. These three are believed to be the most common cause of generalized intellectual impairment in the elderly.

Cerebral hypoxia is the reduction of oxygen supply to the brain. There are many causes, including ischemic anoxia, as in cardiac arrest; anoxic anoxia, as in impaired respiratory function; and histotoxic anoxia, resulting from the effects of toxins. Gray matter is always damaged more than white matter. The behavioral deficits vary so widely that dementia may be an improper diagnosis for impairment resulting from anoxia. Depending on the severity, duration, and type of anoxia, deficits may be complete or partial. Although dementia may occur in the early stages, the patient may eventually display aphasia, apraxia, or dysarthria.

Metabolic diseases, including myxedema, hypoglycemia, chronic hepatic disease, uremia, and Wilson's disease, are included in Barrett's classification of symptomatic dementias. Again, these may result in other behavioral disorders (aphasia, language of confusion) rather than dementia. Two, myxedema and Wilson's disease, have been discussed previously under the language of confusion. Hypoglycemia usually occurs in labile diabetics. Damage results from repeated episodes of lowered blood glucose, and this may evolve into impairment of memory and general intellectual functions. Chronic hepatic disease results when there is an elevation of blood ammonia or a low tolerance for ammonia. Behavioral signs may include dementia, dysarthria, or the language of confusion. Uremia is commonly seen in the late stages of progressive renal failure. Dementia also may occur along with other speech and language disorders. These have been reported by Rosenbek et al. [203].

Nutritional diseases, including Wernicke-Korsakoff syndrome, vitamin B_{12} deficiency, and pellagra, may result in dementia or the language of confusion. These were discussed previously as disorders that result in the language of confusion.

Heavy-metal intoxication and drug intoxication may result in dementia or other neuropathologies of speech and language. The ultimate speech and language diagnosis depends on where and how much damage occurs. If damage is focal, aphasia or apraxia of speech or both result. If damage is generalized, the language of confusion may result if destruction has not been permanent or the patient responds to treatment. If damage is generalized and permanent, the language of generalized intellectual impairment and other signs of dementia result.

Normal-pressure hydrocephalus may create a slowly progressing dementia and an apraxia of gait. The assumed pathology is ventricular enlargement subsequent to obstruction of the normal spinal fluid pathway. Spinal fluid pressure remains or returns to normal levels, but excessive force is exerted on the lateral ventricular walls. Treatment involving introduction of a low-pressure ventriculoatrial or lumboperitoneal shunt frequently has a dramatic effect in relieving these symptoms.

Neoplasms, trauma, or infection may result in dementia or one of the other neuropathologies of speech and language. Again, the size and location of damage dictate the behavioral deficits. Further, the effectiveness of treatment (surgery, medication, etc.) dictates whether dementia, if present, persists or subsides into a more focal neurogenic speech and language disorder.

Probably the most recent and carefully compiled list of etiologies is provided by Cummings and Benson [41]. They separate cortical dementias from subcortical dementias, as has been noted. Further, they classify and discuss dementia in vascular and infectious disorders; dementia in metabolic and toxic conditions; hydrocephalic dementia; dementia associated with psychiatric disorders, the "pseudodementias"; and dementias associated with other acquired (e.g., trauma) and inherited disorders (e.g., leukodystrophies).

APPRAISAL. Dementia is a medical diagnosis made by the primary care physician. The language of generalized intellectual impairment is a language diagnosis made by the speech pathologist. The latter diagnosis is supportive evidence for the former. Appraisal of the patient suspected of being demented requires collection of the biographical, medical, and behavioral data listed in Tables 1-4, 1-5, and 1-6. In addition, more elaborate appraisal of the patient's verbal and nonverbal intelligence is done, and a psychiatric interview may be obtained to rule out psychosis. The additional intellectual appraisal is typically carried out by a psychologist or a neuropsychologist.

Roth and Meyers [209], Wells [251], and Cummings and Benson [41] present detailed outlines of the appraisal procedure used to assess the presence of dementia. A condensation of these is shown in Table 1-12. When taking the history, the physician becomes suspicious if the patient's complaints fit no discernible pattern of physical disease; if the patient presents a variety of psychiatric symptoms, such as depression, anxiety, and irritability; or if the patient presents a story that remains vague and unclear even after exhaustive questioning. If dementia is suspected, the patient's history has to be examined carefully. First, a precise description of the initial symptoms is essential. For example, has there been memory loss, difficulty concentrating, keeping facts and schedules in order, or dealing with complex materials? Second, the onset and

progression of the problems are important, because these may suggest an etiology. For example, abrupt onset and a stuttering course imply vascular disease. Third, a complete history of cerebral functioning is obtained. For example, have there been headaches, changes in level of consciousness, or seizures?

Much of the mental status evaluation is accomplished during history taking. The formal portion documents the presence of dementia, provides a quantitative baseline of ability, and identifies specific dysfunctions (e.g., amnestic, agnostic, apractic, and aphasic) that may have focal significance. Evaluation of appearance and behavior includes observation of the patient's dress and grooming, alertness and responsiveness, ability to attend to questions, speed and range of movements, and cooperativeness. Orientation is evaluated by asking the patient's name, where he or she is, the time of day, the day of the week, the date, the year, and the season. Speech and language evaluation includes observation of the amount of speech used, intelligibility of articulation, syntax, word-finding problems, and logical content of the patient's discourse. Evaluation of mood is an attempt to get at the patient's "spirits," fears, anxieties, manias, and depressions. Four areas of memory—immediate recall, recent memory, remote memory, and general grasp and recall—are evaluated. Tests for immediate memory include repetition of digits, forward and backward, or repeating three unrelated words immediately and again 5 minutes later. Recent memory is tested by having the patient explain how he or she got to the examiner's office, when and what he or she ate last, or three things the

Table 1-12. Appraisal battery for evaluating dementia

Examination	Areas evaluated
History	Primary complaint, onset of complaint, specific symptoms
Mental status evaluation	Appearance and behavior, orientation, speech and language, mood, memory (immediate, recent, remote, general grasp, and recall)
General intellectual evaluation	General information, calculation, discrimination, and judgment
Special preoccupations and experiences	Hallucinations; illusions; delusions, obsessions, phobias, compulsions, rituals; understanding
Physical examination	Complete medical
Neurologic examination	Complete routine examination
Laboratory tests	Chest x-ray; skull x-ray; CT scan; EEG; brain scan; electrocardiogram; urinalysis; Schilling test; complete blood studies (serologic, drug levels, electrolytes, urea, liver function, protein-bound iodine); cerebrospinal fluid

patient has done that day. Remote memory testing involves asking the patient's date of birth, parents' names, schools attended, jobs held, names of children, etc. General grasp and recall testing involves asking the patient to perform a series of tasks that increase in difficulty. For example, "Raise the right arm, put the left index finger on the nose, put the right index finger on the left eye," and so on. Recalling a story read to the patient also measures general grasp and recall.

The general intellectual evaluation is designed to determine whether patients can perform at a level consistent with their social, occupational, and educational status. It includes tests of general information (e.g., Who is president of the United States? Who is governor of your state? Name the states that border on your home state, and so on); calculation (e.g., subtract 7 from 100, then continue subtracting 7 from each remainder obtained; compute 2 times 3, 5 times 8, 9 times 12); discrimination and judgment (e.g., explaining analogies, interpreting proverbs, solving problems).

The special preoccupations and experiences portion of the mental status evaluation is designed to uncover whether the patient experiences hallucinations, sees or hears things that are not there; has illusions, misinterprets sensory stimuli (e.g., sees shadows as animals); has delusions, false beliefs about poverty, guilt, health, etc.; has obsessions, compulsions, phobias, and rituals (e.g., habits that bother him or her, recurrent thoughts or ideas, compulsions to perform certain acts); and has an understanding of the current situation (e.g., knows he or she is ill, understands why he or she is being examined).

The physical examination is administered to identify systemic disorders (infection, hypertension, endocrine dysfunction, malnutrition, or cardiovascular disorders) that might cause dementia. The neurologic examination is administered to identify evidence of neurologic disease and, if it is present, to determine whether it is focal or diffuse. Laboratory tests are run to identify specific disorders. For example, a chest x-ray may indicate the primary site of a tumor that has metastasized to the brain. Skull x-ray, EEG, brain scan, and CT scan give evidence of possible focal lesions. The electrocardiogram may indicate recent or remote myocardial infarction. Urinalysis explores the possibility of renal or hepatic disease. The Schilling test can reveal impaired vitamin B_{12} absorption. Blood studies test for anemia; infection; syphilis; drug intoxication; and renal, endocrine, hepatic, or thy-

roid dysfunction. Cerebrospinal fluid workups are done to identify intracranial disease, such as degeneration, chronic infection, and syphilis.

An expanded battery of verbal and nonverbal intellectual tests administered by a psychologist or a neuropsychologist might include the Wechsler Adult Intelligence Scale (WAIS), which yields verbal and performance IQs, the Goldstein-Scheerer Test of Abstract and Concrete Thinking, the Rorschach Ink Blot Test, Draw a Person, Bender-Gestalt, Wechsler Memory Scale, and the Thematic Apperception Test (TAT). Some of the nonverbal intelligence measures listed in Table 1-6 (Coloured Progressive Matrices, Symbol Digit Modalities Test, Wisconsin Card Sorting Task) are also appropriate for detecting the presence of dementia. Finally, Alexander [2] has demonstrated an attention deficit in demented patients. His demented subjects performed without error on a simple stimulus-response recognition task. However, they demonstrated deficits in short-term retention on a response-contingent task. He concluded that dementia may be, in part, a disorder of selected attention, and he recommends such tasks be included when appraising the disorder. Smith [230] offers a complete discussion of neuropsychological tests appropriate for evaluating dementia.

Appraisal of a demented patient's speech and language should include at least one general language measure (e.g., PICA, BDAE, MTDDA), a measure of functional language ability, a motor speech evaluation, assessment of orientation and general information, and special tests of auditory comprehension and verbal fluency. Halpern, Darley, and Brown [92] report that overall communicative adequacy, reading comprehension, arithmetic, auditory comprehension, auditory retention, naming, and syntax show mild to moderate involvement in patients demonstrating the language of generalized intellectual impairment. Espir and Rose [73] observe that the speech of demented patients may be affected, but vocabulary ability may be retained until late in the course of the illness. They suggest the Babcock sentence: "There is one thing a nation must have to be rich and great, and that is a large, secure supply of wood." This is a quick test for detecting the presence of dementia. The examiner repeats the sentence until the patient says it perfectly. Failure after several attempts is indicative, according to Espir and Rose, of dementia. Critchley [38] suggests a task that requires the patient to list alternatives for a given dimension. For example, "Tell me five girls' names." The demented patient, according to Critchley, responds in a concrete and specific manner by giving only names of females he or she knows. Finally, Rochford [198] observes that demented patients are particularly poor in naming pictures. They give an inordinate number of "misrecognition" responses (e.g., calling a picture of a whale "vegetable marrow"). He contrasted this performance with naming body parts, where the demented patients' naming ability improved.

Bayles [13, 14] and Bayles and Boone [15] have developed a battery of language measures to detect the presence and to rate the severity of dementia. These include tests of receptive pragmatics, vocabulary, sentence error correction, visual-spatial abilities, story retelling, sentence disambiguation, verbal description, and picture naming. Discriminant function analyses conducted by Bayles [14] and Bayles and Boone [15] indicate these language measures are extremely sensitive in detecting the presence of dementia.

Evaluation of speech and language behavior in dementia requires a knowledge of the patient's premorbid educational achievement and language ability. In mild cases, language ability begins to deteriorate on the most difficult language tasks, reading and writing. These are the things we learn in school, and unless the speech pathologist knows that patient's educational achievement, he or she may diagnose a lack of education or illiteracy as the language of generalized intellectual impairment. Further, a patient's high school diploma may be misleading. If the patient tells you he or she "never was much of a reader or writer," this information must be used when evaluating performance.

DIAGNOSIS. The physician looks for confirmation for his or her definition of dementia to make the diagnosis. Therefore the physician is interested in signs of disorientation, memory deficits, impaired intellectual functioning, disrupted judgment, and change in affect. The speech pathologist looks for evidence to satisfy his or her definition of the language of generalized intellectual impairment. Therefore deterioration of performance on more difficult language tasks; reduced efficiency in all communicative modalities; problems on language tasks requiring better retention, close attention, and powers of abstraction and generalization are significant signs. Roth and Meyers [209] observe that the physician must differentiate dementia from other syndromes of organic brain disease (clouding of consciousness, amnestic syndrome, aphasia, apraxia, and agnosia). The speech pathologist must differentiate dementia from other neuropathologies of speech and language (aphasia, language of confusion, apraxia of speech, and dysarthria). Kral [130] believes that both have a difficult task, since neither knows how to differentiate between symptoms and signs of dementia and the patient's reaction to stress and the disease. Finally, since dementia is typically seen in older adults, Jackson [115] offers two additional cautions. First, we do not know that individuals who are unsuccessful on tasks used to appraise dementia ever attained the ability to complete the tasks premorbidly. Second, we do not know whether we are observing mild dementia or the signs of aging.

No single tool in the physician's armamentarium permits him or her to make a diagnosis. For example, Levy [144], discussing neurophysiologic data in dementia, observes that EEG, cerebrocirculation, oxygen uptake, and conduction velocity in peripheral nerves may change in dementia. However, he concludes that the overlap between different forms of dementia and between normal and pathologic conditions diminishes the value of neurophysiologic data. Also, there is no tool to differentiate between doubtful cases. The physician must rely on clinical data supplemented by psychological test scores. Paulson [181] believes that the neurologic examination of demented patients indicates a release of primitive activity. Thus diffuse brain damage may be eroding cerebral inhibition. Signs of motor impersistence; perseveration; and immature gait, posture, and reflexes suggest that dementia is a reversal in the phylogenetic process. Unfortunately, Paulson observes, we see many of the same signs in the aged who are not demented. Thus, Shakespeare's "once a man, twice a child" observation, cited by Hughlings Jackson, may indicate age, dementia, or a combination of both.

The speech pathologist's task of differentiating dementia from other neuropathologies of speech and language is equally difficult. Frequently this difficulty arises because of the range of severity seen in dementia. Figure 1-14 shows PICA profiles for two patients, one diagnosed as demonstrating severe dementia and another diagnosed as demonstrating moderate dementia. The patient with severe dementia displayed literally no verbal, gestural, or written responses. Only his ability to match identical objects on subtest XI differentiated him from the obtunded. His neurologic diagnosis was chronic brain syndrome resulting from cerebral vascular disease and syphilis. He responded correctly but inconsistently with "yes," and "no," and "all right." His longest verbal responses were "I don't know" and "H-A-R-R-Y" when asked what his name was. A problem in these cases, of course, is whether the patient will not or cannot communicate. We sided with the neurologist who had diagnosed dementia. Diagnosis of the language of generalized intellectual impairment is equally difficult in the other patient shown in Figure 1-14. His neurologic diagnosis was cerebrovascular disease, chronic alcoholism, and an episode of carbon monoxide poisoning. His speech, vocabulary, and syntax were too good to entertain a diagnosis of aphasia, and his reading and writing were too poor for his educational background. He was oriented for time and place, but his fund of general information was lacking. Language was concrete, and he had difficulty explaining proverbs and analogies. Both verbal and nonverbal intelligence were impaired. We noted no tendency to confabulate or to be irrelevant. On the basis of these observations, we diagnosed the language of generalized intellectual impairment.

Several reports offer information to assist in differentiating the language of generalized intellectual impairment from aphasia. Critchley [38] reports that demented patients demonstrate aposiopesis, the tendency to start a sentence but not finish it. Rochford [198] has contrasted naming errors made by aphasic patients with those made by demented patients. Aphasic patients tend to make no response or to describe objects when confronted with a naming task, whereas demented patients misname the objects. He concludes that aphasic patients recognize the objects but cannot name them, while demented patients fail to recognize them and, therefore, misname them. Halpern, Darley, and Brown [92] observed that the language of generalized intellectual impairment is characterized primarily by deficits in reading comprehension, and to a lesser extent, auditory retention span. Conversely, aphasia is characterized by impairment of auditory retention span and fluency. Our own observations are that patients demonstrating the language of generalized intellectual impairment frequently meet Porch's three criteria for bilateral involvement [189]—poorer performance on primary visual tests (matching objects, matching pictures with objects) than on primary auditory tests (pointing to objects when named, pointing to objects when described by their function); inordinately high verbal scores compared with gestural

and writing ability; and inordinately low writing scores compared with gestural and verbal ability. Further, these patients show deficits on the two reading tasks (reading the names of objects, and reading the functions of objects) that cannot be explained by a premorbid lack of education. Watson and Records [247] have used the PICA to differentiate dementia from aphasia.

Schwartz, Marin, and Saffran [224] and Bayles and Boone [15] report semantic knowledge deteriorates first in dementia, but there is relative preservation of syntactic and phonologic abilities. Horner and Heyman [111] agree; however, they suggest that as severity increases, demented patients begin to show syntactic errors, and when dementia is severe, phonologic errors are present. In aphasia, semantic errors are present in all types of aphasia and in all levels of severity. Phonologic and syntactic errors may be present at all levels of severity and vary as a function of type of aphasia.

Differentiating the language of generalized intellectual impairment from confusion is a bit more difficult. However, demented patients tend to show deficits on more difficult language tasks (reading and writing) while, if they can be kept tuned into the task, patients with the language of confusion perform without deficits. Further, on more open-ended language tasks, orientation tasks, and tasks requiring general information, demented patients tend to express an inability to perform (e.g., "I don't know"). Conversely, patients demonstrating the language of confusion tend to give a response that is confabulated or irrelevant.

We experience little difficulty in differentiating the language of generalized intellectual impairment from apraxia of speech or dysarthria. Both disorders, particularly dysarthria, may coexist with the language of generalized intellectual impairment because of the diffuse damage. However, this is a situation in which disorders coexist rather than one being a symptom of the other.

PROGNOSIS. The future for patients suffering dementia is influenced by the precipitating cause and the patient's age. Espir and Rose [73] summarize the range of possible outcomes dictated by the disorder. They establish a continuum ranging from progressive and untreatable to treatable if diagnosed early. Bergmann [19] summarizes the negative influence of advanced age by reporting that 50 percent of patients suffering senile dementia die within 6 months after admission to the hospital. Of the remainder, 80 percent die within 2 years after ad-

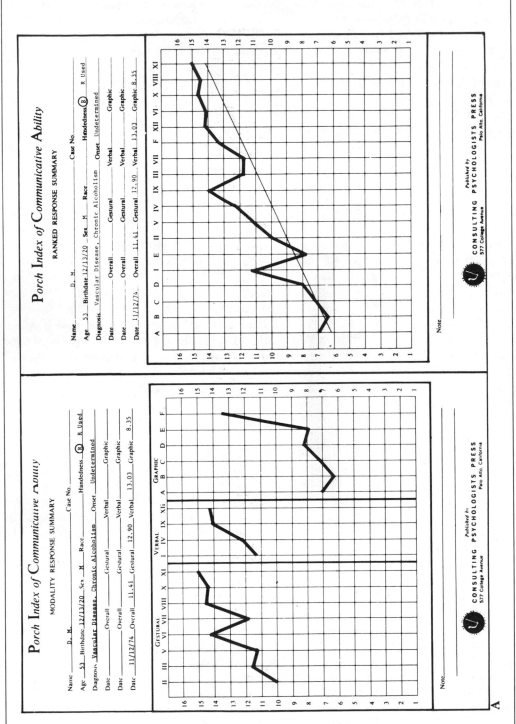

Fig. 1-14. PICA profiles on two patients demonstrating the language of generalized intellectual impairment. The patient shown in (A) demonstrates mild to moderate impairment; the patient in (B) displays severe impairment. The difference in severity between the two patients demonstrates the wide range of impairment possible in patients suffering the language of generalized intellectual impairment.

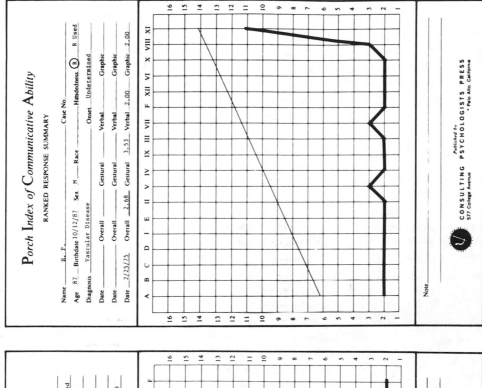

Porch Index of Communicative Ability

MODALITY RESPONSE SUMMARY

Name H. P.   Case No. _____

Age 87   Birthdate 10/12/87   Sex M   Race _____   Handedness ⓇR Used _____

Diagnosis Vascular Disease   Onset Undetermined _____

Date _____ Overall _____ Gestural _____ Verbal _____ Graphic _____

Date _____ Overall 2.68 Gestural _____ Verbal _____ Graphic _____

Date 2/25/75 Overall 2.68 Gestural 3.53 Verbal 2.00 Graphic 2.00

Note _____

CONSULTING PSYCHOLOGISTS PRESS
Published by
577 College Avenue   Palo Alto, California

B

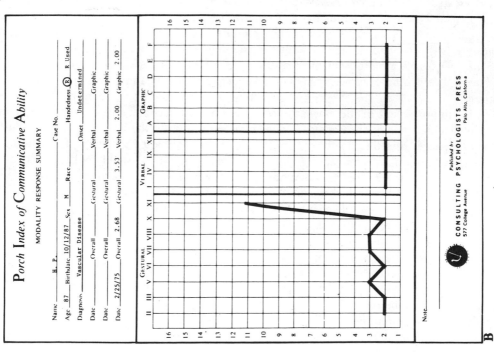

Porch Index of Communicative Ability

RANKED RESPONSE SUMMARY

Name H. P.   Case No. _____

Age 87   Birthdate 10/12/87   Sex M   Race _____   Handedness ⓇR Used _____

Diagnosis Vascular Disease   Onset Undetermined _____

Date _____ Overall _____ Gestural _____ Verbal _____ Graphic _____

Date _____ Overall _____ Gestural _____ Verbal _____ Graphic _____

Date 2/25/75 Overall 2.68 Gestural 3.53 Verbal 2.00 Graphic 2.00

Note _____

CONSULTING PSYCHOLOGISTS PRESS
Published by
577 College Avenue   Palo Alto, California

Fig. 1-14 (CONTINUED)

mission, and the other 20 percent survive for longer periods. Roth and Meyers [209] agree that advanced age is a poor prognostic sign if for no other reason than patients under 65 have a greater proportion of treatable diseases. However, dementia is no longer a hopeless diagnosis. Horenstein [109] believes that diffuse involvement of the brain does not necessarily indicate an untreatable or irreversible disorder. Espir and Rose [73] list benign intracranial tumors, neurosyphilis, and vitamin B_{12} deficiency as causes now considered treatable. Roth and Meyers [209] cite normal-pressure hydrocephalus as a rare, but possibly treatable, cause of dementia.

Dementias resulting from Alzheimer's disease, Pick's disease, Jakob-Creutzfeldt disease, Huntington's chorea, progressive supranuclear palsy, and spinal cerebellar degeneration have poor prognoses [9], because all are progressive. Senile dementia also carries a poor prognosis, and it is associated with the additional negative influence of advanced age. Conversely, some arteriopathic dementias (e.g., lacunar state, Binswanger's subcortical encephalopathy, granular cortical atrophy); cerebral hypoxia; some metabolic diseases (e.g., myxedema, hypoglycemia, chronic hepatic disease, uremia, Wilson's disease); some nutritional diseases (e.g., Wernicke-Korsakoff syndrome, vitamin B_{12} deficiency, pellagra); heavy-metal or drug intoxication; normal-pressure hydrocephalus; some neoplasms; and some infections have a more favorable prognosis [9]. Favorable outcome, however, implies an early diagnosis.

Prognosis for improvement in the language of generalized intellectual impairment accompanying dementia is influenced, therefore, by the precipitating disorder, and control or elimination of the cause may result in improved language. Beyond this gross observation, no established prognostic indicators for the language of generalized intellectual impairment exist. However, there are some rare observations. For example, Espir and Rose [73] believe that speech therapy will not help if there is a significant degree of dementia. Bergmann [19] speculates that the presence of dysphasia and parietal lobe types of disabilities may have prognostic significance. The implication here is that a focal symptom may indicate a focal lesion, and dementia, if present, is not sufficiently severe to mask the dysphasia or parietal lobe signs.

FOCUSING THERAPY. Treatment for the demented patient is both specific and nonspecific. Specific treatment is administered for disorders known to respond (e.g., medication for syphilis and vitamin B_{12} deficiency, shunts for normal-pressure hydrocephalus); and nonspecific treatment is administered for dementia without a treatable cause. The goals of the latter are restitution of lost function that is susceptible to restitution, reduction of the patient's need to employ functions that have been lost, and maximum utilization of residual functions. Wang and Busse [246] categorize dementia as a sociopsychosomatic disorder that involves physical health, socioeconomic status, environment, and personality. All these areas present opportunities for intercession by medical and rehabilitative personnel, including speech pathologists.

Restitution of lost function ranges, in medicine, from direct treatment to reverse the course of symptomatic dementia to correction of medical and physical limitations in primary dementia. Even though the progression of dementia cannot be stopped or slowed, the patient's other medical ailments may be relieved, and efforts can be made to preserve ambulation and maintain mobility. Wells [251] reports that physical, psychiatric, and social problems are more common in bedridden or wheelchair-bound demented patients.

Reducing the patient's need for functions that have been lost requires careful assessment to determine which functions have been irretrievably lost. Denial or lack of awareness of his or her deficits sets the demented patient up for failure. The battle to perform the impossible may generate such stress that the patient's ability to perform the possible is diminished; and refusal to give up the fight may continue into the terminal stages of the disease. Therefore those in the patient's environment must eliminate the possibility of hopeless combat. Patients with intellectual deficit no longer need to solve such socioeconomic problems as paying bills, balancing a checkbook, and filling out forms. Social workers can organize the family and hospital personnel to eliminate these activities from the patient's routine. Disoriented patients may profit from the reality orientation program described previously for patients suffering the language of confusion [75, 186]. Remembering where one is or the date is not difficult for them if the information is close at hand on a reality orientation board or if ward personnel are constantly giving them this information. Also, simplification of the surroundings may assist in reducing the patient's anxiety. For example, if there is only one place to put things, a lapboard on a wheelchair or a single bedside table, the search for missing material is shortened. Thus these and other efforts can be made to reduce the number of times a patient must face his or her inadequacies.

The primary care physician guides attempts to ensure that the patient utilizes his or her residual functions. The physician serves the patient as both personal physician and as the organizer of health care delivery by other disciplines. He or she keeps the patient as healthy as possible by administering appropriate medical care and prescribing medications to relieve symptoms. Also, the physician ensures that physical therapy keeps the patient as mobile as possible. Social service workers coordinate the family's help to solve the patient's social problems; and other care personnel create an environment that permits the patient to use residual abilities.

Medications are administered to the patient to relieve anxiety, improve mood, reduce paranoid symptoms, and improve sleep. However, no drug improves cerebral functions in demented patients. Westreich, Alter, and Lundgren [266] reported that cyclandelate was no more effective than placebos in improving higher cortical function in demented patients, which is an example of the lack of effectiveness of drug therapy. In fact, drug treatment may be inappropriate for demented patients. Wells [251] observed that sedatives are poorly tolerated in patients with structural brain disease, and a damaged nervous system may be hypersensitive to psychotropic agents. He cautions that barbiturates and similar medications should be avoided, and treatment, if employed, should begin with extremely small doses. Finally, certain drugs (phenothiazines) may induce postural hypotension, which is an extremely unfortunate side effect in demented geriatric patients. Thus medication may counterachieve the desired results.

By organizing other rehabilitation disciplines, the patient's residual abilities can be maximized and the progression of dementia may be slowed. For example, patients involved in a physical therapy stand-up or exercise program maintain ambulation and mobility longer than those allowed to sit or lie down. Range-of-motion programs for bedridden or wheelchair-bound patients impede the progression of reduced mobility. Occupational therapy programs can provide activities within the patient's range of ability to utilize intellectual and manual skills to produce projects that provide some personal satisfaction. Social workers involve family members and acquaint them with services that may help to solve the patient's social problems. Recreational therapy may fill vacant hours: Games, entertainment, and social activities appropriate for a demented patient's level of functioning provide enjoyment, remind the patient that he or she is still a person, and help him or her maintain some contact with reality. Finally, ward personnel (nurses, nursing assistants, custodians) can be employed to provide reality orientation. Each person who comes in contact with the patient calls him or her by name, identifies himself or herself, and gives reality data, for example, the time, date, place, next activity, and next meal. These interpersonal contacts are supplemented by a calm, nontaxing, structured environment to create a setting to maximize the patient's use of residual abilities.

The same three avenues—restitution of lost functions, reduction of the patient's need for functions that have been lost, and utilization of residual functions—constitute the approach in focusing speech and language therapy for the patient demonstrating the language of generalized intellectual impairment. Although diseased neurons cannot be restored, efforts are employed to permit the neurons that are still functioning to perform optimally. Patients may not accept the fact that they have a speech or language disorder. This may be an insurmountable problem for the speech pathologist, because direct speech and language intervention is rejected. Confronting the patient with speech and language deficits and recommending a remedial program is seldom effective. However, therapy disguised as interest, social interaction, and friendliness is usually acceptable to demented patients.

Since speech pathologists spend a good deal of time with patients in a one-to-one setting, they may have an opportunity to discover lost functions that are restorable. For example, demented patients with a hearing loss may profit from a hearing aid. Amplification will not improve intellect, but it may eliminate the overlaid deficits resulting from hearing loss. Further, missing or poorly fitting dentures may place an additional burden on the patient's oral communication. The speech pathologist can intervene by requesting dental consultation. Similarly, missing or inappropriate glasses may reduce visual input beyond the reduction created by the primary disorder. Too often demented patients are not taken seriously enough. For example, one of our patients, after a visit to an ophthalmologist, complained he was given the wrong glasses. Everyone knew the patient was demented and considered his complaint an additional sign of his intellectual deficit. Unfortunately, it took 2 days to discover he was right. He had been given the wrong glasses. This episode convinced us that demented patients, no matter how severe their disorder may be, are capable of some understanding. Finally, perceptual classification of a coexisting dysarthria might lead the speech pathologist to inquire about medication for improving the patient's speech. For example, dementia associated with or coexisting with Parkinson's disease will not improve from administration of a dopa derivative; however, it may cause the patient's intelligibility to improve.

Speech pathology can assist in reducing the need for lost function by contributing baseline data on the functions lost. For example, other medical and rehabilitative disciplines can be acquainted with the patient's level of listening, reading, speaking, and writing abilities. They can be told which stimulus modes are best for presenting information and demands, and they can be told which ones to exploit for obtaining a response. For example, nurses can be informed that a demented patient will perform better if verbal instructions are accompanied by gesture, or the dietician may be told that the patient cannot read the menu but will select appropriate items if they are presented in a multiple-choice manner. Further, the speech pathologist may provide means for alternative modes of communication. Communication boards containing stimuli the patient can identify, point to, and occasionally needs can be designed and provided.

Finally, speech pathology can help the patient utilize his or her residual abilities by discovering them and communicating them to other personnel. The considerations in focusing aphasia therapy listed in Table 1-9 are useful in organizing the collection of these data. For example, the length and complexity of stimuli the patient can handle can be determined and communicated to those around him or her. Further, emphasis should be placed on meaningful, extremely concrete stimuli. Finally, redundancy and the number of alternatives a demented patient can handle can be determined. Rather than giving the patient a choice among three alternatives or between two, each individual alternative may need to be presented, a response obtained, and then the next single alternative may be presented. Similar considerations must be given to stimulus modes. Speech pathology can determine the best input modality—auditory, visual, or tactile. Some demented patients may profit from auditory stimuli or a combination of auditory and visual stimuli. Patients with impaired auditory and visual acuity may require tactile input. This information can be used in the reality orientation program. For example, patients who maintain some reading ability but have difficulty in auditory comprehension profit more from visual orientation information rather than auditory. Generally, focusing therapy for the language of generalized intellectual impairment is designed to maintain function, for as long as possible, rather than to improve function. Unlike treatment for aphasia, treatment hierarchies are constructed in reverse. The patient must be monitored constantly to determine his or her level of disability. As the disorder progresses, communicative interaction must be simplified.

Wells [251] observes that the field of dementia is strewn with discarded remedies; and there is a paucity of information on how to treat patients with generalized intellectual impairment. These patients are not everyone's favorite rehabilitation candidates. Their prognosis is poor, and we have yet to discover effective means of therapeutic intervention. However, a demented patient is more than just an "old crock." Our failure to have known them as the wonderful people they once were should not prevent attempts at treatment that may uncover a part of their former selves, if only fleetingly and rarely.

CLINICAL EXAMPLE. L. C. was a 69-year-old man with a 6-year history of cerebrovascular disease. He was transferred to the Veterans Administration Hospital from a nursing home after suffering an apparent right hemisphere CVA. He had been residing in the nursing home for 3 years after retiring as a marina attendant. The onset was undetermined, and his diagnosis was chronic brain syndrome. Speech and language evaluation showed a moderate auditory comprehension deficit, severe reading deficit, mild to moderate speaking problems, and a severe writing deficit. His PICA scores are shown in Figure 1-15. His initial overall performance was at the 37th percentile. The profile resembles Porch's "W-J" profile [190], which indicates premorbid illiteracy. L. C.'s premorbid education of 12 years and his former employer's report that he could read and write did not support premorbid illiteracy. The PICA profile also meets Porch's criteria for bilateral involvement—poorer performance on one of the primary visual tests than on the primary auditory tests, inordinately high verbal performance compared with gestural and graphic performances, and inordinately low graphic

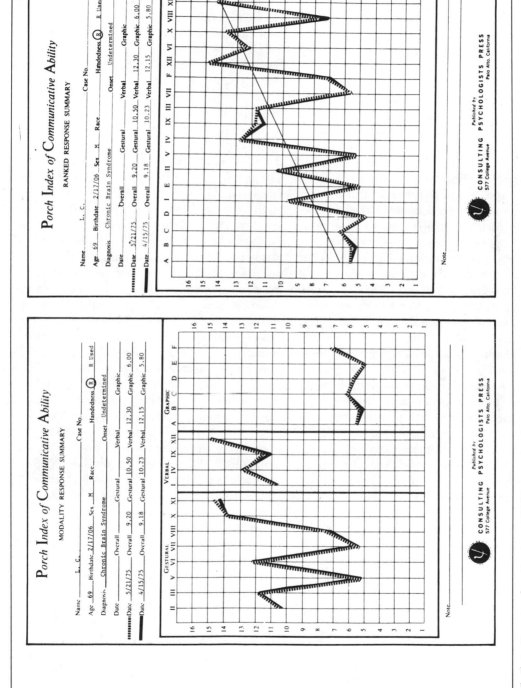

Fig. 1-15. Pretreatment and posttreatment PICA profiles for a patient suffering from the language of generalized intellectual impairment. Essentially no change occurred during 1 month of daily therapy.

abilities. MTDDA results classified him in Schuell's group IV [218], aphasia with scattered findings compatible with generalized brain damage. His Token Test performance was 16 correct on the 61-item test; his Coloured Progressive Matrices performance was 8 correct on the 36-item test; and he produced 16 total words on the Word Fluency Measure. The Peabody Picture Vocabulary results indicated that he had an IQ below 55, below 1st percentile performance for 18-year-olds, and a mental age of 7 years. L. C. demonstrated no apraxia of speech or dysarthria. His language was extremely concrete; he had no obvious word-finding problems, and his syntax was normal. He admitted to no speech or language problems other than that people did not understand what he said at times. He explained his reading problems by "blurred vision" and did not see any errors in his totally incomprehensible writing. He was disoriented for date and place and possessed a very limited fund of general information. He demonstrated mild hemiplegia in his left arm and leg, left visual neglect, incontinence, and emotional lability. Generally, he was in good spirits and was congenial except to those who "make fun of me." To test the generally held opinion that patients with the language of generalized intellectual impairment do not profit from speech and language therapy, we instituted daily treatment sessions with him. He could not understand why he needed help in these areas; however, he was willing to "help you in any way I can." Treatment to restore residual functions involved daily physical therapy to improve use of the involved left extremities, an ophthalmology evaluation, and locating his missing dentures. The visual evaluation showed his present prescription was correct for his peripheral visual deficit. Treatment designed to reduce the need for lost function included simplifying the patient's environment by providing a lapboard for his wheelchair to keep all of his immediate needs (e.g., cigarettes, glasses, tissues) within reach, establishing a rigid daily schedule, checking and informing the patient that his financial situation was secure, instituting an orientation program involving all personnel, and placing a reality orientation board on his wheelchair lapboard. Therapy to ensure maximum use of residual function included assisting him to explore his left visual field and requesting that all hospital personnel keep instructions short, simple, and concrete. Speech and language–specific therapy included tasks designed to force the patient to explore his left visual field (e.g., constant re-minders to look for visual stimuli placed to the left), intensifying visual stimuli following auditory instructions, matching visual stimuli, orientation drill requiring verbal responses, and copying simple, visually presented materials.

After 1 month of treatment, L. C. was reevaluated before his return to a nursing home. Reevaluation PICA scores are shown in Figure 1-15. No obvious improvement was noted. His overall performance remained at the 37th percentile. MTDDA performance, Token Test, Coloured Progressive Matrices, Word Fluency Measure, and Peabody scores were unchanged. L. C. remained in the nursing home, and his generalized intellectual impairment was reported to have progressed.

Apraxia of Speech

If nothing else, apraxia of speech is controversial. The arguments vary from Martin's contention [157] that the articulatory characteristics described by Johns and Darley [117] represent linguistic impairment and should be considered as manifestations of aphasia through Johns and LaPointe's [118] plea for identifying and describing apraxia of speech to improve scientific communication and design appropriate treatment to Geschwind's [79] contention that an isolated apraxia seldom, if ever, exists. Darley [48] and Johns and LaPointe [118] observe this argument is over a century old. It began with Broca's description of aphemia, defined as a disorder of the faculty of articulated language and not as a deficit in the general faculty of language. Unfortunately, as Critchley [39] explains, Trousseau introduced the term aphasia, and Broca's aphemia has since been identified as Broca's aphasia. Others have seen what Broca saw and choose to supply their own terminology. These terms are reviewed by Johns and LaPointe [118] and described by Darley [48] as over 100 years of proliferation of confusion.

Regardless of the theoretical differences (language disorder or motor speech disorder), most clinicians agree that a clinical syndrome exists and is characterized by a specific pattern of articulatory behavior. Since the emphasis here is on patient management, theories are only interesting. For convenience, we use the term apraxia of speech to describe disruption of the second requirement for oral-expressive communication described by Darley, Aronson, and Brown [50], programming of speech skills for the volitional production of speech sounds, and their combination into sequences to form words.

Darley's [48] definition, listed in Table 1-1, considers apraxia as an articulatory deficit that results from brain damage. The patient has difficulty programming the positioning of speech muscles and sequencing muscle movements to produce phonemes. There is no significant weakness, slowness, or incoordination of these muscles in reflexive or automatic acts. Darley suggests that prosodic alterations may be associated with the articulatory problem and perhaps exist as an attempt to compensate for it. Wertz, LaPointe, and Rosenbek [262] have modified Darley's definition as follows:

Apraxia of speech is a neurogenic phonologic disorder resulting from sensorimotor impairment of the capacity to select, program, and/or execute in coordinated and normally timed sequences, the positioning of the speech musculature for the volitional production of speech sounds. The loss or impairment of phonologic rules of the native language is not adequate to explain the observed pattern of deviant speech, nor is the disturbance attributable to weakened or misdirected actions of specific muscle groups. Prosodic alteration . . . may be associated with the articulatory disruption either as a primary part of the condition or in compensation for it.

The major differences between this definition and Darley's are addition of *sensori-* to *motor* and an emphasis on prosody. Apraxic patients do appear to display a range of disrupted oral sensation [137, 208] and prosodic disturbances [12, 124, 125] are prominent.

The articulatory programming problems do not result from disruption of language; however, a language disorder, typically aphasia, may coexist and usually does [265]. In addition, the patient may have a coexisting weakness, slowness, restricted range, and incoordination in muscular activity that can be identified as dysarthria [265]. However, this coexists with apraxia of speech rather than causing it.

Johns and Darley [117], Shankweiler and Harris [225], Wertz et al. [262], and others provide signs for identifying apraxia of speech. Specifically, apraxia is an articulatory disorder, and oral apraxia is commonly found in association with it. Prosodic disturbances may reflect the patient's attempts to compensate for the articulatory problems. Errors are highly inconsistent and unpredictable. They are off-target approximations of the desired production, and they vary with stimulus length; there are more errors on multisyllabic words than on monosyllabic words. Further, errors vary with the complexity of the articulatory adjustment; there are more errors on fricatives and affricates and consonant blends than on vowels or plosives. The apraxic

patient's automatic-reactive speech is better than his or her volitional-purposive speech, or, as Darley [48] described it, the apraxic patient produces "islands of error-free production." Imitative responses in apraxia of speech may be especially poor. Finally, the apraxic patient is aware of his or her errors but typically is unable to anticipate or correct them. Wertz, LaPointe, and Rosenbek [262] have summarized recent investigations [12, 56, 135, 243] that permit revision of these earlier observations. Presently, behavior demonstrated by patients with apraxia of speech can be classified according to phonetic, prosodic, and nonphonetic characteristics.

Phonetic characteristics are listed in Table 1-13. While errors of omission, distortion, addition, and prolongation may appear in the speech of apraxic patients, substitution errors are more frequent than any other type. However, these are slightly off-target approximations. The error sounds are more likely to differ from the target productions by one phonetic dimension (e.g., place, manner, voicing, and so on) than by two or more. Errors may be either anticipatory or perseverative; however, anticipatory errors occur more frequently. Place errors are more common than errors of manner, voic-

Table 1-13. Phonetic characteristics in apraxia of speech

Substitution errors are more frequent than other error types.

Error sounds are more likely to differ from the target by one phonetic dimension than by two, three, or four.

Some errors are anticipatory, some perseverative, and some metathetic with anticipatory errors probably predominating.

Errors are more likely errors of place than of manner, voicing, or oral-nasal.

Errors of place are more than half the time off by only one unit.

Apicoalveolar and bilabial sounds are more often correct than sounds produced at other places.

Voiceless for voiced substitutions are more frequent than voiced for voiceless ones.

Errors are more likely on consonant clusters than on singletons.

Affricatives and fricatives tend as classes to be more often in error than plosives, laterals, nasals, and vowels, although the error may vary with position in utterance.

Consonants are more likely to be in error than vowels, but some patients may make no more consonant than vowel errors.

Many substitutions appear to be more difficult combinations for easier ones.

Source: Adapted from J. C. Rosenbek and R. T. Wertz, Veterans Administration Workshop on Motor Speech Disorders. Madison, Wis., 1976.

ing, or nasalization. Place errors, however, remain "in the ballpark," because they are typically off by only one unit (e.g., an intended bilabial production is more likely to be a labiodental production rather than a linguovelar error). Sounds produced in the front of the mouth, bilabial and apico-alveolar, are more likely to be correct than sounds produced at other places. If a voicing error is made, the error is more likely to be a voiceless sound substituted for a voiced sound (e.g., /p/ for /b/) rather than the reverse. Also, production of consonant clusters results in more errors than production of single consonants. Affricatives and fricatives yield more errors than other classes, although the position of the sound in the utterance will influence its production. In some patients, consonants are more likely to be in error than vowels; however, in other patients, the reverse is true. Finally, many substitutions appear to be substitution of more difficult combinations for easier ones. This suggests that apraxia of speech is not a "phonemic disintegration." While individual patients may vary, as a group, apraxic patients demonstrate the following hierarchy of phonetic difficulty from least to most difficult: vowels, plosives, nasals, glides, semivowels, fricatives, affricatives, and blends.

Other influences on articulation in apraxia of speech have been observed. For example, in consonant-vowel-consonant (CVC) stimuli, an initial sound is more likely to be in error than a final one; and frequently occurring sounds are more likely to be correct than infrequently occurring ones. Also, articulatory accuracy is better for meaningful than for nonmeaningful utterances, and, similarly, articulatory accuracy is better for frequently occurring words than for rare ones. Apraxic errors increase as words increase in length, but this increase is not linear; and errors increase as the distance between successive points of articulation increases. For example, moving from a bilabial sound to a linguopalatal sound is more likely to result in an error than moving from a linguoalveolar sound to a linguopalatal sound. Finally, grammatical class, especially when combined with length, influences the probability of an error.

Several prosodic disturbances have been observed in patients demonstrating apraxia of speech [12, 117, 126, 207]. These are listed in Table 1-14. First, apraxic patients tend to give words equal stress. Second, they use inappropriate intersyllabic pauses. Third, there are restrictions and alterations of normal intonational contours. Fourth, the normal durational relationships between vowels and

Table 1-14. Prosodic characteristics in apraxia of speech

Apraxic patients tend to use equal and even stress.

Apraxic patients insert inappropriate intersyllabic pauses.

Restriction and alteration of normal intonational contours occur in speech apraxia.

Normal durational relationships of vowels and consonants are distorted.

Effortful groping and repetitive attempts are observed in the patient's attempts to produce a sound accurately.

Rate of production is slowed overall.

Prosodic disturbances probably reflect the effects of the primary motor deficit as well as the patient's efforts to compensate.

Source: Adapted from J. C. Rosenbek and R. T. Wertz, Veterans Administration Workshop on Motor Speech Disorders. Madison, Wis., 1976.

Table 1-15. Nonphonetic influences on articulation in apraxia of speech

Within narrow limits, articulatory accuracy is better for automatic-reactive speech than for volitional-purposive speech.

Articulatory accuracy is better with auditory-visual stimulation than with auditory or visual stimulation alone.

Imitative accuracy is better than spontaneous accuracy.

Some patients improve if given more than one consecutive attempt at a production.

Motivating instructions, within very narrow limits, have no influence on articulatory accuracy.

Delay intervals of 0, 3, and 6 seconds do not significantly influence articulatory accuracy.

Source: Adapted from J. C. Rosenbek and R. T. Wertz, Veterans Administration Workshop on Motor Speech Disorders. Madison, Wis., 1976.

consonants are distorted. Fifth, apraxic patients exhibit effortful groping and make repetitive attempts to produce sounds accurately. Sixth, the overall rate of production is slower than normal. And, seventh, prosodic disturbances probably reflect the effects of the primary motor deficit as well as an effort to compensate for it. These prosodic alterations differentiate apraxia of speech from the oral-expressive manifestations of aphasia. Further, different prosodic alterations are seen in dysarthria.

Nonphonetic influences on articulatory accuracy in apraxia of speech are listed in Table 1-15. These observations have been provided, primarily, by Johns and Darley [117] and Deal and Darley [56]. Within normal limits, patients demonstrating apraxia make fewer errors in automatic-reactive productions than in volitional-purposive productions. Articulatory accuracy is better with auditory-visual stimulation than with auditory or visual stimulation alone. However, the study done by

LaPointe and Horner [134] failed to support this observation. Imitative accuracy is better than spontaneous accuracy, which conflicts with earlier observations [48] and requires empirical support. Similarly, some patients improve if given more than one consecutive attempt at production [117], but more recent evidence makes us question this statement [134]. Motivating instructions, within very narrow limits, have no influence on articulatory accuracy [56]. Finally, delay intervals of 0, 3, and 6 seconds do not result in a significant improvement in articulatory accuracy [56]. Other observations of the nonphonetic characteristics influencing apraxia include the following: individual patients may anticipate their errors at a level significantly greater than chance [50]; auditory discrimination is usually superior to verbal production [7]; and performance in other modes is usually better than that in speech. The latter observation, of course, depends on the amount of coexisting aphasia.

Apraxia of speech, therefore, is a label given to an identifiable pattern of performance. Whether or not it is a manifestation of aphasia is not important. What is important is that it requires a different treatment approach from that employed with aphasia or dysarthria. Thus it is discussed here as a separate neuropathology of speech.

Fig. 1-16. Theoretical clinical profile of apraxia of speech, indicating no impairment in language, impaired programming of motor speech, no muscle involvement, no intellectual deficits, and no orientation problems.

Figure 1-16 shows a theoretical clinical profile of apraxia of speech. No language, intellectual, or orientation deficits exist as part of the problem. The primary disorder is an inability to program articulatory movements. Since these problems cannot be explained by significant slowness, weakness, restricted range of movement, or incoordination of the articulators, apraxia is not dysarthria, and no significant muscle involvement exists. Although language problems may be present, these are believed to result from coexisting aphasia rather than as symptoms of apraxia. Halpern, Darley, and Brown [92] observed minimal language impairment in their group of apraxic patients. These patients were marked by their lack of fluency.

Recent instrumental investigations have provided information on the acoustic [124, 125] and physiologic correlates [77, 113, 114] of apraxia of speech. These are summarized by Wertz, LaPointe, and Rosenbek [262]. The acoustic characteristics of apraxia of speech include: slow speaking rate with prolongations of transitions and steady states as well as intersyllabic pauses; restricted variations in relative peak intensity across syllables; slow and inaccurate movements of the articulators to spatial targets for both consonants and vowels; frequent mistiming or dyscoordinations of voicing with other articulatory movements; occasional errors of segment selection or sequencing including intrusion, metathesis, and omission; initiation difficulties often characterized by false starts and restarts; and complex sound sequences associated with an

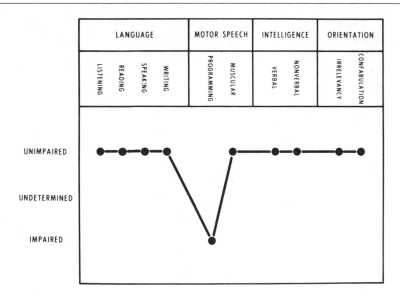

apparent search for the intended targets. The physiologic characteristics include the presence of antagonistic muscle cocontraction; continuous, undifferentiated electromyographic (EMG) activity; instances of movement without appropriate voicing; dyscoordinated, added, and groping movements; and reduced peak expiratory flow in some patients.

LOCALIZATION. Most agree that apraxia of speech results from a unilateral, left hemisphere lesion involving the third frontal convolution. Johns and LaPointe [118] review over 20 reports, and all localize the lesion in essentially the same area. Since Broca was the first to report a case of apraxia of speech (aphemia), the site of lesion has been designated Broca's area. Thus much of the localization data for apraxia comes from reports on what is called, by some, Broca's aphasia. Mohr [167, 168] presents a detailed analysis of localization in Broca's aphasia and concludes that, typically, what is called Broca's aphasia results from a larger lesion involving more than Broca's area. This is consistent with the observation that apraxia typically coexists with aphasia.

Wertz, Rosenbek, and Deal [265] discussed the difficulty in obtaining precise localization information. Their localization data, which they report as inadequate, do not discount the importance of a Broca's area lesion. However, a large proportion of their patients appeared to suffer lesions involving other areas of the left hemisphere. Halpern, Darley, and Brown [92] report that all 10 of their patients demonstrating apraxia of speech suffered lesions anterior to the central fissure. Some [31, 153] postulate two types of motor aphasia. Luria [153] suggests an efferent motor aphasia resulting from a lesion in the frontal lobe and an afferent motor aphasia resulting from more posterior lesions. Similarly, Canter [31] differentiates a primary Broca's aphasia resulting from anterior lesions from a secondary Broca's aphasia resulting from more posterior lesions. Deutsch [63] presents empirical evidence to support this view. Finally, Kertesz [126] has discussed the possibility of apraxia of speech resulting from subcortical lesions.

Based on the current evidence, apraxia of speech probably results from involvement of the third frontal convolution, Broca's area. However, there is a possibility of apraxia following more posterior, probably parietal, lesions. More importantly, lesions that result in apraxia, like lesions that result in aphasia, are not discrete and create a situation where apraxia and aphasia coexist.

CAUSE. Possible causes of apraxia of speech are listed in Table 1-2. Essentially, the same things that will cause aphasia will cause apraxia. These causes include CVA, neoplasms, trauma, infection, and perhaps, diffuse CNS disease, such as Alzheimer's, Pick's, and Jakob-Creutzfeldt disease.

Halpern, Darley, and Brown [92] report that 9 of their 10 patients demonstrating apraxia of speech had suffered a CVA. The other patient had suffered trauma. Johns and Darley [117] studied 7 apraxic patients who had suffered a CVA and 3 whose onset was traumatic. Analysis of the 176 adults in the sample reported by Wertz, Rosenbek, and Deal [265] showed that 68 percent suffered CVAs, 13 percent had a neoplasm, 7 percent suffered trauma, 1 percent had an infectious disorder, 5 percent suffered miscellaneous disorders (e.g., Jakob-Creutzfeldt disease), and 6 percent had an undetermined disorder.

The cause is probably not all that important. However, the more diffuse the problem, the more likely it is that there are coexisting disorders. For example, a CVA will probably result in coexisting apraxia of speech and aphasia. Further, the more diffuse the lesion, the more severe the coexisting aphasia.

APPRAISAL. Because patients demonstrating apraxia of speech have brain injuries, they require collection of biographical, medical, and behavioral data, such as those listed in Tables 1-4 through 1-6. Further, since aphasia typically coexists with apraxia, the aphasia appraisal battery listed in Table 1-7 is appropriate for patients suspected of suffering from apraxia.

The primary purposes of appraisal for apraxia of speech are the same as for other disorders— measure the patient's symptoms and establish their hierarchy; determine the patient's diagnosis, the severity of the disorder, and the prognosis; and focus the therapy. Since apraxic patients typically have coexisting aphasia, it is important to specify the stimulus modes being appraised. The continual question is whether errors in the patient's response represent a verbal output problem, apraxia or aphasia, or whether they represent an auditory, visual, or tactile input problem. Porch's cautions regarding specifying instructional modality, stimulus modality, and response modality must be followed [188]. Further, the clinician must remember the phonetic conditions that affect articulatory accuracy in apraxia of speech. These include: manner of articulation, position of the phoneme in the utterance, difficulty of the initial phoneme, distance between successive points of articulation in the utterance, word length, and word frequency. These influences are built into appraisal tasks and assist in differential diagnosis.

A basic battery for appraising apraxia should include the following: a general language measure (e.g., PICA, MTDDA, BDAE), motor speech evaluation, and, if time and personnel permit, oral sensory measures (e.g., two-point discrimination, oral-form identification, mandibular kinesthesia). The general language measure appraises the presence and severity of coexisting aphasia and may indicate the presence of apraxia [264]. The motor speech evaluation permits appraisal of apraxia and possible coexisting dysarthria. Oral sensory measures give some indication of deficits in oral sensation and perception [208]. Most oral sensory measures, however, tap both sensation and motor ability, and they are extremely time consuming.

The nucleus of the appraisal for apraxia of speech is the motor speech evaluation shown in Table 1-16. It manipulates the influences suspected to affect apraxia of speech. The tasks have been drawn from reports by Johns and Darley [117], Darley, Aronson, and Brown [50], Wertz and Rosenbek [263], and Wertz, LaPointe, and Rosenbek [262], among others. Vowel production, in most apraxic patients, should be intact. Similarly, repetition of single phonemes should be intact, since the patient is not required to sequence any motor movements. Repetition of combined monosyllables, however, should demonstrate some errors. Multisyllabic words (e.g., *snowman, catastrophe, artillery*, and so on) contain difficult sounds for apraxic patients and should induce errors [204]. Words of increasing length (e.g., *please, pleasing, pleasingly*) should show more errors on longer words than on shorter ones. Words with the same initial and final phoneme (e.g., *coke, gag, dad, sis*) should show more errors on the initial phoneme than on the final phoneme. And repetition of sentences should elicit errors (e.g., "Please put the groceries in the refrigerator"), because the stimuli are loaded with difficult sounds and multisyllabic words. Unfortunately, these also tap auditory comprehension deficits that may exist as part of the coexisting aphasia.

Picture description permits the patient more

Table 1-16. Motor speech evaluation

Apraxia of Speech

Vowel production: /ɑ/, /i/, /u/

Diadochokinetic tasks:
  Repeating monosyllables: /p/, /t/, /k/
  Repeating combined monosyllables: /p -t -k/

Multisyllabic words: *snowman, gingerbread, impossibility,* etc.

Words of increasing length: *please, pleasing, pleasingly*

Words with the same initial and final phoneme: *coke, dad, gag,* etc.

Repeating sentences: "Please put the groceries in the refrigerator," etc.

Describing a picture:
  Repeat "error" sentences made in spontaneous picture description.

Counting: 1–20
  Forward and backward

Days of the week:
  Forward and backward

Oral-Nonverbal Apraxia

Tongue movements: "Stick out your tongue," "Lick your lips," etc.

Lip movements: "Smile," "Show how you would kiss a baby," etc.

Miscellaneous: "Cough," "Make your teeth chatter," "Clear your throat," etc.

Source: Adapted from R. T. Wertz and J. C. Rosenbek, Appraising apraxia of speech. *J. Colo. Speech Hear. Assoc.* 5 : 18, 1971.

freedom to make errors. For example, the "cookie thief" picture from the BDAE or the MTDDA Card 11 are good sources of stimuli, and repetition of "error" sentences observed in picture description permits a look at the patient's consistency or the lack of it. Serial tasks such as counting and saying the days of the week, permit a comparison of the patient's automatic speech with the more volitional-purposive speech observed in picture description. Requesting the patient to count forward and then backward or say the days of the week forward and then backward also permits comparison between automatic and volitional speech tasks. Tests of oral-nonverbal apraxia measure the patient's ability to make volitional, nonverbal oral movements. Deficits here frequently coexist [61] with apraxia of speech, and the presence of an oral-nonverbal apraxia has prognostic and treatment significance. Oral movement tasks can be single movements (e.g., "Stick out your tongue") or sequential tasks (e.g., "Touch your upper lip with your tongue, protrude your lips, and lick your lips") discussed by LaPointe and Wertz [136] and Johns and LaPointe [118].

Scoring is typically binary: plus or minus. We have experimented with a variety of scoring systems; however, all have flaws and few are reliable. Probably the best method of determining the severity of the patient's disability is to rate behavior on a one-to-seven, equal-appearing interval scale. This is a surprisingly reliable method [264]. Most importantly, the clinician must obtain clean data. If a response is uninterpretable, we have found that a three-step approach may resolve ambiguity. First, we ask a patient to "Say snowman." If the response is ambiguous, we repeat it: "Listen! Say snowman." If the response remains uninterpretable, we use a cue: "Listen! Watch me! Say snowman." This sequence usually provides interpretable data. Finally, the intent is not to seek a specific score on the motor speech evaluation but rather to determine the presence or absence of the pattern of behavior we call apraxia of speech.

DIAGNOSIS. Documenting the presence of apraxia of speech and differentiating it from aphasia and dysarthria are the two primary tasks of diagnosis. Apraxia may coexist with the language of confusion or the language of generalized intellectual impairment; however, such coexistence is rare. Wertz, Rosenbek, and Deal [265] report that apraxia of speech frequently coexists with aphasia, and the presence of one disorder may mask the presence of the other. Further, since apraxia is a motor speech disorder, its symptoms may be confused with those of dysarthria. Thus diagnosis is based on whether the patient demonstrates the phonetic and prosodic characteristics listed in Tables 1-13 and 1-14, and whether the patient is influenced by the nonphonetic variables listed in Table 1-15. Difficulty in diagnosing apraxia occurs when there is a moderate to severe amount of coexisting aphasia. The clinician must determine whether the patient's oral-expressive deficits result from auditory comprehension or visual input deficits, or whether they represent apraxic errors. Further, when apraxia is severe, the patient may produce an extremely limited verbal sample, making it almost impossible to apply the phonetic and prosodic criteria.

Differentiating apraxia of speech from aphasia requires scrutiny of the patient's oral-expressive productions. Typically, diagnostic difficulty arises in differentiating apraxia from the paraphasias described by Goodglass and Kaplan [86]. Rosenbek and Wertz [207] have listed several differential di-

agnostic characteristics for separating apraxia from paraphasia. First, apraxia results in a higher proportion of errors that are "on target." Conversely, paraphasia results in a lower proportion of such errors. The apraxic patient responds *figerette* to the stimulus *cigarette*, while the paraphasic patient may offer *didicus*. Second, the apraxic patient, in an attempt to program and sequence speech sounds, may produce non-English speech sounds, whereas paraphasic patients tend to produce only English speech sounds. Third, the direction of substitutions may be more predictable in apraxia compared with the lack of prediction for substitutions seen in paraphasia. Fourth, apraxic patients tend to produce more errors in the initial position, while paraphasic patients may be somewhat more likely to produce errors in the final position. Fifth, suprasegmentals are distorted in apraxia of speech, and they tend to be preserved in paraphasia. And, sixth, depending on the amount of coexisting aphasia, apraxic patients make overt efforts to correct their errors, while paraphasic patients, also depending on the severity of aphasia, demonstrate a lesser tendency to self-correct.

Pertinent data for differentiating apraxia of speech from aphasia come from the verbal tests on the general language measure and the motor speech evaluation. On the PICA, for example, depending on the severity of apraxia, one may see a predominance of the scores 7 (related productions) and 14 (distorted productions). These are observed as individual responses and may be submerged in the overall test means. On the MTDDA, the repetition of monosyllables and repetition of phrases are useful. On the BDAE, patients with apraxia of speech usually display a Broca's aphasia profile with deficits in melodic line and articulatory agility. On the motor speech evaluation, patients reveal the phonetic and prosodic characteristics of apraxia and are influenced by the nonphonetic variables built into the tasks.

Finally, if one collects oral sensory data, apraxic patients are prone to show oral sensation and perception deficits. Rosenbek, Wertz, and Darley [208] report that apraxic patients make significantly more errors on oral sensation and perception tasks than normal persons and aphasic patients without coexisting apraxia.

Johns and Darley [117] have listed the significant criteria for differentiating apraxia of speech from dysarthria. These criteria include more substitution errors in apraxia of speech compared with more distortion errors in dysarthria; less consistency of error type in apraxia of speech compared with more consistency of error type in dysarthria; greater effect of nonphonetic variables in apraxia of speech compared with lesser effect of nonphonetic variables in dysarthria; more normal resonance balance in apraxia compared with disrupted resonance balance in dysarthria; typical absence of consistent dysphonia in apraxia compared with the frequent presence of consistent dysphonia in dysarthria; and cranial nerves near their normal limits in apraxia compared with involvement of cranial nerves in dysarthria. Wertz, LaPointe, and Rosenbek [262] list four salient, clinical characteristics of apraxia of speech: effortful trial and error, groping articulatory movement, and attempts at self-correction; dysprosody unrelieved by extended periods of normal rhythm, stress, and intonation; articulatory inconsistency on repeated productions of the same utterance; and obvious difficulty initiating utterances. Application of these criteria usually accomplishes differentiation; however, the task is more difficult when disorders coexist or apraxia of speech is extremely severe, resulting in a paucity of analyzable speech.

PROGNOSIS. Since apraxia of speech typically results from a unilateral left hemisphere lesion, and since it typically coexists with aphasia, many of the prognostic variables, listed in Table 1-8, that influence recovery from aphasia can be applied in predicting the future for patients demonstrating apraxia. For example, younger patients in good health, with small lesions and a brief duration of impairment, have a better prognosis for recovery than older patients in poor health, with diffuse lesions and long duration. There is a limited number of variables that may be specific to prognosis in apraxia. These include oral-nonverbal ability, severity, duration, severity of associated aphasia, and failure to learn or generalize in treatment. Few reports exist to document the influence of any of these variables.

Rosenbek [200] reports that oral-nonverbal apraxia has a negative influence on recovery in apraxia of speech. Similarly, Butfield [29] cited severe "mouth apraxia" as a deterrent to recovery of oral communication skills. Webb and Love [248] observed that patients with oral-nonverbal apraxia fail to profit from cues administered in therapy tasks designed to improve apraxia. Severe oral-nonverbal apraxia, especially if it persists, is a poor prognostic sign. Vignolo [245] listed oral apraxia and anarthria, probably severe apraxia of speech, continuing beyond 2 months as an extremely unfavorable prognostic sign. Severity of coexisting aphasia limits the apraxic patient's ability to respond to stimuli. In mild to moderate apraxia, patients attempt to self-correct errors, which is identified as a favorable prognostic sign by Wepman [253]. However, severe coexisting aphasia reduces the patient's ability to identify and correct his or her verbal errors. Finally, failure to demonstrate learning and generalization is a poor prognostic sign. As in aphasia, the clinician does not have time to teach the apraxic patient every sound in every combination necessary for functional communication. Therefore the apraxic patient with no coexisting oral-nonverbal apraxia, a short duration, mild to moderate severity, minimal coexisting aphasia, and demonstrated learning and generalization has a better prognosis for recovery than apraxic patients displaying the converse of each feature.

FOCUSING THERAPY. The clinician's roles in managing apraxic patients include development of improved, usually, compensated speech; providing a setting for successful practice; and providing a knowledge of results. Unlike treatment for aphasia, speech therapy of apraxia emphasizes drill. Therefore environmental stimulation and the rapport, socialization, psychotherapeutic, and interest approaches that may have their place in aphasia therapy have little influence on remediating the speech of apraxic patients. Like aphasia, focusing therapy for apraxic patients requires consideration of those variables listed in Table 1-9 (stimuli, stimulus modes, response modes, temporal relations of stimulus and response, facilitators, reinforcements, and methods). Further, since most patients demonstrating apraxia of speech also have a coexisting aphasia, treatment for both is necessary. Rosenbek's discussion of treating apraxia (Chap. 7) and Wertz, LaPointe, and Rosenbek's [262] discussion of treatment need no elaboration here. Therefore the following discussion on focusing therapy in apraxia will consider management of the disorder as it coexists with aphasia.

First, and probably last and always, apraxia of speech is a motor speech disorder that requires a different treatment approach from that employed with the language problems constituting aphasia. The general stimulation techniques appropriate for improving aphasia will, it is hoped, do that—improve aphasia. However, they will have little influence on remediating apraxia. Focusing therapy for apraxic patients is influenced by the amount of coexisting aphasia. The influences include where the emphasis of treatment is placed, on the aphasia or the apraxia; when the emphasis is placed, on the aphasia early or until sufficient auditory and visual input abilities are developed for the patient to profit from techniques designed to improve apraxia; and what the ultimate goal is—an alternative mode of communication through the use of gestures or a communication board, improved language with persisting apraxia, or improving motor programming deficits when aphasia is mild and sufficient language is available.

Consider the three patients shown in Figure 1-17. Patient A demonstrated severe aphasia and severe apraxia of speech. His initial PICA overall score placed him at the 15th percentile, and his verbalization was limited to unintelligible, undifferentiated responses. Patient B demonstrated marked aphasia and marked apraxia. His initial PICA overall performance was at the 51st percentile, and his verbal performance was characterized by a small group of nouns, essentially no verbs, and a meager syntax. All verbal attempts featured the phonetic and prosodic features typical of apraxia of speech. Patient C demonstrated moderate aphasia and moderate apraxia. His initial PICA overall performance placed him at the 79th percentile. He was able to repeat words, complete sentences, name objects, and describe objects by their function. However, all his responses demonstrated the phonetic and prosodic characteristics of apraxia of speech. Each patient, therefore, demonstrated apraxia with coexisting aphasia. However, the severity of both disorders varied greatly among patients and required different treatment. Thus methods effective for one patient are inappropriate for others.

Table 1-17 lists methods for treating apraxia of speech and places a different emphasis on the effectiveness of the methods, depending on the amount of coexisting aphasia. For example, patients with severe apraxia of speech and severe coexisting aphasia may profit from imitation, phonetic derivation, or phonetic placement. Because of the paucity of verbal output, melodic intonation therapy or intersystemic gestural reorganization is less appropriate. Unless the patient's verbal output improves with imitation, phonetic derivation, or phonetic placement therapies, an alternative mode of communication must be considered. Two possibilities are the Amerind gestures of Skelly et al. [229] or the use of a communication board. When marked aphasia and apraxia coexist, imitation, phonetic derivation, phonetic placement, melodic intona-

tion therapy, and intersystemic reorganization gestures are appropriate methods. Even though aphasia is marked and influences auditory and visual input, typically the patient has sufficient awareness and understanding to profit from one or more of these methods. When mild to moderate aphasia and apraxia of speech coexist, imitation, phonetic derivation, phonetic placement, melodic intonation therapy, and intersystemic reorganization through gestures are all possibilities. However, if the patient has sufficient syntax, contrastive stress drills that manipulate loudness, pitch, articulation time, and pause time are effective in reducing prosodic disturbances. Further, treatment hierarchies designed to improve programming of articulatory movements can be inserted into the stress drill format. For example, sentences can begin with sounds the patient is able to produce (e.g., "*Bob* bit Bill") and progress to error-causing combinations (e.g., "*Stripes* are stimulating"). Manipulating loudness, pitch, articulation time, and pause time by appropriate questions (e.g., "Did you say spots are stimulating?") and having the patient respond (e.g., "No! *Stripes* are stimulating") uses these elements to improve motor programming.

Methods, of course, are comprised of the other dimensions important in focusing therapy. In severe aphasia and severe apraxia of speech, stimuli should be meaningful, short, simple, and occur frequently in the language. The length, complexity, frequency of occurrence, and number present in the task must be appropriate for the severity of aphasia coexisting with the apraxia. Stimulus modes include auditory, visual, or tactile possibilities. In severe aphasia and apraxia, visual input is usually best. Oral sensation and perception may be impaired, negating the use of oral-tactile cues. The presence of severe aphasia may eliminate or, at least, greatly restrict the use of auditory stimuli. Patients with marked to mild aphasia and coexisting apraxia will indicate which stimulus modes are best by their performance. For patients with severe aphasia and apraxia of speech, response modes may be limited to pointing and simple gesturing. Complex gesturing, writing, and speaking are possible response modes in marked to mild aphasia and apraxia. For patients with severe apraxia, responses made in unison with the examiner and immediate responses represent the best temporal relations between stimulus and response. As the severity of the condition decreases, delayed responses and consecutive responses can be introduced. Thus while treatment techniques for apraxia differ from those

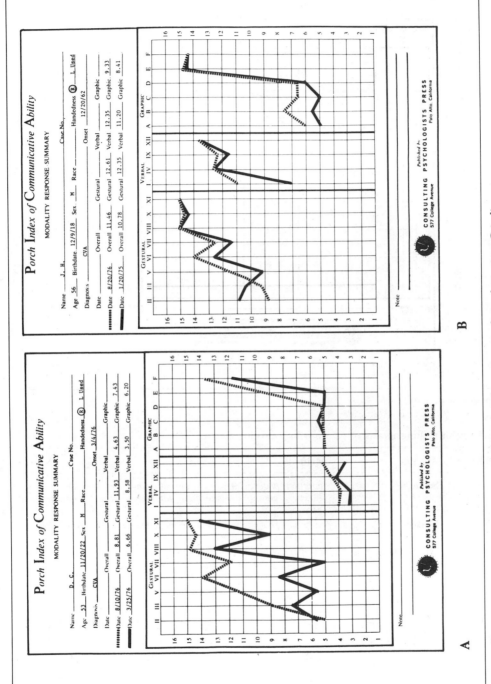

Fig. 1-17. PICA modality response summaries for three patients with apraxia of speech. The severe verbal deficits demonstrated by patient A, the marked verbal involvement displayed by patient B, and the moderate verbal impairment shown by patient C indicate the range of severity seen in patients with apraxia of speech.

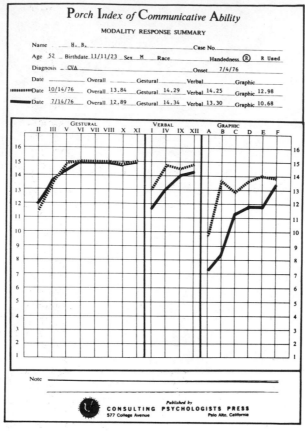

C

Fig. 1-17 (CONTINUED)

Table 1-17. Methods for treating apraxia of speech with coexisting aphasia

Apraxia of speech	Aphasia	Methods*
Severe	Severe	*Imitation, phonetic derivation, phonetic placement*, melodic intonation therapy, gesture (reorganization, *alternative mode*), *communication board*
Marked	Marked	*Imitation, phonetic derivation, phonetic placement, melodic intonation therapy*, gesture (*reorganization*)
Mild to moderate	Mild to moderate	Imitation, phonetic derivation, phonetic placement, melodic intonation therapy, gesture (reorganization), *contrastive stress*

*Italics indicate most effective method(s).

employed with aphasia, the same dimensions must be considered in focusing the therapy.

Given this information, we can return to the three patients listed in Figure 1-17. Patient A demonstrated severe aphasia, severe apraxia of speech, and severe oral-nonverbal apraxia. Three months of daily speech and language therapy failed to produce any usable verbal communication. Thus gesture, as an alternative mode of communication and supplemented by a communication board, became the method of choice. Some improvement was noted in auditory comprehension, reading, and written copying. Rosenbek describes patient A's treatment in detail in Chapter 7. Follow-up evaluation approximately 5 months after onset indicates persisting severe aphasia and severe apraxia. Patient B was approximately 13 years after onset when we met him. He demonstrated marked aphasia and marked apraxia of speech. His verbal output was characterized by a small group of nouns and severe agrammatism. His insistence on wanting to talk in complete sentences led us to eschew methods for improving articulatory programming and to opt for a method that would increase his language and improve his syntax. Intersystemic reorganization, using combined gestures and speech, was the method of choice. A lesser emphasis was placed on improving auditory comprehension, reading, and writing. Because his home was a great distance from our clinic, he was seen once a week for a year and a half. His initial one-word responses increased to a limited, but functional, group of complete syntactical statements accompanied by appropriate gestures. There was minimum, but noticeable, improvement in his apraxia. The patient's desire and his paucity of speech influenced us to work on his language rather than his motor speech. Patient C demonstrated mild to moderate aphasia that coexisted with a mild to moderate apraxia on his initial evaluation. Imitation, phonetic derivation, and phonetic placement methods were used to combat the apraxic deficit. We employed the eight-step task continuum reported by Rosenbek et al. [201]. Auditory-visual stimulation was emphasized initially, and, as the patient's ability to read improved, we moved to visual stimulation. Simultaneous treatment for auditory comprehension deficits experienced on longer and more complex stimuli, reading problems, and writing deficits was undertaken. After approximately 1 month of daily treatment, the patient was discharged. His most recent reevaluation indicated improvement in all communicative abilities, particularly in writing and speaking.

Focusing therapy for patients demonstrating apraxia of speech is influenced by the severity of coexisting aphasia. Treatments for both apraxia and aphasia are administered simultaneously. While methods differ for treating apraxia, the amount of coexisting aphasia influences the method selected.

CLINICAL EXAMPLE. E. S. is a 56-year-old, left-handed man who suffered a CVA in the left hemisphere. He was seen 10 days after his stroke and presented a diagnostic enigma. E. S., on our first meeting, assumed his reading and writing were normal; however, he admitted to speaking and listening problems. Evaluation indicated severe aphasia crossing all communicative modes. His initial PICA performance is shown in Figure 1-18. Overall performance was at the 39th percentile, gestural at the 55th, verbal at the 25th, and graphic at the 51st. He obtained a total score of 12 on the 61-item Token Test, produced no words on the Word Fluency Measure, and was correct on 25 of the 36 Coloured Progressive Matrices problems. He demonstrated severe oral-nonverbal apraxia and marked limb apraxia. There was no indication of hemiplegia, peripheral vision deficits, or peripheral auditory deficits. His verbal output was a combination of literal paraphasia and apraxic articulation errors. If he attempted to repeat auditory stimuli, the result was paraphasia. Conversely, if he attempted to read written stimuli aloud, the result was apraxia of speech.

The favorable prognostic signs included his relatively young age, good health, closeness to onset, and his motivation to improve his speech and language deficits. An intensive daily treatment program was initiated.

Early treatment involved a natural language program similar to that described by Kushner [131] and the Rosenbek et al. [201] eight-step task continuum for treating apraxia. The patient was entered at step 5, written stimuli (V_2) and simultaneous production, because of his poor auditory comprehension and his good reading ability. This quickly progressed to step 6, written stimuli (V_2) with delayed production. Treatment was administered twice daily and supplemented by evening assignments involving written work on the verbal stimuli used during the daily session. After approximately 10 sessions, his auditory comprehension improved sufficiently to permit stimuli being presented in the auditory mode. A "key word" technique was introduced for drill on different phonemes.

For example, E. S. typically could produce a phoneme correctly in at least one monosyllabic word (e.g., /s/ produced correctly in the word six). The key word was printed and placed before the patient for him to use as a landmark when drilling on specific sounds.

Reevaluation was done after approximately 1 month of treatment. His PICA performance (Fig. 1-18) showed performance at the 63rd percentile overall, 66th percentile in the gestural modality, 41st percentile in the verbal modality, and 88th percentile in the graphic modality. Token Test scores had improved to 32 correct on the 61-item test. Both Oral-nonverbal apraxia and limb apraxia were mild.

Treatment continued for 6 more months. E. S.

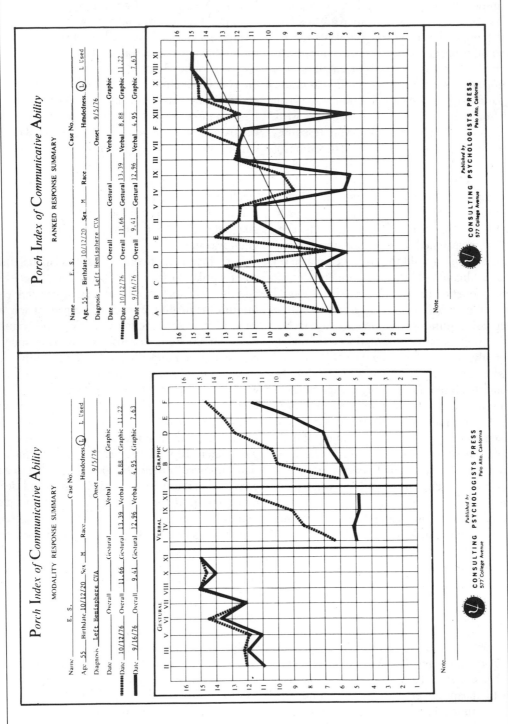

Fig. 1-18. PICA modality and ranked response summaries for E. S., who demonstrated severe apraxia of speech. Comparison of his initial performance and performance after 1 month of daily therapy shows significant improvement.

progressed through steps 7 and 8 on the task continuum. Stimulus length and phonetic difficulty were gradually increased as he progressed. Contrastive stress drill was introduced to improve prosody. Treatment ended at 7 months after onset. PICA performance was at the 90th percentile overall, 95th percentile gestural, 80th percentile verbal, and 95th percentile graphic. His Token Test score was 53 correct on the 61-item test, Word Fluency performance was 35 words produced, and the Coloured Progressive Matrices score was 33 correct on the 36-item test. Oral-nonverbal apraxia and limb apraxia had vanished. E. S. spoke functionally though not entirely normally.

Dysarthria

Disruption of the third requirement for oral communication described by Darley, Aronson, and Brown [50], ability to produce normal respiration, phonation, resonance, articulation, and prosody, results in dysarthria. The problem may occur in children or adults; and it may be present in isolation or coexist with other neuropathologies of speech and language, transient or persistent, mild or severe, and amenable to remediation or unchangeable. The speech pathologist is charged with managing the dysarthric patient's abnormal speech.

Darley's [48] definition of dysarthria (Table 1-1) transcends the literal meaning of the term, *dys-* (representing faulty) and *-arthria* (signifying articulation). Further, it expands the medical dictionary definition, "imperfect articulation in speech" [65].

First, Darley implies that dysarthria refers to a group of disorders rather than a single disorder. Dissimilar types of deviant speech (distorted articulation, resulting from a weak, slow-moving tongue; breathy voice quality and hypernasality, resulting from weak laryngeal and palatal muscles; a rapid rate of articulation, resulting from muscular rigidity and a paucity of movement) should not receive the same diagnostic label. Therefore we are discussing a group of disorders, and it is more appropriate to pluralize the problem and refer to the dysarthrias rather than to dysarthria.

Second, Darley emphasizes that the dysarthrias are speech disorders. They should not be confused with the oral-expressive manifestations seen in language disorders: aphasia, confusion, or generalized intellectual impairment. The clinical relevance of this distinction, of course, is in patient management. Treatment for dysarthria differs from that employed for language disorders.

Third, Darley specifies that dysarthrias result from disruption of muscular control as a result of damage of the central or peripheral nervous system or both. There is some involvement of the basic motor processes used in speech, and this results in a movement disorder. Speech movements may show abnormal speed, range, strength, or coordination. Thus dysarthria differs from apraxia of speech, another motor speech disorder. Further, Darley's specification that dysarthrias represent impaired muscle activity distinguishes them from speech defects resulting from developmental problems (dyslalia), structural abnormalities, dental defects, and psychogenic influences.

Fourth, Darley's inclusion of possible disruption of all the basic motor processes of speech (respiration, phonation, articulation, resonance, and prosody) cautions against overemphasizing disordered articulation. Slow, restricted, weak, or uncoordinated muscle activity used in breathing for speech (respiration); producing sound in the larynx (phonation); selectively amplifying sound by changing the size, shape, and number of cavities through which it must pass (resonance); and varying intonation, stress, and rhythm during speech (prosody) may contribute more to overall severity than does disrupted articulation. This view is consistent with previous observations [27, 88, 89, 182].

The term *prosody* must be qualified. There is a tendency to consider prosody as a basic motor speech process on a par with respiration, phonation, articulation and resonance. It is not. Prosody— intonation, stress, and rhythm—refers to vocal effects constituted by variations in pitch, loudness, duration, and silence. These variations occur by manipulating the basic speech processes. Pitch is changed primarily in the larynx by shortening and lengthening the vocal folds; loudness variation results from respiratory activity with a minor assist from the larynx; and duration and silence are regulated by checking or releasing respiratory and articulatory muscles. Variations of these four features of prosody lend intelligibility, interest, and meaning to what is said.

Figure 1-19 is a theoretical clinical profile of dysarthria. Language, intellectual, and orientation abilities are unimpaired. Further, there is no involvement of the ability to program articulatory movements for the volitional production of phonemes. The problem is an impaired ability to make movements necessary for speech; and muscle involvement results in speed, range, strength, and coordination deficits. Dysarthria may coexist with

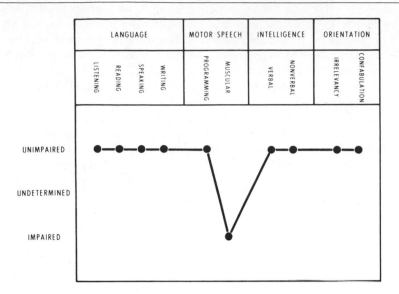

LANGUAGE				MOTOR SPEECH		INTELLIGENCE		ORIENTATION	
LISTENING	READING	SPEAKING	WRITING	PROGRAMMING	MUSCULAR	VERBAL	NONVERBAL	IRRELEVANCY	CONFABULATION

UNIMPAIRED

UNDETERMINED

IMPAIRED

Fig. 1-19. Theoretical clinical profile of a patient with dysarthria, indicating no language involvement, no motor speech programming problems, impaired muscles for producing motor speech, no intellectual deficits, and no orientation problems.

language, programming, intellectual, or orientation disorders, but it is a separate disorder rather than a symptom.

CLASSIFICATION: LOCALIZATION, CAUSE, PERCEPTUAL ANALYSIS. Formulating a system that classifies what one observes is a historic, scientific technique. It permits taking the poorly understood whole and breaking it down into its more easily understood parts. This is essential in managing dysarthric patients. Darley, Aronson, and Brown [50] discuss several approaches for classifying the dysarthrias. These approaches are listed in Table 1-18. Each system has advantages and disadvantages.

Classification by age of onset suggests that dysarthria in a state of evolution (child) may require different remedial approaches from those used with dysarthria in a state of dissolution (adult). Typically, the symptoms, course, and causes differ between congenital dysarthria and acquired dysarthria. Unfortunately, this system promotes an artificial dichotomy. For example, injuries to the nervous system that cause dysarthria in children are frequently pooled under the term *cerebral palsy*. Similar injuries resulting in dysarthria in adults direct one in search of a specific cause.

The most popular historic approaches for classifying the dysarthrias are those that focus on the general cause, disease process, neuroanatomic area, or the cranial nerves involved. These efforts attempt to use the dysarthric patient's speech and voice characteristics either to localize the damage in the nervous system or to identify the cause. Froeschels [76], Luchsinger and Arnold [150], and Brain [27] formulated systems that classified the dysarthrias according to the neuroanatomic site of the lesion; and Peacher [182] and Grewel [89] developed classifications that combine both the neurologic system involved and the specific cause. While these approaches are useful in confirming localization of the lesion or the system involved and possible identification of what caused the dysarthria, they are limited in providing useful information for the speech pathologist charged with evaluating and treating the dysarthric patient.

Systems that are used to classify the dysarthrias according to the speech processes, valves, and events involved overlap. The three approaches can be arranged into a hierarchy of increasing precision and yield of information.

First, the dysarthrias can be classified in terms of the speaking process (or processes) that is involved. Is the patient's respiratory activity adequate for speech? Are the abdominal and thoracic muscles functioning to produce and regulate adequate air pressure for talking? Or, as is the case in the spinal form of multiple sclerosis, does the patient display weak respiratory muscles inadequate for obtaining and controlling air supply? If so, the dysarthria can be classified as having a significant res-

Table 1-18. Possible classification systems for the dysarthrias

Types	Examples
Age at onset	Congenital or acquired
General cause	Vascular, neoplastic, traumatic, infectious, etc.
Disease processes	Multiple sclerosis, myasthenia gravis, parkinsonism, etc.
Neuroanatomic area involved	Cerebral, cerebellar, brainstem, etc.
Cranial nerves involved	V, VII, IX, X, XI, XII
Speech processes involved	Respiration, phonation, resonance, articulation, prosody
Speech valves involved	Respiratory, laryngeal, pharyngeal, velar, lingual, dental, labial
Speech events involved	Neural, muscular, structural, aerodynamic, acoustic, perceptual
Perceptual characteristics	Pitch, loudness, voice quality, respiration, prosody, articulation, general impression

Source: Adapted from F. L. Darley, A. E. Aronson, and J. R. Brown, *Motor Speech Disorders*. Philadelphia: Saunders, 1975.

piratory component. Similarly, appropriate questions can be asked about phonation: Do laryngeal muscles permit adequate voice production and pitch change? In terms of resonance, do pharyngeal and palatal muscles contract to manipulate the size, shape, and number of cavities needed for normal selective amplification of sound? And in articulation, are tongue, lip, and facial muscles adequate to permit the speed, range, strength, and coordination of movement necessary to produce adequate intelligibility? In prosody, do respiratory, laryngeal, and articulatory muscles act in sequence to provide pitch, intensity, and time variations needed for normal stress? Typically, a dysarthria will involve more than one speech process. When it does, the speech pathologist attempts to determine the relative contribution of each to the overall severity of dysarthria.

Second, classifying by the integrity of the muscular valves used in speech permits more precision than is possible with the speech process system. Netsell [176, 177] has described the speaking mechanism as being comprised of a series of functional components. This is illustrated in Figure 1-20. Each component represents an area in which muscle activity interrupts (valves) or releases the air used in speech. Dysarthria results when a neurogenic disorder disrupts the speed, range, strength, and coordination of movement necessary for normal valving of the airstream. Each numbered component represented in Figure 1-20 can be assimilated into the speech process classification just discussed. For example, abdominal muscles (one), diaphragm (two), and rib cage and associated muscles (three) comprise respiration. Laryngeal muscles (four) produce phonation. Velopharyngeal muscles (five), tongue-pharynx (six), and tongue muscles (seven and eight) create resonance. And, velopharynx (five), tongue-pharynx (six), tongue

muscles (seven and eight), jaw (nine), and lips (ten) produce articulation. Prosody is the result of coordinating valving by one or more of the ten functional components. This system permits greater precision in determining the location of disordered speech movements (e.g., weak diaphragmatic contraction) than is possible with a speech process classification (e.g., respiratory involvement). More precise classification leads to highly focused remedial efforts that are more effective.

Finally, Kent [121] and Hixon's [101] model (Fig. 1-2) organizes motor speech activity into events occurring on several levels. These events are reproduced in Figure 1-21. Internal events include neural and muscle activity, structural movements,

Fig. 1-20. Functional components of the speaking mechanism, showing areas where the airstream may be valved. Adapted from Netsell [176, 177].

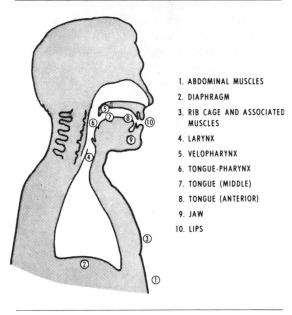

1. ABDOMINAL MUSCLES
2. DIAPHRAGM
3. RIB CAGE AND ASSOCIATED MUSCLES
4. LARYNX
5. VELOPHARYNX
6. TONGUE-PHARYNX
7. TONGUE (MIDDLE)
8. TONGUE (ANTERIOR)
9. JAW
10. LIPS

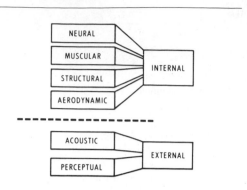

Fig. 1-21. Two ways of observing different levels of speech events. Internal events are observed by appropriate instrumentation (e.g., EMG, cinefluorography). External observation includes analysis of the speech signal or perceptual classification by the clinician. (Adapted from R. D. Kent, Study of vocal tract characteristics in the dysarthrias. Presented to the Veterans Administration Workshop on Motor Speech Disorders, Madison, Wis., 1976; T. Hixon, Respiratory-laryngeal evaluation. Presented to the Veterans Administration Workshop on Motor Speech Disorders, Madison, Wis., 1976.)

and the aerodynamics of air pressure and air flow. As we descend through these four levels, our knowledge about dysarthria increases, and the need for interdisciplinary interaction and elaborate instrumentation decreases. Hardy [95] has discussed most of these events and has offered several suggestions for physiologic research in dysarthria.

Neural and muscular events are observed by EMG. This technique looks at the integrity of the nervous system by recording the electrical activity in muscles used for speech. The cooperation of a neurologist and elaborate instrumentation are necessary. Leanderson, Meyerson and Persson [138, 139], Leanderson, Persson, and Ohman [140], Netsell [176], Netsell and Cleeland [178], and Netsell, Daniel, and Celesia [179] have studied EMG activity in dysarthric patients.

Structural events, particularly movements of the lip, jaw, tongue, velum, pharynx, and larynx, are observed by cinefluorography (x-ray). This technique permits a look at the range and speed of structural movement during speech. It requires collaboration with a radiologist and x-ray technician and availability of elaborate, expensive equipment. Kent and Netsell [122]; Kent, Netsell, and Bauer [123]; Netsell [175]; Netsell and Kent [180]; and Logemann et al. [147, 148] have provided evidence of structural movement abnormalities in dysarthric patients.

The aerodynamics of speech may be measured by the elaborate instrumentation described by Hixon [102] or by more basic instruments, such as the U-tube manometer. Measurements range from lung volume and breath pressure to oral and nasal air flow. Marquardt [156], Netsell [175], Netsell, Daniel, and Celesia [179], and Putnam and Hixon [194] have reported volume, pressure, and flow characteristics in dysarthric patients.

Two speech events, acoustic and perceptual, are observed externally. Acoustic analysis requires instrumentation to obtain a visual representation of the speech signal. Primary measurements include observation of the physical properties of sound: frequency, intensity, and temporal relations. Kent and Netsell [122]; Lebrun, Buyssens, and Henneaux [141]; Lehiste [143]; and Ludlow and Bassich [151] have used acoustic analysis to describe dysarthric speech.

Perceptual analysis requires the trained ears of experienced clinicians, a variety of talking tasks to obtain a speech sample, and a system for classifying what is heard. Because most speech pathologists do not have access to the instrumentation or interdisciplinary personnel necessary for evaluating and classifying dysarthrias according to neural, muscular, structural, aerodynamic, and acoustic events, perceptual classification is convenient and popular.

Darley, Aronson, and Brown [50–52] conducted what have come to be known as the Mayo Clinic studies. By listening to speech samples collected from over 200 dysarthric patients with unequivocally diagnosed neurologic lesions or disease, they concluded that dysarthrias resulting from damage in different parts of the nervous system sound different and can be differentiated according to specific perceptual dimensions. Utilizing 38 dimensions of speech and voice, Darley, Aronson, and Brown [51, 52] developed a perceptual classification system composed of six different types of dysarthria. Each has specific perceptual characteristics, each indicates the probable origin of nervous system disruption, each is associated with specific causes, and each results from specific abnormal neuromuscular conditions.

Table 1-19 lists the six different types of dysarthria. The first five are relatively "pure" types, distinguished by specific perceptual characteristics that specify the probable location of nervous system involvement. Each results from discernible causes and each is characterized by specific neuromuscular conditions that result in abnormal speech movements. Experienced speech pathologists can use their trained ears to listen to neurologically impaired patients and classify what is heard. If, for example, a patient displays breathy voice quality, hypernasality, and consonant imprecision, he or she is classified as having a flaccid dysarthria. This classification implies that the lesion involves the lower motor neuron system and results from infection, tumor, CVA, congenital condition, a specific lower motor neuron disease, or trauma. The information is conveyed to the patient's physician, who compares it with the results of his or her neurologic evaluation and special tests. Typically, the speech classification will agree with the medical information, and the physician will diagnose the patient as having bulbar palsy, which is a medical diagnosis consistent with involvement of the brainstem. If the patient demonstrates spastic dysarthria, and if the physician agrees, the diagnosis would be pseudobulbar palsy, implying a lesion of the upper motor neuron system. Other pure types are ataxic dysarthria, resulting from cerebellar involvement; hypokinetic dysarthria (Parkinson's dysarthria), resulting from extrapyramidal involvement; and hyperkinetic dysarthria, also resulting from extrapyramidal involvement.

The mixed dysarthrias listed in Table 1-19 occur as frequently as the pure types. The first three mixed dysarthrias listed are based on empirical evidence collected in the Mayo Clinic. The final type, others, permits classification of dysarthrias involving multiple systems; for example, a spastic-ataxic-flaccid dysarthria resulting from a tumor that has metastasized to involve upper motor neurons, the cerebellum, and lower motor neurons.

The three mixed types, based on perceptual data, demonstrate the validity of the system. Darley, Aronson, and Brown [51, 52] verified the perceptual characteristics in amyotrophic lateral sclerosis (ALS). The perceived characteristics combine what is heard in pure flaccid dysarthria and pure spastic dysarthria. The neuromuscular condition represents movement problems seen in both. Therefore ALS involves both upper and lower motor neurons and is classified as a mixed, spastic-flaccid dysarthria. Similarly, Berry et al. [23] demonstrated that the perceived characteristics in patients suffering from Wilson's disease imply upper motor neuron, cerebellar, and extrapyramidal involvement. Finally, Darley, Brown, and Goldstein [53] found that the movement disorders and the perceptual characteristics in multiple sclerosis (MS) varied according to which system or systems (upper motor neuron, cerebellar, or lower motor neuron) were involved.

Thus dysarthrias can be classified in numerous ways. Until the availability of and our sophistication with instrumentation improve sufficiently to classify according to Kent's [121] and Hixon's [101] levels of speech events, the perceptual classification system developed in the Mayo Clinic is useful. The different types of dysarthrias can be identified by their perceptual characteristics. These predict the cause, the localization of neurogenic involvement, and the neuromuscular condition. It must be remembered that the dysarthrias listed in Table 1-19 are speech diagnoses. Medical diagnoses (e.g., bulbar palsy) differ in vocabulary, but they can be compared with speech diagnoses.

APPRAISAL. The purposes of appraisal in dysarthria are essentially the same as those in apraxia of speech. Appraisal is designed to measure the patient's symptoms and establish their hierarchical relation; to determine the patient's speech diagnosis, not only dysarthria but also the type of dysarthria; to determine the severity of the disorder; to determine the patient's prognosis; and to focus the therapy. Appraisal can be done perceptually or instrumentally. Since the perceptual approach does not require availability of or experience with instrumentation, it will be emphasized here.

Complete appraisal of dysarthria is a team effort. The biographical, medical, and behavioral data listed in Tables 1-4 through 1-6 are supplied by a variety of disciplines, including neurology, orthopedics, physiatry, psychology, social work, physical therapy, occupational therapy, and speech pathology. The neurologic workup may be expanded, depending on the solution obtained in the search for a cause. EMG and more elaborate laboratory studies may be required. Since many dysarthrias result from disorders that affect the entire being (e.g., MS), physical therapy will appraise range of motion, strength, and so on in the affected limbs, and occupational therapy will survey the patient's ability to perform activities of daily living. Speech pathology, of course, appraises the patient's communicative behavior. For the patient, team appraisal should result in the best possible description, labeling, and treatment planning. For the professional, team diagnosis requires becoming familiar with potential contributions of each specialty, their technical vocabulary, and their appraisal techniques.

Appraisal of communicative deficit in dysarthria

Table 1-19. Mayo clinic perceptual classification of dysarthrias

Type	Perceptual characteristics	Localization	Causes	Neuromuscular condition
Flaccid dysarthria	Breathy voice quality, hypernasality, consonant imprecision	Lower motor neuron	Viral infection (e.g., poliomyelitis), tumor, CVA, congenital conditions, disease (e.g., myasthenia gravis), palsies (e.g., bulbar, facial), trauma	Flaccid paralysis, weakness, hypotonia, muscle atrophy, fasciculations
Spastic dysarthria	Strained-strangled-harsh voice quality, hypernasality, slow rate, consonant imprecision	Upper motor neuron	CVA, tumor, infections (e.g., encephalitis), trauma, congenital conditions (e.g., spastic cerebral palsy)	Spastic paralysis, weakness, limited range of movement, slowness of movement
Ataxic dysarthria	Imprecise consonants, excess and equal stress, irregular articulatory breakdown	Cerebellar system	CVA, tumor, trauma, congenital condition (e.g., ataxic cerebral palsy, Friedreich's ataxia), infection, toxic effects (e.g., alcohol)	Inaccurate movement, slow movement, hypotonia
Hypokinetic dysarthria	Monopitch, monoloudness, reduced stress, imprecise consonants, inappropriate silences, short rushes	Extrapyramidal system	Parkinson's disease, drug induced (e.g., reserpine or phenothiazine)	Slow movements, limited range of movement, immobility, paucity of movement, rigidity, loss of automatic aspects of movement, resting tremor
Hyperkinetic dysarthrias Predominantly quick	Imprecise consonants, prolonged intervals, variable rate, monopitch, harsh voice quality, inappropriate silences, distorted vowels, excess loudness variation	Extrapyramidal system	Chorea, infection, Gilles de la Tourette's syndrome, ballism	Quick involuntary movements (e.g., myoclonic jerks, tics, etc.), variable muscle tone

Predominantly slow	Imprecise consonants, strangled-harsh voice quality, irregular articulatory breakdown, monopitch, monoloudness	Extrapyramidal system	Athetosis (e.g., acquired or congenital, infection, CVA, tumor, dystonia, drug induced (e.g., tranquilizers), dyskinesia (e.g., torticallis, or tardive dyskinesia)	Twisting and writhing movements, slow movements, involuntary movements, hypertonia
Mixed dysarthria Spastic-flaccid	Imprecise consonants, hypernasality, harsh voice quality, slow rate, monopitch, short phrases, distorted vowels, low pitch, monoloudness, excess and equal stress, prolonged intervals	Upper and lower motor neurons	Amyotrophic lateral sclerosis, trauma, CVA	Weakness, slow movement, limited range of movement
Spastic-ataxic-hypokinetic	Reduced stress, monopitch, monoloudness, imprecise consonants, slow rate, excess and equal stress, low pitch, irregular articulatory breakdown	Upper motor neuron, cerebellar, extrapyramidal	Wilson's disease	Intention tremor, rigidity, spasticity, slow movement
Variable (spastic-ataxic-flaccid)	Variable (e.g., slow rate, harsh voice quality, irregular articulatory breakdowns)	Variable (e.g., upper motor neuron, cerebellar, lower motor neuron)	Multiple sclerosis	Variable (e.g., spasticity, weakness, slow movement, limited range of movement, inaccurate movement)
Others	Variable	Variable	Multiple CVAs, tumor, trauma, disease, etc.	Variable

Source: Adapted from F. L. Darley, A. E. Aronson, and J. R. Brown, *Motor Speech Disorders*. Philadelphia: Saunders, 1975.

requires documenting the presence of, or ruling out, a coexisting language disorder and collecting sufficient data to meet the purposes of appraisal. The former is accomplished by administering a battery of measures similar to those listed in Table 1-6. The latter is accomplished by appraising muscles and structures used in speaking on speech and nonspeech tasks. Sources of data range from observation of structures to timed productions and phonetic transcriptions. We employ a variety of tests, including the Motor Speech Evaluation, a Structural Functional Evaluation, Speech Valve Analysis, and Articulation Inventory. However, we seldom administer all these measures. The number given increases as dysarthria becomes less apparent and more difficult to detect. Thus it is usually the normal suspect who receives our entire battery.

The Motor Speech Evaluation already described is an adequate screening device for gaining a quick impression of whether additional testing is necessary. Specifically, the tasks—conversation, vowel prolongation, rapid alternating movements in production of monosyllables, repetition of multisyllabic words, and reading a passage—can be administered in almost any environment. If possible, we attempt to record the patient's responses for later analysis and to serve as a baseline comparison with reevaluations. Unless the dysarthria is extremely severe or extremely mild, the motor speech evaluation may be adequate for making a diagnosis (e.g., flaccid, spastic, or ataxic) and for estimating severity. It is an insufficient sample to determine all symptoms and their hierarchy, formulate a prognosis, or focus therapy.

The Structural Functional Evaluation is a battery of nonspeech, speech, and sensory tests designed to evaluate the integrity of cranial nerves V, VII, IX, X, XI, and XII and two groups of special tests for respiration and laryngeal function. Again, completion of the entire battery is seldom necessary. Nonspeech testing to evaluate the fifth cranial nerve involves palpation of the temporalis and masseter muscles after the patient is instructed to "bite down hard," manipulation of the mandible against resistance, and observation of the mandible during mouth opening. Weakness, atrophy, groping, and deviation are noted. Speech testing involves rapid production of /pʌ/. Three trials are elicited, and the number of syllables produced in 5 seconds is determined. Fifteen to 20 are considered within a normal range. Articulatory accuracy and evenness of rate are observed. Sensory testing includes inquiries about numbness of the face and testing light touch with cotton on each cheek.

Evaluation of the seventh cranial nerve involves nonspeech evaluation, including observation of ptosis; rigid or masked facies; tremor; facial weakness; facial movement in automatic activities (e.g., laughing); lip movements on lip retraction (e.g., "Show me your teeth"), puckering, alternating puckering and smiling, and lip compression against force (e.g., "Close your lips and don't let me open them"); and wrinkling the forehead (e.g., "Look at the ceiling without moving your head"). On movement tasks, weakness, slowness, reduced range, asymmetry, and groping are observed. Speech tasks involve rapid production of /pʌ/ with a bite block inserted to eliminate mandibular participation in the task. Three trials are elicited, and the number of syllables produced during 5 seconds is determined. While no normative data are available for comparison, an overt discrepancy between the number of syllables produced in the blocked and unblocked conditions will determine the patient's need for mandibular participation in the task and indicates some involvement in the lip muscles.

Nonspeech evaluation of cranial nerves IX, X, and XI includes observation and questioning about dysphagia and drooling, cough and throat clearing, and palatal conditions and movements. Speech evaluation includes observation of palatal movement during production of sustained and interrupted /ɑ/, listening to resonance changes during production of /u/ while alternating pinching and releasing the nares, observing clouding of a mirror held under the nose during production of /u/, and rapid production of /i-i-i/ on three consecutive 5-second trials. The observations include determining the presence or absence of hypernasality or hyponasality and deviant voice qualities, including breathiness, strained-strangled harshness, and hoarseness.

Nonspeech testing for evaluating the twelfth cranial nerve includes observing atrophy or fasciculation in the tongue at rest; range, speed, and symmetry of tongue movement on protrusion, lip licking, and lateral movement; and strength of the tongue against resistance. Speech tasks include rapid production of /tʌ/, /kʌ/, and /pʌ-tʌ-kʌ/ in blocked and unblocked conditions.

Respiration tests include timed maximum duration of /ɑ/, ability to increase loudness rapidly and dramatically, loudness patterning on a sequence provided by the examiner, and observation of abdominal movement during sniffing and panting. Prolongation gives an indication of vital capacity and ability to control exhalation with the respiratory muscles. Rapid increase of loudness and loudness patterns is another indicator of respiratory control. Sniffing and panting should be brisk and show movement in the abdominal area.

Laryngeal tests include rapid production of /i-i-i/ as a measure of the patient's ability to valve quickly with the vocal folds, rapid pitch change (e.g., *à la* Tarzan), pitch patterning with a model provided by the examiner, and estimation of the patient's pitch range. Since pitch is primarily controlled by the laryngeal muscles, all tasks are designed to determine the integrity of phonatory muscles.

Analysis of speech valves involves having the patient produce a series of phonemes designed to test how quickly the patient can valve the airstream at different points in the speech tract. In addition, the quality of response indicates the strength of valving at the level tested. Testing begins at the level of the glottis. The patient is asked to produce /i-i-i/ as rapidly and clearly as possible for 5 seconds. Testing of the palatopharyngeal valve requires 5-second production of /ŋ-ɑ, ŋ-ɑ, ŋ-ɑ/. Linguopalatal valving is tested by production of /kʌ-kʌ-kʌ/; linguoalveolar valving is tested with /tʌ-tʌ-tʌ/; linguodental valving is tested with /θʌ-θʌ-θʌ/; labiodental valving is tested with /fʌ-fʌ-fʌ/; and bilabial valving is tested with /pʌ-pʌ-pʌ/. This approach analyzes how strongly and rapidly the patient can put structures into and out of the airstream. It should indicate where air is being wasted and, therefore, assist in focusing therapy.

The traditional approach to appraising dysarthria involves articulation testing. It has much to recommend it. We employ several articulation tests, including a phonetic inventory, such as the Templin-Darley Test [240] or the McDonald Deep Test [160], Sentence Tests of Articulation from both these measures, Tikofsky's 50-Word Intelligibility Test [242], and the Sound by Syllable Test discussed earlier and elaborated by Rosenbek in Chapter 7. Phonetic inventories assist in determining symptoms and arranging these into a hierarchy, provide an estimate of severity, and direct focusing therapy. Sentence Tests of Articulation provide the same data collected in a more useful environment. Tikofsky's intelligibility lists yield a numerical indication of severity in percent correct. Finally, the Sound by Syllable Test tells us not only where a patient fails but also where he or she succeeds and, therefore, provides a useful tool for focusing therapy. Articulation testing provides the data for doing more elaborate articulation analyses. These include analysis of error type, error frequency, error distribution, and the reason for errors.

Three additional appraisal techniques—perceptual dimensions evaluation, prosody analysis, and oral sensation testing—are useful. The first assists in determining the speech diagnosis, and the second yields information on prosody that may be exploited in treatment. The motor speech evaluation should provide sufficient information to classify the dysarthria (e.g., flaccid, spastic, or ataxic). If it does not, the procedure employed by Darley, Aronson, and Brown [51, 52] can be used. This involves listening for specific dimensions, determining the presence or absence of each, and, if present, rating its prominence on a scale of 1 (mild) to 5 (severe). Clusters of prominent dimensions can be compared against the salient dimensions and clusters provided by Darley, Aronson, and Brown [51, 52]. Appraisal of prosody involves having the patient manipulate the suprasegmentals (e.g., pitch, loudness). This can be done on individual sounds, words, or within sentences. Natural manipulation of these can be accomplished by establishing a basic utterance (e.g., "Bob bit Bill") and asking appropriate questions (e.g., "Did Jack bite Bill?") and observing the patient's manipulations of stress (e.g., "No! *Bob* bit Bill") in the response. Finally, the third technique, oral sensation and perception testing, can be done by administering the standard tasks: two-point discrimination on the tongue and lip, oral-form identification, and mandibular kinesthesia. Creech, Wertz, and Rosenbek [37] and Rutherford and McCall [212] report methods and the use of these techniques with dysarthric patients. Kent [121] cautions that so-called oral sensory testing is really oral sensorimotor testing, since most tasks require the patient to make movements and the sensory results are probably affected by motor deficits.

Two recent perceptual measures of dysarthria, Enderby's Frenchay Dysarthria Assessment [72] and Yorkston and Beukelman's Assessment of Intelligibility of Dysarthric Speech (AIDS) [268], expand the clinician's appraisal tools. The former uses a nine-point rating scale to examine a variety of behaviors, structures, and influences. Enderby [71, 72] has discussed its development, reliability, and clinical use. The latter provides measures of single-word and sentence intelligibility and speaking rate. It is an excellent tool to establish baseline performance and evaluate change resulting from treatment.

DIAGNOSIS. Dysarthria receives both a medical and a speech diagnosis. Medical diagnosis is typically made by cause (e.g., myasthenia gravis, MS) and is listed in medical terminology (e.g., pseudobulbar palsy, bulbar palsy). Speech diagnosis is twofold. First, dysarthria is differentiated from other neuropathologies of speech and language, and second, the type of dysarthria is identified.

Differentiating dysarthria from the language disorders of aphasia, language of confusion, and language of generalized intellectual impairment is not overly difficult, but two complications can arise. First, if the language disorder is sufficiently severe to reduce the patient's verbal output to a small number of utterances or total jargon, it is difficult to elicit a sufficient sample to identify or rule out dysarthria. In these cases, diagnosis is sometimes based on nonspeech movement, and the presence or absence of dysarthria is assumed. Even a nonspeech evaluation may be difficult if the patient is unable to follow directions. Second, when dysarthria coexists with a severe language disorder, the interaction between the two may create bizarre verbal output that is difficult to label. It is a rare case, however, in which the clinician cannot determine the presence or absence of coexisting dysarthria. It is slightly more difficult to differentiate dysarthria from apraxia of speech. The procedure was discussed earlier under the diagnosis of apraxia. The steps and rationale are essentially the same when the process is reversed, and the same literature [117, 118] and principles apply. Generally, dysarthria involves all speech levels (respiration, phonation, articulation, resonance, and prosody), while apraxia is primarily a disorder of articulation and prosody. Usually, dysarthria is characterized by distortion errors, while apraxia is characterized by substitution errors. Within the narrow limits established by the severity of the patient's condition, dysarthric errors are probably more consistent than apraxic errors; however, mild dysarthria is probably less consistent than severe apraxia of speech. Finally, dysarthria is a disorder of muscle and movement, resulting from cranial nerve involvement, while apraxia is a disorder of cortex and programming, with no significant cranial nerve involvement. As always, the two disorders may coexist.

Determining the specific type of dysarthria requires a knowledge of the literature, sensitive ears, and clinical experience. We attempt to classify according to the Mayo Clinic system: flaccid, spastic, ataxic, hypokinetic, hyperkinetic, or mixed dysarthria. Patients with the pure causes of dysarthria of moderate severity (e.g., myasthenia gravis) are easiest to classify. Those with causes that result in mixed dysarthrias and represent a severity at either end of the continuum (e.g., mild or severe multiple sclerosis) are more difficult to classify. And patients with mixed causes (e.g., a patient with Parkinson's disease who suffered bilateral CVAs or who has undergone unsuccessful bilateral thalamotomy) are sometimes impossible to classify. Perceptual classification is done by listening and comparing what one hears with the salient dimensions elaborated by Darley, Aronson, and Brown [51, 52].

PROGNOSIS. The future for the dysarthric patient must be qualified with an answer to the question "Prognosis for what?" The qualification can range from prognosis for developing an alternative mode of communication in progressive, severe dysarthria, such as amyotrophic lateral sclerosis, through improved intelligibility in moderate, slowly progressive dysarthria, such as MS, to normal speech in dysarthria that is expected to subside, such as in Guillain-Barré syndrome. Prognostic signs in dysarthria are influenced by the patient's speech and speech-related symptoms.

Medical influences on prognosis include the cause and the patient's general health. Considerations of the cause include the specific disorder and its duration, nonspeech symptoms and complications, availability and effectiveness of nonspeech treatment, and the influence of nonspeech treatments on speech. Prognosis is specific for each disorder. For example, amyotrophic lateral sclerosis is a progressive disorder without remission. Average duration of the patient's life is approximately 3 years from the appearance of the first symptom. There is no treatment that will evoke improvement or even influence the course of the disease. Prognosis for improvement in speech symptoms is, of course, extremely bleak. Conversely, Guillain-Barré syndrome is a disorder in which symptoms progress to their maximum extent within a week to 3 weeks after onset. Mortality is between 15 and 60 percent, with death resulting from respiratory failure or intercurrent infection within 3 weeks of onset. If the patient survives beyond the acute stage of respiratory involvement, the rate of recovery varies from days to months. Although return to normal is frequent, residual effects may persist in the form of slight weakness of facial and extremity muscles. There is no specific therapy for these symptoms. A respirator is used in patients with respiratory muscle paralysis, and good results have been reported with the administration of corticosteroids. If the patient survives the acute respiratory stage, prognosis for improvement of dysarthria is quite good. Therefore the prognosis for improvement in dysarthria must be based on the cause in each individual patient.

Prognostic signs in dysarthria that can be determined by speech or speech-related symptoms include: whether primary function is impaired, overall severity of dysarthria, whether a change in intelligibility can be made easily and quickly, the results of medical management on speech, and the patient's ability to become his or her own clinician.

If primary function (breathing to sustain life, swallowing, and so on) is impaired, the prognosis is poorer than if function is sufficient for biological necessities. For example, the patient with bilateral trauma who remains on the critical list because of respiratory involvement has a poorer prognosis for speech improvement than the patient with bilateral trauma whose tracheotomy has been closed and in whom essentially normal aerodynamics for speech have been reestablished.

Generally, the poorer a dysarthric patient's intelligibility, the poorer the prognosis. A 20 percent intelligibility score on Tikofsky's 50-Word Intelligibility Test [242] implies a less favorable future than a 70 percent intelligibility score. However, the influence of cause, stage of recovery, and availability of medical treatment may negate severity of dysarthria as a prognostic indicator.

If changes in a patient's intelligibility can be made quickly and easily, the prognosis is better than it is for the patient who displays no easily manipulated symptom. For example, insertion of a palatal lift may result in a marked increase in intelligibility by reducing hypernasality. Similar results may be obtained by positioning the patient and giving him or her a better posture for speech. Further, dramatic results may be obtained with brief therapeutic trials using a voice amplifier, delayed auditory feedback, or auditory masking. If improved intelligibility is noted with the use of these devices, prognosis is good, since all can be made portable.

The influence of medical management on speech has prognostic significance. Three possibilities exist: There is no known medical management that improves speech, medical management has been tried and is unsuccessful, and medical management has been tried and is successful. An example of the first possibility is dysarthria resulting from MS. There is no successful treatment program that will improve MS, including the speech symptoms. An example of the second condition is surgical intervention to relieve parkinsonian symptoms. An example of the third condition is a successful medication program to relieve myasthenia gravis. Obviously, prognosis in the first two situations is poor, and prognosis in the latter is favorable.

Finally, if the patient demonstrates the ability to become his or her own speech therapist, he or she has a better prognosis for improving the dysarthria than the patient who improves in the speech clinic but cannot take charge of his or her treatment outside the therapy room. Three questions must be answered. First, can the patient apply therapeutic techniques that result in improved intelligibility? Second, will the patient apply these techniques beyond the influence of the clinician? And, third, does change occur when the patient becomes his or her own clinician? If the answer is yes to all three, the prognosis is good.

Unlike the prognosis for recovery from aphasia, in which we can list several speculations in search of empirical support, prognosis in dysarthria still awaits the discovery of reasonable speculations. Further, many of the causes of dysarthria are not static like those of aphasia. Recovery from aphasia subsequent to a CVA permits a starting point from which to predict the future. Predicting recovery from dysarthria associated with some disorders (e.g., MS) requires constant revision, since the patient's status is continually changing. Thus prognosis in dysarthria is frequently tentative, undetermined, and generally not very exact.

Netsell [173] has listed several factors that may influence a dysarthric patient's response to treatment. He mentions neurologic status and history, age, "automatic" adjustments, treatment effects, personality and intelligence, and support systems. Netsell cautions that these are clinical observations in search of data. Again, while many of us have become aficionados of perceptual classification of the dysarthrias, few of us are adroit in giving dysarthric patients an accurate prognosis.

FOCUSING THERAPY. Dysarthria therapy could be focused according to cause (e.g., myasthenia gravis, MS, bilateral CVAs); the type of dysarthria (flaccid, spastic, ataxic, and so on); or the primary functions involved (e.g., respiration, phonation, articulation). Each method of organizing treatment can be justified. For example, Hanson and Metter [94] report the use of delayed auditory feedback (DAF) with a patient suffering from Parkinson's disease, Simmons [228] elaborates the use of acoustic analysis in the treatment of ataxic dysarthria, and Perkins [184] has edited a collection of treatments suggested for each of the perceptual types of dysarthria. However, any method of organizing treatment is bound to overlap and interact with other methods. Rosenbek and LaPointe discuss treatment for dysarthria in detail in Chapter 2. Only general considerations for focusing dysarthria therapy will be considered here. Focusing dysarthria therapy involves developing a philosophy of treatment, the different types of management available, the goals to be achieved, and applying general and specific principles.

Three considerations, similar to those discussed in therapy for the language of generalized intellectual impairment, constitute a philosophy for dysarthria therapy. First, every attempt is made to restore lost function (e.g., medication, surgery, prostheses). Second, the dysarthric patient's life is structured to eliminate the need for lost function (e.g., situations requiring 100 percent intelligibility, maximum intensity, and lengthy production on one respiratory cycle are avoided). Third, efficient use of residual function is maximized (e.g., length of utterance is reduced to that which can be supported by residual respiratory ability, appropriate stress is used to compensate for impaired articulation, and proper positioning is employed to improve tone).

Three approaches for managing the dysarthric patient exist. First, medical management provides medication, surgery, and other treatments designed to combat the basic disorder and to keep the patient's general health at its best possible level. Second, behavioral management includes all the techniques employed in traditional speech therapy for dysarthria and all the techniques provided by physical and occupational therapies. Third, instrumental management utilizes equipment to provide feedback or administer treatment programs in a more systematic or efficient manner than can be accomplished by a speech clinician.

From the speech pathologist's point of view, the philosophy of treatment and the managements available are designed to achieve specific goals in speech. These include improving posture, strength, and tone; improving respiration; improving phonation; improving resonance; improving articulation; improving prosody; and improving communication through the use of alternative modes.

The specific principles for dysarthria therapy, whether behavioral or instrumental, influence the selection and administration of treatment tasks. First, dysarthria therapy is symptomatic. The symptoms are manipulated to bring about an overall improvement in speech. Second, dysarthria therapy is supportive. The goal is, typically, not to obtain normal speech or, in some cases, even to improve speech above its present level. The speech pathologist supports patients through counseling and feedback to perform as well as possible at their present level, urges them forward, or, if this is impossible, assists them in accepting their limitations. Third, dysarthria therapy is compensatory. Rather than having the patient attempt to perform normally, the speech pathologist urges him or her to perform differently. This may require trading the aesthetics of speech for improved intelligibility. Fourth, dysarthria therapy should demand less than maximum effort. None of us can maintain continuous performance at our physiologic ceiling, and, certainly, the dysarthric patient cannot. Therefore the desired habitual speaking level should be somewhere below the patient's ceiling for physiologic support of speech. Fifth, dysarthria therapy strives for maximum intelligibility. To sound good is desirable, but to be understood is essential. Treatment tasks are selected that first evoke improvement in intelligibility and, second, improve quality.

Therapy begins by selecting a symptom for treatment. There are two primary rules. First, a symptom is selected that is low on the hierarchy of the patient's range of responses and, second, a symptom is selected that, when manipulated, makes a significant change in the patient's intelligibility. For example, one of our patients with MS was elevating his shoulders during inhalation and maintaining his posture during exhalation as an inefficient compensatory attempt to obtain more air for speech. Since he was able to obtain sufficient air to produce short utterances without these gymnastics, impaired inhalation was a symptom low on his hierarchy of respiration symptoms. Further, when we prevented the inappropriate compensatory activity, we observed a marked improvement in his strained-strangled voice quality and improvement in his less effortful articulation. Thus elimination of shoulder elevation and drill on short utterances resulted in improved use of breathing for speech, elimination of abnormal voice quality, and more intelligible articulation. A list of examples for focusing therapy to achieve the seven goals follows.

Improving posture, strength, and muscle tone may result in improved intelligibility. Management may be medical through surgery, behavioral through positioning and bracing, or instrumental through the use of appliances (e.g., palatal lift). Postural adjustments are made to improve speech; however, the physician may override these efforts if they threaten the patient's health (e.g., girdling may improve posture for respiration but can create a perfect setting for the development of pneumonia). Further, postural adjustment does not refer to the most aesthetic positions. For example, turning the head to one side, supporting the neck with a collar, and supporting the trunk with overhead slings may have little eye appeal, but they may result in better speech. Contributions are made by the physical therapist, the rehabilitation team's expert on posture, the occupational therapist who provides the mechanical equipment, and the speech pathologist whose ear measures the result of postural adjustments on speech. Prosthetics can be used to improve posture. For example, improving the posture of the velum with a palatal lift may result in improved intelligibility through reduction of hypernasality. Gonzalez and Aronson's report [84], Aten et al.'s [8] suggestions, and Johns' discussion in Chapter 3 support the effectiveness of using a palatal lift in some dysarthric patients. Strengthening exercises have their advocates and their adversaries. Cole [35] recommends palatal strengthening exercises; Darley, Aronson, and Brown [50] view strengthening exercises as appropriate for severely weakened speech muscles after all other methods have failed; and Shelton [226] cites the lack of data to support the influence of muscle strengthening on speech. Many physical therapists employ muscle strengthening, and numerous patients will testify that strengthening has improved their speech. Netsell [174] suggests that strengthening techniques utilizing instrumental feedback may be more appropriate than traditional behavioral methods. Finally, improved muscle tone can be obtained in some patients medically (e.g., reduction of parkinsonian rigidity by administration of L-dopa); behaviorally, by relaxation exercises (e.g., shaking the jaw to "loosen it"); and instrumentally, with EMG feedback as demonstrated by Netsell and Cleeland [178] in their modification of lip hypertonia in a patient with Parkinson's disease.

Treatment designed to improve respiration is focused on one or more of three problems. First, the patient may have inadequate respiratory drive. Second, he or she may display impaired coordination of respiration. And, third, he or she may display inappropriate compensatory attempts to improve respiration. These conditions do not exist in every dysarthric patient. Many have adequate respiration for speech, but they waste their adequate air supply by inefficient valving at some point or points in the vocal tract. Hixon and Hardy [103] demonstrated this situation in patients with cerebral palsy, and it is true of many adult dysarthric patients. If the patient has inadequate respiratory drive, his or her condition may be improved with medication; for example, reduction of muscle rigidity in parkinsonism or improved strength in myasthenia gravis. A behavioral approach combines proper positioning, girdling, and muscle strengthening with assistance from the physical therapist. Instrumental approaches include those suggested by Hixon [101] and Netsell [174] that employ a U-tube manometer or more elaborate equipment in tasks designed to increase the patient's air pressure over longer periods. Approximately 5 cm of water sustained for 5 seconds is adequate air pressure for normal speech. Having the patient blow into a U-tube manometer and observe his or her efforts as elevation of a water level is effective and, some patients tell us, enjoyable. Finally, the patient can be taught to make the most efficient use of the respiratory ability he or she has. This involves strong inhalations (e.g., "Blow yourself up" in clinical terminology) before each utterance, controlled exhalation by appropriate valving with the patient's most intact structures, and reducing the length of the utterance. Inappropriate coordination can be remedied by focusing attention on the defective valve (e.g., laryngeal, velopharyngeal, or linguovelar). If a clinician has access to a respirometer, the patient can be instructed to inflate and observe valving efficiency during a rapid alternating motion task that is displayed on the respirometer drum (Hixon [101]). The goal is to increase the slope of the write-out when producing sounds with the defective valve (e.g., /tʌ-tʌ-tʌ/ for defective linguoalveolar valving). Inappropriate compensatory activity with the respiratory muscles can be observed, explained, and modified. Using a direct therapeutic technique such as visual feedback from a mirror, the clinician can point out the inappropriate compensation and contrast improved function when the inappropriate movements are eliminated.

Improving phonation can employ medical management involving medication or, possibly, surgery. For example, an effective medication program may eliminate the breathiness of patients with myasthenia gravis. Or, a paralyzed fold may be injected with Teflon, studied by Hammarberg, Fritzell, and Scheratzki [93], thus increasing the likelihood of contact with the other fold. Behavioral techniques include positioning the head to obtain improved phonation, relaxation, and laryngeal valving exercises (e.g., production of /i-i-i/) employing the respirometer technique already described. In dysarthria, the three primary laryngeal deficits are hyperadduction, hypoadduction, and incoordination. These result in the perceptual symptoms of breathiness, strained-strangled harshness, and so on. "Breathy" onset techniques may combat hyperadduction. Exploitation of primary laryngeal valving involved in lifting or exerting pressure with the arms during phonation may change hypoadduction. And patterning drills designed to put the larynx in and out of the airway may improve incoordination. The laryngeal symptoms need to be included in the patient's overall hierarchy of deficits. The question asked is, what contributions do laryngeal symptoms make to overall unintelligibility? Typically, we find that modification of respiration, articulation, and resonance influence intelligibility more than techniques designed to change phonation.

Improving resonance focuses on reduction of hypernasality. This condition is seen in flaccid, spastic, and mixed spastic-flaccid dysarthria. There are three approaches for improving resonance resulting from poor velopharyngeal valving. First, a palatal lift can be fitted. Gonzalez and Aronson [84] report lifts can be effective regardless of the type of dysarthria. Some patients may not be able to tolerate a lift because their teeth are in poor condition or because they are edentulous. A second treatment technique involves articulation drill. Typically, oral and nasal sounds are contrasted (e.g., **pop-mop**), and the patient uses auditory feedback in an attempt to reduce hypernasality in his oral productions. Different degrees of visual feedback are becoming popular. Sprintzen, McCall, and Skolnick [238] have employed a "scape scope," consisting of a nasal olive, tubing, and a cylinder with a piston to provide visual feedback on the presence or absence of hypernasality. The more elaborate oral panendoscope reproduces activity of the soft palate on a screen and permits the patient to see the movement or the lack of it. Shelton et al. [227] report that normal persons can develop volitional palatal control using feedback from the oral panendoscope. Third, palatal strengthening exercises suggested by Cole [35] can be employed. These include blowing, sucking, mirrors under the nose, and so on. It is remarkable how elimination of hypernasality can improve intelligibility. This makes resonance a tempting level for intervention in dysarthria therapy.

Improving articulation would seem to be the primary focus of dysarthria therapy, since the literal definition of the disorder is faulty articulation. It is hoped that this notion has been dispelled. Similar, if not more, improvement in intelligibility may be evoked by intervening at a different level. However, there are some techniques that may result in improved articulation. The first step in focusing therapy is to determine the cause of the articulation error. Articulatory muscles may be weak, move slowly, be restricted in range of movement, or move in an uncoordinated fashion. Some of these deficits are associated with particular types of dysarthria, for example, weakness in flaccidity, incoordination in ataxia, and reduced range in hypokinesia. Therefore the reason for articulation errors may be predicted by the type of dysarthria present. Articulation therapy begins after every effort has been made to obtain the best postural adjustments. If errors result from weakness, muscle-strengthening techniques are appropriate. If errors result from rigidity, medication may relieve this or behavioral relaxation may be employed. The second step in focusing articulation therapy requires an error analysis. Test data should permit creation of a hierarchy of error sounds. Treatment begins with those that are produced correctly in some contexts and proceeds systematically to include those more frequently or seriously involved or both. Our method of choice is integral stimulation (e.g., "Watch me, listen to me, and do what I do") and drill on carefully constructed hierarchies. Most patients require immediate knowledge of their results, auditory training, and explanation of reasons for their errors. Appropriate compensatory techniques (e.g., putting things in "neutral" by pausing before target sounds) may help. The technique of contrastive drill, mentioned in the discussion of hypernasality, is equally effective in articulation therapy. Selection of minimally different pairs (e.g., **pay-bay**) reduces the difficulty of the task, provides contrastive feedback, and permits systematic progression to more difficult contrast, requiring wider ranges of articulatory excursion. When error sounds are stabilized, the length and complexity of practiced stimuli are gradually increased and, it is hoped, end in intelligible, connected speech.

Improving prosody requires manipulation of pitch, loudness, articulation time, and pause time. Prosody is disrupted in most types of dysarthria, and it can be manipulated successfully in most. In addition, improvement of prosody typically results in improved intelligibility. All four elements can be treated behaviorally or instrumentally. Pitch problems in dysarthria are either too low, too high, unchanging, or inappropriate pitch. Instrumentation designed to give digital readout of pitch is available. When pitch is too high or too low, the patient is requested to decrease or increase the numerical values appropriately while reading a passage or repeating stimuli. Behavioral modification involves ear training and constant feedback of results. Of the four elements comprising prosody, pitch is probably the one we treat least often, because a change in pitch alone typically does not constitute a significant improvement in intelligibility. Loudness problems occur when the volume is too loud, too soft, unchanging, or inappropriate. Instrumentation for providing feedback ranges from digital readout of intensity to peaking a V-U meter. Behavioral methods are similar to those used with pitch problems: ear training and knowledge of results. If inadequate loudness is a continuing, unchangeable problem, a portable voice amplifier can be used to compensate. Articulation time refers to the time spent in sound production, and pause time refers to the time devoted to silence. These require manipulation when rate—too fast, too slow, or uneven—is a primary symptom of the dysarthria (e.g., ataxic and hypokinetic conditions). Instrumental approaches range from manipulating rate with a metronome to drills under the influence of delayed auditory feedback. Behavioral methods include timed syllable production by manual tapping or having the patient produce a word each time he or she is signaled by the clinician. Instrumental feedback is probably best for all disorders of prosody because, unlike most therapists, it is consistent. Telling the patient to raise his or her pitch, speak louder, and slow down is not very effective. If these admonitions worked, the patient probably would not be our patient, because he or she has heard them all before. An effective method is to control the patient's stress (simultaneous manipulation of

pitch, loudness, and rate). The contrastive stress drill used with dysarthric patients is similar to that used with patients demonstrating apraxia of speech. A basic utterance is established (e.g., "Pat paid Bob"), appropriate questions are asked (e.g., "Did Bill pay Bob?"), and the patient provides stress in his response (e.g., "No! *Pat* paid Bob"). Not only can stress be manipulated but also target sounds can be inserted as the patient is ready to work on them. For example, the easily produced plosives in one patient's hierarchy of phonetic difficulty progressed to use of more difficult, for him, sibilants (e.g., "Sam saw Sue"). Contrastive stress drill, we believe, is an effective means of improving intelligibility.

Finally, some dysarthrias are sufficiently severe to render intelligible speech impossible, even following intensive therapy. In these cases, adoption of an alternative mode of communication, as rapidly as possible, is the treatment of choice. Several possibilities exist. If the patient has a useable upper extremity, gestural communication can be taught to the patient and those in his or her environment. Skelly et al. [229] have employed a modification of Amerind with severe dysarthric patients. This can be supplemented with writing to convey specific information that cannot be converted to gestures. Another possibility is a communication board designed to fit the individual patient's needs. Typically, these boards contain a set vocabulary of pictures or words, an alphabet for spelling out words to enlarge the set vocabulary, and a list of numbers. If blank space is provided, special vocabulary sheets for special situations can be attached to the board. Further, if the board has a washable surface, non-permanent information can be added in grease pencil and easily removed. In some cases, removing one requirement for speech may be sufficient to result in useful oral communication. If aphonia or dysphonia is a significant symptom, an artificial larynx can provide the raw voice and, perhaps, result in usable speech. Adams [1] has discussed this possibility for patients with amyotrophic lateral sclerosis. Finally, when residuals eliminate the use of arm and hand movements, the creative collaboration of a speech pathologist, bioengineer, and occupational therapist can combine head pointers, electric typewriters, and variations of communication boards that do not require hand control to cope with the patients' limitations, their level of language competence, and their communicative needs. Linebaugh et al. [146] have discussed microcomputer-based augmentative communication systems for dysarthric patients, and Beukelman et al. [24] suggest the use of the Canon Communicator, a portable typewriter, as an alternative means of communication for the severely dysarthric.

CLINICAL EXAMPLE. B. H., a 53-year-old man, suffered a brainstem CVA in July, 1976. He was in a coma for several months. When he regained consciousness, he could not walk or talk, and he could not turn over or control his bodily functions. He was quadraplegic, could not chew foods, and choked when fed. He required total nursing care. B. H.'s communication consisted of responding to commands by blinking. Using this mode of response, we found no indication of severe aphasia, confusion, or dementia. Since he could understand most of what went on around him, he was sensitive to his plight.

Therapy began in October and continued daily for the next 10 months. Neurologists, nurses, occupational and physical therapists, speech pathologists, dentists, social workers, psychologists, and internists were involved in B. H.'s rehabilitation. Occupational and physical therapy and speech pathology filled six of his waking hours. Occupational therapy provided him with slings and special utensils so that he might feed himself. He eventually did. Physical therapy worked to improve his strength so that he would be easier to transfer from bed to chair and back again. He learned to transfer and sit unsupported, but not to walk. Speech pathology worked to improve his speech, which was characterized, originally, by weak, hypernasal approximations of single words. Our diagnosis was mixed flaccid-spastic dysarthria with primarily flaccid characteristics.

Speech intervention was designed to improve his posture for speech, respiration, articulation, resonance, and prosody. A dentist made and fitted a palatal lift that reduced a large proportion of B. H.'s hypernasality. His unintelligibility resulted from severe sound distortions, omissions, and substitutions; for example, a voiceless plosive was substituted for a voiced plosive in the final position. He was hypernasal, his voice was breathy and hoarse, and his respiratory support for speech was significantly reduced. At first, he could produce only one or two syllables on any exhalation. All valves and processes were significantly impaired.

Postural adjustments, obtained by positioning and bracing B. H. and providing overhead slings, attached to his wheelchair and through which he put his arms, gave him better position for respiration and speech. In addition, it created a situation in which improved strength developed by physical therapy could be employed in speech. Finally, postural adjustments appeared to improve his tone by creating a "better background" for his speaking efforts.

Respiration therapy involved teaching B. H. to make the most efficient use of what he had. He was taught to begin each utterance with a strong inhalation and to control exhalation. This involved longer and longer exhalations of vowels and voiced or voiceless fricatives. Initial attempts were less than 1 second in duration, but these were gradually increased to approximately a 4-second duration.

Treatment for phonatory involvement included proper positioning of B. H. to increase his background of effort. We had him place his arms on the armrests of his wheelchair and lean slightly forward while talking. This was combined with a conscious effort to "trap" the air in his throat. We guessed that this advice resulted in a generalized increase in tone. No attempt was made to correct errors of voicing (e.g., voiced /b/ for voiceless /p/) in the phonation phase of treatment. This was managed with articulation therapy.

Resonance imbalance, primarily hypernasality, was managed with the use of a palatal lift. We employed contrast drill (e.g., contrasting **pop** with **mop** and other oral nasal contrasts) to check the efficiency of the lift. It seemed to work, since hypernasality was markedly reduced with the lift in place.

B. H.'s articulatory errors appeared to result from weakness and slowness of all articulators. Treatment began with work on the plosives and progressed to sound productions that were more difficult for him. Using the facts of normal speech sound production, we were able to select and arrange appropriate stimuli. For example, voiced and voiceless plosives differ in characteristics of aspiration, duration, and air pressure and flow. These differences were determined and explained to B. H. He finally achieved perceptually different /k/ and /g/ by first learning strong aspiration of the /k/. A contrastive drill pattern was employed. B. H. drilled on *Pete—beet* and other plosive contrasts. Gradually the length and complexity of the practiced units were increased until they were intelligible in connected speech. He ended therapy by producing intelligible three- and four-word utterances, and, if the utterance happened to be loaded with plosives, he could produce as many as 13 syllables.

Manipulation of prosody emphasized pitch and loudness. Since B. H. spoke very slowly, and since we had little hope of increasing his rate, we accepted whatever he could produce. A contrastive stress drill was employed as soon as he could combine the two words "I do." By manipulating stress, first on the first word and then on the second, B. H. was able to emphasize one or the other using pitch or loudness changes.

Treatment began with no intelligible speech and progressed to the day when B. H. recorded his first 11-syllable utterance, "I can do it today or tomorrow too." Almost 1 year to the day after entering the hospital, he was discharged. When he left, he could talk intelligibly in three- and four-word sentences if given time and tolerance. His wife, 13 years younger than he and determined, was confident she could care for him with the help of a visiting nurse. She has succeeded in doing this.

Final Considerations

There is a traditional belief that each clinician is the final authority for his or her patient. The fecundity of effort between the first and second editions of this book requires this traditional belief be modified. Clinicians may exercise final authority only if they, as Rosenbek [199] suggests, "keep up." Failure to do so is internecine. I have attempted to purge my original attempt (done less than a

decade ago) of dross, and to incorporate recent contributions on the management of neurogenic communication disorders. The result is typified more by its omissions than its inclusions; too much has happened to capture it all.

Some of what we know now, that we did not know 10 years ago, is new. Some represents our ability to understand the efforts of our predecessors. We continue to discover that Mark Twain was correct when he observed that although the past does not repeat itself, it does rhyme with the present.

We understand some disorders better than others. For example, what we know about aphasia and dysarthria is sufficient to permit refining rather than refurbishing. Studies of other disorders, for example, apraxia of speech, remain controversial. Nevertheless, while we continue to debate the theoretical issues, language impairment or motor speech disorder, we have evidence that what we do for some apraxic patients does some good. Appreciation of the remaining two disorders, the language of confusion and the language of generalized intellectual impairment, has moved from mysterious to puzzling. Table 1-20 is a compilation of the clinical profiles presented earlier, and it is reintroduced to indicate where we are.

How we define aphasia continues to be debated. The position taken here is that aphasia is a general language disorder crossing all communicative modalities. Salient symptoms in some patients may

Table 1-20. Theoretical clinical profiles of five neuropathologies of speech and language

Behaviors	Disorders				
	Aphasia	Language of confusion	Language of generalized intellectual impairment	Apraxia of speech	Dysarthria
Language					
Listening	−	?	−	+	+
Reading	−	?	−	+	+
Speaking	−	?	−	+	+
Writing	−	?	−	+	+
Motor speech					
Programming	+	+	+	−	+
Muscular	+	+	+	+	−
Intelligence					
Verbal	?	?	−	+	+
Nonverbal	?	?	−	+	+
Orientation					
Irrelevancy	+	−	?	+	+
Confabulation	+	−	?	+	+

−, impaired; +, unimpaired; ?, undetermined impairment.

permit classification of aphasia into specific types. However, approximately 40 to 60 percent of the aphasic patients we see in our clinic cannot be classified. Motor speech deficits, apraxia of speech or dysarthria, are not a part of the symptom complex. While the patient may display orientation deficits, these result from a lack of language rather than irrelevant or confabulated behavior. Whether aphasic patients suffer intellectual deficit remains obscure. Collecting data on aphasic patients with existing intelligence tests has not provided an answer. Perhaps new measures are necessary. Or, perhaps a different approach would be more successful. For example, an analogue of intelligence testing, the purpose of which is to predict ability to do well in school, is an appropriate beginning. Maybe a task that measures an aphasic patient's ability to learn, hence to do well in therapy, would serve as a measure of intellect, resolve the dilemma, and provide prognostic information. More pertinent needs in the study of aphasia are easily applied criteria for differentiating it from the language of confusion and the language of generalized intellectual impairment; a method for formulating an early, exact prognosis; further demonstration that clinical speech and language tests measure functional communicative behavior; therapeutic techniques that are appropriate for the disorder but also can be adapted for use with individual patients with different levels of severity; and additional empirical evidence supporting the clinical belief that aphasia therapy is effective. Since 1978, efforts to understand aphasia and to do something about it have generated at least five books. Benson [17], Chapey [33], Darley [43], Davis [54], and Sarno [215] document where we are and where we need to go.

The language of confusion and the language of generalized intellectual impairment have been poorly understood. Both are confused with aphasia and with one another. Thus they present diagnostic dilemmas. The presence of a language deficit in confusion may depend on the severity of the patient's condition and the tests used. Structured tasks may yield no language deficits, while open-ended tasks may show severe language impairment. Perhaps a test that compares the two—structured versus nonstructured—would be a useful diagnostic tool. Similarly, identifying the language of generalized intellectual impairment is influenced by severity, and lack of knowledge of premorbid intelligence and education may make diagnosis difficult. Mildly to moderately demented patients may

go undetected on routinely administered speech and language tests. Tasks that require using language abstractly (explanation of proverbs, analogies) must be included in appraisal batteries to detect the presence of the language of generalized intellectual impairment. Bayles [13, 14] and Bayles, Tomoeda, and Caffrey [16] made significant contributions to our ability to appraise the language of generalized intellectual impairment, and Cummings and Benson [41] have improved our ability to diagnose it. However, prognostic indicators are almost nonexistent, and the effectiveness of any treatment approach is a mystery.

Information about and interest in apraxia of speech have been abundant during the past decade. The question regarding its status as a motor speech or language disorder has generated more controversy than answers. The theoretical issue, if one is interested, remains to be solved. Clinical necessities are methods for formulating an exact, early prognosis; establishing the acoustic and physiologic correlates; and empirical tests of the effectiveness of different therapeutic techniques. Since apraxia of speech usually coexists with aphasia, all efforts to provide the clinical necessities must consider not only the relative contribution of each disorder but also interaction between the two. Application of acoustic analysis by Kent and Rosenbek [125, 126] and instrumental analysis by Fromm et al. [77], Itoh and Sasanuma [113], and Itoh et al. [114] have permitted both confirmation and questioning of earlier perceptual studies. Wertz, LaPointe, and Rosenbek [262] have collected where we appear to be in our management of apraxia of speech into a single volume, and Rosenbek, McNeil, and Aronson [202] have edited contributions that represent the "state of the art."

Understanding of and ability to manage the dysarthrias have rapidly improved during the last 10 years. Not only are we able to determine the presence of a dysarthria but also we experience a high success rate in differentiating among the various types. Order has been created in our perception of dysarthrias, and there is an increasing amount of physiologic data to explain what we hear. Clinical needs may be fewer in the area of dysarthria, but they may be more difficult to meet. Unlike aphasia or apraxia, where physiologic status is typically stable or improving, the dysarthric patient may be stable, improving, or regressing. The dynamic nature of the disorder influences the approach to providing two clinical necessities, developing a method to determine prognosis, and testing the effectiveness of different behavioral and instrumental therapeutic techniques. Collections by Berry [21]; McNeil, Rosenbek, and Aronson [163]; and Perkins [184] indicate efforts are underway to meet these necessities.

We continue to await apocalyptic disclosures, but we have moved from necromancy to knowledge. The approach emphasized (definition, appraisal, diagnosis, prognosis, and focusing the therapy) is potentially probative for differentiating among and managing patients suffering different neuropathologies of speech and language. It helps us to learn what our patients have to tell us about their disorders and to permit our limitations to point out the direction in which we should go. As we travel, it will be important to remember that management of neurogenic communication disorders is not like a globe. One can go the wrong way even if one goes far enough. Thus, as we learn more and more, we need to avoid a food processor approach in managing our patients. Sometimes, knowledge generates a process where patients are not only quartered but also diced. All of our efforts to assist persons to make language are less important than assisting them to make a life.

References

1. Adams, M. R. Communication aids for patients with ALS. *J. Speech Hear. Disord.* 31 : 274, 1966.
2. Alexander, D. A. Attention dysfunction in senile dementia. *Psychol. Rep.* 32 : 229, 1973.
3. Alexander, M. P., and LoVerme, S. R. Aphasia after left hemispheric intracerebral hemorrhage. *Neurology* 30 : 193, 1980.
4. American Psychiatric Association. *DSM III: Diagnostic and Statistical Manual of Mental Disorders* (3rd ed.). Washington, D. C.: American Psychiatric Association, 1980.
5. Anderson, P. P., Bourestom, N., and Greenberg, F. R. *Rehabilitation Predictors in Completed Stroke: Final Report.* Minneapolis: American Rehabilitation Foundation, 1970.
6. Aten, J. L., Caligiuri, M. P., and Holland, A. L. The efficacy of functional communication therapy for chronic aphasic patients. *J. Speech Hear. Disord.* 47 : 93, 1982.
7. Aten, J. L., Johns, D. F., and Darley, F. L. Auditory perception of sequenced words in apraxia of speech. *J. Speech Hear. Res.* 14 : 131, 1971.
8. Aten, J. L., McDonald, A., Simpson, M., and Gutierrez, R. Efficacy of Modified Palatal Lifts for Improving Resonance. In M. R. McNeil, J. C. Rosenbek, and A. E. Aronson (eds.), *The Dysarthrias: Physiology, Acoustics, Perception, Management.* San Diego: College-Hill, 1984.
9. Barrett, R. E. Dementia in adults. *Med. Clin. North Am.* 56 : 1405, 1972.
10. Basso, A., Capitani, E., and Vignolo, L. A. Influence of rehabilitation on language skills in aphasic patients: A controlled study. *Arch. Neurol.* 36 : 190, 1979.
11. Bateman, F. *On Aphasia or Loss of Speech in the Localization of the Faculty of Articulate Language.* London: Churchill, 1890.
12. Bauman, J. A. Durational measurements of vowels in the speech of apraxic adults: A comparative investigation on the basis of selected words and logatoms in structured sentences. University of Colorado Master's Thesis, 1975.
13. Bayles, K. A. Language and Dementia. In A. L. Holland (ed.), *Language Disorders In Adults.* San Diego: College-Hill, 1984.
14. Bayles, K. A. Language function in senile dementia. *Brain Lang.* 16 : 265, 1982.
15. Bayles, K. A., and Boone, D. The potential of language tasks for identifying senile dementia. *J. Speech Hear. Disord.* 47 : 210, 1982.
16. Bayles, K. A., Tomoeda, C., and Caffrey, J. Language and dementia producing diseases. *Commun. Disord.* 7 : 131, 1982.
17. Benson, D. F. *Aphasia, Alexia, and Agraphia.* New York: Churchill Livingstone, 1979.
18. Benson, D. F. Aphasia rehabilitation. *Arch. Neurol.* 36 : 187, 1979.
19. Bergmann, K. The epidemiology of senile dementia. *Br. J. Psychiatry* 9 : 100, 1975.
20. Berry, M. F. *Language Disorders of Children.* New York: Appleton-Century-Crofts, 1969.
21. Berry, W. R. (ed.). *Clinical Dysarthria.* San Diego: College-Hill, 1983.
22. Berry, W. R. A psychometric reconsideration of the Token Test. Presented at the Third Conference on Clinical Aphasiology, Albuquerque, N.M., 1973.
23. Berry, W. R., Darley, F. L., Aronson, A. E., and Goldstein, N. P. Dysarthria in Wilson's disease. *J. Speech Hear. Res.* 17 : 169, 1974.
24. Beukelman, D., Yorkston, K., Gorhoff, S., Mitsuda, P., and Kenyon, V. Canon communicator use by adults: A retrospective study. *J. Speech Hear. Disord.* 46 : 374, 1981.
25. Boller, F., and Vignolo, L. A. Latent sensory aphasia in hemisphere-damaged patients: An experimental study with the Token Test. *Brain* 89 : 815, 1966.
26. Borkowski, J. G., Benton, A. L., and Spreen, O. Word fluency and brain damage. *Neuropsychologia* 5 : 135, 1967.
27. Brain, W. R. *Speech Disorders: Aphasia, Apraxia, and Agnosia.* London: Butterworth, 1965.
28. Brookshire, R. H. *An Introduction to Aphasia.* Minneapolis: BRK Publishers, 1973.
29. Butfield, E. Rehabilitation of the dysphasic patient. *Speech Pathol. Ther.* 1 : 60, 1958.
30. Butfield, E., and Zangwill, O. L. Re-education in aphasia: A review of 70 cases. *J. Neurol. Neurosurg. Psychiatry* 9 : 75, 1946.
31. Canter, G. Dysarthria, apraxia of speech, and literal paraphasia: Three distinct varieties of articulatory behavior in the adult with brain damage. Presented to the American Speech and Hearing Association, Detroit, Mich., 1973.

32. Carhart, R. (ed.). *Human Communication and Its Disorders, An Overview*. Bethesda, Md.: National Advisory Neurological Diseases and Stroke Council, 1969.

33. Chapey, R. (ed.). *Language Intervention Strategies in Adult Aphasia*. Baltimore: Williams & Wilkins, 1981.

34. Chédru, F., and Geschwind, N. Disorders of higher cortical functions in acute confusional states. *Cortex* 8 : 395, 1972.

35. Cole, R. M. Direct Muscle Training for the Improvement of Velopharyngeal Function. In K. R. Bzoch (ed.), *Communicative Disorders Related to Cleft Lip and Palate*. Boston: Little, Brown, 1971.

36. Cox, J. R. Double-blind evaluation of naftidrofuryl in treating elderly confused hospitalized patients. *Gerontology* 17 : 160, 1975.

37. Creech, R. J., Wertz, R. T., and Rosenbek, J. C. Oral sensation and perception in dysarthric adults. *Percept. Mot. Skills* 37 : 167, 1973.

38. Critchley, M. *Aphasiology and Other Aspects of Language*. London: Edward Arnold, 1970.

39. Critchley M. Aphasiological nomenclature and definitions. *Cortex* 3 : 3, 1967.

40. Culton, G. L. Spontaneous recovery from aphasia. *J. Speech Hear. Res.* 12 : 825, 1969.

41. Cummings, J. L., and Benson, D. F. *Dementia: A Clinical Approach*. Boston: Butterworth, 1983.

42. Dabul, B. *Apraxia Battery for Adults*. Tigard, Oregon: C. C. Publications, 1979.

43. Darley, F. L. *Aphasia*. Philadelphia: Saunders, 1982.

44. Darley, F. L. (ed.). *Evaluation of Appraisal Techniques in Speech and Language Pathology*. Reading, Mass.: Addison-Wesley, 1979.

45. Darley, F. L. A retrospective view: Have the major issues and questions of 25–50 years ago been answered in speech pathology? Presented to the American Speech and Hearing Association, Washington, D. C., 1975.

46. Darley, F. L. Treatment of Acquired Aphasia. In W. J. Friedlander (ed.), *Current Reviews of Higher Nervous System Dysfunction, Advances in Neurology*. New York: Raven, 1975. Vol. 7.

47. Darley, F. L. The efficacy of language rehabilitation in aphasia. *J. Speech Hear. Disord.* 37 : 3, 1972.

48. Darley, F. L. Aphasia: Input and output disturbances in speech and language processing. Presented in dual session on aphasia to the American Speech and Hearing Association, Chicago, Ill., 1969.

49. Darley, F. L. *Diagnosis and Appraisal of Communication Disorders*. Englewood Cliffs, N.J.: Prentice-Hall, 1964.

50. Darley, F. L., Aronson, A. E., and Brown, J. R. *Motor Speech Disorders*. Philadelphia: Saunders, 1975.

51. Darley, F. L., Aronson, A. E., and Brown, J. R. Clusters of deviant speech dimensions in the dysarthrias. *J. Speech Hear. Res.* 12 : 462, 1969.

52. Darley, F. L., Aronson, A. E., and Brown, J. R. Differential diagnostic patterns of dysarthria. *J. Speech Hear. Res.* 12 : 246, 1969.

53. Darley, F. L., Brown, J. R., and Goldstein, N. P. Dysarthria in multiple sclerosis. *J. Speech Hear. Res.* 15 : 229, 1972.

54. Davis, G. A. *A Survey of Adult Aphasia*. Englewood Cliffs, N.J.: Prentice-Hall, 1983.

55. Davis, G. A., and Wilcox, J. Incorporating Parameters of Natural Conversation in Aphasia Treatment. In R. Chapey (ed.), *Language Intervention Strategies in Adult Aphasia*. Baltimore: Williams & Wilkins, 1981.

56. Deal, J. L., and Darley, F. L. The influence of linguistic and situational variables on phonemic accuracy in apraxia of speech. *J. Speech Hear. Res.* 15 : 639, 1972.

57. Deal, J. L., and Deal, L. A. Efficacy of Aphasia Rehabilitation: Preliminary Results. In R. H. Brookshire (ed.), *Clinical Aphasiology: Proceedings of the Conference*. Minneapolis: BRK Publishers, 1978.

58. Deal, J. L., Wertz, R. T., and Spring, C. Differentiating Aphasia and the Language of Generalized Intellectual Impairment. In R. H. Brookshire (ed.), *Clinical Aphasiology: Proceedings of the Conference*. Minneapolis: BRK Publishers, 1981.

59. Deal, L. A., Deal, J. L., Wertz, R. T., Kitselman, K., and Dwyer, C. Statistical Prediction of Change in Aphasia: Clinical Application of Multiple Regression Analysis. In R. H. Brookshire (ed.), *Clinical Aphasiology: Proceedings of the Conference*. Minneapolis: BRK Publishers, 1979.

60. DePasquet, E. G., Gaudin, E. S., Bianchi, A., and DeMendilaharsu, S. A. Prolonged and monosymptomatic dysphasic status epilepticus. *Neurology* 26 : 244, 1976.

61. DeRenzi, E., Pieczuro, A., and Vignolo, L. A. Oral apraxia and aphasia. *Cortex* 2 : 50, 1966.

62. DeRenzi, E., and Vignolo, L. A. The Token Test: A sensitive test to detect receptive disturbances in aphasia. *Brain* 85 : 665, 1962.

63. Deutsch, S. E. Predictions of Site of Lesions from Speech Apraxic Error Patterns. In J. C. Rosenbek, M. R. McNeil, and A. E. Aronson (eds.), *Apraxia of Speech: Physiology, Acoustics, Linguistics, Management*. San Diego: College-Hill, 1984.

64. DiSimoni, F. G., Keith, R. L., Holt, D. L., and Darley, F. L. Practicality of shortening the Porch Index of Communicative Ability. *J. Speech Hear. Res.* 18 : 491, 1975.

65. *Dorland's Illustrated Medical Dictionary* (25th ed.). Philadelphia: Saunders, 1974.

66. Eisenson, J. *Adult Aphasia: Assessment and Treatment*. New York: Appleton-Century-Crofts, 1973.

67. Eisenson, J. Aphasia: A point of view as to the nature of the disorder and factors that determine prognosis for recovery. *Int. J. Neurol.* 4 : 287, 1964.

68. Eisenson, J. *Examining for Aphasia*. New York: The Psychological Corporation, 1954.

69. Eisenson, J. Prognostic factors related to language rehabilitation in aphasic patients. *J. Speech Hear. Disord.* 14 : 262, 1949.

70. Eisenson, J. Aphasics: Observations and tentative conclusions. *J. Speech Hear. Disord.* 12 : 290, 1947.

71. Enderby, P. The Standardized Measurement of

Dysarthria is Possible. In W. R. Berry (ed.), *Clinical Dysarthria*. San Diego: College-Hill, 1983.

72. Enderby, P. *Frenchay Dysarthria Assessment*. San Diego: College-Hill, 1983.

73. Espir, M. L. E., and Rose, F. C. *The Basic Neurology of Speech*. Philadelphia: Davis, 1970.

74. Ferm, L. Behavioural activities in demented geriatric patients. *Gerontology* 16 : 185, 1975.

75. Folsom, J. C. Reality orientation for the elderly mental patient. *J. Geriatr. Psychiatry* 1 : 291, 1968.

76. Froeschels, E. A contribution to the pathology and therapy of dysarthria due to certain cerebral lesions. *J. Speech Disord.* 8 : 301, 1943.

77. Fromm, D., Abbs, J. H., McNeil, M. R., and Rosenbek, J. C. Simultaneous Perceptual-Physiological Method for Studying Apraxia of Speech. In R. H. Brookshire (ed.), *Clinical Aphasiology: Proceedings of the Conference*. Minneapolis: BRK Publishers, 1982.

78. Gerin, J. Double-blind trial of naftidrofuryl in the treatment of cerebral arteriosclerosis. *Br. J. Clin. Pract.* 28 : 1, 1974.

79. Geschwind, N. The apraxias: Neuromechanisms of disorders of learned movement. *Am. Sci.* 63 : 188, 1975.

80. Geschwind, N. Writing Disturbances in Acute Confusional States. In R. S. Kohen and M. W. Wartofsky (eds.), *N. Geschwind Selected Papers on Language in the Brain*. Boston: Reidel, 1974.

81. Geschwind, N. Brain Mechanisms Suggested by Studies of Hemispheric Connections. In C. H. Millikan and F. L. Darley (eds.), *Brain Mechanisms Underlying Speech and Language*. New York: Grune & Stratton, 1967.

82. Geschwind, N. Disconnection syndromes in animals and man. *Brain* 88 : 237, 1965.

83. Goldstein, K. *Language and Language Disturbances*. New York: Grune & Stratton, 1948.

84. Gonzalez, J. B., and Aronson, A. E. Palatal lift prosthesis for treatment of anatomic and neurologic palatopharyngeal insufficiency. *Cleft Palate J.* 7 : 91, 1970.

85. Goodglass, H., and Kaplan, E. *The Assessment of Aphasia and Related Disorders* (2nd ed.). Philadelphia: Lea & Febiger, 1983.

86. Goodglass, H., and Kaplan, E. *The Assessment of Aphasia and Related Disorders*. Philadelphia: Lea & Febiger, 1972.

87. Grant, D. A., and Berg, E. A. A behavioral analysis of degree of reinforcement and ease of shifting to new responses in a Weigl type card sorting problem. *J. Exp. Psychol.* 38 : 404, 1948.

88. Green, M. C. L. *The Voice and Its Disorders* (3rd ed.). Philadelphia: Lippincott, 1972.

89. Grewel F. Classification of dysarthrias. *Acta Psychiatr. Neurol. Scand.* 32 : 325, 1957.

90. Haase, G. R. Diseases Presenting as Dementia. In C. E. Wells (ed.), *Dementia*, Contemporary Neurology Service No. 9. Philadelphia: Davis, 1971.

91. Hagen C. Language Disorders in Head Trauma. In A. L. Holland (ed.), *Language Disorders in Adults*. San Diego: College-Hill, 1984.

92. Halpern, H., Darley, F. L., and Brown, J. R. Differential language and neurological characteristics in cerebral involvement. *J. Speech Hear. Disord.* 38 : 162, 1973.

93. Hammarberg, B., Fritzell, B., and Scheratzki, H. Teflon injection in 16 patients with paralytic dysphonia: Perceptual and acoustic-evaluation. *J. Speech Hear. Disord.* 49 : 78, 1984.

94. Hanson, W. R., and Metter, E. J. DAF Speech Rate Modification in Parkinson's Disease: A Report of Two Cases. In W. R. Berry (ed.), *Clinical Dysarthria*. San Diego: College-Hill, 1983.

95. Hardy, J. C. Suggestions for physiological research in dysarthria. *Cortex* 3 : 128, 1967.

96. Hecaen, H., and Ajuriaguerra, J. *Left-Handedness*. New York: Grune & Stratton, 1964.

97. Hecaen, H., and Sauget, J. Cerebral dominance in left-handed subjects. *Cortex* 7 : 19, 1971.

98. Helm, N. Criteria for selecting aphasia patients for melodic intonation therapy. Paper presented to the American Academy for the Advancement of Science, Washington, D.C., 1978.

99. Helm-Estabrooks, N. Severe Aphasia. In A. L. Holland (ed.), *Language Disorders in Adults*. San Diego: College-Hill, 1984.

100. Helm-Estabrooks, N., Fitzpatrick, P., and Barresi, B. Visual action therapy for global aphasia. *J. Speech Hear. Disord.* 47 : 385, 1982.

101. Hixon, T. Respiratory-laryngeal evaluation. Presented to the Veterans Administration Workshop on Motor Speech Disorders, Madison, Wis., 1976.

102. Hixon, T. Some New Techniques for Measuring the Biomechanical Events of Speech Production: One Laboratory's Experiences. In R. T. Wertz (ed.), *Orofacial Function: Clinical Research in Dentistry and Speech Pathology*. ASHA Reports, No. 7, Washington, D.C., 1972.

103. Hixon, T., and Hardy, J. C. Restricted motility of the speech articulators in cerebral palsy. *J. Speech Hear. Disord.* 29 : 293, 1964.

104. Holland, A. L. (ed.). *Language Disorders in Adults*. San Diego: College-Hill, 1984.

105. Holland, A. L. When is aphasia aphasia: The problem of closed head injury. In R. H. Brookshire (ed.), *Clinical Aphasiology: Proceedings of the Conference*. Minneapolis: BRK Publishers, 1982.

106. Holland, A. L. *Communicative Abilities in Daily Living*. Baltimore: University Park, 1980.

107. Holland, A. L. Some Practical Considerations in Aphasia Rehabilitation. In M. Sullivan and M. S. Kommers (eds.), *Rationale for Adult Aphasia Therapy*. Omaha: University of Nebraska Medical Center, 1977.

108. Horenstein, S. The Clinical Use of Psychological Testing in Dementia. In C. E. Wells (ed.), *Dementia*, Contemporary Neurology Service No. 9. Philadelphia: Davis, 1971.

109. Horenstein S. Amnestic, Agnostic, Apractic, and Aphasic Features in Dementing Illness. In C. E. Wells (ed.), *Dementia*, Contemporary Neurology Service No. 9. Philadelphia: Davis, 1971.

110. Horner, J. Moderate Aphasia. In A. L. Holland

(ed.), *Language Disorders in Adults*. San Diego: College-Hill, 1984.

111. Horner, J., and Heyman, A. Aphasia associated with Alzheimer's dementia. Paper presented to the International Neuropsychological Society, Pittsburgh, Pa., 1982.

112. Isaacs, B., and Walkey, F. A. The measurement of mental impairment in geriatric practice. *Gerontol. Clin.* 6 : 114, 1964.

113. Itoh, M., and Sasanuma, S. Articulatory Movements in Apraxia of Speech. In J. C. Rosenbek, M. R. McNeil, and A. E. Aronson (eds.), *Apraxia of Speech: Physiology, Acoustics, Linguistics, Management*. San Diego: College-Hill, 1984.

114. Itoh, M., Sasanuma, S., Hirose, H., Yoshioka, H., and Ushijima, T. Abnormal articulatory dynamics in a patient with apraxia of speech: X-ray microbeam observations. *Brain Lang.*, 11 : 66, 1980.

115. Jackson, D. W. Relationship of residence, education, and socialization to cognitive tasks in normal people of advanced old age. *Psychol. Rep.* 35 : 423, 1974.

116. Jakobson, R. Toward a Linguistic Typology of Aphasic Impairments. In A. DeReuck and M. O'Connor (eds.), *Disorders of Language*. London: Churchill, 1964.

117. Johns, D. F., and Darley, F. L. Phonemic variability in apraxia of speech. *J. Speech Hear. Res.* 13 : 556, 1970.

118. Johns, D. F., and LaPointe, L. L. Neurogenic Disorders of Output Processing: Apraxia of Speech. In H. Whitaker and H. A. Whitaker (eds.), *Studies in Neurolinguistics*, New York: Academic, 1976. Vol. 1.

119. Jones L. V., and Wepman, J. M. Dimensions of language performance in aphasia. *J. Speech Hear. Res.* 4 : 220, 1961.

120. Joynt, R. J., and Goldstein, M. N. The Minor Cerebral Hemisphere. In W. J. Friedlander (ed.), *Current Reviews of Higher Nervous System Dysfunction. Advances in Neurology*. New York: Raven, 1975. Vol. 7.

121. Kent, R. D. Study of vocal tract characteristics in the dysarthrias. Presented to the Veterans Administration Workshop on Motor Speech Disorders, Madison, Wis., 1976.

122. Kent, R. D., and Netsell, R. A case study of an ataxic dysarthric: Cineradiographic and spectrographic observations. *J. Speech Hear. Disord.* 40 : 115, 1975.

123. Kent, R. D., Netsell, R., and Bauer, L. Cineradiographic assessment of articulatory mobility in the dysarthrias. *J. Speech Hear. Disord.* 40 : 467, 1975.

124. Kent, R. D., and Rosenbek, J. C. Acoustic patterns of apraxia of speech. *J. Speech Hear. Res.* 26 : 231, 1983.

125. Kent, R. D., and Rosenbek, J. C. Prosodic disturbance and neurologic lesion. *Brain Lang.* 15 : 259, 1982.

126. Kertesz, A. Subcortical Lesions and Verbal Apraxia. In J. C. Rosenbek, M. R. McNeil, and A. E. Aronson (eds.), *Apraxia of Speech: Physiology, Acoustics, Linguistics, Management*. San Diego: College-Hill, 1984.

127. Kertesz, A. *Western Aphasia Battery*. New York: Grune & Stratton, 1982.

128. Kertesz, A. *Aphasia and Associated Disorders: Taxonomy, Localization, and Recovery*. New York: Grune & Stratton, 1979.

129. Kertesz, A., and McCabe, P. Recovery patterns and prognosis in aphasia. *Brain* 100 : 1, 1977.

130. Kral, V. A. The psychopathology and neuropathology of senile and presenile psychoses. *Laval Med.* 38 : 584, 1967.

131. Kushner, D. Extended Comprehension Training Leading to Improved Verbal Production: A Treatment Program for an Aphasic Patient. In R. H. Brookshire (ed.), *Clinical Aphasiology: Conference Proceedings*, 1975. Minneapolis: BRK Publishers, 1975.

132. LaPointe, L. L. Base-10 Program Stimulation: Task Specification, Scoring, and Plotting Performance in Aphasia Therapy. In B. E. Porch (ed.), *Proceedings of the Conference on Clinical Aphasiology*. New Orleans, La.: Veterans Administration Hospital, 1974.

133. LaPointe, L. L., and Horner, J. *Reading Comprehension Battery for Aphasia*. Tigard, Oregon: C. C. Publications, 1979.

134. LaPointe, L. L., and Horner, J. Repeated Trials of Words by Patients with Neurogenic Phonological Selection-Sequencing Impairment (Apraxia of Speech): Stimulus, Mode, and Response Condition Revisited. In R. H. Brookshire (ed.), *Clinical Aphasiology: Proceedings of the Conference*. Minneapolis: BRK Publishers, 1976.

135. LaPointe, L. L., and Johns, D. F. Some phonemic characteristics in apraxia of speech. *J. Commun. Disord.* 8 : 259, 1975.

136. LaPointe, L. L., and Wertz, R. T. Oral-movement abilities and articulatory characteristics of brain-injured adults. *Percept. Mot. Skills* 39 : 39, 1974.

137. Larimore, H. W. Some Verbal and Non-Verbal Factors Associated with Apraxia of Speech. University of Denver Ph.D. Thesis, 1970.

138. Leanderson, R., Meyerson, B., and Persson, A. Lip muscle function in Parkinsonian dysarthria. *Acta Otolaryngol. (Stockh.)* 74 : 271, 1972.

139. Leanderson, R., Meyerson, B., and Persson, A. The effect of L-dopa on speech in Parkinsonism: An EMG study of labial articulatory function. *J. Neurol. Neurosurg. Psychiatry* 34 : 679, 1971.

140. Leanderson, R., Persson, A., and Ohman, S. Electromyographic studies of the function of the facial muscles in dysarthria. *Acta Otolaryngol. (Stockh.)* 263 : 89, 1970.

141. Lebrun, Y., Buyssens, E., and Henneaux, J. Phonetic aspects of anarthria. *Cortex* 9 : 126, 1973.

142. Lebrun, Y., and Hoops, R. (eds.). *Intelligence and Aphasia, Neurolinguistics II*. Amsterdam: Swetz & Zertlinger B.V., 1974.

143. Lehiste, I. Some Acoustic Characteristics of Dysarthric Speech. In *Bibliotheca Phonetica*, FASC. 2, Basel: Karger, 1965.

144. Levy, R. The neurophysiology of dementia. *Br. J. Psychiatry* 9 : 119, 1975.

145. Linebaugh, C. W. Mild Aphasia. In A. L. Holland (ed.), *Language Disorders in Adults*. San Diego: College-Hill, 1984.

146. Linebaugh, C. W., Baird, J. T., Baird, C. B., and Armour, R. M. Special Considerations for the Development of Microcomputer-Based Augmentative Communication Systems. In W. R. Berry (ed.), *Clinical Dysarthria*. San Diego: College-Hill, 1983.

147. Logemann, J., Blonsky, E., Fisher, H., and Boshes, B. Vocal tract control in neurologic disease: A profile of function. Presented to the American Speech and Hearing Association, Las Vegas, Nev., 1974.

148. Logemann, J., Blonsky, E., Fisher, H., and Boshes, B. A cineradiographic study of lingual function in Parkinson's disease. Presented to the American Speech and Hearing Association, Detroit, Mich., 1973.

149. Lomas, J., and Kertesz, A. Patterns of spontaneous recovery in aphasic groups: A study of adult stroke patients. *Brain Lang.* 5 : 388, 1978.

150. Luchsinger, R., and Arnold, G. E. *Voice-Speech-Language: Clinical Communicology—Its Physiology and Pathology*. Belmont, Calif.: Wadsworth, 1965.

151. Ludlow, C. L., and Bassich, C. J. Relationships between Perceptual Ratings and Acoustic Measures of Hypokinetic Speech. In M. R. McNeil, J. C. Rosenbek, and A. E. Aronson (eds.), *The Dysarthrias: Physiology, Acoustics, Perception, Management*. San Diego: College-Hill, 1984.

152. Luria, A. R. *Traumatic Aphasia: Its Syndromes, Psychology, and Treatment*. The Hague: Mouton, 1970.

153. Luria, A. R. *Higher Cortical Functions in Man*. New York: Basic Books, 1966.

154. Luria, A. R. Factors and Forms of Aphasia. In A. DeReuck and M. O'Connor (eds.), *Disorders of Language*. London: Churchill, 1964.

155. Luria, A. R. *Restoration of Function After Brain Injury*. New York: Macmillan, 1963.

156. Marquardt, T. P. Aspects of speech motor control in Parkinsonian dysarthria. Presented to the American Speech and Hearing Association, Detroit, Mich., 1973.

157. Martin, A. D. Some objections to the term "apraxia of speech." *J. Speech Hear. Disord.* 39 : 53, 1974.

158. Martin, A. D. A Proposed Rationale for Aphasia Therapy. In B. E. Porch (ed.), *Proceedings of the Conference on Clinical Aphasiology*. New Orleans, La.: Veterans Administration Hospital, 1974.

159. Mayo Clinic. *Procedures for Language Evaluation*. Unpublished test.

160. McDonald, E. T. A *Deep Test of Articulation: Sentence Form*. Pittsburgh: Stanwix House, 1964.

161. McNeil, M. R., and Prescott, T. E. *Revised Token Test*. Baltimore: University Park, 1978.

162. McNeil, M., and Prescott, T. Assessment of auditory deficits associated with aphasia: The revised Token Test. Presented to the Third Conference on Clinical Aphasiology, Albuquerque, N. Mex., 1973.

163. McNeil, M. R., Rosenbek, J. C., and Aronson, A. E. (eds.). *The Dysarthrias: Physiology, Acoustics, Perception, Management*. San Diego: College-Hill, 1984.

164. Mills, R. H., and Drummond, S. S. Analysis of impaired naming in language of confusion. Paper presented to the American Speech-Language-Hearing Association, Detroit, 1980.

165. Milton, S. B., Tunstall, C. M., and Wertz, R. T. Dysnomia: A Rose by Any Other Name May Require Elaborate Description. In R. H. Brookshire (ed.), *Clinical Aphasiology: Proceedings of the Conference*. Minneapolis: BRK Publishers, 1983.

166. Mitchell, J. Speech and language impairment in the older patient. *Geriatrics* 13 : 467, 1958.

167. Mohr, J. P. Revision of Broca Aphasia and the Syndrome of Broca's Area Infarction and Its Implications in Aphasia Therapy. In R. H. Brookshire (ed.), *Clinical Aphasiology: Proceedings of the Conference*. Minneapolis: BRK Publishers, 1980.

168. Mohr, J. P. Broca's Area and Broca's Aphasia. In H. Whitaker and H. A. Whitaker (eds.), *Studies in Neurolinguistics*. New York: Academic, 1976. Vol. 1.

169. Moss, C. S. *Recovery with Aphasia: The Aftermath of My Stroke*. Urbana: University of Illinois Press, 1972.

170. Mountcastle, V. B. (ed.). *Interhemispheric Relations and Cerebral Dominance*. Baltimore: Johns Hopkins Press, 1962.

171. Myers, P. S. Right Hemisphere Impairment. In A. L. Holland (ed.), *Language Disorders in Adults*. San Diego: College-Hill, 1984.

172. Naeser, M. A., Alexander, M. P., Helm-Estabrooks, N., Levine, H. L., Laughlin, S. A., and Geschwind, N. Aphasia with predominantly subcortical lesion sites: Description of three capsular/putamenal syndromes. *Arch. Neurol.* 39 : 1, 1982.

173. Netsell, R. A Neurobiologic View of the Dysarthrias. In M. R. McNeil, J. C. Rosenbek, and A. E. Aronson (eds.), *The Dysarthrias: Physiology, Acoustics, Perception, Management*. San Diego: College-Hill, 1984.

174. Netsell, R. Instrumentation in the Rehabilitation of Dysarthria. Presented to the Veterans Administration Workshop on Motor Speech Disorders, Madison, Wis., 1976.

175. Netsell, R. Evaluation of velopharyngeal function in dysarthria. *J. Speech Hear. Disord.* 34 : 131, 1973.

176. Netsell, R. Lip electromyography in the dysarthrias. Presented to the American Speech and Hearing Association, San Francisco, Calif., 1972.

177. Netsell, R. A *Developing Framework for Research in Speech Production. Progress Report No. 1*. Madison: Speech Research Laboratory, Neurological and Rehabilitation Hospital, University of Wisconsin, 1971.

178. Netsell, R., and Cleeland, C. Modification of lip hypertonia in dysarthria using EMG feedback. *J. Speech Hear. Disord.* 38 : 131, 1973.

179. Netsell, R., Daniel, B., and Celesia, G. Acceleration and weakness in Parkinsonian dysarthria. *J. Speech Hear. Disord.* 40 : 170, 1975.

180. Netsell, R., and Kent, R. Paroxysmal ataxic dysarthria. *J. Speech Hear. Disord.* 41 : 93, 1976.

181. Paulson, G. W. The Neurological Examination in Dementia. In C. E. Wells (ed.), *Dementia*, Contemporary Neurology Service, No. 9. Philadelphia: Davis, 1971.

182. Peacher, W. G. The etiology and differential diagnosis of dysarthria. *J. Speech Hear. Disord.* 15 : 252, 1950.

183. Penfield, W., and Roberts, L. *Speech and Brain-Mechanisms.* Princeton, N.J.: Princeton University Press, 1959.

184. Perkins, W. H. (ed.). *Dysarthria and Apraxia.* New York: Thieme-Stratton, 1983.

185. Perkins, W. H. (ed.). *Language Handicaps in Adults.* New York: Thieme-Stratton, 1983.

186. Phillips, D. F. Reality orientation. *J. Am. Hosp. Assoc.* 47 : 191, 1973.

187. Porch, B. E. *Porch Index of Communicative Ability* (3rd ed.). Palo Alto, Calif.: Consulting Psychologists Press, 1981.

188. Porch, B. E. Introduction to the Porch Index of Communicative Ability (PICA). Presented to the American Speech and Hearing Association, San Francisco, Calif., 1972.

189. Porch, B. E. A comparison of unilateral and bilateral PICA profiles on brain-damaged adults. Presented to the American Speech and Hearing Association, Chicago, Ill., 1971.

190. Porch, B. E. *Porch Index of Communicative Ability.* Palo Alto, Calif.: Consulting Psychologists Press, 1967.

191. Porch, B. E., Collins, M. J., Wertz, R. T., and Friden, T. Statistical prediction of change in aphasia. *J. Speech Hear. Res.* 23 : 312, 1980.

192. Porch, B. E., Wertz, R. T., and Collins, M. J. A Statistical Procedure for Predicting Recovery from Aphasia. In B. E. Porch (ed.), *Proceedings of the Conference on Clinical Aphasiology.* New Orleans, La.: Veterans Administration Hospital, 1974.

193. Prins, R., Snow, C., and Wagenaar, E. Recovery from aphasia: Spontaneous speech versus language comprehension. *Brain Lang.* 6 : 192, 1978.

194. Putnam, A. H. B., and Hixon, T. J. Respiratory Kinematics in Speakers with Motor Neuron Disease. In M. R. McNeil, J. C. Rosenbek, and A. E. Aronson (eds.), *The Dysarthrias: Physiology, Acoustics, Perception, Management.* San Diego: College-Hill, 1984.

195. Raven, J. C. *Coloured Progressive Matrices.* London: H. K. Lewis, 1962.

196. Reyes, M. G., Chokroverty, S., and Masdeu, J. Thalamic neuroaxonal dystrophy and dementia in Hodgkin's disease. *Neurology* 26 : 251, 1976.

197. Robinson, K. A double-blind clinical trial of naftidrofuryl in cerebral vascular disorders. *Med. Digest* 17 : 50, 1972.

198. Rochford, G. A study of naming errors in dysphasic and in demented patients. *Neuropsychologia* 9 : 437, 1971.

199. Rosenbek, J. C. Some Challenges for Clinical Aphasiologists. In J. Miller, D. Yoder, and R. Schiefelbusch (eds.), *Contemporary Issues in Language Intervention.* Rockville, Md.: American Speech-Language-Hearing Association, ASHA Reports No. 12, 1983.

200. Rosenbek, J. C. The prognostic significance of oral-nonverbal apraxia. Presented to the American Speech and Hearing Association, Detroit, Mich., 1973.

201. Rosenbek, J. C., Lemme, M., Ahern, M., Harris, E., and Wertz, R. T. A treatment for apraxia of speech in adults. *J. Speech Hear. Disord.* 38 : 462, 1973.

202. Rosenbek, J. C., McNeil, M. R., and Aronson, A. E. (eds.). *Apraxia of Speech: Physiology, Acoustics, Linguistics, Management.* San Diego: College-Hill, 1984.

203. Rosenbek, J. C., McNeil, M. R., Lemme, M. L., Presscott, T. E., and Alfrey, A. C. Speech and language findings in a chronic hemodialysis patient: A case report. *J. Speech Hear. Disord.* 40 : 245, 1975.

204. Rosenbek, J. C., and Merson, R. M. Measurement and prediction of severity in apraxia of speech. Presented to the American Speech and Hearing Association, Chicago, Ill., 1971.

205. Rosenbek, J. C., Messert, B., Collins, M. J., and Wertz, R. T. Cortical stuttering. *Brain Lang.* 6 : 82, 1978.

206. Rosenbek, J. C., and Wertz, R. T. Treatment of Apraxia of Speech in Adults. In R. T. Wertz and M. J. Collins (eds.), *Proceedings of the Conference: Clinical Aphasiology, 1972.* Madison, Wis.: Veterans Administration Hospital, 1976.

207. Rosenbek, J. C., and Wertz, R. T. Veterans Administration Workshop on Motor Speech Disorders. Madison, Wis., 1976.

208. Rosenbek, J. C., Wertz, R. T., and Darley, F. L. Oral sensation and perception in apraxia of speech and aphasia. *J. Speech Hear. Res.* 16 : 22, 1973.

209. Roth, M., and Meyers, D. H. The diagnosis of dementia. *Br. J. Psychiatry* 9 : 87, 1975.

210. Rubins, A. B. Aphasia with infarction in the territory of the anterior cerebral artery. *Cortex* 11 : 239, 1975.

211. Russell, W., and Espir, M. L. E. *Traumatic Aphasia.* London: Oxford University Press, 1961.

212. Rutherford, D., and McCall, G. N. Testing Oral Sensation and Perception in Persons with Dysarthria. In J. F. Bosma (ed.), *First Symposium on Oral Sensation and Perception.* Springfield, Ill.: Thomas, 1967.

213. Sands, E., Sarno, M. T., and Shankweiler, D. Long-term assessment of language function in aphasia due to stroke. *Arch. Phys. Med. Rehabil.* 50 : 202, 1969.

214. Sarno, J. E., Sarno, M. T., and Levita, E. Evaluating language improvement after completed stroke. *Arch. Phys. Med. Rehabil.* 52 : 73, 1971.

215. Sarno, M. T. (ed.). *Acquired Aphasia*. New York: Academic, 1981.

216. Sarno, M. T. The Functional Communication Profile. *Rehabilitation Monograph 42*, Institute of Rehabilitation Medicine, New York University Medical Center, 1969.

217. Sarno, M. T., Silverman, M., and Levita, E. Psychosocial factors in recovery in geriatric patients with severe aphasia. *J. Am. Geriatr. Soc.* 18 : 405, 1970.

218. Schuell, H. *Differential Diagnosis of Aphasia with the Minnesota Test*. Minneapolis: University of Minnesota Press, 1965.

219. Schuell, H. *The Minnesota Test for Differential Diagnosis of Aphasia.* Minneapolis: University of Minnesota Press, 1965.

220. Schuell, H. A short examination for aphasia. *Neurology* 7 : 625, 1957.

221. Schuell, H. Aphasic difficulties understanding spoken language. *Neurology* 3 : 176, 1953.

222. Schuell, H., Jenkins, J. H., and Jiménez-Pabón, E. *Aphasia in Adults: Diagnosis, Prognosis, and Treatment*. New York: Hoeber-Harper, 1964.

223. Schultz, M. C., and Carpenter, M. A. The bases of speech pathology and audiology: Selecting a therapy model. *J. Speech Hear. Disord.* 38 : 395, 1973.

224. Schwartz, M. F., Marin, O. S. M., and Saffran, E. M. Disassociation of language function in dementia: A case study. *Brain Lang.* 7 : 277, 1979.

225. Shankweiler, D., and Harris, K. S. An experimental approach to the problem of articulation in aphasia. *Cortex* 2 : 277, 1966.

226. Shelton, R. L. Therapeutic exercise and speech pathology. *ASHA* 5 : 855, 1963.

227. Shelton, R. L., Paesani, A., McClelland, K. D., and Bradfield, S. S. Panendoscopic feedback in the study of voluntary velopharyngeal movements. *J. Speech Hear. Disord.* 40 : 232, 1975.

228. Simmons, N. N. Acoustic Analysis of Ataxic Dysarthria: An Approach to Monitoring Treatment. In W. R. Berry (ed.), *Clinical Dysarthria*. San Diego: College-Hill, 1983.

229. Skelly, M., Schinsky, L., Smith, R. W., and Fust, R. S. American Indian sign (Amerind) as a facilitator of verbalization for the oral verbal apraxic. *J. Speech Hear. Disord.* 39 : 445, 1974.

230. Smith, A. Neuropsychological Testing in Neurological Disorders. In W. J. Friedlander (ed.), *Current Reviews of Higher Nervous System Dysfunction, Advances in Neurology*. New York: Raven, 1975. Vol. 7.

231. Smith A. *Symbol Digit Modalities Test*. Los Angeles: Western Psychological Services, 1973.

232. Smith, A. *Diagnosis, Intelligence, and Rehabilitation of Chronic Aphasics: Final Report*. Ann Arbor: Department of Physical Medicine and Rehabilitation, university of Michigan, 1972.

233. Sparks, R., Helm, N., and Albert, M. Aphasia rehabilitation resulting from melodic intonation therapy. *Cortex* 10 : 303, 1974.

234. Sparks, R., and Holland, A. L. Method: Melodic intonation therapy for aphasia. *J. Speech Hear. Disord.* 41 : 287, 1976.

235. Spellacy, F. J., and Spreen, O. A short form of the Token Test. *Cortex* 5 : 390, 1969.

236. Sperry, R. W., and Gazzaniga, M. S. Language Following Surgical Disconnection of the Hemispheres. In C. H. Millikan and F. L. Darley (eds.), *Brain Mechanisms Underlying Speech and Language*. New York: Grune & Stratton, 1967.

237. Spreen, O., and Benton, A. L. *Neurosensory Center Comprehensive Examination for Aphasia* (ed. A). Victoria, British Columbia: Neuropsychology Laboratory, University of Victoria, 1969.

238. Sprintzen, R. J., McCall, G. N., and Skolnick, M. L. A new therapeutic technique for the treatment of velopharyngeal incompetence. *J. Speech Hear. Disord.* 40 : 69, 1975.

239. Stoicheff, M. L. Motivating instructions and language performance of dysphasic subjects. *J. Speech Hear. Res.* 3 : 75, 1960.

240. Templin, M. C., and Darley, F. L. *The Templin-Darley Tests of Articulation*. Iowa City: Bureau of Educational Research and Service, Extension Division, State University of Iowa, 1960.

241. Thomas, L. *The Lives of a Cell: Notes of a Biology Watcher*. New York: Viking, 1974.

242. Tikofsky, R. S. A revised list for the estimation of dysarthric single word intelligibility. *J. Speech Hear. Res.* 13 : 59, 1970.

243. Trost, J. E., and Canter, G. J. Apraxia of speech in patients with Broca's aphasia: A study of phoneme production accuracy and error patterns. *Brain Lang.* 1 : 63, 1974.

244. Van Buskirk, C. Prognostic value of sensory defect in rehabilitation of hemiplegics. *Neurology* 6 : 407, 1955.

245. Vignolo, L. A. Evolution of aphasia and language rehabilitation: A retrospective exploratory study. *Cortex* 1 : 344, 1964.

246. Wang, H. S., and Busse, E. W. Dementia in Old Age. In C. E. Wells (ed.), *Dementia*. Contemporary Neurology Service, No. 9. Philadelphia: Davis, 1971.

247. Watson, J. M., and Records, L. E. The Effectiveness of the Porch Index of Communicative Ability as a Diagnostic Tool in Assessing Specific Behaviors of Senile Dementia. In R. H. Brookshire (ed.), *Clinical Aphasiology: Proceedings of the Conference*. Minneapolis: BRK Publishers, 1978.

248. Webb, W. G., and Love, R. J. The efficacy of cueing techniques with apraxic-aphasics. Presented to the American Speech and Hearing Association, Las Vegas, Nev., 1974.

249. Wells, B. B. The Long-Term Implications of Reality Orientation. In *Reality Orientation*. Washington, D. C.: The Hospital and Community Psychiatric Service, American Psychiatric Association, 1969.

250. Wells, C. E. The Clinical Management of a Patient with Dementia. In C. E. Wells (ed.), *Dementia*. Contemporary Neurology Service, No. 9. Philadelphia: Davis, 1971.

251. Wells, C. E. The Symptom and Behavioral Manifestations of Dementia. In C. E. Wells (ed.), *De-

mentia. Contemporary Neurology Service, No. 9. Philadelphia: Davis, 1971.

252. Wepman, J. M. Aphasia: Language without thought or thought without language? *ASHA* 18:131, 1976.

253. Wepman, J. M. The relationship between self-correction and recovery from aphasia. *J. Speech Hear. Disord.* 23 : 302, 1958.

254. Wepman, J. M. A conceptual model for the process involved in recovery from aphasia. *J. Speech Hear. Disord.* 18 : 4, 1953.

255. Wepman, J. M. *Recovery from Aphasia.* New York: Ronald, 1951.

256. Wepman, J. M., and Jones, L. V. *Studies in Aphasia: An Approach to Testing.* Chicago: University of Chicago Education-Industry Service, 1961.

257. Wepman, J. M., Jones, L. V., Bock, R. D., and Van Pelt, D. Studies in aphasia: Background and theoretical formulations. *J. Speech Hear. Disord.* 25 : 323, 1960.

258. Wertz, R. T. Language Intervention Context and Setting for the Aphasic Adult: When. In J. Miller, D. Yoder, and R. Schiefelbusch (eds.), *Contemporary Issues in Language Intervention.* Rockville, Md.: The American Speech-Language-Hearing Association, ASHA Reports No. 12, 1983.

259. Wertz, R. T. Appraisal and Diagnosis in Aphasia: Evaluating the Effects of Treatment. In M. Sullivan and M. S. Kommers (eds.), *Rationale for Adult Aphasia Therapy.* Omaha: University of Nebraska Medical Center, 1977.

260. Wertz, R. T., Collins, M., Weiss, D., Kurtzke, J., Friden, T., Brookshire, R., Pierce, J., Holtzapple, P., Hubbard, D., Porch, B., West, J., Davis, L., Matovitch, V., Morley, G., and Resurreccion, E. Veterans Administration cooperative study on aphasia: A comparison of individual and group treatment. *J. Speech Hear. Res.* 24:580, 1981.

261. Wertz, R. T., Keith, R. L., and Custer, D. D. Normal and aphasic behavior on a measure of auditory input and a measure of verbal output. Presented to the American Speech and Hearing Association, Chicago, Ill., 1971.

262. Wertz, R. T., LaPointe, L. L., and Rosenbek, J. C. *Apraxia of Speech in Adults: The Disorder and Its Management.* New York: Grune & Stratton, 1984.

263. Wertz, R. T., and Rosenbek, J. C. Appraising apraxia of speech. *J. Colo. Speech Hear. Assoc.* 5 : 18, 1971.

264. Wertz, R. T., Rosenbek, J. C., and Collins, M. J. Identification of Apraxia of Speech from PICA Verbal Tests. In R. T. Wertz and M. J. Collins (eds.), *Clinical Aphasiology: Conference Proceedings, 1972.* Madison, Wis.: Veterans Administration Hospital, 1976.

265. Wertz, R. T., Rosenbek, J. C., and Deal, J. L. A review of 228 cases of apraxia of speech: Classification, etiology, and localization. Presented to the American Speech and Hearing Association, New York, N.Y., 1970.

266. Westreich, G. Alter, M., and Lundgren, S. Effect of cyclandelate on dementia. *Stroke* 6 : 535, 1975.

267. Yarnell, P., Monroe, P., and Sobel, L. Aphasia outcome in stroke: A clinical neuroradiological correlation. *Stroke* 7 : 514, 1976.

268. Yorkston, K. M., and Beukelman, D. R. *Assessment of Intelligibility of Dysarthric Speech.* Tigard, Oregon: CC Publications, 1981.

2

The Dysarthrias: Description, Diagnosis, and Treatment

John C. Rosenbek
Leonard L. LaPointe

Complete loss of articulatory speech is known as anarthria, while partial impairment is spoken of as dysarthria. [Test phrases] especially employed . . . [include] Constantinople was the capital of Turkey, third riding artillery brigade, Lillibulero, irretrievable, Peter Piper picked a peck of pickled peppers, 'round the rugged rock the ragged rascal ran.'

I. S. Wechsler
Clinical Neurology (9th ed.)

Definition

In contemporary speech pathology, the ragged rascal has made his last revolution around the rugged rock, and Peter Piper tongue twisters are no longer regarded as effective means of testing speech proficiency. The above quotation, however, is a rather typical traditional view both of the definition of dysarthria and of speech evaluation strategies of the dysarthric person, as evidenced by reports in many clinical neurology textbooks and by some writers in speech pathology. Current usage of the term *dysarthria* is more comprehensive and precise than the traditional definition: *imperfect articulation of speech caused by nervous system damage.* The concept of a unitary dysarthria is being refined to the dysarthrias—a group of related motor speech disorders resulting from disturbed muscular control over the speech mechanism. These dysarthrias are manifested as disrupted oral communication caused by paralysis, weakness, abnormal tone, or incoordination of the muscles used in speech, and encompass coexisting motor disorders of respiration, phonation, resonation, articulation, and prosody. Movements and synchrony of the components of the speech system may be impaired in direction, range, force, endurance, and timing. In addition to negative signs, such as reduced range of movement or reduced muscle tone, some neurologic problems with dysarthria as a symptom are also characterized by positive manifestations, such as inappropriate or involuntary movements because of uninhibited activity of intact parts of the nervous system [95].

Motor impairment of the articulatory system, including the lips, tongue, mandible, and velum, often produces a more devastating effect on the intelligibility of speech than do dysfunctions of the laryngeal or respiratory systems. Thus the most prominent acoustic features that affect the intelligibility of speech are those that result from imprecise consonant production, repeated or prolonged phonemes, distorted vowels, or irregular articulatory breakdown.

Darley, Aronson, and Brown [35] have honed the definition of dysarthria even further. They delimit the boundaries of the definition in a manner that is useful for our purposes.

The term will encompass coexisting motor disorders of respiration, phonation, articulation, resonance, and prosody. It will also comprise isolated single-process impairments, such as an isolated articulation problem due to cranial nerve XII involvement, an isolated palatopharyngeal incompetence of neurogenic origin, or an isolated dysphonia due to unilateral vocal fold paralysis (p. 3).

Historic Perspective

Tracing the evolution of this process of clarification and refinement of the definition of dysarthria is relevant because it lends perspective to the development of principles of evaluation and treatment, which are the subject of this chapter.

The human capability for oral communication probably evolved in parallel with the evolution of the brain. A precise record of the emergence of this singularly human faculty is lost in the fog of prehistory, but we can assume that as long as humans have possessed oral speech, they have been susceptible to its disturbance or loss. Trauma and diseases have disrupted our ability to communicate and have repeatedly underscored the dependence of this skill on the integrity of the central and peripheral nervous sytems.

Descriptions of neurogenic speech loss appear in early Egyptian hieroglyphics and can be traced periodically through the medical literature of several civilizations. A manuscript in a surgical papyrus, composed at about 3500 B.C., contains the first use of the word *brain* and presents 13 case descriptions of skull fractures that probably resulted from war injuries. Bleeding from the nose and ears following fractures is cited, as are disturbances of speech. One case is presented with perhaps the earliest description of neurogenic speech loss, although the disorder could be either dysarthria or aphasia.

A man having a wound in his temple . . . perforating his temporal bone . . . ; if thou ask of him concerning his malady . . . he speak not to thee, . . . copious tears fall from both his eyes, so that he thrusts his hand often to his face that he may wipe both his eyes with the back of his hand as a child does, and he knows not that he does so [110, pp. 3–4].

The medical writings of the Greeks also contain such descriptions. Only scattered references to the nervous system are found among the Homeric Greeks (pre-Hippocratic); but with Hippocrates, an ancient clinical descriptive neurology, including references to speech loss, was born. In *Epidemics* Hippocrates describes hemiplegia, convulsions, paralysis of the right arm, and loss of speech, which could have been aphasia, dysarthria, or a combination of both.

A woman who lived on the sea-front was seized with a fever while in the third month of pregnancy. She was immediately seized with pains in the loins. On the third day, pain in the head, neck, and around about the right clavicle. Very shortly, the tongue became unable to articulate and the right arm was paralyzed . . . Her speech was delirious . . . fourth day: speech was indistinct but she was no longer paralyzed . . . [110, p. 11].

During the Middle Ages and Renaissance, few advances were made from the original descriptions of the Greeks in understanding neurogenic speech loss. The seventeenth and eighteenth centuries also were somewhat barren of detailed reports on the topic, but by the nineteenth century the rivulets of interest and curiosity merged into a coalescence of scientific inquiry and clinical writing. Most of the observations and detailed case reports during this time revolved around the disturbances of speech, auditory comprehension, reading, and writing, which were eventually called aphasia, but it was also during this fruitful period that investigators such as Jackson [83] suggested that many disturbances of speech were not necessarily linked to symbolic impairment.

Neuropathologies

A wide variety of congenital and acquired neuropathologies can affect the speech production system and result in one of the dysarthrias. Damage can be located in cortical areas, the cerebellum, the brainstem, or in the peripheral nervous system, which comprises the cranial and spinal nerves with their associated ganglia. The nature of the speech disruption caused by neurologic damage not only depends on the site and extent of the lesion, but it also depends on when the insult occurs in the development of the individual [95].

Conditions responsible for this damage represent an array of congenital injuries and anomalies as well as a variety of acquired conditions, such as infections, toxic processes, space-occupying neoplasms, demyelinating diseases, neuromuscular diseases, trauma, and the multiple varieties of cerebrovascular disturbances. Relative newcomers to the list include leukemia [85] and a variety of drugs [18, 46]. Inherited conditions are also being studied [41, 166, 170]. Wertz's chapter (Chap. 1 in this book) presents a more detailed presentation of disorders related to the dysarthrias.

Classification

Approaches to classification are dependent on the theoretical and clinical orientation of the classifier, and a number of systems have emerged. Some of these are based on causal factors, the predominant aspect of speech involved, a specific associated disease, or the site of the lesion.

Peacher [133] was one of the first to indicate that the dysarthrias can encompass more than just the articulatory process, and he called for integration of the principles of neurophysiology, psychology, experimental phonetics, and speech pathology in the study of the disorder. Peacher stressed a holistic approach to the study of motor disorders of speech, both central and peripheral, and presented a classification of speech defects based on neuroanatomic principles. He attempted to correlate neurophysiology with the disrupted processes underlying the motor speech disorders. Peacher's article seems to mark a turning point in attention to dysarthria and was followed by several other comprehensive studies in the 1950s.

Morley [115] discussed the symptoms and prognosis of dysarthria secondary to Parkinson's disease, multiple sclerosis, chronic progressive bulbar palsy, poliomyelitis, and trauma. This classification scheme associated the dysarthrias with causative factors and is one of the few that offers specific recommendations on examination and treatment strategies.

Grewel [61] reviewed the disorder historically and also based his classification system on neuroanatomic principles. He cites Kussmaul as probably the first to attempt a classification of speech disturbances into distinct groups. Fourteen types of dysarthria are listed by Grewel, including cortical, subcortical, peduncular, supranuclear, bulbar, cerebellar, diencephalic, mesencephalic, peripheral, and others. He concludes that his system is based on the principle that the dysarthrias are, by definition, neurologic symptoms, and therefore a classification must reflect neurophysiologic factors. Grewel stopped short, however, of describing the subtle differences in symptoms among the various forms of dysarthria he listed.

Another attempt to bring order to the array of motor speech disorders is provided by Canter [27]. He classified these disorders as being either peripheral or central, and he lists three subtypes under each category.

I. Peripheral dysarthria
    A. Myopathic
    B. Myoneural
    C. Lower motor neuron
II. Central dysarthria
    A. Spastic
    B. Dyskinetic
    C. Ataxic

Canter suggested that predictable alterations in the resulting speech pattern exist according to the level of the lesions, and he outlined some characteristics for each of the categories listed.

Mayo Clinic Research in Motor Speech Disorders

In the work of Peacher and of Grewel, one can see the seeds of contemporary principles of dysarthria, which were later to germinate and be experimentally realized in work by Darley and his associates at the Mayo Clinic.

In meticulous investigations that are laced with diagnostic and therapeutic implications, Darley, Aronson, and Brown [36, 37] outlined clusters of deviant speech dimensions that are characteristic of various types of dysarthria. These authors also classify the dysarthrias on the basis of the underlying disturbed neurophysiology.

Darley, Aronson, and Brown presented two articles [36, 37] in 1969. These articles formed the basis for a subsequent book on motor speech disorders [35], which serves as the most comprehensive analysis of the dysarthrias to date. These studies have strongly influenced contemporary thinking on motor speech disorders and will probably achieve a prominent place as historic milestones on the topic. Much of what we present in this chapter is a reflection of the clarification and refinement of fundamental concepts of motor speech disorders that have been provided by the Mayo Clinic research.

Darley, Aronson, and Brown attempted to establish differential diagnostic patterns among the dysarthrias by identifying clusters of deviant speech dimensions associated with specific neurologic disorders. Thirty-second speech samples were analyzed on at least 30 subjects in each of seven neurologic groups. The authors state that each subject was unequivocally diagnosed as being representative of his or her assigned neurologic group. The groups represented were bulbar palsy, pseudobulbar palsy, amyotrophic lateral sclerosis, cerebellar disorders, parkinsonism, dystonia, and chorea. Three judges independently rated each speech sample on 38 dimensions of speech and voice, using a seven-point scale of severity.

Table 2-1 is a list of some of the deviant speech dimensions used in the Mayo Clinic research. This table is presented in checklist form to indicate how the dimensions can be categorized and adapted to clinical use in evaluating dysarthric speech.

Correlational matrices based on computer analysis of the ratings on each subject revealed that each of the seven neurologic disorders had a unique pattern of clusters of deviant speech dimensions. Analysis of these clusters led to deductions about the neuromuscular substrate for each group and permitted the application of an appropriate name for each type of dysarthria based on the defective neurophysiology responsible for the cluster. From this analysis, five types of dysarthria were delineated: flaccid dysarthria (in bulbar palsy), spastic dysarthria (in pseudobulbar palsy), ataxic dysarthria (in cerebellar disorders), hypokinetic dysarthria (in parkinsonism), and hyperkinetic dysarthria (in dystonia and chorea). In addition, mixed dysarthrias were described that result from disorders of multiple motor systems and are associated with such conditions as amyotrophic lateral sclerosis, multiple sclerosis, and Wilson's disease.

Table 2-2 presents a summary of some of the salient information provided by the Mayo Clinic studies on motor speech disorders. For additional detail and appreciation of the scope of these studies, the reader is urged to consult the appropriate references.

Physiologic Research in Motor Speech Disorders

An orientation to dysarthria, often referred to as the physiologic approach [123] was emerging at the same time as the Mayo approach. Netsell [119, 120] has recorded the history of the physiologic approach. Its advocates consider the dysarthrias to be movement disorders rather than speech disorders. Their research tools are the spectrograph [168, 178] and a variety of instruments such as the x-ray microbeam [70, 92]. The diagnostic and therapeutic implications of the physiologic orientation have been discussed at some length in a variety of other publications [119, 142].

Table 2-1. Checklist of deviant speech dimensions

Voice
  Pitch characteristics
    _____Pitch level overall
    _____Monopitch
  Loudness characteristics
    _____Loudness level overall
    _____Alternating loudness
    _____Excess loudness variation
  Quality characteristics
    _____Harsh voice
    _____Breathy voice (continuous)
    _____Strained-strangled voice
    _____Nasal emission

    _____Pitch breaks
    _____Voice tremor

    _____Monoloudness
    _____Loudness decay

    _____Hoarse (wet) voice
    _____Breathy voice (transient)
    _____Voice stoppage
    _____Hyponasality

Respiration
    _____Forced expiration-inspiration
    _____Grunt at end of expiration

    _____Audible inspiration

Prosody
    _____Rate overall
    _____Increased rate overall
    _____Variable rate
    _____Intervals prolonged
    _____Short rushes of speech

    _____Phrases short
    _____Increased rate in segments
    _____Reduced stress
    _____Inappropriate silences
    _____Excess and equal stress

Articulation
    _____Imprecise consonants
    _____Phonemes repeated
    _____Irregular articulatory breakdown

    _____Phonemes prolonged
    _____Vowels distorted

Source: Adapted from Darley, F. L., Aronson, A. E., and Brown, J. R.: *Motor Speech Disorders*. Philadelphia: Saunders, 1975; Clusters of deviant speech dimensions in the dysarthrias. *J. Speech Hear. Res.* 12:462, 1969; Differential diagnostic patterns of dysarthria. *J. Speech Hear. Res.* 12:246, 1969.

One aim of the physiologic orientation has been to discover the relationships of underlying pathophysiology to the perceptual symptoms identified in the Mayo Clinic and other perceptual studies. Some researchers have argued that such relationships must be discovered if clinical practice is to be advanced. Hunker and Abbs [78] suggest, for example, that

Without such analyses, motivated by specific hypotheses concerning underlying neural dysfunction, advances beyond surface classifications of global symptoms or new treatment techniques beyond 'black box' trial and error are unlikely to be forthcoming [p. 70].

That sentiment is a bit strong. Refinements in evaluation and treatment techniques designed to enhance the quality of life of dysarthric speakers can no more await complete understanding of underlying neurophysiology than can prescription of antiinflammatory and painkilling drugs await total appreciation of how they work. On the other hand, continued physiologic research is a necessity. Acoustic analyses, for example, will help clinical researchers understand the relationships between abnormal movements and perceptual symptoms [168]. Movement and electromyography (EMG) data will clarify the relationship of such conditions as weakness, abnormal tone, and tremors to specific perceptual abnormalities. An example of one important finding already published (others are to be discussed in subsequent sections) is the discovery that different speech structures may be involved in different ways, even in the same patient [1]. The clinical implication is that a single approach to the entire speech mechanism of a dysarthric talker may be totally inappropriate and indeed may even make the patient's speech sound worse.

It is obvious from this introduction that American speech pathology has spent more of its energy and resources on defining and describing the dysarthrias than on developing treatments for them. As recently as 1968, Sarno [148] could observe, and truthfully, that few speech pathologists treated patients with Parkinson's disease; and that treatment, if it was completed at all, had its major effect on the patient's psyche rather than on his or her speech. All the efforts spent in description are to be applauded, because they have not only enriched our understanding of the relation of neural function and speech, but they have also spawned a general, clinical interest in the dysarthrias and have created a basis for an expanding treatment literature. Even now treatment of a wide variety of dysarthric patients is commonplace, and speech as well as psyches is being influenced.

The authors are clinicians, representatives of a generation of speech pathologists forced by what Boone [20] identifies as "times of immediacy and relevance" to eschew rigid experimental control for intuition—for what seems to work. Boone is right; clinical hunches, no matter how carefully conceived and no matter how forthright and sincere the hunchmaker, can never replace rigid pure and applied research. As clinicians we take consolation in the words of Sir Arthur Quiller-Couch: "Remember there is no harm in guessing so long as we do not pretend our guesswork to be something else" [137, p. 201]. It should be emphasized that much of this chapter is guesswork: Experimental investigation of the methods and explanations does not exist. We are, however, reporting the guesses we are happy with. Future research will demonstrate where we guessed wrong and where we were prematurely and indiscriminately pleased. The growth of dysarthria treatment will be stunted if chapters such as this one are viewed as more than they are—if they are viewed as ends rather than beginnings.

The rest of this chapter is divided into five sections. The first develops an orientation for treatment; the second describes the medical context of dysarthria therapy; the third describes what can be called a behavioral context; the fourth describes diagnosis as a focuser of treatment; and the fifth, and largest portion, outlines the specific goals of dysarthria therapy and procedures for achieving them.

An Orientation to Treatment

The majority of writers [3, 47, 51, 80, 115, 122, 134, 139] assume that dysarthria treatment is effective; and some like Farmakides and Boone [47], Ince and Rosenberg [80], and Sarno [148] even portray the focus of influence—whether on the rate, articulation, or psyche. We share the optimism of these authors, and although it is difficult to tell because some (although certainly not all) of them talked more about procedures than about principles, we probably share many of their attitudes about the conceptual framework of dysarthria treatment as well. Brief comments on what dysarthria treatments accomplish and how they accomplish it constitute an orientation to the more extensive diagnostic and treatment sections that follow.

Table 2-2. Summary of Mayo Clinic research on motor speech disorders

Dysarthria type	Neurologic conditions	Location of neuropathology	Neuromuscular movement-tone deficit	Clusters of deviant speech dimensions	Most distinctive speech deviations
Flaccid	Bulbar palsy	Lower motor neuron	Muscular weakness; hypotonia	Phonatory incompetence; resonatory incompetence; phonatory-prosodic insufficiency	Marked hypernasality, often with nasal air emission; continuous breathiness; audible inspiration
Spastic	Pseudobulbar palsy	Upper motor neuron	Reduced range, force, speed, hypertonia	Prosodic insufficiency; articulatory-resonatory incompetence; phonatory stenosis	Very imprecise articulation; slow rate; low pitch; harsh strained-strangled voice
Ataxic	Cerebellar ataxia	Cerebellum	Hypotonia; reduced speed; inaccurate range, timing, direction	Articulatory inaccuracy; prosodic excess; phonatory-prosodic insufficiency	Excess and equal stress; phoneme and interval prolongation; dysrhythmia of speech and syllable repetition; slow rate; some excess loudness variation
Hypokinetic	Parkinsonism	Extrapyramidal system	Markedly reduced range; variable speed of repetitive movements; movement arrest; rigidity	Prosodic insufficiency plus four uncorrelated dimensions	Monopitch, monoloudness, reduced overall loudness; variable rate; short rushes of speech; some inappropriate silences
Hyperkinetic 1. Quick	(a) Chorea (b) Myoclonus (c) Gilles de la Tourette's syndrome	Extrapyramidal system	Quick, unsustained, random, involuntary movements	Nearly all clusters of speech dimensions	(a) Highly variable pattern of imprecise articulation; episodes of hypernasality; sudden variations in loudness; (b) Rhythmic hypernasality; rhythmic phonatory interruption; (c) Sudden ticlike grunts, barks, coprolalia

102

			Neuromuscular condition	Speech characteristics	Distinctive speech dimensions
2. Slow	(a) Athetosis (b) Dyskinesias (c) Dystonia	Extrapyramidal system	Sustained, distorted movements and postures; slowness; variable hypertonus	Clusters unreported Articulatory inaccuracy; prosodic excess; prosodic insufficiency; phonatory stenosis	(a) Distinctive deviations unreported (b) Distinctive deviations unreported (c) Prolongations of phonemes, intervals; unsteady rate, loudness
3. Tremors	Organic voice tremor	Extrapyramidal system	Involuntary, rhythmic, purposeless oscillatory movements		Rhythmic alterations in pitch, loudness; voice stoppages
Mixed	(a) Amyotrophic lateral sclerosis (b) Multiple sclerosis (c) Wilson's disease	Multiple motor systems	Muscular weakness; limited range, speed	Prosodic excess; prosodic insufficiency; articulatory-resonatory incompetence; phonatory stenosis; phonatory incompetence; resonatory incompetence	(a) Grossly defective articulation; extremely slow, laborious rate; marked hypernasality; severe harshness, strained-strangled voice; nearly complete disruption of prosody (b) Impaired control of loudness; harshness (c) Reduced stress; monopitch; monoloudness; similar to hypokinetic dysarthria except no short rushes of speech

103

Compensated Intelligibility

Only if a dysarthric patient's nervous system returns to normal will speech return too. The return to normal—either because of natural or physiologic recovery or because of medical treatment—is a rare circumstance indeed. Therefore the aim of all dysarthria treatment is compensated intelligibility. With professional guidance and by dint of individual effort, many dysarthric patients can learn to talk better. They can do so for two reasons: (1) physiologic support for a patient's speech can be enhanced; or (2) they can learn to make better use of whatever residual support is left to them. A total treatment program probably—and this has never been demonstrated experimentally—accomplishes both.

Physiologic Support for Speech

Physiologic support for speech is the cumulative effect of the potential to produce speech that resides within the speech structures and their neural supply. Normal speakers possess a range of physiologic support (Fig. 2-1) that is only partially tapped by daily speaking requirements. For example, normally loud speech requires only a portion of a speaker's respiratory vital capacity. The loudness required to be heard in the back of a large auditorium after the microphone has gone dead may require more air. A shouted warning may demand even more. Normal speaking taxes the range of support only minimally, and even the most excessive speaking demands either leave a normal talker with a margin of support or are sufficiently brief so that the speaker is successful even though taxed to the maximum.

Dysarthric speakers have a much-reduced range of physiologic support [28], which is also shown in Figure 2-1. For most—at least of those who end up in a speech clinic—the range is reduced so severely that normal speech under any condition is impossible, although one occasionally diagnoses a hypokinetic dysarthric person whose soft speech would be essentially normal in those conditions when soft speech is appropriate. The majority of dysarthric speakers, because of their reduced support, are frustrated by *all* speaking and, especially, they have little or no reserve of support for special demands, including those made by the clinician. Frequently, however, the dysarthric patient's range is not so drastically narrowed as his or her unintelligible speech and inability to meet communication demands might suggest. Rather, the dysarthric patient is more involved than necessary, because he or she has not learned to make the best use of the remaining function. Dysarthric patients are like persons plunged suddenly into the sea so deep they cannot see the sky. These patients struggle erratically and impotently without knowing if their efforts will cause them to reach the surface or even where that surface is.

Increasing Physiologic Support

A patient's range of physiologic support may be expanded (Fig. 2-2), although data confirming the speech pathologist's ability to create such expansions are woefully few [13, 19, 25, 130, 144]. Probably there is only minimal agreement among clinicians and researchers even about the kinds of changes in behavior that could appropriately be used as evidence of increased physiologic support. For Canter [28], expanded pitch range as the result of treatment is an example of increased physiologic support. For us, increasing physiologic support means modifying posture, increasing strength, improving tone, or enhancing coordination. In-

Fig. 2-1. Ranges of physiologic support for speech in normal and dysarthric patients.

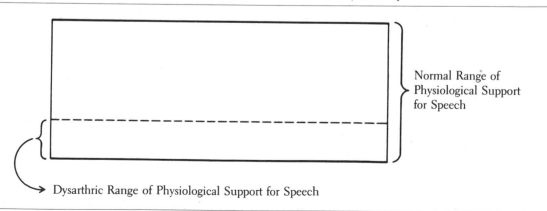

Normal Range of Physiological Support for Speech

Dysarthric Range of Physiological Support for Speech

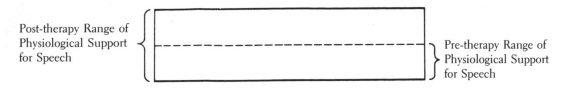

Post-therapy Range of Physiological Support for Speech

Pre-therapy Range of Physiological Support for Speech

Fig. 2-2. Pretreatment and posttreatment ranges of physiologic support for speech. Treatment has expanded the range.

creased pitch range, then, is merely symptomatic of improved support.

We do agree with Canter [28], however, when he says that physiologic support should be increased whenever possible as a first order of clinical business. His reasoning is straightforward: Why teach patients to make the best use of what they have if they can have more? And to Canter's position that efforts to improve physiologic support should occur first in treatment, we would add that these efforts to improve physiologic support are usually a team responsiblity. The speech clinician and physical therapist combine to change the patient's posture or strength; the physician prescribes a drug that reduces rigidity, which may be reduced further by exercise; surgery modifies the patient's posture; and so on. Enhancing coordination of muscle movements used in speech is more nearly the speech clinician's exclusive responsibility; but even here, the patient is helped—if only indirectly—by other professionals working to modify his or her posture, strength, or muscle tone.

Exploiting Residual Physiologic Support
Failure to exploit what they have is common to most dysarthric patients. This failure provides the

speech pathologist wth a second major therapeutic emphasis: teaching patients to exploit their physiologic support for speech.

Physiologic support may go unexploited for several reasons. Ignorance is one: patients do not know how to use what they have. Normal speaking is inadequate preparation for dysarthric speaking. Another, occasionally overlapping, reason for support to go unexploited, is that many dysarthric speakers struggle doggedly to talk as they did premorbidly. They race pell-mell through their speech seemingly unaware that their lips, tongue, jaw, and lungs are incapable of keeping up. These patients need to learn that conscious control must replace automaticity: they must begin substituting closed-loop control, where preceding events influence subsequent oncs, for open-loop control, where a string of events is preprogrammed. Physiologic support may also go unused because a patient's anxiety, depression, or abdication leave him or her unequal to the task. To reduce these negative emotions and stances, the clinician counsels the patient and demonstrates that change is possible. Finally, some patients lack sufficient mentation. They cannot learn the necessary lessons, try as they might; these patients are probably not treatment candidates.

Figure 2-3 shows what happens when a patient profits from treatment by increasing the use of physiologic support. The lower line depicts the pa-

Fig. 2-3. Pretreatment and posttreatment use of residual physiologic support for speech. Treatment has improved the use of residual support.

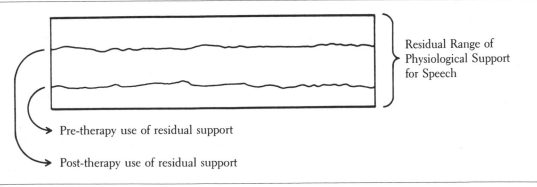

Residual Range of Physiological Support for Speech

Pre-therapy use of residual support

Post-therapy use of residual support

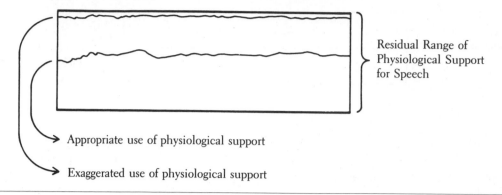

Residual Range of
Physiological Support
for Speech

Appropriate use of physiological support

Exaggerated use of physiological support

Fig. 2-4. Exaggerated and appropriate use of physiologic support. Improvement from exaggerated use is
impossible to maintain.

tient's failure to realize potential before therapy;
the upper line is the posttreatment utilization. The
implication, lest we forget, is that speech improves:
It is louder, phrases are longer, pitch is more normal, or intelligibility is greater.

The upper line in Figure 2-4 identifies a potential therapeutic hazard for any patient undergoing treatment. That line, bumping as it does against
the upper margin, represents a patient talking at
the upper limits of support. Such speech, while
the patient may be able to force it for short periods
both in and out of therapy, is impossible to maintain. Even a normal speaker's voice would eventually fail if every speaking task was the equivalent
of shouting "Fire!" We have included this figure
principally to alert clinicians to avoid conclusions
about a dysarthric patient's potential for permanently compensated intelligibility solely because of
short-term positive results from special manipulations such as binaural masking or delayed auditory
feedback. Both the clinician and the patient can
be seduced into believing that something is permanently possible when it is not, and all because
a patient talked louder for a few seconds under
masking or slower under delayed auditory feedback. The ability to judge the upper limit of physiologic support and how close a patient is to it on
any given task is one critical component of the
clinical art.

Sharp distinctions between improving what a patient has and improving the use of it are impossible
to draw. Even methods that improve support by
improving posture, strength, or tone probably also
(if they are successful) spur the patient to more
efficient use of what he or she has. Training in
skilled movements (articulation drills, for example)
probably serve both therapeutic aims simultaneously.

Medical Context of Dysarthria Treatment
The medical diagnosis, the availability and success
of medical treatment, and the involvement of other
health care personnel constitute the medical context. Whether or not the speech pathologist treats
a dysarthric patient, the type and timing of treatment, and the expectations for that treatment are
all governed in part by these constituents of the
medical context.

Medical Diagnosis
Medical diagnosis usually ends with a label: multiple sclerosis, myasthenia gravis, cerebrovascular
accident, or parkinsonism. The label leads the physician to a set of treatments, if treatment is available, and to a prognosis. The medical diagnosis
aids the speech pathologist as well. Knowing the
diagnosis allows for prediction of the course of the
disease, a major influence on the speech pathologist's decision to treat, and the timing and expectations of that treatment. * Consider five examples.
(1) *Amyotrophic lateral sclerosis* is a rapidly degenerative disease, and the average life expectancy of
a patient who has it is only 3 years after the onset
of the first symptom [111], although some patients
may live for considerable periods and even experience a remission of symptoms [116]. (2) *Parkinson's disease* is degenerative but generally less
rapidly so than amyotrophic lateral sclerosis. (3)
Remission and exacerbation of the symptoms of
multiple sclerosis make that disease different from
either amyotrophic lateral sclerosis or parkinsonism
even though, like them, it is usually degenerative.

Expectation refers to prognosis for development of compensated intelligibility.

(4) In *cerebrovascular accident* and *trauma* the onset of symptoms is acute, and physiologic recovery is accompanied by a return of at least a portion of normal function over a period of days and months. (5) *Guillain-Barré syndrome* is characterized by acute, profound, flaccid paralysis that improves, often very rapidly, so the majority of patients have few or no residual effects after a period of weeks or months.

Opinions differ about the appropriateness, timing, and prognosis of speech therapy in each of these diseases. Peacher [134] says that treatment is inappropriate in degenerative diseases such as amyotrophic lateral sclerosis. Certainly, if speech treatment—other than that to fit the patient with an alternative mode of communication—is undertaken, its purely palliative goals and narrow limits must be understood by both the patient and the clinician. No error is more egregious than to promise what cannot be realized, and the patient's prognosis in rapidly degenerative diseases like amyotrophic lateral sclerosis, whether or not a speech pathologist intervenes, is abysmal. On the other hand, early treatment is encouraged as a way of retarding the inevitable degeneration of function in more slowly progressing diseases, such as parkinsonism [35, 115] and multiple sclerosis [47], although speech treatment of patients with parkinsonism is described as a lifelong obligation [3] and as having its effect on the patient's psyche, not on his or her speech [148], conditions that, if true, discourage many practitioners. In the disorders characterized by remission and exacerbation, such as multiple sclerosis, therapy can be saved profitably for the periods of remission and stability; otherwise the prognosis is poor. In cerebrovascular accident, trauma, or any other condition characterized by acute onset and some physiologic recovery, treatment can begin when the patient is medically stable. Returning physiologic support for speech may account for spectacular early gains, and while data are nonexistent, a common clinical expectation is that such patients can learn to make maximum compensated use of this support. Probably these patients, more often than any other group, are referred for speech treatments by our medical colleagues. In conditions such as Guillain-Barré syndrome, where improvement is rapid, the speech pathologist may never be consulted, and, if so, may do no more than oversee the patient's recovery.

The number and severity of nonspeech symptoms (including language deficit), which, with the exception of the potential language deficits, will be recorded by the physician on the way to a final diagnosis, also influence speech treatment decisions and expectations. The rule is: The more severe and numerous patients' symptoms are, the less likely that they will be treated, and the poorer their prognosis for compensated intelligibility if they are treated. In multiple sclerosis, for example, a patient may begin with progressive leg weakness that is joined by increasing weakness of the trunk and arms; the patient is first confined to a wheelchair, then to a bed. The disorder may extend to the bulbar system and cortex so that the patient develops difficulty with chewing and swallowing and, finally, behavioral and conceptual abnormalities. The further into this decline the patient is, the less likely it is that the clinician will treat or that treatment will be successful.

General intellectual deficit, psychiatric disturbance, and aphasia are especially potent influences on decisions about speech treatment. Again, consider selected examples. Certain diseases, such as Huntington's chorea, are accompanied by mental and behavioral deficits; the speech pathologist can do little for these patients because speech therapy requires active patient participation, participation that is baffled by reduced intelligence and psychiatric distress. Farmakides and Boone [47], as part of their treatment study, felt compelled to withhold treatment from eight multiple sclerosis patients because of the patients' intellectual involvement. Unfortunately, the authors did not describe the amount of deficit they considered prohibitive. They only observed that "success of therapy depends on the degree of deterioration. With little or no (intellectual) deterioration, considerable improvement may be achieved in a short period of time" (p. 287). Brainstem trauma often leaves the patient emotionally incapable of profiting from therapy at least for a period, and the speech pathologist plans the therapy for such patients accordingly [146]. Profound aphasia, such as might accompany dysarthria resulting from trauma or cerebrovascular accident, may cause the clinician to delay work on the dysarthria until the aphasia has resolved or been modified, and, if resolution or modification of the aphasia is impossible, the patient's dysarthria most probably will also remain immune to change. A lesser amount of linguistic deficit, as in surgically managed patients with Parkinson's disease [38], is probably not as handicapping.

Regardless of the number and type of symptoms accompanying a dysarthria, the majority of speech pathologists will continue their generations-old tradition of allowing the patient's response to short-term treatment to determine whether a longer period of treatment is appropriate. This is probably as it should be. However, one danger exists: Speech pathologists cannot afford to assume that all dysarthric patients are potential treatment candidates merely because they have speech problems or because they respond to diagnostic treatment.

Finally, knowing the medical diagnosis also helps to focus the speech treatment. Muscle weakness is symptomatic of both myasthenia gravis and injury to lower motor neurons. Exercise to strengthen weakened muscles is contraindicated in myasthenia gravis, but it may be appropriate for the weakness induced by injury. In this instance, as in others, the medical diagnosis helps the speech pathologist decide not only whether to treat but also provides some insight into possible appropriate treatments.

Medical Treatment

The availability and success of medical treatment for the disorder creating each patient's dysarthria also influence speech treatment decisions. Amyotrophic lateral sclerosis, besides being rapidly degenerative, is representative of a group of disorders for which medicine has no treatment. These patients have little or no hope for improvement. The speech pathologist can offer support and perhaps, in some instances, a few suggestions for temporarily improved speech or an alternative mode of communication. It is for each rehabilitation team and each patient to decide the appropriateness of such treatments. As a general rule, patients for whom medicine has nothing to offer are poor candidates for speech treatment as are those who have undergone a period of unsuccessful medical treatment. Unsuccessful medical treatments may leave the patient defeated and resistant to alternative treatments, especially if the alternatives are viewed as second best—a justifiable view of speech treatments when compared to some surgical or medical treatments. An example of this kind of patient is the hypokinetic dysarthric speaker whose parkinsonism fails to respond to medication [138] or for whom the medicine has ceased to be effective. Such patients deserve speech pathologists' best counseling efforts and, if the symptoms are not too severe, their best teaching efforts. However, if an indifferent attitude emerges, treatment of any sort is doomed. The same is true for patients whose symptoms, including speech symptoms, are worse after medical management, as in some cases of surgically modified parkinsonism [4, 147], where the surgery increases the severity of dysarthria. These patients give the clinician little cause for optimism. This is not to say that such patients should never be treated, but only that both the clinician and the patient are permitted a large dose of well-tempered cynicism.

The best treatment candiates are those whose disease is treatable and whose speech is improved by that treatment. Patients with Wilson's disease [12] and parkinsonism [26, 96] are examples. These patients are left with a more normal background of physiologic support and usually with an enthusiasm that increases the likelihood of benefit from speech treatment.

Another issue raised by the availability of medical management—and it is as crucial as whether to treat—is that of timing. Ideally speech treatments should follow medical treatments. The reasons are simple: The patient has a better chance of succeeding, and the clinician can be more sanguine about taking credit for the patient's gains in intelligibility. In reality, however, the majority of medical and speech treatments probably proceed simultaneously. Such simultaneity demands that the clinician be versatile; a patient beginning a drug regimen may change daily or even within a single day, and the clinician must change with the patient. Simultaneous treatment is also difficult because the patient's neurologic status often fails to provide a stable basis for learning; goals and procedures must change as posture, strength, tone, and timing do. Also, when speech treatments are given simultaneously with other treatments, the speech pathologist can never be confident of his or her influence. Treatment is possible, but accountability is difficult. Finally, giving speech treatments before medical ones, if medical ones are possible, is reprehensible.

Other Health Care Professionals

Speech treatment is influenced by the availability and activities of other health care professionals: vocational counselors, nurses, physical and occupational therapists, and social workers. A legitimate organization of dysarthria treatment is the simultaneous, cooperative involvement of as many ancillary personnel as the patient's symptoms warrant. If other professionals are involved, the self-evident implications are that cooperative scheduling will have to be accomplished, and that each will have to let the others know and see what he or she is doing with the patient. In such a cooperative environment, areas of mutual interest will likely be trenchant. For example, the physical therapist and speech pathologist will discover their mutual concern for facial or trunk-muscle strengthening, and this discovery can lead them into a joint effort with a shared treatment plan. The social worker and speech pathologist both may be counseling patients about their reduced but active role in the family. Other examples of cooperation are commonplace and need not be listed here.

Behavioral Context of Dysarthria Treatment

Patients are unique, as are clinician-patient relationships. The context, which we call a *behavioral context*, within which treatment is conducted, regardless of the patient's disorder, however, is not unique. All clinicians provide drill, although the structure of that drill differs widely; all clinicians provide knowledge of results, and again the forms differ; all clinicians decide issues about the scheduling and organization of sessions and whether treatment is to be individual or group. Taken as a whole, these constitute the behavioral context of, in this case, dysarthria therapy.

Drill

Dysarthria therapy is *drill* or the *systematic practice of specially selected and ordered exercises*. Drill requires successful repetition of progressively more difficult tasks: It involves task continua. Consider as an example the patient with flaccid dysarthria who frequently substitutes /t/ for /d/ in the final position of a word. The first step in treatment might require repeated imitation of single-word pairs, such as /at/ and /ad/, with very slow articulation time. When the patient can make perceptually different plosives and can recognize success and failure, the next step might be to decrease the articulation time, followed by movement of the target words into short sentences created from words the patient says correctly. Drill takes its toll, but only of the clinician, not of the patient—not of the patient, that is, if the materials are correctly organized. Patients will realize that they must practice assiduously if they are to improve; and if they are practicing successfully, they will not mind repetition. Clinicians, however, may well find the repetition wearing even if (as they should) they try to make the patients their own best critics. We hope it is not facile to

conclude that if drills are fun for the clinician, something is wrong.

The creativity and joy in dysarthria treatment for clinicians comes with planning the continua and responding to the unforeseen within sessions. The danger in constructing ordered tasks is that the steps will be insignificant, so the patient is not challenged, or so great that the patient constantly stumbles, gets discouraged, and finally abandons the journey altogether. Therefore steps must be neither insignificant nor gigantic. Similarly, tardiness in responding to the unexpected can result in failure, so the clinician must learn to anticipate future events and must maintain an unflagging respect for Murphy's law, which says that if something can go wrong, it will. The clinician must be ready to discard, substitute, alter, and repeat tasks.

Knowledge of Results

Most patients become independent of their clinicians when they learn to distinguish adequate and inadequate responses. One prerequisite for such learning is *knowledge of results*, provided either by a clinician or by special instrumentation. Independence, however, demands more; it demands that patients be able to judge the new and the old—the adequate and the inadequate—for themselves.

The majority of speech pathologists get patients to do something, watch and listen while they do it, then tell them how they have done. This method of supplying knowledge of results is inexpensive and flexible, but it burdens both the clinician and the patient. The clinician must be able to identify good and bad responses and do so quickly and reliably. Speed and consistency are fragile: A late night, disappointment, the previous patient's behavior, and so on all influence how a clinican will respond each moment. No clinician is immune to the effects of such daily realities. His or her only hope is that firm goals, clear criteria of success or adequacy, and orderly clinical experience will prevent the clinician from becoming part of the disorder rather than part of the cure. The patient is burdened, even if the clinician is a good one, by the familiarity of such knowledge of results. Countless others have no doubt told the patient that something in his or her speech was good or bad, better or worse. This is not to condemn the traditional method, but only to underline the burdens it creates and provide the rationale for another method of providing knowledge of results, which is *instrumental.*

Instruments can be made to monitor what a patient is doing, thereby expanding the clinician's repertoire of methods for providing knowledge of results. This process can be called *biofeedback.** Instruments, such as the pressure transducer, the spirometer, and the electromyograph, sensitive to the results of structural and muscle events whose cumulative effect is speech, register these events and return them to the patient in visual (e.g., oscilloscope) or auditory (e.g., buzzer) forms. The machine does not replace the clinician, who still must select the one most appropriate for the patient's symptom complex and the one most likely to help the patient achieve each therapeutic goal. The clinician must teach the patient how to use the machine and how to interpret the results. Practice sessions must be structured and the patient must be provided with methods for improving performance if mere repetition with biofeedback is insufficient to behavior change. The clinician can even complement the biofeedback by adding "Good!" to what the instrument has already provided.

Because we want to avoid fomenting speech pathology's very own battle between John Henry and the Steel Driving Machine, we will not come out in defense of biofeedback over other methods. Biofeedback does, however, possess virtues that recommend it, especially in dysarthria therapy. The ability to provide reliable, immediate, unequivocal, and unique information is the advantage of biofeedback over all but the most assiduous clinicians. Uniqueness is especially critical in speech rehabilitation. As we will observe many times, if normal auditory feedback were sufficient to speech behavior change, few hearing patients would come under our tutelage: they would self-correct. Another virtue is that biofeedback puts both the patient and the clinician much closer to the primary events of speech production, thereby reducing the errors that plague perceptual judgments. For example, therapeutically improved palatal function may be concealed from the ear by continuing articulation errors, but a nasal airflow transducer would detect the improvement, allowing the clinician to reward the patient and perhaps spur him or her to even greater change. Biofeedback expands rather than threatens the clinical art and science.

Scheduling of Sessions

A clinician's goals and a patient's responses are superior to a text's dictates about scheduling. A few general guidelines may be useful, especially to newer clinicians, however.

Sessions can be scheduled frequently in the early days of therapy and when new goals are introduced; twice a day at such times is good. The sessions, regardless of how many there are, should be scheduled when patients have their best chances of doing well: when they are rested, when they are nourished, and when their medication has had an effect (if medication is important to speech treatments). Everyone wants them at those times, so, of course, team members must compromise. Profitable sessions can be of any length, depending on what is to be accomplished and how the patient is responding. If a patient is responding correctly, a session need not be stopped. If a patient passes through success and begins to fail, a session or that portion of it devoted to the now unsuccessful task was too long. Within obvious limits the patient rather than the clock governs the length of the session. Even these minimum guidelines are more often "should have been" than "were." Proctology, dentistry, the late bath, the lost escort, the out-of-town visitor, illness, and the fates all force cancellation, tardiness, and abrupt termination.

Organization of Sessions

Most sessions involve a warm-up, a time for practice, a time for counseling, a time for interim and progress testing, and a time for closing. Clinicians should always attempt to include each of these activities in a typical session. However, crises may mean that a session is all counseling; an impending decision about placement may dictate an entire session of progress testing; and so on. Perhaps the most important thing is to attempt to end each session with success. Testing, therefore, seldom is the last activity, and time spent with a new response comes from the early rather than the late part of the session.

Individual and Group Therapy

Like Peacher [134], we schedule individual rather than group therapy with dysarthric patients because individual sessions are efficient. Patients no doubt profit from groups, however. A group consisting of clinician, patient, and family can cooperate in solving personal problems, such as a patient's lack of confidence or embarrassment, and in preparing for carryover activities in the home. Two patients

---

*Rubow [143] has discussed biofeedback in detail and has distinguished it from simple knowledge of results.

moving toward the same goal may help each other for short periods. A patient with certain skills might exhort another one or two with equal potential. Carryover of learned compensations can begin in controlled group meetings. That a clinician has three or 20 dysarthric patients, however, does not mean he or she has the makings for a group. Labels and head counts are weak criteria for organizing persons into a group. Rather, group members, because of their ages, interests, needs, or accomplishments, should be of service to one another. The benefit of groups (like the benefits of so much that speech pathologists do) for dysarthric patients is yet to be demonstrated experimentally.

Assessment in the Dysarthrias

Darley, Aronson, and Brown's book [35] is replete with methods and suggestions for accomplishing identification; therefore, how one identifies a dysarthric patient will not be discussed. Rather this section describes assessment as an online process [150] of focusing treatment. The focus of treatment results from: (1) determining the type and locus of the patient's speech symptoms and determining, where possible, any neuromuscular abnormalities; (2) organizing these speech and nonspeech symptoms into a set of hierarchies; (3) determining each symptom's contribution to the patient's speech intelligibility; and (4) diagnostic therapy.

Models for Assessment

Unless speech pathologists have models to guide their ears as they listen to the seeming jumble of dysarthric speech symptoms, they will have no efficient, effective way of winnowing those symptoms, that is, no way of satisfying the requirements of focusing the treatment. The model we have found the most useful is one we adapted from Netsell [126], a short history of which appears in Rosenbek and LaPointe [141]. We called it the *point-place* system (Fig. 2-5). The 1 refers to the muscles and structures of respiration; 2, to the larynx; 3, to the soft palate; 4, to the tongue blade; 5, to the tongue tip; 6, to the lips; and 7, to the jaw. These numbers identify places where important speech activities occur and thus remind us where to look for abnormalities.

The point-place system is complemented by a *process model*. Motor speech can be divided into articulation, resonation, phonation, respiration, and prosody. The process model is traditional and thus has the strength of history; however, it also has

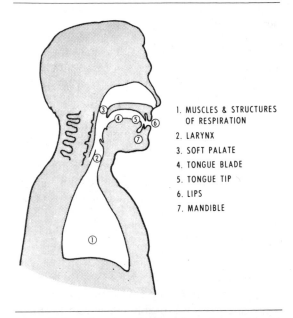

1. MUSCLES & STRUCTURES OF RESPIRATION
2. LARYNX
3. SOFT PALATE
4. TONGUE BLADE
5. TONGUE TIP
6. LIPS
7. MANDIBLE

Fig. 2-5. Line drawing of points along the vocal tract where therapeutically important speech activities occur. (Adapted from R. Netsell, Speech Physiology. In F. D. Minifie, T. J. Hixon, and F. Williams (eds.), *Normal Aspects of Speech, Hearing, and Language.* Englewood Cliffs, N. J.: Prentice-Hall, 1973.)

certain shortcomings. A complete discussion of these would be long and therefore damaging to this chapter, so brief mention of what is wrong with the process model will suffice. First, it is arbitrary; articulation and resonation might as logically be combined as separated. In addition, prosody is as appropriate a member of the list as chocolate cake is in a list of baking supplies. Taken together, the prosodic features of American English (intonation, stress, and rhythm) are the acoustic results of activity in the respiratory structures, larynx, velopharynx, and articulators. For example, the larynx, which is primarily responsible for phonation, also is responsible for intonation and stress; and loudness differences, which also contribute to perceived stress, are the primary result of changes in respiration. In spite of these limitations, the process model is useful because, like the point-place system, it focuses the diagnostician's attention. Predictably, place and process systems overlap. Respiration is accomplished at point 1; phonation at point 2; resonation* at point 3; articulation at points

---

*The entire vocal tract is a resonator, and abnormal resonance can result from structural or movement abnormalities along any part of it. Hypernasality is the most frequently recorded dysarthric resonance abnormality and the one of greatest therapeutic interest in this chapter.

4, 5, 6, and 7; and prosody reflects simultaneous activity at all points.

Determining the Symptoms

Symptoms can be determined perceptually, instrumentally, or both. *Perceptual evaluation* requires that a trained speech pathologist listen to selected samples of a patient's speech and make judgments about the type and distribution of abnormalities. *Instrumental evaluation* requires that a trained speech pathologist make similar interpretations from the readouts of instruments sensitive to the neural, movement, acoustic, and aerodynamic events associated with speaking.

Most classic publications in the dysarthrias describe perceptual symptoms [36, 37, 61, 177], although some early publications [152] and much of modern work [62, 70–73, 77–79, 87–91, 102, 103, 107, 132, 158, 169, 176] are instrumental. The majority of clinicians probably prepare for treatment using perceptual data because such data are relatively inexpensive to collect, and clinicians, if they are taught anything at all about dysarthrias, are taught how to test for and identify perceptual symptoms.

Unfortunately, while perceptual evaluation has almost single-handedly rekindled a dangerously moribund modern interest in the dysarthrias, its popularity threatens to obscure its hazards. First, perceptual judgments are difficult. Memorizing the symptom definitions provided by Darley, Aronson, and Brown [37] is not enough, just as knowing the definition of a footprint is inadequate to track a fleeing felon. An extensive, structured experience in listening is mandatory, preferably with the tutelage of a specially trained clinician. Berry and LaPointe [14] and Darley, Aronson, and Brown [35] describe symptoms, stimuli, and methods for symptom analysis that may be useful to a clinician trying to learn how to listen.

For several reasons, however, errors can occur in perceptual analysis, no matter how experienced the clinician is. First, a patient's speech will reflect his or her age and premorbid medical and social history as well as the effects of neurologic problems. Second, symptoms may be present under certain conditions but not under others, as in the tendency noted by Sarno [148] for hypokinetic pitch and loudness changes to be inadequate only in extraclinical speech, or for articulation in hypokinetic dysarthria to be adequate or nearly so in single words but impaired in connected speech. Third, certain speech symptoms influence the perception of other speech symptoms, as when severe articulation problems influence judgments of hypernasality. Next, what one has just seen or heard will influence subsequent evaluation. A person with mild hypernasality may be evaluated differently, depending on the severity of the previous patient's hypernasality. Probably the greatest hazard of perceptual data, especially as a basis for focusing management, is that similar perceptual symptoms can result from very different abnormal conditions— from different disease processes (e.g., distorted consonants can result from myasthenia gravis and stroke), from different neuromuscular deficits (e.g., flaccidity and spasticity can cause hypernasality), and from different patterns of interaction within a patient's overall symptom complex (e.g., consonant distortion can result form reduced respiratory support for speech, from poor velopharyngeal valving, and from poor laryngeal valving). Of course, an exhaustive history, an extensive list of different stimuli, and careful online procedures will reduce but not extinguish these threats to verity in perceptual analysis; but even the most careful history and perceptual evaluation may not satisfactorily expose the neuromuscular abnormalities underlying the perceptual symptoms.

Alone, instrumental evaluation is far from a panacea. A history and clinical acumen are as mandatory in instrumental as in perceptual evaluation if dysarthric symptoms are to be separated from those of old age, alcoholism, previous trauma, and the rest. The responses one evaluates must be as carefully selected as in perceptual evaluation if all symptoms are to be flushed out of hiding. The greatest contributions of instrumental evaluation are that (1) it is little influenced by preceding evaluations, (2) it brings us closer to events in the peripheral speech mechanism, and (3) it leaves us guessing less about the neuromuscular deficits underlying the perceptual symptoms (EMG, for example, may reveal whether a muscle is flaccid or spastic) and about the presence or absence of symptoms that are easily masked by other symptoms (oral and nasal air-pressure measurements, for example, may reveal an otherwise undetectable palatal dysfunction).

The future may find us content with perceptual evaluation because we will have discovered that instruments confirm what the clinician hears and that if the clinician's hearing is confused, machines will be too. A more likely scenario, however, is that different systems of evaluation will be used for different tasks. Until we can judge the truth of this projection, the diagnostician would do well to learn all forms of evaluation or at least be sensitive to their strengths and to when each is appropriate. Ludlow and Bassich [102] have speculated on the uses of perceptual and acoustic measures. Hypotheses about the relative merits of perceptual [34], physiologic [119], and acoustic [168] measures have been discussed at length [139]. The present discussion emphasizes perceptual evaluation in the interest of space and because the greatest number of clinicians, including the authors, have easiest access to perceptual symptoms by reason of their reading, experience, and education.

EVALUATION OF RESPIRATION (NUMBER 1). Basic to the speech process is its driving force—respiration—which is number 1 in Fig. 2-5. Since loudness is manipulated primarily by the muscles and structures of respiration,* the best perceptual cues to adequacy of respiration are the loudness characteristics of a patient's connected speech. An inadequately loud voice or one characterized by inadequate or inappropriate loudness variation may implicate the respiratory mechanism. We hypothesize—and these are guesses rather than conclusions—that weakness and abnormal tone will be manifested as reduced overall loudness, and a tendency toward monoloudness and incoordination will be betrayed by inappropriate loudness changes.

Inadequate respiration for speech resulting from weakness, abnormal tone, and incoordination can also be diagnosed with reasonable confidence by the patient's history, observation of nonspeech performance, and perceptual evaluation of specially selected imitative speech tasks.† A weak, rigid, or spastic patient may complain that shouting is now impossible, that he or she has shortness of breath for talking, or that he or she has to exert great effort to capture enough air for speech. The patient may report and be observed to have difficulty rolling over, sitting without support, and standing, especially if the weakness is severe. Also, respiratory structures can be observed as a patient breathes

quietly. Unilateral weakness may be betrayed by asymmetries of movement, which may or may not be clinically significant.

Breathing for speech, however, offers the best evidence for clinically significant respiratory abnormalities. Before a quick speech inhalation, most normal speakers assume a "belly-in" position; the abdominal muscles are contracted and the diaphragm is domed. On inhalation, the normal diaphragm contracts and the belly protrudes. Weak patients and patients with abnormal tone may have difficulty achieving the belly-in position or in taking a quick speech inhalation without resorting to compensatory movements, such as elevating the shoulders in an attempt to enlarge the thoracic cavity. Special tests of strength, tone, and coordination of diaphragm, chest, and belly muscles include asking the patient to: (1) sniff, (2) pant, (3) make an abrupt loudness change on a prolonged /a/ (from very soft to very loud) without changing pitch or opening his or her mouth wider, and (4) produce a loudness pattern by gradually increasing and then decreasing the loudness of a sustained vowel [74]. Weak, hypotonic, and hypertonic patients may be able to muster only minimum performance on these four, and the incoordinated patient will have special difficulty with (2), (3), and (4).

The clinician interested in using any of these observations, and especially the last four, needs to spend considerable time evaluating normal performance. Dysarthric speakers seldom fail because they cannot perform the tasks. The majority perform less rapidly, more clumsily, or through a narrower range than normal persons. The differences may be subtle; their detection requires experience.

In pathology confined to the spinal cord, respiration deficiencies may be the only primary speech abnormality. The treatment decision is simple: modify respiration, perhaps in cooperation with the physical therapist. Typically, however, respiration abnormalities coexist with other symptoms, and the significance of the differences in respiration to the total symptom complex will have to be judged before treatment can begin. Just as typically, if the abnormality in respiration is reduced respiration for speech resulting from weakness or abnormal tone, attempts to improve the patient's respiration will occur very early in treatment. Even the grandest articulatory gestures are for naught if the vocal tract is not energized by the exhaled airstream. Occasionally impaired processes other than respi-

---

*Amount of mouth opening and force of laryngeal contraction also influence loudness. Evaluation of these will be discussed at the appropriate time.
†Hixon's [73] and Putnam and Hixon's [136] approach to evaluating and treating respiratory disorders goes well beyond anything contained in this or similar volumes and can profitably be studied by clinicians.

ration will masquerade as poor breathing. Unless the masquerade is exposed, time and energy will be wasted.

EVALUATION OF PHONATION (NUMBER 2). The larynx, number 2 in the point-place scheme, is the primary pitch-changing mechanism and also is a major determinant of voice quality. Therefore, to test its adequacy perceptually, one must listen to pitch and quality characteristics of the patient's speech. Severely reduced pitch range, inappropriate pitch, or pitch change in connected speech suggests laryngeal involvement as do the dysphonias, such as breathiness, harshness, and strained-strangled voice. Again, hypothetically, one can suggest that weakness and reduced tone will be signaled by breathiness and hoarseness; increased tone by strained-strangled dysphonia, harshness, and abnormally high pitch (although all three are not inevitable); and incoordination by inappropriate pitch changes, inconsistent dysphonia, and voicing errors, such as the substitution of voiced for voiceless cognates (these last may be present in weakness and reduced tone as well).

A number of simple perceptual tests may allow the clinician to separate what is specifically laryngeal or phonatory in the disturbed speech signal from symptoms of involvement of other systems and may help determine the type of neuromuscular deficit underlying the perceptual symptoms. Laryngeal weakness is likely if the patient has a weak cough or a laryngeal stridor. Spasticity may be signaled by a strained-strangled voice quality on prolonged /a/ although strained-strangled voice quality may also be the manifestation of a speaker's attempt to compensate for weakness [121]. Laryngeal coordination and coordination of laryngeal and respiratory movements can be measured by asking the patient to (1) make an abrupt pitch change on a prolonged /a/ without changing loudness (the patient begins at a comfortable pitch and then shifts pitch rapidly upward); (2) produce several very rapid pitch changes from low ·to high, reminiscent of Tarzan; and (3) pass unphonated air out the vocal tract and then gradually and smoothly add voicing [74]. Kruel [93] includes rapid, alternate productions of /i/—performance of which requires coordinated activity of tongue tip, larynx, and respiratory structures—as part of his examination for neuromuscular control in hypokinetic dysarthric patients, and he provides normative data from patients with Parkinson's disease and older, normal subjects.

Experimental data must be gathered before the interpretation of performance on all these special perceptual tests for planning treatment is known. Even in the absence of data, however, certain general therapeutic guidelines can be suggested. At the very least, if a laryngeal abnormality is suspected or confirmed, the speech pathologist will want to refer the patient to a physician for further diagnosis and management. Aronson [6] is only one author who has demonstrated the contribution of laryngeal symptoms to proper (in this case medical) treatment. Flaccidity, abnormalities of tone (both too much and too little), and incoordination of the larynx and other speech structures are also directly treatable by the speech pathologist, so treatment may be well served by discrete analysis of the type and distribution of phonatory symptoms and their neuromuscular bases. Finally, if the larynx is normal, or nearly so, the clinician knows there is a valve available that may be useful as the patient tries to compensate for other abnormalities, as when the force of laryngeal adduction compensates for weakness of respiratory structures in producing loudness increments.

EVALUATION OF RESONATION (NUMBER 3). The most frequent resonance abnormality in dysarthria is overriding or inconsistent hypernasality because of palatal weakness or incoordination. The resistance of the soft palate to disturbed tone can only be guessed at, but the relative mildness of hypernasality in a high proportion of hypokinetic and ataxic dysarthric patients—patients whose tone is frequently disturbed—is striking (spasticity is apparently accompanied by hypernasality, but the hypernasality is usually less severe than that in flaccid weakness, and it can be hypothesized that weakness rather than spasticity is responsible for the hypernasality in spastic dysarthria).

To determine the presence and severity of hypernasality, perceptual judgments of connected speech are preferable. To determine specific loci of resonance abnormality and phonetic influences on it, such as the effect of nasal consonants on the resonance characteristics of neighboring, nonnasal consonants, specially designed words and sentences can be tested: e.g., *pants* and "Make me a Hong Kong cookie." Many clinicians also determine velopharyngeal adequacy for consonant-vowel (CV) syllables and for single vowels, such as /i/, /u/, and /a/. A popular test is to have the patient prolong a vowel or a vowel combination, such as /i-u/, while the clinician alternately squeezes and releases the patient's nares or occludes and unoccludes the nostrils. Resonance should not change if the soft palate is normal. Experienced clinicians also know that sometimes resonance does not change even when the palate is abnormal. A mirror placed under the nose during the performance of sound and syllable tasks will fog up if nasal airflow is present. The palate can also be observed directly. A weakened palate will droop, for example. If one sees the effect of velar involvement but cannot hear it, chances are good that the incompetence will be more important diagnostically than therapeutically.*

Many clinicians also evaluate velar function on gag and on such tasks as whistling and blowing. The most compelling reason for testing velopharyngeal adequacy during nonspeech performance is probably prognostic. While it is undocumented as far as we know, popular opinion has it that a patient is a better candidate for a number of therapies to improve velopharyngeal function if he or she has velopharyngeal adequacy during vowel production and, at very least, during some nonspeech activity, such as blowing.

To prepare for therapy, the clinician needs to determine what contribution, if any, the patient's velopharyngeal problem is making to the patient's total dysarthric pattern. Next, it must be decided if prosthetic (palatal lift) or behavioral management is preferable. Discussions of both treatments are forthcoming.

EVALUATION OF ARTICULATION (NUMBERS 4, 5, 6, AND 7). The object of articulation testing is to determine the patient's articulation errors, their locus, and where possible, the reason for them (Chap. 1 describes dysarthric articulation in detail). Such diagnosis usually requires both speech and nonspeech tests. The speech tests can include both single-word and sentence testing, because the patient's articulation may be intact in single words but defective in connected speech. The sentence form of the McDonald Deep Test [109] or of the Templin-Darley Tests of Articulation [163] suits the purpose of sentence testing. Single-word articulation tests for adults have not come to our attention: adaptation of children's tests given imitatively will suffice until something better is developed. Table 2-3 shows selected stimuli from a clinical test to evaluate speech sounds in the initial, medial, and final positions of words. Its construction was

*See Schweiger, Netsell, and Sommerfeld [150] for a different opinion.

Table 2-3. Selected items from a clinical measure of speech sound integrity in initial, medial, and final positions

paᴵ	aᴵp	ʌpaᴵ
peᴵ	eᴵp	ʌpeᴵ
pam	map	ʌpam
bim	mib	ʌbim
bam	mab	ʌbam
ban	nab	ʌban
toᵁ	oᵁt	ʌtoᵁ
taᴵm	maᴵt	ʌtaᴵm
tim	mit	ʌtim
doᵁm	moᵁd	ʌdoᵁm
dæn	næd	ʌdæn
dɛf	fed	ʌdɛf
kaᴵt	taᴵk	ʌkaᴵt
kᴵm	mᴵk	ʌkᴵm
kab	bak	ʌkab
goᵁt	toᵁg	ʌgoᵁt
geᴵm	meᴵg	ʌgeᴵm
gaᵁn	naᵁg	ʌgaᵁn

prompted by the knowledge that position in an utterance may be a potent influence on the adequacy of a sound, especially in dysarthric speech. That test can be given imitatively and admits to any scoring (plus-minus, multidimensional, phonetic transcription) the clinician wishes to employ. The results will provide data on which sounds are easy and which are difficult in relation to their position in the word.

Because articulation errors, their location, their significance to speech adequacy, and how they may be influenced by propositionality are sometimes unrevealed even by a sentence test, we also recommend reading and spontaneous speech samples. Finally, an intelligibility measure [172] can be a valuable addition to the test battery.

The traditional oral-peripheral examination and swallowing examination [99], including evaluation of both articulator structure and function, may contribute additional information on which of the articulators are impaired (in all dysarthric types except flaccid, all articulators are likely to be involved, although the relative severity of involvement may differ) and the reason for that impairment [149]. Structures can first be evaluated by direct examination. Does the mouth droop, is the face expressionless, is the tongue wasted? Function can be checked with a series of nonspeech tests requiring each of the articulators to reveal its force, range, speed, coordination, and symmetry of movement. For example, the patient can open his or her mouth to its fullest extent, pucker, smile, protrude the tongue, and elevate it to the alveolar ridge; the patient can make all these movements

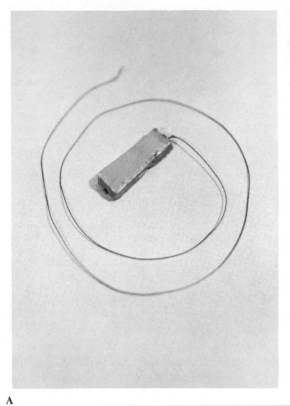

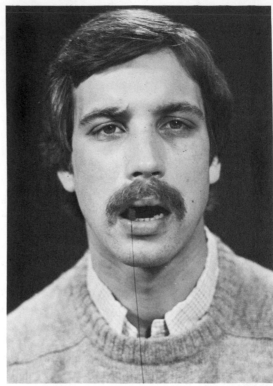

A

B

Fig. 2-6. (A) A bite block for propping the mouth open; (B) bite block in place.

rapidly several times and can make them against resistance. These observations can be combined with diadochokinetic tasks requiring the patient to repeat several productions of /pʌ/, /tʌ/, and /kʌ/. For all such diadochokinetic testing there is a useful rule: *Whenever possible, test points one through four independently.* Having the patient produce /pʌ/, /tʌ/, and /kʌ/ normally and with a bite block between his or her teeth (Fig. 2-6) will allow for such independence.

Important to treatment is what such structural-functional testing reveals about the underlying neuromuscular deficit; the relative integrity of lips, tongue tip, and tongue blade; and whether the jaw helps or hinders lip and tongue movements. The patient with weakness and spasticity is usually slow, but the patient with weakness and reduced tone may be nearly normal in rate. However, both may be limited in range and force of movements. The neuromuscular problems associated with ataxia and parkinsonism may be manifested in the first instance as slowness and incoordination, and in the second as weakness, accelerated rate, and limited range with the effect that movements are blurred.

Nonspeech tasks are more helpful in determin-

ing if the patient is abnormal than in planning the treatment. Generally, the focus of speech treatment comes primarily from the speech data unless the nonspeech tests reveal something unique about the underlying neuromuscular abnormality. Relative integrity of lips and tongue, as measured by both speech and nonspeech testing, supplement other articulation data as the clinician chooses stimuli for treatment. Comparison of the blocked and unblocked conditions may give the clinician an idea about the importance of the jaw to speech and some postural adjustments (to be described) that compensate for this neurologic deficit.

EVALUATION OF PROSODY (ALL NUMBERS). Changes in loudness, pitch,* articulation time, and pause time combine to yield the prosodic features of intonation, stress, and rhythm, or what Lehiste [97] calls tonal features, stress, and quality. Prosodic

---

*A partial evaluation of both loudness and pitch was discussed in the sections on respiration and phonation.

116

features are complex and hence are bothersome and controversial even in normal speech. Their systematic evaluation in dysarthria is just beginning [174]. For now, most clinicians content themselves diagnostically with decisions based on their perceptions about whether (1) the patient's overall loudness, pitch, and pattern of loudness and pitch changes are appropriate to the context; (2) whether the pattern of stressed and unstressed syllables is normal; and (3) whether the pattern of rate change, duration of sounds, and location and length of pauses are right for the context.

These diagnostic judgments can be made of spontaneous speech, although this leaves the clinician at the mercy of whatever vagaries of language the patient happens to reveal. Perhaps better is a set of sentences calculated to force the patient to produce contrastive prosodic patterns. At present, we have such a diagnostic tool only for stress.* We call this a contrastive stress drill after Fairbanks [42], and it works like a question-answer dialogue.

CLINICIAN	PATIENT
Bob bit Bill.	Bob bit Bill. (In imitation of the clinician)
Who bit Bill?	*Bob* bit Bill.
Did Bob hit Bill?	No, Bob *bit* Bill.
Did Bob bite Jon?	No, Bob bit *Bill*.

We take the patient through this series of questions and answers and make perceptual judgments about the use of pitch, loudness, articulation time, and pause time. The patient's performance on this task may be somewhat better than in connected speech, so judgment of both can be profitable. Yorkston et al. [174] are developing a more rigorous and quantified system of perceptual and acoustic analysis of stress.

Evaluation, especially of stress and rhythm, can be important to diagnosis and treatment planning. The type of abnormality helps determine each patient's proper classification. Hypokinetic dysarthria and flaccid dysarthria, for example, have different patterns of abnormal stress and rhythm. In addition, each patient's ability to manipulate stress and rhythm can influence treatment target selection. If stress and rhythm are abnormal and contributing to unintelligibility or bizarreness, they can be treated. Also, if a patient can be taught to enhance rhythm

*Both articulation time and pause time can be evaluated by these materials, so the clinician makes simultaneous judgments about both stress and rhythm.

and stress profiles, it may be that other symptoms such as consonant imprecision and breathiness will improve as a result. Using the contrastive stress drill to enhance such profiles will be described in a later section.

Hierarchical Organization of Symptoms
After the diagnostician has determined the abnormalities in each of the important points in the speech tube (if one uses the point-place system), or in each of the speech processes (if ones uses the process model), he or she prepares for treatment by *organizing these symptoms into hierarchies*. A *hierarchy* is an ordering of symptoms reflecting the clinician's best guess about their causative relationships. Several hierarchies of nonspeech and speech abnormalities can usually be generated for each dysarthric talker's total pattern of abnormalities.

For a given patient, one or more hierarchies will relate muscle and speech symptoms—hierarchies to which Darley, Aronson, and Brown [36] have devoted considerable attention as part of their research on dysarthric types. Consider a clinical example: R. R. had parkinsonism; inadequate loudness was his major speech symptom, and truncal rigidity was his major neuromuscular symptom, although he did have tremor as well. Rigidity of the respiratory muscles seemed to account for the inadequate loudness. The hierarchy for this patient then was:

Decreased loudness
↑
Rigidity

The team treatment plan was to attempt reduction of the rigidity with medication and physical therapy, while at the same time teaching the patient to coax greater loudness from his impaired system with specific speech drills.

Consider a more complex example, that of a 41-year-old patient with multiple sclerosis. On initial evaluation he had a high-pitched, strained-strangled voice, poor loudness control, inconsistently inadequate loudness, short phrases, significant clavicular breathing, and mildly increased articulation time and inconsistent sound distortion. Neuromuscular symptoms were weakness, slowness, and incoordination. We hypothesized that most of his speech symptoms were related to respiratory muscle weakness. To test the hypothesis, we wrapped him tightly around the middle, so the wrap (a girdle) replaced or shored up his weakened abdominal muscles. In the girdled condition, his speech improved significantly except that articulation errors and some loudness control problems persisted. Especially significant was a reduction in clavicular movements and in the strained-strangled dysphonia. Our conclusion was that weakness of respiratory muscles had led to clavicular breathing and to abnormal tensing of the vocal tract both as a result of the clavicular pattern and in a conscious effort to provide maximum control over the minimal amount of air available for speaking. Because the inconsistent sound distortions and abnormal prolongations were unchanged, we assumed they had a different explanation. One of this patient's hierarchies might be diagrammed as follows:

High pitch, strained-strangled dysphonia, inadequate loudness

↑ ↑

Clavicular breathing → abnormal vocal-tract tensing

↑ ↑

Weakness of respiratory muscles

Another of his hierarchies also could be diagrammed:

Inconsistent sound distortion

↑

Incoordination of movements

And finally we hypothesized a third hierarchy:

Increased articulation time, sound distortion

↑

Slowness of movement

Hierarchies limited solely to speech symptoms can also be created. For example, patients with basal ganglia disease often have a rate disturbance that increases the number and severity of their speech sound distortions. Slow them down, and their articulatory precision increases.

Finally, hierarchies relating perceptual symptoms and the speech structures are often easily constructed because of the lawful relationship of structures to aspects of the speech signal. R. H., a primarily flaccid dysarthric man, had inadequate respiratory drive, breathiness, sound distortions and omissions, hypernasality, and speech limited to one or two nearly inaudible and unintelligible syllables. The patterns of influence in his speech were complex, but one hypothesized hierarchy was as follows:

Sound distortion, reduced respiratory support

↑ ↑

Velopharyngeal incompetence

This patient was fitted with a palatal lift and his speech improved, suggesting the reality of this hierarchy.

Why would one want to go to the trouble of hierarchy construction? Hierarchies can tell clinicians where to start treatment—as close to the bottom of each hierarchy as possible. Common clinical wisdom has it that such treatment is most efficient. Examples attesting to that wisdom abound. Rate change is more efficient than articulation training for dysarthric talkers whose consonant imprecision results primarily from abnormal rate. Training to improve respiratory support for speech is often more efficient than treatment of other components of the speech mechanism even if other components are also involved [130]. Treatment of underlying neuromuscular abnormalities such as hypertonicity, rather than of the speech abnormalities resulting from them, can sometimes have a profound influence on the efficacy of a treatment because such a procedure can make subsequent speech treatment unnecessary [144]. The common clinical wisdom is not appropriate in all cases, however. One reason is that the relationship of neuromuscular abnormalities to speech abnormalities has not been satisfactorily established [119], although progress is being made [9, 78]. Therefore hierarchies relating speech and neuromuscular abnormalities are sometimes impossible to create. Sometimes even when they can be created, the clinician will have insufficient time to undertake the often protracted treatment necessary to improve an abnormal condition like muscle weakness. In such cases, in the interest of time, treatment will have to be directed against traditional perceptual symptoms. If a clinician has any doubts about the appropriateness of a given hierarchy, he or she has only to test it in treatment.

Contribution to Intelligibility
The focus of therapy comes also from determining the relative contribution of symptoms to the patient's overall intelligibility: the contribution of symptoms is unequal. Symptoms that contribute little to intelligibility need not be changed as long as they do not threaten the patient. Dysarthria treatment is often arduous under the best of conditions, and speech pathologists seldom have unlimited ac-

cess to a patient; we cannot, therefore, afford wasted time. Like a person besieged by painful boils and dry skin, the dysarthric patient has a right to expect relief from the greatest evil. The judgment about relative contribution to intelligibility is a perceptual and judgmental one in clinical practice. It comes from experience. Darley, Aronson, and Brown [36] have provided some correlative data from selected groups of dysarthric patients.

Diagnostic Therapy

Finally, focus comes from diagnostic measures aimed at determining which, if any, of the symptoms are relatively easily modified. While one logically expects organically based abnormalities to require extensive therapy, such an assumption is sometimes inappropriate, especially about the symptoms of individual patients. Netsell and Cleeland [129], for example, published an interesting report in which they demonstrate modification of lip hypertonia in one short session. They were quick to observe that the explanation for the lip abnormality was unclear. While simplification is to be avoided, it is perhaps legitimate to recall that sometimes patients will be able to modify a symptom by being told only that it is present and that they can rid themselves of it by doing one thing or another. That universal aphorism whose origin is somewhere in a previous century, "Slow down and think before you talk," is not as successful in modifying speech differences as family folklore would have us believe but, used sparingly by a talented clinician, it may work limited wonders.* Other diagnostic measures include postural adjustments, delayed auditory feedback, contrastive stress drills, and most of the other procedures to be described in the next section.

Specific Treatment Goals

It is tempting to describe specific treatment for specific cases from one's own clinical experience, because such an approach shows how it was really done and what did and did not work. Such an approach, however, is endangered by the sundry

---

*At the risk of seeming to flog a moribund horse, it is worth reminding even, or especially, a beginning clinician that it is too easy to get buried under puny details and forget to give patients the whole story and the most straightforward and simplest of explanations of what they must do if they want to sound better.

differences among dysarthric speakers. So, instead of describing specific patients we will outline eight specific treatment goals in the hope that information about goals generalizes more widely than does information about patients. The goals are

1. Help the person to become a productive patient.
2. Modify abnormalities of posture, tone, and strength.
3. Modify respiration.
4. Modify phonation.
5. Modify resonation.
6. Modify articulation.
7. Modify suprasegmentals and prosody.
8. Provide alternative or augmentative modes of communication.

The ordering of these goals does not imply an immutable order of progress or of importance, with one exception: *The patient must accept an active role in treatment before meaningful changes in speech are possible.* A willingness to be active is one attribute of a productive patient. Neither should it be assumed from this list that the goals are discrete. Activities within several of them may be identical or similar, which is to say that certain activities may move the patient toward several goals simultaneously. Even when the drills within each goal are very different, progress toward two or more goals may occur at the same time, as when the clinician is spending one portion of each session in tongue-strengthening activities and another portion in teaching the patient to slow down. The goals merely bound the potential territory of dysarthria treatment; the plat to be occupied by a particular patient and his or her clinician is determined by the patient's needs.

Goal 1: Helping the Person to Become a Productive Patient

Until clinician and patient have agreed on the necessity and value of treatment, what is to be accomplished, and the treatment procedures, dysarthria treatment has almost no chance for success. Patient gains, should they appear, will be gossamer and transient. Getting the patient to agree, then, is what we mean by helping him or her become a productive patient. Most clinicians doubt their ability to make a stone talk, an ability credited to several founding fathers of speech pathology; equally many, however, have no doubt that they could convince a stone to give it a try. As a result, we will discuss only generally the procedures appropriate to goal 1.

The first necessity is knowledge on the clinician's part that not all patients with a dysarthria, even those who show up in the speech pathologist's office, are willing to attempt change. Early treatment sessions then can be used for educating the patient about what he or she has, what can be done about it, and what the short-term and long-term expectations can be. Cooperation is most likely if the patient has a chance to help create and order specific behavioral goals, although all working clinicians no doubt have treated patients who were incapable of formulating productive goals. The clinician is justified in formulating goals for such patients and in convincing them of their value. Counseling so that the patient can begin to feel good about whatever level of compensated intelligibility he or she will attain is also essential to productivity. If possible, the family can be included in all education and counseling, because their cooperation usually makes a difference in the patient's progress [142]. When patients accept where they are going and what they must do to get there, specific behavior change can begin. While patients need not be accepting when treatment begins, that acceptance must evolve or the clinician might as profitably spend time molding clay—statues talk as functionally as passive patients.

Goal 2: Modification of Posture, Muscle Tone, and Strength

Speech performance is influenced by a structural and neuromuscular background, including posture, muscle tone, and strength.* Speech treatment can unashamedly begin with attempts to modify this background, if such modification will improve speech or enhance the possibilities for the success of techniques aimed specifically at the speech signal.

---

*This triad is obviously arbitrary and limited. Netsell [125] would add timing, and other writers might add coordination as well. In addition, weakness and abnormal tone can create postural abnormalities; and therapeutic modification of tone and strength can have a positive effect on posture, and vice versa. We have chosen to discuss posture, muscle tone, and strength, because we wanted to distinguish a class of *passive therapeutic manipulations* of the speech structures, such as surgery, bracing, and girdling (postural adjustments), from *active therapeutic manipulations*, such as increasing strength with exercise. Timing or coordination are not listed because we consider that timing and coordination are influenced by traditional methods of speech therapy that concentrate on speech movements per se and that are discussed at length in subsequent portions of this chapter.

GENERAL POSTURE: CONTEXT FOR TREATMENT. Speaking is done most efficiently during standing, sitting, or lying on one's back, so the spine is straight and the head is in a straight line with the body's midline. Normal speakers, however, can talk twisted around, bent over, or folded up. Unfortunately, dysarthric speakers lack the normal speaker's immunity to postural influences. Therefore an early clinical task is to analyze the dysarthric speaker's posture and decide whether or not to modify it.

The interaction of posture and speech yields six conditions for the clinician's consideration. These are shown in Table 2-4. The first condition requires nothing further of the speech pathologist. The normal posture in the second and third conditions may be modified to an abnormal one if the modification improves the patient's speech, is acceptable to the patient, and is not harmful to the patient's health. The abnormal posture of the fourth condition can be changed if it threatens the patient's health and if a change improves the patient's appearance, as it almost surely will. The fifth condition must be changed because health, appearance, or communication demands it; and the sixth condition can be tolerated and even taught if the patient agrees and if the abnormal posture does not threaten the patient's health.

GENERAL POSTURE: TREATMENT PROCEDURES. Patients can assume or be placed in the posture that is accompanied by the best speech as long as the best speech posture is acceptable and safe. If the head and neck are invaded by involuntary movements or if the neck is weak, patients may profit from a neck brace (Fig. 2-7), and weakened neck muscles may also be aided by merely having patients brace their heads with their hands. Similarly, trunk weakness can sometimes be compensated for by braces. Patients with arm weakness may be helped to perform the activities of daily living by overhead slings, such as those shown in Figure 2-8, and one of our patients discovered for himself

Table 2-4. Six postural considerations important to treatment planning

Posture	Effect on Speech
Normal	Speech improved
Normal	Indifferent effect
Normal	Speech adversely affected
Abnormal	Indifferent effect
Abnormal	Speech adversely affected
Abnormal	Speech improved

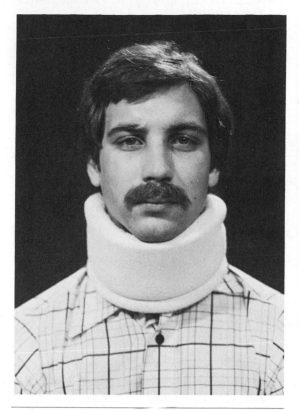

Fig. 2-7. Cervical collar for stabilizing the head.

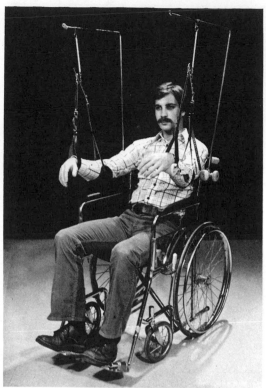

Fig. 2-8. Overhead slings. Patient with limb weakness can exert downward pressure against the slings, thereby improving his or her background of effort.

that he could talk best if he spoke while forcing his arms downward against the slings. All such postural adjustments must be supervised by a physician.

The supine position may be the optimum general posture for some patients, especially those with movement disorders or with weakened respiratory muscles (to whom we will return). Tremor may be reduced in the supine position, for example, especially if relaxation can also be induced. We cannot demand too much of patients in the supine position, however. If the patient has an intention tremor, and if this intention tremor has invaded the speech muscles as well as the trunk and limbs, speech will continue to be disturbed when the patient talks, even if the patient is on his or her back. Nonetheless, the disturbance may be reduced in the supine position, perhaps because the body housing the speech muscles and structures is more stable.

POSTURE FOR RESPIRATION: CONTEXT FOR TREATMENT. Respiration for speech depends on the interaction of three muscle groups: the single muscle

dividing the torso in halves (the diaphragm); the belt or belly muscles; and the muscles of the chest or thorax. The usual posture for a quick speech inhalation is with the belt muscles contracted, the viscera compacted, and the chest wall elevated and moved outward—all accomplished by these three muscle groups. Controlled speech exhalation also requires a delicate interaction of these muscles. Weakness or abnormal tone may prevent patients from assuming the posture for a quick, adequate speech inhalation and reduce their control of the exhaled airstream.

POSTURE FOR RESPIRATION: TREATMENT PROCEDURES. Weakened muscles can sometimes be compensated for by girdling the patient in the area of the abdominal muscles, thereby shoring up the respiratory structures and providing a more normal posture for speech [74]. A number of wraps and girdles, including the extrawide elastic bandage shown in Figure 2-9 and the Posey girdle, can be wrapped around the patient's midsection. The cli-

Fig. 2-9. Girdling with an extrawide elastic bandage.

nician will need to experiment with the best material, tension, and location, and only a short trial will tell the clinician if a palliative effect is to be expected. Whether girdling influences the volume of air that the patient can inhale, increases the patient's control of the exhaled airstream, or both has apparently not been determined. Successful girdling should be reserved for times when improved speech is desirable: during treatment and selected conversations, for example. A word of caution: *Girdling can cause pneumonia, so it must be limited to short periods and must be permitted and supervised by a physician* [74].

Preferable to girdling is a flat surface that the patient can lean into as he or she prepares to speak. A board, for example, could be attached to a patient's wheelchair by means of a moveable brace that would allow it to be swung into position in front of the patient at the level of the belt muscles [74]. As the patient prepares to speak, he or she can lean into the board; and like the girdle, the board will stabilize the patient's posture for respiration and act like a piston to force air out of the lungs. The board could be swung to the side when the patient is entering or leaving the chair or when the patient is silent.

Besides being less risky than girdling, this postural adjustment is more flexible. Patients may find it best to lean into the board (1) only as they inhale, (2) only as they exhale for speech, or (3) only during the last part of exhalation. Clinician-supervised experimentation determines the best use. Occasionally, patients with sufficient arm strength can clutch themselves around the middle to provide surrogate abdominal muscles [74]. Timing and amount of arm activity can be adjusted.

POSTURE FOR PHONATION: CONTEXT FOR TREATMENT. Normal voice requires normal vocal-fold mass and rapid delicate adjustments in the intrinsic and extrinsic laryngeal muscles. Vocal-fold mass may be reduced in flaccid dysarthria of long duration; and muscle function, because of weakness, abnormal tone, or incoordination may be (and usually is) abnormal in all the dysarthrias.

POSTURE FOR PHONATION: TREATMENT PROCEDURES. Injecting a flaccid vocal fold with Teflon or some other substance is a traditional treatment for isolated vocal-fold or recurrent nerve paralysis. Smith et al. [162] report on the success of this procedure with one patient with severe flaccid weakness of all speech structures. The patient, a 60-year-old woman with dysphagia and loss of speech, was given an injection of silicone lateral to the left vocal fold. Improved cough and control of secretions and reduced danger of aspiration were reported; vowel phonation improved, but speech remained unintelligible as other cranial nerves were also involved. This is very significant because it describes results in a patient with more than unilateral vocal-fold paralysis. The patient's unaltered intelligiblity is informative: Symptoms unrelated or trivially related to abnormal laryngeal function are minimally influenced by alteration of the larynx.

As part of a behavioral approach to changing the posture for phonation, some clinicians have wrapped the patient's throat, thereby causing a mechanical approximation of the folds and, presumably, improved voice. Others have encouraged patients to turn their heads to the side of the weakness, thereby distorting the larynx and in some cases bringing about an approximation of the folds. We have not tried these postural adjustments and would recommend them only if supervised by a physician. The head turning seems especially difficult to

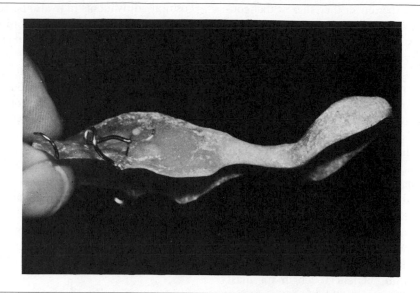

Fig. 2-10. Palatal-lift prosthesis (Photograph courtesy of Ronald Netsell, Ph.D.).

maintain, and we fail to see the reason why patients should eventually be able to abandon it. No training of the vocal folds should result from discovering a position that mechanically distorts the larynx and causes approximation. One has to weigh the disadvantages (here, cosmetic and perhaps medical) and advantages. Both fundamental frequency and vocal quality make little contribution to unintelligibility; the number of dysphonic persons operating otherwise normally in society argues against a major contribution of fundamental frequency and quality to bizarreness or to what society (excluding the speech pathologist) calls acceptable or normal.

POSTURE FOR RESONATION: CONTEXT FOR TREATMENT. Oversimplification is the greatest threat to any discussion of resonation abnormalities; abnormal resonance can result from any supralaryngeal abnormality and need not result exclusively from velopharyngeal incompetence or from modification of the nasal resonance cavities resulting from a deviated septum, nasal polyps, or edema. This section, however, is limited to postural adjustments to modify hypernasality resulting from palatal weakness, because inconsistent or consistent hypernasality is the most frequently reported resonance abnormality in the dysarthrias. Resonance abnormalities resulting from abnormal tongue positioning can be influenced by the articulation therapy to be described, and hyponasality does not appear to constitute a significant dysarthric symptom.

POSTURE FOR RESONATION: TREATMENT PROCEDURES. In severe velopharyngeal paralysis, the palate fails to approximate the posterior pharyngeal wall and consistent hypernasality results. With lesser weakness, the palate may be slow in contacting the posterior wall, may leave it prematurely, or may move in some other abnormal way with inconsistent resonance imbalance as the result [128]. All such inadequacies can sometimes be modified dramatically with a palatal-lift prosthesis. A palatal lift (Fig. 2-10) typically consists of a palatal portion with hooks that attach to the patient's teeth and a posterior extension that elevates the soft palate to the posterior pharyngeal wall, thereby producing a mechanical obstruction between the oral and nasal cavities. Schweiger, Netsell, and Sommerfeld [151] describe the construction and fitting of the palatal lift. Like Kerman, Singer, and Davidoff [91], they also describe the improvements in dysarthric speech resulting from lift management; they base their discussion on both perceptual and instrumental measurement. Shaughnessy, Netsell, and Farrage [153] describe the case of a child fitted with a lift. Chapter 3 details a variety of prosthetic managements.

Gonzalez and Aronson [58] report successful palatal lift management of 35 patients, 19 of whom were dysarthric—5 with flaccidity, 10 with spasticity, and 4 with both flaccid and spastic symptoms. Hypernasality and nasal emissions were reduced, but facial and lingual weakness continued to interfere with normal articulation. Some patients with progressive disease lost their gains. The authors recommend speech therapy to help patients use the lift maximally once it is fitted. As a result of their clinical experience, they suggest that contraindications for prosthetic management are the presence of "a very spastic or stiff palate that does not tolerate elevation" (p. 101), failure to retain the lift, and a lack of patient cooperation. Importantly, they do not consider degenerative disease or tone that is mildly to moderately increased as contraindications of lift management. Gibbons and Bloomer [54] also noted "instantaneous improvement" in speech after a flaccid dysarthric patient was fitted with a lift. The literature leaves one sanguine about palatal lifts in dysarthria treatment.

We have fitted five edentulous, flaccid dysarthric patients with lifts and one was successful. Four patients could not retain the prostheses that were attached to the posterior margins of their dentures. The one successful patient required that the dentist sacrifice maximum, beneficial length for maximum retention. The prosthesis's lift portion was not long enough to carry the soft palate to the posterior pharyngeal wall, but it was long enough to improve velopharyngeal function so that work could begin on other parts of the speech tube. Aten et al. [7] have reported on a lift for edentulous patients.

A few general guidelines for palatal-lift management of the dysarthric patient can be suggested. First, a palatal lift should be considered immediately as a treatment for the dysarthric patient with significant overriding hypernasality, although the clinician will want to wait for the patient to return to sufficient health, so the he or she can cope with the evaluation, fitting, and daily use of the lift. The clinician may want to wait for return (either because of physiologic recovery or with treatment) of sufficient respiratory and articulatory competence to allow for production of at least a limited number of vowels and nasal consonants. In the absence of data, proper timing must be resolved for each patient. Second, neither the patient nor the clinician should expect more of the prosthesis than the patient's symptom complex will allow. If, as is generally the case, processes other than resonation are involved, the lift may help improve all speech dimensions; however, deficits will remain and these may require additional therapy. Third, extremely spastic palates may frustrate lift management, as may toothlessness. Fourth, if the patient's disease is degenerative, gains may be lost. Fifth, maximum benefit from the lift may require continued adjustment by the prosthodontist and therapy by the speech clinician. Often competence with the lift evolves slowly as the patient also works to improve articulation, modify rate, and so on.

Postural adjustments may also be accomplished surgically or with mechanical distortion, although Gonzalez and Aronson [58] argue that a palatal lift is superior to surgery. Lewy, Cole, and Wepman [98] report successful management of one flaccid dysarthric with injection of Teflon along Passavant's line. Johns, in Chapter 3 of this volume, discusses pharyngeal flap management at some length. Mechanical distortion of the palate occasioned by turning the head to the side of weakness may also reduce hypernasality. None of our patients have transferred gains received in this way, just as they have not transferred gains received by lying down with the head back so that gravity causes the palate to fall back against the pharyngeal wall. Such mechanical distortions may have a primarily diagnostic rather than therapeutic importance.

POSTURE FOR ARTICULATION: CONTEXT FOR TREATMENT. Articulation requires normal function of the jaw, lips, and tongue. Abnormalities of any one can disrupt the speech signal; and if the damage is specific, the speech disruption can be also. For example, facial weakness may affect /p/, /b/, /m/, and /u/ but not /t/ and /k/. Probably the majority of dysarthric speakers have disturbed articulation unless they have a lesion which spares the neural supply to face and tongue.

POSTURE FOR ARTICULATION: TREATMENT PROCEDURES. Postural adjustments are not as numerous as one might expect. The jaw can be artificially elevated by a support extending from under the chin to over the head, a postural adjustment reminiscent of a child receiving the home cure for mumps. Darley, Aronson, and Brown [35] describe inhibiting hyperkinetic movements of the articulators by having patients hold something between their teeth. Putting a bite block between the jaws, thereby propping them apart, may improve articulation by stabilizing the jaw [105, 118]. The most esoteric suggestion of all would be to install a false palate in patients with significant lingual weakness, thereby reducing the distance a weakened tongue must travel. To our knowledge this has not been reported with dysarthric patients, although a variety of devices are being developed for patients with oral, structural differences [40]. Also, it may be possible to begin training of dysarthric patients' articulators by placing them with head bent forward or backward so that gravity aids lingual movements.

Postural adjustments may improve the patient's physiologic support for speech, but their primary effect is to allow the patient to make more effective use of what he or she has. Time spent evaluating and manipulating posture is seldom, if ever, wasted.

MUSCLE TONE: CONTEXT FOR TREATMENT. Muscle tone, described by Darley, Aronson, and Brown [35] as resistance to passive movement, is a consistent background of muscle readiness reflecting, at least in part, the influence of the extrapyramidal system, or what those authors call "the indirect motor system." As such, muscle tone offers a kind of support for skilled movements, or what Darley, Aronson, and Brown describe as "the quick, unsustained, phasic movements" of the direct system.

Muscle tone may be abnormally increased more or less equally across antagonist muscle groups, in which case it is called *rigidity*; or it may be limited to certain muscle groups, usually the flexors, creating a condition called *spasticity*. It may be abnormally reduced, yielding *flaccidity* or *hypotonia*; and, finally, it may wax and wane, being irregularly too great and too little—a condition identified as *dystonia*. Darley, Aronson, and Brown [35] hypothesize that abnormalities of muscle tone almost exclusively affect the phonatory aspects of speech. This may be true, but Kent and Netsell [88] think not and propose instead that all speech movements, and therefore the entire speech process may be affected by abnormal muscle tone. Hunker, Abbs, and Barlow [79] have data suggesting a relationship of rigidity to hypokinesia or reduced range of movement in Parkinson's disease. They are quick to point out, however, that the relationship of rigidity to speech errors has not been established. Spasticity's relationship to coexisting speech abnormalities, such as dysphonia and consonant imprecision, has also not been established [9]. Understandably, treatment is also controversial. A limited treatment literature, mostly anecdotal, describes a variety of methods reputed to have a therapeutic influence on tone, however.

MUSCLE TONE: TREATMENT PROCEDURES. Netsell and Cleeland [129] published a provocative account of successfully using EMG feedback to reduce chronic upper lip hypertonia in one patient with parkinsonism. The patient's upper lip contracted, revealing her gum line and making the production of bilabial sounds impossible. The treatment goal was to teach her normal lip positioning during connected speech. Instrumentation included surface electrodes placed over the levator labii superioris and obicularis oris. Muscle poten-

tials from these sites were fed to a voltage-to-frequency convertor and then to an audio speaker. As electrical activity in these muscles increased, so did an EMG analogue tone permitting instant, unique feedback of the amount of muscle contraction. Nonspeech and speech tasks were specially selected to help the patient learn to inhibit the lip hypertonia systematically while talking. After 5 minutes in the first session, she was able to inhibit the abnormal hypertonus if she was not talking, and at the end of 2½ hours she was beginning to show more normal bilabial gestures even during connected speech. A carryover treatment program is described.

Hand, Burns, and Ireland [63] also had success with a similar type of program and patient. Finley and colleagues [48, 49] found that a program to modify the frontalis muscle hypertonus of children with cerebral palsy had a positive influence on the speech of 7 of the 10 subjects. Rubow et al. [144] reported that modifying the hemifacial spasm of one geriatric speaker was accompanied by significant speech improvement.

Presumably, traditional behavioral methods may also influence both hypertonicity and hypotonicity: Certainly any number of such methods have been recommended. Methods of progressive muscle relaxation [84] for treating spasticity and rigidity have generally enjoyed wider currency in Europe than in America; nonetheless, one can read in American publications about methods for relaxing the articulators, including a method called, simply enough, *jaw shaking* [51]. Reserved for moderate spastic conditions, jaw shaking is nothing more than creating rapid lateral movements of a depressed mandible by shaking one's head. Froeschels [51] says that articulation training should follow the relaxation that moderately hypertonic patients can achieve with the jaw-shaking exercise. Froeschels even describes methods for relaxing the healthy half of the genioglossus muscle (responsible for tongue protrusion), so it is less likely to overwhelm the weakened half in patients with unilateral lingual weakness. Froeschels also defends his familiar "chewing method" for the treatment of mild and moderate hypertonia. That method, which the interested reader can learn about by consulting one of Froeschels' major works [50], exploits the primary function of eating as a way of increasing the patient's physiologic support for speech.

Few would deny that patients (especially if they have abnormally increased muscle tone) perform best if they are at ease, but the majority of American speech pathologists probably limit their treatment of hypertonia to attempts at putting the patient at ease and then get right on with the more comfortable task, for them, of changing skilled movements. We occasionally go beyond building rapport to training in massage and relaxation and have even begun to include jaw shaking and chewing as the first step in modifying articulation deficits that appear clinically to be related, at least in part, to increased muscle tone. Objectively, some patients report the palliative effect of all these activities, but we have not confirmed the results experimentally.

The effects of hypotonia, and probably weakness, can sometimes be modified by teaching the patient to use *increased speaking effort.* Presumably, increased effort is related in both normal and dysarthric speakers to an increased amount of neuromuscular activity across the entire voluntary motor system, although the exact mechanisms of increased effort, even in normal persons, have apparently not been described. Regardless of whether increased speaking effort changes muscle tone or strength or something else, it is accompanied by improved articulatory placement and increased duration of sounds [127]. Our clinical experience suggests that getting dysarthric patients to increase their speaking effort improves their intelligibility if flaccidity and weakness are prominent neuromuscular symptoms.

Treatment begins with a search for proper positioning.* Positioning may mean merely having patients sit more erectly; but more frequently it means having them bear down with their arms against the armrests of their chairs as they begin to speak. It may even involve overhead slings, such as those shown in Figure 2-8, against which the patient can exert a downward force. In early sessions the patient may be aided if the clinician places his or her own hands under the patient's arms (or arm, if the patient can only use one side effectively) and exerts an upward pressure or resistance, while simultaneously telling the patient to push against the clinician. Besides giving the patient a better idea of what is required, such a "hands-on" procedure tells the clinician how much pressure the patient is producing and what, if any, effect increased effort has on the speech signal. Explanations of what the patient is to do accompanied by admonitions to "increase your effort," "pinch off your air," "force your speech," or whatever other

*The treatment of posture and tone overlap.

image seems to help will usually accelerate the patient's learning and carryover. If speech is improved in the increased tone condition, the patient can learn to identify the cues associated with increased speaking effort and to delay speaking until he or she has achieved the optimum background of tone. If the posture or appliances can be abandoned, so much the better; but transfer is infrequent at least in our experience. Being forced permanently to lean forward during speech is not a bad fate if speech is improved.

STRENGTH: CONTEXT FOR TREATMENT. Strength refers to the ability of a muscle to do work, move structures, and hold them against resistance. Reduced strength contributes to impaired speech in patients with flaccid, spastic, spastic-flaccid, and hypokinetic dysarthria [131]. Except in patients with flaccid dysarthria, where only one cranial nerve may be involved (for example, Bell's palsy or recurrent nerve paralysis), the weakness in the dysarthrias (including flaccid dysarthria) is usually generalized and thereby is an influence on all parts of the speech production system. Unfortunately, while the importance of muscle strengthening can hardly be denied, the speech pathologist's role in such strengthening and the proper methods for accomplishing it remain controversial.

Shelton [154] opposed muscle strengthening by speech pathologists, primarily because the efficacy of strengthening exercises had not been demonstrated. He would assign muscle strengthening to the physical therapist and restrict the speech pathologist to the treatment of such skilled activities as articulation. In addition, he enjoined speech pathologists to help measure the effectiveness of strengthening exercises, and a limited number of speech researchers have taken Shelton's admonishment to collect hard data seriously. For example, the results of efforts to strengthen the soft palate have been reported by Powers and Starr [135], Lubit and Larsen [101], Berry et al. [11], Yules and Chase [175], and Massengill et al. [108]. Netsell and Daniel [130] report on three lip-strengthening sessions with one dysarthric person. These representative studies are inadequate to the task of resolving our ignorance, however, because the authors studied few dysarthric subjects, used very different techniques, and produced a handful of inconsistent results. Massengill et al. [108] showed a therapeutic effect, as did Netsell and Daniel [130]. Powers and Starr [135] did not. Nonetheless, the studies are important because they blaze the trail other research must take. In the interim, some clinicians will continue to use muscle-strengthening exercises on faith; others will scorn them for the same reason.

Faith is not the weakest of all possible bases for use of a procedure as long as the faithful do not act as if they had proof. We have no proof, but we do use a number of muscle-strengthening activities in cases of weakness if the weakness is contributing to the speech symptom complex—if it is evident from trial treatment that change in posture, muscle tone (effort), and the various speech processes (respiration, phonation, resonation, articulation, and prosody) will not leave the patient satisfactorily intelligible, if we have a reasonable assurance that the patient can remain in treatment for several weeks, and if the patient demonstrates an ability to carry out assignments independently. While our clinical experience prepares us to accept the observation of Powers and Starr [135]—that the greater the inadequacy (they were speaking of velopharyngeal inadequacy), the poorer the prognosis—we do not reserve muscle strengthening with such patients until after all other methods have failed, as is recommended by Darley, Aronson, and Brown [35]. Nor do we follow Froeschels [51] and delay work on speech symptoms until "the best possible training of the muscles involved has been achieved" (p. 313). Instead we make simultaneous efforts to improve strength and speech. Patients with severe dysarthria and very little physiologic support for speech, however, experience many more strengthening exercises than speech drills.

For muscle strengthening we rely on isotonic and isometric exercise. *Isotonic* exercises are repetitive movements without resistance and are especially useful in early sessions with severely involved patients, when the clinician is glad to be able to elicit any movement, no matter how limited in range and force. *Isometric* exercises are movements against resistance; for example, the patient opens his or her mouth while the clinician applies upward pressure against the bottom of the jaw. The goal is increased strength, resulting from overcoming systematically increased resistance. Both types of exercise are appropriate for all the articulators, although the palate, because of its relative inaccessibility and limited sensory system, is somewhat difficult to treat. Very experienced clinicians may want to follow Cole's [29] lead and resist palatal elevations with a specially shaped device that can be inserted in the mouth, behind and above the soft palate, to resist the palate's upward move-

Table 2-5. Summary of the structures and movements potentially requiring muscle strengthening

Structure	Movements
Jaw	Protrusion
	Elevation
	Depression
Lips	Lip rounding
	Lip spreading
	Lip closing
	Lip opening
Tongue	Protrusion
	Retraction
	Elevation of tip
	Elevation of blade
Palate	Elevation

ments. We have no experience with this method, nor do we use electric stimulation. The interested reader can consult Brodnitz [23], Baker and Sokoloff [8], and Yules and Chase [175] for descriptions of that treatment. The lips are more accessible and the instrumentation and methodology for their strengthening have been described by Netsell and Daniel [130].

The muscles to be strengthened are determined by the distribution of each patient's weakness and the requirements of speech. If a patient's lips are adequately strong for undisturbed speech, they need not be strengthened. If the tongue tip is adequate to the production of apicoalveolar sounds but the tongue blade is overmatched by the requirements of producing /k/ and /g/, then only the tongue blade needs to be treated. Table 2-5 shows the structures and speech-related movements that might be treated with exercise.

STRENGTH: TREATMENT PROCEDURES. Muscle strengthening begins with an explanation of rationale, methods, and possible outcome along with a demonstration of any special tools. Baseline testing, perhaps in the form of videotaping, should precede drill. Ideally, the muscle activity required by the exercises should exceed that required by nontherapy activities [69]. However, since speech pathologists generally have no way of knowing the forces and ranges characteristic of the patient's chewing and swallowing, they usually must be content with merely exhorting the patient to extend the articulators as far as possible (in the case of isotonics) and to move against the resistance as vigorously as possible (in the case of isometrics). If resistance is used, the *amount* and *duration* are systematically increased as is the *number of repetitions* of a given movement. The patient should not be exhausted by the drill, but the majority of clinicians probably err on the side of too little rather than too much. Generally patients can tell the clinician whether they have had too much or too little; we need only remember to ask.

For reasons no more sophisticated than convenience, we usually begin the actual strengthening movements in groups of 5 to 10 with a short pause between each member of the group and longer pauses between sets. Each muscle group receives 1 or 2 minutes of therapy at a time unless the patient is very weak, in which case only a few seconds may be spent with each structure. If several muscle groups are being treated simultaneously, the therapy can be rotated among them several times in a session.

Accessibility of the jaw makes it easy to treat. An isotonic exercise can be created by merely instructing the patient to lower or protrude the jaw as far as possible. The clinician can place his or her hand under the patient's chin to resist opening, in front of the chin to resist protrusion, and in the middle to resist closing. An elastic band over the head and under the chin can be used for home practice.

The lips are also relatively easy. The patient can begin with a series of active puckering and smiling movements. Clinicians can then use their fingers to actively oppose any of the four basic lip movements: rounding, spreading, closing, and opening. Devices more ingenious and portable than fingers have sometimes been used in lip strengthening as well. According to Peacher [134], Froeschels, for example, had a set of different-sized corks that the patient was required to hold firmly between the lips. The drill began with small ones and advanced to large ones as the patient's strength increased. We have also seen plastic lip-shaped devices that can be placed in the buccal cavity between the lips and cheeks laterally and the teeth medially. A string fastened to the device will allow the clinician to pull against it while the patient tries to retain the device behind the lips.

If lingual training begins with passive movements, the patient can be instructed to protrude and elevate the tongue. Tongue movements can be resisted by a tongue blade or a device specially shaped to the contours of the tongue. Protrusion and elevation of the tip and blade are the easiest movements to strengthen with systematically increased resistance. Resisting retraction is harder,

but possible. Unilateral weakness may be reduced by having the patient push against a tongue blade placed along the margin of the stronger side. (See Froeschels [51] for a more elaborate discussion of lingual strengthening.)

The palate has received the greatest attention, probably because the child with a cleft palate has long been a popular candidate for treatment. Massage and stimulation of the soft palate to increase its activity may be accomplished by a device such as the Lubit palatal exerciser [101]. The exerciser is an inflatable bulb attached to a bite block, which allows the bulb to be positioned below the palate and alternately inflated (thereby stretching and lifting the palate) and deflated. Berry et al. [11] report improved velar function and intelligibility in two dysarthric patients after a period of treatment like that recommended by Lubit and Larsen [101]. The palate can also be exercised manually. First the clinician and then the patient can massage and lift the palate with gentle anterior to posterior, medial to lateral movements of a finger ensheathed in a finger cot. A period of desensitization before actual massage may be necessary. The efficacy of massage has seldom been reported for a group of dysarthric patients, and the exact mechanisms by which increased function is achieved have not been described, at least to our knowledge. Cole [29] does explain that such exercises attempt "to bring under voluntary control motor acts which are essentially involuntary and reflexive in nature" (p. 253).

Respiratory muscles can be strengthened by the physical therapist as part of the total program to improve balance, transferring, sitting, and walking. Nothing more will be said about strengthening of respiratory muscles.

Behavioral methods, such as those just described, lack specificity because a clinician and patient have to make judgments about fleeting, tenuous changes in muscle activity. Often neither the clinician nor the patient has any very good notions about whether one response was weaker or stronger than another unless the two responses differed considerably. Instrumentation can reduce this subjectivity and hasten the learning, as Netsell [124] and Netsell and Daniel [130] have demonstrated in an experimental lip-strengthening program using EMG. Netsell and his colleagues [124, 130] place electrodes on the upper lip and with special, reasonably inexpensive equipment convert the muscle potentials into an audible tone; the greater the muscle potential, the higher the sound. The patient's task is to compress the lips and keep the tone in the high-frequency part of the range for progressively longer periods. The instrument can be adjusted so that it takes increasingly greater activity to produce the high-frequency sound. In training the lips, a bite block is placed between the teeth so the mastication muscles do not contribute to the EMG signal. Presumably other clinicians are developing similar programs for other articulators. Until such programs become popular, clinicians and patients will have to rely on their own capricious criteria and sensorimotor systems, a fate preferable (in our opinion) to the abandonment of attempts to improve the patient's physiologic support for speech by increasing strength.

Muscle-strengthening exercises are easily abused, and this abuse takes many forms: (1) trying to improve muscle strength when the medical diagnosis, as in myasthenia gravis, makes it inappropriate; (2) delaying direct speech training until muscle strengthening is "finished"; (3) failing to require systematic homework and using muscle-strengthening methods when other potentially more useful ones are available; (4) further reducing a patient's physiologic support by increasing the strength of certain muscles, so that they overwhelm the efforts of the others.

With Froeschels [51] and Canter [28] we believe that dysarthria treatment should first concentrate on improving the patient's physiologic support for speech: improving posture, muscle tone, and strength. We would not think of forcing a hearing-impaired patient to sit with his or her ear pasted to a loudspeaker if the patient's hearing could be improved by surgery or a hearing aid. The dysarthric person is no different. When physiologic support is improved or at least improving, training in skilled movements can begin.*

Goal 3: Modification of Respiration

CONTEXT FOR TREATMENT. Respiration supplies the energy for speech. According to Hixon [75], "the respiratory pump participates in speech by displacing structures, creating pressures behind valves, and generating flows through constrictions within the larynx and upper airways" (p. 99). Hixon's excellent chapter on normal respiration is useful clin-

ical reading, and the facts of normal respiration as he outlines them will not be reviewed here with four exceptions—exceptions of considerable treatment significance. In normal speakers the muscles of inhalation continue to contract well into the exhalation phase of breathing as a check against the nonmuscle forces of exhalation. Nonmuscle forces during the first part of the exhalation stage of respiration can contribute significantly to respiratory drive, especially at high lung volumes. Vital capacity in normal speakers is not significantly related to speech adequacy; if one has enough air for life, one has enough for some speech. No one pattern of speech respiration is best; but a pattern, regardless of type, should be efficient and not productive of abnormal tensions.

These observations on respiration are provided as a rationale for what we have chosen to emphasize (which is to say, what we do clinically) and what we try to avoid in the treatment of dysarthric respiration. We will scrupulously eschew reference to vital capacity, for example, for as Hardy [66] has suggested, reduced vital capacity is less crucial in the dysarthrias than is inefficient use of the exhalatory airstream because of weakness or incoordination of all speech structures. Also, we have earnestly avoided references to breathing types (with one exception, which will be discussed) in the hope of producing a relevant treatment for respiration that does not spark a déja vu of lying on one's back while counting to 100 and watching a descending book placed beforehand on one's belly.

TREATMENT PROCEDURES. If the patient has reduced respiratory support for speech because of muscle weakness (as is frequently encountered in severe dysarthria after cerebrovascular accident and trauma and in the later stages of degenerative disease) or incoordination, the clinician is faced with choices. Phonatory, resonatory, and articulatory valves can be improved, thereby reducing the demands on respiration; muscle strengthening (a physical therapist may handle the strengthening) can be started, while the patient is simultaneously taught how to make the best use of his or her residual respiratory support; or a frontal assault can be planned against all portions of the speech-production mechanism. We usually opt for the frontal assault but spend the largest portion of each session on improving respiratory muscle function.

Several tasks proceed more or less simultaneously. One is to make all appropriate postural

*If a patient can only be seen for a few days, as is frequently the case, the clinician's only alternative may be to teach a few postural adjustments and how the patient can increase his or her own background of tone. Brief stays generally frustrate the learning of skilled movements.

adjustments;* especially important is the fitting of a palatal lift if the palate is weak and if the patient is well enough and strong enough to tolerate the procedure. Another task is to begin trunk and speech muscle strengthening, perhaps in cooperation with the physical therapist; and another is to increase the patient's background of effort. Patients with significant respiratory muscle weakness will usually be confined to a wheelchair or bed. If they are in a wheelchair, they can learn to bear down against its arms as they begin practice and, even better, the clinician can take one of the patient's hands and then encourage the patient to push. Such pushing can be reflexive if the clinician exerts significant but controlled force against the patient's own hand and arm.

With these steps begun,† the patient can begin learning *controlled exhalation*: control means predictable production of consistent, low-pressure exhalation over a period of time. The three previously described steps are an appropriate beginning, primarily for those patients with severe weakness; the patient whose problem is primarily or exclusively incoordination may well profit from beginning treatment with the learning of controlled exhalations.

A number of reasonably simple biofeedback devices can be summoned to the fray. Netsell [124] introduced us to what was once the simplest of these instruments, a water manometer consisting of a polyethylene tube, ¼ inch in inside diameter, which is filled with colored water and attached along a centimeter rule or graph paper calibrated in centimeters (Fig. 2-11). The simplest use of this instrument is to have the patient blow into one end of the tube, thereby displacing the water. The centimeter rule allows the patient and the clinician to know the amount of air pressure in centimeters of water being generated. A bleed valve, 1½ inches long with an inside diameter of ⅜ inch, can be positioned in the corner of the patient's mouth, so that he or she has to continue blowing and cannot merely imprison the water after it has reached a certain pressure. A Y-shaped fitting with the bleed tube leading from one branch of the Y and the water-filled tube leading from the other is prefer-

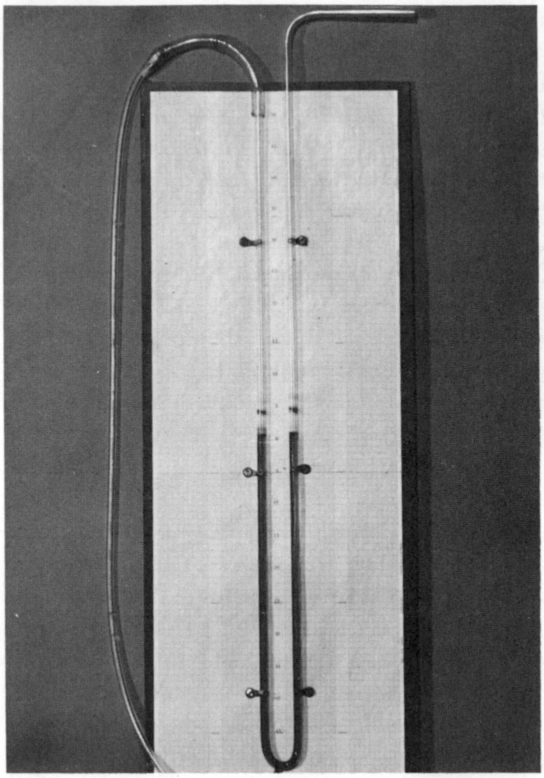

Fig. 2-11. Water manometer for measuring the amount of air pressure in centimeters of water the patient can generate.

able for most dysarthric patients, because it reduces the number of tubes they must hold between their lips from two to one. By blowing into the bottom of the Y, a dysarthric patient's breath stream is automatically divided, so a portion flows out of the bleed valve and a portion flows into the tube containing the water. Hixon, Putnam, and Wilson [76] have assembled an even simpler device using a glass of water and a straw.

Whichever device one uses, the treatment involves having the patient systematically increase the amount of air pressure he or she can produce and the duration of time in which it can be produced. Normal speech is produced with a subglottal breath pressure of 5 to 10 cm of water, and normal breath groups are typically less than 5 seconds in duration. Five centimeters of water pressure for 5 seconds ("five for five") then becomes the patient's goal as he or she works with the manometer [124]. If the patient can already produce normal values, he or she probably does not need this program, because sufficient respiratory support for speech exists. The

---

*We do not resort to girdling or other previously described postural aids until active methods to improve respiratory function have failed. We can imagine instances in which a clinician might want to teach the patient to use these prostheses in between treatment sessions, however.

†Muscle strengthening and even the fitting of a palatal lift take time, and we do not want to imply that controlled exhalations must wait.

patient's speech probably will not be normally loud but it will be loud enough to allow the clinician to change the therapeutic focus to other targets. If the patient does not approximate these normal values, the clinician settles for the patient's best production and tries systematically to help him or her expand both pressure and duration.

An air-pressure transducer coupled to an oscilloscope is more elaborate and more expensive; it is also superior to the water manometer. The oscilloscope screen can provide the patient with a pressure target, which he or she then tries to match by exhaling into the bleed tube and the tube leading to the pressure transducer. The airstream flowing into the pressure transducer can be made to deflect a signal on the oscilloscope screen, and the amount of deflection represents the amount of air pressure generated by the patient. The oscilloscope can be adjusted so that another signal representing the amount of air pressure the patient is trying to achieve sweeps across the screen at regular intervals. The patient tries to bring the signal responsive to his or her own air pressure to the level of the target (Fig. 2-12). The grid lines on the face of the oscilloscope can be calibrated to represent a number of different pressures and durations. Feedback, as provided by the oscilloscope, is more trenchant than that provided by the manometer.

The unique visual feedback of results provided by the manometer or the oscilloscope helps patients improve control of respiratory muscle activity without their ever having to be told about the mechanics of respiration. If a patient fails to make rather rapid gains in pressure and duration, he or she may be helped by instructions to take in more air. The clinician may even have to resort to placing his or her hands on the patient's belly and chest and "guiding" these structures with manual pressure. The carryover of increased respiratory support from nonspeech tasks to speech tasks may be enhanced by having the patient begin attending to the look and feel of control. Nothing guarantees that a patient producing 5 cm of water pressure for 5 seconds will be able to transfer that ability to speaking automatically. In the absence of data, one can only hypothesize that training with the manometer improves strength and coordination of the respiratory muscles and improves the patient's use of whatever background of strength and coordination is left.

Oral weakness, incoordination, abnormal reflexes, or involuntary movements may frustrate some patients' attempts to use instruments. Such patients

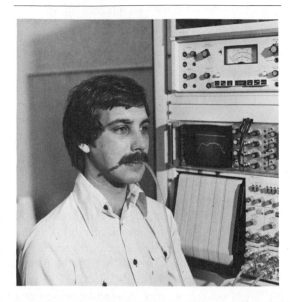

Fig. 2-12. Pressure-matching task with visual feedback provided by an oscilloscope.

may learn controlled exhalation by trying systematically to increase the length of isolated speech sounds while keeping their intensity and quality constant; this can also be the first carryover step for patients whose initial training was instrumental. A stopwatch, a tape recorder, and the patient and clinician's ears replace the manometer as a provider of the knowledge of results.

The stimuli should be sounds over which the patient has at least some articulatory control; the /f/ is sometimes a good first sound perhaps because the jaw, which is a resilient articulator, contributes a major portion of /f/'s production. Some patients will be so severely involved that /a/, some other vowel, or nasals /m/ and /n/ are the only sounds they can prolong. The procedure is to teach the patient to produce the sound at a constant intensity and quality for increasingly longer periods. Severely disabled patients will be capable of only a second or so of prolongation with significant fluctuations in loudness and quality. It is unnecessary (probably even contratherapeutic) to turn this training into an endurance contest; durations of 30, 40, and 50 seconds, even if our patients could produce them (which they cannot), are not essential to adequate speech—*control is*. And again, it is control that the clinician tries to teach.

During speech training as well as during nonspeech training, clinicians should make free use of their hands as they try to coax patients to greater control. Systematic manual pressure against the belly may aid the patient in exhalation, and an initially strong pressure that is systematically reduced may help the patient with inhalation.

Earlier we said that biofeedback seems to help patients improve respiratory support even if they understand nothing specifically of respiratory mechanisms; the same is true of a program using speech. If patients are to hold their gains from an instrumental program or from a program using sound prolongation and then transfer them to connected speech, they can profit from learning to identify the cues associated with improved function. The patient may be thrusting the sternum forward and letting it relax very slowly, or may be thrusting the belly outward on inhalation. These are movements that can be monitored visually or with the hands. Any manifestation of normal "checking" or controlling of exhalation, such as a feeling of increased tension in the larynx or articulators or a change in body posture, can also be highlighted.

The amount of air the patient takes in may be important therapeutically, although we have not experimented much with this. According to Hixon [75], at high lung volumes the natural recoil forces of the breathing mechanism exert significant drive to force air from the lungs. If these forces are not checked by continued contraction of muscles used for inhalation, the result can be an inefficient burst of air through the speech system, because the mechanism's recoil drives the air forcefully from the lungs. It may make sense, therefore, for some patients to learn to use mid rather than high lung volumes for speaking. At mid volumes, recoil forces are decreased, and the demand on the muscles used for inhalation is also decreased. All this is to say that teaching patients themselves to "blow up like a puffer" may be the wrong thing to do. Trial and error will tell you how much air patients can control during both nonspeech and speech drills.

Probably no more than 30 or so sessions should be spent in trying to improve controlled exhalation with either the biofeedback or speech methods, and even then simultaneous muscle-strengthening and articulation training programs can be proceeding. After about 30 sessions the patient will have developed an idea of control and will be working up to a level sufficient to support at least some speech or will have demonstrated that, for whatever reason, he or she can muster no more respiratory support for speech.

After the patient has learned what appears to be his or her maximum stable exhalation on non-speech or sound-in-isolation speech tasks, he or she can begin learning to carry over the gains to connected speech by expanding the number of sounds practiced, by producing sounds in series (/f-f-f-f-f/), by combining consonants with vowels (/f:: a::/, /f:: a:: f::/), and by combining several sounds (/f: a: z: a: θ/). That the durations of sounds in isolation and the numbers of syllables that can be produced will vary because of differences in the air pressure and flow characteristics among sounds is important for both patient and clinician to know, because the idea is to help the patient learn consistent quality rather than constant length. After the patient exhibits control of sound combinations, these combinations can be practiced with different stress and intonation patterns, thereby reinforcing the importance of the suprasegmentals and of prosody early on. During this carryover stage, the clinician and the patient will learn how many syllables can be produced per exhalation; this number (plus or minus a few syllables) may well be transferred to meaningful, connected speech.

Much has been made of *abnormal breathing patterns* in patients with dysarthria and in those with most other disorders as well. The one pattern we try to modify by direct work on exhalation is the one we have most frequently encountered in the spinal form of multiple sclerosis. Occasionally these patients, in an apparent effort to continue producing phrases of normal length, may adopt a pattern of upper thoracic and clavicular breathing and extreme neck, laryngeal, and face tension. The result is a harsh, high-pitched voice that is inadequately loud and one that is characterized by pitch variations.

The therapy with these persons is variable but has three general steps. We discussed the first in the section on posture. A girdle or a device that the patient can lean forward into can replace weakened belt muscles. The second step is to shift the patient back to a more central form of inhalation, even though there may be less air for talking as a result. This shift will be aided by the postural adjustment. The third step is to help the patient learn to inhale oftener and produce fewer syllables on each exhalation. As one patient said, "You want me to speak a page, not a book." These changes may cause a reduction in the facial and laryngeal tensions, and voice and resonance may improve.

These compensations are not easily learned. First, the patient needs counseling to help him or her understand what is being traded: length will be sacrificed, quality will be enhanced. Then the patient needs systematic drill in transferring the inhalatory function more centrally. This can be learned by instruction and by the clinician's placing his or her hands on the patient's abdomen and pressing and releasing with each inhalation and exhalation. Once the more central pattern is established, it can be practiced with short utterances. Words and phrases made of laterals, plosives, and low front, mid, and back vowels may be good materials for this practice, just as they are for transferring improved respiratory support to connected speech. When the patient learns the central control, he or she then needs to learn the maximum number of syllables he or she can produce. Finally, practice is needed in learning the best phrasing for a wide variety of sentence types. We cannot emphasize enough that these are difficult lessons to learn.

Lessons about improved respiratory support are also difficult to carry over outside the clinic. Rubow and Swift [145] may have solved the problem. They report on a wearable microcomputer that samples voice intensity via a throat microphone, informs the speaker when intensity has fallen below a criterion level, and accumulates the percent of speaking time that a speaker spends above any given loudness criterion. They tell of its successful use with one patient having parkinsonian dysarthria. The patient's loudness was first improved in the clinic with instrumental methods like those already described. Transfer outside the clinic was accomplished with the microcomputer.

Training in respiration becomes speech training as soon as speech responses replace nonspeech. And, because all dysarthria treatment emphasizes coordination of subsystems, training in respiration continues with greater or lesser emphasis until treatment is discontinued. As treatment advances and as the patient achieves the best respiratory support for speech his or her system will tolerate, the emphasis shifts; articulation or some other process is emphasized. Even then, however, refresher courses in controlled exhalation can be useful.

Goal 4: Modification of Phonation

CONTEXT FOR TREATMENT. Because of the complexity of the larynx or because of some dimly recalled tradition of differentiating isolated vocal-fold paralysis from the more often generalized paralytic conditions encountered in the dysarthrias, the description and treatment of voice defects secondary to vocal-fold paralysis have appeared almost solely in books devoted exclusively to voice disorders. Generally these discussions have been lim-

ited to unilateral flaccid paralysis. We will neither summarize that material, nor expand it; rather this section proposes limited guidelines about therapy for those dysphonias that are part of a broader dysarthric symptom complex. The reader should consult standard voice textbooks [5, 21, 31, 59, 165] to supplement the content of this section.

The main laryngeal movement abnormalities in the dysarthrias are hyperadduction, hypoadduction, and poorly coordinated laryngeal movements. The type of therapy employed depends on the type of abnormality and on the importance of the laryngeal abnormality to the entire symptom complex, to the patient, and to the intelligibility of his or her speech.

TREATMENT PROCEDURES. What Darley, Aronson, and Brown [35] call strained-strangled dysphonia in spastic dysarthria and the harshness that may also be present in some dysarthric types are not especially disruptive of intelligibility, and our tendency has been to ignore these dysphonias with only one or two exceptions, which will be described. Weakness and laryngeal hypoadduction may be more disruptive to the speech signal, so our own and other writers' techniques for treating these deficits are reviewed briefly. Incoordination seldom seems to produce significant perceptual symptoms, and therefore just as seldom warrants therapy. An exception is laryngeal incoordination resulting in voiced-voiceless substitutions. Treating voiced-voiceless substitutions is discussed in the section on articulation. More thorough discussions of instrumental and behavioral treatments for the dysarthric larynx appear in Rosenbek and Netsell [142] and in Murry [117].

If the harsh or strained-strangled voice is symptomatic of extreme laryngeal tension, relaxation of supralaryngeal muscles can be given a trial. Short periods of simple manual massage or vibratory massage in the area of the genihyoid, mylohyoid, and digastric muscles may be especially useful. After a period of massage, and at such time as the larynx feels "loose" and vowels can be produced with improved quality, syllables, words, and phrases can be practiced. If better voice results, massage and relaxation techniques, such as those discussed by Moncur and Brackett [114] and Boone [21], may be employed for short periods each day and especially at the beginning of each treatment period.

Because bilateral adductor paralysis is frequently part of the total flaccid dysarthria symptom complex, some discussion of its treatment is warranted.

Writers generally are pessimistic about the efficacy of treatment for bilateral adductor paralysis [21], and most seem to recommend a more or less common set of methods. Froeschels, Kastein, and Weiss [52] recommend a pushing exercise for such cases and report good success in about 40 patients. Their push method is simple: The patient raises clenched fists to the level of the chest and then is instructed to "push his arms down in one quick, elastic sweep" (p. 365). Boone [21] also discusses the push method and recommends vigorous downward movements paired with selected speech sound production. To cooperate, a patient quite obviously needs arm strength, and many patients who might otherwise profit from the treatment lack this crucial prerequisite.

Our own approach is very similar in that we first try to place the patient in a posture characterized by as much tone as possible. Depending on upper-extremity strength, the best posture may be one of pushing down against the arms or pulling up against the bottom of a chair. If a patient's extremities are severely weakened, overhead straps, such as those shown in Figure 2-8, can be employed. As shown, the patient's arms can be elevated and he or she can then exert some downward pressure against these slings by using gravity and perhaps proximal arm strength. Such activities may heighten reflexive laryngeal adduction, as it does in the normal person when lifting or straining for any other purpose.

If the laryngeal valve is the only defective one, the patient can begin adding sound production as soon as the background of tone is set. Then the patient can be moved systematically through a series of traditional steps, wherein he or she gradually abandons the facilitating posture while trying to hold voice quality constant. If the patient requires an overhead sling, he or she can continue using it as a facilitator, although perhaps to progressively lesser degrees as treatment progresses.

If speech processes in addition to phonation are involved, the patient can be encouraged to prepare for speaking by "bearing down" with all the speech production muscles. Practice can then center on all processes simultaneously. Good speech materials for this practice are the voiced plosives, especially the /b/ and /d/, and the vowels. Other sound combinations can be added, beginning with the other plosives if the patient can produce them relatively well. If not, the patient can move to fricatives, such as the /f/ and /v/ or /s/ and /z/, depending on which are produced most competently.

The goal is to help the patient learn the maximum control of exhaled air by exploiting basic physiologic processes (the sphincteric action of the larynx) and by forcing all speech valves to perform with as much strength as possible. Getting the patient to produce longer strings of controlled syllables systematically is an easily identified and measured goal. An example of such a systematic progression is this: /aɪ/ /aɪdu/ /aɪdʊlt/ /aɪdʊlttudeɪ/ /aɪdʊlttudeɪtu/.

We avoid trying to increase the background of effort with spastic patients, unless they have significant weakness, and with flaccid patients who have myasthenia gravis. Exertions of the type described may cause further reduction in the physiologic support of speech for these groups.

Laryngeal and respiratory control of air for speech may be improved with a matching task similar to that described for modifying air pressure. Using a pneumotachygraph coupled to an airflow transducer, the patient's airflow can be amplified and displayed on an oscilloscope screen. The patient can be instructed to match target airflows while producing selected speech stimuli (because airflow differs for different sounds, the target flows will also). Some patients will be forced to learn to produce reduced airflows, while others may have to learn to achieve increased airflows. Because it is possible to control airflow using only respiratory muscles, clinicians experienced in this treatment monitor respiratory function simultaneously with laryngeal function.

Goal 5: Modification of Resonance

CONTEXT FOR TREATMENT. What a listener defines as normal resonance results primarily from the volume, shape, and surfaces of the vocal-tract structures; the size of the mouth opening; and the linkage of the nasal cavity with the rest of the vocal tract. Abnormal tongue positioning, too much or too little tension in the articulatory muscles, and inappropriate or incomplete action of the velopharyngeal mechanism produce the resonance abnormalities characteristic of the dysarthrias.

If the palate is weak or incoordinated, hypernasality results either as a constant or intermittent symptom. Important therapeutically are the cause and severity of the hypernasality and its contribution to the patient's total symptom picture. If the hypernasality is severe and is contributing to deficits in other speech processes, a palatal lift is indicated. If the palatal dysfunction is mild or inconsistent, muscle strengthening may be tried concurrently with other activities to improve palatal function. Resonance abnormality resulting from faulty tongue positioning can be modified by traditional articulation therapy and will be discussed only briefly in this section.

If a postural adjustment is unsuccessful or impossible, and if the clinician chooses to do anything specifically about the velopharyngeal dysfunction, the clinician is left with biofeedback or behavioral methods. We have often opted for increasing background of effort and improving articulation, the suprasegmentals, and prosody, all the while ignoring the velopharynx, although we might be influencing it indirectly. It seems important for clinicians who would modify dysarthric palatal function to remind themselves constantly that most of what is known about modifying resonance has been provided by clinicians and researchers of children with cleft palates. As a result, clinicians working with dysarthric patients must try to generalize to their patients from data collected on persons different in age (often) and very different in velopharyngeal anatomy and physiology. Such generalizations, including our own, are tenuous indeed.

TREATMENT PROCEDURES. A palatal training program typically begins wtih increasing the patient's awareness of the velopharyngeal system and activity in that system. Shelton et al. [155] argue that the palate is meagerly supplied with sensory end organs, that awareness of palatal movement is skimpy, and that programs depending on developing palatal awareness are risky.

The methods for supplementing or circumventing meager tactile-kinesthetic cues are many and often ingenious. Consider these examples. Yules and Chase [175] discuss developing awareness of the palate and palatal movement by stimulating the patient's palate and anterior pillar with an ac electric current as the patient says /a/. In their program patients also learned to watch themselves in a mirror during the stimulation. They report that patients with cleft palates developed palatal awareness with these methods, which was then transferred to connected speech tasks. A method that may help in very mild cases of weakness and that requires only inexpensive props is palatal massage combined with speech attempts. In this therapy the clinician and then the patient massage—

anterior to posterior and medial to lateral—and gently lift the soft palate while the patient attempts a series of palatal elevations either with or without accompanying vowel production. The massage and lifting should be done gently with a finger dressed in a finger cot. After a short period of massage, the patient can be instructed to elevate the palate away from the stroking finger and to try to perceive both the broken contact between finger and palate and the reduced hypernasality if the elevation is accompanied by speech. The palatal massage can be complemented by observation in a mirror.

A number of visual feedback devices (other than the mirror) may be used to help the patient improve velopharyngeal function. Visual feedback devices range in sophistication and cost, and while only a few of them have been used in controlled treatment studies with dysarthric patients, all have promise.

The simplest visual feedback devices responsive to airflow have existed in the clinical repertoire for decades: a piece of fluff on a flat surface or a metal mirror that will fog in the presence of nasal airflow. The difficulty with such devices is their lack of calibration and their insensitivity. It is patently impossible to agree on units of fluff displacement, for example, and both fluff and mirror have to be positioned just so to register airflow. Finally, the image of nasal flow they project is fleeting.

More sophisticated instruments, some of them inexpensive, are preferred. The simplest is the "scape-scope" described by Shprintzen, McCall, and Skolnick [157]. The scape-scope is a polyethylene cylinder containing a piston. One end is perforated and a long Y-shaped hose enters the cylinder at the other. The hose is fitted with nasal olives that allow it to be inserted into the patient's nostrils. Nasal airflow causes the piston to rise in the cylinder, and if the cylinder has marks at intervals, the relative amount of flow can be noted across trials. Such a device can be assembled for a few dollars and has the advantage of being quantifiable.

More elaborate airflow and air-pressure transducers, if attached to an oscilloscope or some other display device, accomplish the same ends as the scape-scope but have the advantage of being more accurate and versatile. Collins et al. [30] simultaneously monitored nasal airflow and intraoral air pressure for single words as produced by two patients with mixed dysarthria and hypernasality. A single sensor that represented both flow and pressure was presented on an oscilloscope, and the patients were given a progression of targets for both flow and pressure that required them to maintain their respiratory support at one level while simultaneously reducing their nasal flow. The two patients improved on both trained and untrained items.

The panendoscope is demonstratedly effective in teaching normal speakers discrete, volitional palatal control [156]. The panendoscope allows for projection of an image of the soft palate onto a screen that the subject can then watch. It is like watching oneself on videotape, and its potential in dysarthria therapy may be great.

Regardless of the feedback aid used, stimuli appropriate to each patient will need to be selected and ordered. The continuum described by Shprintzen, McCall, and Skolnick [157] is a good model of stimulus selection and ordering. They use their scape-scope only with persons capable of achieving velopharyngeal closure during whistling or blowing. They begin their treatment by having the patient (with scape-scope in place) combine either a whistle or blow with voicing. If nasal flow is zero, they drop the whistle or blow and try to teach the patient prolonged, nonnasal /i/. This sound is next joined by other nonnasal sounds in words and phrases.

Since velopharyngeal incompetence in dysarthric patients is by no means unitary, exact stimulus selection is ill advised. As a natural inclination, most clinicians would probably begin with stimuli on which the patient had only a bit of inadequacy and try, with practice, to move the patient to progressively more taxing stimuli, while all the time keeping him or her successful. Plosives and low vowels may be good early stimuli; fricatives and high vowels and consonant clusters, such as /sn/ and /sm/, might better be reserved until later. Learning of improved velar function can also be enhanced by the contrast drill, which requires the patient to produce pairs of words, such as *meat-pete*; *me-pea*; *my-pie*, first in isolation and then in phrases.

Improving velopharyngeal competence is usually complicated by the presence of other, sometimes more serious, symptoms. One major implication of multiple symptoms is that the prognosis for improving velar valving is guarded unless the coexisting symptoms are few. Another implication is that one seldom has the leisure of working on the palate to the exclusion of other valves. Our compromise is first to get patients in the best posture and teach them to enhance their background of effort. When this is accomplished and respiration is improved (if it needs to be, and if improve-

ment is possible) a treatment to improve articulation, the suprasegmentals, prosody, and resonation can be initiated more or less simultaneously. In actual practice, the resonance abnormality usually receives the least attention, because by itself it seems to have a less potent influence on intelligibility* than do articulation, the suprasegmentals, and prosody.

Regardless of the methods, stimuli, or place of the velopharyngeal treatment emphasis in the overall treatment plan, velar control must be transferred to the auditory system. The transfer can result from traditional behavioral methods: The patient must learn to hear the difference, with all this implies about the pairing of auditory and visual (if a visual program was used) feedback.

Goal 6: Modification of Articulation

In patients with dysarthria, a favorite target of speech pathology has been and continues to be defective articulation. Two forces are responsible for this attention: Speech pathology departments heavily emphasize articulation, and dysarthria has usually been equated with defective articulation. Change is in the air: Articulation is being forced to share its popularity with other speech processes and especially with prosody, and dysarthria has come to mean speech—not articulation—deficit. It is hoped that what follows reflects at least something of the emerging attitude.

CONTEXT FOR TREATMENT. Articulation is the process of changing the size and shape of the vocal tract with movements of the larynx, pharynx, velum, jaw, tongue, cheeks, and lips. Since respiration supplies the airstream necessary to make these changes in size and shape audible, articulation as a process results from activity of the entire speech production system. This contribution of the entire system to what is called *articulation* serves as a reminder to clinicians that neuromuscular deficits anywhere along the system can disturb articulation and that repair of articulation may require at least

---

*Netsell [128] is only one author who has demonstrated that velopharyngeal inadequacy may directly influence articulation. Such observations force clinicians to make hard and usually compromising decisions about proper therapeutic targets. Expediency is usually the final arbiter. Most dysarthric patients are unavailable for long-term treatment; the clinician does what he or she can most rapidly. We seem to have had our quickest successes with articulation and suprasegmental training, a pattern no doubt reflecting more on our training than on anything inherent in the dysarthric speech process.

as much attention to points 1, 2, and 3 as to points 4, 5, 6, and 7.

The view that speech results from the combination of individual speech sounds, like a chain created from separate links, is increasingly less popular, but no basic speech unit to replace the sound has the unanimous endorsement of speech scientists [86]. While debate, generation of hypotheses, and testing of hypotheses are the foreground for researchers into normal processes, they can be no more than a muted background for the workaday clinician who is forced to help patients immediately; so clinicians are gamblers. They select certain ideas and the treatment implications of these ideas, then translate them into clinical practice. Fortunately for the patient, the treatment process, including the selection and ordering of stimuli and the specific methods, is much like the human body in that it has a margin of safety: It can survive the mishandling and excesses that come from believing things that are partly or even wholly untrue. What we have selected to emphasize in articulation treatment and the explanations we use to support our decisions are no doubt at least partly wrong. We can only hope that our patients are not endangered by our ignorance.

In our clinical practice we generally emphasize speech movements rather than static postures; we treat syllables rather than sounds. Work with sounds is reserved for severely disabled patients or for patients who may be having atypical difficulty achieving even an approximation of the correct posture for a sound. We recognize and try to capitalize on the influence that sounds exert over each other and on the unequal demands placed on the production system by different movement patterns; we therefore attend to the makeup and ordering of speech stimuli. We try to exploit not only the facilitating interaction of sounds or segments but also the facilitating interaction of the segments and suprasegments: pitch, loudness, articulation time, and pause time. One view of segment and suprasegment relations hold that, like icing on a cake, the suprasegmentals are added as a final touch to the segments. Another view, and perhaps a more satisfactory one because of its concordance with the facts, is that like the herbs in a marinade, the suprasegments and segments blend and mutually influence one another. This interaction view guides much of our discussion of articulation treatment and, in fact, our approach to all dysarthria therapy.

Articulation therapy in the dysarthrias is perhaps more difficult than in some other disorders, because there is no simple set of errors or abnormalities. Symptoms vary among patients and among diagnostic categories. Even when symptoms are similar, the movement deficits underlying them may be different: spasticity and weakness causing the symptoms in one patient and rigidity causing a similar set of symptoms in another, for example. Similarly, dysarthric errors may be independent of phonetic environment in one patient and profoundly influenced by environment in another. The inconsistent articulatory errors of hyperkinetic dysarthria are related to the patient's random, abnormal movements and apparently are little influenced by phonetic variables. On the other hand, phonetic conditions are probably especially potent in spastic, flaccid, hypokinetic [100], and ataxic dysarthria. Finally, stimulus conditions such as imitation may exert unequal influences on the articulation of individual patients. Patients with parkinsonism and dysarthria are often especially good imitators, for example.

All this is by way of orienting the reader to our philosophy of articulation treatment and of convincing or reminding him or her that the therapy to be described will have to be modified, sometimes radically, to fit individual patients. Generalization of anything but a framework and a limited number of techniques for articulation therapy is well-nigh impossible.

TREATMENT PROCEDURES. The aim of articulation treatment with dysarthric patients is to *improve the patient's volitional-purposive control of speech sound production to the limits imposed by his or her physiologic support for speech.* The procedures are only a little different from those for treating other articulation deficits. Dysarthric patients need a set of conditions that allow them to produce the sounds correctly; these conditions can be provided by a series of tasks. The methods for moving the patient along these continua are traditional and include: (1) integral stimulation that is essentially a "Watch me, listen to me, and do what I do" approach; (2) phonetic derivation wherein a target is derived from an intact gesture, behavior, or sound; and (3) phonetic placement, a method accommodating a number of different activities, including using pictures to show articulatory gestures, using description of a gesture, and actually moving the patient's articulators into the correct position for the sound. In all forms of articulation therapy, decisions about methods are reasonably standardized; and a clinician's preference is determined primarily by education and the patient's symptoms. A good rule is *to employ the simplest and most effective method.* Simple integral stimulation is frequently the method of choice.

In addition, clinicians complete all the other activities of traditional behavioral therapy. They provide knowledge of results; they help patients become their own best clinicians; they modify and reorder tasks in response to patient performance; they counsel patients; and they supply explanation, simile, metaphor, and imagery so patients have a better understanding of their goals. Because dysarthric articulation errors are usually part of a larger symptom complex, however, the task continua for treating articulation in patients with dysarthria differs from those appropriate for patients with apraxia and functional articulation problems. The next section describes such task continua construction and emphasizes target and environment selection.

Target refers to both the *nonspeech* (posture, tone, and strength) and *speech symptoms* to be modified. Altering posture, muscle tone, and strength (according to methods already described) will often influence speech, including articulation. What the speech pathologist does best, however, is to modify articulation by concentrating directly on improving skilled movements. Picking the speech targets for such direct work is difficult because more is required than that the clinician merely establish a hierarchy of sounds on which the patient has difficulty and then begin working with the easiest.

The speech targets one chooses depend on the position of articulatory errors in the patient's symptom complex. Seldom will the articulatory errors exist independently of other symptoms; instead, errors will be influenced by the patient's respiratory support, velopharyngeal and laryngeal (the articulatory function of these two valves has been discussed) integrity, suprasegmentals, and prosody. So it may be, as with posture, strength, and tone, that changing respiration, laryngeal and velopharyngeal valving, the suprasegmentals, and prosody will in turn improve articulation. If so, articulation treatment may actually begin as respiratory training or with the effort to slow the patient down.

The speech targets (and this point overlaps with the preceding one) will also be influenced by activities that have come before. If, for example, the patient's respiratory support has been improved and the clinician wants next to transfer the patient's gains to speech, the transfer can be accomplished by speech stimuli heavily laden with plosives. Our experience has been that many dysarthric patients find plosives easier to produce than fricatives, so a dysarthric respiratory system may be less burdened by plosive sounds. If, to take another example, the soft palate has been strengthened, improved velopharyngeal function may be carried over to speech by stimuli that contrast nasal and oral cognates: *pea, me, be; pay, may, bay; pie, my, by;* and so on. In the meanwhile, the rest of articulation training might exclude sounds like /ʃ/ and /s/, which are especially taxing of velar competence and concentrate instead on more forgiving sounds, such as /l/ and /a/.

Especially in patients with severe spastic, flaccid, and spastic-flaccid dysarthrias (and less frequently in other types), the clinician, sooner or later, will have to focus directly on improving the patient's points of articulation. Dysarthric patients will not have forgotten how sounds are made (a frequent observation in apraxia of speech), but their impaired systems will frustrate their attempts to do what they know they should. They will omit sounds; but more frequently they will distort them because in inadequate valving, inappropriate voicing, or generally uncoordinated activity up and down their vocal tract. It is in such cases as these that environment is especially crucial.

Environment refers specifically to the *phonetic context of the target speech sound*: Whether the sound is to be worked on in isolation, in a syllable, word, phrase, or sentence; whether (if in any environment except isolation) the target should release or arrest a syllable; whether nonsense or meaningful stimuli should be used; and what other sounds (vowels and consonants) should be combined with the target sound. The clinician can ill afford to ignore the target's environment. Realities of clinical practice dictate, however, that the clinician not become overly concerned about whether /I/ or /i/ is a better vowel and whether /t/ should be combined with /t/ or /d/ in words such as *tight* and *tide.* However, fine-graded articulation testing need not dominate all sessions. Clinicians must do only enough in-depth testing so the patient's journey from unintelligible speech to intelligible speech is successful, and neither patient nor clinician is left prostrate, weighted down with the baggage of insignificant details.

A task continuum for stabilizing voiceless /p/ in the speech of a primarily flaccid dysarthric patient follows. The data that permitted us to construct the continuum were collected by analyzing the patient's imitative productions of the sound-by-position test described earlier (p. 115). The patient imitated such utterances as *pat, tap,* and *ʌpat,* with the /p/ in word initial, final, and medial positions. The overall adequacy of /p/ by position and as compared to that of all other speech sounds was determined. Since it was more often correct than any other sound, it was chosen as the first articulation target. The specific ordering was:

Step 1: /p/ in final position of VC syllables.
Step 2: /p/ in final position of CVC syllables.
Step 3: /p/ in medial position of VCV syllables.
Step 4: /p/ in initial position of CV syllables.
Step 5: /p/ in varying positions in other words, in phrases, in sentences, and finally, in controlled conversation.

One recognizes from the continuum that /p/ was best in the final position and weakest in initial position of the word, so treatment began with what the patient did best. Testing also demonstrated that certain vowels were easy (correct) and others were not; /i/ and /a/ were easy, /I/ and /aᵁ/ were not; thus /p/ was combined first with the easy vowels.

Our experience has been that dysarthric patients can profit not only from an orderly progression of tasks but also from practice that allows them to contrast the target with the error. The patient whose task continuum has been described did not make random errors; initial /p/ was usually produced as /b/—voicing was begun prematurely. The strategy, and it can be employed with other sounds in other environments, was to have the patient produce minimum contrasts. To help him stabilize initial /p/, the patient was required to practice pairs of words: *pete-beet, pea-bee, pie-by, pay-bay,* etc.

Repetition of such contrasts accompanied by careful evaluation of response adequacy by both the patient and the clinician may be enough; the patient may regain control. Often enough, however, the patient's weakness or incoordination will continue to frustrate correct production. At such times the clinician will need to do more than provide a model: He or she will have to mine the literature on normal speech production for facts pertinent to treatment.

Consider some observations about the differences between normal /p/ and /b/ as summarized in Table 2-6. These differences are often statistical ones only (every /p/ does not differ from every /b/ on all these features), some of the differences disappear entirely in certain positions in normal utterances [161], and some of the hypothesized differences, such as the fortis-lentis difference, have

Table 2-6. Differences between /p/ and /b/

/p/	/b/
Voiceless	Voiced
Aspirated	Unaspirated
Greater intraoral breath pressure	Lesser intraoral breath pressure
Greater airflow	Lesser airflow
Longer duration	Shorter duration
Greater perceived difficulty	Lesser perceived difficulty
Fortis	Lentis
Greater force of bilabial contact	Lesser force of bilabial contact

not escaped rigorous experimental investigation unscathed [67]. Others, such as the differences in flow and pressure, are more acceptable [24, 82]. All the differences are probably related more or less directly to the differences in laryngeal function for the two sounds. The larynx begins to vibrate during the hold phase of the voiced plosive but is silent during the hold phase of the /p/. None of this matters to the therapist if a patient can use some of these idealized distinctions between /p/ and /b/ to make real distinctions in speech.

To make perceptually different sounds, dysarthric patients may be forced to compensate; that is, they may be forced to exaggerate some characteristics of the target sound. One of the best cues clinically seems to be aspiration. Patients can learn to detect the burst of unaspirated air characteristic of /p/ and absent or reduced in /b/. None of this is new: For generations clinicians have been holding fluff in front of mouths and having patients feel the buzzing of their own larynxes during voicing. The aim here is only to reinforce the need for clinicians to learn facts of normal production and apply them to treatment. Vowel durations vary before voiceless and voiced plosives, being longer before voiced ones [97]; such differences may be taught. Listeners can identify voiced plosives in the final position even if they are not released [106]. A patient having difficulties differentiating final voiced and voiceless plosives (as was the case with our primarily flaccid patient) may be taught strong aspiration on final, voiceless plosives and to avoid releasing final, voiced plosives. Such a patient might succeed in making all voiceless plosives longer than their voiced cognates by learning to increase the hold phase of the voiceless sounds. Occasionally patients seem to learn contrasts by violating the "facts" of normal. For example, more than one of our patients has learned voiced-voiceless distinctions by producing the voiced of the pair with greater rather than lesser effort.

Implicit in the suggestion to produce paired contrasts of the target sound and its error is the attitude that a thoroughgoing analysis of error types can guide the specifics of all articulation treatment. Describing all possible articulation errors and the treatment of them is outside our ability even if space allowed for it, however. Two common error types and suggestions for their management may be mentioned profitably. Dysarthric patients often produce plosives that sound like fricatives. Weismer [169] has discussed such errors at length. Or they do the reverse: Their fricatives tend toward plosives. The first type of error may result from weakness and poor timing. The patient cannot valve tightly and is slow in releasing the sound. Muscle strengthening, increasing the background of effort, and slowing the speech (especially with intelligent use of pauses) may reduce such errors. The second type of error—fricatives becoming plosives—may result from overshooting. For an /s/ the patient's tongue may contact the alveolar ridge rather than approximate it, and a distorted /t/ is the result. Altering the speed of speech and contrasting plosives and fricatives that show a common place of production may be helpful.

In sum, articulation therapy requires that the patient's errors and the reason for them be analyzed. Armed with this information, the clinician then places patients in the best posture for speaking; teaches them to increase their background of effort or at least of conscious control; teaches them to begin speaking with what is for them the proper respiratory support for speech, and with the best combination of suprasegmental and prosodic features; and then moves them from shorter, easier articulatory units to longer, more demanding ones with the help of specially designed *contrast drills*. Facts of normal production may be a useful source of cues that patients can use as they struggle to produce perceptually different sounds.

Goal 7: Modification of the Suprasegmentals and Prosody

According to Crystal [33], "From the phonetic point of view, prosodic features may be defined as vocal effects constituted by variations along the parameters of pitch, loudness, duration, and silence" (p. 128). These four characteristics will be referred to as the *suprasegmentals* throughout this section. English has three prosodic features: rhythm, stress, and intonation. Rhythm, or the timing of speech, results in part from changes in pause time. Because we consider that stress results from changes in pitch, loudness, articulation time, and pause time, we do not describe different therapies for rhythm and stress: we treat both with a common method. In addition, we describe a separate therapy for intonation and for each of the suprasegmentals, although we have almost nothing to say about pitch for reasons that will be discussed.

Suprasegmental and prosodic disturbances are present in all dysarthric speech. In spite of this universality, much less has been written about treating these disturbances than about treating dysarthric respiration, phonation, resonation, and articulation, although the literature [10, 25, 158, 173] is expanding. The paucity appears to result from a limited understanding of the suprasegmentals and prosody and the peculiar status of both vis-à-vis segment production or articulation.

It was usual, although not inevitable, to view the suprasegmentals and prosody as something added onto the speech signal but not crucial to its intelligibility. They were speech's "formal wear" and could be done without. That attitude no longer enjoys currency. More typical of the present feeling is this statement by Darwin [39]: "There is little doubt that prosodic variables make a significant contribution to the intelligibility of speech" (p. 103). Darwin's conclusion is based on normative studies, such as that by Wingfield and Klein [171], demonstrating that immediate recall is negatively affected by imposing inappropriate intonational contours on American English sentences.

Data support the hypothesis that abnormal suprasegmentals and prosody contribute to dysarthric unintelligibility. Darley, Aronson, and Brown [35], for example, report a correlation of 0.78 for overall intelligibility and reduced stress in hypokinetic dysarthria. The correlation of intelligibility and variable rate was 0.73 and, with monoloudness, 0.60 for that same group. Significant correlations of intelligibility with suprasegmental and prosodic features—the exact features differing according to the type of dysarthria—are reported for all dysarthric types.

Evidence for the influence of treatment on the suprasegmentals and prosodic features is beginning to appear [25, 117, 173] as are data confirming that modifying the suprasegmentals and prosody improves intelligibility, even when segment production remains unchanged. Our own practice suggests that articulation can be improved by work on suprasegmentals and prosodic features. While confirming data from dysarthric speakers are limited, a tantalizing literature on normal speakers focuses especially on the relations of changes in stress to changes in articulation. Netsell [126] observes that articulation in stressed syllables is more precise; for example, vowels more adequately approach their ideal position.

This disproportionately long introduction reflects our concern that dysarthria therapy not be focused solely on attempts to improve articulation. Equally important are palliative efforts directed at the suprasegmentals and at prosody. Unfortunately, few speech pathologists are prepared for such therapy. For the uninitiated, the terminology is arcane. Conflicts about definition* and significance abound, and each writer's status in his or her colleague's eyes is as hard to evaluate as the validity of his or her theories and data. As our profession grows more catholic, however, we will suffer less from the insecurities bred of ignorance, and eventually we will have learned as much about the suprasegmentals and prosody and how to treat them from phoneticians and linguists, as we have learned about aphasia and dysarthria from neurologists. The beginning is now. Minifie, Hixon, and Williams [113], for example, have compiled an impressively complete discussion of normal communication intended for the speech pathologist in which Netsell [126], in a chapter on speech physiology, defines the prosodic features of English and places them in perspicuous outline.

PITCH: CONTEXT FOR TREATMENT. Overall pitch and pitch change are accomplished primarily by laryngeal activity. As Wertz has discussed (see Chap. 1), abnormal pitch, monopitch, and inappropriate pitch changes occur in several of the dysarthrias. Because abnormal pitch level (too high or too low) does not seem to make a major contribution to intelligibility, and because problems of pitch variation can be handled more efficiently by concentrating treatment on rate, stress, and intonation, we have included no specific exercises for modifying pitch. If previously described techniques for changing muscle strength and tone and subsequent ones to modify the other suprasegmentals and

*Separating the suprasegmentals—pitch, loudness, articulation time, and pause time—from prosody may disconcert some readers. What we interpret as patterns of error in the dysarthrias, such as inadequate loudness in a patient with essentially normal pitch, articulation time, pause time, stress, and intonation, lead us to the distinction.

prosody do not simultaneously alter overall pitch, and if the clinician judges it to be in need of treatment, the clinician can consult standard voice textbooks [21, 31] for methods.

LOUDNESS: CONTEXT FOR TREATMENT. Overall loudness and loudness changes are primarily controlled by respiration; the greater the respiratory drive, the greater the loudness. Additionally, loudness can be controlled by the degree of mouth opening [44] (the wider the jaw and tongue's excursion, the louder the voice) and by the force of laryngeal adduction [81]. Diagnosis will have determined if a specific patient's voice is inadequately loud and why. The culprit will most often be respiration, but the influence of the mouth and larynx cannot be overlooked.

LOUDNESS: TREATMENT PROCEDURES. If the posture for respiration has been modified, if speaking effort has been increased, and if respiration training has been completed (assuming these steps were necessary), the patient's loudness will have been substantially altered already. This section outlines methods for further increasing loudness and transferring previous gains to volitional-purposive communication.

Our usual procedure is totally behavioral. We explain how loudness can be increased: by increased respiratory drive, increased laryngeal adduction, and increased mouth opening. Depending on the patients' performance of these three activities (we do not ask them to do more of what they cannot do or of what they are already doing normally or supranormally), we concentrate on getting them to "blow themselves up to a bigger size," which means to take in more air for speech. We get patients to produce nonpropositional speech that is heavy on plosives ("Do it today") to the accompaniment of exaggerated (or at least extensive) jaw movements. We continue this process until we get a number of productions that seem to be the best that patients can consistently produce; and these we identify as the *target*. The patients then spend their time trying to approximate the target and judging, along with the clinician, whether each response is adequate.

Getting patients to the right size is the most interesting part of the treatment. Too much air, and they will overwhelm upstream valves (larynx, palate, tongue, lips); too little, and they are less loud than necessary. Placing one's hands on the patients' bellies and directing the inhalations with manual pressure reminds patients that they must increase their inhalation. Getting their hands to join the clinician's may attune them to what is necessary more efficiently than forcing them to rely solely on the clinician's guidance. Mottoes work occasional wonders: "Breath-talk" may be just the reminder a patient requires.

If a patient's jaw is making small movements, he or she can be taught to open the jaw wider. Training may start with relaxation followed by practice in front of a mirror. Not to be overlooked is the simple "Open your mouth wider." It may even help to block the patient's jaw by placing a bite block between the upper and lower teeth. If nothing else, talking with the block in place may convince the patient of a payoff from increased mouth opening.

Instruments can be coordinated with traditional behavioral methods to help a patient increase loudness. Using the V-U meter on the tape recorder is the most practical because the majority of clinicians have one; some clinicians are also using instruments such as Talk Time.* Boone [21] recommends using an audiometer capable of delivering a binaural masking signal as a way of getting a reflexive increase in loudness. If binaural masking is used, knowledge of results will have to be provided by yet another machine or by the clinician. If a tape recorder is used either alone or in addition to the binaural masking unit, the patient's task is to bring the needle of the V-U meter into the red zone during the production of target utterances. The demand for increased loudness can be systematically increased by reducing the volume on the tape recorder. Regardless of the instrument used, it is as useless in correcting functionally increased loudness as pin-the-tail-on-the-donkey is in correcting fine motor coordination unless patients are helped to understand what they are doing right and to recognize the cues associated with good performance.

Successful patients probably inhale a greater amount of air and increase their background of effort (manifested in speech production as more forceful adduction of the vocal folds and more vigorous mouth movements). The cues to increased inhalation will be greater excursion of respiratory structures, and the patient can learn to recognize these. Greater effort may be signaled by changes in posture, such as a straightening of the spine and

a wider open mouth; the patient can be alerted to these too. When the patient is consistently generating normal loudness, or all the loudness he is capable of, the next step can be initiated—production of pairs of utterances, the first with the V-U meter or other instrument as a cue to success, and the second without it. At first patients may need to listen to recordings of both utterances to be sure of how they did. Eventually, patients must learn to evaluate adequacy by the auditory and tactile cues of their own ongoing speech.

Most important, if our experience is typical, patients must next learn to use the increased loudness "out there." Repetition, self-evaluation, and the clinician's constant admonition and support will aid that process. In spite of all these, carryover will be a perpetual goal rather than a reality if patients lack normal mentation or if they fail to learn what has to be done to be loud and how to identify that they have done it.

Amplification is a last resort if all else fails or if something has worked for a while, but no longer does. A number of small amplifiers [35] are available, and Greene and Watson [60] have described one as it was employed with a hypokinetic dysarthric patient. They describe a portable amplifier with a microphone that attaches to the glasses or on a headband if the person has normal vision. The gains for their patient were emotional and social as well as phonetic.

It is probably a truism, but we will repeat it anyway. An amplifier will do nothing at all for other speech parameters. For this reason it is best suited for the patient with hypokinetic dysarthria, whose major symptom is inadequate loudness but whose articulation is essentially intact. It will only make the unintelligible patient more obviously so. As in the case of any other prosthesis, an individual patient may be reluctant for a number of reasons to wear it. Counseling, demonstrations, and systematic desensitization are necessary if the patient is to use the device upon leaving the clinic.

ARTICULATION TIME AND PAUSE TIME: CONTEXT FOR TREATMENT. Many generations of speech pathologists have admonished their patients to slow down, and such durable advice has much to recommend it. The problem as we see it is in taking rate change too casually. Few, indeed, are the patients capable of therapeutic rate modification without careful systematic instruction. Rate change, when it is appropriate—and it by no means is universally so—must be taught.

*Voice Identification Incorporated, P. O. Box 714, Somerville, New Jersey 08876.

Speaking rate has two components: articulation time and pause time. *Articulation time* is time spent in producing the segments or speech sounds; *pause time* is silence. Both obey phonetic laws. For example, the duration of a vowel varies systematically with the following consonant, being longer before a voiced than before a voiceless cognate [97]; and pauses vary in length depending on the nature of the following phrase [56]. Both components can be modified with practice [57], but as Minifie [112] warns:

The regulation of the rate of utterance is primarily controlled by the number and extent of pauses distributed throughout the discourse. Only limited variations in the rate of utterance may be achieved by altering the durational characteristics of the speech sounds themselves. Durationally, the pauses are the most free to vary (p. 281).

Rate probably affects intelligibility primarily by influencing articulation. The relation between the two is complex, however. Heffner [68] has pointed out that rate fails to impair articulation if the speaker is a normal adult obeying the demand for intelligibility. Minifie [112], on the other hand, describes a condition of *undershoot*, whereby at fast rates a signal for one speech gesture (or set of gestures) arrives at the periphery before a preceding gesture (or set of gestures) is complete. The result is that gestures may be aborted before their completion, and articulation suffers as a result. As he says, "Lower speeds of movement mean less strain" (p. 207).

Because rate of articulation, which varies from approximately two syllables and five segments per second to eight syllables and 18 to 20 segments [68], can at its upper limits strain even a normal speech-production mechanism, abnormal articulation, as in dysarthria, is especially vulnerable to rate differences [57]. If a dysarthric patient tries to maintain his or her premorbid rate, articulation and intelligibility will suffer inordinately. For this reason a majority of speech pathologists have tried to slow down the majority of dysarthric patients.*

ARTICULATION TIME AND PAUSE TIME: TREATMENT PROCEDURES. The first step is convincing the patient of the need for changing his or her rate. We usually tell patients that their thinking is as good as it always was (if it is), but that their troubled tongues and lips are incapable of keeping up with

*Some patients with slowed articulation time can benefit from increased speed. Rate increases can be achieved with contrastive stress drills to be described.

their healthy brains. (Surely, some of them must feel they have come full circle if they "thought faster than they could talk" as children.) An analogy of speaking and walking may be useful. We point out that a person with weak legs falls when trying to run: the "crash" is a reminder not to run again. The speaking crash comes when persons continually say, "huh?" Just as a person with weak legs can no longer run, so can the dysarthric patient no longer talk fast. However, this counseling can never be perfunctory. The difficulty most patients have with slowing down tempts one to speculate that most would rather risk being identified as persons who are sick and talking poorly than as persons who are sick and doing something peculiar (talking slowly) with their speech. Goldman-Eisler [57] seems to suggest that difficulty in slowing down is related to the ease or automaticity with which persons can produce most daily speech. Such speech can be programmed so rapidly that the limits on rate of utterance are imposed by the response characteristics of the peripheral speech mechanism and by the need for intelligibility rather than by higher nervous centers.

Occasionally the clinician will want to exert a dramatic and immediate influence on the patient's rate. This can be done by altering pause time, perhaps with a metronome. By adjusting a metronome to an appropriate rate and instructing the patient to utter a word or syllable on each beat, a slowed, equal, and even stress pattern can be achieved. The achievement takes some teaching and the use of familiar materials so that the patient can practice following the metronome's beat. The influence on rate, and therefore on other aspects of speech, can sometimes be spectacular and especially convincing to the patient who may think that slow speech is hardly worth the effort. Occasionally, similar spectacular results can be achieved with simple reading tasks. Key sentences can be prepared, and then a slit card can be used to reveal only one word at a time. Placing each word of a key utterance on a card and presenting them to the patient one at a time is sometimes appropriate. Stimuli containing a high percentage of plosives can be most effective. Teaching the patient to speak in time with a flashing light or with a continual sound fits into the same general therapeutic pattern.

Pairing speaking with another behavior, such as button pushing, ball squeezing, or tapping, is a form of therapy which Luria [104] calls intersystemic reorganization. Intersystemic reorganization may also be useful in treating rate in dysarthric patients by influencing the number and length of pauses. We have tried several variations of such reorganization, depending on the patient's limb integrity. If the patient is relatively free of tremors and dyskinesia and is sufficiently strong, then he or she can tap on a leg or on a chair or table and accompany each tap with a spoken word or syllable. Any other simple, repetitive activity capable of being repeated with a minimum of energy is also alright. Movements governed by a pacing board fit these criteria. The pace of the tapping may be directed either verbally ("Do it slower") or in imitation of the clinician. If limb muscle deficits prevent the patient from moving his or her arms, the clinician can deliver the taps. The tapping can be faded systematically once the patient begins to speak more slowly.

Metronomes, slit cards, and tapping primarily influence pause time and, in the process, wreak havoc with speech prosody. Their principal use, then, is to cause a dramatic short-term influence on rate. Careful behavioral methods will wean the patient from them and help to transfer the slower rate to volitional-purposive talking. Combining the intersystemic reorganization (tapping) with the contrastive stress drill (to be described) may aid the carryover.

Articulation time can be modified by delayed auditory feedback (DAF) [17, 43, 45]; DAF occupies a paradoxical position in rehabilitation. Depending on the delay interval, intensity, material, and subject, normal speech may be slowed or disrupted entirely by stuttering like repetitions and articulation errors during DAF, yet a palliative effect on the speech of stutterers has been described [164], and reports of DAF with dysarthric patients have appeared [64, 65, 159].

We give the majority of our dysarthric patients a trial period of DAF [140] as part of ongoing clinical research and have reached several tentative conclusions. It appears to have its major influence on articulation time and articulatory adequacy, although loudness, pitch, and prosody may be influenced as well. A delay interval of approximately 50 milliseconds has a beneficial effect on the articulation and prosody of certain patients with ataxic or hypokinetic dysarthria, although Hanson and Metter [64, 65] used delays of 100 and 150 milliseconds. Delay intervals longer than 150 milliseconds are especially disastrous for the speech of most dysarthric patients, regardless of type. Flaccid patients do not seem to benefit and may be handicapped by the DAF, regardless of the delay interval. Why it helps some and not others, even though they may belong to the same diagnostic category, is unclear. Finally, the effect of DAF varies with the stimuli. The effect seems to be most dramatic for less propositional materials. Delay intervals, intensity, and stimuli need to be varied systematically with each patient before one can conclude that DAF does or does not help.

If DAF is palliative, it can be included as part of a traditional behavioral treatment. The goal is to wean the patient from the machine while preserving any improvements in articulation and prosody, although Hanson and Metter's patients wore their DAFs outside the clinic. One procedure for weaning appropriate patients is to have them concentrate on the feel of the improved speech as they practice selected stimuli under the condition of DAF and then strive for the same effect for short periods without it. Recordings of speech under both conditions can also be compared. Patients can move from reading to more propositional speaking, all the time preserving whatever improved speech the DAF helped give them. The clinician will need to be as active as in any other behavioral therapy, because carryover can only be achieved if the clinician not only selects the stimuli and helps provide knowledge of results, but also supervises the transition from DAF to none.

As with other rate-influencing devices, DAF may be useful only to bring about a dramatic change in speech capable of convincing the patient that change is indeed possible. Perhaps it will form the core of an extensive rate-modifying therapy. Either way, the time comes when the patient must transfer the gains. This transfer can be accomplished by contrastive stress drills.

STRESS: CONTEXT FOR TREATMENT. *Stress*, as defined by Netsell [126], is the relative prominence of a speech unit compared to that of companion units. Heffner [68] defines three *stress levels*: fully stressed, half-stressed, and unstressed. For therapeutic purposes, we can talk profitably about two levels (stressed and unstressed) and two units (word and group stress). Word stress is illustrated by the difference between protest as a verb, with stress falling on the second syllable, and protest as a noun, with stress on the first syllable. Group stress unequivocally identifies the type of attack in the sentence "Leonard hit Donnell." Two utterances with identical segments can have different meanings because of *contrastive stress patterns*: Stress, therefore, is phonemic. The crow would be chagrined if all black birds (/black /birds) were blackbirds (/black birds).

Stress is accomplished differently in different normal speakers [129], but a reasonably safe generality is that stressed syllables differ from unstressed ones* in pitch, loudness, and articulation time (the suprasegmentals). Stressed syllables have a higher fundamental frequency, greater intensity, and increased duration. In normal speakers, pitch appears to be the most important cue to stress, and loudness the least [97]. For this reason Broad [22] is probably correct in stating that "the laryngeal voice source is the primary physiological locus for producing prosodic variations" (p. 148). Group stress depends on additional contributions of pause time† and articulation time. One or more pauses exist between consecutive primary stresses [55], and the tendency is to reduce articulatory rate before a stressed element.

We know very little with surety about stress in dysarthric speakers, and what we do know serves differential diagnosis more satisfactorily than treatment, although we are learning more of both diagnostic and therapeutic importance. Inevitably, then, our therapy continues to spring primarily from clinical hunches very much in need of controlled investigation. Our first hunch—although it is really more than that because of research by Darley, Aronson, and Brown [36, 37] and others [174]—is that stress abnormalities in the dysarthrias are potentially as dissimilar as are the neuromuscular abnormalities underlying them. Our second hunch is that nearly all dysarthric speakers are capable of producing some stress differences. Our third hunch is that all but the profoundly involved are capable of learning improved stress, although patients will differ in the way they accomplish this improvement. After studying 14 dysarthric patients, Murry [117] concludes that "dysarthrics use a neuromotor processing system to produce word stress based on compensation rather than enhancement" (p. 80). Studies like his will eventually provide clinicians with even more details about those compensations and how effective they are.

Stress, and the prosodic features in general, are often viewed as late rather than early therapeutic targets; their manipulation represents a kind of "mopping up" action. Because stress drills may improve respiratory performance, phonatory performance, resonatory performance, and articulatory performance, and because improved stress may enhance intelligibility even when segment production remains unchanged, stress is necessarily an early therapeutic target. At the latest, stress drills can begin after respiration and articulation are sufficiently intact to support a few connected utterances.

STRESS: TREATMENT PROCEDURES. The method for improving dysarthric stress patterns is called a *contrastive stress drill* after Fairbanks [42]. The nucleus of the drill is composed of two or more stimuli that are different in meaning because of differences in stress. For example, the meaning of "Bill bit Bob" depends on whether primary stress falls on the first, second, or third word.

An example of a complete contrastive stress drill, which is usually conducted as a dialogue, follows:

CLINICIAN	PATIENT
'bab/ /'bIt/ /'tad	'bab/ /'bIt/ /'tad
Who bit Tod?	'ba:b/ /bIt/ /tad
Did Bob hit Tod?	no^U: bab/ /'bI:t/ /tad
Did Bob bite Don?	no^U: bab/ /bIt/ /'ta:d

Phonetic symbols are provided for the speech pathologist, not the patient, where ' shows primary stress, / / indicates the amount of pause time, and : shows articulation time. Not shown are elevated pitch and increased loudness on the stressed syllables. Not all normal speakers would achieve the stress difference as shown in the example, nor do dysarthric speakers need to. The model is provided primarily for orientation.

The stimuli are created for each patient depending on his or her symptoms and needs. We usually try to create contrastive stress drills as soon as a patient can combine even a few vowels and consonants. If, for example, a patient can produce plosives, sentences such as "I do it" can be practiced as a contrastive stress drill. Even mildly distorted sounds can be used, because they may be improved in stressed environments. Length of utterance can be controlled but is apparently less important than speech sound makeup.

After the stimuli have been selected, therapy begins with an explanation of the contrastive stress drill and what it can accomplish for the patient's

*We probably should talk about comparison of greater and lesser stress rather than of some and none, but tradition supports the stressed-unstressed dichotomy in such discussions.
†Because we include pause time in our consideration of stress, we have not included a section on the treatment of rhythm, which is primarily the result of pause time. Our treatment of stress intends to alter both stress and rhythm.

speech. Patients differ in the amount of explanation they need about how stress is achieved. Usually, stress differences occur as the natural result of answering the question. If they do not, the clinician can explain to the patient that he or she is to stress, or accent, certain words and not stress others; and the clinician can follow up these explanations by having the patient imitate his model.

Practice begins when the patient understands. The patient can first imitate the clinician's equal and even stress production of the target utterance or—once the patient has the idea of the way the drill works—the clinician can merely provide the sentence and then begin asking questions. If the patient achieves what the clinician perceives as adequate stress contrasts, nothing more is involved in the practice than helping patients become their own best critics and motivating them to continue making volitional stress contrasts outside the clinic.

Absent, inadequate, or incorrect stress complicates the clinician's task. Usually all but grossly inadequate stress responds to reinstruction; perhaps some changes can be made in the stimuli (making them shorter, using more stable sounds, making them more meaningful, asking the questions in a different way) and continued practice helps. Perceptually, it appears that some successful patients signal stress in the normal way, primarily with pitch changes, but that many patients need to be taught to emphasize loudness or, even more frequently, articulation time and pause time. It does not matter that these more difficult patients may already be talking slowly compared to normal. The only requirement is that they learn to produce something that is faster than something else. A method emphasizing only rate would encourage slowed articulation time on stressed elements, preceding each with a longer pause than precedes unstressed elements. If the stressed unit is first in the utterance, it can be followed by a longer pause than separates the other parts of the utterance.

Once a patient has learned to make stress differences, carryover can be begun with what we call a *preplanning activity*. In this stage of the therapy, biographical or high-interest stimuli are used. The therapy goes something like this: "Where were you born?" "I was born in Mazomanie." "You say you were born in Madison?" "No, I was born in Mazomanie." Each answer is preceded by a silent period, during which the patient is instructed to prepare and rehearse the answer. We set the limits of that rehearsal period by not allowing the patient to begin an answer until an agreed-upon signal is given. The next stage is to maintain the preplanning period but to conduct real dialogues involving new information. If questions are used that resemble those asked of the patient daily by ward personnel, carryover may be more prompt. Finally, the contrast drills can be sent home as homework.

Articulation and stress can be improved simultaneously by careful placement of target (treated) sounds. A patient, for example, may have been practicing /t/ and /k/ in the final position of single words. The gains can be transferred to more useful speech by having the patient practice sentences such as "I like it." At first, the patient may be required to put primary stress on the second or third words as in answer to the questions, "Do you hate it?" and "Do you like them?" The increased aspiration normally associated with stressed, voiceless plosives may be enhanced, making these target sounds more normal. Later on the sentences can be made longer, and /t/ and /k/ can be moved into the initial and medical positions of words.

INTONATION: CONTEXT FOR TREATMENT. Intrepid is the clinician who would write confidently about modifying intonation. As Fry [53] has said, most of the work necessary to understand intonation in normal persons remains to be done; the same is true in patients with dysarthria. This short section is included more to provoke clinical experimentation than to describe a developed successful treatment.

Netsell [126] defines intonation as "the perception of changes in the fundamental frequency of vocal fold vibration" (p. 225). Fry [53] identifies three uses of such changes. The first is *phonemic*. A tone difference may be the single contrast that identifies differences in meaning between two words; however, tone phonemes do not occur in English. The second is what he calls a *grammatical* or *syntactic* use. Difference in tone can signal the difference between a statement and a question. American English makes this use of tone, and it is the only one for which we will suggest treatment. The third use is *affective*, wherein tone is used to communicate the speaker's feeling.

A speaker's fundamental frequency is constantly changing, yielding an *intonational contour*. The change in this intonational contour at the end of an utterance is the *terminal intonation* [42]. According to Fairbanks, in simple declarative and imperative sentences, the terminal intonation is falling. He diagrams it thus:

I am going home ↓ .

Special questions unanswerable with yes or no often have a similar final contour. The contour at the end of yes or no questions is a rising one.

Am I right ↑ ?

INTONATION: TREATMENT PROCEDURES. This section is confined to the modification of terminal contour. Because the contour is primarily related to laryngeal activity and secondarily to subglottal breath pressure, i.e., to respiratory forces, the first step is to get the optimum postural adjustment for the larynx and for respiration. The second, as always, is to increase the background of effort. The third step is to provide contrastive intonational drills. For example, "I want to go," "I want to go?"

The same rules for stimulus selection, drill, feedback, and the rest that were described for contrastive stress are in effect here. Few clinicians ever employ contrastive intonational drills. Dysarthria therapy is usually short, and distorted intonational contours are seldom significant enough in the symptom complex to warrant therapy. Even in long-term therapy when one might get to intonational contours, time is usually spent in holding the line with rate, loudness, stress, and articulation drills. At least it has been so in our experience.

Goal 8: Providing an Alternative Mode
If dysarthria is profound, the patient can be offered an alternative mode of communication. Most such alternatives have been discussed by specialists in educating patients with cerebral palsy, although publications describing alternative modes for adults are beginning to appear in large numbers [2, 15, 16, 94]. Skelly et al. [160] have developed a system of gestural communication (Amerind) based on American Indian sign language. This system requires control of at least one arm. The signs are easily recognizable even by naive observers, making their use easier than would be the use of a set of idiosyncratic signs or a complex set, such as deaf sign. If a patient has sufficient arm integrity for Amerind, he or she probably can write. Teaching the patient to use a telegraphic written mode is legitimate, as is providing the patient with an alphabet board.

Often the speechless dysarthric patient will have severe limb involvement as well. For these patients any number of relatively simple or more complex electric communication boards are available. Head pointers, electric typewriters, and electric boards operated with foot pedals have all been described [32]. Computers are solving the problems of even the most involved [16].

The major problem with alternative modes is not methodology. The clinician selects an appropriate mode and uses traditional behavioral methods to make the patient skilled in its use, while soliciting the patient's acceptance. The joy of communication may not be nearly as compelling for the patient as for the speech pathologist. If patients are offered an alternative mode in the early days of treatment, they need to understand that their use of it may well be temporary—an alphabet board is not evidence that a tongue is permanently paralyzed. If a period of treatment fails to establish functional speech, patients need to understand that an alternative mode may be superior to the imprisonment and dependency that is the fate of persons with no mode of communication. Finally, however, patients must be allowed to do what they want. If they choose not to communicate, that choice is to be respected.

Netsell [120] posits that most speech treatments for dysarthric talkers help. But success, especially if general and easily won, too easily becomes an opiate. Speech pathologists can ill afford to cease daily efforts to improve their management of dysarthric people. The approach to dysarthria presented in this chapter is not to be a goal for other practitioners. Instead, it is meant to be but a portion of the foundation for enriched, more effective future practice.

References
1. Abbs, J. H., Hunker, C. J., and Barlow, S. M. Differential Speech Motor Subsystem Impairments with Suprabulbar Lesions: Neurophysiological Framework and Supporting Data. In W. R. Berry (ed.), *Clinical Dysarthria*. San Diego: College-Hill, 1983.
2. Adams, M. R. Communication aids for patients with amyotrophic lateral sclerosis. *J. Speech Hear. Disord.* 31 : 274, 1966.
3. Allan, C. M. Treatment of nonfluent speech resulting from neurological disease—treatment of dysarthria. *Br. J. Dis. Commun.* 5 : 3, 1970.
4. Allan, C. M., Turner, J. W., and Gadea-Ciria, M. Investigations into speech disturbances following stereotaxic surgery for parkinsonism. *Br. J. Dis. Commun.* 1 : 55, 1966.
5. Aronson, A. E. *Clinical Voice Disorders: An Interdisciplinary Approach.* New York: Thieme-Stratton, 1980.
6. Aronson, A. E. Early motor unit disease masquerading as psychogenic breathy dysphonia: A clinical

case presentation. *J. Speech Hear. Disord.* 36 : 115, 1971.

7. Aten, J. L., McDonald, A., Simpson, M., and Gutierrez, R. Efficacy of Modified Palatal Lifts for Improving Resonance. In M. R. McNeil, J. C. Rosenbek, and A. E. Aronson (eds.), *The Dysarthrias: Physiology-Acoustics-Perception-Management.* San Diego: College-Hill, 1984.

8. Baker, E. E., Jr., and Sokoloff, M. S. Therapy for speech deficiencies resulting from acute bulbar poliomyelitis infection. *J. Speech Hear. Disord.* 16 : 337, 1951.

9. Barlow, S., and Abbs, J. Orofacial fine-motor control impairments in congenital spasticity: Evidence against hypertones-related performance deficits. *Neurology* 34: 145, 1984.

10. Barnes, G. J. Suprasegmental and Prosodic Considerations in Motor Speech Disorders. In W. R. Berry (ed.), *Clinical Dysarthria.* San Diego: College-Hill, 1983.

11. Berry, R. A., Masters, J. J., Pepa, L. D., and Pickard, R. G. The use of biofeedback to improve velopharyngeal closure with chronic encephalopathy. Presented to the American Speech and Hearing Association, Las Vegas, Nev., 1974.

12. Berry, W. R., Aronson, A. E., Darley, F. L., and Goldstein, N. P. Effects of penicillamine therapy and low-copper diet on dysarthria in Wilson's disease (hepatolenticular degeneration). *Mayo Clin. Proc.* 49 : 405, 1974.

13. Berry, W. R., and Goshorn, E. L. Immediate Visual Feedback in the Treatment of Ataxic Dysarthria: A Case Study. In W. R. Berry (ed.), *Clinical Dysarthria.* San Diego: College-Hill, 1983.

14. Berry, W. R., and LaPointe, L. L. *The Adult Dysarthric Patient: Part I. Evaluation.* Washington, D. C.: Video Cassette, Medical Media Service, Veterans Administration, 1974.

15. Beukelman, D. R., and Yorkston, K. A communication system for the severely dysarthric speaker with an intact language system. *J. Speech Hear. Disord.* 42 : 265, 1977.

16. Beukelman, D. R., Yorkston, K. M., and Dowden, P. A. *Communication Augmentation: A Casebook of Clinical Management.* San Diego: College-Hill, 1984.

17. Black, J. W. The effect of delayed sidetone upon vocal rate and intensity. *J. Speech Hear. Disord.* 16 : 56, 1951.

18. Bond, W. S., Carvalho, M., and Foulks, E. F. Persistent dysarthria with apraxia associated with a combination of lithium carbonate and haloperidol. *J. Clin. Psychiatry* 43 : 256, 1982.

19. Booker, H. E., Rubow, R. T., and Coleman, P. J. Simplified feedback in neuromuscular retraining: An automated approach using electromyographic signals. *Arch. Phys. Med. Rehabil.* 50 : 621, 1969.

20. Boone, D. R. Our profession—where is it? *ASHA* 18 : 415, 1976.

21. Boone, D. R. *The Voice and Voice Therapy.* Englewood Cliffs, N.J.: Prentice-Hall, 1971.

22. Broad, D. J. Phonation. In F. D. Minifie, T. J. Hixon, and F. Williams (eds.), *Normal Aspects of Speech, Hearing, and Language.* Englewood Cliffs, N.J.: Prentice-Hall, 1973.

23. Brodnitz, F. S. *Vocal Rehabilitation.* Rochester, Minn.: Whiting Press, 1967.

24. Brown, W. S., McGlone, R. E., Tarlow, A., and Ship, T. Intraoral air pressures associated with specific phonetic positions. *Phonetica* 22 : 202, 1970.

25. Caligiuri, M. P., and Murry, T. The Use of Visual Feedback to Enhance Prosodic Control in Dysarthria. In W. R. Berry (ed.), *Clinical Dysarthria.* San Diego: College-Hill, 1983.

26. Calne, D. B. *Parkinsonism: Physiology, Pharmacology, and Treatment.* London: Edward Arnold, 1970.

27. Canter, G. J. Neuromotor pathologies of speech. *Am. J. Phys. Med.* 46 : 659, 1967.

28. Canter, G. J. Speech characteristics of patients with Parkinson's disease: II. Physiological support for speech. *J. Speech Hear. Disord.* 30 : 44, 1965.

29. Cole, R. M. Direct Muscle Training for the Improvement of Velopharyngeal Function. In W. C. Grabb, S. W. Rosenstein, and K. R. Bzoch (eds.), *Cleft Lip and Palate.* Boston: Little, Brown, 1971.

30. Collins, J. J., Rubow, R. T., Rosenbek, J. C., and Gracco, V. An instrumental approach to reduction of nasal emission in dysarthria. Paper presented to the American Speech and Hearing Association, Los Angeles, Calif., 1981.

31. Cooper, M. *Modern Techniques of Vocal Rehabilitation.* Springfield, Ill.: Thomas, 1974.

32. Copeland, K. *Aids for the Severely Handicapped.* London: Grune & Stratton, 1974.

33. Crystal, D. *Prosodic Systems and Intonation in English.* London: Cambridge University Press, 1969.

34. Darley, F. L. Perceptual Analysis of the Dysarthrias. In J. C. Rosenbek (ed.), *(Current Views of Dysarthria) Nature, Assessment and Treatment: Seminars in Speech and Language.* New York: Thieme-Stratton, 1984.

35. Darley, F. L., Aronson, A. E., and Brown, J. R. *Motor Speech Disorders.* Philadelphia: Saunders, 1975.

36. Darley, F. L., Aronson, A. E., and Brown, J. R. Clusters of deviant speech dimensions in the dysarthrias. *J. Speech Hear. Res.* 12 : 462, 1969.

37. Darley, F. L., Aronson, A. E., and Brown, J. R. Differential diagnostic patterns of dysarthria. *J. Speech Hear. Res.* 12 : 246, 1969.

38. Darley, F. L., Brown, J. R., and Swenson, W. M. Language changes after neurosurgery for Parkinsonism. *Brain Lang.* 2 : 65, 1975.

39. Darwin, C. J. On the dynamic use of prosody in speech perception. *Status Report of Speech Research.* New York: Haskins Laboratories SR-42/43, 1975.

40. Davis, J. W., and Logemann, J. A. Development of intraoral prostheses to improve speech and swallowing. Short course presented to the American Speech Langauge Hearing Association, San Francisco, Calif., 1984.

41. Eldridge, R. Twin Studies and the Etiology of Complex Neurological Disorders. In C. L. Ludlow and J. A. Cooper (eds.), *Genetic Aspects of Speech*

and Language Disorders. New York: Academic, 1983, p. 109.

42. Fairbanks, G. *Voice and Articulation Drillbook.* New York: Harper & Row, 1960.

43. Fairbanks, G. Selective vocal effects of delayed auditory feedback. *J. Speech Hear. Disord.* 20 : 333, 1955.

44. Fairbanks, G. A physiological correlative of vowel intensity. *Speech Monogr.* 17 : 390, 1950.

45. Fairbanks, G., and Guttman, N. Effects of delayed auditory feedback upon articulation. *J. Speech Hear. Res.* 1 : 12, 1958.

46. Fakeem, A. D., Brightwell, D. R., Burton, G. C., and Struss, A. Respiratory dyskinesia and dysarthria from prolonged neuroleptic use: Tardive dyskineses? *Am. J. Psychiatry* 139 : 517, 1982.

47. Farmakides, M. N., and Boone, D. R. Speech problems of patients with multiple sclerosis. *J. Speech Hear. Disord.* 25 : 385, 1960.

48. Finley, W. W., Niman, C. A., Standley, J., and Wansley, R. A. Electrophysiologic behavior modification of frontal EMG in cerebral-palsied children. *Biofeedback Self Regul.* 2 : 59, 1977.

49. Finley, W. W., Niman, C. A., Standley, J., and Ender, P. L. Frontal EMG-biofeedback training of athetoid cerebral-palsy patients. *Biofeedback Self Regul.* 1 : 169, 1976.

50. Froeschels, E. Chewing method as therapy. *Arch. Otolaryngol.* 61 : 427, 1952.

51. Froeschels, E. A contribution to the pathology and therapy of dysarthria due to certain cerebral lesions. *J. Speech Disord.* 8 : 301, 1943.

52. Froeschels, E., Kastein, S., and Weiss, D. A. A method of therapy for paralytic conditions of the mechanisms of phonation, respiration, and glutination. *J. Speech Hear. Disord.* 20 : 365, 1955.

53. Fry, D. B. Prosodic Phonomena. In B. Malmberg (ed.), *Manual of Phonetics.* Amsterdam: North-Holland, 1970.

54. Gibbons, P., and Bloomer, H. A supportive-type prosthetic speech aid. *J. Prosthet. Dent.* 8 : 362, 1958.

55. Gleason, H. A. *An Introduction to Descriptive Linguistics.* New York: Holt, Rinehart & Winston, 1961.

56. Goldman-Eisler, F. *Psycholinguistics. Experiments in Spontaneous Speech.* New York: Academic, 1968.

57. Goldman-Eisler, F. The significance of changes in the rate of articulation. *Lang. Speech* 4 : 171, 1961.

58. Gonzalez, J. B., and Aronson, A. E. Palatal lift prostheses for treatment of anatomic and neurologic palatopharyngeal insufficiency. *Cleft Palate J.* 7 : 91, 1970.

59. Greene, M. C. L. *The Voice and Its Disorders.* New York: Macmillan, 1957.

60. Greene, M. C. L., and Watson, B. W. The value of speech amplification in Parkinson's disease patients. *Folia Phoniatr. (Basel)* 20 : 250, 1968.

61. Grewel, F. Classification of dysarthrias. *Acta Psychiatr. Neurol. Scand.* 32 : 325, 1957.

62. Haggard, M. P. Speech waveform measurements in multiple sclerosis. *Folia Phoniatr. (Basel)* 21 : 307, 1969.

63. Hand, C. R., Burns, M. O., and Ireland, E.

Treatment of hypertonicity in muscles of lip retraction. *Biofeedback Self Regul.* 4 : 171, 1979.

64. Hanson, W. R., and Metter, E. J. DAF Speech Rate Modification in Parkinson's Disease: A Report of Two Cases. In W. R. Berry (ed.), *Clinical Dysarthria.* San Diego: College-Hill, 1983.

65. Hanson, W. R., and Metter, E. J. DAF as instrumental treatment for dysarthria in progressive supranuclear palsy: A case report. *J. Speech Hear. Disord.* 45 : 268, 1980.

66. Hardy, J. C. Intraoral breath pressure in cerebral palsy. *J. Speech Hear. Disord.* 26 : 309, 1961.

67. Harris, K. S., Lysaught, G. F., and Schvey, M. M. Some aspects of the production of oral and nasal labial stops. *Lang. Speech* 8 : 135, 1965.

68. Heffner, R-M. S. *General Phonetics.* Madison: University of Wisconsin Press, 1969.

69. Hettinger, T. *Physiology of Strength.* Springfield, Ill.: Thomas, 1961.

70. Hirose, H., and Kiritani, S. Velocity of articulatory movements in normal and dysarthric subjects. *Ann. Bull. RIPL* 13 : 105, 1979.

71. Hirose, H., Kiritani, S., and Sawashima, M. Patterns of dysarthric movement in patients with amyotrophic lateral sclerosis and pseudobulbar palsy. *Folia Phoniatr. (Basel)* 34 : 106, 1982.

72. Hirose, H., Kiritani, S., Ushijims, T., and Sawashima, M. Analysis of abnormal articulatory dynamics in two dysarthric patients. *J. Speech Hear. Disord.* 43 : 96, 1978.

73. Hixon, T. J. Speech Breathing Kinematics and Mechanism Inferences Therefrom. In S. Grillner, B. Lindblom, and J. Lubker (eds.), *Speech Motor Control.* New York: Pergamon, 1982.

74. Hixon, T. J. Respiratory-laryngeal evaluation. Presented at the Veterans Administration Workshop on Motor Speech Disorders. Madison, Wis., 1975.

75. Hixon, T. J. Respiratory Function in Speech. In F. D. Minifie, T. J. Hixon, and F. Williams (eds.), *Normal Aspects of Speech, Hearing, and Language.* Englewood Cliffs, N.J.: Prentice-Hall, 1973.

76. Hixon, T. J., Hawley, J. L., and Wilson, J. L. An around-the-house device for the clinical determination of respiratory driving pressure: A note on making simple even simpler. *J. Speech Hear. Disord.* 47 : 413, 1982.

77. Hixon, T. J., Putman, A. H. B., and Sharp, J. T. Speech production with flaccid paralysis of the rib cage, diaphragm, and abdomen. *J. Speech Hear. Disord.* 48 : 315, 1983.

78. Hunker, C., and Abbs, J. Physiological Analyses of Parkinsonism Tremors in the Orofacial System. In M. McNeil, J. Rosenbek, and A. Aronson (eds.), *The Dysarthrias: Physiology, Acoustics, Perception, Management.* San Diego: College-Hill, 1984.

79. Hunker, C. J., Abbs, J. H., and Barlow, S. M. The relationship between parkinsonian rigidity and hypokinesia in the orofacial system: A quantitative analysis. *Neurology* 32 : 749, 1982.

80. Ince, L. P., and Rosenberg, D. N. Modification of articulation in dysarthria. *Arch. Phys. Med. Rehabil.* 54 : 233, 1973.

81. Isshiki, N. Regulatory mechanism of voice intensity variation. *J. Speech Hear. Res.* 7 : 17, 1964.
82. Isshiki, N., and Ringel, R. Air flow during the production of selected consonants. *J. Speech Hear. Res.* 7 : 233, 1964.
83. Jackson, J. H. On affections of speech from disease of the brain. *Brain* 1 : 304, 1978.
84. Jacobson, E. *Progressive Relaxation.* Chicago: University of Chicago Press, 1938.
85. Kanyike, F. B., and Kigonya, R. M. Nerve deafness, dysarthria, and ataxia in chronic granulocytic leukaemia: A case report. *East Afr. Med. J.* 59 : 420, 1982.
86. Kent, R. D. Models of Speech Production. In N. J. Lass (ed.), *Contemporary Issues on Experimental Phonetics.* New York: Academic, 1976.
87. Kent, R. D., and Netsell, R. Articulatory abnormalities in athetoid cerebral palsy. *J. Speech Hear. Disord.* 43 : 353, 1978.
88. Kent., R. D., and Netsell, R. A case study of an ataxic dysarthric: Cineradiographic and spectrographic observations. *J. Speech Hear. Disord.* 40 : 115, 1975.
89. Kent, R. D., Netsell, R., and Abbs, J. H. Acoustic characteristics of dysarthria associated with cerebellar disease. *J. Speech Hear. Res.* 22 : 627, 1979.
90. Kent, R. D., Netsell, R., and Bauer, L. L. Cineradiographic assessment of articulatory mobility in the dysarthrias. *J. Speech Hear. Disord.* 40 : 467, 1975.
91. Kerman, P. C., Songef, L. S., and Davidoff, A. Palatal lift and speech therapy for velopharyngeal incompetence. *Arch. Phys. Med. Rehabil.* 54 : 271, 1973.
92. Kiritani, S., Itoh, K., and Fujimura, O. Tongue pellet tracking by a computer-controlled x-ray microbeam system. *J. Acoust. Soc. Am.* 57 : 1516, 1975.
93. Kruel, E. J. Neuromuscular control examination (NMC) for parkinsonism: Vowel prolongations and diadochokinetic and reading rates. *J. Speech Hear. Res.* 15 : 72, 1972.
94. Lagerman, U., and Hook, O. Communication aids for patients with dysarthria. *Scand J. Rehabil. Med.* 14 : 155, 1982.
95. LaPointe, L. L. Neurologic Abnormalities Affecting Speech. In D. B. Tower (ed.), *The Nervous System* (Vol. 3): *Human Communication and Its Disorders.* New York: Raven, 1975.
96. Leanderson, R., Meyerson, B. A., and Persson, A. Effect of L-dopa on speech in parkinsonism: An EMG study of labial articulatory function. *J. Neurol. Neurosurg. Psychiatry* 34 : 679, 1971.
97. Lehiste, I. *Suprasegmentals.* Cambridge, Mass.: M.I.T. Press, 1970.
98. Lewy, R. B., Cole, R., and Wepman, J. Teflon infection in the correction of velopharyngeal insufficiency. *Ann. Otol. Rhinol. Laryngol.* 74 : 874, 1965.
99. Logemann, J. *Evaluation and Treatment of Swallowing Disorders.* San Diego: College-Hill, 1983.
100. Logemann, J. A., Fisher, H. B., and Boshes, B. A distinctive feature analysis of articulation in Par-

kinson patients. Presented to the American Speech and Hearing Association, San Francisco, Calif., 1972.
101. Lubit, E. C., and Larsen, R. E. The Lubit palatal exerciser: A preliminary report. *Cleft Palate J.* 6 : 120, 1969.
102. Ludlow, C. L., and Bassich, C. J. Relationships between Perceptual Ratings and Acoustic Measures of Hypokinetic Speech. In W. R. Berry (ed.), *Clinical Dysarthria.* San Diego: College-Hill, 1983.
103. Ludlow, C. L., and Bassich, C. J. The Results of Acoustic and Perceptual Assessment of Two Types of Dysarthria. In W. R. Berry (ed.), *Clinical Dysarthria.* San Diego: College-Hill, 1983.
104. Luria, A. R. *Traumatic Aphasia: Its Syndromes, Psychology, and Treatment.* The Hague: Mouton, 1970.
105. Lybolt, J., Netsell, R., and Farrage, J. A bite-block prosthesis in the treatment of dysarthria. Paper presented to the American Speech and Hearing Association, Toronto, Canada, 1982.
106. Malecot, A. The role of releases in the identification of released final stops. *Language* 34 : 370, 1958.
107. Marquardt, T. P. Characteristics of speech production in Parkinson's disease: Electromyographic, structural movement, and aerodynamic measurements. University of Washington Ph.D. dissertation, 1973.
108. Massengill, R., Quinn, G. W., Pickrell, K. L., and Levinson, C. Therapeutic exercise and velopharyngeal gap. *Cleft Palate J.* 5 : 44, 1968.
109. McDonald, E. T. A *Deep Test of Articulation: Sentence Form.* Pittsburgh: Stanwix House, 1964.
110. McHenry, L. C., Jr. *Garrison's History of Neurology.* Springfield, Ill.: Thomas, 1969.
111. Merritt, H. H. A *Textbook of Neurology.* Philadelphia: Lea & Febiger, 1970.
112. Minifie, F. D. Speech Acoustics. In F. D. Minifie, T. J. Hixon, and F. Williams (eds.), *Normal Aspects of Speech, Hearing, and Language.* Englewood Cliffs, N.J.: Prentice-Hall, 1973.
113. Minifie, F. D., Hixon, T. J., and Williams, F. *Normal Aspects of Speech, Hearing, and Langauge.* Englewood Cliffs, N.J.: Prentice-Hall, 1973.
114. Moncur, J. P., and Brackett, I. P. *Modifying Vocal Behavior,* New York: Harper & Row, 1974.
115. Morley, D. F. The rehabilitation of adults with dysarthric speech. *J. Speech Hear. Disord.* 20 : 58, 1955.
116. Mulder, D. W., and Howard, F. M. Patient resistance and prognosis in amyotrophic lateral sclerosis. *Mayo Clin. Proc.* 51 : 537, 1976.
117. Murry, T. Treatment of Ataxic Dysarthria. In W. H. Perkins (ed.), *Current Therapy of Communication Disorders: Dysarthria and Apraxia.* New York: Thieme-Stratton, 1983.
118. Netsell, R. Construction and use of a bite block for evaluating and treating speech disorders. *J. Speech Hear. Disord.,* 1985.
119. Netsell, R. Physiologic Studies of Dysarthria and Their Relevance to Treatment. In J. C. Rosenbek (ed.), *Current Views of Dysarthria: Nature, As-*

sessment and Treatment; Seminars in Speech and Language. New York: Thieme-Stratton, 1984.

120. Netsell, R. A Neurobiologic View of the Dysarthrias. In M. R. McNeil, J. C. Rosenbek, and A. E. Aronson (ed.), *The Dysarthrias: Physiology-Acoustics-Perception-Management.* San Diego: College-Hill, 1984.

121. Netsell, R. Personal communication, 1984.

122. Netsell, R. Speech Motor Control: Theoretical Issues with Clinical Impact. In W. R. Berry (ed.), *Clinical Dysarthria.* San Diego: College-Hill, 1983.

123. Netsell, R. Physiological bases of dysarthria. Research Grant NS 09627, NIH, 1976.

124. Netsell, R. Instrumentation in the rehabilitation of dysarthria. Presented at the Veterans Administration Workshop on Motor Speech Disorders, Madison, Wis., 1975.

125. Netsell, R. Personnal communication, 1975.

126. Netsell, R. Speech Physiology. In F. D. Minifie, T. J. Hixon, and F. Williams (eds.), *Normal Aspects of Speech, Hearing and Language.* Englewood Cliffs, N.J.: Prentice-Hall, 1973.

127. Netsell, R. A Physiological-Acoustic-Perceptual Study of Syllable Stress. Ph.D. dissertation, University of Iowa, 1969.

128. Netsell, R. Evaluation of velopharyngeal function in dysarthria. *J. Speech Hear. Disord.* 34 : 113, 1969.

129. Netsell, R., and Cleeland, C. S. Modification of lip hypertonia in dysarthria using EMG feedback. *J. Speech Hear. Disord.* 38 : 131, 1973.

130. Netsell, R., and Daniel, B. Dysarthria in adults: Physiologic approach to rehabilitation. *Arch. Phys. Med. Rehabil.* 60 : 502, 1979.

131. Netsell, R., Daniel, B., and Celesia, G. G. Acceleration and weakness in parkinsonian dysarthria. *J. Speech Hear. Disord.* 40 : 170, 1975.

132. Okaga, M. Measurement of speech patterns in neurologic diseases. *Med. Biol. Eng. Comput.* 2 : 145, 1983.

133. Peacher, W. G. The etiology and differential diagnosis of dysarthria. *J. Speech Hear. Disord.* 15 : 252, 1950.

134. Peacher, W. G. Speech disorders in World War II. VII. Treatment of dysarthria. *J. Nerv. Ment. Dis.* 106 : 66, 1947.

135. Powers, G. L., and Starr, C. D. The effects of muscle exercises on velopharyngeal gap and nasality. *Cleft Palate J.* 11 : 28, 1974.

136. Putnam, A. H. B., and Hixon, T. J. Respiratory Kinematics in Speakers with Motor Neuron Disease. In M. R. McNeil, J. C. Rosenbek, and A. E. Aronson (eds.), *The Dysarthrias: Physiology-Acoustics-Perception-Management.* San Diego: College-Hill, 1984.

137. Quiller-Couch, A. *The Art of Writing.* New York: G. P. Putnam's Sons, 1916.

138. Rigrodsky, S., and Morrison, E. B. Speech changes in parkinsonism during L-dopa therapy: Preliminary findings. *J. Am. Geriatr. Soc.* 18 : 142, 1970.

139. Rosenbek, J. C. (ed.). *Current Views of Dysarthria: Nature, Assessment, and Treatment: Semi-*

nars in Speech and Language. New York: Thieme-Stratton, 1984.

140. Rosenbek, J. C., Collins, M. J., and Wertz, R. T. Delayed auditory feedback in the treatment of dysarthric adults. Presented to the American Speech and Hearing Association, Houston, Tex., 1976.

141. Rosenbek, J. C., and LaPointe, L. L. A physiological approach to the dysarthrias. *Speech Hear. Dis.* 47 : 334, 1983.

142. Rosenbek, J. C., and Netsell, R. Treating and Dysarthrias. In J. Darby (ed.), *Speech and Language Evaluation in Neurology: Adult Disorders.* Orlando, Fla.: Grune & Stratton, 1984.

143. Rubow, R. Role of feedback reinforcement, and compliance on training and transfer in biofeedback-based rehabilitation of motor speech disorders. In M. R. McNeil, J. C. Rosenbek, and A. E. Aronson (eds.), *The Dysarthrias: Physiology-Acoustics-Perception-Management.* San Diego: College-Hill, 1984.

144. Rubow, R. T., Rosenbek, J. C., Collins, M. J., and Celesia, G. G. Reduction of hemifacial spasm and dysarthria following EMG feedback. *J. Speech Hear. Disord.* 49 : 26, 1984.

145. Rubow, R. T., and Swift, E. Microcomputer-based wearable biofeedback device to improve treatment carry-over in parkinsonian dysarthria. *J. Speech Hear. Disord.* 50 : 178, 1985.

146. St. Onge, K. R., and Calvert, J. J. The brain stem damage syndrome: Speech and psychological factors. *J. Speech Hear. Disord.* 24 : 43, 1959.

147. Samra, K., Riklan, M., Levita, E., Zimmerman, J., Waltz, J. M., Bergmann, L., and Cooper, I. S. Language and speech correlates of anatomically verified lesions in thalamic surgery for parkinsonism. *J. Speech Hear. Res.* 12 : 510, 1969.

148. Sarno, M. T. Speech impairment in Parkinson's disease. *Arch. Phys. Med. Rehabil.* 49 : 269, 1968.

149. Schliesser, H. Alternate motion rates of the speech articulators in adults with cerebral palsy. *Folia Phoniatr. (Basel)* 34 : 258, 1982.

150. Schultz, M. C. The bases of speech pathology and audiology: Evaluation as the resolution of uncertainty. *J. Speech Hear. Disord.* 38 : 147, 1973.

151. Schweiger, J. W., Netsell, R., and Sommerfeld, R. M. Prosthetic management and speech improvement in individuals with dysarthria of the palate. *J. Am. Dent. Assoc.* 80 : 1348, 1970.

152. Scripture, E. W. Records of speech in disseminated sclerosis. *Brain* 39 : 455, 1916.

153. Shaughnessy, A. L., Netsell, R., and Farrage, J. Treatment of a Four-Year-Old with a Palatal Lift Prosthesis. In W. R. Berry (ed.), *Clinical Dysarthria.* San Diego: College-Hill, 1983.

154. Shelton, R. L. Therapeutic exercise and speech pathology. *ASHA* 5 : 855, 1963.

155. Shelton, R. L., Knox, A. W., Elbert, M., and Johnson, T. S. Palate Awareness and Nonspeech Voluntary Palate Movements. In J. F. Bosma (ed.), *Second Symposium on Oral Sensation and Perception.* Springfield, Ill.: Thomas, 1970.

156. Shelton, R. L., Paesani, A., McClelland, K. D., and Bradfield, S. S. Panendoscopic feedback in

the study of voluntary velopharyngeal movements. *J. Speech Hear. Disord.* 40 : 232, 1975.

157. Shprintzen, R. J., McCall, G. N., and Skolnick, M. D. A new therapeutic technique for the treatment of velopharyngeal incompetence. *J. Speech Hear. Disord.* 40 : 69, 1975.

158. Simmons, M. N. Acoustic Analysis of Ataxic Dysarthria: An Approach to Monitoring Treatment. In W. R. Berry (ed.), *Clinical Dysarthria.* San Diego: College-Hill, 1983.

159. Singh, S., and Schlangzer, B. B. Effects of delayed sidetone on the speech of aphasic, dysarthric, and mentally retarded subjects. *Lang. Speech* 12 : 167, 1969.

160. Skelly, M., Schinsky, L., Smith, R. W., and Fust, R. S. American Indian sign (Amerind) as a facilitator of verbalization for the oral verbal apraxic. *J. Speech Hear. Disord.* 39 : 445, 1974.

161. Slis, I. H., and Cohen, A. On the complex regulating the voiced-voiceless distinction. II. *Lang. Speech* 12 : 137, 1969.

162. Smith, R. O., Sands, C. J., Goldberg, N. M., Massey, R. U., and Gay, J. R. Injection of silicone lateral to a vocal cord in a patient with progressive bulbar palsy. *Neurology* 17 : 1217, 1967.

163. Templin, M. C., and Darley, F. L. *The Templin-Darley Tests of Articulation.* Iowa City: Bureau of Educational Research and Service Extension Division, State University of Iowa, 1960.

164. Van Riper, C. *The Nature of Stuttering.* Englewood Cliffs, N.J.: Prentice-Hall, 1972.

165. Van Riper, C., and Irwin, J. V. *Voice and Articulation.* Englewood Cliffs, N.J.: Prentice-Hall, 1958.

166. Ward, C. D., DuVoisin, R. C., Ice, S. E., Nutt, J. D., Eldridge, R., and Calne, D. B. Parkinson disease in 65 pairs of twins and in a set of quadruplets. *Neurology* 33 : 815, 1983.

167. Wechsler, I. S. *Clinical Neurology* (9th ed.). Philadelphia: Saunders, 1963.

168. Weismer, G. Acoustic Descriptions of Dysarthric Speech: Perceptual Correlates and Physiological Inference. In J. C. Rosenbek (ed.), *Current Views of Dysarthria: Nature, Assessment and Treatment; Seminars in Speech and Language.* New York: Thieme-Stratton, 1984.

169. Weismer, G. Articulatory Characteristics of Parkinsonian Dysarthria: Segmental and Phrase-Level Timing, Spirantization, and Glottal-Supraglottal Coordination. In M. R. McNeil, J. C. Rosenbek, and A. E. Aronson (eds.), *The Dysarthrias: Physiology-Acoustics-Perception-Management.* San Diego: College-Hill, 1984.

170. Williams, A., Eldrige, R., McFarland, N., Houff, S., Krebs, H., and McFarlin, D. Multiple sclerosis in twins. *Neurology* 30 : 1139, 1980.

171. Wingfield, A., and Klein, J. F. Syntactic structure and acoustic pattern in speech perception. *Perception and Psychophysics* 9 : 23, 1971.

172. Yorkston, K., and Beukelman, D. *Assessments of Intelligibility of Dysarthric Speech.* Tigard, Or.: CC Publications, 1982.

173. Yorkston, K. M., and Beukelman, D. R. Ataxic dysarthria: Treatment sequences based on intelligibility and prosodic considerations. *J. Speech Hear. Disord.* 46 : 398, 1981.

174. Yorkston, K. M., Beukelman, D. R., Minifie, F. D., and Sapir, S. Assessment of Stress Patterning. In M. R. McNeil, J. C. Rosenbek, and A. E. Aronson (eds.), *The Dysarthrias: Physiology-Acoustics-Perception-Management.* San Diego: College-Hill, 1984.

175. Yules, R. B., and Chase, R. A. A training method for reduction of hypernasality in speech. *Plast. Reconstr. Surg.* 43 : 180, 1969.

176. Zemlin, W. R. A Comparison of the Periodic Function of Vocal Fold Vibration in a Multiple Sclerosis and a Normal Population. Ph.D. disseration, University of Minnesota, 1962.

177. Zentay, P. J. Motor disorders of the central nervous system and their significance for speech. Part 1. Cerebral and cerebellar dysarthrias. *Laryngoscope* 47 : 147, 1937.

178. Ziegler, W., and von Cramon, D. Vowel distortion in traumatic dysarthria: A formant study. *Phonetica* 40 : 63, 1983.

3

Surgical and Prosthetic Management of Neurogenic Velopharyngeal Incompetency in Dysarthria

Donnell F. Johns

Dysarthria is the generic term used to identify motor speech disorders associated with loss or impairment of neuromuscular control because of lesions of either the central or peripheral nervous system. I view the dysarthrias just as Darley, Aronson, and Brown [15, 16] view them and as they are presented in Chapters 1 and 2 of this book. The purpose of this chapter will not be to refine and polish the differentiating characteristics, important as they are, but to focus on management and treatment procedures that have received little attention in speech pathology textbooks.

The speech pathologist is faced with the task of making a comprehensive evaluation of patients with dysarthria and is charged with the responsibility of analyzing and describing not only the acoustic end product but also the underlying dynamics of the problem. Arriving at a differential diagnosis, the speech pathologist can then prescribe a course of treatment and offer a prognosis. The selection of the most appropriate remedial procedure(s) for a particular problem is at times difficult because of the dearth of systematic investigation of the various therapies, or "systems," that are currently available and receiving attention in the literature.

Since each patient requires individual evaluation, it follows that each patient requires individual, specially designed, remedial procedures. There is a glaring deficiency of reported systematic "therapeutic" research in the literature. Subjective clinical interpretations of positive behavioral changes resulting from these various therapeutic approaches are often claimed by the authors of these articles, but empiric evidence supporting the results of many of these various treatment strategies is meager. Given that the problems inherent in research to improve management and treatment procedures are difficult ones, it is obvious that such research is necessary in treating dysarthric patients if we are to make any evaluation of the results of procedures beyond gross clinical impressions.

The specific remedial procedures and therapeutic techniques offered in this book have direct clinical application. However, remedial procedures must be evaluated in terms of their effectiveness as a consequence of the clinical intervention. This type of evaluation must consider the myriad factors that contribute to the success or failure of individual cases, and the extremely complex interaction among these factors must be considered. This type of evaluation can be accomplished only over a considerable period. Even if such longitudinal studies are systematically undertaken, it is inevitable that there will be subjective factors in the research because of the great complexity of variables and individual variations within and between patients.

To succeed in the role that speech pathologists have been encouraged to become engaged in, which is the restoration of these individuals to communicative efficiency [14], requires a process of sifting and selecting management procedures that might transcend the boundaries of any given speech clinic. If rehabilitation programs are to be effective, frequent consultation with professionals in other disciplines and generous use of their expertise is often necessary before a management program can be chosen. I feel compelled to reiterate the necessity of clearly delineating clusters of deviant speech dimensions and their relations to underlying anatomic and physiologic dysfunction. The reader of this chapter is urged to consult the excellent works of Darley, Aronson, and Brown [15–17], most especially their 1975 publication [17]; another good reference is the 1980 historical review by Dworkin and Johns [21].

Resonatory Incompetence:
Hypernasality and Nasal Emission

The entire vocal tract is a resonating cavity, and abnormal resonance can result from various interactions, including abnormal coupling or uncoupling of cavities due to structural or physiologic dysfunction. The primary valving mechanism responsible for normal resonatory competency is the velopharyngeal valving mechanism. In considering the dysarthrias, several assumptions are made for the purposes of this chapter: (1) velopharyngeal incompetency is directly related to neurogenic paresis or paralysis of the oropalatopharyngeal muscles; (2) velopharyngeal incompetency is not due to gross anatomic tissue deficiency, disproportions of the oropharyngeal area, and so on; and (3) in adult patients with acquired velopharyngeal incompetency, relatively normal resonance balance is assumed to have been present before the onset of their neurogenic disorder. That is, it is assumed that these patients had functional integrity of the velopharyngeal mechanism prior to their neurogenic insult.

LaPointe [41], in reviewing the meticulous investigations of Darley, Aronson, and Brown [15, 16], describes the deviant speech dimensions of flaccid dysarthria as consisting of the following three clusters:

1. Phonatory incompetence (hypernasality, nasal emission, audible inspiration, short phrases);
2. Resonatory incompetence (hypernasality, nasal emission, imprecise consonants, short phrases); and
3. Phonatory-prosodic insufficiency (harsh voice, monopitch, monoloudness) (pp. 494–495).

It is commonly accepted that the most frequent abnormal resonatory characteristic in dysarthria is hypernasality due to paralysis, paresis, or incoordination of the muscles involved in velopharyngeal closure. It is recognized that listeners' perceptions of resonance characteristics are influenced by speakers' vocal-tract structures and functions associated with the variable shapes, length, volume, and linkages aside from the velopharyngeal coupling of the pharyngeal and nasal cavities. It is also recognized that the velopharyngeal valving mechanism is the single most important complex that contributes to these resonatory abnormalities (Fig. 3-1).

Thus the most obvious reason for hypernasality, with or without nasal emission, is inadequate func-

Fig. 3-1. Sagittal view of a normal speaker, showing direction of the breath stream through the oral cavity as depicted by the arrows.

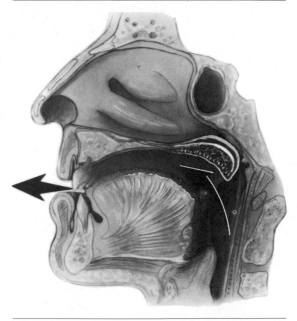

tion of the palatopharyngeal port. However, other aspects of phonatory, articulatory, or prosodic breakdowns are often considered as deviations that are not necessarily directly related to the competency of the velopharyngeal valving mechanism. It is our thesis that many articulatory, phonatory, prosodic, and, of course, resonatory dysfunctions are *directly* associated with dysfunction of the velopharyngeal port mechanism. We believe, as do Randall, Bakes, and Kennedy [62], that vocal-tract dysfunction in one portion affects and influences all portions of the vocal tract and thereby modifies the speech process and acoustical result. As mentioned in Chapter 2, an inadequate velopharyngeal valving mechanism places increased burden on the respiratory system, which could lead to short phrases and phonatory abnormalities affecting the quality of vocal production, pitch, and loudness as well as causing articulatory disturbances, e.g., imprecise consonant production. Therefore the mutual interplay between velopharyngeal valving and other vocal-tract structures undoubtedly influences vocal-tract functioning as a whole. The hierarchic organization of symptoms, as suggested in Chapter 2, needs further analysis, especially as it relates to the integrity of function in the entire vocal tract. Another aspect of viewing the relations of parts to the whole in evaluating symptom complexes will be offered in the following sections.

In Chapter 2, Rosenbek and LaPointe emphasized the construction of a hierarchy of speech symptoms not only for establishing relations between disordered (dysarthric) speech and its underlying neuromuscular dysfunction, but also for the implications of constructing such a system of organization for the purposes of instituting management programs. They suggest that therapy should be directed to the "bottom line" or lowest common denominator in a graded series of symptoms. One example they offered concerned the frequent symptom of inadequate loudness exhibited by patients with hypokinetic dysarthria. They indicate that inadequate loudness reflects limited range of movement of respiratory muscles and that this limited range of movement, in turn, is related to rigidity. They provide an example of a patient who had weak respiratory muscles that were responsible for abnormal respiratory patterns, which in turn were responsible for a harsh, high-pitched, strained-strangled voice quality. Their approach was to improve respiratory support for speech by girdling the patient's abdominal muscles. This approach re-

sulted in essentially normal speech except for persistent speech-sound prolongations and a harsh voice quality that was described as being very mild.

In the true sense of constructing a hierarchy, however, the bases for the dysarthrias lie in higher centers that control neuromuscular activity. The approach used by Rosenbek and LaPointe is directed toward the most basic anatomic part or process affected, and rightly so. The *most* direct approach would be toward neuromuscular junctions, peripheral nerves, the basal ganglia, motor nerve nuclei, or cortical centers, depending on which of the various systems were involved in the dysarthria. As an example, pharmacologic tests are often employed by neurologists as aids in the diagnosis of a number of degenerative disease conditions. In confirming or excluding the diagnosis of myasthenia gravis, Tensilon (edrophonium chloride) has been found suitable [17, 46]. Intravenous administration (2 to 10 mg) of Tensilon has been used, and the resultant muscle-strengthening action can be readily observed within 20 to 60 seconds following the injection, and a significant degree of improvement persists from 1 to 2 minutes. Marked speech improvement following Tensilon administration has a dramatic effect on all dimensions of speech production, including reduction or complete elimination of hypernasality and nasal emission. The effect is shortlived however, and fairly rapid regression and deterioration of speech and return of the preexisting flaccid dysarthric condition become evident because of the short action of the drug. Therefore, because of its brief action, among other reasons, Tensilon is used diagnostically and not therapeutically. Needless to say, we do not have knowledge available to us that will allow significant modification or cure of these patients in a lasting or therapeutic sense.

The velopharyngeal port mechanism can be thought of as the most common denominator in terms of therapy for higher (neural) center damage or it might be considered a higher level system when one thinks of respiratory-laryngeal-phonatory systems. That is, a lower-level mechanism may be repaired to compensate for the lack of higher-level (neural) control and, at the same time, reduce or eliminate dysfunction at lower levels in the vocal tract. Thus elimination of velopharyngeal incompetency might allow reduction of dysfunction up and down the hierarchy simultaneously, with the end result being a qualitative, quantifiable improvement in functional speech. As Wertz wrote in Chapter 1, "It is remarkable how elimination of hypernasality can improve intelligibility. This makes resonance a tempting level for intervention in dysarthria therapy." As it will be seen, we found this temptation compelling, and we found that we had remarkably little resistance to it.

Neurogenic Velopharyngeal Incompetency

Neurogenic velopharyngeal incompetency (NVPI) can be either congenital or acquired. Paresis or paralysis of the palatopharyngeal muscles can be the result of a number of congenital central or peripheral nervous system abnormalities, including such disorders as myotonic dystrophy, bulbar poliomyelitis, Möbius syndrome, and, of course, cerebral palsy. The latter condition is sometimes called *congenital suprabulbar paresis* when the impairment is confined to the upper motor neurons. Many disease entities, processes, and other conditions, such as trauma, invasive neoplasms, cerebrovascular anomalies, occlusions, or hemorrhages can cause acquired neurogenic incompetency of the velopharyngeal valving mechanism (Fig. 3-2). It has been suggested that neurologic

Fig. 3-2. A speaker with normal anatomy but with palatal paresis as a result of brainstem dysfunction. Oral and nasal emission of the breath stream during phonation because of the abnormal coupling between the oral and nasal cavities is depicted by the arrows.

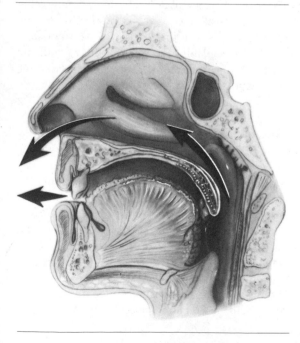

disorders account for the largest number of patients with acquired velopharyngeal incompetency [7].

NVPI has long been recognized by practitioners in the fields of speech pathology, medicine, and dentistry as a serious condition that must be fully investigated to discover ways to reverse its disabling effects on speech and vegetative activities. As stated by Dworkin and Johns [21], "Unfortunately, as we examine the literature in this area, we discover that there are limited data available regarding this condition and its treatment in individuals with dysarthria" (p. 71). In 1983, a symposium entitled "Treatment of the Velopharynx for Individuals with Dysarthria" was chaired by Netsell [51] at the Boys' Town National Institute in Omaha, Nebraska. The purpose of this symposium was to examine the effectiveness of various treatments for NVPI, including surgical, prosthetic, and behavioral procedures. This symposium served as a catalyst for a resurgence of interest in developing treatment criteria for individuals with dysarthria with concomitant velopharyngeal incompetence.

Isolated single-process impairments, such as an "isolated palatopharyngeal incompetence of neurogenic origin" are included under the generic term *dysarthria* [14]. These authors point out that velopharyngeal incompetency as a result of cleft palate and other problems of structural relations of the oropharyngeal area (short palate or congenitally deep pharynx) is *not* included in their definition. Similarly, this chapter is solely concerned with the deviant speech patterns associated with NVPI, whether they are congenital or acquired. In some cases, the palatal paresis or paralysis may be found in isolation; in others, with involvement of other muscle complexes of the oral-facial-pharyngeal-laryngeal complex.

The reader is referred to other chapters in this book and elsewhere [17, 21] for more complete descriptions of diagnostic and evaluative tools available for assessing the disordered speech of the dysarthric patient and, more specifically, for the evaluation of the integrity of the velopharyngeal valving mechanism in the neurogenic patient. The methods discussed by us are thought to be parsimonious and are directed toward a specific management of the disorder.

Speech Therapy/Behavioral Treatment
The goal of speech therapy for individuals with velopharyngeal incompetence, regardless of the underlying pathophysiologic mechanism, is to in-

duce greater velopharyngeal activity, thereby improving resonance balance by reducing or eliminating nasal emission of the breath stream and abnormal nasality. Additional goals in the restoration of these individuals to communicative efficiency also include improving articulatory precision, increasing volume while decreasing the physical energy to achieve more vocal intensity, and increasing phrase length. If improvement in all of these foregoing speech dimensions is realized, it follows that overall speech intelligibility will be greatly enhanced.

Although most of the data available concerning the effects of speech therapy on velar dysfunction were collected from individuals with anatomically deficient palates, certain inferences may be drawn with regard to the efficacy of speech therapy in individuals with neuromuscularly impaired palates as well. A number of therapeutic techniques have been proposed for improving velopharyngeal functioning and speech, including various muscle stimulation programs and articulation exercises. These exercises were designed to induce more effective voluntary control of the velopharyngeal musculature as well as to increase its strength, tone, bulk, and mobility. Although some investigators have reported varying degrees of success in eliminating or reducing hypernasal resonance and associated speech symptoms using one or more of these exercise techniques, others have reported that they do not bring about significant improvement in velopharyngeal functioning [21, 35, 55]. In view of the conflicting evidence, the speech pathologist who uses such exercises should offer a more guarded prognosis, especially if working with an individual whose disorder may involve more than just the velopharyngeal component of the speech mechanism. Data support the contention that it is legitimate to make certain generalizations when applying a traditional speech therapy format for the improvement of articulation, phonation, and/or resonance difficulties in individuals with different types of dysarthria. However, these generalizations cannot as easily be made when applying certain neuromuscular facilitation techniques for the improvement of velar dysfunction associated with different types of dysarthria. For example, whereas facilitation techniques such as application of pressure, icing, brushing, stroking, and electrical stimulation or vibration to the velar musculature may occasionally be successful in eliciting and developing hidden potentials of the weak velopharyngeal mechanism in individuals with *flaccid* dysarthria,

as reported by Dworkin and Johns [21], inhibition techniques such as prolonged icing, pressure to muscle insertion points, slow and irregular stroking, and brushing and desensitization of hyperreflexias of the velar musculature may be prescribed to help bring about more cooperative agonistic-antagonistic velopharyngeal muscle activity in individuals with spastic dysarthria. Thus, the neuromuscular treatment approach for the individual with NVPI associated with mixed dysarthria may vary in accordance with whether such incompetence is characterized by a predominance of flaccid or spastic velopharyngeal muscle activity. Dworkin and Johns [21] further suggest that if a neuromuscular treatment regimen does not result in significant reductions in velopharyngeal incompetency and hypernasality after a period of two months of intensive therapy, it is unlikely that continuing the program will be of further help. However, even if significant mitigation of velopharyngeal incompetency is accomplished through neuromuscular training, the individual may still require prosthodontic and/or surgical intervention to establish a more fully functioning mechanism. Further, since these rehabilitative measures may be of some assistance in effecting improved velopharyngeal functioning, any associated speech symptoms that existed prior to these management procedures will probably require continued attention by the speech clinician. It should be remembered that those patients whose conditions severely affect the velopharynx as well as other components of the speech mechanism may never be able to develop the delicately coordinated movements of the speech musculature necessary for normal speech production. It can be seen that there are several nonsurgical and prosthetic methods designed to ameliorate the problems associated with velopharyngeal incompetency. However, the reduction of abnormal breath stream wastage through the velopharyngeal port mechanism as a result of more traditional speech therapy techniques has been of limited success at best, or has fallen disappointingly short of the desired goal.

Modification of resonatory disorders through the use of various therapeutic behavioral methods, palatal massage, and clinician and biofeedback methods has been described in detail by Dworkin and Johns [21] and in Chapter 2. Mixed reports as to the effectiveness of stimulation and muscle exercises, both voluntary and involuntary, that include blowing, sucking, swallowing, gagging, and, of course, articulation programs are replete, especially in the literature on cleft palate. The general consensus seems to be that these exercises are disappointing and generally ineffective [2, 61]. Other reports, however, claim some success by using variations of rather novel and unique therapy approaches in cases of velopharyngeal incompetency that are *not* associated with neurologic dysfunction [60, 64].

Prosthetic and/or Surgical Management

Prosthetic management has gained a good deal of attention in literature that addresses the management of neurogenic velopharyngeal dysfunction in children (Hardy et al. [26]) and in adult patients

Fig. 3-3. Lateral cephalometric radiographs of two patients (A and B) with neurogenic velopharyngeal incompetency secondary to brainstem trauma. For each patient, the left-hand side shows initial fitting with a palatal-lift prosthesis. The right-hand side of parts A and B shows a modification of the height and length of the prosthesis to effect velopharyngeal closure.

with acquired neurogenic incompetency as reported, for example, by Gonzales and Aronson [25]. In both these reports, the authors indicate that prosthetic management is more successful and desirable than surgical management of neurogenic incompetency. Gonzales and Aronson [25] referred to surgical procedures designed to ameliorate velopharyngeal incompetency as yielding "disappointing results in the management of patients with neurologic palatopharyngeal insufficiencies" (p. 91). Similarly, in management of velopharyngeal dysfunction in children with cerebral palsy, Hardy et al. [26] compared the results of surgical management versus prosthetic management and concluded that "clearly, prosthetic management of palatal paresis in children with cerebral palsy is the procedure of choice. Not only is there no surgical risk to the child, but there appears to be greater probability of success with the prosthetic program than with the surgical procedure" (p. 136).

The use of palatal-lift prostheses (Fig. 3-3) has

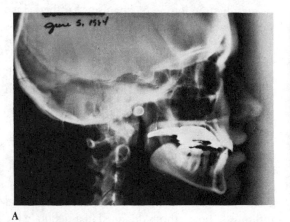
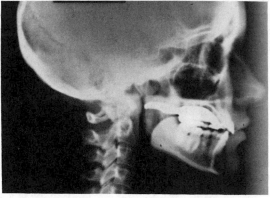

A

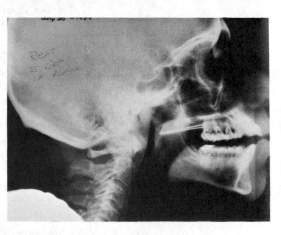
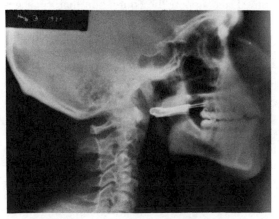

B

been highlighted in several articles [24, 25, 26, 39, 45], all of which reported good results. Methods of constructing palatal-lift prostheses have been discussed in a number of publications, including one by Lawshe et al. [42], who reported on an edentulous patient with velopharyngeal incompetency of undetermined origin who was successfully managed with a palatal-lift prosthesis. These authors generalized that if the prostheses are properly constructed, retention of palatal-lift prostheses may be possible even in edentulous patients with palatal paresis. Other investigators, however, encountered problems with retention [25]. For example, in Chapter 2, Rosenbek and LaPointe reported fitting five edentulous flaccid dysarthric patients with palatal lifts and found that four of them could not retain their prostheses. A more recent (1984) study by Aten et al. [1] reports improved hypernasal resonance in 16 patients with dysarthria of heterogeneous causes after they were fitted with a modified palatal-lift prosthesis. Nine of these patients were edentulous and were fitted with a complete upper denture, which was constructed with an attached light acrylic lift portion connected by wires.

As will be seen, our interdisciplinary team in Dallas has no objection to the use of palatal-lift prostheses, and in fact we have utilized palatal lifts in selected patients as part of a treatment regimen for NVPI that culminates in surgical correction. Since the first edition of this book, we have increased the use of palatal-lift prostheses in our treatment protocol, especially in those patients in whom surgery is judged to be contraindicated based on risk-benefit ratios.

Treatment of NVPI through the use of a "speech-aide prosthesis" (palatal lift) is reported in an excellent article by Lange and Kipfmueller [40]. These authors present findings on six patients with NVPI, all of whom had soft palate structures that were clinically and anatomically normal, who realized improvement in speech intelligibility through prosthetic management. Additionally, they report stimulation of increased movement of the posterior and lateral pharyngeal walls as a result of their patients' wearing prostheses. They indicate that "if stimulation of additional muscle movement can be obtained with the palatal-lift prosthesis and its modification, its use may be indicated to achieve maximum pharyngeal wall movement *prior to secondary surgery*" (italics added) (p. 475). The phenomenon of improved lateral pharyngeal wall motion as a result of mechanically stimulating the muscles of the pharynx by a prosthesis has also

been observed by other investigators [4, 5, 21, 26, 33].

In Dallas, we have observed increased muscle motility after the fitting and wearing of a palatal-lift prosthesis; however, we have observed this phenomenon on a differential basis. That is, frontal cineradiographic views of a patient at rest and during phonation are studied, and lateral pharyngeal wall displacement is measured on an equal-interval psychophysical rating scale of 0 (no medial motion) to 5 (maximum medial motion) in the same manner as reported by Kelsey et al. [38]. These measurements are made both before the patient has been fitted with a prosthesis and after a period of at least 3 months of wearing it (Figs. 3-4 and 3-5). We have noted little to no improved motion in the soft palate per se as a result of wearing the prosthesis as observed on lateral cineradiographic views, but at times we have noted greatly improved mesial movement of the lateral pharyngeal walls (Fig. 3-6). For example, we have observed patients, with 0 to 1 displacement before fitting, increase to ratings of 3 to 4 of lateral pharyngeal wall motion after wearing the palatal lift. As an aside, this differential phenomenon raises a question regarding our knowledge of the nerve supply to the velopharyngeal muscles that has been described in modern texts. It is simply this: Is there significantly different innervation of the superior constrictor and pala-

Fig. 3-4. Frontal view of the velopharyngeal area at rest.

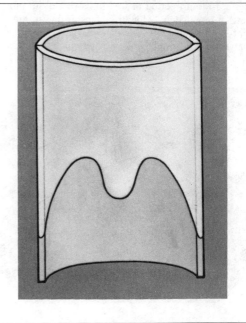

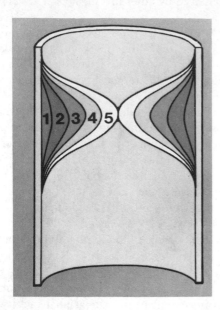

Fig. 3-5. Frontal view of the oropharynx with the velum removed. An equal-interval psychophysical scale is drawn depicting gradations of mesial motion of the lateral pharyngeal walls. No motion at rest to a maximal medial displacement of 5 is depicted.

Fig. 3-6. A patient phonating /ɑ/ before being fitted with a palatal-lift prosthesis is shown by the black arrows on the left. Arrows in right-hand radiograph show lateral pharyngeal wall displacement of 3.5/5 after a 3-month period of wearing a palatal-lift prosthesis. Immediately below the black arrows in the right-hand radiograph, one can see increased lateral pharyngeal wall displacement as compared to the arrows in the radiograph on the left.

topharyngeus as opposed to the levator veli palatini? The association of nerve supply with differential innervation has received little attention, and there is a need to sort out origins and distribution of the supply to the velopharyngeal area, as suggested by Dickson et al. [18, 19]. Such studies could provide a clearer understanding of the physiologic parameters of velopharyngeal closure and could ultimately result in more effective treatment of NVPI (Nishio et al. [53, 54]).

Surgical Management

While paresis, paralysis, and incoordination resulting in incompetency of the velopharyngeal port mechanism have been recognized for many years, until recently this condition has received little attention in the surgical literature. In a 1933 textbook on cleft palate, Dorrance and Shirazy [20] mentioned in passing what one could observe regarding the function of "palsy of the palate." Surgical management of palatal paresis gained some recognition in the early 1950s [12, 49]. In 1960, Randall, Bakes, and Kennedy [62] published the first definitive article on the evaluation and diagnosis of palatal paresis and reported their results in a series of nine patients. Their surgical approach was through the use of an inferiorly based posterior pharyngeal flap in the majority of their cases. While they offered no strong feelings for the preference of this procedure, they did offer reasons to support its use. They suggest that perhaps it would be better to decide on a given procedure and to "develop it thoroughly and to study the results carefully rather than to gain inadequate experiences with a number

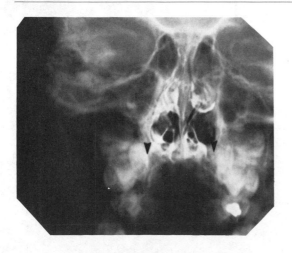
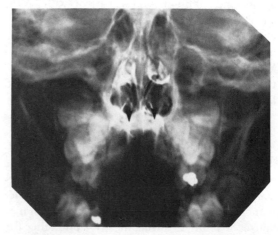

of procedures." They caution that "when neurologic deficits are present, a definite diagnosis is desirable to determine whether the condition is stable or whether it is likely to progress or regress" (p. 494).

Randall, Bakes, and Kennedy [62] indicated that as a result of the surgical correction in their selected cases, significant speech improvement was realized, reporting that "hypernasality and articulatory errors have been consistently diminished or abolished" (p. 494). Other investigators have also reported success in reducing hypernasality through the use of a pharyngeal flap [11, 27].

Under the section Adjuncts to Therapy, by Darley, Aronson, and Brown [17], two methods are offered for approaching velopharyngeal incompetence: palatal lifts and Teflon injection. They cite studies by Lewy, Cole, and Wepman [43] and Bluestone et al. [6]. In the Lewy, Cole, and Wepman study, a Teflon and glycerin mixture was injected along the area of Passavant's line in one patient with NVPI with reported improved speech as a result of this implantation technique. In the study by Bluestone et al., Teflon was injected into the nasopharynx in 12 patients, with reported improvement in voice quality following this procedure. These authors concluded that the results from their study "indicate that Teflon is an excellent implant material for the correction of velopharyngeal insufficiency in selected cases," (p. 22). However, it appears that none of these 12 patients had NVPI, since the criteria for patient selection were limited to "patients with hypernasal speech but with good levator activity . . . patients with poorly defined or erratic levator action . . . were excluded from this treatment" (p. 20). The implantation or injection of other alloplasts, including silicone rubber and Silastic pillows, has been reported. Implantation of fascia, bone, and cartilage into the posterior pharyngeal wall has received some attention in the literature as well [29]. Currently, there are a great variety of techniques for secondary correction of velopharyngeal incompetency, and the reader is referred to Yules [71], who reviews the different surgical procedures, pharyngeal wall implants, dental prostheses, and speech therapy methods used in the management of velopharyngeal incompetency.

For surgical correction of velopharyngeal incompetency, the posterior pharyngeal flap procedure appears to be the most popular approach at this time. While there has been a considerable amount of conflicting information as to the man-

ner in which the flap functions (dynamic versus static) and the type of flap used (inferiorly based versus superiorly based, for example), the literature has, for the most part, been focused on secondary procedures used in patients with cleft palates [8, 10]. A resurgence of renewed interest in surgical correction of NVPI is evidenced by a number of articles and reports [28, 33, 34, 37, 47] and more recently by Tebbetts and Johns [69] and Johns, Tebbetts, and Cannito [36].

In the investigation by Heller et al. [28], 70 patients were studied, 42 possessing velopharyngeal incompetency caused other than by cleft palate. Of these, 15 patients had idiopathic velopharyngeal insufficiency associated with neurologic impairment because of central nervous system dysfunction ranging from severe cerebral palsy to minimal brain dysfunction (p. 352). After careful evaluation, 8 of the 15 patients in this category were considered good surgical candidates, and in all cases the procedure of choice was "a broad, superiorly based pharyngeal flap . . . which included the entire posterior wall of the pharynx" (p. 353). The authors reported that their neurologic patients achieved either improved or acceptable voice quality after pharyngeal flap surgery. The authors suggested criteria for determining candidacy for surgery that focused not so much on the diagnostic label of the disability but on the "degree of severity of the anatomic condition and of the physiologic dysfunction associated with the disability" (p. 357). In their opinion prosthetic devices have severe limitations; they maintain that with thorough evaluation, careful patient selection, and the proper timing of the surgery, a large number of patients can have significant improvement in their speech and voice quality. They conclude that the results of their study "suggest that previous criteria for performing surgery on the multi-handicapped patient may have been too conservative and need to be reexamined" (p. 358).

In 1975 Kaplan [37] studied 41 patients with submucous clefts of the palate and 32 with "occult" submucous clefts. Five of the occult cases were in patients described as having palatal paresis as a result of primary neuromuscular disease. After evaluation at the time of surgery, the procedure was by "levator muscle sling reconstruction, palate push-back, and pharyngeal flap. Excellent speech results are obtained *except with patients having palatal paresis*" (italics added) (p. 368).

Also in 1975, Minami et al. [47] presented their experience with 98 patients without overt cleft palate and related their experience to the relevant literature. These authors used a modified classification system [9, 62] and their cases fell into groups of what they called the "big four." Of these, patients in group 3, palatal paresis, are of special interest. Palatal paresis fell under the heading of dynamic disorders of velopharyngeal incompetency; the authors broke down their classification further in terms of the mechanism involved and their diagnosis in terms of whether it was congenital or acquired. There were 19 patients in this group and of these, five were diagnosed as simply dysarthric. They operated on nine patients, ranging in age from 4 to 60 years, and reported that "all had speech therapy prior to their surgery without significant improvement. Preoperative cineradiography revealed palatal paresis varying from a markedly diminished quickness and amplitude to a total paralysis" (p. 581). They reported that for this group, the patients' preoperative hypernasality was worse than that found in their other three groups and that, in general, the results of their surgical treatment were disappointing regardless of the operation used. The procedure they most frequently used was a combined palatal pushback with a superiorly based pharyngeal flap. Two of the nine patients operated on had implants; one received a silicone rubber pillow and the other received a cartilage implant placed behind the posterior pharyngeal wall with reported minimal benefits. Of the 10 patients who were not operated on, whose nasality ranged from minimal to moderate, minimal or no improvement with time was found on follow-up examinations. However, they also reported that the surgical results in patients with palatal paresis were poor regardless of the procedure, and the authors consider that the combination of palatal pushback and superiorly based pharyngeal flap is inappropriate for these patients. Minami et al. do a masterful survey of the literature and consider a wide spectrum of disorders resulting in NVPI, including upper motor neuron disorders, nuclear disorders, peripheral nerve disorders, myoneural junction disorders, primary muscle disorders, and disorders that are nonspecific or have an undetermined cause. Their diagnosis of palatal paresis in addition to neurologic consultation is by physical examination, speech evaluation, and radiography. As to the management of patients with palatal paresis, they indicate that palatal lifts and obturators may be the treatment of choice, at least in patients with cerebral palsy. They go on to say, "We think that patients with palatal paresis need obturation—and that good results may be achieved

by using wide, lined pharyngeal flaps or the 'lateral port control' pharyngeal flap recently described by Hogan" (p. 583). Minami et al. offer several factors that might adversely influence the result of surgical treatment, and they include "the advanced age at which these patients are first seen, often after years of unsuccessful speech therapy [and] misdiagnosis and/or inappropriate treatment by health professionals" (p. 585).

In the dysarthric patient, frequently there is a long, flaccid soft palate that is immobile because of a lack of proper innervation. Surgical correction of these patients has to be differentiated from that of the incompetent patient with a cleft palate, who may have a short velum with a large space between the soft palate and the posterior pharynx during phonation. In this patient, it is often necessary to use methods that lengthen the palate as well as close the velopharyngeal space. Thus, on the basis of a deficiency of tissue, palatal lengthening is clearly indicated in many of these patients. In patients with neurogenic incompetency, surgical correction of the velopharyngeal port can be attained by a properly designed and executed superiorly based pharyngeal flap [33, 69]. All the patients in our series have been treated by these procedures. Also, levator dissection and retrodisplacement should be considered when a pharyngeal flap is done in patients with cleft palates; however, it is unnecessary and probably should not be considered when the procedure is performed in patients with neurogenic disorders.

Evaluation of Physical Management Results
Patients with cleft palates offer a very large corpus of data from which the effects of secondary surgical procedures, especially pharyngeal flaps, have been studied. Although results obtained through surgical treatment of NVPI have been reported by some to be disappointing in general [47, 55], recent reports are encouraging regarding pharyngeal flap surgery [28, 33, 34, 36, 69]. It would appear to be unscientific to dismiss a therapeutic procedure summarily or, conversely, to accept one uncritically. Thus we must restrain our enthusiasm regarding a particular therapeutic approach until it has been subjected to critical scientific analysis (Lindsay [44]). Such temperance is advised by Spriestersbach et al. [68] who state that "Unsolved problems of clinical management are numerous, and an evaluation of the state of the art . . . is particularly frustrating because there is inadequate evidence from which

to assess the relative value of different therapeutic procedures" (p. 142). Moreover, as Hogan [31] has pointed out, "there is a remarkable lack of objective evaluation of surgical results in all series of recently reported approaches to the treatment of velopharyngeal incompetency" (p. 322).

Various investigators have reported on some of the factors that influence the success or failure of physical management techniques [21, 26, 35, 36]. Hardy et al. [26], while recommending that prosthetic management of palatal paresis in children may be the procedure of choice, reviewed histories of children with neurogenic velopharyngeal incompetency who had undergone pharyngeal flap surgery. The first patient reviewed was a high school student who "demonstrated dramatic improvement in articulation skills and an increase in mean length of response. . . . He made this progress despite generalized neuromuscular problems, and his academic success is attributed in great part to his ability to communicate orally" (p. 130). At the time of this report the authors indicated that this young man had maintained this level for approximately 5 years after surgery and that the surgical approach permitted him to impound satisfactory amounts of oral breath pressure for longer periods, increasing his ability to produce plosive and fricative sounds. The authors considered his surgery to be highly successful, since the young man continued to maintain gains in articulation. They reviewed cases of other patients who underwent pharyngeal flap surgery, which was judged to be ineffective in reducing the size of the velopharyngeal port. They indicated that cinefluorographic films revealed flap placement to be quite low on the posterior pharyngeal wall and postulated that this positioning may have had the effect of tethering the palate down during speech. They related that such a possibility seems likely and observed in two of their three unsuccessful cases that the pharyngeal flaps were inserted inferiorly to the palate on the posterior pharyngeal wall as demonstrated by cinefluorographic films. They suggest that this anatomic relation might be the cause of the unsuccessful results.

Over the years, Owsley and his associates have published a series of reports regarding the level of attachment of the pharyngeal flap as it relates to speech results. Owsley et al. [56–59], Skoog [67], and Webber, Chase, and Jobe [70] have stressed the importance of maintaining a superior-posterior vector motion of the soft palate as it relates to the base of the flap on the posterior pharyngeal wall.

These authors maintain that a "low-based" pharyngeal flap produces traction in an inferior direction and thus tethers the soft palate. A significant number of patients with postpharyngeal flap velopharyngeal incompetency have been reported by a number of authors, including Blackfield et al. [3]. Fara and Vele [23] found that the superiorly based pharyngeal flap provided far superior speech results as compared to the inferiorly based flap, as derived from speech analyses of 270 patients from 5 to 25 years postoperatively.

Mesial movement of the lateral pharyngeal walls as this movement relates to velopharyngeal closure in normal subjects has been reported in a number of articles. The role of the lateral pharyngeal walls has also been the subject of a number of studies as it relates to pharyngeal flap surgery and the functioning of the velopharyngeal port mechanism. Skolnick and McCall [66] indicated that mesial movement of the lateral walls is essential for closure, and Morris and Spriestersbach [50] submit that mesial movement of the lateral walls is a better predictor of the success of the pharyngeal flap technique. These authors emphasized the need always to "consider function and not simply structure [but] of equal or perhaps greater importance, is an evaluation of the movements of the structures involved which must be employed to close those openings to provide velopharyngeal competence during speech" (pp. 69, 70). To underscore this point, Dickson et al. [18], in discussing the dynamics, or motion, of the pharyngeal flap as seen on lateral cineradiography, suggest the adynamic status of the flap per se and the importance of mesial motion of the lateral pharyngeal walls. "Mechanically, the flap can serve only as an obturator since vertical movement of the flap cannot close the lateral ports around the flap. All of the research in this area has demonstrated that medial movement of the lateral pharyngeal walls is the active mechanism for closure" (p. 481).

The same observation has been noted for prosthetic management as well, as described by Gonzales and Aronson [25], who found improved palatopharyngeal efficiency when prostheses were removed in four patients. They postulated that better closure might have been the result of mechanical stimulation of the velopharyngeal muscles by the prosthesis. They conclude that their experience suggests that the palatal-lift prosthesis can be used to stimulate the pharyngeal muscles, which in turn could considerably improve velopharyngeal closure [4, 5, 25, 40].

Correction of velopharyngeal incompetency in neurogenic patients, as reported in a number of investigations cited in the foregoing sections, has enabled these patients to obtain good results in overcoming hypernasality and nasal emission. However, inferences regarding amelioration of resonatory incompetency, that is, imprecise consonants and short phrases or voice disorders, in addition to the hypernasality and nasal emission, have been sparse. For example, Heller et al. [28] report that a large number of their patients "achieved improved voice and even good voice quality" (p. 358). These authors, in suggesting criteria for determining candidacy for pharyngeal flap surgery, feel that the degree of severity of the anatomic condition and the physiologic dysfunction associated with the disability is the significant factor. They also offered contraindications for surgical correction and include "the intellectually gifted child with severe neurologic impairment of the articulatory musculature, because surgery could not alter his dysarthric articulation or improve his general speech pattern, even though voice quality might be improved" (p. 357). As noted earlier, other investigators have reported not only improved resonance characteristics but also improved articulatory abilities. For example, Randall, Bakes, and Kennedy [62], in their series of neurologic patients with velopharyngeal incompetency, reported consistently diminished or abolished hypernasality *and* articulatory errors. As previously noted, quantifiable increases in articulatory skills of dysarthric children with surgically corrected NVPI have been reported [27]. Also, the data demonstrating positive changes in speech behavior, including improved resonance, articulation, and speech intelligibility because of surgery [33, 36, 38, 69, 71], support the notion that overall speech intelligibility can be improved as a consequence of surgery. These reports and our findings are in direct contrast to Noll's [55] opinion, which he expressed in 1982: "Therefore, neurologic integrity is probably necessary for any kind of palatopharyngeal surgery to achieve its optimal results" (p. 562).

Interaction Between Speech Pathology and Plastic Surgery

As can be seen, there are many instances of velopharyngeal incompetency that pose difficult problems of correction. Clinicians find patients with frank problems secondary to clefting and those with occult, idiopathic, or neurogenic problems who possess velopharyngeal incompetency challenging when they attempt to restore their communicative efficiency. Scattered reports exist regarding surgical or prosthetic management of patients with congenital or acquired NVPI; the following section describes a consecutive series of patients who underwent comprehensive evaluation and surgical management of their velopharyngeal incompetency. While our series includes patients of all ages and varied disorders who had difficult problems of velopharyngeal incompetency, the primary focus is on young adult patients with acquired NVPI. Many of the patients in this group had previously undergone rather prolonged, unsuccessful management regimens, which included combinations of speech therapy, palatal massage, muscle retraining programs, and the wearing of palatal-lift prostheses. All these patients were comprehensively studied and underwent preoperative neurologic, speech, cineradiographic, panendoscopic, manometric, and surgical evaluations.

The surgical management of these patients was accomplished by a tailormade superiorly based posterior pharyngeal flap that was carefully outlined and marked at the time of surgery. In selected patients, catheters were introduced transnasally to maintain lateral port apertures on either side of the flap in the manner described by Hogan [30, 31]. Representative cases will be presented for clarifying the rationale, procedure, and results to the reader, but definitive, exhaustive case studies will not be included, since they are presented elsewhere [34, 36].

Since the goal of surgical intervention in these patients is to provide them with a mechanism for functional speech, the design of the surgical procedure is based on information we have regarding normal anatomic and physiologic functioning of the velopharyngeal port mechanism. In order to assimilate normal structure and function surgically, particular attention is paid to the extent of motion of the lateral pharyngeal walls observed in these patients. Regardless of the cause of the velopharyngeal incompetency, each of our patients undergoes preoperative multiview videofluoroscopic studies [65]. As mentioned earlier, the motility of each lateral pharyngeal wall is rated on an equal-interval scale [38] at rest; during sustained phonation of vowels, fricatives, and sibilants; and during connected speech which consists of test phrases. Lateral pharyngeal wall motion is observed and rated from the frontal projection without the use of contrast medium initially, and again after a

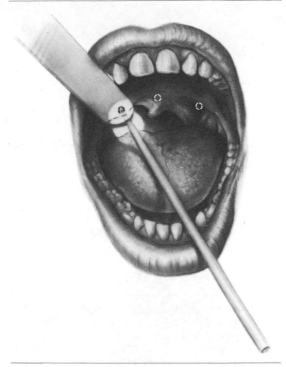

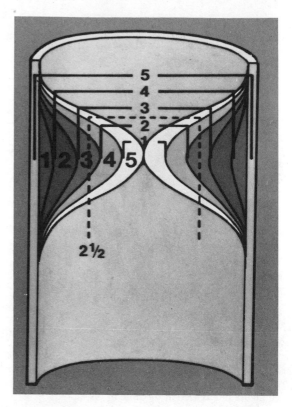

Fig. 3-7. The marking procedure for outlining a proposed tailormade pharyngeal flap. These markings are made during phonation in the operating room. The most medial excursion of each lateral pharyngeal wall is located and marked while the patient is sustaining the /ɑ/ sound. These markings denote the desired width for the lateral incisions of the pharyngeal flap. The midline marking denotes the desired level for the superior attachment of the flap.

Fig. 3-8. Overlay of marked tailormade pharyngeal flaps appropriate for the extent of lateral pharyngeal wall motion. For example, a 4/5 (see top numbers) width would be appropriate for a patient with 1/5 lateral pharyngeal wall motion.

barium mixture is introduced transnasally in order to coat the pharyngeal walls. Lateral pharyngeal wall motion can also be observed clinically by both peroral examination and endoscopic observation.

Once the patient is judged to be a good surgical candidate, the following procedures are carried out in the operating room. With the patient in a seated position on the operating table, a panendoscopic evaluation is made; then the patient is asked to sustain the /ɑ/, and the posterior pharynx is carefully visualized perorally. Mesial movement of the lateral pharyngeal walls is noted and the landmarks are identified. Often, it is necessary to elevate the soft palate with a tongue blade in order to visualize the medial motion of the lateral pharyngeal walls at approximately the level of the palatal plane. Using an atomizer, a solution of 4% Xylocaine is topically sprayed in the pharyngeal area. With the patient sustaining the /ɑ/ sound, the most medial excursion of each lateral pharyngeal wall is located and marked at the level of the palatal plane on the

oral side. (We have used several methods for making the landmarks, including surgical Weck clips, silver nitrate sticks, methylene blue marking pens, and disposable cauterizing units.) A third marking is made in the midline at or above the level of the palatal plane on the nasal side, so it is above the tubercle of the atlas and usually approximates the level of the clivus. These lateral markings denote the desired area for the lateral incisions of the pharyngeal flap, and the midline marking denotes the desired level (height) for the base of the flap. After the marking is complete the patient again sustains the /ɑ/ and the landmarks and lateral markings of the "outlined flap" are easily visualized perorally (Figs. 3-7 and 3-8).

The patient is then administered a general anesthesia by means of an endotracheal tube, a Dingman mouth gag is put into place, and the operative field is easily visualized. The patient, already in a supine position, is further positioned so the head

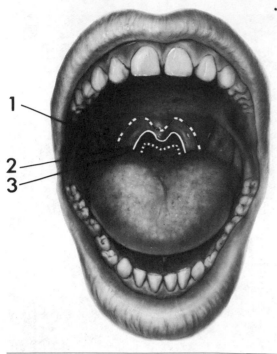

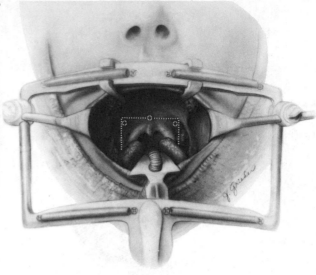

Fig. 3-10. The "ghosted" landmarks and dimensions of an "outlined" tailormade pharyngeal flap. This depicts the patient in a supine position with the head and neck hyperextended, tilted inferiorly, and under a general anesthetic with a mouth gag in place.

Fig. 3-9. Three levels of palatal configurations: (1) during sustained phonation, (2) at rest, and (3) palatal configuration as seen at the time of operation.

and neck are hyperextended and tilted down toward the surgeon. The markings that were made while the patient was awake and in the seated position, before the general anesthesia was administered, are not now visualized unless the mucosa of the soft palate is moved significantly with a surgical hook.

There are several reasons that appear to contribute to this phenomenon: (1) Because of the general anesthetic the muscles are flaccid; (2) because of the patient's supine position and the head and neck being hyperextended and tilted inferiorly, the forces of gravity naturally pull the muscles posteriomedially; and (3) because of the pressive forces of the mouth gag, the palatoglossus and palatopharyngeus muscles mechanically pull the palate in an inferiomedial direction, further decreasing the lateral dimensions of the velopharyngeal lumen. Thus, because of these reasons, the lumen of the palatopharyngeal area is considerably narrowed medially and the anterior-posterior distance between the velum and the posterior pharyngeal wall is reduced as well (Fig. 3-9). Preoperative and intraoperative photographs and movies confirm these observations regarding the placement of the marking ma-

terials that outline the proposed pharyngeal flap. An inexperienced surgeon might well make a much narrower flap with a lower base if the desired landmarks have not been marked and the flap outlined before the patient is put under a general anesthesia (Figs. 3-10 and 3-11). The inadequacy of narrow flaps or flaps based too low in the posterior pharynx, resulting in poor functional speech results, is not an infrequent finding [31, 57, 69]. Some surgeons mark and outline their proposed pharyngeal flaps after general anesthesia has been administered. Based on our experience, we strongly advocate the presurgical marking and outlining while the patient is awake in the seated position, responsive, and most importantly, phonating.

Clinical and Objective Analysis of Postsurgical Speech Results

Velopharyngeal incompetency results in a substantial increase in the damping of the vocal system. Regarding nasalized vowel sounds, Curtis [13] states that "the spectral effects to be expected from this large damping are (1) an increase in the bandwidths of the formants, and a corresponding flattening of the formant peaks; (2) a reduction in the overall energy levels of the vowels" (p. 47). As will be shown, these theoretical predictions are substan-

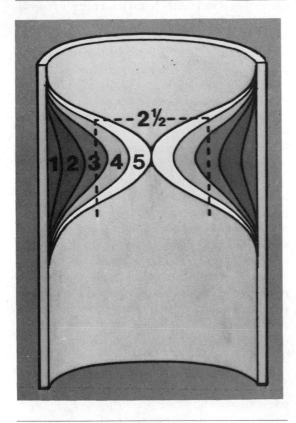

Fig. 3-11. The dotted lines depict the markings for the width (2.5/5) of a proposed tailormade pharyngeal flap. A 2.5/5 width is one-half of the area of the posterior pharynx and would be appropriate for lateral pharyngeal wall motion of 3 to 3.5/5. The width of this flap would be unnecessarily wide for 5/5 motion and too narrow for 2/5 preoperative lateral pharyngeal wall motion.

tiated by the comparison of preoperative and postoperative spectrograms of patients who have undergone pharyngeal flap surgery.

The effect of damping the vocal system has a twofold effect on perceptual judgment. First, the blurring of the resonances may affect the perceptual distinctiveness of the sounds being uttered. Second, the overall intensity of the sound radiated by the speaker will be appreciably reduced, as has been shown by House and Stevens [32]. The reduction in amplitudes of the first formants has been shown to be the greatest. It appears that the individuals with velopharyngeal incompetency are always confronted with the necessity of speaking with vocal tract systems that absorb a considerably greater amount of energy than do those of persons with a normal velopharyngeal mechanism. To compensate for this, the person with velopharyngeal in-

competency can obtain adequate vocal output intensity, as Curtis [13] states, "only by increasing the exciting force from the source, be it the larynx or the noise created by a consonant constriction. Not only will the additional damping of the vocal tract system weaken the vowel sounds and possibly make them less distinct because of the greater formant bandwidths, but the constrictive consonant sounds will be weakened also" (p. 52). While it may be possible for an individual with velopharyngeal incompetency to compensate for this damping of the cavities by driving the vocal system harder, this can only be done by increased expiratory pressure from the lungs and, especially during consonant articulation, by a higher rate of airflow. For example, a person with velopharyngeal incompetency demonstrates the characteristic of his or her speech by pronounced nasalization. Such a speaker will have to expend more than the usual effort to reach an acceptable level of speech intensity [13].

Moll [48], in discussing measurement techniques in assessing nasal voice quality, suggests that it is possible to construct some index of nasality that is shown to have empirical validity with practical advantages in comparison with listener-judgment procedures. He states that "it appears, however, that nasality judgments obtained by some psychological scaling procedure provide a more valid and at least as reliable assessment of this voice quality dimension as is provided by any other technique. By the use of judgment procedures an experimenter recognizes the fact that a listener is always an integral part of the speech communication process. Extreme caution should be exercised in discarding listener judgments for presumably more objective measures which may not be valid or reliable. For as Kantner (1948) pointed out, in the assessment of nasality the 'human ear is the final detector and arbiter' " (p. 100).

The only justification for surgery in these patients is, of course, an expected increase in the intelligibility of the patient's speech. While the literature contains many subjective reports of improvement, more objective evidence is clearly needed before these surgical procedures can be recommended for widespread use in neurologic patients. To this end we have undertaken a study of our own patients with the twofold purpose of evaluating their preoperative speech status and comparing it to their postoperative speech and of identifying the precise nature of the improvement, if any.

In the first part of our ongoing study, a panel of

naive listeners and speech pathologists is asked to identify words when given a closed set. They are also asked to rate the speech samples for intelligibility and nasality. Both preoperative and postoperative speech samples are subjected to the above analysis. The panel's judgments thus provide comparable measures of the intelligibility and quality of these patients' speech before and after the pharyngeal flap surgery.

Valuable as these clinical measures are, it is also desirable to give more objective content to such phrases as "decreased nasality," "more precise articulation," and so on [63]. The second part of the study, therefore, employs the sound spectrograph to examine the speech sounds in detail and to isolate and identify the sources of improvement. Relying on what is known from the acoustic theory of speech production (Fant [22]), it should be possible to infer from changes observed in the acoustic signal what functional physiologic changes have taken place.

CASE HISTORY. On February 16, 1974, T. L., a 35-year-old man, sustained a gunshot wound to the left frontal region as well as the left shoulder and left mandible. The cerebral injury left him with a right-sided hemiplegia, mild aphasia, and severe mixed dysarthria. He possessed bulbar and pseudobulbar palsy with the bulbar component predominating. He underwent a left frontotemporal craniectomy on February 17 with extensive debridement of the wound, regaining alertness by the next day. Postoperatively, he did well and was managed with intensive physical, occupational, and speech therapy. His aphasia cleared, and the major residual speech disorder was a severe flaccid dysarthria with milder spastic dysarthric components. The regimen of speech therapy included palatal massage exercises, and in August he was fitted with a palatal-lift prosthesis. On November 21, multiview cineradiographic studies were done, and on lateral projection the soft palate appeared to be of average length and size and anatomically normal at rest. However, the palate did not move at all while sustaining the sounds /i/, /dɑ/, or /u/. There was some movement noted when he sustained the /s/ sound maximally. The frontal projections were read as having little, if any, motion of the lateral pharyngeal walls, the movement being judged to be 1 on a scale of 5 for both lateral pharyngeal walls. The radiologic impression was gross velopharyngeal incompetence. On November 27, a proposed pharyngeal flap was marked and outlined,

followed by a superiorly based posterior pharyngeal flap procedure. T. L. tolerated the procedure without difficulty. He was discharged 3 days after surgery. A postoperative tape recording was made on January 8, 1975, and it was noted that T. L. had made significant improvement. T. L. returned to the hospital for an elective cosmetic cranioplasty to correct a 6-cm square defect of the left frontal bone. This surgery was done on January 10, and he was discharged on the sixth postoperative day without complaint. In March, T. L. progressed to the point where he was self-sufficient and gainfully employed full-time. A follow-up tape recording was made on September 3 and spectrographic analyses of preoperative and postoperative tape recordings were done.

On October 8, T. L. was discharged from the neurosurgery outpatient clinic with no follow-up planned. On his discharge from the clinic it was noted in his chart that he still possessed a mild right hemiparesis, but he continued to be gainfully employed and well adjusted to his environment (Fig. 3-12).

Figure 3-12 shows broadband sound spectrograms of preoperative and postoperative speech for comparison. The words are *eight*, *nine*, and *ten*, spoken in a counting sequence by T. L. Numbered arrows indicate acoustic characteristics to be compared:

1. Diffuseness of energy in the region of the first formant (i.e., below 1 kHz) found in the preoperative samples is a well-known result of significant oral-nasal coupling. This is in contrast to the postoperative samples, where vowels show sharply defined first formants.
2. Low-frequency nasal formant commonly observed in nasalized vowels with first formants; absent in the postoperative sample.
3. Higher first-formant frequency in nasalized (preoperative) than in nonnasal version of /æ/ in the patient's pronunciation of /næn/ (nine).
4. Generally more intense and better-defined formants in the postoperative sample.

These features all indicate improved postoperative velopharyngeal closure and correlate with perceptual judgments of clarity, improved intelligibility, and decreased nasality. The most important acoustic change is from diffuse, poorly defined formants, especially the first formant, to well-defined formant structure.

To see how these characteristics might be quan-

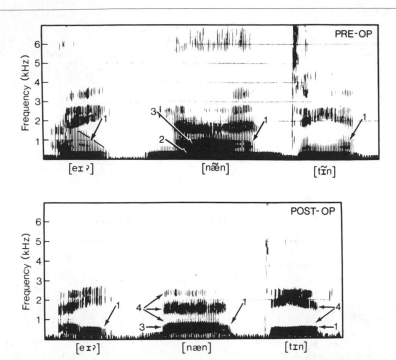

Fig. 3-12. Preoperative and postoperative broadband sound spectrograms (patient T. L.) of the words *eight nine-ten*, spoken in a counting sequence.

Fig. 3-13. Preoperative and postoperative narrow-band (45-Hz) filter setting of the vowels /ei/ in *eight* and /æ/ in *nine* (patient T. L.).

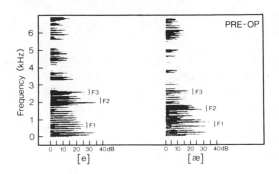

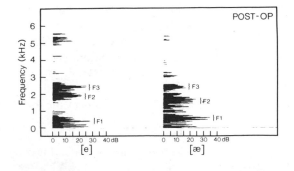

tified, observe the sections in Figure 3-13. Here the vowels /ei/ in *eight* and /æ/ in *nine* are analyzed with the narrow-band (45-Hz) filter setting and displayed as line spectra with all the harmonics shown separately. In the preoperative speech, it can be seen that the energy in the vowels is much more evenly distributed across the harmonics, particularly below 1 kHz, making the formants less distinct (broad band-widths).

Since this characteristic, the distinctness of the lower formants, is the primary auditory cue for vowel identification, it is easy to understand why, perceptually, this patient's intelligibility is greatly improved (Figs. 3-14 and 3-15).

Clinical assessment of T. L.'s speech made it clear, however, that more than just a decrease in nasality was involved. Figure 3-16 is a pair of spectrograms of the utterance "this is the house that Jack built" spoken by T. L. before and after surgery. In this figure a logarithmic frequency scale is used. Note the same overall increase in the distinctness of the formants as noted in Figures 3-14 and 3-15, and several other factors as well:

1. Intense and well-defined frication energy for the /z/ of *is* and /s/ of *house*. This is the direct result of the ability to impound sufficient air behind a vocal-tract constriction to create a strong turbulent sound source.

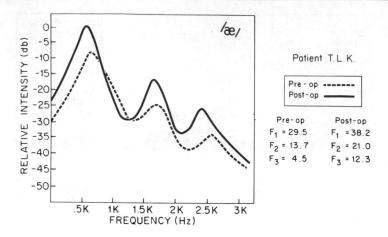

Fig. 3-14. Overall spectra of preoperative (*dashed line*) and postoperative (*solid line*) production of /æ/.

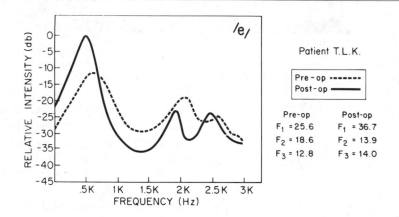

Fig. 3-15. Overall spectra of preoperative and postoperative production of /e/.

2. Transient burst at the beginning of the /dʒ/ in *Jack* is again the result of successful impoundment of air, providing the overpressure needed for plosive release. In the preoperative sample, only weak frication was achieved.

3. Sharp cutoff of vowel amplitude appropriate to voiceless stops in final position in *Jack* and *built*, as compared with overlengthened vowels and "trailing off" of amplitude in the preoperative speech, probably because stop closure did not produce the voicing shutoff that occurs in a properly sealed vocal tract.

Curtis [13] points out an additional implication regarding the speech of a person with velopharyngeal incompetency "that may not be entirely obvious is that both the dynamic intensity range and the vocal pitch range of such a speaker are likely to be significantly reduced" (p. 56), as shown in the preoperative tracing shown in Fig. 3-17.

This last feature brings us from the area of spectral characteristics, roughly what is meant by "resonance," to a consideration of the dynamic features of articulation. Fig. 3-17 compares the same utterances as are in Fig. 3-16, with respect to their overall amplitude over time. The dramatic differences in dynamic range (approximately 10 dB) are immediately obvious and may be attributed to a combination of several factors:

1. Acoustic oral-nasal coupling reduces the intensity of vowels;
2. Venting of air through the velopharyngeal port prevents air-pressure buildup for initial stop consonants; and

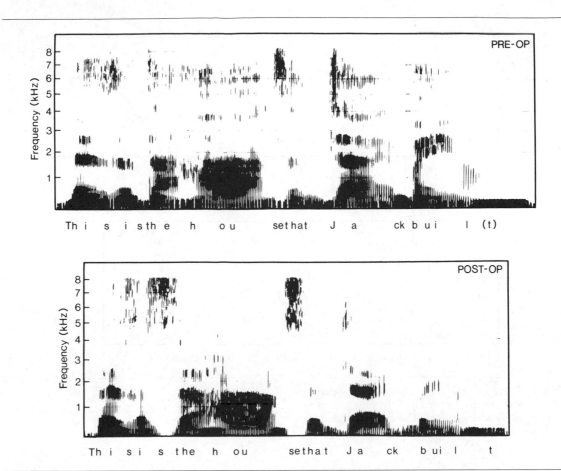

Fig. 3-16. Logarithmic frequency scale of preoperative and postoperative spectrograms (patient T. L.) of the utterance "This is the house that Jack built."

3. Venting of air inhibits rapid shutdown of voicing for final stops, producing a gradual trailing off of amplitude.

We may further speculate whether the loss of the intraoral pressure buildup that normally accompanies stop production causes further problems in timing and articulation. For example, the lengthening and trailing off of the vocalic part of *Jack* and *built* in the preoperative utterance might be attributed in part to the absence of this feedback cue. This is speculative at the present time, given our limited knowledge of the feedback mechanisms in speech, but it cannot be ruled out as one of the factors responsible for the dramatic overall improvement observed in the postoperative speech of many patients.

The following summarizes perceptual data displayed in a histogram and descriptive analyses of the acoustic spectrographic findings for patient

M. M. (Figs. 3-18 and 3-19). In the preoperative nares-open (see Fig. 3-18) condition, frequency by time spectral analysis revealed (1) consonantal energy characterized by intense low-frequency frication representing compensatory velopharyngeal snorting used in lieu of oral plosion of /p/; (2) initial hard glottal attack is indicative of forcefulness of the child's compensatory articulation; and (3) inappropriately distributed vowel resonances are conditioned by abnormal nasal coupling [35, 63]. In this patient, these appear as inappropriate formant frequencies, nasal antiresonances, and a widening of formant bands with associated loss of formant transitions. These deviations are most marked for the diphthong /aɪ/; (4) there is a prolonged, gradual trailing off of formant amplitude for final /i/; (5) amplitude by time tracing reveals a lack of definable syllable structure within and between words, related to continuous airflow through the velopharyngeal port.

In the postoperative condition (see Fig. 3-18) (10) there is distinct oral plosion for /p/ phonemes. (11) Also present is a dramatic redistribution of

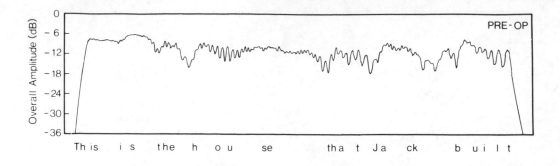

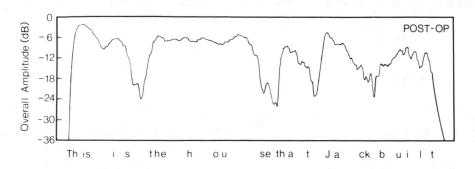

Fig. 3-17. Preoperative and postoperative comparison of the same utterance as in Fig. 3-16 with respect to overall amplitude over time. The dramatic difference in dynamic range is immediately obvious.

Fig. 3-18. Preoperative and postoperative average amplitude by time, and frequency by time displays generated from the utterance "I pet puppies." These acoustic findings confirm the perceptual ratings (see Fig. 3-19) of this patient's speech.

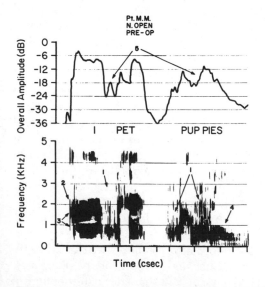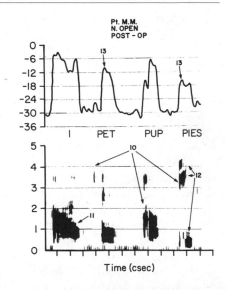

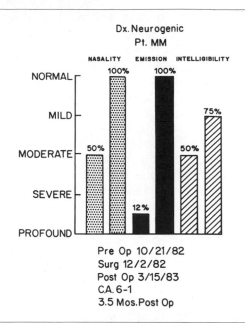

Dx. Neurogenic
Pt. MM

Fig. 3-19. This histogram summarizes the perceptual data compared with the spectrographic findings depicted in Fig. 3-18 for patient M. M. The column on the left for each condition is the preoperative status and the right-hand column is the postoperative result; c.g., preoperatively, nasal emission was judged to be profound (12%), and normal (100%) postoperatively.

vowel resonance, with the initial /aɪ/ appearing as a veritable inverse filter of its preoperative counterpart. That is, a preoperative antiresonance becomes replaced by a resonant peak. The postoperative diphthong approximates a normal /aɪ/ with close association of formants 1 and 2 at onset followed by divergent raising of formant 2 and falling of formant 1. These transitions are less evident in the preoperative nares-open condition, where their reduction may be related to a widening of formant bandwidth. High-frequency periodic energy is now evident for /i/, (12) with more abrupt offset of formant 1 amplitude. Amplitude by time tracing reveals distinct syllabic structure with decreased duration (13).

Acoustic findings confirm the perceptual ratings (Fig. 3-19) of M. M.'s speech, wherein the greatest improvement was a change from severe to profound nasal emission to no impairment. This was associated with distinct but somewhat less dramatic gains in resonance (nasality) and intelligibility (both of which were also less dramatically impaired).

Conclusion

It can be seen that there are several methods designed to ameliorate the problems associated with

NVPI. The reduction of abnormal breath-stream wastage through the velopharyngeal port mechanism as a result of more traditional speech therapy techniques has been of limited success at best, or has fallen disappointingly far short of the desired goal.

The well-trained speech pathologist has significant expertise to bring to bear in the diagnosis through the description, differentiation, and delineation of significant dysarthric symptoms. He or she also possesses the necessary expertise to design management strategies leading to the establishment of treatment approaches and implementation of specific therapeutic procedures in a systematic and rational manner. While there is a rather vast armamentarium of evaluative and remedial techniques available to the speech pathologist, the limitations of these techniques must also be recognized. The goal of restoring the dysarthric patient who possesses significant NVPI to communicative efficiency consists of (1) improving articulatory precision, (2) increasing volume while decreasing the physical energy to achieve more normal intensity, (3) improving resonance balance by reducing or eliminating nasal emission of the breath stream and abnormal nasality, and (4) increasing phrase length. Improvement in all of the foregoing (and more) speech dimensions is possible by restoring the velopharyngeal valving mechanism to a state of competency. If this goal is realized, it follows that overall speech intelligibility will be greatly enhanced. Thus it is important that speech pathologists recognize their important role in the "team approach" to rehabilitating such patients, but they should also be aware of when their techniques are not effective in achieving the primary goal of therapy. In discussing treatment effects in 1984, Netsell [52] pointed out that "obviously, the selection of treatments (whether medical, physical, behavioral, or some combination) can affect speech production. Unfortunately, the selection of treatments usually reflects the educational and experience biases of the clinician as opposed to the most efficacious treatment" (p. 25).

Objective measurement of relevant behavioral changes is considered by Darley [14] to be a fundamental consideration in studying the effectiveness of therapy on the course of recovering from aphasia. I support his belief and I extend his thinking to the area of NVPI when he suggests that supplementary physiologic or psychophysical measurements of behavioral change should be considered whenever possible. He states that "there is no use in even beginning this sort of investigation unless research can be more than an interested clinician's artistic and intuitive reporting of change observed in his patients. Reliable quantitative data must be gathered with rigorous objectivity" (p. 11). Progress is being made; however, this statement is based largely on clinical impressions of effectiveness. I further believe that empirical evidence must supplant or support opinions.

Speech pathologists are also urged to measure changed aspects of a patient's psychological status, that is, "his adaption to his problem and his environment," as objectively as possible [14]. In our young adult patients, we are just beginning to garner such information in a systematic manner, and many report better social adjustment and improved self-esteem. Moreover, there is documentation that our adult patients have been able to secure satisfying employment because of their renewed ability to interact and communicate. For example, T. L. was unable to find employment for more than a year because of his communicative status. He began to think that he was unemployable. However, he gained a satisfying and financially rewarding position 3 months after pharyngeal flap surgery. Another example is the case of M. N., whose acquired NVPI was the result of trauma associated with a motor vehicle accident. M. N. lost her secretarial position because of her inability to communicate over the telephone, but just 6 weeks following surgery she was reestablished in the work force and increased her earning capacity in a higher-paying secretarial position. One year after surgical correction, M. N. was elevated to the position of chief dispatcher for a large metropolitan police department, a prerequisite for the position being "pleasant, clear, and articulate speech." In addition, documentation of children being placed in normal classrooms (some for the first time) following surgery is another way of substantiating the positive psychologic and environmental effects following surgical management of velopharyngeal incompetency.

Such examples lead us to be encouraged by our results to date, but we can only be cautiously optimistic, since we recognize the need for more detailed information regarding long-term results as well as for a more clearly defined and precise protocol for patient selection. We believe that the best hope for obtaining the data that will sufficiently advance our knowledge in the surgical management of NVPI is through longitudinal studies of a sufficiently large number and variety of patients with NVPI.

As this chapter comes to a close, it seems appropriate to reiterate the fact that there are dysarthric patients whose neurologic condition so profoundly affects the velopharynx, as well as other components of the speech mechanism, who may never be able to develop the delicately coordinated movements of the speech musculature necessary for intelligible speech production [21] irrespective of the mode of treatment. The foregoing has compared the efficacy of various behavioral procedures and physical techniques designed to reduce, ameliorate, or eliminate the untoward effects of NVPI in the speech of dysarthric patients. A primary focus of this chapter has been to present the results of a specific surgical procedure—the tailormade pharyngeal flap—as a consideration for inclusion in the choice of treatment alternatives available to the speech pathologist in the management of selected dysarthric patients. It has also presented an approach to evaluate and measure the congruency and validity existing between the perceptual analyses of hypernasality, nasal emission, and overall intelligibility with a detailed examination of the speech sounds designed to isolate and identify the sources of improvement through the use of a sound spectrograph. In combination, it is possible to infer from changes perceived and those observed in the acoustic signal what functional physiologic changes have taken place. Obviously, 100 percent improvement did not always take place across all of the parameters studied in our patient population. However, since the residual speech deficit may be completely unrelated to the anatomic-physiologic mechanism that the surgical procedure is designed to address, namely, the velopharynx, it does not mean that the management procedure failed. For example, limited range of motion because of weakness of the tongue (twelfth cranial nerve involvement) resulting in imprecise lingual consonant and distorted vowel production will affect the overall intelligibility rating of a given speaker, but bears no direct relationship to the competency of velopharyngeal function.

As of this writing our experience is based on more than 70 dysarthric patients whose NVPI was surgically corrected by the method described. While our enthusiasm is tempered pending further systematic investigations and long-term studies, which are imperative before this approach is widely adopted, we believe that surgical management of NVPI, as described in this chapter, holds great promise for a large number of dysarthric patients.

I have attempted to demonstrate that the interaction between two disciplines, speech pathology and plastic surgery, has proved amenable to enhancing the rehabilitative program of select dysarthric patients. There normally are many specialties represented on interdisciplinary rehabilitative teams, all of which are important to various aspects of patient care and none of which alone has the necessary wherewithal to manage *completely* a neurogenically communicatively handicapped patient. Sophisticated referrals to and frequent consultations with members of the team are becoming the norm rather than the exception.

Acknowledgment
My sincere appreciation is extended to Michael P. Cannito and Jack Godfrey, Ph.D., of the Department of Communicative Disorders, University of Texas at Dallas, for their expert assistance in the collection and analysis of the acoustic data.

References
1. Aten, J. L., McDonald, A., Simpson, N., and Guiterrez, R. Efficacy of Modified Palatal Lifts for Improving Resonance. In M. R. McNeil, J. C. Rosenbek, and A. E. Aronson (eds.), *The Dysarthrias: Physiology, Acoustics, Perception, Management.* San Diego: College-Hill, 1984.
2. Baker, E. E., Jr., and Sokoloff, M. A. Therapy for speech deficiencies resulting from acute bulbar poliomyelitis infection. *J. Speech Hear. Disord.* 16 : 337, 1951.
3. Blackfield, H. M., Miller, E. R., Owsley, J. Q., Jr., and Lawson, L. I. Comparative evaluation of diagnostic techniques in patients with cleft palate speech. *Plast. Reconstr. Surg.* 29 : 153, 1962.
4. Blakeley, R. W. Temporary speech prosthesis as an aide in speech training. *Cleft Palate Bull.* 10 : 63, 1960.
5. Blakeley, R. W. The complementary use of speech prostheses and pharyngeal flaps in palatal insufficiency. *Cleft Palate J.* 1 : 194, 1964.
6. Bluestone, C. D., Musgrave, R. H., McWilliams, B. J., and Crozier, P. A. Teflon injection pharyngoplasty. *Cleft Palate J.* 5 : 19, 1968.
7. Bradley, D. P. Congenital and Acquired Palatopharyngeal Insufficiency. In K. R. Bzoch (ed.), *Communicative Disorders Related to Cleft Lip and Palate.* Boston: Little, Brown, 1972.
8. Broadbent, T. R., and Swinyard, D. C. The dynamic pharyngeal flap, its selective use and electromyographic evaluation. *Plast. Reconstr. Surg.* 23 : 301, 1959.
9. Calnan, J. S. The surgical treatment of nasal speech disorders. *Ann. R. Coll. Surg. Engl.* 25 : 119, 1959.
10. Conway, H. Combined use of the push-back and pharyngeal flap procedures in the management of complicated cases of cleft palate. *Plast. Reconstr. Surg.* 23 : 301, 1959.
11. Crikelair, G. F., Kastein, S., and Cosman, B. Pharyngeal flap for post-traumatic palatal paresis. *Plast. Reconstr. Surg.* 45 : 182, 1970.
12. Crikelair, G. F., Kastein, S., Fowler, E. P., and Cosman, B. Velar dysfunction in the absence of cleft palate. *N.Y. J. Med.* 64 : 263, 1964.
13. Curtis, J. F. Acoustics of Speech Production and Nasalization. In D. C. Spriestersbach, and D. Sherman (eds.), *Cleft Palate and Communication.* New York: Academic, 1968.
14. Darley, F. L. The efficacy of language rehabilitation in aphasia. *J. Speech Hear. Disord.* 37 : 3, 1972.
15. Darley, F. L., Aronson, A. E., and Brown, J. R. Differential diagnostic patterns of dysarthria. *J. Speech Hear. Res.* 12 : 247, 1969.
16. Darley, F. L., Aronson, A. E., and Brown, J. R. Clusters of deviant speech dimensions in the dysarthrias. *J. Speech Hear. Res.* 12 : 462, 1969.
17. Darley, F. L., Aronson, A. E., and Brown, J. R. *Motor Speech Disorders.* Philadelphia: Saunders, 1975.
18. Dickson, D. R., Grant, J. C. B., Sicher, H., Dubrul, E. L., and Paltan, J. Status of research in cleft palate: Anatomy and physiology, part I. *Cleft Palate J.* 11 : 471, 1974.
19. Dickson, D. R., Grant, J. C. B., Sicher, H., Dubrul, E. L., and Paltan, J. Status of research in cleft palate: Anatomy and physiology, part II. *Cleft Palate J.* 12 : 131, 1975.
20. Dorrance, G. M., and Shirazy, E. *The Operative Story of Cleft Palate.* Philadelphia: Saunders, 1933.
21. Dworkin, J. P., and Johns, D. F. Management of velopharyngeal incompetence in dysarthria: A historical review. *Clin. Otolaryngol.* 5 : 61, 1980.
22. Fant, G. *Acoustic Theory of Speech Production.* The Hague: Mouton, 1972.
23. Fara, M., and Vele, F. The histology and electromyography of primary pharyngeal flaps. *Cleft Palate J.* 9 : 64, 1972.
24. Gibbons, P., and Bloomer, H. A supportive-type prosthetic speech aide. *J. Prosthet. Dent.* 8 : 362, 1958.
25. Gonzales, J. B., and Aronson, A. E. Palatal lift prosthesis for treatment of anatomic and neurological palatopharyngeal insufficiency. *Cleft Palate J.* 7 : 91, 1970.
26. Hardy, J. C., Netsell, R., Schweiger, J. W., and Morris, H. L. Management of velopharyngeal dysfunction in cerebral palsy. *J. Speech Hear. Disord.* 34 : 123, 1969.
27. Hardy, J. C., Rembolt, R. R., Spriestersbach, D. C., and Jayapathy, B. Surgical management of palatal paresis and speech problems in cerebral palsy: A preliminary report. *J. Speech Hear. Disord.* 26 : 320, 1961.
28. Heller, J. C., Gens, G. W., Moe, D. G., and Lewin,

M. L. Velopharyngeal insufficiency in patients with neurologic, emotional, and mental disorders. *J. Speech Hear. Disord.* 39 : 350, 1974.

29. Hess, D. A., Haggart, R. F., and Mylin, W. K. Velar motility, velopharyngeal closure, and speech proficiency in cartilage pharyngoplasty: An eight year study. *Cleft Palate J.* 5 : 153, 1968.

30. Hogan, V. M. A clarification of the surgical goals in cleft palate speech and the introduction of a lateral port control (L.P.C.) pharyngeal flap. *Cleft Palate J.* 10 : 331, 1973.

31. Hogan, V. M. A Biased Approach to the Treatment of Velopharyngeal Incompetence. In V. M. Hogan (ed.), *Clinics in Plastic Surgery*. Philadelphia: Saunders, 1975.

32. House, A. S., and Stevens, K. N. Analogue studies of the nasalization of vowels. *J. Speech Hear. Disord.* 21 : 218, 1956.

33. Johns, D. F., and Salyer, K. E. A method of correcting difficult problems of velopharyngeal insufficiency. Presented at the Annual Meeting of the American Cleft Palate Association, San Francisco, Calif., 1976.

34. Johns, D. F., and Salyer, K. E. Surgical management of neurogenic speech disorders. Unpublished, 1977.

35. Johns, D. F., and Salyer, K. E. Surgical and Prosthetic Management of Neurogenic Speech Disorders. In D. F. Johns (ed.), *Clinical Management of of Neurogenic Communicative Disorders*. Boston: Little, Brown, 1978.

36. Johns, D. F., Tebbetts, J. B., and Cannito, M. P. Perceptual-acoustic analyses: The self-lined, pull-through pharyngeal flap. *J. Craniofac. Genet. Dev. Biol.* In press.

37. Kaplan, E. N. The occult submucous cleft palate. *Cleft Palate J.* 12 : 356, 1975.

38. Kelsey, C. A., Ewanowski, S. J., Crummy, A. B., and Bless, D. M. Lateral pharyngeal wall motion as a predictor of surgical success in velopharyngeal insufficiency. *N. Engl. J. Med.* 2 : 64, 1972.

39. Kerman, P. C., Singer, L. S., and Davidoff, A. Palatal lift and speech therapy for velopharyngeal incompetence. *Arch. Phys. Med. Rehabil.* 54 : 271, 1973.

40. Lange, B. R., and Kipfmueller, L. J. Treating velopharyngeal inadequacy with the palatal lift concept. *Plast. Reconstr. Surg.* 43 : 467, 1969.

41. LaPointe, L. L. *Neurologic Abnormalities Affecting Speech*. New York: Raven, 1975.

42. Lawshe, B. S., Hardy, J. C., Schweiger, J. W., and Van Allen, M. W. Management of a patient with velopharyngeal incompetency of undetermined origin: A clincial report. *J. Speech Hear. Disord.* 36 : 547, 1971.

43. Lewy, R., Cole, R., and Wepman, J. Teflon injection in the correction of velopharyngeal insufficiency. *Ann. Otol. Rhinol. Laryngol.* 74 : 874, 1965.

44. Lindsay, W. K. Surgical Repair of Cleft Palate. In V. M. Hogan (ed.), *Clinics in Plastic Surgery*. Philadelphia: Saunders, 1975.

45. Marshall, R. L., and Jones, R. N. Effects of a pal-atal lift prosthesis upon the speech intelligibility of a dysarthric patient. *J. Prosthet. Dent.* 25 : 327, 1971.

46. Mayo Clinic Departments of Neurology, Physiology, and Biophysics, *Clinical Examinations in Neurology*. Philadelphia: Saunders, 1975.

47. Minami, R. T., Kaplan, E. N., Wu, G., and Jobe, R. P. Velopharyngeal incompetency without overt cleft palate. *Plast. Reconstr. Surg.* 55 : 573, 1975.

48. Moll, K. L. Speech Characteristics of Individuals with Cleft Lip and Palate. In D. C. Spriestersbach, and D. Sherman, (eds.), *Cleft Palate and Communication*. New York: Academic, 1968.

49. Moran, R. E. The pharyngeal flap operation as a speech aide. *Plast. Reconstr. Surg.* 7 : 202, 1951.

50. Morris, H. L., and Spriestersbach, D. B. The pharyngeal flap as a speech mechanism. *Plast. Reconstr. Surg.* 39 : 66, 1967.

51. Netsell, R. Treatment of the velopharynx for individuals with dysarthria. Symposium, Boys' Town National Institute, Omaha, Nebraska, May, 1983.

52. Netsell, R. A Neurobiologic View of the Dysarthrias. In M. R. McNeil, J. C. Rosenbek, and A. E. Aronson, (eds.) *The Dysarthrias: Physiology, Acoustics, Perception, Management*. San Diego: College-Hill. 1984.

53. Nishio, J., Matsuya, T., Ibuki, K., and Miyazaki, T. Role for the facial, glossopharyngeal and vagus nerves in velopharyngeal movements. *Cleft Palate J.* 13 : 201, 1976.

54. Nishio, J., Matsuya, T., Machida, J., and Miyazaki, T. The motor nerve supply of the velopharyngeal muscles. *Cleft Palate J.* 13 : 20, 1976.

55. Noll, J. D. Remediation of Impaired Resonance Among Patients with Neuropathologies of Speech. In N. J. Lass, L. B. McReynolds, J. L. Northern, and D. E. Yoder (eds.) *Speech, Language, and Hearing* (Vol. 2): *Pathologies of Speech and Language*. Philadelphia: Saunders, 1982.

56. Owsley, J. Q., Jr., Blackfield, H. M., Miller, E. R., and Lawson, L. I. Experience with the high attached pharyngeal flap. *Plast. Reconstr. Surg.* 38 : 232, 1966.

57. Owsley, J. Q., Jr., Creech, B. J., and Dedo, H. H. Poor speech following the pharyngeal flap operation: Etiology and treatment. *Cleft Palate J.* 9 : 312, 1972.

58. Owsley, J. Q., Jr., Lawson, L. I., and Chierici, G. J. The re-do pharyngeal flap. *Plast. Reconstr. Surg.* 57 : 180, 1976.

59. Owsley, J. Q., Jr., Lawson, L. I., Miller, E. R., Harvold, E. P., Chierici, G., and Blackfield, H. M. Speech results from the high attached pharyngeal flap operation. *Cleft Palate J.* 7 : 306, 1970.

60. Peterson, S. J. Nasal emission as a component of misarticulation of sibilants and affricates. *J. Speech Hear. Disord.* 4 : 106, 1975.

61. Powers, G. L., and Starr, C. D. The effects of muscle exercises on velopharyngeal gap and nasality. *Cleft Palate J.* 11 : 28, 1974.

62. Randall, P., Bakes, F. P., and Kennedy, C. Cleft palate-type speech in the absence of cleft palate. *Plast. Reconstr. Surg.* 25 : 484, 1960.

63. Schwartz, M. F. The acoustics of normal and nasal vowel production. *Cleft Palate J.* 5 : 125, 1968.

64. Shprintzen, R. J., McCall, G. N., and Skolnick, M. L. A new therapeutic technique for the treatment of velopharyngeal incompetency. *J. Speech Hear. Disord.* 40 : 69, 1975.

65. Skolnick, M. L. Videofluoroscopic examination of the velopharyngeal portal during phonation, lateral and base projections—A new technique for studying the mechanics of closure. *Cleft Palate J.* 7 : 803, 1970.

66. Skolnick, M. L., and McCall, G. N. Velopharyngeal competence and incompetence following pharyngeal flap surgery: A videofluoroscopic study and multiple projection. *Cleft Palate J.* 9 : 1, 1972.

67. Skoog, T. The pharyngeal flap operation in cleft palate: A clinical study of eighty-two cases. *Br. J. Plast. Surg.* 18 : 265, 1965.

68. Spriestersbach, D. C., Dickson, D. R., Fraser, F. C., Horowitz, S. L., McWilliams, B. J., Paradise, J. L., and Randall, P. Clinical research in cleft lip and palate: The state of the art. *Cleft Palate J.* 10 : 113, 1975.

69. Tebbetts, J. B., and Johns, D. F. The self-lined pull-through pharyngeal flap. Presented at the 40th Annual Cleft Palate Association Meeting, Indianapolis, Ind., May, 1983.

70. Webber, J., Chase, R., and Jobe, R. The restrictive pharyngeal flap. *Br. J. Plast. Surg.* 23 : 347, 1970.

71. Witzel, M. A., Munro, I., and Salyer, K. Treatment of VPI in adults. Success of the superior based pharyngeal flap. Presented at the 42nd Annual Cleft Palate Association Meeting. Bal Harbour, Fla, May, 1985.

72. Yules, R. B. Secondary correction of velopharyngeal incompetence: A review. *Plast. Reconstr. Surg.* 45 : 234, 1970.

4

Aphasia Therapy: Some Principles and Strategies for Treatment

Leonard L. LaPointe

Historic Perspective

For centuries persons who suffered the effects of brain damage, with its often devastating concomitant of aphasia, were treated with remedies based on prevailing principles of alchemy, richly laced with imagination. Until the seventeenth century, diagnosis was frequently unrelated to pathology, and people who possessed the puzzling sequelae of cerebral damage were fed, rubbed, and stuffed with an array of herbs, roots, and other substances.

Mettler's *History of Medicine* [71] lists a prodigious number of substances prescribed during the Middle Ages as beneficial to sufferers of neurogenic disorders, including ". . . cashew (*Anacardium*); recommended for practically all psychiatric and neural affections, especially aphasia" (p. 538).

Polypharmacy, the innovative art of assembling combinations of "medicinal" ingredients, was advocated by Galen and practiced diligently for more than a thousand years after his death. Licht [64], in an informative tracing of the history of stroke rehabilitation, cites a typical prescription for "apoplexy" taken from the work of Theophile Bonét, a prominent French physician.

A most secret and certain remedy against the apoplexy is to take a lion's dung, powdered, two parts, pour spirit of wine till it be covered three finger's breadth, let them stand in a vial stopped three days. Strain it and keep it for use. Then take a crow, not quite pin-feathered and a young turtle, burn them apart in an oven, powder them, pour on the above said spirit of wine . . . then take berries of a linden tree . . . then add as much of the best wine and six ounces of sugar candy . . . Let the patient take a spoonful of it in wine . . . and with the same water, rub the forehead, neck, temples, and nostrils (p. 21).

With the nineteenth century, the shroud of ignorance concerning aphasia began its gradual ascent, and the age of Trousseau, Broca, Wernicke, Bastian, and many others provided a foundation for contemporary thought on the problem. However, the emphasis then, even as in some quarters today, appeared to be on the remarkable and dramatic symptoms of aphasia as opposed to strategies of rehabilitation.

Licht [64] provides perhaps the first reference to specific reeducation of the communication impairment accompanying stroke. He cites the work of Thomas Hun, who in 1851 reported success after recommending exercises in reading, spelling, and repeating words for a 35-year-old blacksmith who was aphasic following a stroke.

Not until World War II, which produced thousands of brain-injured patients, did remediation efforts gain momentum. In 1945 the Surgeon General of the United States Army set up centers for training aphasic patients, and Joseph Wepman carried on this work with the civilian population after the war. Advance in generating principles and specific techniques for treatment of language impairment has been evolutionary, rather than revolutionary, in the years since World War II.

Perhaps one of the reasons for the slow advance of knowledge on the process of recovery from aphasia is related to the apparent enchantment and preoccupation of many aphasiologists with such issues as localization of lesions, neuroanatomic correlates of language behavior, mind-brain debates, and so forth. These neurolinguistic and neuropsychologic issues are a fascinating and legitimate concern of aphasiologists, but the result has been neglect of an adequate balance of attention to another important question: How can we best restore the aphasic person to communicative effectiveness? After the necessary diagnostic and life-prolonging riddle of "Lesion, lesion, where is the lesion?" is solved, someone must be present to address the quality-of-life issue.

An important trend has been gathering momentum in the past 15 years, however. Aphasiologists now appear to be on the threshold of giving long-neglected specific research attention to clinical management issues.

The purpose of this chapter is to summarize and synthesize some of this attention. Emphasis is on principles and strategies of treatment. Excellent sources available elsewhere treat the history of aphasia [83], terminology and symptomatology [35], classification systems, tests, and evaluative strategies [24].

Most chapters on aphasia are restricted by practical considerations, and the omission of reference to some valuable contributions on the subject is inevitable. Most chapters also are a reflection of the training, philosophic orientation, and experience of the writer, and this one is no exception.

Efficacy of Treatment

Most aphasiologists are all too aware of the problem of documenting the effect of language rehabilitation on aphasia. Data on both the course and the ultimate usefulness of language training are not abundant. Active and conscientious clinicians hold very strongly to the view that therapy has a significant and positive effect on language improvement beyond what can be expected from spontaneous recovery of function. However, the hard data and evidence on the efficacy of aphasia therapy are somewhat sparse. As Holland [43] suggested, the scientific community has a right to demand data instead of our word.

Darley [24] devotes an entire chapter to the effect of treatment in his book *Aphasia*. He reviews studies without no-treatment control groups, studies with no-treatment control groups, individual case studies, and other evidence that speaks to the issue of treatment effect. Darley concludes that no single study has proved to be so comprehensive and so creatively designed and carried out as to provide by itself the unequivocal answer to all questions of treatment effect. On the other hand, he states, "But the foregoing collage of studies of groups and individuals collectively provides a series of answers and together lays our doubts about efficacy to rest" (p. 175).

Studies on the Efficacy of Aphasia Therapy

In a review of language rehabilitation in aphasia [22], nine studies of aphasia treatment were analyzed. Some of these are replete with methodologic or interpretive flaws, including failure to attend to the role of spontaneous improvement on recovery and failure to describe important characteristics of the subjects adequately.

Other studies appeared since Darley's review. Smith [89] administered standardized language tests to 80 aphasic adults before and after intensive therapy. Marked improvement in language functions were found in this group. In contrast, negligible changes were reported for 15 untreated aphasics. In this research, Smith concluded that his findings clearly indicate that language rehabilitation results in measurable gains in language function beyond what can be expected to occur as a result of spontaneous recovery.

Additional research on the effect of communication therapy is provided by Hagen [38]. This study concerned the effects of treatment as opposed to no treatment in a group of 20 men with a range of communicative disorders following stroke. Subjects were tested with the Minnesota Test for the Differential Diagnosis for Aphasia, and Hagen concluded that, while both groups exhibited spontaneous improvement during the first 3 months, only the treatment group continued to progress beyond the point of spontaneous recovery. All members of the treated group were reported to have attained functional communication ability.

Basso, Capitani, Vignolo Study

In the *Archives of Neurology*, Basso, Capitani, and Vignolo [5] presented a controlled study of the influence of rehabilitation on language skills. In this study the members of the control group were not randomly assigned but unintentionally selected since personal, family, or transportation problems prevented them from participating in a language rehabilitation program. This design drawback leaves the study open to the criticism that the experimental and control groups may be dissimilar in characteristics that have the potential to influence response to treatment. Nonetheless, the study has converted a few skeptics. In this research, 162 persons with aphasia received intensive treatment and their communication behaviors were compared with 119 untreated patients. Inferential statistics were conducted on the performances of both groups on initial and final tests. The main finding of the study was that language rehabilitation in aphasics does have a positive effect on impairment of the ability to communicate through speaking, listening, writing, and reading; it has a positive effect provided the training is carried out for at least 6 months at a rate of no fewer than three individual sessions per week.

VA Cooperative Studies

In two studies involving several Veterans Administration Medical Centers, Wertz and his colleagues [104, 105] studied issues related to treatment. In the first study [106], the effects of two types of treatment were compared at various times during the treatment course. Subjects were randomly assigned to one of the two treatment groups, and a comprehensive battery of communication, neurologic, and behavioral measures were conducted at regular intervals. Factors that produced attrition resulted in a decreasing number of subjects over the study trial, but equal numbers of persons in each treatment group were studied at 11 weeks ($N = 58$), 22 weeks ($N = 45$), 33 weeks ($N = 39$), and 44 weeks ($N = 34$). Both groups received 4 hours of treatment per week. One group received individual treatment and the other group received treatment in the form of nonspecific small-group activities. Both groups improved significantly on several measures. Thus, significant differences were found [all on Porch Index of Communicative Abilities (PICA) scores] favoring individual treatment, but few other significant differences were found.

The second Veterans Administration Cooperative Study on Aphasia [105] compared clinic, home, and deferred treatment. In this study patients were randomly assigned to three groups: 12 weeks of treatment by a speech-language pathologist followed by 12 weeks of no treatment, 12 weeks of home treatment with a program designed and furnished by a speech-language pathologist followed by 12 weeks of no treatment, or 12 weeks of no treatment followed by 12 weeks of clinic treatment. A wide variety of language, neurologic, and behavioral measures were administered at entry and 6, 12, 18, and 24 weeks postentry. Language measures indicated that clinic treatment resulted in significantly more improvement at 12 weeks than did no treatment. No significant differences were apparent at 12 weeks between the clinic and home groups or the home and deferred groups. At 24 weeks, no significant differences occurred among the three groups. Thus, the authors of this ambitious 5-year study concluded that treatment for aphasia appears efficacious, and delaying treatment for 12 weeks does not appear to reduce ultimate improvement.

Changes in Attitudes

The news used to be mostly bad. A widespread belief was that language treatment was unrelated to recovery; that behavioral changes occurred largely because of the restitution of function that accompanied physiologic change. This rather bleak opinion has changed in the last few years. Refinements in research methodology that allow the determination of treatment effect against the backdrop of spontaneous recovery and continued research effort are contributing to the accumulation of evidence on treatment effect.

Some of this attitudinal direction is reflected in the opinions expressed by neurologists such as Rubens [80]. He states that the brain is not "a totally static and hardwired organ" and suggests several factors that influence recovery, including "specific rehabilitation programs" (p. 31). Benson [6] also commented favorably on the demonstrated effectiveness of language therapy in an editorial in the *Archives of Neurology*. Additionally, the first edition of this book was reviewed by Albert [1] in the *New England Journal of Medicine* and he made the following points:

1. "For a severely impaired aphasic or dysarthric patient, a modest improvement in language or speech may make all the difference in the world . . ."

2. "Therapeutic intervention to rehabilitate pa-

tients with speech and language disorders has now been proved useful."

3. "Something can be done for patients with speech and language disorders, and physicians would be well advised to know that fact" (p. 932).

Darley [23] reviewed most of the published work to date and concluded,

We do not depend on sentiment or intuition in declaring that aphasia therapy works. It works so well that every neurologist, physiatrist, and speech-language pathologist responsible for patient management should refuse to accede to a plan that abandons the patient to neglect (p. 630).

Problems in Aphasia Research

The questions that plague researchers in aphasia have been difficult to answer to the full satisfaction of the scientific community, because the task of answering them is formidable. Several factors contribute to this difficulty.

MULTIPLE, INTERACTING VARIABLES. The influence of multiple, interacting variables on the course of recovery in aphasia means that research in this area is necessarily complex and fraught with risk.

Many aphasiologists are skeptical about the results and interpretations of studies that describe their subjects as being aphasics. People with aphasia are no longer regarded as comprising a homogeneous group, and studies that fail to describe subjects in some detail imply that homogeneity exists. Differences in severity, months after onset, and cause create quite different pictures of aphasia.

Not only is this web of interacting variables problematic for researchers but also it contributes to the hazards involved in establishing a prognosis for individual patients. Table 4-1 lists some of the factors that need to be considered by the researcher studying aphasic individuals and by those who would predict the course of recovery. Certainly, other factors can be generated that have potential significance for recovery, but these appear to be some of the most salient ones.

Even if all the variables important to the course of recovery can be identified and specified, one must appreciate how they interact. For example, certain causes, such as closed head trauma, tend to be much more frequent among younger persons than among older ones with aphasia. It might prove unfounded if a clinician came to conclusions about a patient's recovery on the basis of age alone, without considering the importance of the interaction between the patient's age and the cause of aphasia.

Brookshire [17] recently commented on subject description and generality of results in experiments with aphasic adults. He argues that external validity of studies can be enhanced if certain subject variables are routinely measured and reported. Crucial variables include age, education, subject source, gender, lesion location, handedness, etiology, time postonset, aphasia severity, and aphasia type. Other variables that would aid sample description but may not be crucial include hearing acuity, native language, within-hemisphere lesion location, visual acuity, IQ, mood or alertness, and presence and degree of hemiparesis or hemianopsia. Brookshire suggests that readers who routinely report these subject characteristics will help readers evaluate the generality of findings, assist in resolving conflicts and inconsistencies across studies, and encourage replications and extensions of worthy experiments.

SPONTANEOUS RECOVERY. Another reason why past studies of aphasia have been difficult is the unclear understanding of the natural course of the condition. Nearly everyone acknowledges that spontaneous recovery occurs, and some suggest that it accounts for *all* the recovery from aphasia.

Very few empirical studies have been addressed to this issue in spite of its importance. Vignolo [97] provided insight into the evolution of aphasia by documenting that spontaneous change does exist and that it is in the direction of improvement and restitution of function. Additionally, Vignolo reported a positive association between duration and change of type of aphasia. He found that receptive

Table 4-1. Variables important to aphasia research and prognosis

Subject variables	Medical variables	Speech-language variables	Other variables
Age of onset	Cause	Severity of aphasia	Months after onset
Education	Site of lesion	Type of aphasia	Motivation
Intelligence	Extent of lesion	Coexisting motor speech impairment	Emotional status
Handedness	Concomitant medical problems	Sensory-perceptual deficit	Environment

language functions show greater improvement and remain superior to expressive functions throughout the course of patients' recovery.

A period of spontaneous recovery in recent aphasics was further documented by Culton [20]. He suggested that significant spontaneous recovery may cease much sooner than earlier reports have led us to believe. In his 11 "recent" aphasic subjects (average of 2 weeks since onset), rapid spontaneous recovery of language function was noted in the first month following the onset of aphasia. Although an increase was noted in mean scores on a nonstandardized battery of eight 10-item language tasks, statistically significant change was not evident during the second month. Ten "stable" aphasic subjects (average of 27 months since onset) showed no significant improvement over the 2-month test schedule. Culton's recent group also presented significant recovery of intellectual function, suggesting that there are concomitant intellectual problems with aphasia that are reduced as the language impairment lessens in severity.

Additional insight into the nature of spontaneous recovery is offered by Hagen [38] in an article cited earlier. In a study of 20 men with communication disorders after stroke, he concluded that spontaneous recovery accounts for slight changes in all communication processes during the first 6 months after onset. He also found that certain visual and auditory skills (visual comprehension, visual motor, auditory comprehension, and auditory retention) improved spontaneously to functional levels over time, while reading comprehension, language formulation, speech production, spelling, and arithmetic did not. However, those abilities were eventually improved significantly through language treatment. As Hagen noted, it is of considerable interest to see that the only communication abilities to return spontaneously to functional levels were those that are bilaterally mediated. If this finding is confirmed, it may be unnecessary to treat bilaterally represented (auditory and visual) processes directly. Instead, the speech pathologist could focus on the nuclear problems of language formulation, speech production, spelling, and reading. Recent work on celeration rate, slope measurement of treatment tasks, and trend estimation [56, 67, 68] may prove to be useful in advancing not only our knowledge of extracting treatment effect from the backdrop of spontaneous recovery, but also our ability to predict treatment outcomes.

The studies of Vignolo, Culton, and Hagen provide valuable information, but much still needs to be discovered before we have a comfortable grasp of the effect of treatment when it is superimposed on the backdrop of spontaneous recovery from aphasia.

MEASUREMENT. A third problem in aphasia research that has done little to foster clarity of interpretation across studies has been the lack of objective tests that are sensitive to small changes in behavior. Darley [22] stated, "There is no use even beginning this sort of investigation unless research can be more than an interested clinician's artistic and intuitive reporting of change observed in his patients" (p. 11).

Significant advances have been made in the last 15 years, and several adequate tests have appeared, although some of them pay little attention to psychometric standards of intertester and intratester reliability. An important contribution to quantification of a sample of language behavior is provided by the PICA. The development of this test and others gives us psychometrically sound tools to measure changes in aphasia over time.

Perhaps this review of some of the problems inherent in conducting research on aphasia treatment will explain why studies that provide unequivocal evidence have been slow to emerge. Adequate research designs in this field are very complex.

BETWEEN-GROUP RESEARCH DESIGN. The most frequently encountered strategy employed in studies of aphasia is the "between-group" design. This approach assigns subjects to either a control group or an experimental group and attempts to demonstrate group differences after the introduction of an independent variable, such as treatment. The data usually are comprised of scores for each group derived from the administration of a standardized test battery. These scores are then subjected to statistical evaluation, with the focus frequently on group mean differences rather than on the behaviors of individual subjects. This approach has some disadvantages in aphasia research, not the least of which is the extreme difficulty in matching groups. The medical, subject, and environmental variables outlined previously may make the assumption of subject homogeneity somewhat tenuous, and many studies of recovery from aphasia have neglected to account for these factors.

Further, when experimental findings are evaluated in traditional between-group designs, the statistical procedure used may obscure the lawful effect of experimental or therapeutic intervention.

Problems may arise in assuming that averages from group data are analogous to representing the behavioral progress of individuals. Several subjects in the group may be affected quite differently by therapeutic manipulation, and this effect can be obscured in the statistical treatment of group averages.

TIME-SERIES RESEARCH DESIGNS. Part of the problem in documenting the effect of aphasia treatment may be related to the relative neglect of the so-called time-series, or subjects-as-their-own-controls, approach. This design is not new. For years, behavioral psychologists have demonstrated its principles and usefulness, and some have advocated it as a potent tactic of research in the behavioral sciences [85]. The literature in aphasiology, however, does not inundate us with examples of its application. Reports by Sidman [86], Sidman et al. [87], Salvatore [82], and Bollinger and Stout [11] demonstrate the usefulness and the potential of this approach. The basic logic of the time-series design is to determine the manner in which operations or therapeutic interventions relate functionally to subsequent performance or behavior.

The effect of a selected variable on a person's behavior (for example, requiring an aphasic patient to write or name five pictures 100 times) is demonstrated by the consecutive presentation, removal, and re-presentation of the variable to the person. Control over the patient's behavior exists if his or her performance can be altered by introducing the experimental or therapeutic procedure.

Common to all time-series designs is the process of baseline measurement. A behavior is measured to establish a baseline, which then provides a reference point for predicting what the level of the behavior would be in the future if the experimental or therapeutic procedures had not been introduced.

Any new level of performance is then compared to the baseline, and this strategy is called an A-B design, (A, measurement during baseline; B, measurement during experimental procedures). This approach can establish whether or not the level of performance changed and can determine the approximate magnitude of any change that occurred.

The most frequent elaboration of this design is to reverse the experiment by discontinuing the therapeutic or experimental procedure. If the behavior then returns to baseline levels, or if it reaches a plateau, the initial baseline prediction is supported—that introduction of the experimental or therapeutic procedure has a causal effect on the patient's behavior. This A-B-A design is usually

extended further by reinstating the therapeutic procedure, creating an A-B-A-B design, which further demonstrates that the experimenter or clinician has specified the causal variables and does control them. This design also has been called *reversal technique*, *intrasubject replication*, and *equivalent time samples* [48]. Figure 4-1 illustrates these basic time-series designs.

Modifications of the A-B-A design have been suggested for situations in which effecting a reversal would be undesirable or when a reversal of responses would not be expected, such as in language therapy. The *multiple-element*, or *multiple-baseline*, design is another time-series approach that has valuable potential for contributing to our knowledge of the generalization of communication skills. Using this approach, we can collect data on various types of behavior, individuals, or stimulus modes. For example, baselines on two or more types of behavior can be measured and plotted. After these types of behavior reach stable base rates, the therapeutic or experimental condition is implemented for only one type of behavior, and its effect can be monitored on all types for which baselines were measured.

The multiple-baseline approach seems particu-

Fig. 4-1. Basic time-series research designs with modifications. Ordinate represents performance level and abscissa represents time.

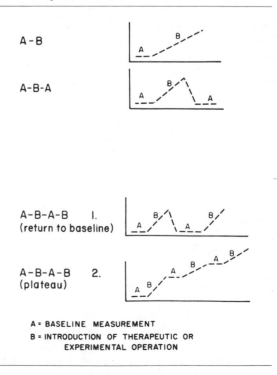

A - B

A - B - A

A - B - A - B 1.
(return to baseline)

A - B - A - B 2.
(plateau)

A = BASELINE MEASUREMENT
B = INTRODUCTION OF THERAPEUTIC OR
      EXPERIMENTAL OPERATION

larly applicable to some of the tasks used in aphasia therapy. We can judge the effect of intervention on similar tasks in all modes. For example, a clinician can plot baselines for both verbal and graphic modes on the production of 10 functional phrases or sentences; then a therapeutic strategy of 20 verbal integral stimulations can be introduced ("Watch me" "Listen to me") for each phrase, with feedback on errors. Finally, measurement can be continued in both modes to monitor the effect, if any, on *writing* the same phrases.

Multiple-baseline designs also can be used to monitor the effect of generalization to different stimulus items within a given mode. For example, on an auditory comprehension task, a clinician can plot baselines or pointing responses on two separate 10-element sets of orally presented commands and then introduce a therapeutic strategy ("Listen again" "Point with me") to the first set of phrases. Finally, the effect of this strategy can be measured on both sets of phrases to plot a generalization of the untreated set.

Some problems exist in using time-series or intrasubject replication design. One interpretive difficulty is embodied in the question: How great does a behavioral change have to be from one treatment to another before it is considered a significant change? Bandura [3] points out that interpretation is not difficult when large successive changes occur rapidly and consistently for many subjects. However, problems arise in interpreting the data of those cases in which behavioral changes are not dramatic. Thus the question of significance of change has been approached statistically to determine if experimental observations are the result of chance. Statistical analysis of the data gathered from individual subjects or small numbers of subjects has been neglected, to a degree, perhaps because of the assumption that inferential statistics are inapplicable to small samples. However, properly conceived studies that collect repeated observations on the same person are appropriate to the analysis-of-variance model and several other statistical strategies. Some work [33] has outlined the rationale for several of these strategies in one-subject designs. Prescott and McNeil [76] also demonstrated the application of inferential statistics to the analysis of an aphasic subject's speech and language change over several test sessions.

Single-subject research designs are gaining favor, and answers to a variety of clinical questions are emerging. The technology of single-case experimentation continues to be refined by such re-

searchers as Hayes [41] and Tryon [94], and the application of time-series research to communication disorders has been comprehensively treated by McReynolds and Kearns [70]. Modifications and varieties of the traditional A-B design now resemble the array one sees when peering at the spectrum of flavors in an ice-cream parlor. Design modifications, each suitable to a specific clinical research issue, have been named multiple baseline, multiple schedule, concurrent schedule, changing criterion, alternating treatment, stratified multiple-N-single-I, and mocha almond fudge.

More and more applications of these unique methods of answering clinical questions are evident in the literature and as Wertz [104] has stated, "we know more about treatments, the conditions under which treatments were administered, and the patient's response to treatment" (p. 258). A positive example of differential performance rates to sequentially manipulated treated versus untreated word lists was presented by LaPointe [58].

The preceding section was designed to give the clinical aphasiologist and the student who anticipates treating aphasic persons a view of some of the problems that have plagued researchers in the area of aphasia treatment. Some may hold the view that the magical and exclusive garden of research cannot be trespassed by mere mortals engaged in clinical endeavors. This idea, that the clinician cannot be the researcher, is not only inaccurate but has probably contributed to the paucity of research on aphasia treatment. Aphasia clinics should be the wellsprings of research on the countless questions related to aphasia treatment. The preceding and following sections are presented partially with the goal of illustrating the clinical adaptability of some traditional research strategies. It is both desirable and practical to incorporate some of these principles into aphasia therapy.

In the view of many, clinicians have paid too little attention to measuring clearly specified tasks during therapy sessions. Risley [77] suggested that incorporating creative strategies of measurement into therapy would serve to improve the service rendered to a client by showing unequivocally when therapy is not being therapeutic (i.e., when it is not correlating with significant improvements in the client's behavior). Measurement alone perhaps would eliminate many of our current routines by demonstrating that no marked improvement occurs when they are followed. How many of our therapeutic strategies would fail this test remains to be seen, and perhaps many would prove to be highly effective. This information should be documented either way.

Measurement can show, in quantified terms, whether or not a patient's behavior is improving; and this is crucial information, assuming that the task is relevant. This information should be available on a session-by-session basis and not merely from monthly retests with a standardized language battery. If a patient is not improving with a given procedure, we can determine this and either modify or discard the task.

Another benefit to be gained by applying more refined measurement systems to aphasia therapy is a clearer understanding of the number of trials that are required before the patient is successful on selected language tasks. How many trials are necessary before an aphasic person can, on command, point to 10 objects with 100 percent accuracy? How many trials are required for an aphasic to verbalize accurately the missing item in a list of 10 paired-associated words? These questions can be extended to almost any specific communication task. Certainly the answers are dependent on clear specification of a number of interacting subject variables, such as the cause, severity, and type of aphasia, months after onset, and several other factors; but application of detailed measurement systems in therapy could contribute much to our knowledge of the number of trials required for aphasic patients to perform these tasks. Knowledge of this sort would enhance our ability to select the most efficient type of therapy and to predict, at least within a specified range, how long treatment must continue for a patient to achieve a selected level of success.

Measurement procedures can be incorporated into activities of therapy with no additional cost in personnel or equipment. Also, these measurements can be charted on tables and graphs in a fraction of the time currently spent writing narrative accounts of each therapy session. No doubt microcomputers will aid us in clinical data management in the near future.

Clinicians must be concerned with the broader perspective of the welfare of patients, which would be enhanced by evaluating current therapeutic procedures. This evaluation would come about through cumulative evidence and would show whether therapeutic strategies are appropriate or irrelevant to improvement in the patient's functional communication. Specific suggestions as to how these measurement systems can be adapted to daily therapy will be detailed in following sections.

Treatment Approaches
Trends and Reasons for Optimism
The challenging picture painted by introspective clinicians some years ago apparently provided some impetus and direction for clinical research. In recent years a few controlled research and clinical case studies have attested to this new direction. Relative neglect of clinical research has been modified, and valid reasons exist for us to be optimistic about renewed vigor and refinement of principles in clinical aphasiology [54].

The application of psychometric principles to the evaluation of aphasia, as exemplified by the development of such tools as the PICA [74], the Boston Diagnostic Aphasia Test [35], the Western Aphasia Battery (WAB) [51], the Communicative Abilities in Daily Living (CADL) [45], and others is a significant trend. From a neurologic point of view, the need for rigorous examination of physiologic and anatomic anomaly is evident. Advances in neurodiagnostic technology have snowballed in the 1980s and the relevance of these new techniques to aphasiology was presented in a special panel discussion at the Clinical Aphasiology Conference. Computerized axial tomography [78], positron emission tomography [40], and nuclear magnetic resonance [28] were among the topics covered by these presentations. However, if correlations between behavioral disturbance and information regarding the site of a lesion and deranged physiology are to be meaningful, the examination and classification of aphasia must maintain the same standards of rigor [86]. Progress in standardizing methods of aphasia examination and classification is very meaningful. Advances in aphasia assessment also have provided means for defining spontaneous recovery and the evolution of aphasia more clearly. Also, standardized methodology is crucial to documenting changes in speech and language behavior during patients' recovery as well as to defining the medical, individual, and speech and language variables that have prognostic significance.

Another reason for optimism is the development and use of careful systems of measurement during speech and language therapy. This trend is based, in part, on the growing utility and refinement of operant procedures in speech pathology. Basic to the operant method is careful measurement and recording of performance, a tenet that has been incorporated in highly individualized programs [37] and specific therapy systems [11].

Recent work in the area of microcomputers is a

genuine reason for cautious rejoicing. Though personal computers will aid us in prediction, data management, and with carefully selected treatment tasks, almost no one predicts that they will ever replace the clinical decision making and interaction of a warm, live clinician. Nevertheless, great strides have been made in the last 5 years in adapting the computer to uses in aphasia. One of the leaders in this area has been Richard Katz [46, 47], who has not only developed relevant software but also has coordinated carefully conceived clinical research.

A further reason for optimism is the emergence of a number of facilitative and compensatory strategies that show great promise of playing a significant role in the rehabilitation of aphasic persons. Some of these strategies are presented in the following section.

Compensatory and Facilitative Strategies
The range of potential prompts and facilitative therapeutic strategies available to the clinician is clearly illustrated in the application of two rather unique intervention techniques, melodic intonation therapy (MIT) [2] and the use of American Indian signs (Amerind) [88].

MIT is a treatment strategy based on rhythm and intonation patterns as facilitators of verbal output. The program progresses from singing in unison to repetition of phrases with normal intonation and, finally, to sentence production in response to questions. The success of MIT in improving the expressive ability of carefully selected aphasic patients has been impressive. Variations on the theme have been composed by Dunham and Newhoff [29].

Amerind, which was originally developed as an alternate means of communication for patients who have had a glossectomy, was adapted for use by aphasic patients who also exhibit severe oral-verbal apraxia. Gestures representing objects, actions, direction, and descriptions were taught to apraxic-aphasic individuals to help them compensate for their expressive handicaps. Some patients developed spontaneous oral production synchronously with their use of sign, indicating that Amerind can be a facilitator of verbalization. Intersystemic reorganization, as defined and detailed in other sections of this book, also has provided a strong case for the use of gestures as facilitators of verbalization.

Amerind as a communicative facilitator in aphasia and apraxia was studied by Dowden, Marshall, and Tompkins [27], and while it was found that gestures may have greater significance as an alternate communication means than as a facilitator, many questions were raised relative to the validity and benefit of gestural training. Some of the original assumptions on the universality of recognition of Amerind have been questioned by Daniloff, Lloyd, and Fristoe [21]. Apparently, controlled studies have resulted in less universal understanding (transparency) of Amerind than originally suspected.

The goals of the clinician in the use of any compensatory-facilitative strategy are (1) to help the aphasic person compensate for the deficit; and (2) to suggest ways in which responding is possible or less difficult. The options available to clinicians to effect these goals are multifaceted: they may standardize and simplify the task instructions; they may restrict the amount of complexity of stimuli; they may provide a wide variety of prompts and cues; they may manipulate the selection of mode of input or output; or they may manipulate the level of response. A basic premise of therapy is that the more normal these dimensions become within the therapy setting, the more prepared the patient is to communicate at a functional level in the real world. Functional communication, and not necessarily the return to premorbid language levels, is a primary goal of therapy. Ideally, this goal will be achieved in modes that are most spontaneous and natural to the aphasic individual (typically, auditory input and verbal output) and to a level comparable to premorbid ability. However, when postmorbid communication is not possible, it is necessary to employ compensatory techniques. Compensatory techniques involve adjusting the patient's level of response to one commensurate with his or her abilities, and utilizing alternative modes of communication. Silent reading may replace auditory input as the chief receptive mode. Similarly, a patient may be able to write words that cannot be retrieved verbally.

Facilitative strategies, in contrast, typically strive to maximize performance in the more natural modes of functioning, and their goal is immediate functional response. For example, auditory deficit may be overcome by reducing the length of stimuli rather than by changing the mode of input. Naming within the verbal mode may be facilitated by phonemic cuing, sentence completion, supra- or subordinate cues, description, or writing the first letter of a word before saying it.

The distinction between compensatory and facilitative techniques is a fine one, and these strategies are not mutually exclusive in their application. Indeed, the cross-mode cuing and deblocking techniques used by Weigl and Bierwisch [101] and Ulatowska and Richardson [96], and the use of alternative modes of communication, such as Amerind, exemplify the deliberate use of compensatory strategies to facilitate the functional return of more disturbed language systems.

The communication behavior that the clinician wishes to stimulate and elicit from the aphasic person is affected as much by task context as by the type or topography of the required response. Defining the relations between the three main behavioral events—antecedent, response, and consequent—and then systematic exploration and manipulation of all relevant dimensions within each are considered by many to be fundamental to therapeutic intervention. A wealth of evidence exists to guide us in our selection of compensatory and facilitative techniques for therapy. Much of this evidence has been derived from experimental studies of aphasic behavior. The purpose of this section is to draw some of these together and to illustrate their adaptability to various approaches to aphasia therapy.

Darley [24] devotes an entire chapter to maximizing the input and output of aphasic persons and presents a wealth of suggestions from the clinical research literature that can readily be adapted to treatment planning. Related to the issue of compensatory or facilitative strategies that either maximize or hinder optimal performance are studies by DeRenzi, Faglioni, and Previdi [26] on the increased susceptibility of aphasic persons to distraction, by Faber and Aten [30] on changes of verbal performance related to altered (broken or distorted) picture stimuli, and the work done on Promoting Aphasics' Communicative Effectiveness (PACE) by Davis and his colleagues [25].

MODALITY CONSIDERATIONS. Verbal errors by aphasic individuals may be affected by a wide variety of stimulus variables. For example, the sensory mode may affect whether or not the patient can name objects. Aphasic patients have shown a uniformity of naming ability in all modes of sensory stimulation [10], and there are similar findings concerning their verbal formulation skills [34]. Other evidence suggests that visual presentation yields more errors than auditory or visual-auditory stimulation [15]. The idea that multimodal presentation facilitates performance in aphasic patients was addressed by LaPointe and Williams [61], who presented a form-recognition task visually, manually, intraorally, and in simultaneous combinations of these three modes. The most conspicuous and potentially significant finding of this study was that simultaneous, multimodal presentation of geometric shapes did *not* facilitate recognition performance. Instead, some subjects seemed to experience stimulus overload, and their performance deteriorated during multimodal presentation. In contrast, multisensory presentation of stimuli was found generally to facilitate performance of a naming task by aphasic subjects [31]. Single-subject analysis in this study, however, yielded the significant qualification that a multisensory approach was not necessarily most efficient for all aphasic patients.

PHYSICAL CHARACTERISTICS OF STIMULI. Naming and recognition performance of aphasic patients may be affected not only by the mode of stimulus presentation but by the physical characteristics of the stimuli as well. A comparison of life-size, realistically shaped, colored objects to reduced size, uncolored line drawings effected no difference in naming performance [18]. In contrast, Bisiach [10], while holding size constant, found poorer performance in responses to line drawings and "mutilated" line drawings when the data were compared with responses to realistic pictures. The size of two-dimensional stimuli had no effect on naming performance, while three-dimensional representations were more effective in eliciting correct naming responses than were two-dimensional ones [7]. One postulate of these studies is that a reduction in redundancy of visual information may be the cause of decrements in naming performance.

STIMULUS CONTEXT. Stimulus context is a potent variable in eliciting verbal responses. The context of open-ended sentences in naming is most effective; response to pictures is less effective; and naming from verbal descriptions is least effective [4]. Similar types of cues were found to be differentially effective in stimulating speech in aphasic patients with phonologic impairment. The following hierarchy of most to least effective cuing techniques was reported by Webb and Love [98]: whole word imitation, initial syllable cue, sentence completion context, and reading the printed word.

Other stimulus variables that may affect responses are word frequency, word length, and phonemic complexity, or "pronounceability."

Such variables also deserve consideration when developing materials for auditory comprehension and verbal tasks. Syntactic structure involves grammatical contrasts (e.g., prepositions: *on* versus *under*); morphemic contrasts (e.g., plurality: "It flies" "They fly"); word order; and properties of words in sentences (e.g., subject versus object: "The train bumps the car" versus "The car bumps the train"). The hierarchy of difficulty of syntactic contrasts on comprehension tasks appears fairly stable for different types of aphasic subjects [62], a finding that should guide clinicians in selecting tasks for syntax programs.

When working at the sentence level in therapy, the clinician must consider the interaction of vocabulary difficulty, sentence length, and syntactic complexity. Syntactic complexity was the greatest source of difficulty on comprehension tasks for several types of aphasic patients, while vocabulary level presented the least difficulty [84].

In selecting vocabulary materials for naming drills or incorporation into sentence tasks, the concepts of "availability" and task difficulty are relevant considerations. A rationale and clinical method for the selection of vocabulary materials for individual aphasic patients provide useful guidance for the clinician [19]. Based on successive pretherapeutic performance, words were designated as "available" if the patient was correct in using it on two trials and "less available" if he or she was correct in using it on only one trial. A clinical implication of this method is that less available responses should be presented first in picture-elicited vocabulary rebuilding exercises. The available words are not used in vocabulary exercises per se, but they are used instead in more abstract verbal contexts (e.g., for the target *bed*, "What do you sleep on?"). Items that are not available (never correct) on pretherapy performance are stimulated last in therapy.

The *ordering* of easy-to-name and difficult-to-name sets of words within sessions also may affect the patient's performance. Brookshire [15] reported that: (1) exposure to difficult-to-name items interferes with the aphasic subject's ability to name subsequent easy-to-name items, and (2) exposure to easy-to-name items facilitates the subject's naming of subsequent difficult-to-name items. On the other hand, the disrupting effect of difficult tasks may decrease after repeated presentations. Specifically, as the patient's performance on difficult-to-name items improves, the effect of interference is less acute. Nevertheless, the potentially disrupting effect of a high proportion of errors as well as the availability of responses should be considered in outlining the therapy tasks.

DEBLOCKING AND TRANSCODING. The interaction of intact and disturbed skills or functions is relatively unexplored. However, the concepts of deblocking and transcoding, as outlined by Weigl [100], Weigl and Bierwisch [101], and Ulatowska and Richardson [96], may provide cornerstones for research in this area. Deblocking essentially refers to the use of intact modes to facilitate the use of modes that are functioning at less than optimum levels.* For example, a functional system (visual recognition of words) was successfully used to "deblock" a deficit in phonemic perception of words. Deblocking, then, concerns the relation between two independent yet functionally overlapping modes, and the technique involves maximizing residual skills by stimulating the channel that is most functional for the patient.

In contrast, transcoding involves the interaction of two language systems or codes. For example, when writing to dictation, auditorily perceived stimuli must be transcoded into graphic units. Reading aloud involves transcoding visually perceived units into an equivalent phonetic structure. In patients with brain damage, the ability to switch from one functional code to another may be impaired even if both systems remain intact. In this case, a goal of therapy would be to reestablish the functional continuity between the related systems.

REPRESENTATIONAL PROMPTS. The broad range of prompts available to the clinician and his or her patient can increase the power and effectiveness of therapy when properly applied. Representational prompts are contrasted with associational prompts by some writers [69]. In assisting a patient's naming or matching response, representational prompts stand for the concepts pinpointed in the responses. Also, representational prompts may be symbolic or realistic. For example, the written, printed, or spoken word *house* is a symbolic representation that prompts naming a picture of a house. Objects and their associated visual, tactual, and olfactory signals, as well as pictures, serve as realistic prompts.

Associational prompts, in contrast, serve to evoke a target concept without actually representing it, e.g., "eyes, nose, and . . ."; "We ride in a. . . ."

*In light of this principle, I feel it is reasonable to suggest that the deliberate alternation of easy and difficult items to facilitate performance on the latter may be considered a type of "intramodal deblocking" strategy.

The model for the use of these prompts in therapy is as follows:

In teaching an aphasic patient to name (or read) a given representation of an object, or to match the representation with its name, the clinician attempts to find a second representation which, when paired with the first, will assist in evoking the desired naming or matching response. In successive naming or matching tasks, both representations are presented simultaneously, but the second, which acts as a prompt, is gradually faded and eliminated. Sometimes it is found helpful to use more than one prompt for the same task in which case each prompt is faded, and eliminated in turn [69, p. 200].

GENERALIZATION. The reestablishment of functional continuity between modes and between language systems has implications for generalization in language retraining of aphasic patients. If one accepts an interference, or performance deficit, explanation of aphasia (which will be discussed subsequently), then our therapeutic goals of facilitation and retrieval are means for acquiring and improving access to linguistic knowledge or competence. With improved access to competence, the potential for generalization is enhanced.

Although we still do not have a comfortable grasp of all its nuances, evidence for generalization in aphasia programs is accumulating relative to a variety of linguistic skills. Carryover of improved comprehension skills following training to standardized measures has been both supported and challenged. In one report [52], training and steady improvement of an aphasic patient's comprehension ability generalized across other modes to untrained verbal production skills. In a naming program, a patient's improvement using untrained skills supports the concept of intramode generalization [87]. Similar generalization effects between trained and untrained skills in aphasic patients have been reported for naming, gestural skills, and syntactic abilities.

In a recent study of generalization across settings [93], a multiple-baseline design was used to explore whether or not aphasic subjects would transfer social greetings, self-disclosures, and questions. Continuous across-setting probes were conducted during subjects' conversations with unfamiliar persons in a nontraining environment. Results indicated the treatment was effective in facilitating generalized production of the social conventions studied. Generalization patterns were different for each subject and questions were more resistant to generalization than other response types in all subjects.

Usually treatment gains were maintained for three months following treatment.

Another recent study [49] used a single-subject (A-B-A-B) research design to study verb generalization. Although auxiliary and copula is verb production was maintained on 2- and 6-week follow-up probes, transfer to spontaneous speech was negligible. The results were interpreted as providing partial support for the existence of a functional or generative response class between verbal auxiliary and the copula is verbs.

Generalization, then, can be viewed as facilitation of performance on untrained items through training of related skills. There is evidence that trained and untrained skills may be similar, or dissimilar, depending on variations in stimulus mode, level of difficulty, and language system (syntactic, semantic, and phonologic). As evidence accumulates with respect to the types of generalization that can occur for specific language tasks, the goal of optimizing the language behavior of the aphasic person will become more efficient. The increasing application of multiple-baseline measurement strategies by clinicians should greatly clarify the nature of generalization. However, even if no generalization can be demonstrated, as is the case with some severely involved speechless patients, the clinician can be comforted that the introduction of several useful words, phrases, or gestures can significantly alter the quality of the aphasic person's life.

TEMPORAL FACTORS. The clinician involved in selecting and manipulating stimulus materials and stimulus contexts that directly or indirectly facilitate language behavior must also consider temporal factors carefully. For example, the length of time a stimulus is exposed has been contrasted with the effect of intervals between stimuli. Some researchers have found that stimulus exposure time was more effective in eliciting correct responses on naming tasks than placing increasing time intervals between constant stimulus exposures [13].

The insertion of pauses in spoken commands improves patients' ability to carry out commands and generally appears to facilitate their auditory comprehension. However, since all pause durations may not be effective with all subjects and with all types of sentences, Salvatore [82] cautions that the use of pausing should be systematically manipulated for each individual.

When a delay is imposed between the presentation of a stimulus and the opportunity for responding, responses of aphasic subjects have been differentially affected, depending on the amount of cues provided. Yorkston, Marshall, and Butler [110] found that the performance of a group of aphasic patients who were given both auditory and visual information on a comprehension task was significantly enhanced by the imposed response delay, while no change in performance was seen under the imposed delay condition for the group receiving auditory information only. Temporal factors and amount and types of cues appear to interact, and the clinician must be careful to assess these interactions with each patient.

The rate of stimulus presentation (normal versus slow) and the amount of redundancy in an auditory cue also appear to facilitate comprehension [62]. Slowed rate of stimulus presentation and reduced task complexity facilitate performance not only on comprehension but on tasks of identification and repetition [32].

SELF-CUING STRATEGIES. The errors that aphasic individuals make in spontaneous conversation or in therapy have two important and distinct characteristics. An error response may *interfere* with the production of the desired or correct response, or it may *facilitate* the correct response [8]. The facilitative type of error is a potentially useful clinical strategy. By making the patient aware of the facilitative aspect of his or her associated error responses, and training him or her to generate and apply them consciously, the aphasic individual can become a more efficient and independent user of language.

Several word-retrieval strategies used by adult aphasic patients in conversational speech have been identified [65]. These include:

1. Delay: filled or unfilled pause.
2. Association: synonyms, opposites, rhymes, and other words with semantic association with the desired word.
3. Description: characteristics or components of the word.
4. Generalization: empty or general words, e.g., "thing."

The degree to which these spontaneously generated word-retrieval strategies are successful may be strongly related to the severity of aphasia. Delay, the most successful approach, is used only by higher-level patients, while generalization, the least successful technique, is most frequently used by the

more severely involved. These findings are readily adaptable to tasks designed to heighten the patient's volitional use of his or her most efficient strategy.

Several other useful self-cuing strategies were presented by Whitney [107]. Conditioning a patient to incorporate self-generated cues systematically involves several steps.

1. Identify and isolate effective cues.
2. Determine the skills necessary to the patient's volitional use of the cues.
3. Heighten the patient's awareness of the utility of the chosen cue for effecting correct responses.
4. Condition the patient to use self-produced cues. This may involve direct instruction of the strategy, indirect prompting, and reinforcement.

A summary of additional work in the area of self-cuing has been presented recently [57], including the suggestion that aphasia may well benefit from studies in normal verbal learning and verbal behavior, such as those on repetition and depth of processing by Nelson [72], and on cue-dependent forgetting by Tulving [95].

Table 4-2 is a summary of a number of compensatory-facilitative and self-cuing strategies. This summary is comprised of both suggestions found in the literature and some facilitative procedures found to be effective in our clinical experience.

Theoretical Rationale Underlying Therapy
Ideally, the choice of a therapeutic intervention strategy is not random; it is guided by a rationale. Several philosophies, or approaches, to aphasia management have been proposed. The approaches that are discussed include direct versus indirect therapy [91, 92]; behavioral versus psycholinguistic approaches [36]; loss versus interference approaches [66]; the preventive method of aphasia rehabilitation [9]; and, finally, cybernetics and PICA theory [74, 75].

DIRECT VERSUS INDIRECT. Aphasia has been viewed as a linguistic disturbance per se and as a deficit of thought process. This distinction is the basis for differentiating direct language-centered therapy from indirect content-centered therapy. While individualized programs of direct stimulus-response training of language have proved to be most popular, Wepman [103] challenged its efficacy for all aphasic patients. In his view, direct approaches fail in some instances to effect transfer of training of specific language skills to spontaneous reception,

Table 4-2. Compensatory-facilitative and self-cuing strategies useful for some aphasic patients

Verbal production (adaptable to other output modes)	Auditory comprehension (adaptable to other input modes)

Delay
  Silent rehearsal
  Pause after error
  Silent self-correction
Association
  Sensory (sight, sound, smell, taste)
  Synonym
  Antonym
  Rhyme
  Stereotyped context
  Category
Description
  Part-whole relation (*sink, kitchen*)
  Whole-part relation (*house, kitchen*)
  Function-object relation (*read, book*)
  Object-function relation (*car, drive*)
Phonologic
  First sound
  Watch clinician's silent placement
Gestural
  Pantomime (action, object, direction, description, place, time)
  Point to object
  "Air-trace" first letter
Written
  First letter
  Partial word
  Whole word
	Generate patient feedback
	  "Yes, I understand"
	  "No, I don't understand"
	  "Please repeat"
	  "Please write it"
	  "Slow down"
	Intersensory supplements
	  Signs-pantomime to indicate feedback
	  Supplement verbalization by gesture, pointing
	Prosodic-temporal factors
	  Increase stimulus time
	  Insert pauses
	  Slow overall rate
	  Exaggerate stress
	Syntactic
	  Reduce length
	  Reduce linguistic complexity
	Semantic-lexical
	  Increase context redundancy
	  Select high-frequency words
	  Reduce abstractions
	  Reduce semantic relatedness

integration, and production of language use. By contrast, in indirect content-centered therapy the ideas underlying communication are the primary focus of therapy. Wepman suggested that the time after onset of aphasia or the length of time in a structured therapy program may be factors influencing the relative efficacy of the direct, as opposed to indirect, approaches for a specific patient.

BEHAVIORAL VERSUS PSYCHOLINGUISTICS. The distinction between behavioral and psycholinguistic approaches to therapy [36] provides new insights into the concepts originally suggested by Wepman's dichotomy. Specifying and measuring carefully defined behaviors as they change over time are the hallmarks of behavioral approaches. Emphasis on content rather than the structure of therapy distinguishes the psycholinguistic approach from a behavioral orientation. The psycholinguistic approach incorporates generalization about the reduced number, variety, and complexity of linguistic operations available to the aphasic patient with respect to both receptive and expressive skills. Such generalizations about language deficit have direct implications for the selection of therapy tasks in aphasia treatment programs.

LOSS VERSUS INTERFERENCE. A third rationale or approach to therapy is based on the view of the nature of aphasia. Aphasia as a *loss* of specific information has been contrasted with the concept that brain damage *interferes* with the operations involved in language. The loss view is traditionally associated with *learning* approaches to therapy, while the interference view is associated with *stimulation* rather than reteaching of disturbed function. Martin [66] offers a refined conceptualization of this traditional dichotomy. In his view, learning approaches have their roots in stimulus-response theory, while stimulation approaches are based on cognitive theory. In the former, learning is viewed as a connection between stimulus and response; thus in therapy the structuring and control of stimulus content to elicit desired responses are of primary concern. In cognitive theory the aphasic person's motivation and interaction with the environment are of primary importance. Thus if one regards learning broadly as involving memory, reproduction, and reorganization skills, the traditional learning approach to aphasia therapy, within the framework of stimulus-response theory, emphasizes *memory* and the *reproduction* of specific content. The stimulation approach, within the framework of cognitive theory, emphasizes *reorganization* of the language system. In both approaches to aphasia therapy, behavior is altered. In the learning approach, the *content* is changed; in the stimulation approach, the *process* of language use is changed.

PREVENTIVE METHOD. A rather unique view of the evolution of aphasia and, subsequently, an approach to aphasia therapy is the preventive method [9]. This method is based on the premise that by regulating the content of the words introduced into the patient's speech, the anticipated emergence of agrammatic or telegraphic speech can be prevented in the patient with severe expressive aphasia. The predictable emergence of telegraphic speech, according to Beyn and Shokhor-Trotskaya [9], is related to the primary pathology of inner speech characterized by disintegration of the predicative system. To counteract this trend, only stimulus words of a predicative character are presented in the initial stages of therapy, i.e., words that express complete ideas, but no substantive meaning (e.g., *ah, here, myself, give, take, yes, no*). Pronouns, adverbs, and verbs are gradually introduced and, finally, nouns. The success these authors report with the preventive method warrants its consideration as a viable therapy approach, although few examples of its use are evident in American speech pathology.

CYBERNETICS AND PICA THEORY. The PICA, a clinical tool designed essentially to measure aphasic disturbance, has also generated a number of principles concerning treatment. Further, clinical use of the PICA with a large number of aphasic patients has spawned several provocative hypotheses about the nature of aphasia. Porch [74, 75] views aphasia as being more than disordered symbolization or linguistic impairment. By drawing analogies among brain function, closed- and open-loop feedback systems, and computer circuitry, Porch reasons that disturbed cybernetic factors are a significant component in impaired communication processing. This view guided the development of a multidimensional scoring system and the selection of subtests comprised of items that are reasonably homogeneous in terms of difficulty. Porch feels that analysis of patterns of scores, within and across subtests, reveals patterns of tuning-in and tuning-out, slow rise time, noise build-up, and other cybernetic disturbances of information processing. The concept has been elaborated on, particularly in the auditory

mode, by Brookshire [16] and by LaPointe et al. [60].

This view of aphasia, coupled with the quantifiable nature of the PICA, allows Porch to suggest underlying principles of treatment based on PICA score profiles and a number of calculations and formulas.

Another concept of PICA theory relates to the selection of tasks to be worked on. Porch suggests that the configuration of a patient's mean subtest scores, when plotted on a ranked response summary, will indicate a sigmoidal curve. That point on a continuum of task difficulty at which performance just begins to show impairment (8s to 13s on the PICA) is considered the fulcrum of the curve and provides a guideline to the types of tasks that should be selected for treatment.

In recent work [75] Porch has elaborated on some of his early applications of PICA theory to treatment. In a chapter on therapy subsequent to the PICA, Porch discusses selecting patients for treatment, choosing treatment tasks, deciding on treatment stimuli, organizing treatment, setting treatment priorities, and implementing criteria for task shift.

Many of the hypotheses generated by use of the PICA remain to be fully documented, but clinical use of the test has suggested some fascinating directions for research.

The stimulation-facilitation approach and the programmed-operant approach emerge from this overview as two main schools of thought in aphasia therapy. These two approaches and a third system that attempts to synthesize concepts from both will be developed in the following sections.

Stimulation-Facilitation Approach
Taylor [92] reviewed some intervention strategies, which she termed *nonspecific stimulation*, or the *spontaneous recovery approach*. In her view these miscellaneous strategies represent "no approach at all." Included in these nonspecific stimulation approaches are:

1. The environment stimulation approach: everybody around the patient talks as much as possible.
2. The rapport approach: a warm relationship is established between the clinician and the patient without regard to the content or method of presentation of stimuli.
3. The socialization approach: also called "coffee-hour treatment," in which group sessions in-

clude singing, crafts, hobbies, games, telling jokes, and playing pranks.

4. The psychotherapeutic approach: group work focusing on problems, such as anxiety and loss of self-esteem, with little direct attempt to retain language.
5. The interest approach: motivating patients by interesting them in subjects related to their previous activities and interests.

Although these general stimulation approaches have been used, and continue to be used in some institutions, they are not to be confused with the *stimulation-facilitation* approach, which was fathered by Wepman [102] and nurtured and refined by Schuell, Jenkins, and Jiménez-Pabón [82].

Proponents of this approach view aphasia as an interference with language processes. The goal of therapy is not to reeducate the aphasic patient but rather to stimulate disrupted processes to function maximally.

Intensive and repeated sensory stimulation, especially through the auditory channel, is a basic characteristic of this approach. This approach has been characterized as *auditory bombardment*. A second characteristic is its emphasis on getting the patient going, talking, responding, listening, and trying.

Specific suggestions for therapy by advocates of this approach include the following:

1. Use intensive auditory stimulation.
2. Use material that is meaningful to the patient.
3. Use abundant and varied clinical material during each session.
4. Use repetitive sensory stimulation.
5. Make sure the patient responds to each stimulus presented.
6. Elicit, do not force responses.
7. Avoid correcting defective responses.
8. Make the stimulus adequate.

After carefully analyzing what is defective in the aphasic person's response, and why, the clinician has several avenues available for manipulating the stimulus to make it adequate. These include altering loudness, length, associational strength, and duration of stimuli; cuing; repetition; gapping; fading; altering tempo and pace; and altering the selection of input mode combinations.

Schuell's [82] conceptualization of the stimulation-facilitation approach has been widely accepted by clinicians, and her concepts have been extended and elaborated on by many.

Programmed-Operant Approach

The programmed-operant approach views language rehabilitation as an educative process. The experimental analysis of behavior and principles of operant conditioning provide the theoretical basis for this approach. This method requires the clinician to analyze the functional relation between environmental events and behavior and then to apply operant procedures systematically to modify behavior.

The chronology of major steps in a programmed-operant approach can be found in many sources, but Brookshire [12] and Holland [44] present them as lucidly as anyone. These steps include the following:

1. Obtain baseline measures. The rate at which behavior occurs before treatment serves as the baseline against which the effects of treatment can be measured. Baseline measurement requires that the patient's behavior be precisely defined in operational terms. In addition, careful scrutiny of the stimulus conditions that control the response is necessary. A few writers have detailed the development of operational specificity and control of stimulus conditions during aphasia treatment [86, 87].
2. Apply behavior-modification procedures. The second procedural step in a programmed-operant approach is modification of the patient's behavior. A precise operational definition of terminal behavior, relative to the rate or topography of response, is prerequisite to application of conditioning procedures. Then procedures designed either to change the response *rate* (such as increasing the frequency of correct naming behavior, or decreasing the frequency of perseverative emissions), or to *establish new responses* must be selected.

In operant learning, the consequent event is the main determinant of the rate of response. For this reason, careful attention to the type of reinforcer used in a program and judicious use of schedules of reinforcement are of central importance when attempting to modify the *rate* of a patient's response.

If the goal of the program is to establish a *new* behavior, the response repertoire of an aphasic person must be carefully analyzed, so a response that shares some characteristics with the terminal behavior, and which the patient can emit, can be modified. From the existing repertoire, the patient's terminal behavior can be shaped or chained into small controlled steps, or *successive approximations*. In some programs, the response requirements may not change; instead, the stimulus conditions that surround the desired response may be faded or subject to variation.

3. Extend stimulus control. The third event in the operant sequence is extension control. This involves carryover or transfer of training from the highly controlled clinical setting to more spontaneous and natural situations of communication. The clinician must manipulate the stimulus-response requirements of the therapy task, including types and schedules of reinforcement, with an ultimate view toward extending the response into the patient's natural communicative environment. Logically, the more closely the stimulus conditions and response contingencies in therapy resemble those found in the natural environment, the more easily carryover will be accomplished. This is the most important step, and one that is often neglected. It does little good to demonstrate adequate communicative performance in the sheltered environment of the clinic if this performance cannot be transferred to the aphasic person's breakfast table or home bathroom needs.

THE CONSEQUENT EVENT. In behavioral psychology the consequent event, or what happens after a response has been emitted, has received a great deal of attention. Aphasia research has not duplicated this attention. Some early studies report successful application of programmed techniques with aphasic subjects in discrimination learning and transfer tasks. Operant methods have been used successfully to effect changes on verbal tasks, such as word and sentence production, when verbal, token, self-reinforcement, self-punishment, delayed feedback, and modeling were employed. Modeling, self-punishment, and delayed reinforcement were found to cause the most marked changes in aphasic subjects' behavior [36, 37]. Delay of reinforcement was studied by Brookshire [14] in a probability learning task, and he found that performance deteriorated with even relatively short delays between patients' responses and the delivery of consequent events. Nonaphasic subjects, however, were not hindered by delayed consequence. Three types of punishment were successfully used

to train aphasic subjects on a visual paired-associate matching task. However, the different types of punishment (time-out, response cost, and presentation of an aversive stimulus) were differentially effective for certain aphasic subjects. Patients learned best when positive reinforcement and punishment were combined [53].

Programmed instruction also has shown promise as a somewhat rewarding approach to aphasia rehabilitation. In a series of case studies, Holland [44] reported success with highly structured and individualized programs for a variety of language problems. Programmed therapy is adaptable to machine-assisted techniques and provides the means for a valuable supplement to face-to-face clinical interaction. The elicitation of naming behavior in aphasic individuals through systematic manipulation of the auditory and visual modes at progressive levels of difficulty was designed by Keenan [50], using the Language Master. A sequence of skills related to auditory recognition, verbal imitation, and verbal naming was adapted by Wilson and Petersen [109] to machine-assisted treatment. These programs are unique in their adaptability to self-administration by the aphasic patient. A good deal of recent research has focused on the adaptation of microcomputer-assisted software to aphasia therapy. Programs developed by Katz [46] are representative and appear to hold great promise in this area.

THE ANTECEDENT EVENT. In contrast to the scanty emphasis on the consequent event in behavior modification, clinical aphasiologists recognize the need for controlling and manipulating the antecedent event. In fact, manipulating the antecedent event, or stimulus control (as it is known in traditional operant terminology), is probably the most potent factor available to the clinician in aphasia therapy. Attention to the antecedent through careful selection and arrangement of tasks, coupled with judicious use of prompts and cues, can provide the optimal environment for the elicitation, facilitation, and shaping of desirable language responses.

The mode and amount of cuing preceding the desired response—specifically, cuing that is designed to facilitate the response—are of primary importance to these systems of therapy. A basis for focusing on the antecedent event is the belief that there is a hierarchy of available cuing techniques that vary in their ability to elicit the efficiently produced communicative responses.

Two processes necessary in planning or manipulating the antecedent event involve data collection and procedural decisions [36]. Data collection is the result of systematic sampling, through either testing or probing of language behavior. In aphasia, testing should differentiate the effects of physiologic damage on behavior from the possible confounding effects of procedures used to measure that behavior. Several variables that may affect the patient's performance and confound task results are the ability of the patient to understand the instructions; irrelevant aspects of the stimuli; effects of response-contingent stimuli (the consequent event); fatigue; and the order of items in the task [82, 83]. A strict behavioral analysis of aphasic responses places special emphasis on the effect of reinforcement and stimulus control during testing.

Premorbid patterns of stimulation and reinforcement exerted by relevant and irrelevant stimuli may be disturbed in the aphasic patient. A baseline probe technique suggested by Salvatore [82] is one method of monitoring task responses. This method involves placing a trained probe item amid task items to separate the effects of fatigue, propagating error, and increasing complexity of items. One can be more confident that responses are valid if the patient is able to respond accurately to the probe item regardless of its position in the task. Other considerations in separating stimulus control deficits from deficits resulting from the aphasia include the meticulous control of input and output modes and the homogeneity of test items [85].

Once behavior is systematically and reliably sampled, procedural decisions are necessary. This is the point at which attention to antecedent factors is crucial and involves choosing modes (e.g., auditory-verbal, visual-motor) and amount of cuing (total, partial, minimal) that are thought to be potentially useful in the therapeutic task [37].

Careful programming of the antecedent event is emphasized in "response contingent small-step treatment" [11]. This treatment involves the presentation of retrieval strategies (the antecedent event)

Fig. 4-2. Base-10 Response Form.

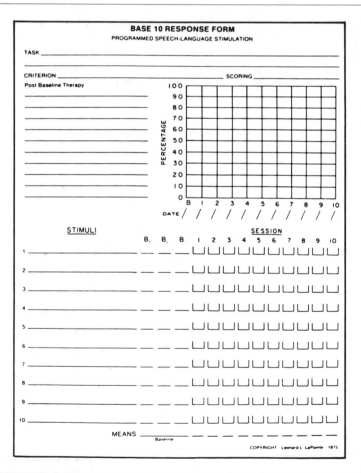

and feedback (the consequent event) within a maximally structured framework, with the ultimate goal of internalization and integration of strategies by the patient. In this system, Bollinger and Stout [11] discuss the concepts of stimulus power and stimulus number, and they suggest methods of identification of task hierarchies. *Stimulus power* refers to the stimulus strength necessary to cue the desired response. *Stimulus number* refers to the number of stimuli in a given response field or the number of items per task or both. The hierarchy is initiated with the most powerful antecedent or cue, i.e., the most facilitative with respect to stimulus power and number. The small-step method is implemented by progressing in small steps in the task hierarchy, to tasks with less powerful antecedents, until errors occur, and then stepping back one level. Performance level and response constancy are used as criteria for moving a patient from task to task within the hierarchy.

Task hierarchies, or task continua, also have been used in treatment of apraxia of speech. This strategy is outlined in more detail in Chapter 7. It is important to emphasize here, however, that the principles underlying this system are as appropriate to aphasic disturbances as they are to phonologic impairment. Steps in the hierarchy vary systematically with respect to the mode of cuing, amount of cuing, and the nature of the patient's response (simultaneous, delayed, or successive). The task continuum of Rosenbek et al. [79] appears to represent a legitimate and useful ordering of tasks by level of difficulty. The steps may be reordered and additional response facilitators may be introduced, when appropriate, without altering the underlying principles or goals of the system.

Base-10 Programmed Stimulation

Many of the concepts related to precise measurement of behaviors, outlined in earlier sections of this chapter, are not only useful strategies for evaluating the efficacy of treatment but are also viable means of organizing daily therapy. Several clinicians and researchers have highlighted some of the fundamental concepts of operant approaches to therapy that emphasize these concepts. These programmed-operant approaches have focused attention on at least four factors that can be applied

Table 4-3. Baseline-10 conversion table. PICA-scored task means to percentages

PICA mean	Percent	PICA mean	Percent	PICA mean	Percent	PICA mean	Percent	PICA mean	Percent
0.1	01	3.1	21	6.1	41	9.1	61	12.1	81
0.2	01	3.2	21	6.2	41	9.2	61	12.2	81
0.3	02	3.3	22	6.3	42	9.3	62	12.3	82
0.4	03	3.4	23	6.4	43	9.4	63	12.4	83
0.5	03	3.5	23	6.5	43	9.5	63	12.5	83
0.6	04	3.6	24	6.6	44	9.6	64	12.6	84
0.7	05	3.7	25	6.7	45	9.7	65	12.7	85
0.8	05	3.8	25	6.8	45	9.8	65	12.8	85
0.9	06	3.9	26	6.9	46	9.9	66	12.9	86
1.0	07	4.0	27	7.0	47	10.0	67	13.0	87
1.1	07	4.1	27	7.1	47	10.1	67	13.1	87
1.2	08	4.2	28	7.2	48	10.2	68	13.2	88
1.3	09	4.3	29	7.3	49	10.3	69	13.3	89
1.4	09	4.4	29	7.4	49	10.4	69	13.4	89
1.5	10	4.5	30	7.5	50	10.5	70	13.5	90
1.6	11	4.6	31	7.6	51	10.6	71	13.6	91
1.7	11	4.7	31	7.7	51	10.7	71	13.7	91
1.8	12	4.8	32	7.8	52	10.8	72	13.8	92
1.9	13	4.9	33	7.9	53	10.9	73	13.9	93
2.0	13	5.0	33	8.0	53	11.0	73	14.0	93
2.1	14	5.1	34	8.1	54	11.1	74	14.1	94
2.2	15	5.2	35	8.2	55	11.2	75	14.2	95
2.3	15	5.3	35	8.3	55	11.3	75	14.3	95
2.4	16	5.4	36	8.4	56	11.4	76	14.4	96
2.5	17	5.5	37	8.5	57	11.5	77	14.5	97
2.6	17	5.6	37	8.6	57	11.6	77	14.6	97
2.7	18	5.7	38	8.7	58	11.7	78	14.7	98
2.8	19	5.8	39	8.8	59	11.8	79	14.8	99
2.9	19	5.9	39	8.9	59	11.9	79	14.9	99
3.0	20	6.0	40	9.0	60	12.0	80	15.0	100

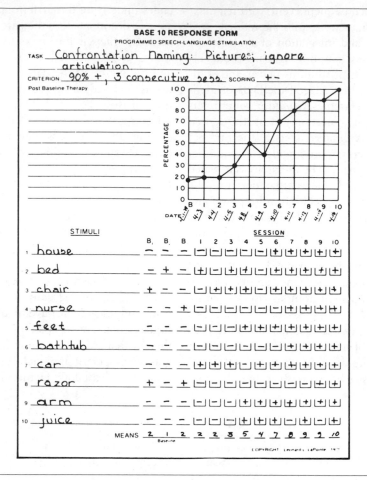

BASE 10 RESPONSE FORM
PROGRAMMED SPEECH-LANGUAGE STIMULATION

TASK Confrontation naming: Pictures; ignore articulation

CRITERION 90% +, 3 consecutive sess.   SCORING + −

Post Baseline Therapy

PERCENTAGE (graph 0–100)

DATE: 4/3, 4/4, 4/5, 4/8, 4/9, 4/10, 4/11, 4/12, 4/15, 4/16

STIMULI	B.	B.	B	1	2	3	4	5	6	7	8	9	10
1 house	−	−	−	−	−	−	−	−	+	+	+	+	+
2 bed	−	+	−	+	−	+	+	−	+	+	+	+	+
3 chair	+	−	−	−	+	+	+	−	+	+	+	+	+
4 nurse	−	−	+	−	−	−	−	−	−	+	+	+	+
5 feet	−	−	−	−	−	−	+	+	+	+	+	+	+
6 bathtub	−	−	−	−	−	−	−	−	−	+	+	+	+
7 car	−	−	−	+	+	+	−	+	+	+	+	+	+
8 razor	+	−	+	−	−	−	−	−	−	−	−	+	+
9 arm	−	−	−	−	−	−	+	+	+	+	+	+	+
10 juice	−	−	−	−	−	−	+	+	+	−	+	−	+
MEANS	2	1	2	2	2	3	5	4	7	8	9	9	10

Baseline

COPYRIGHT Leonard L. LaPointe 19..

Fig. 4-3. Base-10 Response Form example for confrontation naming, using plus-minus scoring.

readily to aphasia therapy: (1) more careful measurement of baseline behaviors, and the predictive value of base-rate performance; (2) attention to the use of reinforcement; (3) definition of terminal behavior and target levels in specific terms; and (4) stimulus control and the value of clearly defining and arranging the stimuli used in a therapy session.

The programmed-operant approach to therapy has been contrasted with the Schuellian, or stimulation, approach. Some basic concepts of each already have been discussed. Apparently, some clinical aphasiologists believe they must adopt only one of these approaches and incorporate it into their philosophy and method of treatment.

The validity of this assumed dichotomy between stimulation and programmed approaches is questionable. Many similarities and areas of overlap exist between the two. Holland [43] suggested that programs can control the amount of stimulation; they can require continuous responding by the aphasic; they automatically allow for restimulation; and they constantly evaluate performance. This pattern closely resembles many of the therapeutic principles of Schuell [83], one of the prime advocates of stimulation and facilitation.

Base-10 programmed stimulation combines some of the principles and concepts of both the programmed-operant and stimulation approaches in a strategy of aphasia therapy [55]. The programmed-operant features of clearly defined tasks, baseline performance measurement, and session-by-session progress plotting are readily adaptable to therapy with the aphasic patient. Just as adaptable are the features of stimulation and facilitation designed to elicit many responses from aphasic subjects. With the programmed-stimulation approach, speech and language tasks are composed of 10 stimulus items, which are scored and plotted during 10 therapy sessions.

Figure 4-2 (p. 196) shows the Base-10 Response Form (available from C. C. Publications, Inc., Tigard, OR; for information call 1-800-547-4800)

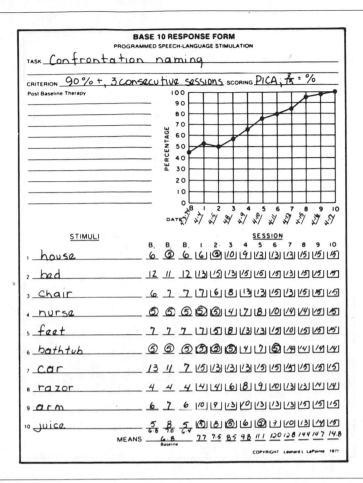

BASE 10 RESPONSE FORM
PROGRAMMED SPEECH-LANGUAGE STIMULATION

TASK Confrontation naming

CRITERION 90% +, 3 consecutive sessions SCORING PICA; $\bar{x}$ = %

Post Baseline Therapy

(graph: PERCENTAGE 0–100 vs DATE/SESSION 1–10)

STIMULI	B.	B.	B.	1	2	3	4	5	6	7	8	9	10
1 house	6	2	6	6	9	10	9	13	13	13	15	15	15
2 bed	12	11	12	13	15	13	15	15	15	13	15	15	15
3 chair	6	7	7	7	6	8	13	13	15	13	15	15	15
4 nurse	5	5	5	5	6	4	7	8	10	14	14	15	15
5 feet	7	7	7	7	5	8	13	13	15	10	15	15	15
6 bathtub	5	5	5	5	5	5	4	7	5	14	14	14	14
7 car	13	11	7	15	13	13	13	15	15	14	15	15	15
8 razor	4	4	4	14	14	6	8	9	10	13	13	14	14
9 arm	6	7	6	10	9	13	10	13	13	13	15	15	15
10 juice	5	8	5	6	6	6	6	6	7	10	13	14	15
MEANS	6.8	7.0	6.7		7.7	7.5	8.5	9.8	11.1	12.0	12.8	14.4	14.7	14.8

Baseline

COPYRIGHT Leonard L. LaPointe 1975

Fig. 4-4. Base-10 Response Form example for confrontation naming, using PICA scoring.

used for each speech and language task. This form allows space for specifying the task, defining and listing an acceptable performance level (criterion), the exact stimulus items used in the task, and the performance score on each item during every session. Finally, the Base-10 Response Form permits a person's performance levels to be converted to a graphic display of progress (or lack of it) in percentage over 10 sessions.

This strategy does not dictate what to work on or how to reinforce responses; but once these decisions are made, it organizes stimulus presentation and provides a medium from which clear judgments of session-by-session progress can be made.

SELECTION OF TASKS. A critical decision in using the Base-10 Response Form in aphasia therapy is task selection. The rationale for selecting therapeutic tasks, of course, is based on evaluation and testing of each individual patient. Several factors

can influence this decision. Clinicians who use the PICA might be guided by the subject's ranked response summary and the fulcrum-of-the-curve concept cited earlier.

Generally, a number of tasks can be used with an aphasic patient in a single session. We use a different response form with each task so progress on each can be plotted. For sessions of 30 to 45 minutes, three or four different tasks are appropriate. These can include such things as sentence completion, naming objects, auditory retention of directions, matching words to sample, and writing from dictation.

The prime guidelines for deciding which tasks to select are functionality and relevance. We try to select tasks meaningful to the patient's functional communication and daily living needs, and we avoid tasks that are marginally relevant, such as naming colors or counting. This means that many of the tasks selected, especially for inpatients, will focus on topics of immediate communicative need

199 Aphasia Therapy: Some Principles and Strategies

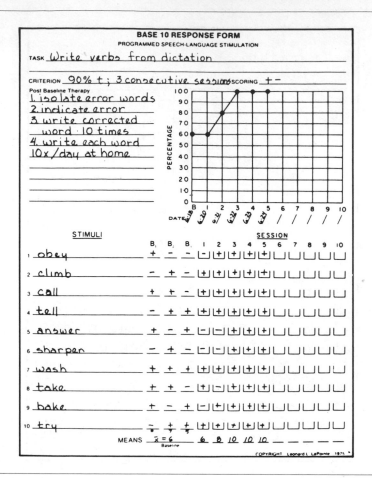

Fig. 4-5. Writing verbs from dictation (patient 1).

related to using the bathroom, grooming, eating, taking medication, indicating pain and discomfort, or anything else we discern as being a pressing communicative need of the individual.

Task selection is an important responsibility of the clinician, since it relates intimately to the overall therapeutic plan and to the goals of therapy. The information relative to the antecedent event presented earlier can serve as a guide to this planning. With some patients, particularly those who are severely involved, the tasks selected may have no immediately obvious relation to functional communication. Many times tasks that are precursors to more complex acts, such as perceptual skills, geometric form matching, letter matching, auditory vigilance, and attentional factors, are part of the processing deficit of aphasia and will require improvement before the patient can progress to more complex language skills.

CRITERION. For the space marked *criterion* a decision must be made about the acceptable level of performance for that task. This decision is guided by the severity of the patient's disorder and by the base rate on the task, and it can be stated as percentage of correct responses for a specified number of sessions. To anticipate 100 percent performance may be unrealistic for many tasks, so we frequently use a criterion (target behavior level) of 90 percent or more for three consecutive sessions as our goal. If a multidimensional scoring system is used, as in the PICA, high scores on individual items within a subtest can serve as a guideline for establishing the criterion.

Target behavior levels on certain tasks are difficult to achieve with some aphasic individuals, and preestablished levels of accomplishment need not be inflexible. Consistency of performance over time is an important key to terminating the task. If, for example, a criterion of 90 percent or greater for three consecutive sessions was established and

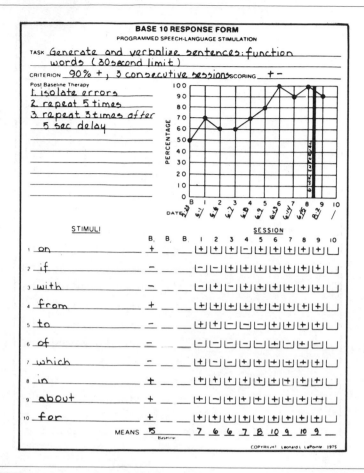

BASE 10 RESPONSE FORM
PROGRAMMED SPEECH-LANGUAGE STIMULATION

TASK _Generate and verbalize sentences: function words (30 second limit)_

CRITERION _90% +, 3 consecutive sessions_ SCORING _+ −_

Post Baseline Therapy
1. isolate errors
2. repeat 5 times
3. repeat 3 times after 5 sec delay

STIMULI	B.	B.	B.	1	2	3	4	5	6	7	8	9	10
1 on	+	_	_	+	+	+	−	+	+	+	+	+	
2 if	−	_	_	−	−	+	+	+	+	+	+	+	
3 with	−	_	_	−	+	−	+	+	+	+	+	+	
4 from	+	_	_	+	+	+	+	+	+	+	+	+	
5 to	−	_	_	+	+	−	−	−	+	+	+	+	
6 of	−	_	_	−	−	−	−	−	+	+	+	−	
7 which	−	_	_	+	−	−	+	+	+	+	+	+	
8 in	+	_	_	+	+	+	+	+	+	+	+	+	
9 about	+	_	_	+	−	+	+	+	+	+	+	+	
10 for	+	_	_	+	+	+	+	+	+	+	+	+	
MEANS	5			7	6	6	7	8	10	9	10	9	_

Baseline

COPYRIGHT Leonard L. LaPointe 1975

Fig. 4-6. Generating sentences with function words (patient 1).

an aphasic subject achieved an 80 percent level and remained on a plateau for five consecutive sessions, the task should probably be terminated or modified on the basis of this performance plateau.

STIMULUS ITEMS. The next decision is to select 10 functional stimulus items for each task and specify them clearly on the Base-10 Response Form, which has adequate space for words, phrases, or sentences. Occasionally, the stimuli selected are too lengthy for the space provided. Then a simple code can be written in the spaces that refer to more extensive word or sentence lists attached to the task sheet.

SCORING. Each stimulus item is presented to the subject and can be scored in one of several ways. Many tasks lend themselves to plus or minus scoring; after each one is scored, the total score for the

session is computed and entered on the percentage graph. However, for many tasks a multidimensional scoring system, such as that used with the PICA, has been found to be much more sensitive to small changes in a patient's performance. The mean of the scores achieved on each of the 10 stimuli is computed, divided by 15 (on the PICA a 15 represents an accurate, prompt, complete, and efficiently produced response), and this conversion to percentage is then entered on the graph. Table 4-3 (p. 197) presents the conversion to percentages for possible PICA-scored task means.

BASELINE MEASUREMENT AND POSTBASELINE THERAPY. Establishing baseline performance on a task can be done in several ways, including measuring performance during successive sessions before initiating any drill or therapy on error items. The baseline may be measured by scoring the 10 items several times during one day or several times within a session, with subsequent plotting of the

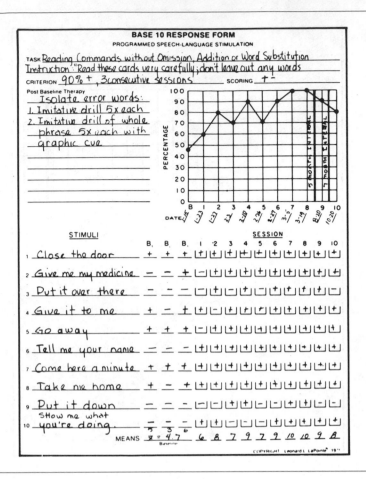

BASE 10 RESPONSE FORM
PROGRAMMED SPEECH-LANGUAGE STIMULATION

TASK Reading Commands without Omission, Addition or Word Substitution
Instruction "Read these cards very carefully; don't leave out any words
CRITERION 90% +, 3 consecutive sessions   SCORING + -

Post Baseline Therapy
Isolate error words:
1. Imitative drill 5x each
2. Imitative drill of whole
   phrase 5x each with
   graphic cue

STIMULI	B.	B.	B.	1	2	3	4	5	6	7	8	9	10
1 Close the door	+	+	+	+	+	+	+	+	+	+	+	+	+
2 Give me my medicine	−	−	+	−	+	+	+	+	+	+	+	+	+
3 Put it over there	−	−	−	−	+	−	+	−	+	+	+	+	−
4 Give it to me	+	−	+	+	−	+	+	+	+	+	+	+	+
5 Go away	+	+	+	−	+	+	+	+	+	+	+	+	+
6 Tell me your name	−	−	−	+	+	+	+	+	+	+	+	+	+
7 Come here a minute	+	+	+	+	+	+	+	+	+	+	+	+	+
8 Take me home	+	−	+	+	+	+	+	+	+	+	+	+	+
9 Put it down	−	−	−	−	−	+	+	−	−	+	+	−	−
10 Show me what you're doing.	−	−	−	+	+	−	−	−	+	+	+	+	+
MEANS	x̄ = 4	7	6	6	8	7	9	7	9	10	10	9	8

Baseline

COPYRIGHT Leonard L. LaPointe 19"

Fig. 4-7. Reading printed commands (patient 2).

mean performance as a base rate. Space is provided on the Base-10 Response Form for recording three baseline measurements (B_1, B_2, B_3). The number of baseline measurements necessary is guided by the stability of these measurements. If baseline performance varies widely from one measurement to another, this usually suggests modification to task difficulty or continued measurement until the patient's performance on that task is stable.

It is important to emphasize that the measurement, or merely scoring the performance on 10 stimulus items, does not constitute the therapy. After baseline performance is established, it is time to introduce the therapeutic variable, or the treatment package, which is the particular strategy selected for improving the patient's performance on the 10 stimulus items. Usually error items are separated, and attention is focused on each one in an attempt to modify the deviant response. This is the point at which all the stimulation and facilitation strategies designed to facilitate and shape the best

possible response are used. Such techniques as integral stimulation ("Watch me," "Listen to me"), additional cuing, cue fading, altering rhythm or tempo, temporal gapping, association, synthesis of stimulus components, explanation and model presentation, and repetition are all effective means of modifying deviant responses. Drill and therapy on each deviant response should be approached with the goal of gradual reduction (fading) of the clinician's facilitative influence. This means that each attack on a deviant response should attempt to increase the patient's volitional control of the response to its maximum. These strategies of therapeutic intervention on the error items are specified and recorded on the Base-10 Response Form under the section labeled *postbaseline therapy*. The continuing measurement of session-by-session performance on the task can then be used to judge effectiveness of therapeutic intervention on each task.

Figure 4-3 (p. 198) exemplifies use of the Base-10 Response Form in a task of confrontation nam-

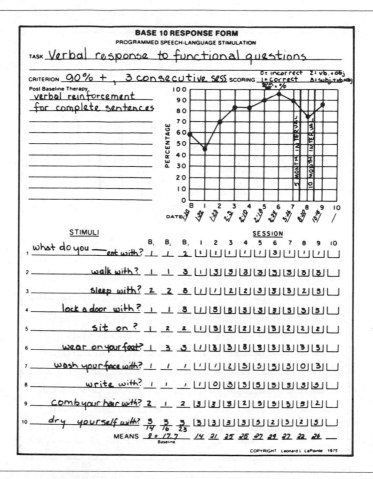

Fig. 4-8. Verbal response to functional questions (patient 2).

ing. On this example, plus-or-minus scoring was used. Figure 4-4 (p. 199) is an illustration of the same task, but on this task a multidimensional PICA scoring system was used.

EXAMPLES OF TASKS RECORDED ON BASE-10 RESPONSE FORMS. The following examples illustrate the performance of a number of aphasic patients. A single communicative task is recorded on each Base-10 Response Form; and these examples represent a variety of tasks, scoring systems, and rates of progress. They are presented to illustrate use of this system in organizing aphasia therapy and to serve as a point of departure to the reader who would generate further creative application of the technique.

Figures 4-5 and 4-6 (pp. 200 and 201, respectively) illustrate two tasks used with a 28-year-old man (patient 1), who sustained traumatic fronto-temporal lobe damage to the left hemisphere. At 14 months after onset, his language impairment was mild (PICA overall, 86th percentile) and included difficulty in spelling verbs during writing and impairment in verbally retrieving and producing connective and functional words. Figure 4-5 illustrates his progress in writing verbs from dictation. He reached criterion in five sessions on this task. This task is representative of several spelling tasks that were plotted using a variety of verb sets.

Figure 4-6 illustrates patient 1's progress on a task of generating and verbalizing sentences with selected prepositions. He reached criterion on this task in eight sessions. Six weeks later he was retested on the same task and performed at the 90 percent level. During each therapy session, after measuring his performance on the task, we selected those items with which he had difficulty and had him practice them in a variety of ways. For example, he was asked to repeat the corrected sentence five times with the clinician, to repeat it five times by himself, or to repeat it several times after an imposed delay.

Figures 4-7 and 4-8 illustrate patient 2's per-

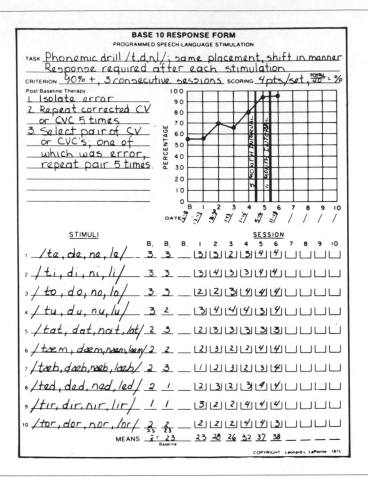

Fig. 4-9. Phonemic drill on manner shift (patient 3).

formance on a reading task and a sentence-formulation task. This patient was a 61-year-old man who suffered a thromboembolic cerebrovascular accident approximately 6 years before arrival at our clinic. He manifested a dense right hemiplegia and moderate to severe aphasia (PICA overall, 47th percentile), with moderate verbal formulation and phonologic selection and sequencing difficulty (PICA verbal, 43rd percentile).

Figure 4-7 illustrates patient 2's performance on a task requiring him to read printed commands aloud without omitting, adding, or substituting words. The mean of these baseline measurements was 47 percent. Postbaseline therapy consisted of isolating the error words in each sentence and repeating them five times with the clinician; saying the complete sentence after the clinician; and then rereading the sentence without being prompted. Criterion performance level was reached after eight sessions, and further work on the task was terminated. After 5 months patient 2 was retested on the

task, and he had maintained performance at the 90 percent level. Two months later his performance had decreased to the 80 percent level. His progress on this task illustrates that efficiency in performing a clearly specified language task can be manipulated. It illustrates further that with a consistent system of measurement, which specifies baseline performance and the nature of therapeutic intervention, the magnitude of progress can be quantified. Since it had been approximately 6 years since the onset of this patient's illness, it is reasonable to assume that his progress was not the result of spontaneous recovery. Further, since he demonstrated no progress on several very similar language tasks, on which performance was measured over the same time span but without a concentrated effort to correct error performance, this progress (see Fig. 4-7) probably did not reflect the "Hawthorne effect," the "placebo" effect, or improvement merely because the patient received the attention of a clinician.

Figure 4-8 represents the performance by patient

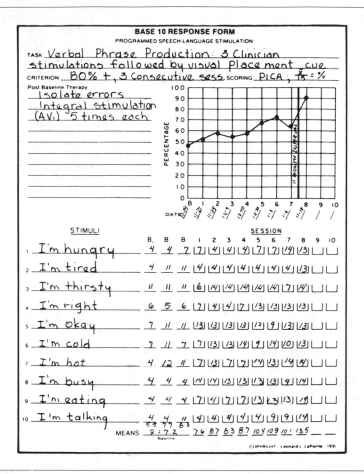

Fig. 4-10. Verbal phrase imitation (patient 3).

2 on a task requiring a spoken sentence response to a series of questions. A four-category scoring system was used on this task, and the postbaseline therapy consisted simply of copious verbal reinforcement of complete sentence responses ("That's right," "Very good," "That's what I'd like you to do," "Use complete sentences") with neutral or no response from the clinician when sentences were less than complete. Mean performance on three baseline measurements was 59 percent, criterion (90 percent or greater) was achieved after seven sessions, and work on the task was terminated. Patient 2 was retested 5 and then 10 months later, and his performance had decreased to 73 percent and 87 percent, respectively. However, maintaining performance at these levels still appears to represent considerably more accurate performance than the mean baseline level of 59 percent.

Figures 4-9 and 4-10 illustrate performance on two tasks by a 42-year-old man (patient 3), who suffered a left middle-cerebral artery thromboem-

bolic episode. At 14 months after onset of illness he exhibited a dense right hemiplegia, right homonymous hemianopia, and moderate aphasia (PICA overall, 57th percentile), which was characterized by unintelligible, differentiated jargon, some neologistic jargon, and moderate phonologic selection and sequencing impairment.

One characteristic of patient 3's speech was frequent substitution of phonemes. Usually placement of the intended phoneme was intact, but a manner change was produced. For this reason, one of the tasks selected for therapy consisted of attempts to produce sets of rhyming CV and CVC words on which the initial phoneme varied in manner but remained constant in place of production. Figure 4-9 illustrates his performance on this task.

Baseline on this task was 58 percent, and he progressed to the 80 percent level after four sessions. Although the task appeared to be beneficial, criterion was never achieved, and the task was terminated because the patient indicated rather convincingly that he did not like the task and preferred working on other things. However, after several months of improvement in verbal formulation skills, patient 3 was retested on this task (at 5 and at 11 months after the task had been terminated), and the impression that he now had less difficulty in manner shifts was confirmed.

Figure 4-10 illustrates the same patient's performance on a verbal imitation task. Therapy on error items consisted of five integral stimulations ("Watch me," "Listen to me," "Say it with me"). Progress on this task was minimal, and after seven sessions the task was changed. This illustrates the guidance that session-by-session measurement can offer in the modification of therapeutic tasks. If performance is not improving, usually a phase change or task alteration is necessary.

In summary, the programmed-stimulation approach to aphasia therapy, using the Base-10 Response Form, has been found useful for several reasons:

1. Stimulus control is emphasized. Our therapy is more organized, and tasks are defined and more clearly specified.
2. Performance is scored and change can be noted on a session-by-session basis.
3. Performance levels can be converted to percentage and plotted graphically. This reinforces the patient and clinician as to the effect of therapy and provides a medium of determining accountability.
4. The system is adaptable to time-series designs and provides a potential medium for furthering our understanding of the efficacy of therapeutic intervention.
5. It is flexible enough to be used with a variety of styles or philosophies of aphasia treatment.

This system is not offered as a panacea or the only approach to treatment of aphasic disturbances. It does not obviate the need for counseling the family, providing realistic hope, providing information, being a source of emotional support, communicating with other professionals, and all the other details that constitute the sum total of efficient patient management. Clinical aphasiologists must remain eclectic. They must also continue to convey humanistic warmth and compassion to the people they deal with, who possess one of life's most devastating, frustrating, and isolating problems. In the past, however, much aphasia management has been long on rapport and warmth and

not too long on specific approaches to treatment. This system is presented as one possible avenue for getting a firm grasp of goals, aiding in therapeutic planning, organizing what goes on in a therapy session, and documenting change in the patient's communication performance.

Darley [22] said, "perhaps ten years [from now] the profession will enjoy substantial agreement about the nature of language breakdown and what can best be done about it." We face a formidable task in demonstrating to the scientific community that therapy has a significant and positive effect on language recovery beyond that which can be expected by spontaneous recovery.

The application of time-series designs and careful measurement and plotting during our daily sessions can help us face this task. If we use these strategies and report our results, not only will our day-to-day therapy be more efficiently organized, but evidence on the effect of language therapy will be cumulative.

Specific Therapy Tasks

Most courses on aphasia treatment and much of what has been written on aphasia end with the nearly universal disclaimer, "There is no cookbook for aphasia therapy." Certainly very little experience is needed to appreciate the variability in performance within and among aphasic individuals, and this dictates that the concepts presented earlier, such as careful selection of tasks and stimulus items, must be carefully considered. Attention to all the factors related to the antecedent event must be meticulously adapted to the individual. This necessitates a firm grasp of the specific communicative needs and of the changing abilities of the person being treated. Failure to underscore the importance of hand-tailoring the goals and techniques of therapy to the individual would be folly. On the other hand, the attitude that specific suggestions or examples of therapy tasks cannot, or must not, be given has left beginning clinicians with the queasy and dually frustrating feeling of being both impotent and empty-handed. Once started, many beginning clinicians confront the aphasic person with a stack of cards on which are line drawings of the 100 most frequent nouns and proceed to leaf incessantly through the stack as the patient attempts to say "cat" or "banana." This approach can be counterproductive.

The purpose of this section is to present a small

sample of the thousands of possible specific tasks that can be used in therapy with the aphasic person. All these tasks have been used, with varying degrees of success, in the Base-10 programmed stimulation approach and are equally adaptable to other approaches to therapy. They are organized according to mode of patient response and reflect rather heavy emphasis on speaking tasks. It will become immediately obvious that many of these tasks can be modified in a number of ways to manipulate difficulty within a mode or to modify appropriateness to other communication modes.

Acknowledgment

I wish to acknowledge the assistance of my past trainees and students at the University of Florida, my current students at Arizona State University, and especially all of my patients, who aided in the preparation of this chapter.

Verbal Tasks

Task
Verbal imitation of functional words

Input
Auditory

Output
Oral

Stimuli

Set 1	Set 2
1. okay	bad
2. soon	hi
3. fine	cold
4. no	go
5. yes	bye
6. here	come
7. later	warm
8. good	give
9. there	up
10. now	take

Task
Simultaneous production of simple words (or imitation of simple words)

Input
Auditory

Output
Oral

Stimuli
1. house
2. rain
3. pants
4. couch
5. shirt
6. milk
7. coat
8. train
9. toast
10. window

Task
Verbalization of bilabial, initial words to picture confrontation

Input
Visual (pictures)

Output
Oral

Stimuli
1. bread
2. money
3. pills
4. bed
5. bus
6. man
7. pen
8. box
9. belt
10. pillow

Task
Verbal imitation of common words

Input
Auditory

Output
Oral

Stimuli

Set 1	Set 2	Set 3
1. book	ashtray	chair
2. boy	apple	church
3. bottle	arm	cigarette
4. box	baby	clock
5. bread	banana	closet
6. bus	bathroom	coat
7. cake	bathtub	coffee
8. cane	bed	comb
9. car	bedroom	couch
10. cat	belt	cup

Task
Verbal imitation of adjective plus noun phrases

Input
Auditory

Output
Oral

Stimuli

Pencil	House
1. old pencil	white house
2. new pencil	big house
3. short pencil	little house
4. long pencil	ugly house
5. broken pencil	pretty house
Book	**Boy**
6. green book	fat boy
7. blue book	thin boy
8. red book	tall boy
9. thin book	young boy
10. thick book	short boy

Task
Verbal paired associates

Input
Auditory

Output
Oral

Stimuli

Set 1	Set 2
1. black and white	bread and butter
2. shoes and socks	pen and pencil
3. dog and cat	winter and summer
4. left and right	up and down
5. hands and feet	sugar and spice (cream)
6. hot and cold	needle and thread
7. ice cream and cake	king and queen
8. high and low	in and out
9. coat and tie	doctor and nurse
10. coffee and tea	red, white, and blue

Task
Verbal production or imitation of short sentences initiated with "I want . . ."

Input
Auditory

Output
Oral

Stimuli
"I want . . ."
1. some coffee
2. my lunch
3. the doctor
4. a drink
5. the nurse
6. to read
7. a pillow
8. a blanket
9. to sleep
10. my medicine

Task
Verbal production or imitation of short sentences initiated with "I'm going . . ."

Input
Auditory

Output
Oral

Stimuli
"I'm going . . ."
1. to PT (physical therapy)

210

2. to the ward
3. to the canteen
4. to watch TV
5. home
6. to eat
7. upstairs
8. to the store
9. to church
10. outside

Task
Verbal imitation of questions

Input
Auditory-visual (watch clinician)

Output
Oral

Stimuli
1. Where are you going?
2. What time is it?
3. Why are you doing that?
4. When are you going?
5. How much did it cost?
6. How many kids do you have?
7. How long did it take?
8. What time are we going?
9. How are you today?
10. What's your name?

Task
Imitation of verb plus noun phrases

Input
Auditory

Output
Verbal

Stimuli

Set 1	Set 2	Set 3
1. open door	I open door	I open the door
2. wear coat	I wear coat	I wear a coat
3. eat lunch	I eat lunch	I eat my lunch
4. drive car	I drive car	I drive my car (a car)
5. drink beer	I drink beer	I drink cold beer (a beer)
6. wear glasses	I wear glasses	I wear my glasses
7. brush teeth	I brush teeth	I brush my teeth
8. drink coffee	I drink coffee	I drink a cup of coffee
9. go bed	I go bed	I go to bed
10. take shower	I take shower	I take a shower

Task
Stimulation of adjective production; or, stimulation of phoneme strings of varied makeup in a meaningful context

Input
Auditory (question)

Output
Verbal (one word)

Stimuli

Set 1
1. Is 100 mph slow or **fast?***
2. Is 20 mph fast or **slow?**
3. Is a feather pillow hard or **soft?**
4. Is soup hot or **cold?**
5. Is a knife dull or **sharp?**
6. Is metal soft or **hard?**
7. Is ice cream hot or **cold?**
8. Is sandpaper smooth or **rough?**
9. At night, is it light or **dark?**
10. Is midnight early or **late?**

Set 2
1. Does a green light mean stop or **go?**
2. Is an elephant little or **big?**
3. Is a feather heavy or **light?**
4. Is a child big or **little?**
5. Is glass rough or **smooth?**
6. Is Alaska close or **far?**
7. Is a boxing champion weak or **strong?**
8. Is a mouse big or **little (small)?**
9. Is a lemon sweet or **sour?**
10. Is rainy weather dry or **wet?**

*Target (correct) word is deliberately placed at the end of the sentence to cue the patient.

Task
Three verbalizations of phrases following three simultaneous productions with clinician

Input
Auditory and visual (watch clinician)

Output
Oral

Stimuli

Set 1
1. I can do it.
2. I like cake.
3. I want my coat.
4. I want a drink.
5. I want a pillow.
6. I want the nurse.
7. I want the doctor.
8. I want a cup of coffee.
9. I want a blanket.
10. I want to take a bath.

Set 2
I'm from _____.
I'm happy.
I'm going to speech.
I'm going to bed.
I'm going to watch TV.
I'm going to read.
I'm eating.
I'm wrong.
I'm a man.
I'm going to PT.

Set 3
I'm hungry.
I'm tired.
I'm thirsty.
I'm getting better.
I'm talking.
I'm busy.
I'm broke.
I'm cold.
I'm hot.
I'm right.

Task
Verbalization of polysyllabic words five times each

Input
Auditory

Output
Oral

Stimuli
1. television
2. ashtray
3. telephone

4. wheelchair
5. catheterization
6. potatoes
7. handkerchief
8. nailfile
9. toothbrush
10. mirror

Task
Verbal stimulation of functional phrases

Input
Auditory

Output
Oral

Stimuli
1. I'm hungry.
2. I'm tired.
3. I'm thirsty.
4. I'm getting better.
5. I'm talking.
6. I'm busy.
7. I'm broke.
8. I'm ___ years old.
9. I'm hot.
10. I'm right.

Task
Verbal production of /CV/ words

Input
Auditory plus graphic

Output
Verbal

Stimuli
1. tie
2. cow
3. new
4. now
5. knee
6. key
7. tea
8. my
9. buy
10. toe

Task
Verbalizing verb-object phrases

Input
Auditory-visual (watch clinician)

Output
Oral

Stimuli
1. want food
2. want money
3. eat lunch
4. open window
5. close door
6. wash face
7. wash hands
8. shave myself
9. drink water
10. go home

Task
Verbalizing possessive phrases (*my* plus noun)

Input
Auditory-visual (watch clinician)

Output
Oral

Stimuli
1. my name
2. my arm
3. my wife
4. my wheelchair
5. my shoes
6. my socks
7. my pajamas
8. my head
9. my legs
10. my feet

Task
Establishing and maintaining phonemic sequencing pattern

Input
Auditory

Output
Oral imitation

Stimuli

Set 1
1. ready
   ready to go
   Are you ready to go?
2. time
   what time
   What time is it?
3. address
   name and address
   Write your name and address.

Set 2
chair
in a chair
I sit in a chair.
water
a drink of water
I want a drink of water.
bath
take a bath
I want to take a bath.

4. breakfast
   a good breakfast
   I had a good breakfast.
5. feeling
   feeling better
   I'm feeling better.
6. soap
   a bar of soap
   I want a bar of soap.
7. sleep
   sleep well
   I didn't sleep well.
8. head
   headache
   I have a headache.
9. chair
   wheelchair
   I want a wheelchair.
10. time
    it's time
    It's time to go.

dark
getting dark
It's getting dark.
TV
watch TV
I like to watch TV.
money
some money
I have some money.
what
what time
What time is it?
breakfast
a good breakfast
I had a good breakfast.
feeling
feeling better
I'm feeling better.
soap
a bar of soap
I want a bar of soap.

Task
Formulate question of "Where is . . .?" pattern after clinician provides the sentence *object*

Input
Auditory

Output
Oral

Stimuli
1. Clinician: ". . . my cane."
   Patient says (or reads cue card if necessary):
   "Where is . . . my cane?" for initiating phrase only
2. Clinician: ". . . my shirt."
   Patient: "Where is my shirt?"
3. my blue shirt
4. the telephone book
5. my pillow
6. my checkbook
7. my supper
8. my belt
9. my razor
10. my toothbrush

Task
Verbal sentence completion to facilitate noun retrieval

Input
Auditory

Output
Oral

Stimuli
1. Apples grow on . . .
2. You eat with a . . .
3. You write with a . . .
4. You cut with a . . .
5. You shoot with a . . .
6. You shave with a . . .
7. You tell time by the . . .
8. You buy things with . . .
9. There is someone at the . . .
10. Milk comes from a . . .

Task
Verbal sentence completion to facilitate verb plus "ing" retrieval

Input
Auditory

Output
Oral

Stimuli
1. I use a razor for . . .
2. I use a spoon for . . .
3. I use a towel for . . .
4. I use a toothbrush for . . .
5. I use soap for . . .
6. I use a handkerchief for . . .
7. I use a hammer for . . .
8. I use a saw for . . .
9. I use a broom for . . .
10. I use a ruler for . . .

Task
Verbal sentence completion (commands)

Input
Auditory

Output
Oral

Stimuli
1. Read a . . .
2. Write a . . .
3. Sing a . . .
4. Drive a . . .
5. Comb your . . .
6. Wind the . . .
7. Open the . . .
8. Mow the . . .
9. Row a . . .
10. Smoke a . . .

Task
Verbal sentence completion: noun retrieval (relatively open-ended)

Input
Auditory

Output
Oral

Stimuli

Set 1	Set 2
1. a cup of . . .	obey the . . .
2. a loaf of . . .	climb a . . .
3. a glass of . . .	sharpen the . . .
4. a gallon of . . .	bake a . . .
5. a drink of . . .	close your . . .
6. a package of . . .	call a . . .
7. a box of . . .	turn on the . . .
8. a piece of . . .	cut the . . .
9. a can of . . .	take a . . .
10. a pair of . . .	pick some . . .

Task
Sentence formulation beginning with "I eat . . ."

Input
Visual (pictures of food)

Output
Oral

Stimuli
1. a hot dog
2. fruit
3. bread
4. potatoes
5. steak
6. sandwich
7. french fries
8. a taco
9. applesauce
10. salad

Task
Verbal sentence formulation following graphic presentation of a noun

Input
Visual (graphic presentation of a noun)

Output
Oral

Stimuli
1. book
2. sun
3. trees

4. jacket
5. car
6. chair
7. comb
8. spoon
9. cup
10. dollar

Task
Verbal sentence formulation following graphic presentation of a verb

Input
Visual (graphic presentation of a verb)

Output
Oral

Stimuli
1. eat
2. drive
3. sleep
4. write
5. built
6. wear
7. cook
8. dry
9. sing
10. fight

Task
Verbal sentence formulation following graphic presentation of a verb and a noun pair

Input
Visual (graphic presentation of a noun and a verb)

Output
Oral

Stimuli
1. read, book
2. drink, cup
3. spent, dollar
4. stir coffee, spoon
5. comb, hair
6. sit, chair
7. drive, car
8. wear, jacket
9. grow, trees
10. sun, shines

Task
Verbal formulation of a complete sentence using given verbs

Input
Auditory

Output
Oral

Stimuli
1. are
2. running
3. caught
4. may
5. look
6. dressing
7. eaten
8. stopped
9. could
10. broken

Task
Verbal formulation of a complete sentence using given function words

Input
Auditory

Output
Oral

Stimuli
1. with
2. or
3. to
4. not
5. and
6. those
7. but
8. both
9. all
10. off

Task
Verbal formulation of a question using given *initial* words

Input
Auditory

Output
Oral

Stimuli
1. Is . . .
2. Where . . .
3. Do . . .
4. What . . .
5. Didn't . . .
6. Who . . .
7. Which . . .
8. When . . .

9. Can . . .
10. How much . . .

Task
Verbally describe function or activity with picture cue only

Input
Visual (pictures)

Output
Oral

Stimuli
1. book/read
2. bottle/put milk in
3. bus/ride, take trip
4. cake/eat
5. car/ride
6. cigarette/smoke
7. closet/hang clothes
8. coat/wear
9. boy/play with
10. cat/play with

Task
Answering questions following model provided by clinician (designed as transition from repetitive skills to volitional verbal skills)

Input
Auditory

Output
Oral

Stimuli
1. Clinician, then patient: I am reading a good book.
   Clinician alone: Are you reading a good book?
   Patient alone: I am reading a good book.
2. I bought a loaf of bread.
   Did you buy a loaf of bread?
3. I had steak for dinner.
   What did you have for dinner?
4. I get up early in the morning.
   Do you get up early in the morning?
5. It is hot in the summer.
   Is it hot in the summer?
6. I went for a walk.
   Did you go for a walk?
7. I write with a pencil.
   Do you write with a pencil?
8. I want a glass of milk.
   Do you want a glass of milk?
9. I read the paper last night.
   Did you read the paper last night?
10. I shave with a razor.
    Do you shave with a razor?

Task
Spontaneous utterance of statement following imitative cue and question prompt

Input
Auditory

Output
Oral

Stimuli
1. Clinician: Say: "I want a drink of water."
   Patient: I want a drink of water.
   Clinician: Do you want a drink of water?
   Patient: I want a drink of water.
2. I want to take a bath.
3. It is getting dark.
4. I'm sitting in a chair.
5. I like to watch TV.
6. I have some money.
7. It is _____ o'clock.
8. I had a good breakfast.
9. I am feeling better.
10. I want a bar of soap.

Task
Verbalizing the function of objects following graphic presentation of noun

Input
Visual (graphic)

Output
Oral

Stimuli
1. chimichanga
2. cup
3. knife
4. book
5. quarter
6. key
7. soap
8. spoon
9. comb
10. bowl

Task
Formulating a statement with the initiating phrase "I want . . ."

Input
Auditory

Output
Oral

Stimuli
1. Clinician: Do you want to watch TV?
   Patient: I want to watch TV.
   After each question, patient says:
   "I want . . ."
2. my cane
3. a new shirt
4. to go to bed
5. my shoes
6. my dark pants
7. steak for dinner
8. to eat now
9. to sleep late
10. to go shopping

Task
Functional response to questions (object; object plus verb;
or complete sentence)*

Input
Auditory

Output
Oral

Stimuli
"What do you . . .?"
1. eat with
2. walk with
3. sleep on
4. lock a door with
5. sit on
6. wear on your feet
7. wash your face with
8. write with
9. comb your hair with
10. dry yourself with after a shower

*Judge correct verb, verb plus object, or complete sentence.

Task
Verbalize sentence with "I like to . . ." initiation (adapt
to individual patient interests)

Input
Auditory

Output
Oral

Stimuli
Require:
  a. Imitation
     Clinician: Say: I like to listen to the radio.
     Patient: I like to listen to the radio.
     Or
  b. Use question prompt
     Clinician: Do you like to listen to the radio?
     Patient: I like to listen to the radio.

"I like . . ."
1. to listen to the radio
2. to watch the news
3. to train my armadillo
4. to watch gymnasts
5. to go to speech therapy
6. to go to the clinic
7. to play cards
8. to visit friends
9. to go to Sedona
10. to drink tequila

Task
Formulate a sentence giving the function of objects depicted in pictures, initiating sentences with "I"

Input
Auditory plus visual (picture)

Output
Oral

Stimuli
Underlined words are presented in picture stimuli:
1. Clinician: What do you do with a cane?
   Patient: I walk . . .
2. a bed
   lie down/sleep/make
3. knife, fork, and spoon
   eat
4. key
   lock/open a door
5. chair
   sit
6. shoes
   wear/put on
7. soap
   wash
8. pencil
   write
9. comb
   comb
10. towel
    dry

Task
Verbalizing appropriately to familiar conversational questions

Input
Auditory (questions)

Output
Oral

Stimuli
1. How are you?
2. What is your name?

3. Where are you right now?
4. Where are you staying?
5. What is your wife's name?
6. What is your home town?
7. What color is your hair?
8. How many kids do you have?
9. How old are you?
10. What kind of therapy are we doing?

Task
Answering questions verbally; written cues can be used

Input
Auditory

Output
Verbal

Stimuli
1. What do you say when you're thirsty?
2. What do you say when you're tired?
3. What do you need to help you walk?
4. What do you need to tell time?
5. What do you say when you're hungry?
6. What do you need to write?
7. What do you need to buy something?
8. What do you say when you need your medicine?
9. What do you say when you want music?
10. What do you say when you're late?

Task
Verbal sentence formulation given a graphic cue (verb)

Input
Graphic cue cards: verbs

Output
Verbal

Stimuli
1. cut
2. lay down
3. eat
4. wear
5. write
6. sit
7. drive
8. tell time
9. clean
10. walk

Auditory Comprehension Tasks

Task
Auditory comprehension: Pointing to objects in a field of three when name is presented

Input
Auditory

Output
Gestural (pointing)

Stimuli

Set 1 (pen, watch, key)	Set 2 (soap, fork, glass)	Set 3 (bowl, toothbrush, glasses)
1. pen	soap	bowl
2. watch	fork	toothbrush
3. key	glass	glasses
4. watch	fork	toothbrush
5. key	soap	glasses
6. pen	glass	bowl
7. pen	glass	bowl
8. watch	fork	toothbrush
9. key	soap	glasses
10. key	soap	glasses

Task
Point to object depicted in the picture, when given the *function*

Input
Auditory plus visual (picture)

Output
Gestural (pointing)

Stimuli
(picture/clinician's cue)
1. spoon/picking up food
2. money/buying things
3. glasses/seeing
4. cup/drinking
5. radio/listening
6. soap/washing
7. pen/writing
8. candy/eating
9. brush/fixing hair
10. shoelace/tying shoes

Task
Auditory comprehension of one-part commands

Input
Visual (objects, field of five)

Output
Gestural (pointing)

Stimuli
"Point to the . . ."
Set 1	Set 2
1. key	cup
2. spoon	glass
3. cigarette	pen
4. matches	pencil
5. fork	soap
6. cigarette	pencil
7. spoon	glass
8. key	cup
9. matches	soap
10. fork	pen

Five objects	*Five objects*
key	cup
fork	glass
spoon	pen
matches	pencil
cigarette	soap

Task
Auditory comprehension of two-part commands (one verb-two objects)

Input
Visual (objects, field of five)

Output
Gestural (pointing)

Stimuli
"Point to the . . . and point to the . . ."
1. key, fork
2. spoon, matches
3. cigarette, key
4. matches, spoon
5. fork, cigarette
6. cigarette, key
7. matches, spoon
8. key, fork
9. cigarette, matches
10. spoon, fork

Task
Auditory comprehension of three-part commands

Input
Visual (objects, field of five)

Output
Gestural (pointing)

Stimuli

"Point to the . . . and point to the . . . and point to the . . ."

Set 1	Set 2
Five objects	Five objects
key	cup
fork	glass
cigarette	pen
spoon	pencil
matches	soap

1. Ky, Fk, Cg	1. Cp, Gl, Pl
2. Sp, Mt, Fk	2. Sp, Pl, Gl
3. Cg, Ky, Mt	3. Pl, Cp, Pn
4. Mt, Sp, Ky	4. Pn, Sp, Cp
5. Fk, Cg, Mt	5. Gl, Pl, Pn
6. Cg, Ky, Sp	6. Pl, Cp, Sp
7. Mt, Sp, Fk	7. Pn, Sp, Gl
8. Ky, Fk, Sp	8. Cp, Gl, Sp
9. Cg, Mt, Ky	9. Pl, Pn, Cp
10. Sp, Fk, Cg	10. Sp, Gl, Pl

Task

Auditory comprehension of object name and association with printed word

Input

Visual and auditory (printed card with object name and auditory cue)

Output

Gestural (pointing)

Stimuli

"Point to the word that says:"

1. soap
2. money
3. cup
4. fork
5. cards
6. house
7. shoes
8. plane
9. pencil
10. car

Task

Decrease the time interval between the stimulus presentation and the patient's focusing of attention; 3-second interval between the patient's name and the stimulus

Input

Auditory and picture

Output

Gestural

Stimuli

"Mr. _____, (3-second delay), point to the _____."

1. stove
2. table
3. watch
4. pillow
5. knife
6. belt
7. car
8. girl
9. coat
10. tie

Task

Retention of subspan lists of words for 3 seconds (delay of 3 seconds between stimulus presentation and the response)

Input

Auditory

Output

Verbal or gestural

Stimuli

1. key, hat, comb
2. car, nail, shoe
3. bus, tack, light
4. fish, soup, can
5. sock, eye, circle
6. letter, pencil, cigar
7. paper, pants, matches
8. table, arm, boy
9. chair, man, house
10. flowers, duck, sun

Task

Retention of subspan lists of words for a period of 6 seconds. (A delay of 6 seconds between the stimulus presentation and the response.)

Input

Auditory

Output

Verbal and gestural

Stimuli

1. apple, coat, coffee
2. baby, egg, dress
3. feet, door, money
4. pen, tie, sink
5. couch, key, bus
6. bathtub, pen, towel
7. train, window, sandwich
8. matches, clock, bread
9. finger, dish, banana
10. lamp, knife, girl

Task

Retention of subspan lists of words for 9 seconds.

Input

Auditory

Output

Verbal or gestural

Stimuli
1. apple, bathtub, cake
2. bottle, chair, hand
3. milk, box, pants
4. teeth, suit, soap
5. mouth, cigarette, doctor
6. cup, bed, radio
7. spoon, dog, house
8. cat, juice, sheet
9. paper, box, light
10. train, belt, ear

Task

Decrease the time interval between stimulus presentation and the patient's focusing of attention; 5-second interval between patient's name and stimulus

Input

Auditory and picture

Output

Gestural; point to the stimulus picture in an array of four pictures

Stimuli

"Ms. _____, (5-second delay), point to the _____."
1. car
2. apple
3. bed
4. chair
5. shoe
6. glass
7. comb
8. toothbrush
9. pencil
10. book

Task

Decrease the time interval between stimulus presentation and the patient's focusing of attention using a 4-second interval between patient's name and the stimulus

Input

Auditory and picture

Output

Gestural; point to the stimulus picture in an array of four pictures

Stimuli

"Ms. _____, (4-second delay), point to the _____."

1. plane
2. nose
3. fork
4. egg
5. toenail
6. girl
7. cat
8. bus
9. television
10. tree

Reading Tasks[*]

Task
Reading or matching single letters

Input
Visual (graphic)

Output
Oral

Stimuli

Set 1	Set 2
1. m	t
2. p	a
3. g	r
4. u	l
5. b	c
6. d	s
7. h	e
8. w	f
9. n	y
10. i	o

Task
Spontaneous verbal reading of single words

Input
Visual (graphic)

Output
Oral (reading)

Stimuli
1. tie
2. chair
3. money
4. car
5. glasses
6. pants
7. comb
8. bed
9. pills
10. shoes

Task
Reading phrases

Input
Graphic

Output
Verbal (reading)

[*]Consult L. L. LaPointe and J. Horner, *Reading Comprehension Battery for Aphasia*. Tigard, Or.: C. C. Publications, 1979.

Stimuli
1. stop
2. canteen
3. sit down
4. go left
5. 10 minutes
6. men's room
7. doctor
8. ladies' room
9. no smoking
10. one hour

Task
Spontaneous verbal reading of phrases

Input
Visual (graphic)

Output
Oral (reading)

Stimuli
(two types: "I'm . . ." and "I need . . .")
1. I'm sick.
2. I'm thirsty.
3. I'm tired.
4. I'm hungry.
5. I'm going home.
6. I need glasses.
7. I need a bath.
8. I need money.
9. I need a shave.
10. I need a car.

Task
Put the card stating object name by the card that says what you do with it

Input
Visual (printed words)

Output
Gestural (reading)

Stimuli
1. soap/wash
2. money/buy
3. cup/drink
4. fork/eat
5. cards/play
6. house/live
7. shoes/wear
8. plane/fly
9. pencil/write
10. car/drive

Task
Reading commands without omission, addition, or word substitution

Input
Visual (written commands)

Output
Oral (reading)

Stimuli
 1. Close the door.
 2. Give me my medicine.
 3. Put it over there.
 4. Give it to me.
 5. Go away.
 6. Tell me your name.
 7. Come here a minute.
 8. Take me home.
 9. Put it down.
10. Show me what you're doing.

Task
Recognizing written phrases (field of five)

Input
Graphic

Output
Gestural (pointing response)

Stimuli
 1. stop
 2. canteen
 3. sit down
 4. go left
 5. 10 minutes
 6. men's room
 7. doctor
 8. ladies' room
 9. no smoking
10. one hour

Task
Reading commands with maximum intelligibility

Input
Visual (graphic)

Output
Oral

Stimuli
 1. Give me my cigarettes.
 2. Take me to Tempe.
 3. Take me home.
 4. Tell me your name.
 5. Show me that.

6. Help me.
7. Give me my lunch.
8. Give me my medicine.
9. Take me to Phoenix.
10. Buy me some Winstons.

Task
Reading commands, length two to five words

Input
Visual

Output
Verbal

Stimuli

Set 1
1. Give me my medicine.
2. Show me what you're doing.
3. Close the door.
4. Put it over there.
5. Go away.
6. Come here a minute.
7. Take me home.
8. Tell me your name.
9. Put it down.
10. Give it to me.

Set 2
1. Give me my cigarettes.
2. Take me to Arizona.
3. Take me home.
4. Tell me your name.
5. Show me that.
6. Give me my medicine.
7. Take me to . . . (speech, PT, OT, etc.).
8. Buy me some salami.
9. Give me my lunch.
10. Help me, please.

Task
Reading sentences of seven or more words in length (containing "series") to facilitate fluency and judicious use of pause

Input
Visual (graphic)

Output
Oral (reading)

Stimuli
1. We ate lunch, went to a movie, and then came home.
2. One son was a lawyer, one a farmer, and the other an engineer.
3. They raise barley, oats, and rye, in the fields by the river.
4. The Red Cross sent food, clothing, and medical supplies.
5. I paid the water, the electric, and the telephone bills.
6. I went to shop at the grocery, the hardware store, and the cleaners.
7. The mines yield silver, gold, and lead.
8. I want a dozen eggs, a pound of butter, and a quart of milk.
9. Do you like your steak rare, medium, or burned?
10. Every mining town had a bar, a pool room, and a grand hotel.

Writing Tasks

Task
Copying of geometric forms and letters

Input
Visual

Output
Graphic

Stimuli
 1. X
 2. △
 3. T
 4. ▭
 5. V
 6. L
 7. O
 8. H
 9. Z
10. ▢

Task
Copy words

Input
Visual (graphic)

Output
Graphic

Stimuli
 1. tie
 2. car
 3. bed
 4. pills
 5. comb
 6. money
 7. pants
 8. chair
 9. shoes
10. glasses

Task
Writing single letters to dictation

Input
Auditory

Output
Graphic

Stimuli

Set 1	Set 2
1. i	o
2. n	y
3. w	f
4. h	e
5. d	s

6.	b	c
7.	u	l
8.	g	r
9.	p	a
10.	m	t

Task
Writing three-letter words to dictation letter by letter

Input
Auditory (letter by letter)

Output
Graphic

Stimuli
Set 1		*Set 2*
1.	top	ham
2.	cat	hot
3.	bad	wet
4.	yes	his
5.	sit	dog
6.	was	bet
7.	fat	bus
8.	run	lot
9.	pan	tin
10.	fan	mop

Task
Writing three-letter words to dictation—whole word

Input
Auditory (whole word)

Output
Graphic

Stimuli
Set 1		*Set 2*
1.	top	ham
2.	cat	hot
3.	bad	wet
4.	yes	his
5.	sit	dog
6.	was	bet
7.	fat	bus
8.	run	lot
9.	pan	tin
10.	fan	mop

Task
Writing two-letter stimuli to dictation

Input
Auditory

Output
Graphic

Stimuli

Set 1: words	*Set 2: nonsense*
1. I'm	ba
2. no	tu
3. we	ca
4. hi	ye
5. do	sa
6. be	wa
7. up	bu
8. go	hu
9. in	fa
10. my	ru

Task
Writing three-letter words to dictation

Input
Auditory

Output
Graphic

Stimuli

Set 1	*Set 2*
1. not	bad
2. wet	top
3. his	cat
4. dog	yes
5. bet	sat
6. got	was
7. hit	bus
8. bed	he's
9. him	fat
10. nod	run

Task
Writing four-letter words to dictation

Input
Auditory

Output
Graphic

Stimuli

Set 1	*Set 2*
1. band	nose
2. tore	went
3. flat	hide
4. sand	hold
5. wait	best
6. bugs	gone
7. heat	beds
8. fast	hire
9. runs	dogs
10. yell	goes

References

1. Albert, M. L. Book review. *New Engl. J. Med.* 300 : 932, 1979.
2. Albert, M., Sparks, R., and Helm, N. Melodic intonation therapy for aphasia. *Arch. Neurol.* 29 : 130, 1973.
3. Bandura, A. *Principles of Behavior Modification.* New York: Holt, Rinehart & Winston, 1969.
4. Barton, M., Maruszewski, M., and Urrea, D. Variation of stimulus context and its effect on word-finding ability in aphasics. *Cortex* 5 : 351, 1969.
5. Basso, A., Capitani, E., and Vignolo, L. A. Influence of rehabilitation on language skills in aphasic patients: A controlled study. *Arch. Neurol.* 36 : 190, 1979.
6. Benson, D. F. Aphasia rehabilitation. *Arch. Neurol.* 36 : 187, 1979.
7. Benton, A. L., Smith, K. C., and Lang, M. Stimulus characteristics and object naming in aphasic patients. *J. Commun. Disord.* 5 : 19, 1972.
8. Berman, M., and Peelle, L. M. Self-generated cues: A method of aiding aphasic and apractic patients. *J. Speech Hear. Disord.* 32 : 372, 1967.
9. Beyn, E. S., and Shokhar-Trotskaya, M. K. The preventive method of speech rehabilitation in aphasia. *Cortex* 2 : 96, 1966.
10. Bisiach, E. Perceptual factors in the pathogenesis of anomia. *Cortex* 2 : 90, 1966.
11. Bollinger, R. L., and Stout, C. E. Response contingent small step treatment: Performance-based communication intervention. *J. Speech Hear. Disord.* 41 : 40, 1976.
12. Brookshire, R. H. Speech pathology and the experimental analysis of behavior. *J. Speech Hear. Disord.* 32 : 315, 1967.
13. Brookshire, R. H. Effects of trial time and intertrial interval on naming. *J. Commun. Disord.* 3 : 289, 1970-1971.
14. Brookshire, R. H. Effects of delay of reinforcement on probability learning by aphasic subjects. *J. Speech Hear. Res.* 14 : 92, 1971.
15. Brookshire, R. H. Effects of task difficulty on naming performance of aphasic subjects. *J. Speech Hear. Res.* 15 : 551, 1972.
16. Brookshire, R. H. Assessing patterns of auditory perception and comprehension impairment in aphasia: II. Paper presented to the Academy of Aphasia, Warrenton, Va., 1974.
17. Brookshire, R. H. Subject description and generality of results in experiments with aphasic adults. *J. Speech Hear. Disord.* 48 : 342, 1983.
18. Corlew, M. M., and Nation, J. E. Characteristics of visual stimuli and naming performance in aphasic adults. *Cortex* 11 : 186, 1975.
19. Croskey, C. S., and Adams, M. R. A rationale and clinical methodology for selecting vocabulary stimulus material for individual aphasic patients. *J. Commun. Disord.* 2 : 340, 1969.
20. Culton, G. L. Spontaneous recovery from aphasia. *J. Speech Hear. Res.* 12 : 825, 1969.
21. Daniloff, J. K., Lloyd, L. L., and Fristoe, M. Amer-Ind transparency. *J. Speech Hear. Disord.* 48 : 18, 1983.

22. Darley, F. L. The efficacy of language rehabilitation in aphasia. *J. Speech Hear. Disord.* 37 : 3, 1972.
23. Darley, F. L. Treat or neglect? *ASHA* 21 : 628, 1979.
24. Darley, F. L. *Aphasia.* Philadelphia: Saunders, 1982.
25. Davis, G. A. *A Survey of Adult Aphasia.* Englewood Cliffs, N.J.: Prentice-Hall, 1983.
26. DeRenzi, E., Faglioni, P., and Previdi, P. Increased susceptibility of aphasics to a distractor task in the recall of verbal commands. *Brain Lang.* 6 : 14, 1978.
27. Dowden, P., Marshall, R., and Tompkins, C. Amer-Ind Sign as a Communicative Facilitator for Aphasic and Apraxic Patients. In R. Brookshire (ed.), *Clinical Aphasiology: Conference Proceedings.* Minneapolis: BRK Publishers, 1981. Pp. 133–140.
28. Duffy, J. Nuclear magnetic resonance. Paper presented at Clinical Aphasiology Conference, Seabrook Island, S.C., 1984.
29. Dunham, M. J., and Newhoff, M. Melodic Intonation Therapy: Rewriting the Song. In R. Brookshire (ed.), *Clinical Aphasiology: Conference Proceedings.* Minneapolis: BRK Publishers, 1979. Pp. 286–293.
30. Faber, M., and Aten, J. Verbal Performance in Aphasic Patients in Response to Intact and Altered Picture Stimuli. In R. Brookshire (ed.), *Clinical Aphasiology: Conference Proceedings.* Minneapolis: BRK Publishers, 1979. Pp. 177–186.
31. Gardiner, B. J., and Brookshire, R. H. Effects of unisensory and multisensory presentation of stimuli upon naming by aphasic subjects. *Lang. Speech* 15 : 342, 1972.
32. Gardner, A. M., and Weintraub, S. Comprehending a word: The influence of speed and redundancy on auditory comprehension in aphasia. *Cortex* 11 : 155, 1975.
33. Gentile, J. R., Roden, A. H., and Klein, R. D. An analysis of variance model for the intrasubject replication design. *J. Appl. Behav. Anal.* 5 : 193, 1972.
34. Goodglass, H., Barton, J. I., and Kaplan, E. F. Sensory modality and object-naming in aphasia. *J. Speech Hear. Res.* 11 : 488, 1968.
35. Goodglass, H., and Kaplan, E. F. *Boston Diagnostic Aphasia Test.* Philadelphia: Lea & Febiger, 1972.
36. Goodkin, R. Case studies in behavioral research in rehabilitation. *Percept. Motor Skills* 23 : 171, 1966.
37. Goodkin, R. Changes in word production, sentence production and relevance in an aphasic through verbal conditioning. *Behav. Res. Ther.* 7 : 93, 1969.
38. Hagen, C. Communication abilities in hemiplegia: Effect of speech therapy. *Arch. Phys. Med. Rehabil.* 54 : 454, 1973.
39. Halpern, H. Effect of stimulus variable on verbal perseveration of dysphasic speech. *Percept. Motor Skills* 20 : 421, 1965.
40. Hanson, W. Positron emission tomography. Paper presented at Clinical Aphasiology Conference, Seabrook Island, S.C., 1984.
41. Hayes, S. C. Single case experimental design and empirical clinical practice. *J. Consult. Clin. Psych.* 49 : 193, 1981.

42. Hedrick, D. L., Christman, M. A., and Augustine, L. Programming for the antecedent event in therapy. *J. Speech Hear. Disord.* 38 : 339, 1973.

43. Holland, A. Some current trends in aphasia rehabilitation. *ASHA* 11 : 3, 1969.

44. Holland, A. Case studies in aphasia rehabilitation. *J. Speech Hear. Disord.* 37 : 3, 1972.

45. Holland, A. *Communicative Abilities in Daily Living.* Baltimore: University Park Press, 1980.

46. Katz, R. C. Using microcomputers in the diagnosis and treatment of chronic aphasic adults. *Semin. Speech Lang.* 5 : 11, 1984.

47. Katz, R., and Nagy, V. T. A Computerized Approach for Improving Word Recognition in Chronic Aphasic Patients. In R. Brookshire (ed.), *Clinical Aphasiology: Conference Proceedings.* Minneapolis: BRK Publishers, 1983. Pp. 65–72.

48. Kazdin, A. E. Methodological and Assessment Consideration in Evaluating Reinforcement Programs in Applied Settings. *J. Appl. Behav. Anal.* 6 : 517, 1973.

49. Kearns, K. P., and Salmon, S. An experimental analysis of auxiliary and copula verb generalization in aphasia. *J. Speech Hear. Disord.* 49 : 152, 1984.

50. Keenan, J. S. A method of eliciting naming behavior from aphasic patients. *J. Speech Hear. Disord.* 31 : 261, 1966.

51. Kertesz, A. *The Western Aphasia Battery.* Orlando, Fla.: Grune & Stratton, Inc., 1982.

52. Kushner, D., and Winitz, H. Extended comprehension practice applied to an aphasic patient. *J. Speech Hear. Disord.* 42 : 296, 1977.

53. Kushner, H., Hubbard, D. J., and Knox, A. W. Effects of punishment on learning by aphasic subjects. *Percept. Motor Skills* 36 : 283, 1973.

54. LaPointe, L. L. The treatment of behavioral disturbances in adults: Current trends and a few reasons for optimism in clinical aphasiology. Paper presented to the Florida Society of Neurology, Orlando, Fla., 1975.

55. LaPointe, L. L. Base-10 programmed stimulation: Task specification, scoring and plotting performance in aphasia therapy. *J. Speech Hear. Disord.* 42 : 90, 1977.

56. LaPointe, L. L. Quantification and Accountability in Aphasia Therapy. In L. Bradford and R. T. Wertz (eds.), *Communicative Disorders: An Audio Journal for Continuing Education* 5, 1980.

57. LaPointe, L. L. Movement toward volitional control in aphasia treatment: Laddering and self-cuing strategies. Workshop presentation, University of Wisconsin–Madison, 1982.

58. LaPointe, L. L. Sequential Treatment of Split Lists: A Case Report. In J. Rosenbek, M. McNeil, and A. Aronson (eds.), *Apraxia of Speech: Physiology, Acoustics, Linguistics, Management.* San Diego: College-Hill, 1984. Pp. 277–286.

59. LaPointe, L. L., and Horner, J. *Reading Comprehension Battery for Aphasia.* Tigard, Or.: C.C. Publications, 1979.

60. LaPointe, L. L., Horner, J., Lieberman, R. J., and Riski, J. E. Assessing patterns of auditory perception and comprehension impairment in aphasia: I. Paper presented to the Academy of Aphasia, Warrenton, Va., 1974.

61. LaPointe, L. L., and Williams, W. N. Recognition of geometric shapes by unimodal and simultaneous multimodal presentation in aphasics. Paper presented at the Annual Convention of the American Speech and Hearing Association, Chicago, Ill., 1971.

62. Lasky, E. Z., Weidner, W. E., and Johnson, J. P. Influence of linguistic complexity, rate of presentation, and interphrase pause time on auditory-verbal comprehension of adult aphasic patients. *Brain Lang.* 3 : 386, 1976.

63. Lemme, M. L., Wertz, R. T., and Rosenbek, J. C. The effects of stimulus modality on verbal output in brain injured adults. Presented at the Convention of the American Speech and Hearing Association, Las Vegas, Nev., 1974.

64. Licht, S. Brief History of Stroke and Its Rehabilitation. In S. Licht (ed.), *Stroke and Its Rehabilitation.* Baltimore: Waverly, 1975.

65. Marshall, R. C. Word Retrieval Strategies of Aphasic Adults in Conversational Speech. In R. Brookshire (ed.), *Clinical Aphasiology: Conference Proceedings.* Santa Fe, N. Mex., 1975.

66. Martin, A. D. A Critical Evaluation of Therapeutic Approaches to Aphasia. In R. Brookshire (ed.), *Clinical Aphasiology: Conference Proceedings*, Santa Fe, N. Mex., 1975.

67. Matthews, B. A., and LaPointe, L. L. Determining Rate of Change and Predicting Performance Levels in Aphasia Therapy. In R. Brookshire (ed.), *Clinical Aphasiology: Conference Proceedings.* Minneapolis: BRK Publishers, 1981. Pp. 17–25.

68. Matthews, B., and LaPointe, L. L. Slope and variability of performance on selected aphasia treatment tasks. In R. Brookshire (ed.), *Clinical Aphasiology: Conference Proceedings.* Minneapolis: BRK Publishers, 1983. Pp. 113–120.

69. McDearmon, J. R., and Potter, R. E. The use of representational prompts in aphasia therapy. *J. Commun. Disord.* 8 : 199, 1975.

70. McReynolds, L. V., and Kearns, K. P. *Single Subject Experimental Designs for Intervention Research in Communicative Disorders.* Baltimore: University Park, 1982.

71. Mettler, C. C. *History of Medicine.* Philadelphia: Blakiston, 1947.

72. Nelson, T. O. Repetition and depth of processing. *J. Verb. Learn. Verb. Behav.* 16 : 151, 1977.

73. Parisi, D., and Pizzamiglio, L. Syntactic comprehension in aphasia. *Cortex* 6 : 204, 1970.

74. Porch, B. E. *Administration, Scoring, Interpretation of the Porch Index of Communicative Ability.* Palo Alto, Calif.: Consulting Psychologists Press, 1967.

75. Porch, B. E. Therapy subsequent to the PICA. In R. Chapey (ed.), *Language Intervention Strategies in Adult Aphasia.* Baltimore: Williams & Wilkins, 1981. Pp. 283–293.

76. Prescott, T., and McNeil, M. Measuring the effects of treatment in aphasia. Paper presented at the Third

Conference of Clinical Aphasiology, Albuquerque, N. Mex., 1973.

77. Risly, T. R. Behavior Modification: An Experimental-Therapeutic Endeavor. In R. Rubin, J. Henderson, H. Fensterhiem, and L. Ullman (eds.), *Advances in Behavior Therapy*. New York: Academic, 1972.

78. Rosenbek, J. C. Computerized axial tomography. Paper presented at Clinical Aphasiology Conference, Seabrook Island, S.C., 1984.

79. Rosenbek, J. C., Lemme, M. L., Ahern, M. B., Harris, E., and Wertz, R. T. Treatment of apraxia of speech in adults. *J. Speech Hear. Disord.* 38 : 462, 1973.

80. Rubens, A. B. The Role of Changes within the Central Nervous System during Recovery from Aphasia. In M. Sullivan and M. S. Kommers (eds.), *Rationale for Adult Aphasia Therapy*. Lincoln: University of Nebraska Medical Center, 1977. Pp. 28–43.

81. Salvatore, A. P. Use of a baseline probe technique to monitor the test responses of aphasic patients. *J. Speech Hear. Disord.* 37 : 471, 1972.

82. Salvatore, A. P. The effects of pause duration on sentence comprehension by aphasic individuals. Paper presented at the Convention of the American Speech and Hearing Association, Washington, D.C., 1975.

83. Schuell, H., Jenkins, J., and Jiménez-Pabón, E. *Aphasia in Adults*. New York: Harper & Row, 1964.

84. Shewan, C. M., and Canter, G. J. Effects of vocabulary, syntax and sentence length on auditory comprehension in aphasic patients. *Cortex* 7 : 209, 1971.

85. Sidman, M. *Tactics of Scientific Research*. New York: Basic Books, 1960.

86. Sidman, M. The behavioral analysis of aphasia. *J. Psychiatr. Res.* 8 : 413, 1971.

87. Sidman, M., Stoddard, L. T., Mohr, J. P., and Leicester, J. Behavioral studies of aphasia: Methods of investigation and analysis. *Neuropsychologia* 9 : 119, 1971.

88. Skelly, M., Schinsky, L., Smith, R. W., and Fust, R. S. American Indian Sign (Amerind) as a facilitator of verbalization for the oral verbal apraxia. *J. Speech Hear. Disord.* 39 : 445, 1974.

89. Smith, A. *Diagnosis, Intelligence and Rehabilitation in Chronic Aphasics: Final Report*. Ann Arbor: University of Michigan, Department of Physical Medicine and Rehabilitation, 1972.

90. Sparks, R. W. Melodic intonation therapy. In R. Chapey (ed.), *Language Intervention Strategies in Adult Aphasia*. Baltimore: Williams & Wilkins, 1981.

91. Sullivan, M., and Kommers, M. S. *Rationale for Adult Aphasia Therapy: Proceedings of a Conference Held at the University of Nebraska Medical Center*. Omaha: University of Nebraska Press, 1977.

92. Taylor, M. L. Language therapy. In H. G. Burr (ed.), *The Aphasic Adult: Evaluation and Rehabilitation*. Charlottesville, Va.: Wayside, 1964.

93. Thompson, C., and Byrne, M. Across setting generalization of social conventions using a "loose training" strategy in agrammatic aphasics. Paper presented at Clinical Aphasiology Conference, Seabrook Island, S.C., 1984.

94. Tryon, W. W. A simplified time-series analysis for evaluating treatment interventions. *J. Appl. Behav. Anal.* 15 : 423, 1982.

95. Tulving, E. Cue-dependent forgetting. *Am. Sci.* 62 : 74, 1974.

96. Ulatowska, H. K., and Richardson, S. M. A longitudinal study of an adult with aphasia: Considerations for research and therapy. *Brain Lang.* 1 : 151, 1974.

97. Vignolo, L. A. Evolution of aphasia and language rehabilitation: A retrospective exploratory study. *Cortex* 1 : 344, 1964.

98. Webb, W. G., and Love, R. J. The efficacy of cueing techniques with apraxic-aphasics. Paper presented at the Convention of the American Speech and Hearing Association, Las Vegas, Nev., 1974.

99. Webb, W. C., and Love, R. J. Reading problems in chronic aphasia. *J. Speech Hear. Disord.* 48 : 164, 1983.

100. Weigl, E. Neuropsychological experiments on transcoding between spoken and written language structures. *Brain Lang.* 1 : 227, 1974.

101. Weigl, E., and Bierwisch, M. Neuropsychology and linguistics: Topics of common research. *Found. Lang.* 6 : 1, 1970.

102. Wepman, J. M. A conceptual model for the processes involved in recovery from aphasia. *J. Speech Hear. Disord.* 18 : 4, 1953.

103. Wepman, J. M. Aphasia therapy: A new look. *J. Speech Hear. Disord.* 37 : 203, 1972.

104. Wertz, R. T. Response to Treatment in Patients with Apraxia of Speech. In J. Rosenbek, M. McNeil, A. Aronson (eds.), *Apraxia of Speech: Physiology, Acoustics, Linguistics, Management*. San Diego: College Hill, 1984. Pp. 257–276.

105. Wertz, R. T., Aten, J. L., LaPointe, L. L., Holland, A., et al. Comparison of clinic, home, and deferred treatment for aphasia. Seminar presented at Annual Convention of American Speech-Language-Hearing Association, San Francisco, 1984.

106. Wertz, R. T., Collins, M. J., Weiss, D., et al. Veterans Administration cooperative study on aphasia: A comparison of individual and group treatment. *J. Speech Hear. Res.* 24 : 580, 1981.

107. Whitney, J. L. Developing aphasics' use of compensatory strategies. Paper presented at the Convention of the American Speech and Hearing Association, Washington, D.C., 1975.

108. Wiegel-Crump, C., and Koenigsknecht, R. A. Tapping the lexical store of the adult aphasic: Analysis of the improvement made in word retrieval skills. *Cortex* 9 : 411, 1973.

109. Wilson, P., and Petersen, D. Machine-assisted, complementary treatment for severe aphasic patients. Paper presented at the Conference of Clinical Aphasiology, Albuquerque, N. Mex., 1973.

110. Yorkston, K. M., Marshall, R. C., and Butler, M. R. Effects of imposed response delays on aphasics' comprehension of material presented with and without visual cues. Presented at the Convention of the American Speech and Hearing Association, Washington, D.C., 1975.

5

Coaching, Self-Coaching, and Rehabilitation of Head Injury

Mark S. Ylvisaker
Audrey L. Holland

Let (the soul) be likened to the union of powers in a team of winged steeds and their winged charioteer. Now all the gods' steeds and all their charioteers are good, and of good stock, but with other beings it is not wholly so. With us men, in the first place, it is a pair of steeds that the charioteer controls; moreover one of them is noble and good, and of good stock, while the other has the opposite character, and his stock is opposite. Hence the task of our charioteer is difficult and troublesome . . .

Plato
The Phaedrus

Plato chose a sports analogy to clarify his model of human personality in his important dialogue, *The Phaedrus*. Knowing his audience, he chose to clarify this theme by relating it to one of the most popular sports of the age, chariot racing. Very generally, the view was that a person consists of relatively independent forces and functions (the steeds: ambition and the appetites), and that to work harmoniously and efficiently, they must be brought under the governance of practical reason (the charioteer).

In head injury rehabilitation, we have long recognized the need for patients to employ consciously this self-governing or charioteer function to facilitate their recovery. In current practice an administrative or executive analogy is often used in place of Plato's image of the charioteer. In this chapter, because victims of head injury are most often 15- to 25-year-old sports-minded males, we return to Plato's method, using one of the most popular sports of our day, football, to clarify the executive functions to both patients and clinicians. Specifically, we use the image of an internalized coach to represent to patients their role in governing their own actions.

We have found that understanding the functions of a coach enables many patients to use the concrete goal of becoming a good self-coach constructively in their rehabilitation. The executive or coaching functions considered in the treatment section of this chapter are defined below:

1. *Self-awareness*: Being cognizant of one's own strengths and weaknesses and of factors that affect one's functioning.
2. *Goal setting*: Setting goals that are realistic, meaningful, and challenging.
3. *Planning-preparing-training*: Putting oneself in a position to complete a task effectively.
4. *Self-instruction*: Giving oneself specific appro-

priate directions about how to carry out a task effectively.

5. *Self-motivation*: "Getting going" and "shutting down" when appropriate.

6. *Self-monitoring*: Attending to one's performance and factors that interfere with success.

7. *Problem solving and practical reasoning*: Taking stock of one's performance and modifying goals, plans, or strategies in response to obstacles.

Each of these functions will be discussed within the coaching metaphor in what follows. Most of our illustrations are taken from football, that grand form of organized violence that both of us secretly espouse as our ultimate career goal. However, for readers with no interest in football, other team sports, drama, music, or even politics could serve as the analogical base. The coaching approach is intended to support two fundamental theses: (1) Effective head injury therapy includes all of the elements of effective team coaching, and (2) the single most useful way to serve head-injured patients is to teach them how to coach themselves.

The reason for this emphasis on executive functions relates to the nature and location of closed head injuries (CHIs). Executive functions are typically associated with the anterior frontal lobes, which are commonly contused in CHI when rotational inertial forces cause the brain to scrape against the orbital ridges inside the skull. Consequently, CHI patients often resemble patients with explicit frontal lobe damage from other causes. The other characteristic injuries in CHI are widespread microscopic shearing lesions and temporal lobe contusions resulting from rotation of the brain within the skull following impact. These injuries relate to the attentional, concentrational, and generalized efficiency problems that exaggerate apparent frontal lobe dysfunction.

There is limited rehabilitation literature relating directly to CHI, and much of it is directed to earlier phases of recovery. For this reason we have chosen to limit the topic to the less well described patients of later phases of recovery, about whom little of explicit clinical application is available and who constitute a significant clinical enigma. Such patients can be described as being in the postconfusional stages of recovery typified as Rancho Los Amigos level VIII and beyond [15]. We will discuss assessment and treatment issues relevant to adolescent and adult patients who are adequately oriented, goal-directed within a structured environment, and capable of some new learning, although they may have severe memory problems. These patients' impairments of language and cognition often elude neurologic assessment either by sophisticated diagnostic procedures like computed tomography (CT) scans and evoked potential measurement, or by language and cognitive assessment tools, which are not specifically designed to detect head injury–related problems. Patients who are aphasic in the sense of traditional syndromes will *not* be discussed. This is because, while aphasia sometimes occurs in CHI, the far more predominant language disturbances are those that result from cognitive impairment itself [33].

Table 5-1 summarizes both the cognitive impairments and their realization in language that our coaching analogy is intended to subserve. Readers are urged to study this table carefully because it specifies the problems on which the rest of our treatment suggestions are focused.

Before discussing the executive functions, there is one more cautionary note. Regardless of the language or cognitive behavior in question, its efficiency can be compromised by external factors, such as rate of presentation of information, complexity of the material presented, and setting in which performance is expected. A patient's behavior may be deceptively appropriate or inappropriate as a result of these factors. For example, a patient may be able to comprehend and produce language adequately, but only when the stimuli are presented at a reduced rate or are restricted in amount. Or, attention, comprehension, and memory may be efficient but only for concrete information. Or even if processing is efficient and at an appropriate conceptual level, this quality of performance may only be obtainable in highly controlled, familiar settings, with little generalization to other settings.

Assessment

A coach's knowledge of prospective players begins with the scouting report, including assessment of the player's height, weight, speed, strength, stamina, and position-related skills (throwing, catching, etc.). In addition, the coach views films or attends games to observe the player under game conditions. The coach also assesses such attributes as leadership, composure under stress, "heart," initiative, team spirit, and desire. Finally, before making selections or position assignments, the coach considers the entire team, the anticipated opposition, and how the most effectively integrated whole can be created.

Table 5-1. Common long-term cognitive and cognitive language deficits following severe closed head injury

Cognitive deficit	Cognitive-language symptoms
Attention related Reduced arousal, attention span, selective attention, maintenance of focus, attentional flexibility	Reduced comprehension and difficulty in maintaining an organized conversational flow

Processing related
  Inefficient perception related to cognitive stress variables (rate, complexity, amount of information)
 	
  Inefficient organization of information: associational organization, sequential organization, part/whole analytic and synthetic organization
	Depressed language comprehension, despite adequate vocabulary, related to rate, amount, and complexity of language to be processed
	Rambling discourse, inefficient word search, poorly organized descriptions or written themes, failure to discern central themes in comprehension tasks

Weak memory (encoding, storage, and retrieval of information): when the problem is at the encoding level, memory problems may simply be symptoms of inefficient attention or perception, or a poorly organized knowledge base into which to integrate the new information; memory problems may also be independent of these other cognitive disturbances; episodic memory (personal experiences) and semantic memory (abstracted information and rules) may be differentially impaired; executive disturbances may also result in a failure to search one's storage system efficiently	Verbal versions of any or all of these memory functions may be impaired.
Reasoning related All forms of higher level inferential, analogic, divergent, and evaluative thinking may be impaired, as well as practical problem solving and social judgment	Verbal versions of all of these forms of thought may be impaired

Executive functions
  Self-awareness
  Goal setting
  Planning, organizing, preparing
  Self-instruction
  Self-initiation/inhibition
  Self-monitoring
  Self-evaluating/adjusting
	Weak awareness of language-related deficits, unrealistic goals, weak initiation, inhibition, or both, weak monitoring and evaluation of language comprehension and expression, and failure to compensate spontaneously for deficits may result in severely impaired communication and psychosocial adjustment problems

In contrast, cognitive-language assessment following head injury often stops with the assessment of component functions analogous to the player's height, weight, speed, strength, throwing and catching skills, etc. These components, as well as their interrelationships, are typically measured by neuropsychologic and language batteries. Component-based treatment, derived strictly from component-based assessment, is as foolish as a coach preparing a team for its first game by focusing only on individual player drill in strength, speed, blocking, tackling, throwing, and catching. Four types of information are essential if the therapist wishes truly to know the patient's capabilities.

Patient History

Pretrauma history and current medical history are important. A head injury rarely creates a wholly different personality. Rather, pretrauma personality characteristics, coping and learning strategies, and interests are exaggerated [25]. Understanding the patient's personality is important in selecting goals, activities, treatment techniques, and interactive style. Pathophysiologic information from the medical records may give clues about expected patterns of strength and weakness and long-term prognosis, but it does not count heavily, because neurologically silent lesions (e.g., widespread, but microscopic, shearing damage) often dominate the recovery picture.

Formal Assessment

The purposes of cognitive language assessment are to describe the patient's intellectual status and cognitive and psychomotor processes and to delineate the components implicated in the disruption of complex functional systems. Adequate neuropsychologic assessments should provide some estimates of strengths so that intact cognitive abilities can be exploited in treatment.

Such assessment should include a core neuropsychologic battery. Some clinicians use a fixed neuropsychologic battery, such as the Halstead-Reitan [16, 29] or the Luria-Nebraska [13]. We prefer a flexible battery administered by several different professionals within an agency. Flexible batteries have the advantage of not overtesting unimpaired processes or undertesting processes where the key disruption is difficult to discern. Language evaluation is a part of the total neuropsychologic assessment. What tests or procedures one selects should be determined by patient-specific hypotheses related to rehabilitation planning that remain unresolved by other assessments. Table 5-2 summarizes some of the problem areas clinicians might wish to test, and some appropriate instruments.

Informal Assessment

The professional scout observes a prospect playing the game, as well as interviewing the player's college coach to discover the person behind the stat sheets. With head-injured patients, some essential information is most appropriately obtained through family interviews and by observation of the patient during testing and in familiar settings.

The clinician must also know what kind of environmental and communicative demands the patient is training for. Without this focus, the clinician is like a coach training a player without knowing that player's position, the nature of the opposition, or the conditions of the game. An important way to achieve this end is through structured but informal assessment of the following areas, some of which can also be measured through formal tests:

1. Attention span, quality of attention, distractibility.
2. Flexibility in task orientation and shifting.
3. Spontaneous or elicited strategy use observed during testing.
4. Awareness of strategies (e.g., answers to questions like "How did you help yourself to that?").
5. Ability to implement strategies when they are suggested.
6. Awareness of deficits (e.g., accuracy of response to questions like "How do you think you did?").
7. Response to stress, whether self-imposed or imposed by the demands of a given test.
8. Appropriateness of functional communication.
9. Spontaneous problem-solving ability.

A sheltered, familiar environment such as the home may provide the setting for the patient's highest level of functioning. Commonly, however, the home setting also reveals problems not apparent in formal assessment sessions, especially regarding judgment, changes in communication style, self-initiated problem solving, endurance, and persistence. Therefore, observations by family members are invaluable sources of information.

Diagnostic Treatment

Even with complete and accurate scouting reports, a coach may not know how to use the players most effectively until beginning to work with them in training camp. The therapist-coach must understand that formal assessments can yield unrealistic predictions regarding a head-injured patient's academic, social, or vocational adjustment [18]. The problem can be mitigated somewhat if the tests used are sensitive to characteristic head injury–related sequelae, are interpreted by an experienced clinician, and are accompanied by relevant informal observation. Done by the unwary, purely formal assessment, because it is geared for optimum performance, may conceal the patient's most functionally debilitating deficits. The following examples are illustrative:

1. A neat, quiet, and isolated test environment may compensate for attention or concentration deficits;
2. Clear test instructions may compensate for difficulties in task orientation, flexibility, initiation, and spontaneous problem solving;
3. Test items that do not include the quantity of information routinely processed in everyday life may compensate for weak integration of information;
4. The *rate* of test item presentation may compensate for generally reduced efficiency of information processing;
5. Independent test sessions paced to fatigue level may allow the patient to compensate for weak long-term storage and retrieval of new information;
6. A supportive and encouraging examiner may provide the patient with a compensation for the inability to cope with interpersonal stress or perception of demands;
7. Tests that tap pretraumatically acquired knowledge or skills may generate false optimism regarding new learning;
8. Tests may fail to evoke a head-injured patient's difficulty in generalizing a newly acquired skill to a novel context.

Table 5-2. Cognitive language assessment

Assessment focus	Suggested instruments
LANGUAGE COMPREHENSION	
Receptive vocabulary	Peabody Picture Vocabulary Test Form L or M [11]
Compare vocabulary level with processing as affected by	
1. Increases in *amount* of language (spoken or written)	Token Test (short form) [9]; paragraphs from aphasia batteries or graded reading tests; high-level patients: Read and summarize book chapters
2. Increases in *complexity* of language	Token Test
3. Increases in *abstractness* of language	Informal: Interpretation of metaphors, figures of speech
4. Increases in *rate* of delivery	Tape-recorded Token Test commands, 200 words per minute
5. Increases in *distractions*	Conversation comprehension in busy environment or with tape-recorded background conversation
Conversational comprehension: Comprehension and integration of extended flow of conversation, contextual cues, speaker's nonverbal behavior, speaker's suprasegmental features	Informal
LANGUAGE EXPRESSION	
Naming	
1. Unstressed confrontation naming	Boston Naming Test [21] or Expressive One-Word Picture Vocabulary Test [12]
2. Word retrieval under time stress	
a. Phoneme cue	Word Fluency Measure [34]
b. Category cue	Category naming from Boston Diagnostic Aphasia Examination [14]
c. Picture cue	Rapid Automatized Naming Tests: colors, random objects [8]
3. Word retrieval in conversation	
Organization (oral and/or written)	1. Picture description (e.g., "Cookie Theft" from [14]), explanation of complex game
	2. Written summary of age and interest-appropriate book chapter; analyze for *presupposition, organization* (main idea, coherence, integration), *completeness* (detail and expansion), *accuracy, redundancy*
Conversational competence	Analyze unstructured conversation for *initiation, relevance, topic maintenance, logical topic shifting, turn taking, "rambling," inhibition, social appropriateness*
VERBAL INTEGRATION, ABSTRACTION, AND REASONING	
Semantic associations	1. The Word Test [19]
	2. Likenesses and differences (Detroit Tests of Learning Aptitude [1])
	3. Analogies tests (completion of analogies may be too automatic to detect subtle problems; it is helpful to request an explanation of the analogic principle)
Concept formation	Concept Formation subtest of Woodcock-Johnson Psychoeducational Battery, Tests of Cognitive Ability [36]; also assesses flexibility in reorientation to changing task format
Verbal reasoning	Use of paragraph or current event *discussion* format to assess the patient's ability to detect main ideas, draw inferences, construct interpretations and explanations, and engage in organized problem solving
VERBAL MEMORY AND NEW LEARNING	
Immediate recall	Digit span or unrelated word list repetition; this is a better measure of concentration or "attention space" than of verbal memory and learning; patients with severe memory and learning deficits often perform normally on tests of immediate recall
Long-term storage and retrieval (no feedback)	Logical Memory subtest of Wechsler Memory Scale [35] (immediate and 30-minute delay norms from Russell [30]); informal—story retelling: immediate vs. 30-minute delay vs. 24-hour delay (*Note:* there is no conclusive way to decide between inefficient processing and encoding, and inefficient storage and retrieval as an explanation for poor performance)

Table 5-2 (CONTINUED)

Assessment focus	Suggested instruments
Verbal learning (with feedback)	Auditory-Visual Learning subtest of the Woodcock-Johnson Psychoeducational Battery: Tests of Cognitive Ability [36]; Selective Reminding Test [6]

STRATEGIC BEHAVIOR

The examiner should note all strategies used by the patient to facilitate comprehension, word retrieval, expressive organization, memory, problem solving, etc. Furthermore, the patient should be interviewed about strategy use. Questioning should begin with open-ended questions ("How did you help yourself do that?") and if necessary, proceed to cued questioning (e.g., "Did you repeat things in your mind?" "Did you draw mental pictures?"). This helps determine if the patient is a spontaneous strategist, is aware of himself or herself as such, and if there is a pattern to the selection of strategies. This is useful in focusing compensatory strategy intervention.

SELF-AWARENESS

Responses to questions such as "How do you think you did on that test?" as well as open-ended interviewing regarding current deficits help the clinician to assess the patient's ability to evaluate his or her own performance and, derivatively, set reasonable goals.

Source: Adapted from Comprehensive Cognitive Assessment. In M. Ylvisaker (ed.), *Head Injury Rehabilitation: Children and Adolescents*. San Diego: College-Hill, 1985.

An initial period of diagnostic therapy often provides the additional necessary information. Diagnostic treatment involves the systematic exploration of the effects on learning and general adaptive behavior of the following:

1. Learning environment: level of activity, type and number of distractions, pace of activities, structure and consistency, level of therapist-supervisor-peer pressure.
2. Patient endurance, persistence, and initiative.
3. Alternate cueing systems.
4. Types of task presented (processing difficulty as well as interest factor).
5. Types of reinforcement, density of success, explicitness of rules and instructions.
6. Use of compensatory strategies and the ability to generalize and maintain the use of strategies.
7. Adaptability to revised educational or vocational goals.

To summarize our position regarding assessment, the sports analogy is appropriate. Coaches know that athletic ability, considered in discrete measurable quantities, is far from synonymous with success in sports. Wayne Gretsky, arguably the world's best hockey player, is well known for the mediocrity of his speed, strength, his size, and aggressiveness. Conversely, preseason cut lists are littered with the names of players whose abilities on paper would predict the high-figure contracts of their agents' dreams. Therapist-coaches must expand their investigation of the total patient beyond formal assessment batteries.

Treatment

Self-Awareness

Once strengths and weaknesses are recognized, the clinician is in a position to share that information with the head-injured patient. Weak awareness of cognitive deficits and their consequences is pervasive following CHI. In addition to organically based failure to perceive deficits, patients' lack of awareness is often also complicated by psychoreactive denial. Reduced self-awareness can severely limit rehabilitation, for if patients are unaware of their deficits, they also likely will lack the ability to set rehabilitation goals and the motivation to improve or compensate. Such patients will be ineffective self-coaches.

We suggest a sequence of four techniques for dealing with this problem:

1. We often begin to teach patients self-awareness indirectly, by having them observe, describe, and discuss other head injured patients. Our patients observe either former patients who have been videotaped to illustrate cognitive or communicative impairments, or other members of a head injury group. Having acquired the ability to describe problems in others, patients are better prepared for more objective observation of themselves.

2. After one or two sessions designed to accustom patients to viewing themselves, we videotape them performing a task that illustrates a targeted deficit. Initially, patients view the tape with no outside commentary. Gradually we introduce replays and ask probing questions to focus attention on the target behavior. Subsequent video sessions combine planned success and planned failure so

that we can provide feedback for guiding patients to be aware of both strengths and deficits.

3. At a later stage, and within generally supportive group therapy sessions, we require patients to describe their own rehabilitation goals and related deficits.

4. Finally, we give patients explicit instruction on CHI, its typical consequences, the presumed effects of the injury on a specific patient's *own* brain, and what that means for rehabilitation.

Goal Setting

The preseason ritual of proclaiming the Super Bowl or the National Championship as this year's single goal belies the coach's true appraisal of the team's potential and the coach's unstated desire simply to improve last year's record. With individual players, the coach may negotiate noble, but realizable goals. Whether team or individual, however, goals pervade the athlete's environment. Contracts are studded with performance incentives; locker-room walls are plastered with goal-oriented motivational slogans.

Head injured patients typically have goal-related problems. They range from setting unrealistic goals ("I was, am, and always will be a truck driver"), to having no goals, to failure to grasp the relationship between current therapy and ultimate goals.

The therapist-coach must begin by persuading the patient to accept provisional goals to give therapeutic activities meaning. Every therapy session begins and ends with "goal talk"; "What are we doing this for?", "What does it mean for you?" Gradually, goal setting is turned over to the patient, at least in part, even if it is inefficient. The time invested is cheap in relation to the value of the patient's learning to set realistic, reachable goals.

With guidance, patients progress from rote recitation of therapist-selected goals, to increasingly spontaneous goal statements, to active participation in discussing realistic versus unrealistic goals. Mutual support and constructive criticism of goals are part of group therapy. Ultimately, the patient should be able to organize and write goals and describe how rehabilitation activities relate to them.

Planning, Preparing, Training

For the head injured patient, the crux of treatment lies in learning to put oneself in a position to behave appropriately and effectively. In what follows, we devote considerable attention to this aspect of head injury rehabilitation as it relates to the ex-

ecutive coaching function. We will critically discuss component training, functional-integrative training, and compensation for cognitive problems in head injury in that order. However, although there is little doubt that component cognitive and language subskills can be improved following brain damage [4], we feel that most therapy materials, programs, and discussions disproportionately emphasize them. Therefore, we choose to focus our attention on the other aspects.

COMPONENT TRAINING. In sports, component training includes strength, speed, quickness, and agility exercises as well as position-specific drill. In therapy, the analogous focus is on strengthening defective underlying cognitive or language components, separated from their natural contexts. The coach must ensure that the players are maximally strong, fast, agile, and efficient in the requisite skills for a position (block, tackle, throw, catch, kick, etc.). Because the heat of the game is no time to isolate and refine these skills, the coach devotes practice time to drills and requires players to exercise and practice on their own. The coach, however, never limits training to isolated skills. Players are also required to integrate these skills in situations increasingly resembling a real game so that they will be prepared when they actually compete.

Unfortunately, cognitive and language rehabilitation often begins and ends with "component drill." A common conceptualization of cognitive language remediation is that it involves only two processes: (1) the identification, through careful and thorough neuropsychologic assessment, of those specific cognitive and linguistic components implicated in a given patient's failure to perform functional tasks; and (2) a remedial program of exercises designed to improve the patient's overall functioning by improving the components thought to be responsible for the functional deficits. Many cognitive training programs provide long lists of component training activities [7]. Many of these resemble training activities that have been widely, and in many cases unsuccessfully, employed by generations of occupational therapists, speech-language pathologists, and special educators. Frequently, training activities are derived from neuropsychologic assessment tasks or from experimental paradigms in cognitive psychology. Considerable interest has been created by the use of custom-designed electronic training machines [3], and more recently by microcomputer-based cognitive remediation [23]. The following are among the more widely used cognitive retraining (CRT) software packages.

1. The cognitive rehabilitation software developed by the staff of the Institute of Rehabilitation Medicine (IRM), New York University Medical Center.
2. The Cognitive Rehabilitation Series (Hartley Courseware, Inc., Dimondale, Mich.).
3. COGREHAB (Gianutsos and Klitzer, Life Sciences Associates, New York, N.Y.).
4. Bracey [5] has developed several cognitive rehabilitation programs.

These programs are designed to remediate a narrow range of basic cognitive and language processes that purportedly underlie more complex and functional activities. The underlying processes include: attention and concentration, reaction time, information organization at a fairly concrete level, and storage and retrieval of rote information. While most of the therapeutic activities incorporated in current microcomputer-based training can be done without electronic assistance, the computer has some advantages, including the following:

1. Computer-based training interests patients, particularly veterans of the video-game parlor.
2. Computers offer infinite patience for practice and drill, often not possessed by therapists.
3. Computers make possible independent cognitive and language drill, although it is often necessary or desirable to have a clinical coach with the patient during these training sessions.

In addition to customized cognitive rehabilitation software, commercial video games have recently been discussed as an adjunct to cognitive and cognitive-perceptual retraining [26]. Unfortunately, such games often begin at a level too demanding for many brain-injured patients and frequently they are not specifically related to deficits. Video games and other high-interest software heighten alertness and attention in some patients. They also prepare patients for more complex interactive tasks and can serve as a context for compensatory strategy training.

For patients who lack initiative, interactive skill, and problem-solving ability in addition to having attentional and organizational weaknesses, passive responses may simply exaggerate passive learning styles. For such patients, Logo-based programs may

be effective because they require both active interaction with the computer and the use of organizational skills. Logo is a simple programming language that allows even very young children to write easy, stimulating computer programs.

Little encouraging evidence exists to suggest that computer-based component training alone effectively improves a patient's performance on complex, functional tasks in the real world. Nevertheless, the drill and practice involved in microcomputer training can be integrated with compensatory strategy intervention. An effective therapist can use this motivating context to heighten a patient's awareness of a deficit, to raise attention to a conscious and deliberate level, and to formulate and practice strategies to improve performance.

Just as successful players spend hours repeating exercises for specific skills, patients can independently practice component drills such as vocabulary, categorizing, and sequencing, with appropriate clinical guidance. Patients can use newspapers or the afternoon soap operas to rehearse separate functions such as stating main ideas, drawing inferences, and constructing explanations. Video games can be used independently to heighten alertness, decrease reaction time, and make information processing more efficient.

Component drill has a legitimate place in cognitive-language rehabilitation, particularly when it can be established that functional impairments result from specifiable component deficits. But over the past 20 years, extensive special education research (reviewed by Kavale and Mattson [22]) supports the conclusion that perceptual and perceptual-motor training alone have little effect on more general and functional cognitive and academic performance. We believe that this finding extends to the rehabilitation of CHI patients and makes other sorts of training imperative. We suggest functional-integrative training and compensatory training.

FUNCTIONAL-INTEGRATIVE TRAINING. In sports, functional-integrative training includes practice sessions under increasingly gamelike conditions culminating in preseason scrimmages or games that differ from the real thing only because the results don't count and therefore the coaches feel free to experiment with new players, plays, and strategies.

No coach would send a team into a game with practice only in the component skills of that game. The coach plans integration systematically, starting with related subgroups of players (e.g., receivers and defensive backs), practicing their interactive roles together and ending with full scrimmages under real-life forms of stress.

Analogously, the therapist-coach rehearses the patients in increasingly integrative and functional tasks under increasingly natural conditions, using as the "opposition" the actual conditions, stresses, people, and demands that patients must face in their vocational, educational, or social lives.

The therapist who fails to progress beyond component drill is similar to the coach whose team has done nothing but lift weights, block, and tackle in preparation for their opening game. Gamelike practice sessions in football are analogous to therapy sessions that emphasize functional behaviors in increasingly natural settings. The following features serve to identify functional-integrative intervention:

1. The targets of treatment are functional behaviors the patient needs in academic, work, or social settings.
2. Training takes place in contexts that increasingly approximate the setting in which the behavior is needed.
3. Components of a complex function can be separated out for special consideration, and possibly even drill, but quickly reintegrated into the functional activity.
4. Functional-integrative practice may or may not incorporate the patient's use of compensatory strategies, discussed later in this section.

Interpersonal process recall (IPR) [20], a technique for improving communicative interaction, illustrates functional-integrative treatment. Its effectiveness with severely head injured adults has recently been demonstrated by Helffenstein and Wechsler [17].

IPR requires videotaping of an interaction between the patient and therapist. Both then view and analyze the tape, solving jointly any interactive problems. The interaction can be spontaneous or structured to evoke specific behaviors. Some alternative behaviors are modeled. Subsequent practice is then videotaped. Ideally, a second therapist serves as an objective third party in the review, analysis, and evaluation of the interaction, but we use this procedure effectively in group therapy with only one therapist acting as both interaction partner and reviewer.

The keystone of the technique is direct feedback at three points: as the patient views the videotaped interaction with no commentary, as all participants comment on the interaction, and from the interaction partner. In addition, the patient is trained to identify inappropriate or otherwise deficient interpersonal skills, to explore actively more appropriate alternatives, and to practice the new skill. Next, the patient practices newly acquired interpersonal skills with a variety of communication partners in a variety of settings.

The value of video therapy has been established by a number of studies in education, rehabilitation, and psychotherapy [31]. For head injury groups, the planning and organizing involved in producing a tape to illustrate a point is itself a therapeutic activity. Other advantages to video-therapy techniques include: self-confrontation without interpersonal confrontation; immediate, concrete feedback; microanalysis of behavior; active patient involvement in stopping the tape for review and analysis; access to feelings and attitudes that emerge during tape reviews; prevention of disputes based on faulty memory or defensive denial; encouragement for patients who have difficulty accepting assurances from others that they are making progress.

COMPENSATORY TRAINING. Unfortunately, some often crucial cognitive and/or linguistic functions impaired by head injury do not respond to "strengthening" exercises (component skills training) and are therefore precluded from functional-integrative training. When a patient requires a crutch to function effectively, we enter the rich domain of compensation. Compensatory approaches take two forms. In the first, the individual is taught compensatory techniques. In the second, the environment itself is modified to provide compensatory alternatives.

The sports analogy remains fitting for both. In the case of personal compensation, a coach with a weak player or two on the team will create a game plan specifically designed to compensate. If the left offensive tackle is a weak link, the coach will help with double-team blocking or will use a preponderance of plays running to the right. A quarterback returning from a serious shoulder operation is not expected to reach preinjury level of efficiency with the long passing game. Rather, the quarterback masters the "short outs" or over-the-middle patterns so that the team still has a viable passing game despite the limited effectiveness of a crucial player. When game time approaches, the coach's question is "How can I succeed with the players I have?", not, "If I yell at him long enough, can I make Bradshaw's elbow better?"

Rehabilitation professionals are familiar with compensatory devices and strategies for sensory and motor impairments. Relatively less attention has been given to compensatory devices and strategies or to environmental modifications for disorders of orientation, attention, learning and memory, organized thinking, efficient information processing, problem solving, and judgment. We will give disproportionate attention to this area, partly because of its neglect and partly because we believe that a large part of rehabilitation involves training in use of compensating strategies and family-teacher-supervisor counseling about environmental compensation.

Compensatory strategies are simply deliberate, self-initiated applications of sometimes unconventional procedures to achieve desired goals. We emphasize "deliberate" and "self-initiated" to distinguish this concept from the so-called instructional strategies invoked by the therapist to teach specific skills.

Compensatory strategies can be either overt or covert. Overt strategies may involve "external aids" such as keeping a log book to compensate for impaired memory, or behaviors such as requesting a speaker to slow down to compensate for an impairment in rate of processing. Covert strategies ("internal aids") range from simple self-cuing instructions to complex mental associations or imagery schemes to enhance comprehension and retrieval.

Three important facts about compensatory strategies are underscored. First, we all use strategies (note taking, schedule books, watches) to extend the limits of our processing mechanisms. The difference is that brain-damaged individuals reach the limits of their processing mechanisms more quickly than non-brain-damaged people. Second, given that most relatively well recovered patients with residual impairments adopt some compensatory strategies, it is a clinical responsibility to facilitate those that are efficient and adaptive. Without guidance, many patients choose inefficient, maladaptive, or escapist strategies. Third, deliberate strategies require attention and thinking in patients whose "attentional space" may already be limited. Hence, strategies should be practiced until they become automatic, so that valuable "space in consciousness" is left for the more mundane perceptual and thinking processes of daily life.

Strategy selection: Patients who are self-aware, relatively realistic about goals, and who see the need for compensation are ideal candidates for

strategy training. To the extent that patients deviate from this ideal they must be viewed as poorer risks. Further, the selection of patient-appropriate individual strategies must reflect the patient's particular strengths and weaknesses: (1) A patient who has a generalized memory impairment but is superior in simultaneous visuospatial processing over sequential-linguistic processing would presumably do better with a visual-imagery mnemonic than with a verbal-rehearsal or verbal-associational strategy; (2) a shy, fearful, noninteractive patient probably would not be a candidate for a strategy involving requests for repetition, clarification or slowing down; and, (3) an impulsive patient with minimal self-awareness and weak self-monitoring would generally do better with an external aid than with an internal procedure.

Table 5-3 summarizes important variables to consider in fitting patients to strategies. Such fitting should precede intervention itself and must be individual. It is invalid to conclude that a given strategy shown to be useful with a large number of patients is necessarily appropriate for an individual patient. Further, occasionally a strategy that is not generally useful may help a particular patient.

Teaching compensatory strategies: Table 5-4 is a

Table 5-3. Some important variables to consider in the selection and training of compensatory strategies

1. Environment-social factors
   A. Pretrauma social, educational, occupational status
   B. Current functional needs and environmental supports
2. Cognitive processes: strengths and deficits
   A. Sensory, perceptual, perceptual-motor abilities
   B. Attention and memory (encoding, storage, and retrieval)
   C. Language abilities
   D. Organization, reasoning, problem solving
   E. Knowledge (level of content and organization)
   F. Metacognitive abilities: Awareness of cognitive function, explanation of own strategies, prediction of performance
   G. Strategic intent and spontaneous strategies used
3. Readiness for new learning: Degree of confusion, disorientation, attentional impairment
4. Executive functions: Self-awareness, self-initiation, self-direction, self-monitoring, self-evaluation, self-adjustment
5. Cognitive style: Impulsive or reflective; persistent; active or passive, flexible; decisive
6. Situational discrimination: Ability to distinguish situations that do and do not require application of a given strategy
7. Personality and social control: Shy or aggressive; fearful or confident; attitude toward rehabilitation
8. Motivation
   A. Presence of goals
   B. Perceived need to use a strategy
   C. Interests

Table 5-4. A sample of compensatory strategies

A. Attention and concentration
  1. External aids: Use a timer or alarm watch to focus attention for a specified period.
  2. Internal procedures: Self-instruct, e.g., "Am I wandering? What am I supposed to do? What should I be doing now?" (May need written cue cards for these during training period.)
B. Orientation (to time, place, person, and event)
  1. External aids: Refer to pictures of persons who are not readily identified (carry pictures attached to log book).
  2. Internal procedures: Select anchor points or events during the week and then attempt to reconstruct either previous or subsequent points in time (as "My birthday was on Wednesday and that was yesterday, so this must be Thursday").
C. Input control
  1. Auditory: Give feedback to a speaker as, "Please slow down, speed up"; break information into smaller chunks.
  2. Visual: Cover parts of a whole and look at exposed areas systematically, as in a "clockwise direction" or "left to right."
D. Verbal processing and comprehension: Use of self-question (e.g., "Do I understand? Do I need to ask a question? How is this meaningful to me? How does this fit with what I know?", etc.).
E. Memory (encoding and retrieval of information)
  1. Use semantic knowledge of basic scripts (e.g., going to a restaurant, buying groceries, etc.) to help reconstruct previous events.
  2. Pigeonholing (spatial arrangement): Remembering things by their location; if they have no typical location, image them in one (e.g., put items to be remembered in different parts of a house or garden and then think of walking through on a planned route).
F. Word retrieval
  1. Organized search of lexical memory according to various categories and subcategories (e.g., person: family, neighbors, friends, workers, professional, etc.).
  2. Circumlocute freely (talk about or around subject).
G. General learning behaviors: Use a tape recorder hooked up to a timer to initiate self-questioning (e.g., "What is my goal? Where am I now? What is left to be done? Have I done it correctly so far?").
H. Problem solving and judgment: Use a problem-solving form or programmed procedure.
I. Organization
  1. Task organization: Lay out task in advance, including materials needed, sequence of steps, time frame.
  2. Thought organization and verbal expression: Construct a "time line" to maintain appropriate sequence of events.

sampling of compensatory strategies and includes both internal and external examples. It is important to understand that these are only illustrations; readers are encouraged to use them as creative springboards for devising others.

Awareness of the deficits to be targeted for compensatory strategy training and some ability to discriminate between successful and unsuccessful performance are mandatory prerequisites for strategy training. The behaviors are never perfected for anyone; the coach is never totally free from feedback concerning fine details of performance, and neither is the therapist. Nonetheless, some baseline self-awareness must precede compensation training.

The first step then is convincing the patient of the usefulness of a particular strategy, and demonstrating or externalizing for the patient how a particular strategy will work in his or her case. One way to accomplish this is through setting up procedures in which success is dependent upon using a particular strategy. For example, if a patient's auditory comprehension is facilitated by slowing down messages, the patient could be taught to request the conversational partner to slow down. The utility of such slowing down would first be demonstrated by having the patient compare his or her slowed-down-rate with normal-rate performance on an auditory task such as complying with commands. Next the patient might be taught specifically to state the direct connection between improved performance, slowed-down rate, and how to achieve that by requesting speakers to slow down. Then, practice is given, with the opportunity both to request "slow-downs" and to experience the differential consequences of requesting and not requesting them. Finally the opportunity is provided for using the strategy in a broader range of verbal and personal contexts.

Therapists should not introduce too many strategies at once or teach strategies that can be confused with one another. It is crucial for therapists to work together in introducing alternative strategies designed to achieve the same goals. The therapy team should systematically track any strategy in use or in training.

Environmental compensation: Obviously, there is another way of achieving the above goal of slower input for the patient: to instruct family and others on the value of it, teaching them not only to slow down when requested, but *as a matter of course* to do so. Such modification of the environment to assist the patient in maintaining the highest level of functioning is an example of environmental compensation. Again, the football analogy applies.

Coaches use the "home field advantage," including support of fans, equipment suited to the specific playing conditions, and referees who can be swayed by home field pressure. The goal is for a weak team to compete optimally under conditions that compensate for that weakness. The therapist-coach similarly counsels teachers, family members, and employers, often suggesting modification of the patients' environment or social interactions to make maximal functioning possible.

Head injured patients whose cognitive and linguistic deficits are unaccompanied by sensory or motor loss often appear normal, and talk and act much as they did pretraumatically. However, processing inefficiency, exaggerated response to stress, memory and learning deficits, fatigue, and psychosocial adjustment problems make performance at pretraumatic levels impossible. Head injury therapists must, therefore, become their patients' counselors and advocates with family members, teachers, work supervisors and other significant figures in their patients' lives.

Efficacy: Although little research has reported on the effectiveness of compensatory strategies with head injured children or adults, the little that does exist (reviewed by Diller and Gordon [10] and Levin, Benton, and Grossman [24]) encourages further clinical exploration and research. Some evidence of the value of compensatory strategies exists in the aphasia literature [32]. Finally, a number of reports in the special education literature show that strategy intervention is useful for a wide range of other impairments. To the extent that findings from other special populations can be generalized to CHI, this research is the basis for optimism.

Motivation

However they felt about them during their playing days, former players typically look back on good coaches as persons who knew how to get the most out of their players, especially when it counted. Coaching styles vary from the emotional fire of a Vince Lombardi to the icy stoicism of a Bud Grant, but in their varying ways, good coaches know how to light a fire under lifeless players while calming and focusing the overaroused.

Applied to head injury and damaged frontal lobe functions, the problem of motivation is a tricky and important one indeed. Compromised by limited self-awareness and often by some degree of faulty self-perception, motivation in CHI directly feeds into the additional problems of initiating behavior in the first place, and often of inhibiting behavior that is inappropriate or that has simply been going on for too long.

Ben-Yishay and Diller [2] advocate the use of a range of motivational techniques, including exhortation, psychodrama, evocative metaphors, and the inspirational style of a revivalist preacher. To this list can be added the motivational tools of the coach. Whatever techniques one uses to increase

or to channel motivation, their success depends upon the development of a strong underlying interpersonal clinical relationship between therapist and head injured patient.

Self-Monitoring

One of us once overheard a high school football coach brag that, after years of practice, he had reached the point where he could attend to six or seven of his 11 players on any given play. He then added wistfully that the local university coach could probably take in all 11. Nevertheless, for even the most perceptive coach, the game film is an essential element in monitoring individual and team performance. The film is reviewed shortly after a game, repeatedly, and frame-by-frame at crucial points. The game film has its analogue in head injury rehabilitation. Perhaps the most effective way to develop increased appropriate self-monitoring in head injured patients is by use of the objective records furnished by videotaped interactions. The most effective programs for increasing self-monitoring skills use these as reviews in which patients learn to describe their own behavior in detail, find examples of behavior on tapes, and so forth. Monitoring can also be increased by keeping log books that require the patient to note his behavior in selected situations. Finally, a good self-monitoring technique involves role switching and having the patient play the roles of both therapist and patient during treatment sessions.

Self-Instruction

Having prepared the team and a game plan beforehand, the coach maintains an instructional role during the game, sending in plays and revising plans. However, team members must be trained to call plays as the situation dictates, to shout out observations to remind themselves and others how to respond, and even to remind themselves covertly of their responsibilities given an opponent's defensive set, the state of the game, and other relevant factors. This set is similar to the important phase of head injury rehabilitation in which transfer of management to the patient is begun. The goal is to train patients to be their own best coaches. Some ways to accomplish this are to

1. Systematically withdraw cues given to the patient.
2. Teach patients in groups to give coaching instructions to other group members.
3. Require patients to begin each task with an ex-

plicit, overt self-instruction (using cue cards as needed).

4. Gradually have patients make their self-instructions increasingly covert [27].

Using such self-instructional techniques, the patient transforms previously automatic activities into deliberate, planned processes. The long-term goal is that practice will permit new strategies to become automatic, making deliberate self-instruction no longer necessary. Until that goal is reached, patients may need self-generated cues as reminders. For example, some patients wear alarm watches that go off at set intervals, signaling the patient to ask himself or herself something like "What should I be doing now?"

Problem Solving and Practical Reasoning
In the heat of a game, the coach must diagnose problems and revise game plans, taking all relevant information and possible solutions into account. Similarly, the therapist must be observant, flexible, and thoughtful in revising therapy plans in response to inadequate progress. Of equal importance, we must give the patient-coach an organized method for addressing problems that arise in his or her life once dismissed from treatment.

While last on the list of skills to be explored directly, problem-solving ability or practical reasoning may be the most important goal for head injured patients. Problem solving is difficult to train because it involves such a variety and complexity of conceptual functions. But with good problem-solving abilities, patients can assume a self-coaching role and achieve independence more easily. Problem-solving training is also important for head injured people because they simply have more problems as a result of their injuries. The irony, of course, is that frontal lobe involvement results in impaired problem-solving abilities.

Organized problem solving is a multistage process involving several distinct types of reasoning. These components are often exercised in workbooks through multiple-trial practice sessions focusing on one form of reasoning at a time. We prefer to integrate remedial reasoning exercises into the context of real-life problem solving. In Table 5-5 we present a small problem-solving guide that patients carry with them and are taught to use for organizing and guiding their problem-solving exercises.

Most of the steps of the outline also exercise one or more component reasoning functions in addition

Table 5-5. Problem-solving guide

   I. Problem: State in a few words exactly what the problem is.
  II. Goal: Why is this a problem? What do you hope to gain by solving this problem?
 III. Relevant information: What do you know or need to know in order to solve the problem?
  IV. Possible solutions: List at least three possible solutions.
   V. Evaluation of solutions: List one or more reasons for and against each solution. Think about the following:
      1. Effective?
      2. Enough time?
      3. Able to do it?
      4. Like to do it?
      5. Break any rules?
      6. Effects on yourself? others? the environment?
      7. Have solutions like this worked in the past with similar problems?
  VI. Best solution: In light of all of the information and reasons, what is the smartest thing to do?
 VII. Plan of action: What do you plan to do?
VIII. Results: Did it work? Are there any new problems?

to their role in the integrated problem-solving process. Specifically, step 1, learning to state the problem, also involves learning to distinguish main ideas from peripheral details. For steps 3 and 4, some practice at divergent thinking is given; for step 5, evaluative thinking and analogical reasoning are exercised; for step 6, convergent thinking skills are practiced; and for the remaining two steps, planning, sequencing, and self-evaluation are stressed.

Targeting these processes within integrative problem-solving sessions using actual problems as they arise in the patient's life has the advantages of (1) explicit integration, (2) allowing the patient to see the importance of the "thinking" components, and (3) increasing motivation by using actual problems.

This outline can be used for group or individual therapy exercises. Often several sessions are required to complete a given exercise. Patients who are familiar with the format can take a problem-solving outline home and complete the reasoning exercises as homework.

Conclusion
In this chapter we have tried to present some explicit approaches to managing the problems of patients at the late stages of recovery from CHI. Generally this is the recovery phase that is most elusive, and at this point the one about which the least is known in terms of management. The ideas presented here may thus soon be outdated. However, the principle upon which they are presented—be-

coming one's own coach—is likely to remain valid for a long time to come. To compromise that discrepancy, we suggest the following.

In the spirit of Chuck Noll, coach of four Super Bowl champion football teams, we propose that therapists do "whatever it takes" to restore head injured patients to lives that are as active, independent, and fulfilling as possible. For some of us, this entails a blurring of professional boundaries; for others, an expansion of a well-defined role within the rehabilitation team. For all of us, it means working ourselves out of a job by teaching our patients to coach themselves.

Acknowledgments
We wish to thank members of the cognitive rehabilitation therapy team at the Rehabilitation Institute of Pittsburgh for their helpful suggestions. In part this work was supported by Department of Education Grant No. 600830010.

References

1. Baker, H. J., and Leland, B. *Detroit Tests of Learning Aptitude.* Indianapolis: Bobbs-Merrill, 1967.
2. Ben-Yishay, Y., and Diller, L. Cognitive Deficits. In M. Rosenthal, E. R. Griffith, M. R. Bond, and J. D. Miller (eds.), *Rehabilitation of the Head Injured Adult.* Philadelphia: Davis, 1983.
3. Ben-Yishay, Y., Rattok, J. and Diller, L. A Clinical Strategy for the Systematic Amelioration of Attentional Disturbances in Severe Head Trauma Patients. In *Working Approaches to Remediation of Cognitive Deficits in Brain Damaged Persons.* New York University Medical Center; Institute of Rehabilitation Medicine, 1979.
4. Ben-Yishay, Y., Rattok, J., Ross, B., Lakin, P., Ezrachi, O., Silver, S., and Diller, L. Rehabilitation of Cognitive and Perceptual Defects in People with Traumatic Brain Damage; A Five Year Clinical Research Study. In *Working Approaches to Remediation of Cognitive Deficits in Brain Damaged Persons.* Rehabilitation Monograph No. 64. New York University Medical Center; Institute of Rehabilitation Medicine, 1982.
5. Bracey, O. Using Computers in Neuropsychology. In M. D. Schwartz (ed.), *Using Computers in Clinical Practice.* New York: Haworth, 1984.
6. Buschke, H., and Fuld, P. A. Evaluating storage, retention, and retrieval in disordered memory and learning. *Neurology* 24 : 1019, 1974.
7. Craine, J. F., and Gudeman, H. E. *The Rehabilitation of Brain Functions: Principles, Procedures, and Techniques of Neurotraining.* Springfield, Ill.: Thomas, 1981.
8. Denckla, M. B., and Rudel, R. Rapid "automotized" naming (R. A. N.): Dyslexia differentiated from other learning disabilities. *Neuropsychologia* 14 : 471, 1976.
9. DeRenzi, E., and Faglioni, P. Normative data and screening power of a shortened version of the token test. *Cortex* 14 : 41, 1978.
10. Diller, L., and Gordon, W. Interventions for cognitive deficits in brain-injured adults. *J. Consult. Clin. Psychol.* 40 : 822, 1981.
11. Dunn, L., and Dunn, L. *Peabody Picture Vocabulary Test-Revised.* Circle Pines, Minn.: American Guidance Service, 1981.
12. Gardner, M. D. *Expressive One-Word Picture Vocabulary Test.* Novato, Calif.: Academic Therapy Publications, 1979.
13. Golden, C. J., Hammeke, T. A., and Purisch, A. D. *The Luria-Nebraska Neuropsychological Battery: Manual.* Los Angeles: Western Psychological Services, 1980.
14. Goodglass, H., and Kaplan, E. *The Assessment of Aphasia and Related Disorders* (2nd ed.). Philadelphia: Lea & Febiger, 1983.
15. Hagen, C. Language Disorders in Head Trauma. In Holland, A. (ed.), *Language Disorders in Adults.* San Diego: College Hill, 1984.
16. Halstead, W. C. *Brain and Intelligence.* Chicago: University of Chicago Press, 1947.
17. Helffenstein, D. A., and Wechsler, F. S. The use of Interpersonal Process Recall (IPR) in the remediation of interpersonal and communication skill deficits in the newly brain-injured. *Clin. Neuropsychol.* 4 : 139, 1982.
18. Jennett, B., and Teasdale, G. *Management of Head Injuries.* Philadelphia: Davis, 1981.
19. Jorgenson, C., Barrett, M., Huisingh, R., and Zachman, L. *The Word Test.* Mokine, Ill.: Lingui Systems, 1981.
20. Kagan, N. Interpersonal process recall. *J. Nerv. Ment. Dis.* 148:365, 1969.
21. Kaplan, E., Goodglass, H., and Weintraub, S. *Boston Naming Test.* Philadelphia: Lea & Febiger, 1983.
22. Kavale, K., and Mattson, P. "One jumped off the balance beam." Meta-analysis of perceptual-motor training. *J. Learn. Dis.* 16 : 165, 1983.
23. Kurlychek, R. T., and Glang, A. E. The Use of Microcomputers in the Cognitive Rehabilitation of Brain-Injured Persons. In M. D. Schwartz (ed.), *Using Computers in Clinical Practice.* New York: Haworth, 1984.
24. Levin, H., Benton, A., and Grossman, R. *Neurobehavioral Consequences of Closed Head Injury.* New York: Oxford University Press, 1982.
25. Lishman, W. A. The psychiatric sequelae of head injury: A review. *Psychol. Med.* 3 : 304, 1973.
26. Lynch, W. J. TV games as therapeutic interventions. Paper presented at American Psychological Association Annual Conference, Los Angeles, Calif., 1981.
27. Meichenbaum, D. *Cognitive Behavior Modification: An Integrative Approach.* New York: Plenum, 1977.
28. Pressley, M., and Levin, J. R. *Cognitive Strategy Research: Educational Applications.* New York: Springer-Verlag, 1983.

29. Reitan, R. M., and Davison, L. A. *Clinical Neuropsychology: Current Status and Applications.* New York: Hemisphere, 1974.
30. Russell, E. W. A multiple scoring method for the assessment of complex memory functions. *J. Consult. Clin. Psychol.* 43 : 800, 1975.
31. Sanborn, D. E., Pyke, H. F., and Sanborn, C. J. Videotape playback and psychotherapy: A review. *Psychotherapy: Theory, Research and Practice* 12:179, 1975.
32. Salvatore, A. P. The effects of pause duration on sentence comprehension by aphasic individuals. Paper presented at the conference of the American Speech and Hearing Association, Washington, D.C., 1975.
33. Sarno, M. T. The nature of verbal impairment after closed head injury. *J. Nerv. Ment. Dis.* 168 : 685, 1980.
34. Sprecn, O., and Benton, A. *Neurosensory Center Comprehensive Examination for Aphasia, Edition A., Manual of Instructions.* Victoria, B.C.: Neuropsychological Laboratory Department of Psychology, University of Victoria, 1969.
35. Wechsler, D. A standardized memory scale for clinical use. *J. Psychol.* 19:87, 1945.
36. Woodcock, R. W., and Johnson, M. B. *The Woodcock-Johnson Psycho-educational Battery, Part One: Tests of Cognitive Ability.* Hingham, Mass.: Teaching Resources, 1977.

6

Developmental Apraxia of Speech: Symptoms and Treatment

Sara Haynes

The diagnosis of developmental apraxia of speech is difficult compared with that of apraxia of speech resulting from an identified and documented cortical insult. Moreover, the paucity of well-defined research on developmental apraxia has led to persisting controversy over the existence of this disorder. While many investigators have made reference to the entity of developmental apraxia under a variety of names, including articulatory dyspraxia [25–28] and developmental verbal dyspraxia [12, 24], descriptions of characteristics clearly differentiating it from the plethora of functional articulation disorders have been most clearly enumerated only in recent investigations [5, 19, 32, 34, 46, 47]. Similarly, specific rationales for the treatment of developmental apraxia of speech, as differentiated from therapeutic programs designed to remediate functional disorders of articulation, are limited. Such rationales do, however, exist. Yoss [46], in a comprehensive review of the literature on developmental apraxia in children, concluded that there have been "no systematic studies delineating characteristic behaviors which would distinguish children with developmental apraxia from the conglomerate of 'functional articulation' disorders" (p. 95). Yet because functional articulation problems constitute the majority (60 percent) of speech disorders in the United States [31], the necessity for identification of subgroups within this population of more than 6 million persons is apparent. A group of individuals undoubtedly persists within the population who, in the absence of known organic or neurologic pathology, exhibit hard-core articulation disorders that are extremely resistant to traditional methods of remediation. A review of the literature describing this population and suggestions for therapeutic intervention provide the basis for this chapter.

Symptoms and Differential Diagnosis

As early as the late 1800s, investigators were beginning to discuss "defects of articulation in children of good mental capacity . . . associated neither with mechanical conditions in the mouth, nor with disease of the auditory apparatus, but almost certainly dependent on some fault in the central nervous system" [18, p. 103]. Dr. W. B. Hadden [18], in his descriptions of an 11-year-old boy admitted to a London hospital, further describes the child as having no diseases but reportedly not speaking until the age of 3. At age 11, his speech was unintelligible and errors in articulation were somewhat inconsistent. After several months of intensive therapy, his speech had improved but was labeled as having a "scanning" character (p. 100).

From this early description in 1891 through the mid-1980s, speech pathologists, pediatricians, and neurologists, among others, have added to and amplified many speech and nonspeech characteristics in an attempt to describe a developmental apraxia of speech. Unfortunately, few of these characteristics have proved to be valuable in arriving at a differential diagnosis of the disorder.

Research from Great Britain and Europe over the past 30 years has contributed significantly to the literature on developmental apraxia. Morley and her colleagues, in several longitudinal investigations, describe *developmental articulatory dyspraxia* [26–29], which is defined as "the failure or limited ability to control and direct the movements and coordinations of the respiratory, laryngeal and oral muscles for articulation when muscle tone is otherwise adequate" [26, p. *vii*]. In differentiating the disorder from both aphasia and dysarthria, Morley [25] lists several characteristics, including a limitation of the consonants produced, less frequent misarticulation of vowels, consistent or inconsistent consonant substitutions, consonant clusters more difficult to produce than singletons, transpositions of sounds and syllables, and the substitution of voiced for unvoiced consonants. She further states that the movements of the tongue, lips, and palate are normal during isolated voluntary acts carried out on request, but that they are clumsy and awkward when attempted in rapid, complex speech [27]. Ingram and Reid [22] described similar characteristics in children with articulatory apraxia: distortion of speech sounds, substitutions, irregularities of rhythm, and, in severe cases, disturbances in intonation. Ingram and Reid objected to the term developmental articulatory apraxia, finding it too difficult to differentiate from functional disorders of articulation.

Other authors [3, 9–11, 16, 36, 40, 43] list characteristics of developmental apraxia and include an inability to imitate speech sounds in the absence of abnormalities of the tongue, lips, or palate; difficulty in initiating speech movements; unawareness of articulator positions; impairment in production of sound sequences; improved performance with visual feedback; occasional telegraphic speech; disturbances in repetition of speech as well as in conversation; inconsistency of articulatory output; and difficulty increasing with word length. In addition, investigators often seem to describe apraxiclike conditions in their characterizations of developmental, or congenital, aphasia [3, 7, 9, 30, 38, 45]. A clear differentiation between developmental apraxia of speech and functional articulation disorders has, to the chagrin of the diagnostician and clinician, continued to prove somewhat elusive. Some European authors [29] suggest that diagnosis should be based not only on speech symptoms but also on the longevity of the rehabilitation process [9]. Numerous reports of therapy regimens with this population do, in fact, mention prolonged remediation programs. A differential diagnosis must, however, be far more objectively based than the suggestion that "the experienced therapist is . . . aware that the child's difficulty in response to treatment is indicative of . . . some basic organic condition" [28, p. 156].

Eisenson [14] describes the early oral activity of the developmentally apraxic child, which includes little sound play. "Early vocal play is often notably absent or present only in token form" [14, p. 192] even though auditory discrimination and auditory perception are intact.

The works of Yoss and Darley [46, 50] and Rosenbek and Wertz [35] have more clearly defined the parameters of developmental apraxia. Rosenbek and Wertz [35] outlined primary speech characteristics after studying 50 children ranging in age from 2 years and 9 months to 14 years. Symptoms included delayed or deviant speech development; receptive abilities far superior to expressive abilities; the possible presence of an oral apraxia; phonemic errors more often in the form of sound omissions; metathetic errors; an increase in errors with increased word length; connected speech much poorer than single-word productions; errors more frequently occurring on the more complex fricatives, affricatives, and consonant clusters; highly inconsistent error patterns; prosodic disturbances; and groping or trial-and-error behavior or silent posturing. Yoss [46], while also describing many of these speech symptoms, observed groping or trial-and-error behavior only in those children who were either older or had had extensive therapy. Rosenbek and Wertz [36] emphasize four symptoms as high-probability indicators to diagnose developmental apraxia of speech differentially from functional disorders of articulation. These include (1) the presence of vowel errors; (2) an increasing number of errors on longer responses; (3) an oral apraxia; and (4) groping postures of the speech muscles. Yoss [46–48] also recognizes two- and three-feature errors in articulation, possibly encompassing difficulties in place, voicing, and continuancy, as well as prolongations of both sounds and syllables, distortions, and additions most prominently observed in repeated speech tasks. She reports that more than twice as many errors involving voiced/voiceless features were made by patients with developmental apraxia in her study than by children with other articulation disorders.

In addition to overt speech symptoms, difficulty in executing volitional movements of the oral musculature appears to be of diagnostic significance [14, 32, 36, 46, 48]. More demonstration is required for successful performance of sequenced volitional oral movements (i.e., "Puff out your cheeks, stick out your tongue"), because the correct performance of these movement patterns often is impossible. Rates of oral diadochokinesis are also slower than normal [46, 48].

The role of gross and fine motor abilities has been extensively studied in both functional articulation disorders and developmental apraxia of speech [6, 39, 44, 46, 48]. Winitz [44] describes the results of investigations that suggest positive relationships between articulation disorders and general motor deficits as inconclusive, but clinical observation continues to lend support to a correlation between the two. In a 5-year investigation of preschool children enrolled in a daily, half-day program for delayed speech and language, over 50 percent of those children with hard-core articulation disorders were also described by physical therapists as having difficulty with coordination of the extremities [21]. A high incidence of "soft" neurologic findings, including difficulty in fine motor coordination, gait, and alternate movements of the extremities has been observed as a primary characteristic in developmental apraxia [20, 46, 48]. Similarly, children described as having developmental apraxia of the extremities also exhibit motor planning problems of the oral muscles in both speech and nonspeech activities [45].

In a more recent investigation designed to delineate diagnostic characteristics of developmental apraxia, Williams, Ingham, and Rosenthal [44] failed to confirm significant evidence of previously reported characteristics, including presence of soft neurologic signs, inability to maintain syllabic integrity, and use of slower speech accompanied by prosodic alterations. Moreover, their population of 30 subjects exhibited no more difficulty in the sequencing of volitional oral movements than matched controls. These findings are at variance with data reported by Yoss and Darley [48] and others. Similarly, Aram and Horowitz [1] were unable to demonstrate manual-gestural, constructional, or oral apraxias for single nonspeech, volitional movements in a population of six subjects diagnosed as developmentally apraxic. They did, however, report that sequences of nonspeech, volitional movements were impaired in their subjects.

The presence of orosensory deficits has been suggested as an indicator of developmental apraxia of speech [12, 19, 32]. In a case study describing speech and nonspeech behaviors of a 36-year-old man with a developmental apraxia, Haynes, Johns, and May [19] describe not only inconsistent articulatory errors, prosodic alterations, struggle behavior, and minor neurologic signs, but significant difficulties on tasks of oral-form identification and two-point discrimination as well. Their investigation lends strong support to the need for evaluating orosensory perceptual abilities before therapy is initiated for patients with either functional or apraxic articulation disorders.

Attempts to differentiate developmental speech apraxia from a so-called congenital, or developmental, aphasia are well documented [14, 15, 28, 29, 35, 46]. Eisenson [14] describes a "small number of children who do seem to understand spoken language but . . . are unable to acquire productive language. Such children are . . . erroneously designated as motor expressive aphasics" (p. 187). Use of the term *apraxia*, which emphasizes the motor planning disorder in these patients, differentiates them from those with a central language impairment [35]. Delay in the development of either speech or language is not inherent as a sequela of the disorder. While a developmental aphasia or language delay may accompany it, and therefore complicate a diagnosis, children with developmental apraxia do understand language; their receptive skills appear accelerated in relation to their expressive ability.

Based on the literature discussed here, the clinician should include, within a diagnostic battery, tools to assess the following skills:

1. Language ability
2. Articulatory proficiency: comparison and analysis of isolated phonemes, both simple and complex; polysyllabic words; connected speech utterances
3. Rates of oral diadochokinesis
4. Volitional movements of the oral muscles, both in isolation and in sequence
5. Orosensory perception and oral awareness

Blakeley [4], in developing a screening test for developmental apraxia of speech in children, first addresses the assessment of receptive and expressive language. He then provides stimuli to assess high-probability error parameters, including (1) vowel and diphthong production, (2) volitional oral movements, (3) verbal sequencing, (4) speech sound development, (5) imitation of motorically complex words, (6) production of multisyllabic words, and (7) prosody in connected speech.

The disciplines of audiology and psychology should be considered to rule out possible auditory deficits or cognitive difficulties. Neurologic examination and physical therapy may be implemented to provide information regarding general motor planning skills as well as gross motor abilities.

Suggestions for Remediation

"The therapeutic significance of differentiating the apraxic child" or the developmentally apraxic adult "from the one with a functional articulation disorder is difficult to determine because little is known about proper articulatory training procedures with apraxic children" [36, p. 32]. However, information regarding specific therapeutic techniques for the person with developmental apraxia of speech can be gleaned not only from direct references to the disorder itself, but also from a study of literature on acquired apraxia of speech as well as many of the general principles included in articulation therapy. The following suggestions have been drawn from the available literature [2, 5, 12–14, 17, 19, 33, 35, 45, 48].

CONCENTRATED DRILL ON PERFORMANCE, BOTH IN IMITATION AND ON COMMAND, OF TONGUE AND LIP MOVEMENTS. Movements in isolation and in sequence should be utilized. Moreover, motor planning exercises of oral movement patterns, using mouthwash or foods, have proved beneficial [19]. The patient in the investigation by Haynes, Johns, and May [19] was required to move the tongue to designated targets in and around the oral cavity. For example, a patient's tongue tip and right buccal area were swabbed with mouthwash; the patient was then instructed to move the tongue tip to the designated target site in the right buccal area. In addition, he was instructed to remove foodstuffs with his tongue from designated areas within the oral cavity; and he was required to use his tongue to remove small quantities of food placed on a tongue depressor held at various distances and angles outside the oral cavity. These exercises were incorporated into a 5-minute segment of each therapy session. Accompanying visual feedback is strongly recommended, as is an emphasis on the heightening of visual awareness of articulatory positions. Edwards [13] reports an inadvertent improvement in the articulation skills of a child experiencing difficulties in voluntary movements of the tongue. The child, who was also being seen for orthodontic treatment, was fitted with an appliance that had a small screw immediately behind the upper central incisors. This reportedly served as a focusing point; in 4 weeks, the child was producing alveolar stops correctly. Edwards, as a result of this experience, suggests the use of small acrylic plates with roughened surfaces as aids to improve orosensory awareness as well as motor planning skills.

IMITATION OF SUSTAINED VOWELS AND CONSONANTS FOLLOWED BY PRODUCTION OF SIMPLE SYLLABLE SHAPES. Visible voiceless phonemes may give rapid initial success, and isolated phonemes may then be paired in consonant-vowel (CV) or VC combinations. It is sometimes beneficial to introduce voiced consonants in VC combinations [34]. CVC configurations should follow VC and CV shapes. Yoss [47] suggests real and nonsense rhyming words in minimal pairs (*pat, bat*) with the simultaneous use of body movements to accent stress patterns.

MOVEMENT PATTERNS AND SEQUENCES OF SOUNDS. Because, by definition, the individual with developmental apraxia exhibits marked difficulty in motor planning of movement patterns, emphasis on the production of sounds in isolation should not be belabored. The clinician should attempt a rapid transition from the imitation of sustained vowels and consonants to the production of syllables and words. For the patient with less severe apraxia, words, and indeed, phrases, may be an appropriate beginning point for therapy. Rosenbek and Wertz [36] suggest teaching of the intrusive *schwa* to help the patient produce phonemes in consonant clusters, as well as to ensure appropriate sound ordering; the schwa should then be dropped after a sound has been stabilized. Word lists requiring back-to-front and front-to-back movements (*took/cart*) also help to stabilize the accurate production of movement sequences [19].

AVOIDANCE OF AUDITORY DISCRIMINATION DRILLS.
The inclusion of drills designed to heighten patients' auditory discrimination ability should be used with caution. Drills are not necessarily beneficial in remediation of disordered articulation [35, 47]. While ear training does constitute a major step in more traditional programs of articulation therapy, descriptions of apraxia emphasize that most of these patients are able to demonstrate knowledge of the acoustic properties of phonemes they misarticulate. Thus intensive ear training warrants consideration only if deficits in discrimination have been clearly identified.

SLOW RATE, SELF-MONITORING. Because increased intelligibility is of paramount concern, early introduction to and heightening of self-monitoring ability is essential. As movement sequences are introduced, a slower rate, often utilizing an even stress pattern, increases the patient's intelligibility while sound sequences and motor patterns are being stabilized. "A slow but accurate effort is generally more desirable than a more rapid one that impairs correct sequential articulation" [14, p. 199].

CORE VOCABULARY. The introduction of a keyword vocabulary has been suggested [8] and has proved particularly beneficial in cases of severe developmental apraxia [19]. The reinforcement of intelligible verbal communication often provides the impetus for maintaining the patient's motivation and interest over a prolonged period of time.

CARRIER PHRASES. The use of carrier phrases, such as "I want a . . ." or "I see the . . .", has been emphasized [14, 47]. Such phrases may successfully serve to extend sequencing efforts and provide the basis for the generation of many appropriate utterances that can be incorporated into meaningful and useful sentences.

RHYTHM, INTONATION, AND STRESS PAIRED WITH MOTOR INVOLVEMENT. Singing has been a useful therapeutic device in the treatment of aphasics [38] and adults with acquired apraxia of speech [47]. The use of songs has also proved beneficial in the treatment of developmental apraxia. The rhythm and stress patterns involved apparently assist in facilitating motor sequencing. This activity has proved most successful when singing has been paired with motor movements of the extremities, such as foot

tapping or finger tapping. Inclusion of a pause between syllables also increases the accuracy of patients' responses. If the patient can read, Rosenbek and Wertz [35] suggest writing words and phrases, accompanied by stress and intonation indicators. A clarification of this technique may be heightened by comparing it to teaching an individual the tune of a song he or she is unsure of, for example, "way down upon the Swanee Ri-ver."

INTENSIVE, FREQUENT, AND SYSTEMATIC DRILL. Just as intensive therapy programs have been advocated and successfully used in treatment of the patient with acquired apraxia of speech (Johns and Darley [23]), daily drill sessions appear most appropriate for the person with a developmental apraxia [5]. It has been suggested [47] that this intensive drill should be interrupted by rest or a shift in activities within each therapy session to decrease the possibility of perseverative behavior. Because the goal of therapy is the ingraining and habituation of accurate motor planning for speech, the necessity for frequent drill sessions to aid in this habituation is apparent.

OROSENSORY PERCEPTUAL AWARENESS. Since several investigations [8, 12, 19] have identified diminished orosensory integrity as a characteristic of developmental apraxia of speech, a multisensory therapeutic program should be considered. Because utilization of specific orosensory awareness activities is a recent addition to the literature on developmental apraxia, it will be dealt with in some detail. Edwards [12, 13] advocates a program based on the principles of proprioceptive neuromuscular facilitation (PNF) and reports that such programs appear to be successful in improving sensorimotor patterning and feedback. Additional and more recent literature [19, 20] specifically outlines techniques designed to heighten oral awareness. If deficits in orosensory awareness are identified through careful diagnostic procedures, attempts can then be made to increase the patient's awareness of the orosensory mechanism by bombarding it with multisensory stimuli. Since tactile stimulation reportedly has a facilitating effect on the pyramidal tract, which, in turn, is responsible for more skilled or planned motion [2], it would then appear reasonable to use tactile stimulation to improve the patient's orosensitivity and awareness. Such techniques have previously been used in the treatment of cerebral palsy [33, 34, 37, 41] and include such activities as icing, brushing, rubbing, or touching with such instruments as toothbrushes. Additional stimulation techniques using textures, such as cotton or sandpaper, could be applied to the patient's upper lip, tongue, palate, and buccal area. Application of deep pressure and resistance techniques further facilitates oral awareness.

In view of the close relation between taste and smell, noxious odors, such as ammonia and alcohol, might also serve to increase the patient's oral sensitivity [33], as would the taste of unpleasant or bitter foods, such as grapefruit or lemon. The manufacturing of candy of various sizes, shapes, and textures has been suggested for prolonged stimulation and utilization in home management programs.

Haynes, Johns, and May [19] reported significant improvement in patients' oral awareness as well as notable gains in articulation skills following a 3-month intensive oral awareness program that was instituted in conjunction with standard phonetic-articulatory drills. These authors outline a 5-minute program to be used at the onset of each therapy session, including:

1. The application of various textures of sandpaper to stimulate oral sites, including the lips, tongue tip, and tongue blade.
2. The swabbing of sites within and around the oral cavity with sour food, including lemon and grapefruit juice.
3. The smelling of noxious odors, including ammonia and rubbing alcohol.
4. Probing of various areas on the patient's tongue and lips, followed by the instruction to identify the stimulated sites by pointing to corresponding areas on diagrams of the tongue and lips.

PHYSICAL THERAPY. Since "soft" neurologic signs are a high-probability characteristic of developmental apraxia, consultation with physical therapists, who could assist in the design and implementation of programs to increase skills in motor planning activities of the extremities as well as to improve coordination, should be considered. Clinical impressions of several preschool children diagnosed as having developmental apraxia of speech revealed improvement in articulation only when speech therapy regimens were coupled with programs of physical therapy [21].

Many of the therapeutic techniques suggested here are beneficial to patients with a functional articulation disorder as well as for those with developmental apraxia. This overlap has needlessly served to confuse some clinicians and raise questions as to the efficacy of the term developmental apraxia. However, such an overlap should be neither confusing nor surprising. Many techniques successfully employed in therapy programs for patients with acquired lesions are also used efficiently in programs for those with so-called functional, or delayed, disorders of communication. The clinician who has treated patients with acquired aphasia or delayed language can well attest to this.

The therapy guidelines outlined have proved successful in creating positive changes in the articulation of children diagnosed as developmentally apraxic. There does seem to exist, however, a population of children whose motor planning deficits are so severe as to preclude functional verbal communication, even following intensive speech therapy programs. It is hoped that this population is small in number. Consideration of adjunct communication systems such as Rebus and Bliss symbolics may warrant consideration in such cases. Many clinicians advocate the use of adjunct communication systems as soon as the child reaches the cognitive-receptive language age of 18 months. This does not imply that systematic drill to increase articulatory proficiency should be abandoned; rather that methods to assist the child in functionally communicating in his or her environment be employed as soon as possible, and in conjunction with an articulation regime designed to attack the motor planning deficit.

The diagnosis of developmental apraxia should be made cautiously. It has been suggested that the population is only a small subgroup among those disorders most frequently labeled as functional [33, 46–48]. However, careful examination of patients with persisting single-sound substitutions, such as the /r/ or /s/, as well as those with multiple articulation errors, may reveal motor planning deficits that are in greater numbers than previously suspected.

The effects of therapy for the individual with developmental apraxia of speech are optimal only if the original diagnosis has been accurate. Moreover, the need for continued research and clinical emphasis on treatment as well as diagnosis of this disorder is paramount. As Rosenbek [35] aptly states, "the apraxic child (and adult) is a rarity; knowledgeable therapies should not be" (p. 21).

References

1. Aram, D. M., and Horowitz, S. J. Sequential and non-speech praxic abilities in developmental verbal apraxia. *Dev. Med. Child Neurol.* 25 : 197, 1983.

2. Ayres, J. *Sensory Integration and Learning Disorders.* Los Angeles: Western Psychological Services, 1972.

3. Benton, A. L. Developmental aphasia and brain damage. *Cortex* 1 : 40, 1964.

4. Blakeley, R. W. *Screening Test for Developmental Apraxia of Speech.* Tigard, Ore.: C. C. Publications, 1980.

5. Blakeley, R. W. Treatment of Developmental Apraxia of Speech. In W. H. Perkins (ed.), *Dysarthria and Apraxia.* New York: Thieme-Stratton, 1983.

6. Brenner, M. W., Gillman, C., Zangwill, O. L., and Farrell, M. Visual-motor disability in school children. *Br. Med. J.* 4 : 259, 1967.

7. Broadbent, W. Cerebral mechanisms of speech and thought. *Med. Chir. Trans.* 55 : 145, 1872.

8. Chappell, G. E. Childhood verbal apraxia and its treatment. *J. Speech Hear. Disord.* 38 : 365, 1973.

9. Court, D., and Harris, M. Speech disorders in children—part I. *Br. Med. J.* 2 : 345, 1965.

10. Court, D., and Harris, M. Speech disorders in children—part II. *Br. Med. J.* 2 : 409, 1965.

11. Daly, D. A., Cantrell, R. P., Cantrell, M. L., and Aman, L. A. Structuring speech therapy contingencies with an oral apraxic child. *J. Speech Hear. Disord.* 37 : 22, 1972.

12. Edwards, M. Developmental verbal apraxia. *Br. J. Disord. Commun.* 8 : 64, 1973.

13. Edwards, M. Personal communication, 1976.

14. Eisenson, J. *Aphasia in Children.* New York: Harper & Row, 1972.

15. Eisenson, J. Developmental aphasia: A speculative view with therapeutic implications. *J. Speech Hear. Disord.* 33 : 3, 1968.

16. Eisenson, J. Developmental patterns of nonverbal children and some therapeutic implications. *J. Neurol. Sci.* 3 : 313, 1966.

17. Gubbay, S. The management of developmental apraxia. *Dev. Med. Child Neurol.* 20 : 643, 1978.

18. Hadden, W. B. On certain defects of articulation in children with cases illustrating the results of education of the oral system. *J. Ment. Sci.* 37 : 96, 1891.

19. Haynes, S. M., Johns, D. F., and May, E. B. Assessment and therapeutic management of an adult patient with developmental apraxia of speech and orosensory perceptual deficits. *Tejas* 3 : 6, 1978.

20. Haynes, S. M., Johns, D. F., Richardson, S. M., and May, E. B. Orosensory perception and apraxia of speech: A diagnostic approach with therapeutic implications. *Tejas* 2 : 6, 1977.

21. Hirsch, S. H. Longitudinal study of a preschool language development program. Unpublished data, 1976.

22. Ingram, T. T. S., and Reid, J. F. Developmental aphasia observed in a department of child psychiatry. *Arch. Dis. Child.* 31 : 161, 1956.

23. Johns, D. F., and Darley, F. L. Phonemic variability in apraxia of speech. *J. Speech Hear. Res.* 13 : 556, 1970.

24. McLaughlin, J. F., and Kriegsman, E. Developmental dyspraxia in a family with x-linked mental retardation (Renpenning syndrome). *Dev. Med. Child Neurol.* 22:84, 1980.

25. Morley, M. Defects of articulation. *Folia Phoniatr. (Basel)* 11 : 65, 1959.

26. Morley, M. *Development and Disorders of Speech in Childhood* (2nd ed.). Baltimore: Williams & Wilkins, 1965.

27. Morley, M. E., Court, D., and Miller, H. Developmental dysarthria. *Br. Med. J.* 1 : 8, 1954.

28. Morley, M., Court, D., Miller, H., and Garside, R. Delayed speech and developmental aphasia. *Br. Med. J.* 2 : 463, 1955.

29. Morley, M. E., and Fox, J. Disorders of articulation: Theory and therapy. *Br. J. Dis. Commun.* 4 : 151, 1969.

30. Myklebust, H. R. Childhood Aphasia: An Evolving Concept. In L. E. Travis (ed.), *Handbook of Speech Pathology & Audiology.* New York: Appleton-Century-Crofts, 1971.

31. National Institute of Neurological Diseases and Stroke. *Human Communication and Its Disorders: An Overview.* Monograph 10. Washington, D.C.: Government Printing Office, 1970.

32. Prichard, C. L., Tekieli, M. E., and Kozup, J. M. Developmental apraxia: Diagnostic considerations. *J. Commun. Disord.* 12 : 337, 1979.

33. Rood, M. Neurophysiological reactions as a basis for physical therapy. *Phys. Ther. Rev.* 34 : 446, 1954.

34. Rosenbek, J., Hansen, R., Baughman, C. H., and Lemme, M. Treatment of developmental apraxia of speech: A case study. *Lang. Speech Hear. Serv. Schools* 5 : 13, 1974.

35. Rosenbek, J. C., and Wertz, R. T. A review of 50 cases of developmental apraxia of speech. *Lang. Speech Hear. Serv. Schools* 3 : 23, 1972.

36. Savage, V. A. Childhood autism: A review of the literature with particular reference to the speech and language structure of the autistic child. *Br. J. Dis. Commun.* 3 : 75, 1968.

37. Stockmeyer, S. A. An interpretation of the approach of Rood to the treatment of neuromuscular dysfunction. *Am. J. Phys. Med.* 46 : 930, 1967.

38. Travis, L. W. (ed.). *Handbook of Speech Pathology & Audiology.* New York: Appleton-Century-Crofts, 1971.

39. Walton, J. N., Ellis, E., and Court, S. D. M. Clumsy children: A study of developmental apraxia and agnosia. *Brain* 85 : 603, 1962.

40. Weiner, P. S. The perceptual level functioning of dysphasic children: A follow-up study. *J. Speech Hear. Res.* 15 : 423, 1972.

41. Westlake, H., and Rutherford, D. *Speech Therapy for the Cerebral Palsied.* Chicago, Ill.: National Society for Children and Adults, 1961.

42. Williams, R., Ingham, R. J., and Rosenthal, J. A further analysis for developmental apraxia of speech

in children with defective articulation. *J. Speech Hear. Res.* 24 : 496, 1981.

43. Wilson, L. F. Characteristics of Aphasia in Children. In S. R. Rappapord (ed.), *Childhood Aphasia and Brain Damage.* Narberth, Penn.: Livingstone, 1964. Vol. 1.

44. Winitz, H. *Articulatory Acquisition and Behavior.* New York: Appleton-Century-Crofts, 1969.

45. Worster-Drought, C. Report: Failure in normal language development of neurological origin. *Folia Phoniatr. (Basel)* 5 : 130, 1953.

46. Yoss, K. A. Developmental apraxia of speech in children with defective articulation. Florida State University Ph.D. Thesis, 1972.

47. Yoss, K. A. Therapy in developmental apraxia of speech. *Lang. Speech Hear. Serv. Schools* 5 : 23, 1974.

48. Yoss, K. A., and Darley, F. L. Developmental apraxia of speech in children with defective articulation. *J. Speech Hear. Res.* 17 : 399, 1974.

7

Treating Apraxia of Speech

John C. Rosenbek

An extensive general literature on treatment for the apraxic patient exists [1, 27, 36, 44, 53, 56, 66, 74, 84, 106, 118, 132, 136, 137], yet the demand for new treatment ideas persists. If clinicians are aware of the existing literature, as they doubtless are, then why the demand? A few possible answers may provide a context for the subsequent development of a philosophy of management, for the description of management strategies, and for the presentation of representative case histories.

Clinicians are always looking for something new, something to improve the quality of future service over past service. Unfortunately, the search for new behavioral treatment is bound to be futile. Until drug or surgical breakthroughs revolutionize treatment of brain-damaged patients in general, nothing really new will emerge for treating patients with apraxia of speech. Although modifications and expansions of existing techniques will continue to appear, these will reflect more of the author's ingenuity than creativity, because the seeds for present behavioral techniques were sowed generations ago. Being forced to share the chagrin of that late-nineteenth-century patent official who suggested closing down the patent office because nothing new could possibly be invented would be welcome.

Johns and Darley [63] and Johns and LaPointe [64] have attempted to reduce the confusion caused by the existing proliferation of labels by suggesting that the descriptions of a number of different diagnoses, including aphemia, cortical dysarthria, Broca's aphasia, motor aphasia, and phonetic disintegration, are similar to the present-day descriptions of apraxia of speech. They conclude, therefore, that perhaps apraxia is a synonym for all those labels and that the terminology can be simplified. However, the drawback is that some clinicians have assumed that all expressive problems are apraxic and, as a result, treatment for apraxia of speech has been wasted on nonapraxic patients and on patients whose apraxia was, and would always be, less severe and thus less important than their aphasia.

All expressive difficulties, whether they are called Broca's aphasia, motor aphasia, aphemia, or something else, do not result from disturbed volitional, oral movements [29, 53, 84]. If Goldstein [53], Conrad [29], and Luria [84] are correct, treatment for apraxia should not be equally effective for all expressive problems—and in fact it is not. The inevitable failures introduce a second reason why clinicians want more new ideas for treatment. The programs they have used have not worked. However, in part, and only in part, their failure has resulted from misapplication of the existing methods rather than from weakness in the methods themselves.

One other reason for wanting more treatment programs can be hypothesized. Discussions of methods are more popular and more numerous than discussions of theory, even though several writers [3, 36, 44, 118, 135] have developed conceptual frameworks for apraxia of speech therapy. Methods without a conceptual framework are vulnerable to misuse. They may be given an inadequate trial, they may be applied in the wrong order, or they may be applied at the wrong time. In such instances it is the rationale, not the methods, that is inadequate. It is hoped that this chapter will sufficiently identify apraxic patients, develop the theory, and describe the methods of treatment so readers will know when, how, and how much treatment to use. Nothing so presumptuous as silencing the demand for new methods is intended. Perhaps the clinician will know, as a result of reading this chapter once, when to consult it again or turn to a more complete source, such as the book by Wertz, LaPointe, and Rosenbek [137].

The Apraxic Patient

Patients with mild to moderately severe apraxia are easily identified unless they have severe aphasia. They understand the stimulus until it gets complex, and they may understand even difficult material if they have no aphasia. Their internal speech is reasonably intact [98]; and they read and write, although not perfectly. Their speech is dysprosodic and is characterized by articulatory errors described in detail by Wertz (Chap. 1) and more recently by Rosenbek, Kent, and LaPointe [106]. They grope inconsistently for the correct sound and may struggle awkwardly but determinedly through sequences. Their nemesis is the five-syllable, rare word, whose accent falls toward the end and whose syllables are made of fricatives grouped in clusters and unrelieved by plosives. Their automatic-reactive speech may be completely normal. In diagnosis and in therapy they give clear evidence of recognizing their errors, and much of their grouping appears to result from attempted self-correction. They know what they want to say and may communicate their intentions by gestures and by writing. They may return to work if normal speech is not required; and they are capable of decision making and of running many of their own and their families' daily affairs.

Severe apraxia of speech is harder to describe because severely apraxic patients often have severe aphasia across all modalities, making all test interpretations extremely difficult. They may be reduced to a limited repertoire of sounds and to a sparse stock of meaningful or meaningless recurring utterances [2]. Their reading, writing, and listening may be severely disrupted, although some patients may have profound deficits of speaking yet have reasonably intact reading, writing, listening, and gesturing abilities. Figure 7-1 shows a severely apraxic patient's performance on the Porch Index of Communicative Ability (PICA) [103]. This patient's speech was characterized by unintelligible, recurring utterances; but reading, writing, and gesturing were relatively well preserved. How much the patients with severe apraxia understand is demonstrated by their recognition of errors, at least during the acute and early chronic stages. However, after years of chronic, severe apraxia, some patients cease to listen, perhaps because their ability to do so degenerates.

Articulatory characteristics in severe apraxia of speech are infrequently described because, for any number of experimental reasons, patients with severe apraxia are excluded from descriptive studies. The literature, therefore, is of little help and may even be misleading. For example, the observation that apraxic errors approximate the target is true only if patients have a large repertoire. If their repertoires are limited, as they are in severe apraxia, they will approximate targets only when the targets resemble sounds they have already. Clinically, patients with severe apraxia may be speechless or they may have a limited repertoire of meaningful and meaningless recurring utterances. They generally have an oral, nonverbal apraxia and their deficit in oral, verbal, and nonverbal tasks is more severe than can be explained on the basis of motor weakness or aphasic difficulty in understanding.

Diagnosis of some patients with severe apraxia may have to await the outcome of therapy. Apraxic patients will learn to produce new sounds with proper teaching methods, but these sounds and combinations of them will retain a learned, dysprosodic quality. Their acquisition will be accomplished by much groping and trial and error. Patients with severe apraxia will not ignore the clinician nor will they ignore their own errors, unless the therapy dictates that patients should ignore their errors. They will not have large numbers of fluent asides. Speech, even speech sounds, exacts a toll in concentration and effort each time it is produced.

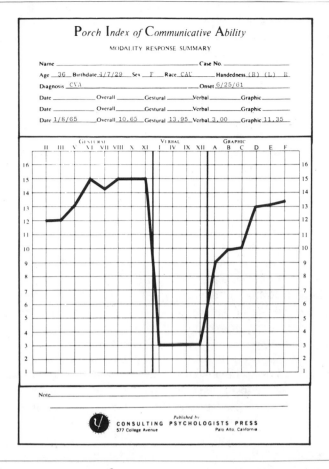

Fig. 7-1. PICA modality response summary for a patient with severe apraxia of speech. Writing, reading, and listening are much better than speaking. Speaking is unintelligible. (All PICA forms shown are from Porch, B. E. *The Porch Index of Communicative Ability.* Palo Alto, Calif.: Consulting Psychologists Press, 1967. With permission.)

The therapy discussed in this chapter is designed for apraxic patients, regardless of the severity of their condition. The presence of aphasia, general intellectual deficit, hearing loss, and dysarthria will dictate modifications in the program and even different methods entirely. Among the many other influences on the effectiveness of methods about to be described is the clinician. What works for one clinician fails for another, and the difference is not easily accounted for. One warning is appropriate. The greatest possible misuse of this chapter would be its uncritical acceptance and application. It can be for the clinician what an abridged dictionary is for the writer—a limited source. Good treatment, like good writing, requires extensive and creative reading, listening, and practice.

A Philosophy of Apraxia of Speech Rehabilitation

No matter how detailed, a catalog of techniques is of limited usefulness unless it is prefaced by a philosophy of management. This next section sets forth a management philosophy that reflects both the nature of apraxia in its acute and chronic forms and the changes in nervous system function hypothesized to result from successful treatment. Nothing in the philosophy is original. Its sources are the definitions and descriptions of apraxia emanating from America and Europe and the management philosophies of Goldstein [53], Alajouanine and Lhermitte [3], Kreindler and Fradis [72], Beyn [11], Luria [84], and others. Thus this section is transductive, not creative.

Apraxia of speech* is a nondysarthric, nonaphasic sensorimotor disorder of articulation and prosody. Aphasia and dysarthria may coexist with

---

*Martin [87] objects to this term. The interested reader may want to note his objections and the research [88, 89] he uses to support them as well as the first published objections to his objections [4].

apraxia of speech but language deficits and deficits in muscle strength or endurance do not account for apraxic errors. Therefore apraxia is probably not most efficiently managed with general stimulation techniques or therapy directed toward thought processes [134], although these approaches have a place in the overall treatment program. Nor are muscle strengthening and other methods tailored to the neuropathologies underlying dysarthric symptoms appropriate to treating apraxia of speech.

Severe apraxia of speech is loss or impairment of the ability to position the articulators consistently for production of speech sounds or to move them consistently to produce speech sound combinations. In milder apraxia, individual gestures may be preserved, but the automaticity of coarticulation will be lost or impaired.* Regardless of the severity of apraxia, the deficits may result from temporary inhibition of the cortical programmer of articulatory movements because of edema or damage to surrounding tissue, in which case improved function will accompany physiologic recovery. The deficit may also result from damage directly to the motor programmer rather than from the programmer's inhibition, in which case the loss is likely to be permanent unless special therapy is undertaken.

Talk of speech sound production and programming of movements is traditional in discussions of apraxia of speech. Recently [18, 70, 94], different models and concepts of motor performance, and hence different vocabularies for talking about deficits, have begun to appear. Their influence on treatment procedures and the way treatment is discussed is yet to be determined. It seems inevitable, however, that they will eventually have an influence, if not on practice, then at least on the way that practice is viewed and discussed.

In the acute stage of apraxia the clinician's primary roles are those of a *facilitator*,† or *deblocker*, and of a *prophylactic*, or *preventor*. As *facilitator*, the clinician systematically elicits and reinforces speech, using whatever stimuli, modes, and methods are most effective. He or she establishes the conditions so an intact, or nearly intact, phonologic system is deblocked, i.e., so the patient's access to it is improved. If speech is temporarily inhibited during the acute stage, the deblocking will

be easy and the clinician may well have difficulty keeping abreast of the patient's sometimes daily changes. The speech pathologist may do no more than oversee and structure the return by getting the patient to work systematically on certain stimuli in certain modes. As *prophylactic* for the patient with acute apraxia, the clinician attempts to influence the patient's attitude about the traumatic episode and resulting communication deficits so the patient is prevented from bad habits, such as frustrated groping and inordinate silence, and so the patient can invest the energy and emotion necessary for improvement. As a prophylactic measure, the clinician counsels family and friends so they learn to create a relaxed, helpful environment, and so they are capable of maintaining that environment without fear and frustration as the patient begins the struggle toward recovery.

In the chronic stage of apraxia, when physiologic recovery has provided what it can, facilitating and prophylactic functions continue. They are joined by (1) efforts to improve the speech programmer by specific concentration on programmer function, and (2) efforts to reorganize speech function by systematically incorporating intact or relatively intact systems into the function of the speech programmer [11]. Both these efforts may be accomplished by what Luria [84] calls *intrasystemic and intersystemic reorganization*.

Reorganization
Luria [84] defines *intrasystemic reorganization* as the improvement in a system (e.g., the speech system) accomplishable in two ways. "One can shift a disturbed function down to a lower level within its own system, i.e., have it carried out at a more primitive, automatic level and thus avoid the effects of disorders involving the voluntary execution of the motor acts"; or one can "shift the function up by giving it new meaning and transferring its execution to the level of higher cortical processes" (p. 385). Intrasystemic reorganization, then, is an attempt to improve the function of a system by manipulation within the system. Using a nonverbal gesture, such as tongue protrusion as a basis for helping a patient learn /θ/, and making speech more volitional or conscious are both examples of intrasystemic reorganization, which attempts to improve the speech programmer by concentrating solely on that programmer. As such, it is like facilitation. The two differ in that reorganization improves the phonologic system, whereas facilitation improves merely the patient's access to it. Reor-

*Luria [84] seems to believe that these differences are unrelated to severity and instead are indicative of different symptom complexes.
†Beyn [11] and Luria [84] describe drug therapy as a primary facilitator, but medical managements of any sort are not discussed in this chapter.

ganization takes a long time because it involves relearning; facilitation takes a short time because it is only deblocking.

Luria [84] calls the second form of reorganization *intersystemic*. In this reorganization, a behavior or a system is improved by involving elements of intact or more nearly intact systems. Beyn [11] calls this form of reorganization "round-about," an adjective that has a memorable lucidity about it. Intersystemic reorganization can be understood by example. Consider one provided by Luria. A patient with parkinsonism could not squeeze a ball rhythmically. He was taught to pair an eye blink, which Luria describes as a "semiautomatic motor act," with the voluntary squeeze. According to Luria, the patient "was told to repeat to himself, 'Blink and press, blink and press'" (p. 383). Under these conditions squeezing was more normal. Luria observes that "objectively the movements were the same as those he had performed before, but now they were carried out on the basis of a new functional system" (p. 384).

Speaking is a total-body response, and finding a functional system uninvolved in it is difficult. If we assume that speaking is primarily an auditory-vocal activity, however, then any use of *visual information* to treat the apraxic patient is intersystemic reorganization, as would be any use of certain *limb gestures* to aid the patient in speaking. However, since both vision and limb gestures are part of speaking, the definition of intersystemic reorganization has been revised for purposes of this chapter.

Intersystemic reorganization is accomplished when a system or set of behaviors is introduced into the act of speaking in an unprecedented form or with an unprecedented regularity. For example, limb gestures accompany normal speech but seldom are elaborate; they are not pantomimes of the activity being discussed. However, if oral production of words, such as *eat*, *drink*, and *sleep*, could be improved by pairing their oral production with a pantomime of eating, drinking, and sleeping, this would be a form of intersystemic reorganization. Similarly, introducing a number of visual cues into speech, as when the patient watches the clinician, is also intersystemic reorganization, according to the modified definition, even though vision has at least casual significance in normal speech performance.

Beyn [11] argues that a system, portion of a system, or a behavior to be used in reorganization will itself need strengthening even if it is normal

or nearly so. This is especially true for apraxic patients both because the majority seem to have deficits in all systems and because successful reorganization cannot be created from damaged parts. If, within the context of intrasystemic reorganization, nonverbal movements are to be integrated into volitional speech gestures, these nonverbal movements must be strengthened. For example, a gossamer blow will not support a vigorous /p/. If tapping or vision is to be integrated into the act of speaking as part of the intersystemic reorganization, tapping must be practiced, and what to look for and how to evaluate what is seen must be taught. Deal and Darley [37] explain their finding that looking in the mirror failed to aid apraxic articulation significantly by stating that the patient had received too little instruction. Thus it might be predicted that, in fact, considerable instruction and even practice in looking must be accomplished before any guarantee can be made that vision will aid speaking.

A final observation about reorganization is that speech so modified is obviously reorganized, and it usually retains a permanently conditioned quality. For example, the special effort to produce a /k/ remains reflected in a tensely protruded mandible. The patient undergoing successful reorganization may move from a system of obvious external controls to a system of less obvious internal controls, however. For some patients, these self-generated cues can be shortened and speech may become less "conditioned." Just as reorganized speech is conscious and effortful, so also is it limited. The reorganized speaker generally has only a portion of what is needed to be normal, although Beyn [11] suggests that generalization is possible. The *unenviable alternative* to *effortful* and *limited* speech, however, is a *persisting, more severe* deficit, for it seems to be true, as Luria [84] has said, that, "The 'rebirth' of speech can come about only as a result of special retraining" (p. 388).

Beyn [11] says that therapy in apraxia, whether it is facilitation or reorganization, can never concentrate on anything less than the total speech-language process, including even those portions that are not used in reorganization. Other writers [118, 137] agree. The major reasons are that apraxia of speech probably can be improved by improving language function and that patients seldom have pure disorders. Patients are rarely purely apraxic or purely aphasic. Thus disruption of one part of the patient's speech-language performance will frequently be accompanied by disruptions of other parts, either because the lesion is extensive enough to involve multiple systems or because speech-language processes and brain areas interact to such a degree that the entire system is disrupted by a lesion, no matter how circumscribed it is. *An adequate therapy for apraxia of speech, then, involves speaking, listening, reading, writing, and gesturing.*

Reorganization has its conceptual counterparts in American speech pathology. American speech pathologists, for example, distinguish between improving a function by working on it directly, and improving a function by pairing it with other, more intact ones. In addition, they would probably agree with Beyn's [11] warning that improved function requires more than the pairing of a healthy function and an unhealthy one.

Other parallels between American and European concepts can be traced also. Berman and Peelle [10] discuss self-generated cues in apraxia therapy and mention, for example, the patient who could elicit a word once he had written the first letter. Helping the patient build internal cues is another definition of reorganization, and reliance on writing is a form of intersystemic reorganization. In addition, most American speech pathology methods fit within the reorganization concept. Since imitation is probabaly carried out at a different level in the nervous system than is spontaneous speech, an imitative program results in intrasystemic reorganization. Also, phonetic placement using diagrams of speech-sound gestures is an intersystemic reorganizer. Melodic intonation therapy (MIT) [121, 122] may be either intersystemic or intrasystemic. As will be demonstrated, an aggressive rehabilitation program, whether here or abroad, will involve myriad methods and both types of reorganization simultaneously.

Regardless of the clinician's nationality; whether the patient's condition is acute or chronic, severe or mild; or whether the overall goal of treatment is facilitation or reorganization, the use of *intensive drill* can be profitable. The word *intensive* means that the patient and clinician meet each day if possible, especially during the acute stage. Unfortunately in these cost-conscious days, clinicians in private hospitals cannot afford to deliver such intensive treatment. Thus daily sessions, and especially less frequent sessions, must be supplemented with *homework*. The patient's success depends on specially trained family and home programs that are carefully created and monitored.

Drill means the systematic practice of an orderly set of tasks. In spite of its unfortunate connotations, it does not have to be either mindless or bloodless. It means working at high levels of success and at a pace suited to the patient's health and ability to respond. Hale and hearty patients are met with a vigorous and varied set of activities to move them to whatever level of volitional-purposive communication their battered nervous systems will support. If a patient is reluctant, ill, or depressed, he or she does not drill, but rests and listens. Drill should evoke images of order rather than of repetition.

The philosophy of this chapter is that the clinician helps patients to regain whatever volitional-purposive communication their nervous systems will support. When speech is possible, the primary focus of apraxia therapy is articulation and prosody, but all parts of the speech-language system are treated from the beginning of therapy. The type of therapy chosen for the apraxic patient will be primarily prophylactic and facilitating in the acute stage and prophylactic, facilitating, and reorganizing in the chronic stage. Reorganization can be intrasystemic, intersystemic, or both. Intensive drill is crucial in both the acute and the chronic stages and is especially important in reorganization.

Assessment of Apraxia of Speech

Prophylaxis, facilitation, and reorganization are planned in the traditional way—with assessment. While the exact goals of assessment differ with each clinician's purposes, five goals can be described: (1) determine the symptoms, (2) fix the label, (3) establish the severity, (4) establish the prognosis, and (5) focus the treatment. All these goals are not equally important for each patient. For example, establishing severity may be unimportant in one instance, and circumstances may conspire to obviate focusing the therapy in another. These goals are offered to delimit a potential diagnostic territory. How much of that territory is occupied by a given patient and clinician cannot be predicted.

Determining the Symptoms

Because apraxia of speech most often coexists with aphasia, dysarthria, or both, and because the whole speech-language system is treated, complete diagnostic testing must include measures of the entire speech-language system. LaPointe (Chap. 4) described aphasia testing, and Rosenbek and LaPointe (Chap. 2) have described an approach to evaluation of dysarthria. Those discussions will not be repeated here. Rather, this section focuses on specific methods of testing the apraxic patient.

The raw materials for determining the symptoms of apraxia are automatic, imitative, and spontaneous utterances of varying complexity. Traditional aphasia tests, such as the Boston Diagnostic Aphasia Test [54], the Minnesota Test for Differential Diagnosis of Aphasia [112], and the PICA [103], and specific batteries such as that by Dabul [32] provide most of these raw materials. Wertz, Rosenbek, and Collins [140] have even demonstrated that portions of one such test, the PICA, are as sensitive to the presence of apraxia of speech as is a specially designed test for the disorder. Standard language tests reveal symptoms in all modes: reading, writing, listening, gesturing, and speaking.

Specially selected stimuli can supplement the data on articulation and prosody. Some possible tasks are given in Table 7-1. These tasks were designed as a result of what the early experimental [64, 116] and clinical literature [31, 35, 48] revealed about the phonetic variables that influence articulatory and prosodic errors in apraxia of speech. Sources of the specific stimuli are Schuell, Jenkins, and Jiménez-Pabón [113], Johns and Darley [63], Wertz and Rosenbek [139], and Darley, Aronson, and Brown [36]. The serial, imitative, reading, and spontaneous tasks listed in Table 7-1 are just a beginning to total diagnosis in apraxia. Actually, such a battery is adequate to do little more than fix a label, although it contains sufficient variety so a busy clinician with a need to treat something immediately could do so after listening to the patient perform the tasks.

The battery can be supplemented with the McDonald Deep Test [90], the Templin-Darley Sentence Articulation Test [124], or any other articulation test, so as to have more data on a hierarchy of difficult speech sounds and selected clusters. If these tests do not yield that hierarchy, specially created stimuli can complete the picture. A sound-by-position test, administered as a word or sentence test, is given in abbreviated form in Table 7-2, which allows comparison of the relative integrity

Table 7-1. Selected tasks for diagnosing speech apraxia

Repetition of /pʌ/, /tʌ/, /kʌ/, and /pʌtʌkʌ/
Imitation of polysyllabic words
Imitation of monosyllabic words
Imitation of sentences
Reading
Spontaneous speech

Table 7-2. Selected stimuli for determining articulatory ability on stop-consonants in initial, medial, and final positions

pæt	*tæp*	*ʌpæt*
pad	*dap*	*ʌpad*
pɪk	*kɪp*	*ʌpɪk*
bæt	*tæb*	*ʌbæt*
bɛd	*dɛb*	*ʌbɛd*
bɪf	*fɪb*	*ʌbɪf*
tⁱn	*nɪt*	*ʌtⁱn*
tʌb	*bʌt*	*ʌtʌb*
teⁱm	*meⁱt*	*ʌteⁱm*
dip	*pid*	*ʌdip*
dɛn	*nɛd*	*ʌdɛn*
dak	*kad*	*ʌdak*
kʌm	*mʌk*	*ʌkʌm*
koᵘt	*toᵘk*	*ʌkoᵘt*
kan	*nak*	*ʌkan*
guf	*fug*	*ʌguf*
gʌt	*tʌg*	*ʌgʌt*
gat	*tag*	*ʌgat*

of the six English plosives in initial, medial, and final positions. The patient produces the consonant-vowel-consonant (CVC) and vowel-consonant-vowel-consonant (VCVC) syllables by imitating the clinician. Some of the combinations are meaningful and some are meaningless. The patient's responses can be transcribed immediately or tape-recorded for later analysis.

Because of the prosodic deficits in apraxia [7, 66], a clinician can also look more or less systematically at the apraxic patient's ability to control loudness, pitch, articulation time, pause time, stress, and the effect that variation in these has on articulation. Appropriate stimuli are contrastive stress materials; these are described extensively in Chapter 2.

Oral, nonverbal movements can be measured with any number of adequately described tests [39, 78]. The most complete battery would appear to be that described by Moore, Rosenbek, and LaPointe [96]. This test employs picturable oral responses, such as puckering, and it samples the patient's ability to perform these gestures under four stimulus conditions. Moore's multidimensional scoring system, which depends extensively on that of Poeck and Kerschensteiner [102], captures a significant amount of apraxic performance and eventually may find itself in common clinical practice. Such data have prognostic [2, 129] and therapeutic [84, 113, 131] significance.

Instrumental measures are increasingly common. Spectrographic analysis has been used to measure sound durations, including voice onset time [16, 28, 40, 42, 46, 60, 70, 117] and other features such as the intonational and loudness contours of connected speech [70]. Fiberscopic observation of the palate [58, 61]; x-ray microbeam evaluation of the lower lip, tongue, and velum [58, 59]; and electromyographic (EMG) and movement data from a variety of articulators [47] have also begun appearing. One conclusion from these studies is that apraxic speech contains a high proportion of sound distortions in addition to the previously recognized sound substitutions. Another conclusion is that apraxic talkers are slow, depending on their severity and on the stimuli they are asked to produce. Instrumental studies, therefore, have expanded and refined the traditional descriptions of apraxic speech. Subsequent research should combine several kinds of analyses so that another generation of speech clinicians will profit from an even more complete profile of the apraxic talker and from an enriched set of hypotheses about why apraxic talkers make the errors they do.

Once the language, articulation, prosody, and nonverbal symptoms have been determined, the clinician has the raw material for satisfying the other diagnostic obligations.

Fixing the Label

Apraxia of speech can be differentiated from confusion, general intellectual deficit, psychiatric distress, aphasia, and dysarthria. The symptoms of these distinct diagnoses have been discussed by Wertz (Chap. 1) and, for the most part, are not repeated here. The clinician's purpose is to select formal and informal tests that will reveal the pattern of the patient's errors. The patient's pattern is then compared to ideal patterns associated with each of the labels, and the diagnostic label, or labels, of best fit is selected.

If one wants to improve the fit, one can draw on the history; physical and neurologic examinations; and special tests, including acoustic and physiologic. If the history reveals a steady decline of long duration in memory and social grace, but no acute illness, general intellectual deficit is suspected. If the history and physical examination show acute onset of difficulty in understanding directions and in naming, reading, and writing, aphasia is suspected. Also, the brain scan may reveal a left frontoparietal lobe tumor. If a speech problem is present, it may well be apraxia.

As long as apraxia is regarded primarily as an articulatory disorder, with prosodic disturbances being nothing more than reflections of the patient's attempt to cope with articulation problems, the diagnostic function, including labeling, will rely exclusively on segment error data. Such a reliance is revealed in numerous studies differentiating apraxia of speech from aphasia [20, 22, 45, 81] and from dysarthria [63]. An expanded definition, including prosodic disturbance among the primary symptoms, urges study of prosodic abnormalities for their differential diagnostic significance. After completing a traditional comparison of articulatory patterns in Broca's and Wernicke's aphasics, Blumstein [14, 15] concluded that the patients did not differ in their patterns of articulation errors; however, prosodic disturbance did differentiate the groups. Other authors [8, 71] have reported similar conclusions for so-called nonfluent and fluent aphasic subjects. However, Blumstein [15] referred only to the "dysarthric" quality of prosody in Broca's aphasia, which does little for the struggle to maintain distinctions between aphasia, apraxia, and dysarthria. Unfortunately as well, there are no guarantees that apraxic patients constitute more than a portion of the groups labeled *Broca's* and *nonfluents* in these studies. As a hypothesis for subsequent testing, an apraxic dysprosody profile can be posited including abnormal articulation and pause time; inappropriate stress; and effortful, groping, trial-and-error attempts at normal articulation [70]. A nascent literature on the prosodic profiles of all neurologically based speech-language disorders, including apraxia, aphasia, and dysarthria, deserves considerable nurturing by speech pathologists, speech scientists, and linguists.

Generally, it is simple to differentiate between apraxia of speech and dysarthria. Specifically, however, two problem groups need to be recognized, although only briefly, so as not to divert this chapter too far from its primarily therapeutic emphasis. The first group consists of patients with apraxia of speech and what might appear to be a spastic dysarthria. If a persisting spastic dysarthria results only from bilateral upper motor neuron damage, then a frequently encountered group of apraxic patients with what seems to be a persisting dysarthria must have bilateral damage. Otherwise, it may be that subgroups of apraxic patients exist and that one group includes those patients with unilateral damage but with a very high proportion of persisting sound distortions in addition to their apraxic substitutions, omissions, and additions. The reality and significance, if any, of such a group can be determined profitably. Their locus of lesion, prognosis, and treatment may differ from that of more traditionally apraxic talkers like the ones originally described by Johns and Darley [63]. The second problem arises in trying to differentiate apraxia from ataxia, especially if such differentiation must be based primarily or exclusively on speech symptoms. Both groups may have irregular articulatory breakdowns; and both groups may exhibit prolonged sounds and talk with overall slowed articulation time. A tendency for apraxic patients to make more metathetic errors and to attempt more self-corrections may differentiate them from their ataxic counterparts.

Because labels are anathema to some clinicians for reasons that are unfathomable to others, this section ends in defense of labeling. Different disorders are treated with different methods. If a description of the disorder were enough to determine the treatment, labeling would be unnecessary. However, description is inadequate—in part because some disorders have very similar symptoms but can result from very different causes. For example, the speech mechanism has only a limited number of ways in which it can function, and very different conditions, such as apraxia, dysarthria, and aphasia, can result in some common symptoms. Thus if the clinician treats descriptions, he or she might conceivably treat a dysarthric and an apraxic similarly with uncomfortable and disappointing results. The fact that labels are sometimes wrong reflects on the labeler, not the system. Also, it is predictable that a patient may seem to require many labels or that the clinician cannot be confident in excluding all but one. Patients often have more than one disorder, and even if they do not, much research must be done in speech pathology before we can confidently reduce the number of labels for a given patient to one, even if only one label applies. Thus the object is to exclude as many labels as possible and assign relative probabilities to the remaining ones [114]. Treatment begins, or at least proceeds more confidently and effectively, once this has been done.

Establishing the Severity

The majority of aphasia tests yield measures of the severity of the overall communication deficit, but none is specifically designed to determine the severity of apraxia. Apparently the majority of aphasiologists have not been too concerned about measuring the severity of their apraxic patients'

conditions, although one suspects that most clinicians could and do make judgments of severity each day. The questions are How? and How reliably?

As part of a study to predict recovery from apraxia of speech [104], six clinicians were trained in the use of an eight-point equal-appearing interval scale of severity, where 1 represented mild, and 8, severe apraxia. Interjudge reliability was on the order of 0.93 after 6 hours of training, although disagreement occurred for apraxic patients with moderate to severe aphasia. This research demonstrates that persons can agree on judgments of severity if they are trained. However, whether they would agree as well if they were untrained was not studied. It also suggests that an equal-appearing interval scale may be useful as a diagnostic tool.

In an independent study, Rosenbek and Merson [109] determined that judged severity of apraxia of speech was significantly correlated with the total number of articulatory errors and that the most stable judgments of severity occurred with polysyllabic words. Severity might then be based clinically on the number of errors a patient makes on some battery that contains a high proportion of polysyllabic words.

Of all the diagnostic obligations, determining severity is often the least useful, and it may often be made more or less perfunctorily, if at all. Perhaps the major reason for measuring severity is for its potential post hoc contributions to treatment. Speech pathologists may discover that patients with severe apraxia, like those with severe aphasia, make little recovery.

Establishing the Prognosis

Prognostic statements about apraxic patients, whether based on data or clinical intuition, are meaningful only if one specifies "for what." The prognosis for *functional communication* after the period of physiologic recovery and without treatment is very poor. It is fair with intensive therapy, unless the patient is only moderately or mildly disabled, in which case the prognosis is good. However, the prognosis for *return to normal* or even near normal competence after the period of physiologic recovery, with or without therapy, unless the patient is mildly disabled, is poor.

Overall, with therapy the apraxic patient's prognosis is probably better than that of patients with aphasia [85], although there is disagreement on this point [50, 53]. In addition to diagnosis and whether or not the patient has been treated, there are other prognostic signs. Of potential prognostic interest in apraxia are *oral, nonverbal ability; duration of involvement; presence of associated deficits; and failure to learn and generalize.*

The presence of an oral, nonverbal apraxia may well be of prognostic significance. Butfield [21] blames a poor prognosis for recovery of oral communication on severe "mouth apraxia," and he is probably correct. The same principle applies to psychomotor (praxic) functioning and speech as well as to lower levels of motor function and speech. Adequate speech is scarcely possible when bulbar or pseudobulbar deficits invade chewing and swallowing abilities; also, we can predict severe limitations of volitional, oral communication if apraxia invades the primary oral function even on requested tasks. Luria [84], for example, observes that "perseveration on the basic levels is most important for the restoration of articulatory movements in severe disturbances of expressive speech" (p. 389).

Duration of oral, nonverbal apraxia or apraxia of speech is also prognostic. Vignolo [129], for example, considers that anarthria, including oral apraxia that is present after 2 months, is a poor prognostic sign. To this might be added the opinion that initial severity of oral apraxia or apraxia of speech is far less important than the speed with which each resolves. Rapid (within the first few days) resolution is good, no matter how long apraxia has lasted or how severe it is. Slow resolution, unless the patient's strength is sapped by illness, is bad.

Brain-damaged patients seldom have just one deficit: apraxia of speech is often accompanied by aphasia, dysarthria, or both. Because a cerebrovascular accident is more frequent among older persons than young ones, associated medical problems, such as diabetes and dementia, may complicate recovery in many stroke patients. In general, the more extensive the symptoms, the poorer the prognosis. Especially inhibiting are poor health for whatever reason, dementia, and receptive aphasia. The apraxic patient's greatest asset is the ability to monitor and self-correct. Illness dulls the willingness, and dementia and aphasia destroy the ability.

Data on behavioral bases for prognosis are unavailable. That these data are not available is a regrettable oversight, for behavioral data on how patients respond to therapeutic manipulations are among the most sensitive of prognostic signs. With the premature glint that so often streams from the clinician-researcher's eye, we would posit two hypotheses about prognosis for functional recovery with therapy. Poor prognosis is indicated by inconsistent day-to-day performance, or what we have called the *sawtooth profile.* Poor prognosis is signaled also by a patient's failure to generalize from treated to nontreated material. For example, if therapy with /s/ does not generalize to environments with /s/ that have not been treated and even to /z/, the prognosis is poor.

The best data for judging whether a patient can learn are those from systematic treatment within the restraints of the single-case design [92], and speech pathologists must collect these data.

Focusing the Treatment

To focus the therapy, one needs to *discover* the *stimulus length* the patient is *capable of producing imitatively and spontaneously.* If recurring utterances and a patient's occasional, reflexive response are disregarded, one discovers that severely disabled patients may have difficulty even with sounds and syllables. Patients with milder disabilities will produce phrase- and sentence-length responses, although they may have difficulty with certain sounds and clusters, and the rate of the utterance may influence how competently they can perform it. An occasional patient with severe apraxia will be able to produce word and phrase utterances if the stimuli, methods, and facilitators are carefully chosen. For severely disabled patients, an imitative test of consonants in the initial position of consonant-vowel (CV) syllables, in the medial position of VCV syllables, in the final position of VC syllables, and in isolation and of all vowels and diphthongs in isolation may yield a useful hierarchy of difficulty. Sounds the patient cannot produce in isolation or in syllables may be present in words. Thus if one can discover such words, the beginnings of a phonetic derivation therapy are established. If syllables and words are intact, sentence-articulation tests, such as the Templin-Darley Tests of Articulation [124] and the McDonald Deep Test [90], reveal the patient's competence with longer units Usually patients have a variable pattern, breaking down on longer utterances in some instances and shorter ones in others.

Articulatory proficiency can be *compared* for *imitation* and *reading* since both are useful therapeutically. For example, a group of 10 words and 10 sentences can be administered both ways and the results can be compared. It often happens that certain stimuli are imitated better than they are read, others are read better than imitated, and some show no effect of stimulus condition. Written stimuli that are competently produced can be used in facilitation, reorganization, and homework; and stimuli that are equally facilitated by both imitation and reading are useful both inside and outside the clinic.

A trial period with *rhythmic stimulation* may pay dividends. Keith [67], for example, discovered serendipitously that one of his apraxic patients could sing, and subsequently he published a report of that therapy [68]. Any number of clinicians can recount similar fortuitous conditions. If rhythmic stimulation, such as is described for MIT [121], is included as part of focusing the therapy, time can be saved and suitable patients will not be missed. The selection process is also aided by the criteria that Helm [57] uses to predict a patient's success with MIT. The Boston group [121] warns that the effectiveness of MIT may not be reliably established without a long period of treatment. Nonetheless, a diagnostic session of MIT can be considered as part of focusing therapy. At the Madison Veterans Administration Hospital, we test repetition with exaggerated but normal stress, with MIT-type rhythms, and with equal and even stress.

Finally, clinicians may find it useful to determine each patient's facility with a *communication board* and with a *system of gestures*. Both can be used as alternative modes of communication and in reorganization. The patient's ability to use a communication board can be determined in traditional ways and need not be discussed here. On the other hand, in light of an inchoate and developing interest in gesture for apraxic patients, a description of diagnostic procedures may be warranted.

The first step requires the patient to produce spontaneous gestures in response to 20 questions, such as "How would you show me you are hungry and want something to eat?" Many patients have trouble with the role-playing attitude required, so special instructions and explanations may be necessary. The next step is to find out how long it takes the patient to acquire volitional-purposive control of five common gestures, such as *eat* and *drink*. Although the teaching method is not standardized, it involves demonstration, imitation, and the fading of cues; and each response is recorded, if possible, so the shape of the patient's learning curve can be graphed. Finally, the patient's ability to accompany gestures with speech is determined.

These data are useful in planning the type of reorganization that can be undertaken.

A Context For Treatment of Apraxia of Speech

Treatment of apraxia is no more limited to clinician stimulation and patient response than swimming is to holding one's breath. This section describes a complex admixture of environment, decisions, procedures, and attitudes that influence what happens between a clinician and his or her patient. These factors constitute the *context for treatment.*

Team Therapy

The speech pathologist, physical therapist, occupational therapist, social worker, vocational counselor, and physician may be involved as a team in the patient's management. Team size and membership will vary, depending on the setting: hospital, rehabilitation center, university clinic, nursing home, or private home. The presence of a team will influence, among other things, when the patient is seen for speech treatment and for how long. Ideally, these issues are decided by the group in response to the patient and are not arbitrarily imposed by one or a few team members. On the other hand, the speech pathologist, depending primarily on environment and training, is free to decide independently whether he or she will see the patient and what specific goals and methods will be employed. Often, team professionals will include other activities that expand and reinforce the activities of other team members, which is as it should be.

Setting

Patients with acute apraxia usually are treated in the hospital; but patients with chronic apraxia may be seen in hospitals, rehabilitation centers, university clinics, nursing homes, private offices, or even at the patients' homes. Predicting what the setting will mean for treatment is well-nigh impossible, but it will influence it. University clinics can often afford to see chronic patients for protracted periods if prolonged therapy is justified. Hospitals, rehabilitation centers, and nursing homes may allow for more intensive treatment, but of shorter duration. The home may allow for naturally occurring practice in functional communication that is harder to achieve in other settings.

Characteristics of the Patient

MEDICAL DIAGNOSIS. The medical diagnosis is as important to the treatment of apraxia as it is to that of the dysarthrias. The cause of a patient's disorder will influence whether or not he or she is treated and what the expectations will be. For example, the implications for treatment of an inoperable tumor are obviously quite different from those for cerebrovascular accident. Generally, if speech pathology has any role at all in the first instance, it is supportive. The speech pathologist can function as prophylactic, facilitator, and reorganizer in the second. Also, each patient has an important *medical history*. Speech pathologists apparently have not been very concerned about the implications of history for their own treatment decisions, as witnessed by the slighting of this topic in general discussions of treatment. However, this may be an unfortunate oversight. For example, hypertension and diabetes in one stroke patient make him or her different from another stroke patient without these additional problems. It may be that many differences in speech symptoms reflect differences in the patients' histories. In general, the "cleaner" the patient's medical history, the better the prognosis. In addition, an apraxic patient, like a dysarthric one, is a better treatment candidate if any *medical management* has been successful. Among the poorest candidates for speech treatments are persons with untreatable diseases or those with unsuccessfully treated diseases.

It is true that each patient is more than an apraxic. The medical *more than* exerts a powerful influence on face-to-face treatment.

SPEECH DIAGNOSIS. Apraxic patients seldom have a pure disorder. Therefore it must be determined whether treatment is to be directed at the apraxia partially, primarily, exclusively, or not at all. If one agrees with the philosophy of management outlined previously, then the decision is not whether to treat or ignore associated language deficits, but only how much to treat them. A general rule might be that the apraxia should receive one of the primary thrusts of treatment if it is the most *pernicious* influence on the patient's communication. Another primary thrust can be reserved for abilities useful to reorganization. Other abilities can receive relatively less emphasis but cannot be ignored comfortably.

PROGNOSIS. The clinician must decide if the patient is a treatment candidate. Some patients, because of the severity of their conditions, duration of apraxia, living conditions, and associated medical and psychological problems, cannot be treated profitably. Some of these patients can be assigned to periodic follow-up. Others must be dismissed with no follow-up. Two groups of poor treatment candidates, in addition to those identified in the section on medical diagnosis, are those with general intellectual deficit and those who, for whatever reason, reject the goals and procedures necessary to treatment. For the demented patient, the speech pathologist has very little to offer. Experience suggests that prevention, facilitation, and reorganization require intellect and the ability to focus on a task; and speech treatment cannot somehow skirt or cope with dementia. If a patient's intelligence is preserved but he or she rejects the speech pathologist's goals and procedures, treatment is also impossible. Such a patient needs counseling and education. If the patient still refuses, as is his or her right, then all therapy must be stopped.

A final group of patients, those making minimal gains, creates somewhat different problems for the clinician. It is dangerously facile to conclude that these patients should be dropped from the rolls and reevaluated at intervals; neither, probably, should they be kept hanging on, perennially pursuing better speech. It is unconscionable for a clinician to collude with patients who continue to think that good speech awaits them next spring or next year. On the other hand, the clinician must listen to patients' requests. Common sense and individual circumstances may solve the problems created quite inadvertently and unmaliciously by such patients. Many finally leave therapy, much to their credit. Others are content to come in infrequently and to complete homework in between. University clinics serve some who want more therapy and who can cope emotionally with the prospect of little or no improvement.

It should be remembered that, however humane and inexpensive, treatment can become part of the patient's residual symptoms. Going to therapy can become something the patient does, just as groping through consonant clusters is. Before this happens the clinician can make every effort to help the patient and his or her family build the best possible life using the patient's residual abilities. This life need not include speech treatment, even though the patient has a speech defect.

Testing
Part of treatment is systematic evaluation: Patient change needs to be measured. A convenient tool

for recording and storing progress data is LaPointe's Base-10 record [75], which allows the clinician to record baseline and progress scores for 10 items during 10 sessions. Progress toward volitional-purposive control of selected utterances, whether they are sounds, syllables, words, phrases, or something else, can be measured to document the patient's learning and generalization.

If a patient is progressing, the clinician can be reasonably sanguine about methods and can advise the patient and the family that they can continue to hope. If generalization occurs, the clinician, patient, and family can even rejoice. However, failure to learn confirms the need for a reevaluation of procedures and, ultimately, the discontinuation of therapy. Failure to generalize dictates the same conclusion.

Group Therapy

A few discussions of group therapy for apraxic patients have been published [30], but problems of control seem to have precluded any popular experimental studies. Until these appear, practicing clinicians can only recount personal experience and hope that, unwittingly or purposefully, they generate testable hypotheses about what groups accomplish at various stages of treatment. They also can and will continue treating patients in groups. This too is as it should be. If clinicians did only those things of documented efficacy, most of them would be idle.

Apraxic patients, like other handicapped persons, may develop emotional problems as they try to adjust to an altered, restricted life. These and other more mundane problems of recreation, travel, and the like can sometimes be discussed and solved by a group of patients with similar problems, by groups of patients and spouses, or by groups of spouses only. Such problem-solving serves the goal of prophylaxis. Facilitation and reorganization also can be realized within group therapy. For example, patients may be more willing both to talk and to practice in a group. If the groups are organized with patient diagnosis, severity, prognosis, and goals in mind, they can be successful. However, if they are organized for other reasons, such as to meet budgeting requirements, or in ignorance of diagnosis and patient need, they may fail. No matter how carefully patients are chosen, the final ingredient for group success is an experienced clinician who has knowledge of both apraxia and group dynamics.

Homework

The inexperienced clinician is constantly in danger of forgetting homework or of using it perfunctorily. Fortunately, the apraxic patient survives both, but is so admirably suited to homework programs that clinicians can invest as much time in planning them as they do in planning individual sessions. The clinician and patient together cannot possibly practice as much as the patient if he or she is healthy and happy, wants and needs to. Reading, writing, listening, and speaking activities aided by trained family members, a tape recorder, or some other instrument allow the patient to practice as much as he or she will. If the stimuli are carefully arranged, the individuals are carefully selected, the auditor is well trained, and the results are carefully judged, improvement should be forthcoming.

Prophylaxis

Prophylaxis, or the prevention of attitudes and behaviors that threaten face-to-face treatment and patient progress, was earlier identified as a major therapeutic goal. Preventing negative forces in patients with acute apraxia and undoing them in patients with chronic apraxia is best accomplished by restitution of speech competence. Facilitation and reorganization, the other major goals of treatment, therefore serve a prophylactic function. Face-to-face treatment alone, however, is inadequate to the task. The necessary additional ingredient is counseling. Prophylaxis in the form of counseling is only a portion of treatment; in many ways it is the crucial portion. Lucky indeed is the clinician who helps a patient, whether the apraxia is acute or chronic, change permanently by using only facilitation and reorganization.

FAMILY COUNSELING. Families of hospitalized patients may be confused and apprehensive. Changing these negative emotions to positive ones requires a combined effort of the hospital staff. The speech pathologist is the most qualified to inform the family about the communication deficit, the understanding of which may contribute to alleviating negative emotions.

The first step is a meeting with the family, at which time they can be provided with one of several books written for the aphasic's family. They can also receive a summary of any testing; a tentative prognosis; a discussion of what forms therapy can take; an outline of their options, e.g., whether there should be long-term therapy, short-term therapy, or no therapy; and a list of specific suggestions for helping. In the early stages this last item does not mean arming them with methods, and it may never mean so instructing them unless the clinician feels the family can support a patient-spouse–clinician-spouse relationship. This first session is then followed by any number of subsequent sessions to answer questions, give direction, and so on. Much of this is traditional and uncontroversial.

If an apraxic patient is to be prevented from deferring to family or from becoming isolated, he or she must exist in a particular environment—one that only families can create. Coming to understand what the patient has and what can be done about it will help the family create that environment. However, more specific knowledge is mandatory. The family must learn that one crucial element is *patience*. The apraxic patient is non-fluent; syllables come effortfully, but most often they come; errors need to be corrected, and apraxic talkers try to correct them; and the articulators grope tentatively for the proper place of articulation, and, ultimately, they find it. As long as the effortful groping is effective and not frustrating, the clinician encourages it by giving the patient time, which the patient comes to expect. The family must learn to provide the same amount of time, to let the patient know that in this crucial way home or hospital visits are like clinic visits. The result is that the patient is less likely to attempt hiding the apraxia or to become resigned to it. Or, if the patient is a chronic apraxic, he or she may be willing to take a chance in such an atmosphere.

Part of a family's ability to learn patience comes with recognizing when a patient's attempt is, or promises to be, successful and when it is not. This requires helping the family learn to recognize and value whatever level of intelligible, compensated speech the patient is capable of and also to anticipate frustration and failure. These abilities require, in turn, that a family observe therapy. Besides patience, such observation will provide them with another element of the environment, a *hierarchy of cues*, so they can intervene to foil frustration with subtler levels of cuing than merely telling the patient to stop and start again, to slow down, or to repeat an offending word or phrase after them. To this end, observing treatment and discussing cuing are important. The goal is to help families learn a hierarchy of cues and the principles of applying the most powerful, effective cue, which simultaneously preserves as much of the patient's independence as possible.

A frequent clinical observation is the patient who, when asked questions or in some other way required to respond, defers to his or her spouse. This kind of behavior poses a significant challenge. The clinician and family must learn which responses are in the patient's repertoire and which are not. The patient obviously must defer on the absent ones. Families must learn all these subtleties: when to wait, how to cue, and when to speak for the patient. They can do this if they are counseled and taught.

Wertz, LaPointe, and Rosenbek [137] have discussed counseling in depth. They highlight special challenges created by a patient's severity and duration of apraxia of speech.

PATIENT COUNSELING. A patient's behavior is immutable until he or she and the clinician have cooperated to accomplish a number of counseling objectives. Several questions struggle for supremacy in apraxic patients' minds as they begin therapy. "Will I ever be able to talk as I did?" is most frequently asked. If the patient is in the first month after a traumatic episode, the clinician must answer that the patient's return is difficult to predict. The clinician can follow this with reassurance that the first month is often a period of tremendous improvement. If the patient has more than a month's duration of apraxia, the outlook for normal speech is bleaker, depending of course on how far physiologic recovery has carried the patient during the first 30 days. When one is reasonably confident about a patient's potential, no matter how dark the clinician may predict that future to be, the patient and family must be told. Grief cannot be obviated. Seldom is anything of value gained by delaying its occurrence unnecessarily. It is as unconscionable to promise too much as it is to promise too little. When patients have a realistic expectation of their future and have been supported during their grief, they are often ready for work.

Patients entering therapy for the first time also want to know what will be expected of them and why. The clinician can answer these questions by explaining a philosophy of management and a set of methods consistent with that philosophy. He or she can help patients to see that apraxia therapy is hard work that will continue for a long time, and it will continue in some form to the end of the patients' days.

In addition to answering questions, clinicians have other counseling obligations that will, if met, prevent patients from developing maladaptive responses to apraxia in the acute stage or help to reduce such responses in the chronic stage. While many of these are common sense, they can be discussed profitably, if for no other reason than that they are so frequently assumed and therefore ignored.

An early counseling obligation is to prepare the patient for the differences between speech treatments and what presumably are more familiar medical ones. A patient may well expect to feel the effects of medical therapy after only 1 or 2 hours. After all, pain disappears shortly after an aspirin is swallowed, and swelling retreats under the influence of cold compresses. If the patient is not helped to understand that gains may come slowly, his or her motivation in the early stages, which would otherwise be high, may be low. Another related danger to therapeutic progress is letting the patient try out new productions on others after only a few sessions without telling him or her that they will not work as well outside the clinic as inside, and they may even be impossible outside the clinic for some time. Patients ignorant of these facts may lose faith in themselves and in their therapy.

Against this background, the clinician and patient must work out a progression of goals. Goals usually originate with the clinician and are given final shape and organization by the patient and clinician working together. Such a cooperative effort is important if the patient is going to accept the procedures and outcomes. It bears reiteration that behavior change cannot start until the patient and clinician are of a single mind about therapy, so efforts spent in careful planning are seldom wasted.

Before therapy begins, patients need to understand that day-to-day variations in their ability to respond are inevitable and manageable. The patient and clinician need to agree on goals and activities for "bad periods." Comparing the patient's variability with normal variability may help. For example, patients can be told that whether or not one has had a stroke, one gets up on the wrong side of the bed occasionally; and a world champion soccer team is unable to beat all its opponents every day. During low periods, patients need a good deal of support, but less so if they understand that low periods are natural and unavoidable. Drill need not be abandoned completely. In fact, if meaningful tasks can be accomplished, negative emotion may be reduced.

As therapy begins, counseling continues. The clinician highlights successes and mollifies patients about their failures. The reason for failure can be explained, and the failure itself can be reversed by an immediate change in the task. However, frustrations and failures cannot be allowed to accumulate; and successes must rise in trenchant superiority to failures. Counseling, facilitation, and reorganization can make this happen.

Throughout therapy, apraxic patients probably hear more about *time* than about almost anything else. The frustration of apraxia is impossible to exaggerate. Patients recognize their errors, and they read the listener's confusion. Like stutterers, apraxic patients seem to be competing with an internal, accelerated clock. They can be provided with an old-fashioned aphorism: Slow down, don't work so hard. Such advice, if unaccompanied by specific counseling, is useless, of course. But patients can be helped to see that fighting to get a particular utterance out is like flailing about in quicksand; it is unproductive and may make things worse. Instead they can (1) be alert to the appearance of trouble, (2) pause if the correct response is not forthcoming, (3) plan the response, and (4) restart. Such procedures will not be 100 percent successful, but they will almost always be superior to struggle. Patients can be reassured that the procedures will have to be relied on less and less in the course of therapy, and they will become progressively more effective on those occasions when they are necessary. Moreover, they need to know that the clinician and their families will wait.

Additionally, patients need to be taught how to recognize and manage potentially disastrous influences on their speech. They can be counseled about the effects of fatigue, depression, anger, and illness, and they can be advised not to practice when under the influence of any of these conditions. They can be counseled that practice is reserved for early morning, after naps, and at other times when fatigue is minimal. Practice sessions can be short for the same reason. It is important to help patients accept that certain conditions will be destructive and that when these conditions cannot be avoided, silence is a viable response.

As therapy reaches an end, counseling obligations shift. The patient should have been prepared from the start for independence and an end to therapy. If the patient has been, terminating therapy involves no very great threat and little or no negative emotion. Of course, termination is especially painless if the patient has made a nice recovery. The recovered patient has only to be reminded of the conditions that might influence speech and of the techniques that will help him or her through the bad times. The patient can be told that further improvement, however slight, is possible, but that a dip may occur immediately after leaving therapy. Finally, the patient needs to be reassured that return is possible if needed.

Improved but still abnormal patients are more difficult. If the clinician has been counseling them and sharing their goals, the realization that they will never again be normal should come as no great shock. A major obligation to these patients is to do what one can to guarantee that they feel good about the ability they have. Part of the job is helping the patients and their families create a life, perhaps narrowed in its limits, that is complete and allows them to fully exploit their residual levels of function. These patients also need to know they can return at least for counseling and that actually a gradual fading of therapy may be better than "cold turkey."

With severely disabled patients for whom no or very little progress is possible, the counseling obligation is much the same. Our duty is to tell them that no progress is possible, that they will never talk again, that the years will not somehow magically cure them. We must then help place them in an environment in which others understand this, which exploits their other abilities and does not punish their deficits.

Counseling is reinforced by simultaneous treatment. When patients slow down or stop talking and begin planning, they must be able to evoke internal cues. The difference between "stop and think," and "stop and think about your tongue" is significant. Thus prophylaxis, facilitation, and reorganization reinforce one another.

This, then, is context, and the clinician ignores it only at great risk. Coping with its influences is difficult to teach and harder yet to write about instructively. Thus if this section merely alerts the reader, especially the neophyte, to occasionally look up from the stimuli, it will have been worthwhile.

An Outline For Treatment

Before any therapy session and within sessions in response to what a patient does, decisions are made that influence what happens between the clinician and the patient. An outline for treatment includes the broad classes of things about which clinicians decide. These are *stimuli, stimulus modes, response modes, temporal relations of stimulus and response, facilitators, reinforcements*, and *methods*. This section treats each of these factors in detail.

Stimuli

In many ways apraxia treatment soars or flutters depending on the clinician's ability to select and order the stimuli. Fortunately, most of the research on apraxia has implications for stimulus selection and arrangement, and this literature, when combined with observation of the individual patient, lifts and sustains most clinicians.

NONSPEECH MOVEMENTS. Nonspeech movements have a place in apraxia therapy despite concern that certain kinds of nonverbal movements are under a different pattern of neuromotor control than are speech movements. Schuell, Jenkins, and Jiménez-Pabón [113] begin treatment with nonverbal movements, such as tongue protrusion, if the apraxic patient cannot imitate sounds and syllables. These authors urge abandoning nonspeech activities when the "patient can initiate phonation and move the tongue voluntarily" (p. 351). Luria [84] begins with nonverbal, or what he calls the "practical movements of the oral apparatus," and builds speech gestures from these basic gestures. For example, he describes an elaborate set of steps for producing /p/ from blowing.

If oral, nonverbal movements are to serve as stimuli, training in them should emphasize development of skill rather than of strength unless, of course, the patient has significant muscle weakness. Improved skill in their performance is essential if they are to be used for reorganization, and reorganization is the most compelling reason for working on them at all. Next, the movements should be components of speech gestures if they are to be used for reorganization. Legitimate ones include protruding the tongue, puckering the lips, blowing, and biting the lower lip, among many others. The exception to this rule might be the use of any oral movements (no matter how amorphous, but preferably coordinated and replicable) in the early days of therapy as a way of helping the patient get a variety of movements started. Finally, work with nonspeech stimuli should be reserved until direct attempts to help the patient relearn sounds by using speech stimuli have failed, and they should be modified and incorporated into speech sounds as soon as possible.

Patients with severe apraxia rather than those with mild or moderately severe apraxia often work intensively on nonverbal stimuli. In fact, the patient with severe apraxia without speech challenges the clinician's creativity in stimulus selection and ordering. Such a patient may need thousands of repetitions of mouth opening, tongue protrusion, puckering, smiling, and the like. This patient needs to get something going predictably and volitionally, and oral, nonverbal movements may be that something.

SPEECH SOUNDS: MANNER OF PRODUCTION. Within very narrow limits, the manner of production influences articulatory accuracy. LaPointe and Johns [77] report that consonants are more often ravaged by apraxia than are vowels. Lebrun, Buyssens, and Henneaux [80] noted as many vowel as consonant errors in one patient, and Dabul and Bollier [34] suggest that equal vowel and consonant difficulty is a frequent finding. Data on vowel errors are also available in Kent and Rosenbek [70]. LaPointe and Johns [77] report that affricatives and fricatives are significantly more difficult than glides, nasals, and plosives, which do not differ significantly from each other. Other studies generally report similar tendencies [63, 79, 116, 126].

These data then might be used to create the following hierarchy by manner from easiest to hardest:

EASIEST
Vowels
Plosives, nasals, laterals
Fricatives

HARDEST
Affricatives

Such a hierachy is as useful as were early maps of the lands of the Apache. Like those maps, the hierarchy keeps one from wandering aimlessly. However, it does not obviate the clinician's obligation to create a specific hierarchy for each patient. Consider the differences between an individual patient's hierarchy and the statistical one. The following hierarchy was created after two long sessions with a patient with severe apraxia. Easy sounds were those the patient could imitate; moderate sounds arrived after only a few minutes of therapy; hard ones resisted early therapy.

EASY
/i/, /a/, /oᵁ/, /m/, /l/, /w/, /r/, and /θ/

MODERATE
/u/, /ʌ/, /aI/, /f/, /ð/, /p/, /b/, /t/, and /s/

HARD
/ɪ/, /eI/, /æ/, /aᵁ/, /ɛ/, /d/, /k/, /g/, /z/, /v/, /tʃ/, and /dʒ/.

As can be seen, affricatives and fricatives were predictably difficult. Unexpectedly, certain vowels and plosives were also among the hard sounds.

SPEECH SOUNDS: PLACE OF PRODUCTION. The experimental data are reasonably consistent in reporting that sounds made forward in the mouth are more likely to be correct in apraxic speech than those made more posteriorly, although Larimore [79] posits that manner is a more important influence on articulatory accuracy than is place. LaPointe and Johns [77] report a significantly greater proportion of errors on palatal and dental sounds than on others.

The effects of place on accuracy do not suggest specific muscular involvement. Instead, the differences may be at least in part because of the greater visibility of the front sounds over the back sounds. In fact, it may be more useful therapeutically to think of visibility rather than place. Beginning with visible sounds and, most importantly, using that visibility to help the patient regain control of sounds is a frequent suggestion in therapy [36, 53, 97].

SPEECH SOUNDS: VOICING. Markedness theory predicts that apraxic patients will have more difficulty with voiced sounds than with voiceless ones [14]. The data are not in total agreement [77]. The frequency and type of voicing error may depend on phonetic environment, including function in the syllable. The tendency seems to be for individual patients to have greater difficulty with voiced sounds such as /b/ in word-final position, and greater difficulty with the voiceless sounds in the initial position.

SPEECH SOUNDS: SINGLETON OR CLUSTER. Clinical experience suggests that apraxic patients have an easier time with singletons than with clusters. Shankweiler and Harris [116], however, observe that affricatives and some clusters may be equally difficult and that the difficulty of an individual cluster, such as /st/, may not be the same for sounds in the initial and final positions of words. Individual patients produce unique hierarchies, and some clusters may appear easier than some singletons, especially if the cluster is slowed in its production. An ordering along the singleton-cluster dimension, then, would generally have singletons before clusters, but with adjustments to fit individual abilities.

SPEECH SOUNDS: FREQUENCY OF OCCURRENCE. Blumstein [14, 15] says frequency of occurrence is a major influence on speech sound adequacy in patients with apraxia of speech. As the frequency of sounds produced in her experimental group of patients' own speech increased, errors decreased. Trost and Canter [126] report the same relations, but they did not analyze their patients' spontaneous productions, and instead relied upon normative data from nonapraxic talkers. They believe that frequency is a better predictor of the locus of apraxic errors than are manner and place of sound production. A relation between errors and frequency is confirmed by clinical practice. Most clinicians eschew working on infrequently occurring sounds until late in therapy. They prefer to make the immediate change in intelligibility that comes with correcting high-frequency sounds. The literature and experience lead us to believe that manipulating these high-frequency sounds also allows the patient to work at high levels of success.

SPEECH SOUNDS: POSITION IN UTTERANCE. There is an argument about whether apraxic patients tend to make more errors in sounds that are in the initial or final position of words. LaPointe and Johns [77] and Johns and LaPointe [64] report no differences in errors by position. However, Darley, Aronson, and Brown [36] reference data supporting the putative difference. Burns [20] contrasted a group of aphasic patients with the apraxic patients of Trost and Canter [126] and concluded that a significant difference between the two groups was the locus of errors, with aphasic patients tending to make more final-position errors, and apraxic patients, more initial-position errors. The issue remains unresolved for groups but should be resolved for individual patients in treatment. A sound-by-position test, such as that described in the section on diagnosis, can determine where to begin. Therapy should probably be initiated with sounds in positions in which the patient has a high probability for success.

WORDS AND PHRASES: MEANINGFULNESS. Generally, authors [36, 84] advocate beginning with sounds in isolation or in syllables and then moving to meaningfulness as quickly as possible so the patient is making sense as well as sounds. A minority [33, 34] advocate avoiding meaningfulness until the patient's movement sequences in syllables are stable. Their rationale is that the patient is free to concentrate on movement patterns if the stimuli are meaningless. However, one might argue that because meaningfulness helps the patient to elicit the correct response, it can be exploited profitably in the stimuli selected for therapy.

Depending on the severity of the patient's condition, work begins with sounds and syllables if patients fail to use them correctly in words. Occasionally also, unstable target sounds may be practiced in isolation or in syllables for short periods even if they appear in some longer utterances. Such practice seems to increase the sounds' stability. A mistake to avoid is assuming that patients with severe conditions will need to work with sounds and syllables. Often these patients will produce longer, meaningful utterances better than shorter, meaningless ones. If work has had to begin with sounds in isolation or in syllables, however, meaningfulness can be introduced as rapidly as possible, and the patient can be made aware of that meaning. Patients are just as willing to concentrate on movement and position if they are helped to realize that sounds, such as /pi/ and /mi/, mean different things as they are if they are told to utter meaningless units, say, /fa/ and /da/. Meaning seems to help, not hinder.

WORDS AND PHRASES: OTHER LINGUISTIC CHARACTERISTICS. A universal finding is that the length of an utterance influences speech sound adequacy in patients with apraxia of speech [36, 37, 63, 79]. The increase in difficulty with length is not linear, however [110]. Therefore, it is not clear whether it is necessary to fret over the length of stimuli used in treatment. Certainly the use of polysyllabic words early may discourage a patient. On the other hand, by manipulating other variables, such as articulation and pause time, a patient can be helped to produce longer, more useful stimuli than he or she might if special adjustments were not made. Additionally, variables other than length influence whether a word is difficult or easy for the patient. Deal and Darley [37] report that a word can be more or less troublesome for an apraxic patient, depending on its length, its position in the utterance (whether it appears early or late), the part of speech, and the difficulty of the word's initial phoneme. Word weight, or the number of these variables that characterize a word, can be used to predict the occurrence of apraxic patients' difficulties. For example, a four-syllable adjective beginning with /k/, such as cockamamie, appearing as the second word in an utterance, is more difficult for the apraxic patient than is a word that is less highly loaded. Also, it is clear that stimuli cannot be limited to short prepositions beginning with /a/ that are buried toward the end of an utterance. The importance of the research by Deal and Darley is that it alerts the clinician to stimuli that he or she may want to introduce later rather than sooner and that will require greater alacrity of the clinician if the patient is to avoid failure.

Finally, the apraxic patient is likely to have more difficulty with rare words than with common ones. It behooves us to remember, of course, that *puer* and *etui* may be common for some but not others, depending on their jobs or interests. Thus frequency can be considered profitably in work with apraxic patients.

WORDS AND PHRASES: STRESS. The influence of phonetic stress on apraxic patients' performance is as yet unclear. Larimore [79] reports that stress does not have a significant influence on articulatory accuracy. Rosenthal [110] reports a study that controlled the influences of stress to see the effect on apraxic patients' articulation. She found that apraxic patients performed better on stressed than on unstressed syllables. This finding prepares us to accept the clinical impression—reported by Darley, Aronson, and Brown [36]—that "errors occur more frequently when sentences are presented by clinician and imitated by the patient with few variations in stress . . ." (p. 284). The stress patterns of stimuli may have an influence on patients' responses and, certainly, the clinician should be sensitive to the possibility. However, much remains to be done in comparing the effects of normal stress, exaggerated normal stress, and equal and even stress. Stress will be reintroduced in the section on facilitators.

Stimulus Modes

The modes of stimulus presentation are *auditory*, *visual*, and *tactile*. Auditory presentation can be either live voice or recorded voice; visual presentation can be watching the clinician, watching oneself in a mirror or some other monitor, or reading; tactile input has not been studied. The good clinician winnows through all these possibilities and selects those that will help the individual patient with individual stimuli. There is a limited amount of literature to aid in the sorting.

Johns and Darley [63] report that production of single words by 10 apraxic patients was significantly better when the patients heard and watched the clinician than when they produced the words after hearing them on a tape recorder or if they read them. Trost and Canter [126] report that the imitation of single words containing no consonant

clusters was superior to spontaneous production of those same words. Also, words containing consonant clusters were not produced better when patients imitated the clinician. And to make matters worse for those persons wanting consistency, LaPointe and Horner [76] report that words of varying length presented in the auditory mode are articulated better than if they are presented through visual or combined auditory and visual modes. We can only conclude that all these researchers are probably correct. Patients and stimuli are sufficiently different to create differences in research findings.

Imitative therapies usually rely on combining auditory, visual, and even tactile modes in an integral stimulation approach [93]. These imitative programs systematically fade the auditory, visual, and tactile modes. Some patients may be "overloaded" by the multiple inputs of this type of therapy. This does not mean that imitation need be abandoned but rather that the number and combination of modes used in a program should be evaluated for each patient.

Some clinicians [33] advocate sole reliance on the visual mode in a program that is primarily directed toward intersystemic reorganization. However, such an approach is limited to only a portion of the highly visible sounds, as these authors admit. For example, watching a person produce /p/, /b/, or /m/ does not tell the naive subject whether the sound is /p/, /b/, or /m/. Hageman [55] has demonstrated that apraxic and normal subjects make idiosyncratic errors when asked to produce homorganic sounds with only visual cues from a clinician. In addition, his research demonstrated that some sounds, such as /l/ and /r/, are difficult to produce at a level higher than chance with only visual cues. The conclusion from even this brief description of the complications in a visual-only program is that stimuli will influence the selection of the best stimulus mode.

A discussion of stimulus modes would be incomplete without some discussion of the ubiquitous *mirror*. The mirror is highly touted as a therapy device with apraxic patients. Deal and Darley [37] report no significant therapeutic effect for single-word utterances using a mirror, however. As Darley, Aronson, and Brown [36] observed, "apparently, patients with apraxia of speech cannot use the information derived from visual monitoring, at least without specific instructions as to 'how' and 'why' this information should be used" (p. 265). The mirror is like the minor political figure who somehow manages to find a place at every head table. One cannot help but wonder how it was done. One cannot help but wonder about the mirror's success either. Its use at best is limited to very few stimuli, and it may be distressing for the apraxic patient to be confronted with the right-sided facial weakness. Whether or not the patient is disturbed by his or her visage, the image of the articulatory gestures is fleeting. Although we must keep the mirror around, its proper place is toward the back, close to the door leading to the kitchen.

The clinician should be versatile in the use of stimulus modes. The clinician prepares to use all three: auditory, visual, and tactile. Different stimuli at different times in the therapy will require different modes or combinations. It is important that the patient learn to use these modes and to store the data on correct articulation provided by them. Such learning and storing will benefit both facilitation and reorganization.

Response Modes

Apraxic patients have a number of response modes available to them, depending on the severity of their disorder, diagnosis, stage in therapy, and the philosophic bent of their clinician. They can *point*. They can *gesture elaborately* with some form of sign language or more *simply*, such as with a repetitive tapping. They can *write* all or part of a response. They can *speak*. Response modes can be combined, and some modes can be employed for some stimuli but not for others.

Because apraxia of speech is an articulatory-prosodic disorder, and because the management goal is restoration of as much volitional-purposive communication as the patient's physiologic support for speech allows, the traditional assumption has been that oral responses should be the first and most frequently practiced. An apraxic patient learns to speak by speaking, or so goes the argument. In this view, the other modes may substitute for oral responses only while speaking is impossible early in treatment or after intensive therapy has demonstrated that the patient will never speak again. Belief in the reorganization hypothesis requires that the other modes of communication be viewed not only as alternatives but as useful in reorganization as well.

The position that apraxic patients should respond orally, however, has seldom been seriously challenged except in those instances in which speaking is impossible. The result of research on the auditory processing of apraxic patients by Aten, Johns, and Darley [5] has been used [62] to support the contention that at least auditory discrimination need not be treated; and the status of apraxia as a motor speech disorder distinct from aphasia has led any number of authors [36, 108] to spurn the use of auditory processing therapies more appropriate to the aphasias. However, there are no hard data to support the legitimacy of these positions. A number of clinical hypotheses need to be tested. Perhaps it is true that apraxic patients are actually aided in their progress by a period of discrimination training, as were the children reported by Winitz and Preisler [143]. Also, apraxic patients may even be aided by a program requiring active problem solving, such as that involved in Natural Language Learning [144]. This program requires the patient to listen to speech and then to make choices about what has been heard by pointing to one of four pictures. The program is reported to have been successful in increasing the confrontation naming ability of one apparently aphasic patient [73]. It is noteworthy that this patient's speech was not treated directly during the period of the study. He only listened and pointed. If patients identified as having apraxia of speech respond to such a program, therapies emphasizing speaking will need to be reevaluated. Until the data are in, however, the traditional emphasis on speech will no doubt continue.

The treatments outlined in this chapter are traditional in that oral responses are emphasized; however, all response modes are treated both for their own sakes and because of their potential use as alternative response modes, facilitators, and reorganizers. Such a global approach should be seen as orienting rather than as dictating. One does what works until the literature and clinical experience divulge something that works better.

In fairness, even now, clinicians differ in their approaches, especially to the acutely speechless and apraxic patient. Some begin immediately to improve speech. Others delay work on speaking until a more auspicious time, preferring instead to help the patient reestablish some baseline of listening and gesturing skill, perhaps complemented by a communication board. Other clinicians begin simultaneous work on gesturing, speaking, and even writing. For speechless patients entering the chronic period, treatments may continue to differ. Gesturing and a communication board may be substituted outright for speech. Occasionally a patient with severe, chronic apraxia may be encouraged to write rather than speak. Some clinicians continue to treat the speech mechanism with unyielding regularity.

Again, in the absence of data, intuition and patient difference reign.

Finally, depending on whether a patient's apraxia is acute, chronic, mild, moderate, or severe, speech can be reorganized by pairing it with other response modes. Gesture and writing both can be incorporated into speech. As such, these response modes can serve as a source of self-generated cues to correct speech production. Methods for accomplishing such a reorganization will be discussed.

Temporal Relations

Clinician and patient can respond simultaneously, or the patient can delay his or her response for any interval, or the clinician can provide the stimulus and the patient produce it several times in succession. These three temporal relations have been labeled simply *simultaneous, delayed,* and *consecutive* [63]. They describe the major temporal relations of clinician stimulation and patient response manipulable in therapy.

The *simultaneous* condition with patient and clinician speaking together affords strong stimulus control. One can easily test the hypothesis that this temporal relation is more facilitating than the other two for any given patient and for any given stimulus. Ineluctably, some patients, on some stimuli and at some points in their therapies, will be impeded by simultaneity. These patients may find *delay* more to their liking.

Several pages would be required to discuss *delay* adequately. Deal and Darley [37] were among the first to test the effect of delay intervals on speech sound adequacy in patients with apraxia of speech. They report no significant differences in articulatory accuracy for 0-, 3-, and 6-second delay intervals. Wilson [141] studied the influence of no delay, 5-second delay, and 15-second delay on the ability of three severely apraxic-aphasic speakers to imitate words. Responses deteriorated as a function of delay. She used different patients and delay intervals from Deal and Darley. These differences may explain disparities between the two studies. Nonetheless, one can use his or her own patients to test the hypothesis that systematically increasing delay intervals provides for equally systematic progress toward volitional-purposive speech. If amount of delay has no effect, then its control is unnecessary. If it does have an effect, the clinician may want to include Wilson's [141] published hierarchy of temporal manipulation as part of the overall treatment approach.

Potentially as important as the length of the delay

interval is what the patient does during that interval. A patient's speaking may be influenced by whether he or she makes overt articulatory gestures or is silent during the delay intervals. Warren [130] discovered differences in individual apraxic patients' responses to silent and aloud rehearsal. Two of his five patients spoke equally well regardless of whether they rehearsed aloud or silently. Two did best with aloud rehearsal. One did best with silent rehearsal. Bugbee and Nichols [19] suggest that whether the clinician or the patient controls the amount of rehearsal may also have an influence on the apraxic person's speech sound adequacy. A clinician may want to determine, in controlled clinical experiments, if a patient should rehearse, how the patient should rehearse, and who should control the amount and type of rehearsal. It may be that controlled observations on rehearsal during delay will teach speech pathologists something of value about apraxia in general as well as something of specific therapeutic importance for individual patients.

In the *consecutive* condition, the patient hears the stimulus and then responds more than once without intervention by the clinician. The term and procedure are borrowed from Johns and Darley [63], who report a trend for apraxic patients to improve their performance if allowed to make three unobstructed attempts to produce a stimulus. Rosenbek et al. [108] used the consecutive condition as step 4 in an eight-step task continuum on the assumption that the consecutive condition was more difficult for apraxic patients than were simultaneity and brief delay. LaPointe and Horner [76] report no significant difference in response adequacy between a delay and a consecutive condition for a group of seven apraxic patients, although a "trend toward deterioration" was noted in the consecutive condition. Such dissimilarity in research and practice suggests that the entire issue of temporal relations is complex and that the sane clinician should let each patient's reponse indicate what is best. The present value of the consecutive condition is that it provides the good self-corrector a measure of independence from the clinician.

Facilitators

Overlap with other categories makes this one cumbersome. Because *facilitators* are being defined here as those things the clinician does to the production of the speech signal to help the patient, we have set aside a special section for them. A clinician does not merely repeat stimuli like a tape recorder, faithfully reproducing its message. Instead, he or she is constantly and systematically responding to the patient's response adequacy with changes in the loudness, pitch, articulation time, and pause time of his or her own speech; and the clinician may well be requesting similar changes of the patient. It is to *loudness, pitch, articulation time*, and *pause time* and their interaction in *stress* that the term facilitators refers.

Overall loudness can be increased, can be normal, or can be reduced even to a whisper. If a patient hears normally, normal loudness or only slightly increased loudness is usually most appropriate; however, a number of loudness manipulations also may be appropriate. Loudness may be increased on certain troublesome segments, whether or not these would be stressed normally. The dissimilarity of stimuli may be increased by making their loudness characteristics very different. For example, loudness may be decreased as one way of fading auditory cues.

Distinguishing syllables or individual words by distinctive pitch differences may be facilitating. For example, the phrase "I know it" could be produced with a low pitch on *I* and *it* and a somewhat higher pitch on *know*. Such changes are crucial in MIT [121, 122] and can be used by clinicians even though they are not committed to a total MIT approach. The distinctive pitch differences among stimuli can be gradually reduced in magnitude as the patient's articulation improves.

Rate change accomplished by altering articulation time and pause time, both independent of and related to stress, seems to be an especially potent facilitator. Articulation time, or the amount of time spent producing the sounds and segments, can be increased, normal, or decreased. Troublesome sounds and sound clusters may be easier for the patient if they are presented in the context of a reduced rate of articulation. Longer stimuli, including words and phrases, can be introduced earlier in therapy if articulation time is increased. Normal or near normal rate can be regained as the patient's articulatory accuracy improves. Decreased articulatory time is presently being studied with aphasic patients, and its possible facilitating effects should not be ignored in experimentation with apraxic patients as well.

Pauses can be normal in duration and location, longer or shorter in duration, and more or less frequent. Pause time, like articulation time, can exert an energetic influence on speech sound adequacy. In fact, the judicious use of pause length

and location may be one of the best facilitators, because it allows the clinician to use stimuli that might otherwise cause a patient to fail. Longer pauses preceding difficult sounds and words may make it possible for the patient to produce these correctly. Pause length and number can be manipulated independently, and both can approach normal as the patient's articulation improves. Like articulation time, pause time deserves study.

Perhaps the best facilitator is stress, and any research documenting its therapeutic use is promised a warm reception. Studies [17, 49] suggesting possible relations of stress and language function in Broca's aphasia have already begun to appear, as have studies of stress in apraxia of speech [125]. In therapy, the stress of stimuli can be normal, the normal profile can be preserved but exaggerated, or normal stress can be replaced by any approximation of equal and even stress. Rosenbek et al. [108] implied that the stress of stimuli should first be equal and even and then an exaggeration of the normal. Perhaps it is more productive to think of the three general stress types as options that might be exercised more or less simultaneously in any patient's therapy. Clinical experience suggests that primary stress is usual with patients with severe apraxia if they are working on only one syllable, but that stress modifications can begin profitably when the patient can sequence two or more stimuli. In other words, when such syllables as /pa/ and /ma/ can be combined, the patient can repeat the sequence with varied stress: /'pa ma, pa 'ma, 'pa 'ma/. Our present tendency is to use exaggeratedly normal stress as soon as meaningful sequences are begun and to rely on equal and even stress with pauses between words only if the patient is having difficulty. A "perception of stress" may be preserved in aphasic patients [17], but the full implications for therapy of that preservation can only be guessed at, given present knowledge.

In a previous publication [108] these facilitators were called the flesh and blood of therapy, and nothing has since happened to change that opinion. Creative, experienced use of facilitators can redeem incorrect stimuli and inappropriate methods. Most important, these facilitators can help a patient be successful at every step of treatment.

Methods
The state of methodology in apraxia of speech is chaotic. Techniques have been selected, sometimes willy-nilly, from aphasiology, from the literature on articulation problems in children, and

from psychology, education, learning theory, and music. Philosophies of what one tries to do with whatever methods one selects are far less numerous, however. The result is that recommended methods are as disparate as the MIT of Sparks, Helm, and Albert [121], which is a total treatment package complete with theory on the one hand, and the admonition to concentrate solely on the patient's psychological problems, on the other. This section attempts to describe some common treatment methods and to organize and classify some methodologic bits and pieces winnowed from the literature. The relation of these methods to the goals of facilitation and reorganization is also hypothesized.

IMITATION. For the functional articulation case, Milisen [93] described an imitative program of articulation training, emphasizing multiple input modes, especially the visual and auditory, which he called *integral stimulation*. The patient listens and watches the clinician and then attends equally carefully to selected cues provided by the patient's own imitative attempts. Parents and speech pathologists have used this method for decades, and its resiliency attests to its usefulness. Its appropriateness to apraxic problems cannot be merely assumed, however. Darley [35] observed that the apraxic patient's repetitive responses are especially poor. Doubtless he was referring to a patient's attempts to imitate what can be said automatically or reflexively. Indeed, many apraxic patients cannot imitate their automatic-reflexive speech. Clinical experience, however, suggests that some apraxic patients can often imitate utterances that are otherwise impossible for them, and Webb and Love [131] have demonstrated the potency of imitation as a method for eliciting single-word naming responses from apraxic patients.

A crucial question about imitation is What does it accomplish? Imitation is not volitional-purposive speech, it may even require unique patterns of neuromotor control, and transfer of imitative accuracy to volitional-purposive accuracy is not automatic. At best with an acute patient, simple repetition may be facilitating. For reorganization to take place, patients presumably must be taught to watch, listen, feel, and make judgments about their performance and that of the clinician. They must be helped to make the transfer to volitional-purposive speech by a system of fewer and weaker clinician cues; and, finally, internally generated cues or reorganization must replace the clinician

altogether. An eight-step task continuum [108] that is primarily imitative, which more or less meets the requirements for facilitation and reorganization of apraxic patients, follows:

STEP 1. Integral stimulation. "Watch me" (visual [v₁]), "Listen to me" (auditory [a]), and simultaneous production (clinician and patient produce the utterance at the same time). The clinician urges the patient to attend carefully to the auditory, tactile, and especially to the visual cues of correct production as they make the utterance together.

STEP 2. Integral stimulation [v₁, a] and delayed production (the patient imitates the clinician after a delay) with visual [v₁] cue. The clinician provides a model to which the patient attends; then, while the clinician mimes or repeats the utterance without sound, the patient attempts the utterance aloud. In other words, the simultaneous auditory cues are faded, while the visual ones remain.

STEP 3. Integral stimulation [v₁, a] and delayed production with no visual [v₁] cue. This is the traditional "I'll say it first, and you say it after me" approach. No simultaneous cues are provided by the clinician.

STEP 4. Integral stimulation and successive productions without intervening stimulation and without auditory [a] or visual [v₁] cues. After the clinician produces the utterance once, the patient is required to produce it several times consecutively without cues of any kind.

STEP 5. Written stimuli [v₂] and simultaneous production.

STEP 6. Written stimuli [v₂] and delayed production.

In step 5, the patient reads the target utterance from cards or from the blackboard, and in step 6 these cues are provided for the patient but he or she does not attempt the utterance until the written stimuli have been removed.

STEP 7. Appropriate utterance elicited by question. The imitative model is abandoned. The clinician now provides the conditions so the target utterance is used volitionally as the appropriate response to a question.

STEP 8. Appropriate response in a role-playing situation. The clinician, staff, and friends assume roles appropriate to the target utterance and the patient responds.

This continuum aided three severely apraxic patients to regain volitional-purposive control of a set of five utterances. The inadequacies of this continuum, especially because of the introduction of two reading steps (steps 5 and 6), were also clarified by the three patients. The patients could not switch from imitation to reading without great difficulty. Revisions prompted by patient responses have been discussed in another publication [107], which includes removal of reading steps for some apraxic patients and their inclusion, as steps 1 and 2, for still others. In spite of inadequacies, the continuum helps apraxic patients regain volitional control, and the exact ordering and number of steps for a given patient is governed by his or her unique responses. Deal and Florance [38] revised the continuum. They made more rigid criteria for moving from step to step. They deleted some steps, and they used portions of the continuum as a successful home program for three of their four patients.

Imitation is only the bare bones of a method, and to say that a patient regained functional communication because the clinician had the patient imitate, is to say almost nothing at all. The other essential ingredients of an imitative program have been discussed previously and include stimuli, facilitators, and reinforcements. Tasks to aid generalization or carryover also need to be completed. Despite facilitators and generalization tasks, an imitative method is not equally effective with all stimuli or at all times in therapy. Some stimuli may be too long or contain too many difficult sounds. The stimuli may be uttered too fast, or they may be inadequately differentiated by prosodic features from other stimuli. Also, assumed reinforcements may not be reinforcing at all.

When an imitative treatment works, it does so presumably because repetition is facilitating of motor speech behavior, as practicing against a backboard is good for one's forehand or backhand, and probably also because it aids in reorganization. The continuum described combines, as so many methods do, elements of both intersystemic and intrasystemic reorganization. Incorporating the visual (*watch me*) into what is a strong auditory-oral activity is consistent with principles of intersystemic reorganization. Imitation itself may represent a downward shift within the speech system and therefore functions in the main as an intrasystemic re-

organizer. When combined with other methods, repetition or imitation is a useful method for treating apraxic articulation and prosody.

MELODIC INTONATION THERAPY. MIT [57, 121, 122] is one of the few therapy packages available for apraxic patients. This section cannot be considered adequate to the practice of this form of therapy, because we have not had sufficient training or experience with the method to do it justice. If what will constitute more of a commercial than a discussion piques the reader's interest, he or she is well advised to read the authors' own discussions.

MIT consists of four levels with several carefully graded steps at each one. The purpose is to move the patient toward volitional-purposive control of selected, meaningful phrases. Essentially an imitative program, MIT begins with the clinician and patient intoning phrases according to prearranged patterns of stress, rhythm, and pitch. From this beginning, which also requires the patient to tap out the rhythm of target sentences, the patient and clinician begin to approach normal sentence prosody. This approach is aided by a mode of presentation called *Sprechgesang*, a presentation of stimuli that retains "the rhythm and stress of a melodic contour while it substitutes the constantly changing pitch of speech for the constancy of pitch in sung notes" [121, p. 307]. Criteria for moving from one step to another, scoring, what to do if a patient fails, selected stimuli and testing procedures, criteria for selecting people into the program, and dismissal criteria are all provided.

The authors are quick to point out that MIT is not singing and that popular lyrics and melodies must be avoided. Instead, MIT exploits the apparently facilitating effect of normal prosody to aid speech return. Why does it work? Sparks, Helm, and Albert suggest that MIT increases the right hemisphere's participation in speech, a possibility also discussed by Berlin [9].

MIT has elements of both intersystemic and intrasystemic facilitation. Tapping out the prosody is intersystemic. No one can be sure what is happening cortically that makes MIT speech different from normal speaking. Since both activities are primarily auditory-vocal activities, we can hypothesize that MIT stimulation and response moves speaking down or perhaps even laterally (to the other hemisphere) within the same system. Most importantly, it seems to work, and revisions to accommodate individual patient differences have begun to appear [86].

PHONETIC DERIVATION. Phonetic derivation [127, 128] refers to a method of deriving target sounds from intact nonspeech or speech gestures. This method, also called the method of *progressive approximation*, is a traditional tool of articulation clinicians. It is especially useful for patients with severe apraxia who must relearn or stabilize single sounds and syllables.

This method is useful in molding oral, nonverbal gestures into speech gestures. For example, biting the lower lip, if accompanied by a gently exhaled airstream, yields /f/. Adding gently exhaled air to tongue protrusion produces some allophone of /θ/. Adding voice to a pucker may make /u/ or /oᵁ/. A smile may yield /i/. Winitz [142] described a method for deriving the non-English, voiceless, postdorsal-postvelar fricative /x/ from a snorelike inspiration. The apraxic patient does not need /x/, but the interested clinician may profit from careful study of the Winitz procedure.

Luria [84] urges the clinician, when working with nonspeech gestures, to first stabilize the nonspeech gesture until the patient can produce it immediately and without cues. Only then, he says, can the nonspeech gesture be used to derive a speech gesture. Besides being stable, the nonverbal gesture can be a phonetic component of the target sound. Biting the upper lip or licking one's nose is not necessary to produce any English speech sounds, so it does not make a good derivation gesture.

The most popular sources of derivation materials are intact sounds, and speech pathologists have been developing tricks to make one sound yield another for generations. The requirements and methods are the same as for any other kind of derivation. The clinician needs to know the phonetic dimensions of source and target. This knowledge will make the search for sources of derivation materials more efficient. The source must be stable because of either preservation or teaching. The clinician must then provide the stimuli, the environments, the stimulus modes, the facilitators, the reinforcements, and the rest, so the derivation is accomplished with a minimum of failure and so the target sound is stabilized in as near normal a form as the patient's physiologic support for speech allows.

It is unnecessary and probably impossible to go through all the possible derivations. Two examples may serve to demonstrate the uses of phonetic principles. Because /ʃ/ and /s/ differ in large measure because of resonance differences, /s/ can be made to produce /ʃ/ by merely having the patient shape his or her lips in a slightly rounded and protruded position during production of /s/. The sound /u/ yields /oᵁ/ if the patient drops his or her jaw and perhaps eases off on the bilabial tension. All standard textbooks and especially phoneticians and school clinicians are rich sources of other examples.

Possible sources of derivation materials for apraxic patients are their recurring utterances, and serial, automatic-reactive utterances, such as counting. If the recurring utterances are meaningful, the clinician may want to try using their sound constituents as building blocks for new utterances. Our own success has not been great with such attempts, however. Presently we spend more time trying to inhibit these utterances than we do trying to shape them, because their presence seems to disrupt the reappearance of more meaningful speech. Counting and similar responses that may be partly or wholly preserved can be more useful as derivation materials if the patient can produce them reliably. In fact, *reliable production* seems to be the criterion any response must meet if it is to be grist for the "derivation mill." As we have already noted [108] *one, two* can yield *want to*, and the sound sequences of numbers, days, and so on can be systematically dissected away from the rest and used to create new utterances. Certainly such derivation may be useful for at least some utterances, and desperation to show patients some results of their taxing, sweating labors may force the clinician, not improperly, to these ready sources of derivation materials.

Phonetic derivation is primarily intrasystemic reorganization. Luria [84] even uses the example of deriving /p/ from a blow to demonstrate the concept of intrasystemic reorganization. The entire phonetic derivation process, and especially that of consciously manipulating one sound to get another, has elements of intersystemic reorganization also. This consciousness of the act—the wrestling of speech away from automatic control—suggests an upward movement within the same system or processor. If a mirror or other visual feedback device is used, derivation is again intersystemic reorganization. Thus derivation, like most other methods, contains elements of both types of reorganization.

PHONETIC PLACEMENT. Phonetic placement requires that the clinician use any of a number of techniques, including actual manipulation of the articulators to help the patient assume the correct position for producing a speech sound. A special variation of the phonetic placement method is Young and Hawk's [146] motokinesthetic method. In a motokinesthetic approach, the clinician manipulates, strokes, and coddles the patient's articulators into the proper configurations. Europeans have been practicing motokinesthetic therapy for generations and have even developed small tools that allow for specific manipulations of the articulators [83]. Popular American use has been more restrained, however programs, especially for children, are appearing [6, 26].

Phonetic placement includes a number of other techniques besides actual manipulation. According to Van Riper and Irwin [128], phonetic placement begins with description: descriptions of the tongue's proper position, where the patient should feel the contacts, where airflow is to be directed, and the like. Explanation is then supplemented by diagrams or even photographs of the articulators in static positions. School speech pathologists are a rich source of these supplies. Having patients watch themselves, the clinician, or someone else in the mirror, on a videotape monitor, or in person are all traditional procedures that are classified as placement techniques.

All phonetic placement is potentially useful, especially in patients with severe apraxia. Explanations, in the absence of severe aphasia, especially if combined with diagrams, charts, or photographs, may provide a patient all that is needed to produce a correct sound. This is the usual first step in a phonetic placement program. Explanations and visual aids can then be followed with patients watching themselves, the clinician, or both performing the gesture. Many clinicians have created elaborate visual display units for apraxic patients. Pitts [101], for example, has a videotape unit that can be used to film or monitor the "look" of articulatory gestures. A tripod-mounted camera is fixed with a long handle, so the camera's position is easily shifted from the patient to the clinician. Using the visual in this way causes phonetic placement to overlap imitative methods.

The ultimate phonetic placement procedure is manipulation of the patient's articulators. Patients with severe apraxia often require this final step either as the sole procedure or in combination with other methods, such as phonetic derivation and MIT.

Manipulation requires the clinician to know phonetics: in other words, to have a knowledge of place of articulation and the configuration of articulators during sound production. Knowing about the change in the tongue's height as /aɪ/ is produced, for example, provides the clinician with phonetic placement tricks for getting /aɪ/ from /a/. Thus as the patient is producing an /a/, he or she can be instructed to "hump" the tongue, or the equivalent, while the clinician simultaneously presses upward on the tongue from underneath the patient's chin. Also, pressing upward in the same area while depressing the tongue's apex, and simultaneously telling the patient to "make a dam with your tongue," may help the patient begin learning the painfully difficult /k/ and /g/. The clinician can pull the corners of the patient's mouth laterally for /i/, compress and pucker the lips for /u/, and force the jaw down for /a/. A cataloging of these placement tricks is unnecessary, because they are adequately described in most general speech pathology textbooks. These methods, regardless of how mechanical or manipulative they appear, if preceded by explanation and rationale, and if employed only after other methods have failed, are rarely rejected and may provide for extremely efficient learning.

Phonetic placement has a number of nonfatal limitations. The techniques are effective only, if at all, with sounds in isolation or perhaps with syllables; therefore they are useful primarily to patients with severe apraxia. Also, sounds are not equally amenable to placement influence. Front sounds are more easily manipulated than are /ʃ/, /ɝ/, /æ/, and the like. Also, putting hands, tongue blades, or wires in the patient's mouth floods his or her system with a confusing array of tactile cues. Imitation is "clean," manipulation is "dirty." Actual manipulation, then, is best reserved until other methods have failed. If employed, manipulation should be faded rapidly and systematically.

Phonetic placement combines elements of both intrasystemic and intersystemic reorganization. The explanations elevate the articulatory movements to a more volitional, mediated level within the same system. Diagrams and exploitation of the visual mode, in general, involve intersystemic reorganization. When combined with other methods, as it almost inevitably is, phonetic placement significantly expands the apraxia clinician's arsenal.

VISUAL REORGANIZATION. Using visual information to aid speaking is a form of intersystemic reorganization. No completely visual program for reorganizing the apraxic patient has been published, but Dabul and Bollier [32, 33] recommend that visual cues be emphasized over auditory ones, and a majority of treatment discussions describe the visual mode's primacy in apraxia of speech therapy. Making the apraxic patients "visually minded" is to reorganize them. When Berman and Peelle [10], in describing self-cuing techniques for apraxic patients, advocate having the patient first write and then pronounce the initial letter of a difficult word, they are describing a form of reorganization using the visual mode, although writing obviously involves more than the visual mode alone. When patients watch themselves or the clinician, they are, at least potentially, being reorganized just as they are when they try to match the articulatory postures they see in drawings or photographs. The visual mode, then, processes a wealth of information potentially useful to speech reorganization.

Regardless of whether simple visual cues, reading, or even something that might be called relying on the "mind's eye" is used in reorganization, certain requirements must be met. First, it should be established diagnostically that some other input, such as simple auditory input, is not superior to visual stimulation. Second, and this overlaps the first, the patient must have the ability to profit from visual information. If the patient has a visual-field deficit, looking may be difficult and require special positioning and effort. Even if reading is near normal and peripheral vision is intact, the visual mode will require training before it can be used in reorganization. The patient needs to learn how to collect and use visual information. A set of drills and instructions can teach these patients how to watch the clinician or watch themselves, and reading can be strengthened by practice in word selection and the like.

This training to strengthen the patient's ability in the visual mode continues during actual reorganization, which begins when the patient starts making oral responses that are influenced by visual cues. Visual reorganization itself can begin with a variety of procedures, but the majority of clinicians probably use imitation or reading. For example, the patient carefully watches as the clinician protrudes his or her tongue for /θ/, and then the patient and the clinician protrude their tongues together. Or, the patient reads the stimulus from a card and then, with the clinician's help, judges the adequacy of the production. Wertz, LaPointe, and Rosenbek [137] describe reading as treatment in some detail. Or, perhaps the patient just dis-

covers the initial letter of a troublesome word on an alphabet board and uses the visual, written cue to prompt production of the rest of the utterance. Whatever the cue, the drill continues until the reorganization or control is *internal, or patient generated*, rather than *external, or clinician generated*. Internal control means, for example, that patients can consult their mind's eye to discover how a particular sound looks while it is being made correctly. They can then compare what their mind's eye has helped them to produce with tactile-kinesthetic and auditory cues of response adequacy. Or, instead of visualizing the sound, they may be able to visualize the first letter of a word and then produce the word, or they may have to write the first letter or a whole word in the palm of their hands or in the air as a way of cuing themselves as to the first articulatory gesture of a target utterance. Reorganization is incomplete until such internal cues replace external ones.

Visual reorganization is tedious. If it is to succeed, the patient must practice daily. Although it does not need to be the only therapy the patient is receiving, it must consume a major proportion of any therapy in which simple facilitation or reorganization on some other basis is expected to be of limited usefulness.

GESTURE. Several authors [24, 25, 41, 43, 52, 100, 120] have described gestural programs for apraxic patients. These systems of gestures range in complexity from the 20-gesture system described by Goldstein and Cameron [52] to the more complex system, called American Indian sign language (Amerind), by Skelly et al. [120]. In general, all these authors have developed or adapted gestural systems to provide their patients, and in one case [52] one of themselves, with an alternative mode of communication. Such a use is traditional, straightforward, and important. Gesture can be offered as an alternative mode of communication for the profoundly involved and as an augmentative mode in patients with severe involvement.

More interesting because of both its theoretical and practical implications is a controversy about the relation of limb gesturing to oral gesturing, or speaking. In a mordant letter to the editor, Goda [51] expressed concern that limb gestures were equally as difficult as oral ones and that the same difficulties that preclude the apraxic's learning oral communication would affect the learning of limb gestures. In addition, he argued that a limb system would inhibit the return of speech. Chen's equally corrosive reply [23] was that patients could learn her system and that gestures should be only adjuncts to traditional speech therapy.

She did not repeat earlier statements [24, 25] that a manual alphabet "reawakens the power of speech." She might well have done so, and confidently, because other authors have reported similar conclusions. Goldstein and Cameron [52] thought that gestures enhanced the one author's recovery by improving his emotional outlook and helping him regain speech earlier than he might have otherwise. An increase in a patient's speaking after a period of training in combined Indian and deaf sign language moved Eagleson, Vaughn, and Knudson [43] to ask, "Could this have been the result of the exercise of analogic communication which provided carryover toward the development of digital codification and verbal communication?" We continue to be in need of the research suggested by Skelly, et al. [120], who also noticed improved and expanded oral communication as a result of a systematic effort to improve manual gesturing. Skelly et al. end their discussion of Amerind by requesting further exploration of Amerind signs as facilitators of speech. That exploration can be accomplished clinically as the result of systematic treatment.

The gestural program presented by Skelly et al. [120] is a good one for such a clinical study and for treatment in general. Amerind was originally adapted by the senior author as an alternative mode of communication for dysglossic and dysarthric patients, and its use was extended to apraxic patients. Instruction in Amerind begins with a thorough introduction to the signs and their rationale. When practice begins, it does so very systematically with the patient working at a high level of success and with the clinician providing knowledge of the results, all the while teaching the patient to become his or her own best critic. The signs are universal, but they have been modified for one-handed production, making them suitable for the apraxic patient with hemiplegia. With apraxic patients, simultaneous gestures and speaking are practiced at predetermined points in the program.

Gestures, whether Amerind or some other system, may function not only to facilitate speech but also to reorganize it. It may be that the systematic pairing of oral and limb gestures creates a reorganized neural system to support speech [105]. If so, such a reorganization would be intersystemic, because gestures are paired with speaking in a modified form and with an increased intensity and regularity that was not characteristic of the patient's previous gestural accompaniment of speech. Whether the gestures are facilitating or reorganizing is not as crucial as are the continuing development and testing of gestural methods.

Depending on how one classifies them, at least two types of gestures can be used—timing gestures and symbolic gestures. Timing gestures are simple repetitive gestures, such as tapping, that can be made to accompany appropriate speech units. Apraxic patients will occasionally discover timing gestures on their own and will be seen to tap or perhaps gesture rhythmically with fingers, arm, or even body, especially on speech segments with which they are having difficulty. Timing gestures have been employed with both adults [137] and with children [145]. We have also used timing gestures with apraxic patients at all levels of severity. The patient with severe apraxia may tap, pat, squeeze, or bob in accompaniment to productions of vowels, consonants, and words. Patients with milder apraxia can use similar gestures in time with the number and stress of syllables or word units in practice utterances. If nothing else, the gestures may slow these patients down, thereby heightening their chances for successful articulation.* Timing gestures may also accentuate stress and stress differences, which in turn may influence articulatory accuracy. A simple way of achieving this accentuation is to teach the patient harder tapping for stressed than for unstressed syllables.

Alone, tapping or any other timing gesture will accomplish very little, and with the severely disabled patient such gestures may actually interfere. Also, some patients are overloaded by the gestures even if they do practice them, as they should before pairing them with speech, even if the gestures are kept simple. Thus if a patient is overloaded, gestures are simplified even more. If a patient is still overloaded, gestures must perforce be abandoned, and other methods of facilitation and reorganization are sought.

Clinical experience has suggested some general guidelines for the use of timing gestures [105]. The timing gesture, or gestures, should be *simple*. Their *rationale must be explained* and their *use postponed* until the patient *understands and accepts* them and has *learned to perform them predictably*. They then can systematically and repeatedly be paired with articulatory gestures. The patient and clinician can perform unison gestures and speaking; the patient

*Johns and Darley [63] report perceptual data supporting the conclusion that some apraxic patients articulate better when they are urged to talk faster than normal.

can imitate the clinician; the clinician can perform the gestures while the patient talks; and so on. Timing gestures can be systematically faded, if possible, and they are unnecessary if other, simpler methods are more successful.

We have branded another group of gestures as *symbolic*. These gestures are of two types. One type merely corresponds to the direction of articulatory movements. The other type, which includes the Amerind gestures, tends to be more universal in that the meaning of the gestures can often be inferred from a performance of them. Examples of the first type of symbolic gestures are elevation of the shoulders on /u/, dropping the shoulders on /a/, a lateral gesture with the hand on /i/, and a medial gesture on /u/ or /o^U/. A more elaborate example is to open and close the hand, with fingers extended in an impolite gesture for *talks too much*, which resembles the lowering and raising of the jaw on *have*. Examples of the second type of symbolic gestures are laying one's head on one's hand to show *sleepy* or *tired*, cupping one's ear to show *hear*, pretending to lift a cup to one's mouth and then swallowing with the head back for *drink*. As noted, Amerind is a rich source of these meaningful gestures.

The gestures showing direction contain some that resemble the previously described *timing gestures*. We have separated such gestures as shrugging, however, primarily because of the way they can be used. Patients with severe apraxia begin with simple oral gestures that may be no more than components of phonemes; for example, opening the mouth. Others may be able to at least approximate differentiated vowels by rounding or spreading their lips or by lowering their jaws. Such nonspeech and speech oral gestures may be reorganized on the basis of limb gestures that somehow suggest the direction and intensity that the articulators must achieve. As was pointed up earlier, apraxic patients need to sequence. A downward gesture for /a/ and lateral one for /i/, which can be gradually faded, can begin a severely apraxic patient on the road to those sequences [65].

No single method has proved best for reorganizing a patient's speech on the basis of symbolic gestures, because patients differ in abilities. For example, strong gestures can be practiced simultaneously with attempts to speak in any of the following ways. The clinician can say the target stimulus while, at the same time, helping the patient perform the gesture. The clinician can produce the gestures with the patient while the patient attempts the speech target alone. The clinician can say the target while using phonetic placement techniques to help the patient produce the oral portion of the utterance. The clinician can systematically fade the cues. Also, the clinician can increase the amount of delay between what he or she does and what the patient is asked to do. In other words, the clinician can employ traditional behavioral methods.

Regardless of the exact symbolic gestures used, certain rules seem to pertain as they did with simple timing gestures. Gestures will usually need to be strengthened. They can only interfere unless they are under volitional-purposive control. Also, gestures must be as discrete as possible, although the variety of limb gestures seems to be more limited than the variety of oral ones. Their introduction must be preceded by adequate explanation and demonstration, and especially, the patient is told that the gross early form of the gesture may be replaced by speech or by a combination of speech and a much abbreviated form of the gestures. Their practice must be entered into with good-natured vigor.

We are unable to predict the kind of apraxic patient for whom the more elaborate Amerindlike gestures will work. We have been employing a basic set of 10 to 20 gestures with all patients with severe apraxia, most of whom have a severe coexisting aphasia. Some learn the gestures after intensive training; oral production improves for some of these, but it is unaltered for others. Data that might explain who will be helped are unavailable* or have gone unrecognized. Thus we continue to complete clinical research.

CONTRASTIVE STRESS DRILLS. Prosodic features, including rhythm, intonation, and stress are discussed extensively in Chapter 2. The appropriate sections in that chapter can be read for a list of methods equally as useful with apraxic patients as with dysarthric ones. The reader should not conclude, because the material is being only summarized here, that stress drills are of secondary or tertiary importance in apraxia therapy. As was mentioned in the section on facilitators, apraxic articulation errors may result from prosodic abnormalities; therefore they are treatable not as articulation errors per se, but within the context of prosodic manipulations. In addition, articulation

*Using gestures for selected words seems to aid certain agrammatic patients, some of whom have an accompanying apraxia of speech. Agrammatism, however, is a syndrome distinct from apraxia.

errors, whether or not they result from prosodic disturbance, may be directly influenced by manipulation of speech prosody. The primacy of prosody as a therapeutic target is the same in both instances.

A contrastive stress drill consists, on the surface, of nothing more than a phrase or sentence, the meaning of which can be altered by changes in stress. For example, the meaning of the sentence "Sue likes books" varies, depending on whether the first, second, or third word receives the primary stress. As employed with apraxic patients, the basic sentence can be repeated by the patient and clinician simultaneously with equal and even stress or with stress on any of the three words. Next, the patient can imitate the clinician after a delay and then can make consecutive responses. Finally, the whole drill can be practiced as a set of questions and answers. The last step may be the first one for some patients, depending on the symptoms and the severity of apraxia.

Diagrammed, the procedure looks like this:

Clinician
ˈsuː ˈlaɪːks ˈbʊːks
Who likes books?
Does Sue hate books?
Does Sue like magazines?

Patient
ˈsuː ˈlaɪːks ˈbʊːks
ˈsuː laɪks bʊks
ˈnoː suː ˈlaɪːks bʊks
ˈnoː suː laɪks ˈbʊːks

The ˈ indicates primary stress; the ː shows relative vowel length; and the distance between words suggests the relative pause times. Meaningfully different responses result because of differences, not in sounds, but in stress.

If the primary aim of the drill is to improve the patient's stress patterns, all words contain sounds the patient can produce easily. On the other hand, a combined concentration on articulation and stress results from building stimuli with controlled numbers and loci of target sounds. For example, if the target sound is /s/, the clinician may first want to introduce only one CV /s/ word into the drill and then practice that word only in contexts where it will be stressed and logically preceded by a pause.

It is potentially deluding to seem to suggest that contrastive stress is a method of apraxia of speech therapy in the same way MIT [122] is. Contrastive stress drills are really nothing more than a system

for presenting stimuli, and as such they must be conducted with careful attention to the type of stimulus, mode of presentation, temporal relation, and the rest. In the early stages, particularly troublesome sounds and words may have to be extracted from the drill and practiced with other methods until they are stronger. Contrastive stress is included as a separate method to emphasize the opinion that apraxia of speech is both an articulatory and a prosodic disturbance.

Contrastive stress drills may aid intrasystemic reorganization by shifting speech within the same auditory-vocal system. Whether the shift, if it is a shift at all, is upward or downward to a more automatic level can only be guessed. Right or wrong, the guess has little to do with the method's effectiveness. Elements of intersystemic reorganization appear if vision or gesture is added to the drill.

INSTRUMENTAL TREATMENTS. A limited number of instruments have been employed in the treatment of apraxia, although few have yet appeared in popular publications. These include vibrotactile stimulators [111], binaural maskers, delayed auditory feedback (DAF) devices, metronomes, and EMG feedback instruments. Rationales, although limited in number, have also been described.

Birch and Lee [13] and Birch [12] employed a continuous tone of 256 hertz (Hz) presented binaurally at an intensity of 60 decibels (dB). The tone was presented to a total of 35 patients with expressive aphasia for 30 seconds before the beginning of and all during a number of naming and reading tasks. According to Birch [12], approximately 75 percent of the patients improved on at least a portion of the tasks. Naming improved, reading improved, response latencies were reduced, and enunciation was decidedly improved. He even reports some carryover for up to a few hours. As a result of what he interpreted as the method's obvious therapeutic worth, Birch suggested a treatment program. "The possibility exists that by conditioning the auditory stimulation to a clenched hand or to some other self-applied stimulus, the auditory effect may be carried over on a conditioned basis to circumstances in which auditory stimulation is not present" (p. 3852).

Birch's reason for experimenting with masking is interesting because of what is suggested about reasons for expressive (presumably at least in part, apraxic) symptoms. He reasoned that motor speech production was inhibited rather than impossible and that the cerebral auditory system was responsible for that inhibition. Thus binaural masking might inhibit the inhibitor.

This treatment does not seem to have captured the popular imagination, and a subsequent study [133] of 18 patients failed to confirm Birch's findings. Wertz and Porch [138] also were unable to confirm Birch's conclusions with one exception. They did discover reduced response latency in the masked condition. The patients continued to make mistakes, but they made them sooner. Nonetheless, Birch's early observations deserve to be tested further. It is relatively easy and inexpensive clinically to include a masking condition in the diagnostic evaluation.

Various clinics are also experimenting clinically with both DAF and the metronome, and reports of the influence of DAF on aphasic [119, 123] and apraxic [82, 115] speech have been published. However, no conclusions are possible based on these reports. The rationale for these two instruments is not so easily described as it was for the case for masking. Certainly the metronome does not inhibit the cortical auditory analyzer nor presumably does delayed auditory feedback. Instead, it might be posited that the DAF and the metronome influence articulatory accuracy by slowing the patient's speech. If rate has an adverse influence on the patient's articulatory competence, then these two rate-manipulating instruments might contribute to a palliative effect.

DAF can slow speech down because of its primary influence on articulation time. Sounds are produced more slowly during delay. If DAF is to be useful in apraxia treatment, it likely will be so only for patients with mild to moderate apraxia who are capable of phrase and sentence-length utterances; and it will have to be included as part of an overall clinician controlled, behavioral therapy. The patient will need to be instructed in the use of DAF and be allowed to adjust to it. Optimum delay intervals, loudness, and stimuli will need to be discovered.

The metronome primarily influences pause time, depending on its rate and what the patient is instructed to do with it. Probably it is insufficient merely to turn one on and have the patient talk along with it, one syllable at a time. As with purely visual forms of feedback, the patient will need to be taught to use the metronome's timing action. If it works, it may do so because of its influence on stress: Talking along with a metronome forces the patient to put primary stress on each syllable.

If a patient's articulatory gestures are somehow coded cortically as part of a prosodic profile [69], then exaggerating the normal prosodic profile rather than disrupting it completely may be advisable. For this reason, DAF may be superior to a metronome because it is less likely to disrupt overall prosodic profiles. Clinically, speech pathologists may want to add a session with DAF and one with the metronome to their efforts to focus the therapy.

Deep-muscle relaxation accomplished by EMG feedback of muscle potentials is also an instrumental treatment for apraxia. McNeil, Prescott, and Lemme [91] induced deep-muscle relaxation using biofeedback involving muscle action potentials from the frontalis muscle. Their four apraxic patients performed a number of nonspeech and speech tasks before and after relaxation, and their performance in the relaxed condition was superior to that in the unrelaxed condition. For example, verbal performance as measured on the PICA [103] was improved for all four patients. Nielsen et al. [99] reported the clinical effectiveness of progressive relaxation in one patient with pure motor aphasia. These authors state that relaxation prepared their patient to begin speech training. The possible explanation is that tension manifested in increased muscle action potentials inhibits speech performance in apraxia. Thus relaxation may be facilitating. It also may be a useful prerequisite to reorganization. However, additional controlled experiments would be welcome.

In general, if a method or combination of methods is going to work with an apraxic patient, its potential will be revealed quickly. The exception may be MIT, and the creators of that method are making criteria available to help clinicians decide if individual patients are candidates before they begin treatment [57]. As always, the best rule is to use what works most efficiently, and what works will be influenced by the severity of the patient's disorder, duration, coexisting symptoms, and willingness as well as by the clinician's training and preference. If a patient's condition is acute, facilitating methods, such as imitation that is perhaps aided by phonetic placement and derivation, are uncomplicated and signs of their effectiveness follow immediately. If the patient has chronic apraxia, imitation is again a reasonable first method, but the clinician can expect to be forced to undertake reorganization using MIT or the visual or gestural modes or both. Almost all patients, whether they have acute or chronic apraxia, will require a combination of approaches.

Equally or even more important than trying to

describe an ordering of methods is to agree on what the methods, regardless of type, are to accomplish. The clinician's aim is to restore as much volitional-purposive communication as the patient's nervous system can support. Also, the methods must allow the patient independence from the clinician. Regardless of the method or what it does for the patient while under the clinician's guiding, urging hand, if it leaves the patient impotent outside the clinic, it is only manipulation—not facilitation and not reorganization.

REINFORCEMENT. Reinforcement is seldom discussed as part of treatment for apraxia of speech, perhaps for good reason—reinforcement is the least important consideration in most apraxia therapy. Apraxia patients are notoriously hard working. Even small gains in functional communication are enough to make them increase their efforts. Rather than discussing the type, amount, or schedule of reinforcement, this section describes a set of guidelines for responding to errors that occur during apraxia therapy.

Apraxic patients make errors during therapy with even the best clinician, and what the clinician does in response to these will influence how well the patient does. Subsequently, as a general rule, overt punishment of errors is unprofitable, although some patients are strong and can benefit from their clinicians occasionally saying "wrong." Nor should the clinician ignore the errors. Most apraxic talkers are good listeners and will be confused if the clinician seems to be ignoring errors that they themselves can hear. Preferable to punishing or ignoring errors is responding to them with analysis and with stimuli, modes, facilitators, and methods so that errors are followed by correct responses.

What is meant by correct can only be described for each patient, but seldom does it mean normal. It means instead that the patient's response is as adequate as his or her physiologic support for speech will allow. What is possible, and therefore correct, changes as a patient is treated. In the beginning even unintelligible responses, if they are differentiated, may be reinforced, whereas later on the same patient may receive reinforcement only for minimally distorted responses. Thus each patient must learn and accept that the definition of correct can change.

At times and for any number of reasons, clinicians may decide to introduce difficult stimuli with the result that the patient makes a high proportion of errors. The reason for such stimuli can be ex-plained to the patient, and then the patient and clinician can endure the work together. Generally, failure can be limited to a few responses, and quick changes in the task will allow the clinician to surround the patient's failures with successes.

Errors are useful to treatment if patients are helped to learn from them. While it awaits experimental confirmation, it seems that apraxic talkers actually learn more efficiently if they have some errors to analyze than if they are so controlled by the clinician that they merely respond correctly (and perhaps uncritically) time and again. Part of the clinical art is knowing how to control a patient's error rate and how much to analyze each mistake when it occurs.

Case Presentations

This section presents patient treatment programs preceded by brief descriptions of general treatment outlines. The patients were selected to provide a range of duration, severity of apraxia, associated symptoms, and success. These factors allow for consideration of a wide variety of methods. Granting failure equal billing with success breathes reality into what otherwise may be the fervid, purblind atmosphere of a traditional chapter on treatment. It is hoped that the air of reality about failure will nourish equally the reader's self-confidence and subsequent efforts to discover treatments better than those described in this chapter.

Treating the Patient with Severe Apraxia

The difference between the potential progress of a patient with acute, severe apraxia and one with chronic, severe apraxia leads to a very different set of expectations for the clinician. Treatments for the two groups, however, differ only subtly.

The patient with acute, severe apraxia may change rapidly, especially if the lesion is limited to Broca's area [95], and the clinician is left to discover the change rather than cause it. The changes in patients with chronic, severe apraxia may be imperceptible or even nonexistent from day to day. For long intervals, the clinician, perhaps in league with the patient, will be the only one who is aware of the change. The clinician can never be sanguine about his or her influence on the emerging speech of patients with acute apraxia, but can share the patient's relief and can structure that return.

Treatment for patients with acute apraxia *emphasizes prophylaxis* and *facilitation* more than it does reorganization; the chronic patient's treatment, while not ignoring prophylaxis and facilitation, *concentrates* on *reorganization*. Patients with acute apraxia can be prevented from developing maladaptive ways of coping with their deficit by counseling and increased speech competence. This prophylactic function has been discussed in the section on context of therapy. With chronic patients, the concentration is on undoing rather than preventing maladaptive coping behaviors, and to a lesser extent on the prevention of increasingly intense or extensive bad habits, such as deferring constantly to one's spouse.

The patient with severe, acute apraxia may well receive large doses of general facilitation in the form of conversation and a small amount of reorganization. Reorganization, when it occurs, will more likely be intrasystemic than intersystemic. The patient with severe, chronic apraxia and the clinician both know something beyond attempts at talking and listening are required if the patient is to change. If listening and struggling to talk were therapeutic, the patient would have gotten better on his or her own. So, for this patient, the emphasis is on both intrasystemic and intersystemic reorganization.

The rest of treatment is not significantly different. Stimuli may well include nonverbal movements, and phoneme repertoires will need expanding and strengthening. Stimulus modes, temporal relations, facilitators, and reinforcements must be selected to fit individual differences. Most methods will be summoned to the fray at some time. Finally, the severely disabled patient, whether the condition is acute or chronic, will require practice in listening, reading, writing, gesturing, and speaking.

CASE 1. The patient, a man in his fifties, is a farmer with a high school education. He was described by his family and friends as gregarious and considerably above average in intelligence. A cerebrovascular accident left him with a dense right hemiplegia and speechlessness. At the time of the evaluation, 15 days after his stroke, he was alert and cooperative; however, he had not been heard to make a sound. Tests revealed, besides the speechlessness, a profound oral and limb apraxia and severe deficits in reading, writing, and listening. However, he did respond appropriately to yes and no questions with head shakes and gave evidence of retaining concepts about his previous work and hobbies. His PICA overall score of 6.66 placed him at the 15th percentile for aphasic adults. His

gestural performance was at the 13th percentile; verbal was at the 12th percentile; and graphic abilities were at the 31st percentile. His family was understandably very anxious about his speechlessness and would not believe that he might never regain speech, although they did admit it might take many years. They received weekly progress reports and were prepared gradually and as painlessly as possible to cope with a severely involved husband and father.

Initially, treatment concentrated on his listening and speaking deficits. The listening program was traditional. The patient was counseled about the need to watch carefully and to avoid responding until he was sure of the message. He was instructed to request repeats rather than try to guess what was required. Commands involving whole body movements, body parts, his room, and real objects were repeated over and over gain. He was made to solve actively problems presented orally without having to demonstrate that problem solving through speech. He pointed instead. Such active problem solving progressed from pictured stimuli to written words and sentences.

The restoration of speech began with the restoration of volitional phonation. All traditional methods were tried: Singing was unsuccessful; imitation of /a/ was unsuccessful; and getting the patient to sigh, grunt, laugh, yawn, and even exhale noisily were to no avail. We manipulated his larynx while phonating ourselves; we pushed on his abdomen, jiggled his larynx, and phonated with his hand against our own vibrating larynx. We gave explanations and manually manipulated not only his larynx, but his jaw and face as well. We swung his arm, vigorously grunting all the while. Thirty minutes went by; everyone had become light-headed at least once from inhaling too much nonproductive air. Finally, the clinician arrived at the happy notion of getting the patient to try a few animal noises. The patient, a dairy farmer, hummed an imitation of a cow. Within 10 minutes he could hum predictably, and the session ended.

At the next session, the hum was securely bastioned; in fact, it was implacable. No other sound could be elicited and much nonverbal activity was accompanied by a rhythmic, continual /m/ or /n/. The clinician decided to stabilize one oral, nonverbal movement, opening the mouth, as a first step in building an /a/ to compete with the hum. Several minutes' practice over 5 days was necessary before the patient could predictably open and shut his mouth on command. He knew what was required, for he would touch his face in an apparent effort to discover if his own mouth was open. Each time he was urged to phonate, the jaw would come up and out would come /m/ or /n/. He could not lower his jaw once he had initiated sound. Once the lowered jaw was stabilized, however, an oral sound was gotten by allowing the patient to begin his nasal production, which the clinician would then disrupt by pinching the patient's nostrils. Almost immediately an /a/ or nasal /a/ would result as the patient began to direct the airflow orally. First one nostril and then the other was released and, finally, after two sessions, the /a/ was usually oral. Three sessions later, the patient could voluntarily imitate /a/ with only an occasional need for the occluded nostrils trick. Almost immediately, work began on producing sound sequences. The first was /ma/. The patient got this in one session. The meaningfulness of it was reinforced. Fifteen more sessions employing similar methods resulted in reasonably stable /aɪ/ and /oᵁ/. However, in spite of the clinician's best efforts, no other sounds were forthcoming.

A concerted effort to establish gestural communication started after 3 days of traditional therapy. Three gestures, *drink*, *pain*, and *go* were introduced. The patient's ferocious limb apraxia and severe aphasia made it slow going. After five sessions he could approximate the three gestures on command. Watching the clinician was only mildly helpful because of the apraxia, and on almost every trial the patient's hand had to be molded into the proper configurations. After approximately 10 sessions, during which time he got volitional-purposive control of only the *drink* gesture, he indicated he wanted to stop working on gestures. They were replaced by a communication board. After approximately 10 sessions, the patient could answer questions using the board's pictured stimuli. He took the board to his room, and staff and family members were instructed in its use.

Because his speech was severely limited, in spite of the appearance of a few meaningful, recurring utterances, the shift was toward improved listening, reading, and writing skills. It was hoped that careful listening might improve the patient's speech. The principal method for improving his listening and reading was to have him select orally presented words from a display of four written stimuli. A group of 40 words, including functional nouns and verbs, was used. Speaking was not encouraged and, in fact, it seemed clinically that his sound making impaired his listening. After about 10 sessions, the patient began to produce some of the single words correctly. Writing exercises using the same words were also completed, although somewhat erratically and far less frequently—less frequently, that is, until the last month of his treatment. The slow progress of therapy revealed that this patient could write single words after only a little practice, so writing was finally determined to be his best mode of output.

Listening, reading, and writing all improved. After 2½ months of therapy, the patient's PICA overall had shifted from the 15th percentile to the 30th percentile, and his performance was improved in all modes. However, his speech was still unintelligible. Figure 7-2 shows the PICA modality response summary. As can be seen by looking at his performance on subtests I, IV, IX, and XII, the patient was not significantly better in spontaneous or even imitative speaking.

This patient's therapy is typical of what is performed with patients whose apraxia is so severe that they cannot even phonate volitionally. It contains elements of both intrasystemic and intersystemic reorganization. Beginning with basic gestures, in this case, mouth opening, and then building a sound on this gesture is intrasystemic reorganization. Introducing visual cues and the clinician's phonetic placement cues are part of intersystemic reorganization. While it has not been extensively discussed already, reorganization took place within the context of extensive counseling. The patient was told the purpose of each day's work. He was not promised anything but our best efforts, and his family was helped in their efforts to communicate with him. They were told that his speaking ability would never return. It did not. However, he did regain his ability to draw to an inside straight when playing poker.

CASE 2. The patient is a 61-year-old man with chronic, severe apraxia of speech of 8 years' duration. He was referred after all that time because he had expressed an interest in speech rehabilitation. It was agreed to complete eight sessions during 1 month to see if the patient could learn and if his learning would generalize. At the time of testing, he had a mild right-sided weakness, which was greater in the arm than the leg, and he was ambulatory.

Testing with the PICA showed him to be at the 36th percentile overall; his gestural performance was at the 76th percentile; verbal performance was at the 12th percentile; and his graphic ability was

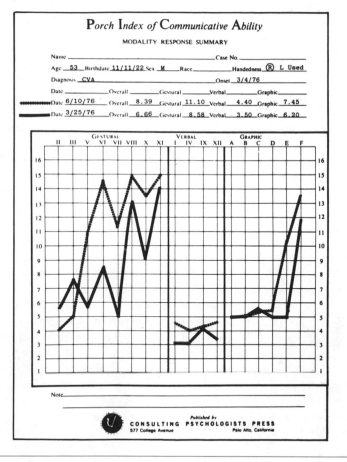

Fig. 7-2. PICA modality response summary for Case 1. Several weeks of treatment failed to improve the patient's speech. Reading, listening, and copying were much improved.

at the 15th percentile. He could easily cope with the comprehension demands imposed by activities of daily living. He had a severe oral, nonverbal apraxia but no limb apraxia, and he had even worked out a crude system of gestures. His speech was limited to "yeah" and a recurring utterance, /'boɪ'baɪ/, that he could and did produce with varying gusto any time an oral response was called for.

Because he had been a chronic apraxic and aphasic patient for some time, the prognosis was poor. His therapy had two goals: to determine his ability to learn a set of 10 limb gestures and as many sounds as possible, and to determine any generalization effects from either program. Limb gestures were to be offered as an alternative mode of communication to expand and improve his own self-taught system. The attempt to teach him speech gesture appeared justified, because he wanted to talk and

had not had any but a general stimulation therapy immediately after his stroke. Because this therapy was to last only eight sessions, no efforts were directed toward reading and writing skills.

Interestingly enough, this patient had developed few maladaptive responses in 8 years. He had a good family, and he enjoyed good fishing year around. He was instructed to listen more carefully, but his recurring utterance was not inhibited except during drill, because he seldom used it outside the clinic and there was no guarantee that some useful speech would replace it. His family was coping well, so no counseling was necessary beyond an explanation of what would happen in eight sessions.

Gestures were taught with an imitative method that required the patient to perform the gestures simultaneously with the clinician, then in delayed imitation of the clinician, and finally in response to appropriate questions. For example, the last step was for the patient to perform the gesture for *drink* in response to the question, "If you were thirsty and needed water, what would you do?" He learned all 10 gestures in less than 1 hour and retained all of them except one for an entire week. It was decided that Amerind could be made available to him and to his family as an alternative mode of communication, if they wanted it, and if the speech program appeared to be limited or doomed.

The process of teaching him oral gestures proceeded according to the guidelines discussed previously in this chapter. Single sounds, both vowels and consonants, were the first stimuli. The method at the outset was imitation with simultaneous production. All the patient's responses were oral. The patient indicated by his behavior that visual information eased his burden, so initial therapy emphasized clear visual cuing. Organized baseline testing showed that the patient could imitate vowels /aɪ/ and /oᵁ/ and the consonant /θ/. He could inconsistently approximate /eɪ/, /b/, /d/, /g/, /s/, /h/, and /j/. Simple integral stimulation was sufficient to stabilize /i/, /b/, /s/, /h/, /ð/, and /v/ in one session. Other vowels were often substituted for by /aɪ/, a formidable opponent to volitional differentiated production. His recurring utterance was unmodifiable and had to be inhibited on every occasion. Just as /aɪ/ intruded on other vowels, so /b/ intruded on other consonants. The sound /p/ came late in the third session because /b/ was so potent.

By the third session and after about 2 hours of drill, the patient had some control over /p b m d g l f v θ ð ʃ z s h i u oᵁ i a aɪ/. Space and interest obviate a discussion of how these were all achieved, although certain special procedures can be mentioned: /p/ was derived from blowing, and /ʃ/ was derived from /s/. Intensive phonetic placement with extensive description and tongue-blade and finger manipulation were necessary to get /a/, /d/, and /g/; and /a/ became /aɪ/ unless the tongue's back was inhibited. His tongue tip had to be elevated for /d/ and inhibited for /g/; and whispered /d/ yielded /t/. As soon as sounds were stable in isolation, selected ones were combined: /si/, /soᵁ/, /fi/, and /faɪ/ were early, and by the fourth session /aɪsi/ and /aɪs ti/ were under reasonable imitative control. He could even produce these in answer to questions if he had minimal simultaneous visual cues. The final session was spent entirely on practice of combinations, and their meaningfulness was stressed by providing their written form on 2- by 5-inch cards along with an explanation or definition of the words.

Intrasystemic and intersystemic reorganization in the form of imitation, phonetic placement, and phonetic derivation characterized this therapy. The resultant speech had an effortful, conditioned quality. After four sessions, it had not extended beyond the clinic. No generalization was evident, but expecting it was probably premature. The patient realized that his road was arduous and he chose fishing over treatment. We congratulated him on his choice even though the rapidity with which he moved to sound combinations suggested he might have unexploited and reorganizable neural support for speech. As he left, he hinted he might be back for gestures, but that gesture seemed to be his way of allowing us to save face.

CASE 3. The patient, a 58-year-old man, was apraxic after surgery for a wound to the chest. At the time of testing, the patient had been apraxic and aphasic for 4 weeks, but he had been very ill for most of that time. His PICA overall score of 5.48 placed him at the 9th percentile; gestural performance was at the 8th percentile; verbal, at the 10th percentile; and graphic, at the 11th percentile. He had no volitional-purposive speech but did utter unintelligible, undifferentiated combinations of bilabial plosives and vowels. He recognized the inadequacy of these utterances and was frustrated by them. His understanding was good for activities of daily living. The diagnosis was profound apraxia of speech and moderate aphasia. In addition, he had profound oral and limb apraxia and right-sided sensory deficit.

This patient's therapy was satisfactorily and exclusively apraxia of speech therapy as described in earlier sections of this chapter. Simultaneously, work began to improve his speaking, gesturing, and listening. While this work was proceeding, the patient used a language board for basic communication. His imitation ability was sufficient to cause the emergence of /a/, /i/, /u/, /oᵁ/, /eɪ/, /m/, /n/, /s/, /z/, /l/, /w/, and /h/. However, the sounds /p/, /b/, /t/, and /d/ required an additional boost from placement methods, including manipulation of lips and tongue; and /f/, /v/, /k/, and /g/ required extensive phonetic placement.

The work done with /s/ can represent what was done with the other sounds. It was introduced in the initial position of CV syllables except for /s/ plus /i/, which was produced normally only in VCV combinations. The most facilitating vowels were /aɪ/ and /oᵁ/. The least facilitating were /i/ and /u/. Practice then began with /saɪ/ and /soᵁ/ before advancing to the rest of the vowels. With /s/, an imitative therapy and extensive explanation of what was required were employed almost exclusively. The patient could not read well enough at first for the written mode to be very useful. In speech, simultaneity of stimulus and response was rapidly replaced by delay. Equal and even stress and increased articulation time on /s/ were the facilitators. The words *see, saw, sue, say, sigh, so* were introduced immediately and practiced in phrases by the third day. Sample phrases are "I say so," "I see Sue," and "I saw Sue." He was able to handle CVC stimuli quickly, so words like *some, same,* and *seem* were introduced and phrases were subsequently expanded. In 1 week of extensive drill, he had volitional-purposive control of these words and phrases. One of his greatest strengths was the ability to judge the adequacy of each production. This ability was consistently rewarded and strengthened from the first day of therapy. After 4 weeks, he was capable of individual work with a language master. The materials he practiced on the machine were those he had successfully conquered in therapy.

Work began simultaneously on other such sounds as /f/ and such words as *hi, we, you, no,* and *yes.* Functional phrases, such as "I want a cigarette," were also practiced almost from the outset. The word and phrase work was begun because the patient could successfully imitate and because we wanted to give him functional communication as quickly as possible. A major component of the phrase work was to establish different stress and timing patterns for each one. Differences in prosody seemed to help him switch from one phrase to another.

CV and CVC words were used to improve his listening and reading as well as speaking. The methods were traditional. Words, for example, were written on cards and then presented in displays of two or three. He would listen and then point to the word the clinician uttered. He also copied the words, although ferocious visual deficits made this frustrating and infrequent work. Then all these manipulations were combined so that he was listening, speaking, reading, and writing the same group of stimuli. Perhaps because of his visual deficits, imitation accomplished the most for his speech, and reorganization using visual information other than watching the clinician was unsuccessful.

Reorganization by pairing gestural and oral responses began the second week, when trial testing demonstrated that he found volitional use of words for which he had gestures easier than volitional use of words unaccompanied by gestures, even though he did not always use the gestures. The method was as described in a previous section. The patient was able to volunteer many reasonably differentiated gestures when they were requested and he was capable of pairing words with gestures almost from the outset, although time had to be spent strengthening his gesturing ability. Words, and sentences in which words and gestures were paired, were practiced twice each day, and these phrases were the first we heard outside the clinic. Extensive reorganization was unnecessary, however, because massed practice of imitative responses helped him regain considerable volitional-purposive communication. Besides, he came to dislike the gestures.

After 3 weeks of therapy (7 weeks after the apraxia began), the patient could produce both practiced and unpracticed sentences. His unintelligible jargon began to break up and to be replaced by a variety of sounds and many approximations of target utterances. The question then is whether the therapy was facilitating or reorganizing. Presumably, it was both. He was both facilitated and reorganized by the extensive imitative drill. Because both his visual and gestural systems were too weak or too little practiced to be the basis for reorganization, the reorganization must have been intrasystemic rather than intersystemic. He could recognize his errors and could make deliberate self-corrections, suggesting that drill was helping him reorganize with auditory and tactile information. The importance of concentrating on the entire language system cannot be documented, but it impressed all this patient's clinicians as being crucial. This patient demonstrates the facilitating effects of meaningful stimuli and the necessity to work with longer, meaningful stimuli simultaneously with shorter ones and, to a degree, he even demonstrates that sounds can sometimes be stabilized in longer units more easily than in shorter ones. After working with such a patient, a clinician will never neglect testing words and phrases even in a patient with profound difficulty in producing sounds and syllables.

The only prevention necessary was occasional morale boosting, because this patient would gladly work 6 hours a day. He had few friends, but the few he did have were very supportive, and just a bit of counseling helped them learn to provide the patient with a facilitating, rewarding environment.

The treatment was successful. After 4 weeks his PICA overall was changed from the 9th percentile to the 22nd, and after 7 weeks he had improved to the 30th percentile. Of special interest was the change in his verbal abilities, as measured by the PICA, because these improved from the 10th percentile to the 45th percentile after 7 weeks. Figure 7-3 shows the modality response summary from the PICA. More importantly, each day the patient expanded his repertoire of functional phrases and intelligible near-misses.

Treating the Patient with Moderate Apraxia

The same differences in prognosis typical of acute and chronic apraxic patients are typical of moderately involved patients. Also, the proportions of prevention, facilitation, and reorganization for patients with acute and chronic, moderate apraxia are the same as for those with severe apraxia. The treatment for patients with moderate apraxia differs in some ways from that of patients with severe apraxia, however. A major difference between the therapies is in the stimuli. Patients with severe apraxia

have a limited repertoire of phonemes. Moderately involved apraxic patients have a more nearly complete repertoire of speech sounds, although they will make errors on many sounds, depending on context, length, stress, rate, and the like. Even in patients with moderate apraxia, certain sounds will be very fragile in a number of environments, and some sounds may be absent or infrequently correct. In patients with moderate apraxia, the clinician will usually be working on words and phrases of varying length, although he or she will have to stabilize some of those unstable consonant or vowel singletons and consonant clusters. While it should not be assumed that severity of apraxia and aphasia are significantly correlated, it would seem to be true clinically that reading and writing are less impaired in patients with moderate apraxia than in those with severe apraxia. Therefore patients with moderate apraxia can use these stimulus modes more readily for reorganization. Moderately involved patients are less likely to require simultaneous production than are severely involved ones,

Fig. 7-3. PICA modality response summary for Case 3. Speaking is significantly improved. Writing is unchanged.

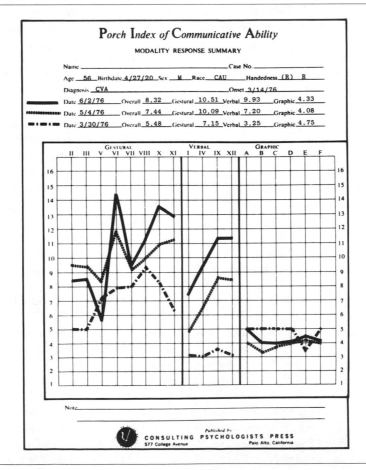

although simultaneity may be a good way of strengthening some demanding utterances. Phonetic placement and derivation will seldom be used; but imitation, contrastive stress, and gesturing will be used extensively. Finally, the moderately involved apraxic patient can often do more homework than the patient with severe apraxia can.

CASE 4. This patient is a spry 84-year-old man who suffered a cerebrovascular accident 3 weeks before our evaluation. His stroke left him with mild right-sided facial weakness, moderate apraxia of speech characterized by inconsistent substitutions, omissions, and stutteringlike repetitions in connected speech, and difficulty with fricatives and consonant clusters in polysyllabic words; and mild aphasia. He could make himself understood if he did not try to hurry, but attempts to hurry and frustration sometimes created a complete deterioration of his speech. Analysis of his sentence and word articulation revealed that words with high proportions of fricatives, especially /s/, /ʃ/, and /θ/ were very difficult for him, and metathetic errors were common. His PICA overall was at the 54th percentile; gestural performance was at the 72nd percentile; graphic abilities were at the 54th percentile; and verbal performance was at the 49th percentile.

Three overlapping goals were set with this patient. We wanted to stabilize certain sounds through reorganization so he could produce them more easily. We wanted to provide him with facilitating practice in programming polysyllabic words, consonant clusters, and phrases. Also, we wanted to teach him to anticipate difficulty or recognize it immediately and then take steps to reduce either the occurrence or the amount of struggle.

To aid reorganization of troublesome sounds such as fricatives /s/, /f/, and /θ/, extensive use was made of explanation and description (Where do you place your teeth for /f/?) and on internalization of visual and tactile-kinesthetic cues to correct sound production. As part of drill, he had to assume static postures for the target sounds and check the accuracy of those placements against the template of visual and tactile-kinesthetic cues being established. He created lists of words beginning with target sounds. He practiced making a word's first sound, holding it, and then producing the rest of the word. He was given words and was asked to create sentences. The effectiveness of this complex pattern of techniques is hard to evaluate, because other forms of practice were going on simultaneously. However, the patient thought it helped.

Polysyllabic word practice began with spondee words containing only one fricative. Phrase and sentence drills began with short phrases that were heavy on words with plosives, such as *can*, *do*, *did*, and *caught* and containing only one monosyllabic word beginning with a fricative. A typical practice sentence was "Sue did it." The sounds /l/ and /r/ were avoided in the early stages, because these were extremely unstable unless produced slowly in short utterances. Polysyllabic words were made more complex by increasing their length, number of clusters, and number of fricatives. Spondees were replaced by polysyllabic words with two or more levels of stress, although these were sometimes practiced first with equal and even stress. From the outset, phrases were practiced with an early form of the contrastive stress drill. Practice usually began with reduced articulation time, increased pause time, and primary stress on the target word or word containing the fricative. This was followed by drills to improve stress and to increase the patient's awareness of normal stress and ability to place stress anyplace in the utterance.

The patient came to therapy with a behavior that slowed his speech and aided his passage through troublesome responses; and we were able to refine this behavior. He would accompany each syllable of a troublesome word with a tap of his finger on the table top. He accompanied each tap with the production of a stressed syllable. The behavior seemed to function as a reorganizer, and it was facilitating as well. In practice, he reported the number of syllables in a troublesome word; then he would simultaneously tap and speak, first in conjunction with the clinician and then in delayed imitation. The rate of production was systematically increased and the amount of clinician help and tapping were systematically decreased.

Increasing this patient's ability to predict trouble and to reduce it was accomplished by practice already completed. The patient came to recognize his difficult utterances, and his ability to cope with length, stress, and the rest improved. He needed special counseling to resist time pressure and to abort his tendency to hurry through an utterance regardless of the toll in struggle and error.

Progress toward all goals was aided by homework. Practice sentences and words were printed and recorded on cards, and the patient practiced these a few minutes each hour. The influence of homework is impossible to calculate accurately. Our feeling is that it hastened increased volitional-purposive control.

In retrospect, much of this patient's therapy appears to have been facilitation. During the first 2 weeks of therapy, each day brought changes in his speech. His brain was obviously improving and speech was improving along with it. Certain troublesome sounds remained troublesome into the chronic period, and visual reorganization of these was effective. This patient is especially interesting, because he discovered tapping, which we could help him refine, and which he could subsequently use in reorganization. Because of his limited aphasia he could also make extensive use of written stimuli and could perform such crucial carryover activities as creating sentences with target words.

He improved significantly in 5 weeks. He made fewer mistakes in connected speech and was capable of correcting the ones he did make without frustration or debilitating struggle. He and his family left the hospital content with their progress and eager to continue a home program.

CASE 5. This 70-year-old patient suffered what was assumed to be a left hemisphere cerebrovascular accident 3 weeks before referral. The only symptoms of this episode, according to his wife, were obvious speech problems that at first did not alarm her because she thought her husband might merely be fatigued by too much work. He had been blind for 20 years and had a moderate, bilateral hearing loss of ill-defined duration. Case 5 resembles Case 4 in many ways except that this patient had a trace of right facial weakness and somewhat more aphasia and general intellectual deficit. His errors were most prominent in connected speech and consisted of multiple sound repetitions and substitutions, including a very high percent of metathetic errors. His answers to questions were generally better than the speech he initiated himself, and his ability to repeat was good, but not errorless. His spontaneous comments were arduous both in speaking and listening. An abbreviated bilabial gesture would intrude on the beginning of any utterance on which he was having difficulty. He would fix on a syllable or sound, repeat it, then substitute a kind of bilabial plosive, and finally trail off into more and more indistinct and unintelligible groping until he gave up with an "oops" or an "oh my." At other times, statements, questions, and answers would be nearly perfect, although deficits in stress might remind the listener of the patient's apraxia. Analysis, especially of imitative utterances, revealed the consistent omission or distortion of unstressed elements in a sentence, but all the individual sounds of

American English were present somewhere in his speech. His blindness prevented most formal testing, but informal testing documented moderate speech apraxia and aphasia.

His blindness created an interesting treatment dilemma. Even though it was not even 1 month after his stroke, facilitation and reorganization were planned against a background of extensive prophylaxis. The first goal was to provide him with at least 1 hour per day of general facilitation in the form of word, phrase, and sentence repetition and volitional production patterned after the eight-step task continuum [108]. The second goal, reorganization, began with timing gestures and "mind's eye" visual images. The gestural and visual reorganizers were used to increase the signal value of the beginning of utterances and of the unstressed elements where most of his trouble predictably occurred. All these maneuvers were intended to make his errors in connected speech less frequent but, more important, to provide him with cues he could rely on when he got into trouble. The motto we taught both him and his wife was "When trouble comes, stop, think, restart." The gestural and mind's eye cues were to give him something to think about.

We talked to the patient and his wife about the motto and what it required and, by doing so, provided the appropriate preventive counseling. It was emphasized again and again that the patient must be willing to search and that his wife must be willing to wait and provide cues that helped him, while preserving his independence. Controlled conversation and therapy with both present provided ample opportunities for him to practice the motto and for his wife to learn to cue him with questions and key words. The patient and his wife counseled their many friends about what was required—careful listening and a minimum of demands. Heated discussions about whether a Republican or a Democrat was best suited to the presidency, so popular before the stroke, had to be shortened and cooled after it. Friends had to learn new activities that allowed the patient more success.

Facilitation and reorganization were worked on simultaneously. Increasing the signal value of initial unstressed elements was accomplished by teaching the patient a system of hard and soft taps to accompany each word in an imitative utterance. Initially, the words were monosyllabic and were heavy on plosives. Later, fricatives, clusters, and polysyllabic words were introduced. High-frequency and nonrhyming words dominated most sentences. Sentences like "Bake a cake" were carefully avoided, because they seemed to promote assimilative errors. A group of approximately 20 sentences was practiced. The patient first had to identify the number of words in an utterance and the letter that began each word. He then practiced each in unison with his clinician, who guided him in the rhythmical tapping. The patient then used the sentences in delayed imitation of the clinician. In the delay condition, the clinician would tap out the rhythm as the patient spoke. The sentences were used to answer appropriate questions, and the questions and answers were worked into contrastive stress drills.

To improve his ability to visualize the initiation of words, he practiced making articulatory gestures in isolation (an activity that proved most difficult) and providing the first sound (letter) of selected words. He also wrote the first sound of selected words in the air and did a number of other tasks to get him focused on the first sound of words with which he was having difficulty. He was never able to create lists of words beginning with particular sounds and, in fact, had great difficulty with all visualization tasks.

For 3 weeks, this patient progressed. Testing and family reports confirmed the clinical impression of improvement. Unfortunately, the patient had a series of seizures and developed a right hemiparesis and more severe aphasia at the end of 3 weeks. An inoperable left parietal lobe tumor was discovered. Therapy, except for family counseling, was discontinued.

Treating the Patient with Mild Apraxia

Therapy with mildly apraxic patients, when they are referred and when they accept treatment, can be compared and contrasted with therapy for the patients with severe and moderate apraxia. If the patient's apraxia is acute, he or she will require general facilitation and perhaps some prevention in the form of counseling about the kind of problem the patient is having, its probable course, and the need to work creatively with that problem. In patients with chronic mild apraxia, the goal will be systematic, controlled practice of certain frail sounds or sound sequences and practice to improve overall prosodic, especially stress, profiles. Intrasystemic reorganization, accomplished by moving speech production to a more conscious, volitional level, can be relied on to the exclusion of intersystemic reorganization. Most of the treatment even with patients with chronic, mild apraxia can be facili-

tating, with the clinician carefully structuring the patient's practice.

Stimuli can usually be words and phrases in questions and answers and spontaneous speech tasks. Occasionally, a particularly troublesome word or even consonant cluster will be practiced in isolation and then quickly reinserted into longer utterances. A majority of therapy time can be spent in improving prosody, especially stress, with contrastive stress drills or their equivalent.

CASE 6. This 58-year-old man suffered a left hemisphere stroke 22 months before our evaluation. At the time of testing, he had a right hemiplegia; he was ambulatory, but his arm was useless. He had right facial weakness, mild apraxia of speech, and mild aphasia. His PICA overall of 12.95 placed him at the 80th percentile for aphasic patients. His gestural abilities were at the 84th percentile, his verbal abilities at the 70th, and his graphic abilities at the 81st. His connected speech was almost always intelligible, but he spoke with abnormal stress and with increased pause time and articulation time. Consonant clusters, /s/, and polysyllabic words gave him his greatest difficulty, but these difficulties were manifested only infrequently: when he was excited, going too fast for some other reason, depressed, or when the idea was complex. Generally, his pattern was one of slow, careful speech and his primary errors were mild apraxic distortions and prosodic disturbances rather than substitution or omission. This entire pattern is reminiscent of other mildly apraxic patients. In addition, this patient had developed a sigmatism on both /s/ and /ʃ/.

The goals of therapy were to repair the sigmatism on /s/, stabilize consonant cluster and polysyllabic word production, and improve prosody, especially stress.

As a first order of business, the patient was taught a "closed-mouth" /s/. This /s/ required closing the mouth and baring the teeth slightly. The resultant, reasonably normal /s/ was introduced into the initial position of CVC words and CV words and syllables. After it was stable, contrast drills opposing /s/ and /θ/ and /s/ and /ʃ/ were practiced with primary stress on each word. For example, thin and sin and shoe and Sue were produced in varying orders, and the distinctiveness of the utterances was evaluated. Contrast drills such as these exploited the facilitating effects of meaningfulness. Then /s/ was combined in clusters, but it was not treated in medial and final positions during the patient's

1-month hospital stay. It started to appear correctly in the medial position after only a few days but never made a correct appearance in the final position. Careful self-monitoring and judgment of correctness based on auditory and visual cues were emphasized from the first day. The major method was imitation and, as such, was primarily intrasystemic reorganization. Sounds like /l/ and /r/ and clusters, such as /str/, were also practiced using an imitative method.

Contrastive stress drills using monosyllabic words constructed first from easy segments and then with never more than one initial position /s/ also began on the first day of therapy. From early on, the best position for /s/ was as an abnormally prolonged initial sound in a stressed word preceded by a longer-than-normal pause. Because of his minimal aphasia, any number of reasonably complex drills could be created for contrastive stress drills. The patient could make up sentences using a provided /s/ word, and the sentences could then be practiced several times in a contrastive stress context. He even became capable of placing his stress where he wished with reasonable facility.

At the time of release, after 1 month of therapy, this patient's performance on a sentence deep test for /s/ had improved from 0 percent correct to 80 percent correct. His connected speech was more normal in articulation and prosody. He was released with a home program. Five-month follow-up showed /s/ production to be even more improved, and more difficult and expanded homework was provided.

Disposition

Apraxia of speech therapy can, but must not, go on indefinitely. All patients leave therapy eventually, and it makes sense for that leaving to be planned and successful rather than inadvertent and perhaps disappointing. As a rule, the patient is pointed toward therapy's exit immediately on appearing at its entrance. This pointing is accomplished in any number of ways—by projecting the patient's eventual amount of recovery and approximate time that recovery will be reached; by sharing short- and long-term goals with the patient; by consistently helping the patient to develop internal or self-generated cues to adequate speech production, which is to say by helping him or her to reorganize speech; by carefully assigned homework; by careful training of family and friends to both treat and respond appropriately to the patient's speech; by patient counseling about the need to create a full life out of residual abilities; by scheduling systematically less frequent sessions; by providing finally for only periodic rechecks, if the patient wants; and by reassuring the patient and family that you are available if it is necessary during the intervals.

Conclusion

This chapter's content need not be summarized, but the writer's attitudes about it and how it can be used should be. Nothing in this chapter is original. For many working clinicians, therefore, the content is only reinforcing. Everything in this chapter must be considered in terms of specific patients and clinicians. Equally as fascinating as each person's uniqueness, whether patient or clinician, is the uniqueness of each patient-clinician relationship. It is perhaps only slightly exaggerated to say that each therapeutic relationship will have as much influence on the application of principles and procedures from this chapter as will the principles and procedures on the therapeutic relationship. Thus nothing in this chapter should be believed unless it works.

References

1. Agronowitz, A., and McKeown, M. R. *Aphasia Handbook*. Springfield, Ill.: Charles C Thomas, 1964.
2. Alajouanine, T. Verbal realization in aphasia. *Brain* 79 : 1, 1956.
3. Alajouanine, T., and Lhermitte, F. Aphasia and Physiology of Speech. In D. M. Rioch and E. A. Weinstein (eds.), *Disorders of Communication*. Baltimore: Williams & Wilkins, 1964.
4. Aten, J. L., Darley, F. L., Deal, J. L., and Johns, D. F. Comment on A. D. Martin's "Some objections to the term apraxia of speech" (letter). *J. Speech Hear. Disord.* 40 : 416, 1975.
5. Aten, J. L., Johns, D. F., and Darley, F. L. Auditory perception of sequenced words in apraxia of speech. *J. Speech Hear. Res.* 14 : 131, 1971.
6. Bashir, A. S., Grahamjones, F., and Bostwick, R. Y. A Touch-Cue Method of Therapy for Developmental Verbal Apraxia. In D. M. Aram (ed.), *Assessment and Treatment of Developmental Apraxia. Seminars in Speech and Language*. New York: Thieme-Stratton, 1984.
7. Bauman, J. A., Waengler, H. H., and Prescott, T. E. Durational aspects of continuous speech: Comparative measurements based on vowel and consonant productions by normal and apraxic speakers. Paper presented to the American Speech and Hearing Association, Washington, D.C., 1975.
8. Benson, D. F. Fluency in aphasia: Correlation with radioactive scan localization. *Cortex* 3 : 373, 1967.

9. Berlin, C. On: Melodic intonation therapy for aphasia by RW Sparks and AL Holland. *J. Speech Hear. Disord.* 41 : 298, 1976.
10. Berman, M., and Peelle, L. Self-generated cues: A method for aiding aphasic and apractic patients. *J. Speech Hear. Disord.* 32 : 372, 1967.
11. Beyn, E. S. Basic principles of restorative therapy of speech in aphasia. *Topical Probl. Psychiatr. Neurol.* 7 : 174, 1969.
12. Birch, H. G. Experimental investigations in expressive aphasia. *N.Y. State J. Med.* 56 : 3849, 1956.
13. Birch, H. G., and Lee, J. Cortical inhibition in expressive aphasia. *A.M.A. Arch. Neurol. Psychiatry* 74 : 514, 1955.
14. Blumstein, S. *A Phonological Investigation of Aphasic Speech.* The Hague: Mouton, 1973.
15. Blumstein, S. Some Phonological Implications of Aphasic Speech. In H. Goodglass and S. Blumstein (eds.), *Psycholinguistics and Aphasia.* Baltimore: Johns Hopkins University Press, 1973.
16. Blumstein, S. E., Cooper, W. E., Goodglass, H., Statlender, S., and Gottlieb, J. Production deficits in aphasia: A voice-onset time analysis. *Brain Lang.* 9 : 153, 1980.
17. Blumstein, S., and Goodglass, H. The perception of stress as a semantic cue in aphasia. *J. Speech Hear. Res.* 15 : 800, 1972.
18. Buckingham, H. W., Jr. Explanation in apraxia with consequences for the concept of apraxia of speech. *Brain Lang.* 8 : 202, 1979.
19. Bugbee, J. K., and Nichols, A. C. Rehearsal as a Self-Correction Strategy for Patients with Apraxia of Speech. In R. H. Brookshire (ed.), *Clinical Aphasiology: Conference Proceedings, 1980.* Minneapolis: BRK Publishers, 1980.
20. Burns, M. S. A phonemic analysis of literal paraphasia. Unpublished paper, 1973.
21. Butfield, E. Rehabilitation of the dysphasic patient. *Speech Pathol. Ther.* 1 : 60, 1958.
22. Canter, G. J. Dysarthria, apraxia of speech, literal paraphasia: Three distinct varieties of aberrant articulatory behavior in the adult with brain damage. Paper presented to the American Speech and Hearing Association, Detroit, Mich., 1973.
23. Chen, L-C. Y. Reply to Goda. *Arch. Phys. Med. Rehabil.* 53 : 345, 1972.
24. Chen, L-C. Y. Manual communication by combined alphabet and gestures. *Arch. Phys. Med. Rehabil.* 58 : 381, 1971.
25. Chen, L-C. Y. "Talking hand" for aphasic stroke patients. *Geriatrics* 23 : 145, 1968.
26. Chumpelik, D. The Prompt System of Therapy: Theoretical Framework and Applications for Developmental Apraxia of Speech. In D. M. Aram (ed.), *Assessment and Treatment of Developmental Apraxia. Seminars in Speech and Language.* New York: Thieme-Stratton, 1984.
27. Collins, M., Cariski, D., Longstreth, D., and Rosenbek, J. Patterns of Articulatory Behavior in Selected Motor Speech Programming Disorders. In R. H. Brookshire (ed.), *Clinical Aphasiology: Conference Proceedings, 1980.* Minneapolis: BRK Publishers, 1980.
28. Collins, M. J., Rosenbek, J. C., and Wertz, R. T. Spectrographic analysis of vowel and word duration in apraxia of speech. *J. Speech Hear. Res.* 26 : 244, 1983.
29. Conrad, K. New problems of aphasia. *Brain* 77 : 491, 1954.
30. Corbin, M. L. Group speech therapy for motor aphasia and dysarthria. *J. Speech Hear. Disord.* 16 : 21, 1951.
31. Critchley, M. Articulatory defects in aphasia. *J. Laryngol. Otol.* 66 : 1, 1952.
32. Dabul, B. *Apraxia Battery for Adults.* Tigard, Ore.: C. C. Publications, 1979.
33. Dabul, B., and Bollier, B. Therapeutic approaches to apraxia. *J. Speech Hear. Disord.* 41 : 268, 1976.
34. Dabul, B., and Bollier, B. Therapeutic approaches to apraxia. Unpublished paper, 1973.
35. Darley, F. L. The classification of output disturbances in neurologic communication disorders. Paper presented in dual session on aphasia to the American Speech and Hearing Association, Chicago, Ill., 1969.
36. Darley, F. L., Aronson, A. E., and Brown, J. R. *Motor Speech Disorders.* Philadelphia: Saunders, 1975.
37. Deal, J. L., and Darley, F. L. The influence of linguistic and situational variables on phonemic accuracy in apraxia of speech. *J. Speech Hear. Res.* 15 : 639, 1972.
38. Deal, J. L., and Florance, C. L. Modification of the eight-step continuum for treatment of apraxia of speech in adults. *J. Speech Hear. Disord.* 43 : 89, 1978.
39. DeRenzi, E., Pieczuro, A., and Vignolo, L. A. Oral apraxia and aphasia. *Cortex* 2 : 50, 1966.
40. DiSimoni, F. G., and Darley, F. L. Effect on phonemc duration control of three utterance-length conditions in an apractic patient. *J. Speech Hear. Disord.* 42 : 257, 1977.
41. Dowden, P. A., Marshall, R. C., and Tompkins, C. A. Amer-Ind Sign as a Communicative Facilitator for Aphasic and Apractic Patients. In R. H. Brookshire (ed.), *Clinical Aphasiology: Conference Proceedings, 1981.* Minneapolis: BRK Publishers, 1981.
42. Duffy, J. R., and Gawle, C. A. Apraxic Speakers' Vowel Duration in Consonant-Vowel-Consonant Syllables. In J. C. Rosenbek, M. R. McNeil, and A. E. Aronson (eds.), *Apraxia of Speech: Physiology-Acoustics-Linguistics-Management.* San Diego: College-Hill, 1984.
43. Eagleson, H. M., Vaughn, G. R., and Knudson, A. B. C. Hand signals for dysphasia. *Arch. Phys. Med. Rehabil.* 51 : 111, 1970.
44. Eisenson, J. *Adult Aphasia: Assessment and Treatment.* New York: Appleton-Century-Crofts, 1973.
45. Farmer, A. A phonemic analysis of literal paraphasia. Paper presented to the American Speech and Hearing Association, Detroit, Mich., 1973.
46. Freeman, F. J., Sands, E. S., and Harris, K. S. Temporal coordination of phonation and articulation in a case of verbal apraxia: A voice onset time study. *Brain Lang.* 6 : 106, 1978.

47. Fromm, D., Abbs, J., McNeil, M., and Rosenbek, J. Simultaneous Perceptual-Physiological Method for Studying Apraxia of Speech. In R. H. Brookshire (ed.), *Clinical Aphasiology: Conference Proceedings, 1982.* Minneapolis: BRK Publishers, 1982.

48. Fry, D. B. Phonemic substitutions in an aphasic patient. *Lang. Speech* 2 : 52, 1959.

49. Gleason, J. B., Goodglass, H., Green, E., Ackerman, N., and Hyde, M. R. The retrieval of syntax in Broca's aphasia. *Brain Lang.* 2 : 451, 1975.

50. Gloning, K., and Quatember, R. Some classification of aphasic disturbances with special reference to rehabilitation. *Int. J. Neurol.* 4 : 296, 1964.

51. Goda, S. Manual communication for aphasics (letter). *Arch. Phys. Med. Rehabil.* 53 : 344, 1972.

52. Goldstein, H., and Cameron, H. New method of communication for the aphasic patient. *J. Arizona Med. Assoc.* 9 : 17, 1952.

53. Goldstein, K. *Language and Language Disturbances.* New York: Grune & Stratton, 1948.

54. Goodglass, H., and Kaplan, E. *The Assessment of Aphasia and Related Disorders.* Philadelphia: Lea & Febiger, 1972.

55. Hageman, C. Sound Production Ability of Apraxic Adults. M.A. thesis, University of Colorado, 1977.

56. Halpern, H. Therapy for Agnosia, Apraxia, and Dysarthria. In R. Chapey (ed.), *Language Intervention Strategies in Adult Aphasia.* Baltimore: Williams & Wilkins, 1981.

57. Helm, N. Assessing candidacy for melodic intonation therapy. Paper presented to the American Speech and Hearing Association, Houston, Tex., 1976.

58. Itoh, M., and Sasanuma, S. Articulatory Movements in Apraxia of Speech. In J. C. Rosenbek, M. R. McNeil, and A. E. Aronson (eds.), *Apraxia of Speech: Physiology-Acoustics-Linguistics-Management.* San Diego: College-Hill, 1984.

59. Itoh, M., Sasanuma, S., Hirose, H., Yoshioka, H., and Ushijima, T. Abnormal articulatory dynamics in a patient with apraxia of speech: X-ray microbeam observation. *Brain Lang.* 11 : 66, 1980.

60. Itoh, M., Sasanuma, S., Tatsumi, I. F., Murakami, S., Fukasaki, Y., and Suzuki, T. Voice onset time characteristics in apraxia of speech. *Brain Lang.* 17 : 193, 1982.

61. Itoh, M., Sasanuma, S., and Ushijima, T. Velar movements during speech in a patient with apraxia of speech. *Brain Lang.* 7 : 227, 1979.

62. Johns, D. F. Application of experimental evidence in the treatment of apraxia of speech. Paper presented to the American Speech and Hearing Association, San Francisco, Calif., 1972.

63. Johns, D. F., and Darley, F. L. Phonemic variability in apraxia of speech. *J. Speech Hear. Res.* 13 : 556, 1970.

64. Johns, D. F., and LaPointe, L. Neurogenic Disorders of Output Processing: Apraxia of Speech. In H. Whitaker, and H. A. Whitaker (eds.), *Studies in Neurolinguistics: Perspectives in Neurolinguistics and Psycholinguistics,* Vol. 1. New York: Academic, 1976.

65. Johnson, G. A case study of an aphasic hemiplegic: To develop an eurythmic approach combining physical therapy and speech therapy. Unpublished paper, 1970.

66. Keatley, M. A. Intonational Contours in Apraxia of Speech. M.A. thesis, University of Colorado, 1975.

67. Keith, R. L. *Speech and Language Rehabilitation.* Danville, Ill.: Interstate, 1972.

68. Keith, R. L., and Aronson, A. E. Singing as therapy for apraxia of speech and aphasia: Report of a case. *Brain Lang.* 2 : 483, 1975.

69. Kent, R. Study of vocal tract characteristics in the dysarthrias. Paper presented at the Neuropathologies of Speech Workshop, Madison, Wis., 1976.

70. Kent, R. D., and Rosenbek, J. C. Acoustic patterns of apraxia of speech. *J. Speech Hear. Res.* 26 : 231, 1983.

71. Kerschensteiner, M., Poeck, K., and Brunner, E. The fluency-nonfluency dimension in the classification of aphasic speech. *Cortex* 8 : 233, 1972.

72. Kreindler, A., and Fradis, A. *Performances in Aphasia: A Neurodynamical, Diagnostic and Psychological Study.* Paris: Gauthier-Villars, 1968.

73. Kushner, D. Extended Comprehension Training Leading to Improved Verbal Production: A Treatment Program for an Aphasic Patient. In R. H. Brookshire (ed.), *Clinical Aphasiology: Conference Proceedings, 1975.* Minneapolis: BRK Publishers, 1975.

74. LaPointe, L. L. Sequential Treatment of Split Lists: A Case Report. In J. C. Rosenbek, M. R. McNeil, and A. E. Aronson (eds.), *Apraxia of Speech: Physiology-Acoustics-Linguistics-Management.* San Diego: College-Hill, 1984.

75. LaPointe, L. L. Base-10 programmed-stimulation: Task specification, scoring, and plotting performance in aphasia therapy. *J. Speech Hear. Disord.* 42 : 90, 1977.

76. LaPointe, L. L., and Horner, J. Repeated Trials of Words by Patients with Neurogenic Phonological Selection-Sequencing Impairment (Apraxia of Speech): Stimulus Mode and Response Condition Revisited. In R. H. Brookshire (ed.), *Clinical Aphasiology: Conference Proceedings, 1976.* Minneapolis: BRK Publishers, 1976.

77. LaPointe, L. L., and Johns, D. F. Some phonemic characteristics in apraxia of speech. *J. Commun. Disord.* 8 : 259, 1975.

78. LaPointe, L. L., and Wertz, R. T. Oral-movement abilities and articulatory characteristics of brain-injured adults. *Percept. Motor Skills* 39 : 39, 1974.

79. Larimore, H. W. Some Verbal and Nonverbal Factors Associated with Apraxia of Speech. Ph.D. dissertation, University of Denver, 1970.

80. Lebrun, Y., Buyssens, E., and Henneaux, J. Phonetic aspects of anarthria. *Cortex* 9 : 126, 1973.

81. Lecours, A. R., and Lhermitte, F. Phonetic paraphasias: Linguistic structures and tentative hypotheses. *Cortex* 5 : 193, 1969.

82. Lozano, R. A., and Dreyer, D. E. Some effects of delayed auditory feedback on dyspraxia of speech. *J. Commun. Disord.* 11 : 407, 1978.

83. Luchsinger, R., and Arnold, G. E., *Voice-Speech-Language.* Belmont, Calif.: Wadsworth, 1965.

84. Luria, A. R. *Traumatic Aphasia: Its Syndromes, Psychology and Treatment.* The Hague: Mouton, 1970.

85. Marks, M., Taylor, M., and Rusk, H. A. Rehabilitation of the aphasic patient: A survey of three years' experience in a rehabilitation setting. *Arch. Phys. Med. Rehabil.* 38 : 219, 1957.

86. Marshall, N., and Holtzapple, P. Melodic Intonation Therapy: Variations on a Theme. In R. H. Brookshire (ed.), *Clinical Aphasiology: Conference Proceedings, 1976.* Minneapolis: BRK Publishers, 1976.

87. Martin, A. D. Some objections to the term "apraxia of speech." *J. Speech Hear. Disord.* 39 : 53, 1974.

88. Martin, A. D., and Rigrodsky, S. An investigation of phonological impairment in aphasia. Part 1. *Cortex* 10 : 317, 1974.

89. Martin, A. D., and Rigrodsky, S. An investigation of phonological impairment in aphasia, Part 2. Distinctive feature analysis of phonemic commutation errors in aphasia. *Cortex* 10 : 329, 1974.

90. McDonald, E. T. *A Deep Test of Articulation: Sentence Form.* Pittsburgh: Stanwix House, 1964.

91. McNeil, M., Prescott, R., and Lemme, M. An Application of Electromyographic Biofeedback of Aphasia/Apraxia Treatment. In R. H. Brookshire (ed.), *Clinical Aphasiology: Conference Proceedings, 1976.* Minneapolis: BRK Publishers, 1976.

92. McReynolds, L. V., and Kearns, K. P. *Single-Subject Experimental Designs in Communicative Disorders.* Baltimore: University Park, 1983.

93. Milisen, R. A rationale for articulation disorders. *J. Speech Hear. Disord.* 4 : 6, 1954.

94. Mlcoch, A. G., and Noll, J. D. Speech Production Models as Related to the Concept of Apraxia of Speech. In N. J. Lass (ed.), *Speech and Language: Advances in Basic Research and Practice.* New York: Academic, 1980.

95. Mohr, J. P., Pessin, M. S., Finkelstein, S., Funkenstein, H. H., Duncan, G. W., and Davis, K. R. Broca aphasia: Pathologic and clinical aspects. *Neurology* 28 : 311, 1978.

96. Moore, W. M., Rosenbek, J. C., and LaPointe, L. L. Assessment of Oral Apraxia in Brain-Injured Adults. In R. H. Brookshire (ed.), *Clinical Aphasiology: Conference Proceedings, 1976.* Minneapolis: BRK Publishers, 1976.

97. Nathan, P. W. Facial apraxia and apraxic dysarthria. *Brain* 70 : 449, 1947.

98. Nebes, R. D. The nature of internal speech in a patient with aphemia. *Brain Lang.* 2 : 489, 1975.

99. Nielsen, J. M., Schultz, D. A., Corbin, M. L., and Crittsinger, A. The treatment of traumatic aphasia of World War II patients at Birmingham General V.A. Hospital, Van Nuys, California. *Milit. Surg.* 102 : 351, 1948.

100. Ostreicher, H. J., and Hafmeister, L. B. The use of simultaneous gestural-verbal technique with aphasic and apraxic adults. *Aphasia, Apraxia, Agnosia* 2 : 31, 1980.

101. Pitts, W. Personal communication, 1975.

102. Poeck, K., and Kerschensteiner, M. Analysis of the sequential motor events in oral apraxia. Paper presented to the Academy of Aphasia, Albuquerque, N. Mex., 1973.

103. Porch, B. E. The Porch Index of Communicative Ability. Palo Alto, Calif.: Consulting Psychologists Press, 1967.

104. Rosenbek, J. C. Unpublished data, 1976.

105. Rosenbek, J. C., Collins, M. J., and Wertz, R. T. Intersystemic Reorganization in the Treatment of Apraxia of Speech. In R. H. Brookshire (ed.), *Clinical Aphasiology: Conference Proceedings, 1976.* Minneapolis: BRK Publishers, 1976.

106. Rosenbek, J. C., Kent, R. D., and LaPointe, L. L. Apraxia of Speech: An Overview and Some Perspectives. In J. C. Rosenbek, M. R. McNeil, and A. E. Aronson (eds.), *Apraxia of Speech: Physiology-Acoustics-Linguistics-Management.* San Diego: College-Hill, 1984.

107. Rosenbek, J. C., Lemme, M., Ahern, M., Harris, E., and Wertz, R. T. Advances in the Treatment of Apraxia of Speech. In R. T. Wertz and M. J. Collins (eds.), *Clinical Aphasiology: Conference Proceedings, 1973.* Madison, Wis.: Veterans Administration Hospital.

108. Rosenbek, J. C., Lemme, M. L., Ahern, M. B., Harris, E. H., and Wertz, R. T. A treatment for apraxia of speech in adults. *J. Speech Hear. Disord.* 38 : 462, 1973.

109. Rosenbek, J. C., and Merson, R. M. Measurement and prediction of severity in apraxia of speech. Paper presented to the American Speech and Hearing Association, Chicago, Ill., 1971.

110. Rosenthal, E. The Effects of Selected Phonetic Variables on Speech Sound Adequacy in Apraxia of Speech. M.A. thesis, University of Colorado, 1974.

111. Rubow, R., Rosenbek, J. C., Collins, M. J., and Longstreth, D. Vibrotactile stimulation for intersystemic reorganization in the treatment of apraxia of speech. *Arch. Phys. Med. Rehabil.* 63 : 150, 1982.

112. Schuell, H. *Minnesota Test for Differential Diagnosis of Aphasia.* Minneapolis: University of Minnesota Press, 1965.

113. Schuell, H., Jenkins, J. J., and Jiménez-Pabón, E. *Aphasia in Adults: Diagnosis, Prognosis, and Treatment.* New York: Harper & Row, 1964.

114. Schultz, M. C. The bases of speech pathology and audiology: Evaluation as the resolution of uncertainty. *J. Speech Hear. Disord.* 38 : 147, 1973.

115. Shane, H. C., and Darley, F. L. The effect of auditory rhythmic stimulation on articulator accuracy in apraxia of speech. *Cortex* 14 : 444, 1978.

116. Shankweiler, D., and Harris, K. S. An experimental approach to the problem of articulation in aphasia. *Cortex* 2 : 277, 1966.

117. Shewan, C. M., Leeper, H. A., Jr., and Booth, J. C. An Analysis of Voice Onset Time (VOT) in Aphasic and Normal Subjects. In J. C. Rosenbek, M. R. McNeil, and A. E. Aronson (eds.), *Apraxia of Speech: Physiology-Acoustics-Linguistics-Management.* San Diego: College-Hill, 1984.

118. Shewan, C. M. Verbal dyspraxia and its treatment. *Hum. Commun.* 5 : 3, 1980.
119. Singh, S., and Schlanger, B. B. Effects of delayed sidetone on the speech of aphasic, dysarthric, and mentally retarded subjects. *Lang. Speech* 12 : 167, 1969.
120. Skelly, M., Schinsky, L., Smith, R. W., and Fust, R. American Indian Sign (Amerind) as a facilitator of verbalization for the oral verbal apraxic. *J. Speech Hear. Disord.* 39 : 445, 1974.
121. Sparks, R., Helm, N., and Albert, M. Aphasia rehabilitation resulting from melodic intonation therapy. *Cortex* 10 : 303, 1974.
122. Sparks, R. W., and Holland, A. L. Method: Melodic intonation therapy for aphasia. *J. Speech Hear. Disord.* 41 : 287, 1976.
123. Stanton, J. B. The effects of delayed auditory feedback on the speech of aphasic patients. *Scott. Med. J.* 3 : 378, 1958.
124. Templin, M. C., and Darley, F. L. *The Templin-Darley Tests of Articulation.* Iowa City: Bureau of Educational Research and Service, University of Iowa, 1960.
125. Tonkovich, J. D., and Marquardt, T. P. The Effects of Stress and Melodic Intonation on Apraxia of Speech. In R. H. Brookshire (ed.), *Clinical Aphasiology: Conference Proceedings, 1977.* Minneapolis: BRK Publishers, 1980.
126. Trost, J. E., and Canter, G. J. Apraxia of speech in patients with Broca's aphasia: A study of phoneme production accuracy and error patterns. *Brain Lang.* 1 : 63, 1974.
127. Van Riper, C. *Speech Correction: Principles and Methods.* Englewood Cliffs, N.J.: Prentice-Hall, 1963.
128. Van Riper, C., and Irwin, J. V. *Voice and Articulation.* Englewood Cliffs, N.J.: Prentice-Hall, 1958.
129. Vignolo, L. A. Evolution of aphasia and language rehabilitation: A retrospective exploratory study. *Cortex* 1 : 344, 1964.
130. Warren, R. Rehearsal for Naming in Apraxia of Speech. In R. H. Brookshire (ed.), *Clinical Aphasiology: Conference Proceedings, 1977.* Minneapolis: BRK Publishers, 1977.
131. Webb, W. G., and Love, R. J. The efficacy of cueing techniques with apraxic-aphasics. Paper presented to the American Speech and Hearing Association, Las Vegas, Nev., 1974.
132. Weisenberg, T. H., and McBride, K. E. *Aphasia: A Clinical and Psychological Study.* New York: Commonwealth Fund, 1935.
133. Weinstein, S. Experimental analysis of an attempt to improve speech in cases of expressive aphasia. *Neurology* 9 : 632, 1959.
134. Wepman, J. M. Aphasia: Language without thought or thought without language? *ASHA* 18 : 131, 1976.
135. Wepman, J. M., and Van Pelt, D. A theory of cerebral language disorders based on therapy. *Folia Phoniatr. (Basel)* 7 : 223, 1955.
136. Wertz, R. T., Response to Treatment in Patients with Apraxia of Speech. In J. C. Rosenbek, M. R. McNeil, and A. E. Aronson (eds.), *Apraxia of Speech: Physiology-Acoustics-Linguistics-Management.* San Diego: College-Hill, 1984.
137. Wertz, R. T., LaPointe, L. L., and Rosenbek, J. C. *Apraxia of Speech: The Disorder and Its Treatment.* New York: Grune and Stratton, 1984.
138. Wertz, R. T., and Porch, B. E. Effects of masking noise on the verbal performance of adult aphasics. *Cortex* 6 : 399, 1970.
139. Wertz, R. T., and Rosenbek, J. C. Appraising apraxia of speech. *J. Colorado Speech Hear. Assoc.* 5 : 18, 1971.
140. Wertz, R. T., Rosenbek, J. C., and Collins, M. J. Identification of Apraxia of Speech from PICA Verbal Tests and Selected Oral-Verbal Apraxia Tests. In R. T. Wertz, and M. J. Collins (eds.), *Clinical Aphasiology: Conference Proceedings, 1972.* Madison, Wis.: Veterans Administration Hospital, 1976.
141. Wilson, P. Temporal Relationships in Therapy for Apraxia. In R. H. Brookshire (ed.), *Clinical Aphasiology: Conference Proceedings, 1977.* Minneapolis: BRK Publishers, 1977.
142. Winitz, H. *Articulatory Acquisition and Behavior.* New York: Appleton-Century-Crofts, 1969.
143. Winitz, H., and Preisler, L. Discrimination pretraining and sound learning. *Percept. Motor Skills* 20 : 905, 1965.
144. Winitz, H., and Reeds, J. *Comprehension and Problem Solving as Strategies for Language Training.* The Hague: Mouton, 1975.
145. Yoss, K. A., and Darley, F. L. Therapy in developmental apraxia of speech. *Lang. Speech Hear. Serv. Schools* 5 : 23, 1974.
146. Young, E. H., and Hawk, S. S. *Moto-Kinesthetic Speech Training.* Stanford, Calif.: Stanford University Press, 1955.

Index